2013-14
EDITION

Indian Economy

Performance and Policies

Also by the same author :

24th Edition: 2013-14
INDIAN ECONOMY SINCE INDEPENDENCE.

5th Edition: 2010-11
INDIA'S ECONOMIC DEVELOPMENT SINCE 1947

The book is essentially, a collection of select articles by some of India's topmost economists and experts. These highly recommended original readings are well supported by comprehensive 'editorial notes' by Uma Kapila

In addition to being a textbook, this volume also serves as an ideal gateway for any interested reader to explore, in a most authentic manner, various aspects relating to India's economic development since 1947.

UMA KAPILA, author/editor of several other books, has taught Indian Economy to undergraduate students for forty two years. She retired as Reader from the Department of Economics, Miranda House, University of Delhi. Presently she is Senior Editor, Academic Foundation.

An Honours Graduate from Miranda House, University of Delhi and M.A. and Ph.D. from Delhi School of Economics, Dr. Uma Kapila has also served on the Planning Commission Study Group on "Agricultural Strategies in the Eastern Region of India for the Seventh Five Year Plan" (Perspective Planning Division).

Dr. (Mrs.) Uma Kapila is the author of the book *Oilseeds Economy of India* (1982) published by the Institute of Economic Growth. She is also the author of two other textbooks on Indian Economy, one meant for B.A. Economics (H), and the other for B.A.(Programme) / B.Com. / Eco.(Subsidiary). She has also co-edited along with Raj Kapila, a number of books on India's economy, banking and finance. Detailed information on these publications is readily available at the publisher's website: **www.academicfoundation.com**

2013-14 Edition

Indian Economy

PERFORMANCE AND POLICIES

Uma Kapila

- Designed to serve as a textbook for B.Com (H) Paper No. CH 4.5: Semester-IV.
- Based on the latest recommended readings and guidelines (Restructured Course) of University of Delhi.
- Recommended text in several other Universities in India.
- Widely used by students preparing for IAS.

ACADEMIC FOUNDATION
NEW DELHI

www.academicfoundation.com

Edition, 2013-14

ACADEMIC FOUNDATION
4772-73 / 23 Bharat Ram Road, (23 Ansari Road),
Darya Ganj, New Delhi - 110 002 (India)
Phones : 23245001 / 02 / 03 / 04
Fax : +91-11-23245005
E-mail : books@academicfoundation.com
www.academicfoundation.com

INDIAN ECONOMY: PERFORMANCE AND POLICIES (2013-14)
by Uma Kapila

ISBN 13: 978-93-327-0085-7

Designed and typeset by Italics India, New Delhi
Printed and bound in India

Guidelines and Syllabus
(December 2012)
for
B.Com. (Hons.)
Paper No-CH 4.5: Semester-IV
Indian Economy: Performance and Policies

(UNIVERSITY OF DELHI)

Duration: 3 hours *Max. Marks: 75*

Section-1: Basic Issues in Economic Development: Concept and Measures of Development and Underdevelopment.

Readings:

(a) Michal P. Todaro and Stephen C. Smiths, *Economic Development* (Pearson Education Asia, 8th edition 2003):
Ch.1 – "Economics, Institutions and Development: A Global Perspective" and Ch.2 – "Diverse Structures and Common Characteristics of Developing Nations."

1.2 Human Development

Readings:

(b) Mahbul-ul-Haq (1996). *Reflections on Human Development* Foreword by Paul Streeten and Ch.1. New Delhi: Oxford University Press.

(c) UNDP, *Human Development Report* 2011—Overview 1-12, Ch.1, p. 13-20..

Section-2: Basic Features of Indian Economy at Independence

Composition of national income and occupational structure, the agrarian scene and industrial structure.

Readings:

(a) Bettleheim. Charles India Independent. Chapters 1, 2 and 3.

Note: No question will be asked from section 2.

Section-3: Policy Regimes

a) The Evolution of Planning and Import substituting Industrialisation

b) Economic Reform and Liberalisation

Readings:

(a) Ahluwalia, Montek Singh (2012)."Planning" in Kaushik Basu and Annemie Maertens (ed.), *The New Oxford Companion to Economics in India* (Delhi: OUP, 2012, Vol. II).

(b) ———. "Prospects and Policy Challenges in the XIIth Plan", in Uma Kapila (ed.), *Two Decades of Economic Reforms*. Delhi: Academic Foundation.

Section-4: Growth, Development and Structural Change

a) The Experience of Growth, Development and Structural Change in different phases of growth and policy regimes across sectors and regions.

Readings:

Kapila, Uma (2012). "Growth and Structural Change Since 1950", Ch. 25, in *Indian Economy Since Independence*, 23rd (ed.) 2012-13.

b) The Institutional Framework: Patterns of assets ownership in agriculture and industry; Policies for restructuring agrarian relations and for regulating concentration of economic power;

c) Changes in policy perspectives on the role of institutional framework after 1991.

Readings:

Ghatak, Maitreesh (2012). "Land Reforms", in Kaushik Basu and Annemie Maertens (ed.), *The New Oxford Companion to Economics in India*. OUP, Vol.II. Pp. 442-445.

d) Growth and Distribution; Unemployment and Poverty;

Readings:

(a) A, Kotwal (2012). "Employment and Poverty", in Kaushik Basu and Annemie Maertens (ed.), *The New Oxford Companion to Economics in India*. OUP, Vol.I. Pp. 166-168.

(b) Papola, T.S. (2012). "Employment Trends", in Kaushik Basu and Annemie Maertens (ed.), *The New Oxford Companion to Economics in India*. OUP, Vol.I. Pp. 169-173.

(c) Subramaniam, S. (2012). "Poverty", in Kaushik Basu and Annemie Maertens (ed.), *The New Oxford Companion to Economics in India*. OUP, Vol. II. Pp. 542-547

(d) Somanathan, Rohini (2012). "Poverty and Exclusion", in Kaushik Basu and Annemie Maertens (ed.), *The New Oxford Companion to Economics in India*. OUP, Vol. II. Pp.547-550.

e) Demographic Constraints: Interaction between population change and economic development

Readings:

(a) Dyson, Tim (2008). "India's Demographic Transition and its Consequences for Development", Third Lecture in the Golden

Jubilee Lecture Series on IEG (Delhi, 2008). Also available in Uma Kapila, *Indian Economy Since Independence,* Ch. 7, 23rd edition, pp. 172-186.

(b) Navaneetham, K (2012). "Demographic Dividend", in Kaushik Basu and Annemie Maertens (ed.), *The New Oxford Companion to Economics in India.* OUP, Vol. I, pp 126-129.

Section-5: Sectoral Trends and Issues

5.1 Agriculture: Agrarian growth and performance in different phases of policy regimes i.e. pre green revolution and the two phases of green revolution; Factors influencing productivity and growth; the role of technology and institutions; price policy, the public distribution system and food security.

Readings:

(a) Dev, S. Mahendra (2012). "Agriculture Development", in Kaushik Basu and Annemie Maertens (ed.), *The New Oxford Companion to Economics in India.* OUP, Vol.I, pp.12-17.

(b) Gulati, Ashok (2012). "Reforming Agriculture", in Uma Kapila (ed.), *Two Decades of Economic Reforms.* Delhi: Academic Foundation, pp.305-314.

(c) Alagh, Yoginder (2012). "Green Revolution", in Kaushik Basu and Annemie Maertens (ed.), *The New Oxford Companion to Economics in India.* OUP, Vol.II. Pp. 301-304.

(d) Jha, Shikha (2012)."Food Procurement Policy" in Kaushik Basu and Annemie Maertens (ed.), The New Oxford Companion to Economics in India (Delhi: OUP, Vol. II), pp.250-254.

5.2 Industry and Services: Phases of Industrialisation – the rate and pattern of industrial growth across alternative policy regimes; Public sector – its role, performance and reforms; The small scale sector; Role of Foreign capital.

Readings:

(a) R. Nagaraj, "Industrial Growth", in Kaushik Basu and Annemie Maertens (ed.), *The New Oxford Companion to Economics in India,* OUP, Vol. II.

(b) Ahluwalia, Isher Judge (2012). "Industry" in Kaushik Basu and Annemie Maertens (ed.), *The New Oxford Companion to Economics in India,* OUP, Vol. II.

(c) Nayak, Pulin B.(2012). "Privatisation", in Kaushik Basu and Annemie Maertens (ed.), *The New Oxford Companion to Economics in India,* OUP, Vol. II.

(d) Kelkar, Vijay (2012). "On Strategies of Disinvestment and Privatisation", in Uma Kapila (ed.), *Two Decades of Economic Reforms.* Delhi: Academic Foundation.

(e) Chakraborty, K.C. (2012). "Empowering MSMEs for Financial Inclusion & Growth-Issues & Strategies", in Uma Kapila (ed.), *Two Decades of Economic Reforms.*

(g) Chanda, Rupa (2012). "Services—Led Growth", in Kaushik Basu and Annemie Maertens (ed.), *The New Oxford Companion to Economics in India*, OUP, Vol. II.

(h) Kumar, Nagesh (2012). "FDI", in Kaushik Basu and Annemie Maertens (ed.), *The New Oxford Companion to Economics in India.* OUP, Vol. I.

5.3 The Financial Sector: Structure, Performance and Reforms

Readings:

(a) Krishnan, K.P. (2012). "Financial Sector Reforms", in Kaushik Basu and Annemie Maertens (ed.), *The New Oxford Companion to Economics in India*, OUP, Vol. I. pp. 229-233.

5.4 Foreign Trade and Balance of Payments: Structural Changes and Performance of India's Foreign Trade and Balance of Payments; Trade Policy Debate; Export policies and performance; Macro Economic Stabilisation and Structural Adjustment; India and the WTO.

Readings:

(a) Kapila, Uma (2012). "India's External Sector: Policies, Developments and Issues", Ch.21, in *Indian Economy Since Independence* 23rd (ed.) 2012-13.

(b) Kapila, Uma (2012). "India and WTO", Ch. 23, in *Indian Economy Since Independence* 23rd (ed.) 2012-13.

Latest *Economic Survey* may be consulted.

Latest edition of text-book may be used.

Chap. 1 of Draft Paper of *Twelfth Five Year Plan* may also be consulted.

Note:
1. Each question of 15 marks will have internal choice.
2. There will $\frac{1}{2}$ question of 7.5 marks from **Section I**.
3. No question from **Section II**.
4. There will be $1\frac{1}{2}$ questions of 22.5 marks from **Section III** and **IV**.
5. There will be 3 questions of 45 marks from **Section V**; one question from each sub unit i.e., Agriculture, Industry and Services, and External Sector.
6. For questions involving data analysis, the relevant data shall be provided along with the examination question paper.

CONTENTS

...contd....

Section - III

Policy Regimes

...contd....

...Contd....

SECTION - IV

Growth, Development and Structural Change

...contd....

...contd....

Section-V

Sectoral Trends and Issues

V.1. Agriculture:

...contd....

...Contd....

...contd....

...contd....

...contd....

...contd....

...contd....

...contd....

Preface

THIS new revised edition (2013-14) of *Indian Economy: Performance and Policies* has been specially brought out for the students of B.Com (Hons.) of University of Delhi for Paper no. 4.5 Semester IV.

The content of the book essentially based on the new revised guidelines and readings recommended is organised in five sections.

Section I, covers the basic concepts and issues in economic development, underdevelopment as well as human development and sustainable human development.

Section II, looks at the basic features of the Indian economy at Independence.

Section III, discusses policy regimes: the evolution of planning, import-substituting industrialisation, economic reform and liberalisation.

Section IV, deals with the experience of growth, development and structural changes in different phases of growth, and policy regimes across sectors and regions; the institutional framework and changes in policy perspectives after 1991. This section also provides a wide coverage of the issues of unemployment, poverty, including demographic aspects of development.

Section V, is devoted to sectoral trends and issues: agriculture, industry and services, financial sector and external sector.

The analyses and discussion, covering these five sections in the various chapters of this book, are based on the latest revised readings recommended for this course. However, where required, I have supplemented from other sources, reference to which is given in the footnotes of the respective chapters.

I owe my debt of gratitude to Montek S. Ahluwalia, Isher Judge Ahluwalia, Y.K. Alagh, T.C.A. Anant, Kaushik Basu, Jagdish Bhagwati, K.C. Chakraborty, Rupa Chanda, Nitin Desai, S. Mahendra Dev, Jean Drèze, Tim Dyson, Maitreesh Ghatak, Jim Gordon, Ashok Gulati, Poonam Gupta, P.D. Jeromi, Shikha Jha, Vijay L. Kelkar, A. Kotwal, K.L. Krishna, K.P. Krishnan, Nagesh Kumar, Rakesh Mohan, R. Nagaraj, K. Navaneetham, Pulin Nayak, D.M. Nachane, Deepak Nayyar, Arvind Panagariya, T.S. Papola, R. Radhakrishna, C. Rangarajan, C.H. Hanumantha Rao, S.K. Ray, Alak Sharma, Amartya Sen, Rohini Somanathan, T.N. Srinivasan, Arvind Subramanian, M.H. Bala Subrahmanya, S.D. Tendulkar (late), A. Vaidyanathan, Pravin Visaria (late) and V.S. Vyas, from whose writings I have been able to draw for the benefit of students.

I am equally grateful to my colleagues teaching in various colleges for making useful suggestions from time-to-time.

I hope this thoroughly revised book on Indian economy will prove handy and useful to students and teachers. I would always welcome any comments and suggestions for further improvement.

September 2013 — *Uma Kapila*

Section - I

Basic Issues in Economic Development

Section - II

Basic Features of
Indian Economy at Independence

Section - III

Policy Regimes

Section - IV

Growth, Development and
Structural Change

1

Economic Development and Under Development

Introduction

The world today presents a picture of sharp contrasts between developed/advanced and backward/underdeveloped/developing countries. At one extreme, there are countries like USA with per capita GNI of $ 46730 (2009) and on the other extreme are countries like Liberia with per capita GNI of $ 290.[1]

According to *World Development Report* (2011), around 16.5 per cent of world population lives in countries which are classified as high income developed countries (like USA, Canada, Australia, countries of Western Europe, New Zealand and some of the Asian countries such as Japan, Singapore, Hong Kong), 83.5 per cent of the population lives in countries which are in the category of low income and middle income developing economies.

The Growth Report 2008[2] states that growth has accelerated in the global economy and in an even wider set of developing countries. Further, the Report projects that the world population is projected to increase by 3 billion people by 2050. Unfortunately, 2 billion of this extra population will live in countries that are currently enjoying little or no growth. Thus, if these trends persist, the proportion of the world population living in low-growth environments might increase.

---

1. The World Bank (2011). *World Development Report.*
2. Commission on Growth and Development (2008). *The Growth Report, Strategies for Sustained Growth and Inclusive Development.*

What Does Development Mean

The term *development* may mean different things to different people. In strictly economic terms, development has traditionally meant a sustained annual increase in GNP (or GDP) at rates varying from 5 per cent to 7 per cent or more.[3]

A common alternative economic index of development has been the rates of growth of per capita GNP i.e., the ability of a nation to expand its output at a rate faster than the growth of population. Thus, per capita GNP is equal to GNP divided by population. However, it is the real per capita GNP which measures the overall economic well-being of a population i.e., monetary growth of GNP per capita minus the rate of inflation. If the rate of growth of GNP per capita is, let us say, 4 per cent and the rate of inflation is say 5 or 6 per cent, there cannot be any improvement in the economic well-being of a population.

Economic Growth and Economic Development

Till the 1960s, the term 'economic development' was often used as a synonym of economic growth, the measure for the latter being the rise in per capita GNP in real terms. According to Kindleberger,[4] "Whereas economic growth merely refers to a rise in output, economic development implies changes in technological and institutional organisation of production as well as distributive pattern of income." *Thus, economic development is a broader concept than economic growth.* Compared to the objective of development, economic growth may be easy to realise. By larger mobilisation of resources and raising their productivity, output levels can be raised. The process of development is far more extensive. Apart from the rise in output, it involves changes in the composition of output as well as a shift in the allocation of productive resources to ensure social justice.

In some of the underdeveloped countries, the process of economic growth has been accompanied by economic development. But this may not be the case always. *While there can be growth without development, development without growth is unconceivable.* A substantial rise in a country's GNP is required before it can hope to expand its industries and the services sectors. Nowhere in the world has the occupational distribution of population changed in the absence of growth.

---

3. Todaro, Michael (2004). *Economic Development in the Third World* (8th edition), ch.1. Delhi: Pearson Education (Singapore) Pvt. Ltd.
4. Kindleberger, C.P. (1965). *Economic Development* (2nd edition) ch. 1.

The New View of Economic Development

During the 1950s and 1960s while many of the Third World nations did realise the economic growth targets, the respective levels of living of the masses remained unchanged. This resulted in the rejection of the narrow definition of economic development by an increasing number of economists who now clamoured for the "dethronement of GNP" and advocated direct attack on widespread absolute poverty, increasingly inequitable income distribution and rising unemployment. Thus, in the 1970s economic development came to be redefined within the context of a growing economy. "Redistribution from growth" became a common slogan. In this context Kindleberger argued that, "economic development is generally defined to include improvements in material welfare, especially for persons with the lowest incomes, the eradication of mass poverty with its corelates of illiteracy, diseases and early death, changes in the composition of inputs and outputs that generally include shifts in the underlying structure of production away from agricultural growth towards industrial activities, the organisation of the economy in such a way that productive employment is general among the working age population rather than the situation of a privileged minority and the correspondingly greater participation of broadly based groups in making decisions about the directions, economic and otherwise, in which they should move to improve their welfare."[5]

Dudley Seers[6] posed three basic questions about the meaning of development:

What has been happening to poverty ?

What has been happening to unemployment ?

What has been happening to inequality ?

If all three of these have declined from high levels, then beyond doubt this has been a period of development for the country concerned. If one or two of these central problems have been growing worse, especially if all three have, it would be strange to call the result 'development' even if per capita income doubled.[7]

This assertion was a hard reality for a number of developing countries which experienced relatively high rates of growth of per

5. Ibid.
6. Seers, Dudley (1969). "The Meaning of Development", paper presented at the Eleventh World Conference of the Society for International Development, New Delhi.
7. Todaro (2004). *op.cit.*

capita income during the 1960s and 1970s but showed little or no improvement or even an actual decline in employment, equality and the real income of the bottom 40 per cent of their population. By the earlier definition of 'growth', these countries were developing but by the new criteria of poverty, equality and employment, they were not. The situation in the 1980s worsened further as GNP growth rates turned negative for many less developed countries and the governments, faced with mounting foreign debt problems, were forced to cut back on their already limited social and economic programmes.

While during the 1980s, the World Bank championed "economic growth" as the goal of development, its *World Development Report of 1991* asserted that "the challenge of development ... is to improve the quality of life. For the world's poor countries, a better quality of life generally calls for higher income ... and it involves much more. It encompasses, as ends in themselves, better education, higher standards of health and nutrition, less poverty, a cleaner environment, more equality of opportunity, greater individual freedom, and a richer cultural life."

Development as a Multi-dimensional Process

According to Todaro, "Development must, therefore, be conceived of as a multi-dimensional process involving major changes in social structures, popular attitudes and national institutions, as well as the acceleration of economic growth, the reduction of inequality and the eradication of absolute poverty." According to Goulet,[8] at least three basic components as core values should serve as a conceptual basis and practical guidelines for understanding the "inner" meaning of development. These core values—sustenance, self-esteem and freedom—represent common goals sought by all individuals and societies. They relate to fundamental human needs that find their expression in almost all societies and cultures at all times.

Three Core Values of Development

Sustenance: The life-sustaining basic human needs include food, shelter, health and protection. When any one of these is absent or in critically short supply, a condition of absolute "underdevelopment" exists.

Self-esteem: A second universal component of good life is self-esteem—a sense of worth and self-respect—of not being used as a tool

8. Goulet, Denis (1971). *The Cruel Choice: A New Concept in the Theory of Development.* New York: Atheneum. pp.87-94.

by others for their own ends. Due to the significance attached to material values in developed nations, worthiness and esteem are now-a-days increasingly conferred only on countries that possess economic wealth and technological power—those that have developed.

Now-a-days the Third World seeks development in order to gain the esteem which is denied to societies living in a state of disgraceful 'underdevelopment'. Development is legitimised as a goal because it is an important, perhaps even an indispensable, way of gaining esteem.[9]

Freedom from Servitude—To be Able to Choose: Arthur Lewis[10] stressed the relationship between economic growth and freedom from servitude when he concluded that "the advantage of economic growth is not that wealth increases happiness, but that it increases the range of human choice." Wealth can enable a person to gain greater control over nature and his physical environment than they would have if they remained poor. It also gives them the freedom to choose greater leisure. The concept of human freedom should encompass various components of political freedom, freedom of expression, political participation and equality of opportunity.

Development, Freedom and Opportunities

According to Drèze and Sen, "In recent years, development economics has been also taking a much more inclusive view of the nature of economic development. One way of seeing development is in terms of the expansion of the real freedoms that the citizens enjoy to pursue the objectives they have reason to value, and in this sense the expansion of human capability can be, broadly, seen as the central feature of the process of development."[11]

The basic objective of development as the expansion of human capabilities was never completely overlooked in the modern development literature, but the focus has been mainly on the generation of economic growth, in the sense of expanding gross national product and related variables.[12] The expansion of human capabilities can clearly

---

9. Goulet Ibid.
10. Lewis, Arthur W. (1963). "Is Economic Growth Desirable?" in Allen and Unwin (eds.), *Theory of Economic Growth*. London. p.420.
11. Drèze, Jean and Amartya Sen (2005). *India Development and Participation*, ch.2. Delhi: Oxford University Press.
12. Arthur Lewis one of the pioneers of development economics, emphasised that the appropriate objective of development is increasing 'the range of human choice', but nevertheless he decided to concentrate specially on 'the growth of output per head', since that 'gives man greater control over his environment and thereby increases his freedom' (Lewis, 1955: pp.9-10, 420-1).

be enhanced by economic growth (even in the limited sense of growth of real income per head), but: (1) there are many influences other than economic growth that work in that direction, and (2) the impact of economic growth on human capabilities can be extremely variable, depending on the nature of that growth (for example, how equitable and employment-intensive it is, and whether the economic gains from growth are used to address the deprivations of the most needy).

The Three Objectives of Development

According to Todaro development is both a physical reality and a state of mind in which society has, through some combination of social, economic, and institutional processes, secured the means for obtaining a better life. Whatever the specific components of this better life, development in all societies must have at least the following three objectives:

1. To increase the availability and widen the distribution of basic life-sustaining goods such as food, shelter, health, and protection.
2. To raise levels of living, including, in addition to higher incomes, the provision of more jobs, better education, and greater attention to cultural and human values, all of which will serve not only to enhance material well-being but also to generate greater individual and national self-esteem.
3. To expand the range of economic and social choices available to individuals and nations by freeing them from servitude and dependence not only in relation to other people and nation-states but also to the forces of ignorance and human misery.

The Millennium Development Goals

In September 2000, the 189 member countries of the United Nations at that time adopted eight Millennium Development Goals (MDGs), committing themselves to making substantial progress toward the eradication of poverty and achieving other human development goals by 2015.

The MDGs were developed in consultation with the developing countries, to ensure that they addressed their most pressing problems. In addition, key international agencies, including the United Nations, the World Bank, the International Monetary Fund (IMF), the

Organisation for Economic Cooperation and Development (OECD), and the World Trade Organisation (WTO) all helped develop the Millennium Declaration and so have a collective policy commitment to attacking poverty directly. The MDGs assign specific responsibilities to rich countries, including increased aid, removal of trade and investment barriers, and eliminating unsustainable debts of the poorest nations.

TABLE – 1.1

Millennium Development Goals and Targets for 2015

Goals	*Targets*
1. Eradicate extreme poverty and hunger	• Reduce by half the proportion of people living on less than $1 a day • Reduce by half the proportion of people who suffer from hunger
2. Achieve universal primary education	• Ensure that all boys and girls complete a full course of primary schooling
3. Promote gender equality and empower women	• Eliminate gender disparity in primary and secondary education, preferably by 2005, and at all levels by 2015
4. Reduce child mortality	• Reduce by two-thirds the mortality rate among children under 5
5. Improve maternal health	• Reduce by three-quarters the maternal mortality ratio
6. Combat HIV/AIDS, malaria, and other diseases	• Halt and begin to reverse the spread of HIV/AIDS • Halt and begin to reverse the incidence of malaria and other major diseases
7. Ensure environmental sustainability	• Integrate the principles of sustainable development into country policies and programs; reverse loss of environmental resources • Reduce by half the proportion of people without sustainable access to safe drinking water • Achieve significant improvement in lives of at least 100 million slum dwellers by 2020

contd...

...contd...

8. Develop a global partnership for development	• Develop further an open, rule-based, predictable, nondiscriminatory trading and financial system; includes a commitment to good governance, development, and poverty reduction—both nationally and internationally • Address the special needs of the least developed countries; includes tariff and quota free access for least developed countries' exports; enhanced program of debt relief for heavily indebted poor countries (HIPCs) and cancellation of official bilateral debt; and more generous official development assistance (ODA) for countries committed to poverty reduction • Address the special needs of landlocked countries and small island developing states • Deal comprehensively with the debt problems of developing countries through national and international measures in order to make debt sustainable in the long term • In cooperation with developing countries, develop and implement strategies for decent and productive work for youth • In cooperation with pharmaceutical companies, provide access to affordable essential drugs in developing countries • In cooperation with the private sector, make available the benefits of new technologies, especially information and communications

Source: United Nations Development Program, "Millennium Development Goals," *http://www.undp.org/mdg/goallist.shtml*, Aug. 16, 2007.

Developed and Underdeveloped Countries

Over 75 per cent of world population lives in the poor underdeveloped countries while just about 25 per cent people inhabit advanced and developed countries. The developed economies have high per capita income that gives their people high standards of living. The

USA, The UK, France, Germany, Japan, etc., are among the developed economies. These countries have well developed and diversified economic structure and high rates of saving and investment that make their growth process self-sustained.

The underdeveloped countries on the other hand have low levels of per capita income and low living standard of their masses. The underdeveloped countries today are also known as developing economies because they are capable of and indeed making efforts towards economic progress through better utilisation of their actual and potential resources. The underdeveloped countries are also known as the Third World countries.

Defining the Developing World

The most common way to define the developing world is by per capita income. Several international agencies, including the Organisation for Economic Cooperation and Development (OECD) and the United Nations, offer classifications of countries by their economic status, but the best-known system is that of the International Bank for Reconstruction and Development (IBRD), more commonly known as the World Bank. In the World Bank's classification system, 208 economies with a population of at least 30,000 are ranked by their levels of gross national income (GNI) per capita. These economies are then classified as low-income countries (LICs), lower-middle-income countries (LMCs), upper-middle-income countries (UMCs), high-income OECD countries, and other high-income countries.

Generally speaking, the developing countries are those with low-, lower- middle, or upper-middle incomes.

Sometimes a special distinction is made among upper-middle-income or newly high-income economies, designating some that have achieved relatively advanced manufacturing sectors as newly industrialising countries (NICs). Finally, the United Nations Development Program (UNDP) classifies countries according to their level of human development, including health and education attainments.

The World Bank in its *World Development Report 2009*[13] classified the various countries on the basis of per capita gross national income (GNI).

13. *World Development Report*, 2009.

(i) Low income countries with GNI per capita $ 578 or less (PPP GNI per capita $ 1,494 or less).

(ii) Middle income with per capita GNI $ 2872 (PPP GNI per capita $ 5952). Within middle income, there are lower middle income and upper middle income countries.

Lower-middle income countries with per capita GNI $ 1,887 (PPP per capita $ 4,543).

Upper middle income countries with GNI per capita $ 6,987 (PPP per capita $ 11,868).

(iii) High income countries with per capita GNI of $ 37,566 or more (PPP per capita $ 36,100 or more).

According to data given in the *World Development Report 2009*, in 2007, low income countries accounted for about 19.6 per cent of the world population but contributed only 2.9 per cent to total world PPP GNI. The middle income countries constituted 64.4 per cent of world population but accounted for about 39 per cent of world PPP GNI. These two groups, popularly described as developing economies or underdeveloped economies, comprise 84 per cent of the world population but account for about 42 per cent of world PPP GNI. Most countries of Asia, Africa, Latin America and some countries of Europe are included in them.

The high income economies, comprising about 16 per cent of world population, contribute around 55 per cent to world PPP GNI.

TABLE – 1.2

Distribution of World Population and World GNI among Various Groups of Countries (2007)

	Population 2010 Million	*GNI 2010 (Billion $) PPP*	*GNI 2007 (per capita) $ PPP*	*Average Annual Growth of Population (2000-2007)*
World	6855	75803	11058	1.2
Low Income Countries	817	1018	1246	2.2
Middle Income Countries	4915	33326	6780	1.2
Low and Middle Income Combined	5732	34344	5991	1.3
High Income Countries	1123	41756	37183	0.7
India	**1171**	**4171**	**3560**	**1.4**

Source: World Development Report, 2012.

One may make the following observation with regard to this UN classifications of developed and underdeveloped/developing countries on the basis of per capita income. There is gross inequality of income between the rich and the poor countries and this gap is widening over the years. All high income countries are not necessarily developed countries as Joan Robinson remarked, "For several of the Arab States, GNP per capita suddenly jumped to levels which exceeded that of the richest western states yet in these countries are found some of the poorest and least developed communities in the world."

According to Todaro (2013) the simple division of the world into developed and developing countries is often useful for analytical and policy purposes. However, the wide income range of the latter serves as an early warning for us not to overgeneralise. Indeed, the economic differences between low-income countries in sub-Saharan Africa and South Asia and between upper-middle-income countries in East Asia and Latin America can be every bit as profound as those between high-income OECD and upper-middle-income developing countries.

As modern development economics defined development as a process involving elimination of poverty, income inequality and unemployment, underdevelopment in this framework would be a situation characterised by the worst kind of deprivation.

Michael Todaro while defining underdevelopment in terms of poverty, states that, "Underdevelopment is a real fact of life for over three billion people in the world."[14]

A different approach to underdevelopment is provided by Jacob Viner. According to Viner, development potential of a country is a much better criterion to judge the extent of its underdevelopment. He defined an underdeveloped country as the one "which has good potential for using more capital or more labour or more available natural resources or all of these, to support its population on a higher level of living." The definition of an underdeveloped country given by the Indian Planning Commission in its Five Year Plan is similar to the one given by Jacob Viner. "An underdeveloped country's economy is characterised by the existence, in greater or lesser degree, of unutilised or underutilised manpower on the one hand and of unexploited natural resources on the other. This state of affairs may be due to stagnancy of techniques or to certain inhibiting socio-economic factors which

---

14. Todaro, P. Michael (2013). *Economic Development*, Tenth edition. New Delhi: Pearson.

prevent the more dynamic forces in an economy from asserting themselves."[15]

Characteristics of the Developing World: Diversity within Commonality

The underdeveloped countries, also known as developing countries or Third World Countries, have some common characteristics. Todaro classifies these common characteristics into Ten broad categories.[16]

There are important historical and economic commonalities among developing countries that have led to their economic development problems being studied within a common analytical framework in development economics. At the same time, however, there is a great deal of diversity across the developing world, even within these areas of broad commonality. Different development problems call for different specific policy responses and general development strategies.

1. Lower Levels of Living and Productivity

In developing nations, general levels of living tend to be low for the vast majority of people. These low levels of living are manifested in the form of low incomes (poverty), inadequate housing, poor health, limited or low education, high infant mortality and low life expectancy.

The GNP per capita is often used as a summary index of the relative economic well-being of people in different nations. On account of low per capita income, population suffers from poor health, low education, high infant mortality and low life expectancy.

Indeed, some star performers among now nearly developed economies such as South Korea and Taiwan were once among the poorest in the world. Some middle-income countries are also relatively stagnant, but others are growing rapidly—China most spectacularly. Indeed, income growth rates have varied greatly in different developing regions and countries, with rapid growth in East Asia, stagnant growth in sub-Saharan Africa, and intermediate levels of growth in other regions.

The lower average levels but wide ranges of income in developing areas are seen in Table 1.3. Even when adjusted for purchasing power parity, and after the impressive recent growth in China and India, the low- and middle-income developing nations, with more than five-sixths

---

15. Government of India, Planning Commission (1952). The First Five Year Plan, Ch. 1, p. 7, New Delhi.
16. Todaro (2013), *op cit.*

(84%) of the world's people, received less than half (46%) of the world's income in 2005, as seen in Figure 1.1.

FIGURE – 1.1

Shares of Global Income, 2005

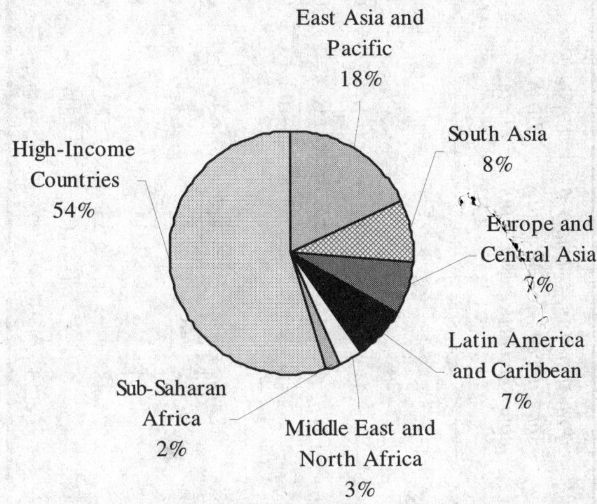

Source: World Bank, World Development Indicators, 2007 (Washington, D.C.: World Bank, 2007), p.17.

At very low income levels, in fact, a vicious cycle may set in, whereby low income leads to low investment in education and health as well as plant and equipment and infrastructure, which in turn leads to low productivity and economic stagnation. This is the well-known vicious cycle referred to variously as the poverty trap or by Nobel laureate Gunnar Mydral as "circular and cumulative causation."

In India, at the time of Independence, the life expectancy at birth was 32 and literacy was only 18 per cent. Poverty ratio i.e., percentage of population below poverty line was above 50 per cent. As a result of planned economic development during the last six decades, expectation of life has improved to 66.1 years in 2010-11 while the average for middle income countries is 67. Literacy rate has improved to 74.04 per cent against the average of 90 in middle income countries and 61 in low income countries. Poverty ratio has also declined considerably from more than 50 per cent to under 20 per cent but the total number of poor is still very high—220 million (10th Plan). Inspite of significant improvement in various human development indicators, India's rank is still low in several of these indicators.

TABLE – 1.3

Commonality and Diversity: Some Basic Indicators

Country or Group	*2005 Income Per Capita (U.S. $)*	*2005 PPP (U.S. $)*	*Life Expectancy (Years)*	*Prevalence of Under-nourishment (%)*	*Under 5 Mortality per 1,000 Live Births*	*Crude Birth Rate*	*Adult Literacy*	
							Male	*Female*
Income Group								
Low	585	2,486	59	24	114	29	71	50
Lower middle	1,923	6,314	70	11	39	16	93	85
Upper middle	5,634	10,931	71	4	27	16	96	93
High	35,264	32,550	79	3	7	10	99	98
Country								
Dem. Rep. Congo (LIC)	120	720	44	74	205	50	81	54
India (LIC)	730	3,460	64	20	74	24	73	48
Egypt (LMC)	1,260	4,440	71	4	33	26	83	59
Brazil (LMC)	3,550	8,230	71	7	33	20	88	89
Malaysia (UMC)	4,970	10,320	74	3	12	21	92	85
United States (high-income)	43,560	41,950	78	<2.5	7	14	99[a]	99[a]

Note: a UNDP estimates.

Source: Data from World Bank, *World Development Indicators, 2007* (Washington, D.C.: World Bank, 2007), various tables.

Throughout the developing world, levels of labour productivity are extremely low compared with those in developed countries. Low level of living and low productivity are self-reinforcing social and economic phenomenon in Third World countries and as such, are the principal manifestation of, and contributors to, their development. Myrdal's well known theory of "circular and cumulative causation" in underdeveloped countries is based on the interaction between low living levels and low productivity.

Low productivity is due to low level of technology. The sharp differences in productivity between developed and underdeveloped nations can be traced to the level of technology in these countries. Productivity level in Indian economy has been low on account of backward or poor technology and this applies to all sectors of the economy—whether it is agriculture, industry or the tertiary sector.

A comparison of productivity levels in Indian agriculture with the levels in other countries shows how low the productivity in Indian agriculture is. Productivity of wheat in India is about 35 per cent of the productivity in France. It is 66 per cent (i.e., less than two-thirds) of the productivity in comparison to another developing country, China. As far as rice is concerned, productivity in India is 46 per cent of the productivity in China and Japan (i.e., less than half). The productivity of cotton in India is one-third of the productivity in China. Even in comparison to Pakistan, productivity of cotton in India is just 61 per cent. As far as groundnut is concerned, productivity in India is 34 per cent of the productivity in USA, 40 per cent of the productivity in China and 51 per cent of the productivity in Argentina. Similar conclusions hold for most of the other crops.[17] The low levels of productivity in Indian agriculture point to the possibilities of increasing productivity by adopting appropriate strategies and policies.

International comparisons reveal a wide gulf in India's performance between achievements in output and productivity. While India compares favourably in terms of total output, it compares poorly in terms of yield per hectare.

Since, about three-fourths of world population lives in underdeveloped countries which have less than one-fifth share in world income, it is obvious that a vast majority of people in these countries must be living under conditions of poverty, malnutrition, disease, squalor, illiteracy, etc. Even basic necessities of subsistence such as

17. Tata Services Ltd., *Statistical Outline of India*, 1998-99.

minimum food, clothing and shelter are not easily accessible to the poor masses. The reasons for this mass poverty and low living standards in these countries are to be found in their stagnating or slow growing economies and rapidly growing population.

2. Lower Levels of Human Capital

Human capital—health, education, and skills—is vital to economic growth and human development. Compared with developed countries, much of the developing world has lagged in its average levels of nutrition, health (as measured by life expectancy), and education (measured by literacy), as seen in Table 1.3. The under-5 mortality is still 15 times higher in low-income countries than in high-income countries.

The well-performing developing countries are much closer to the developed world in health and education standards than they are to the lowest-income countries. While health conditions in East Asia are relatively good, sub-Saharan Africa continues to be plagued by problems of malnourishment, malaria, TB, AIDS, and parasitic infections. Despite progress, South Asia continues to have high levels of illiteracy, low schooling attainment, and undernourishment. Still, in fields such as primary school completion, low-income countries are also making great progress; for example, enrollments in India are up from 68 per cent in the early 1990s to 89 per cent by 2005. Some development economists contend that a country's level and distribution of education is the most fundamental determinant of future development prospects.

3. High Rate of Population Growth and Dependency Burden

Population dynamics is another area of wide variation among developing countries. Populations of some developing countries, particularly in Africa, continue to grow rapidly. From 1990 to 2005, population in the low-income countries grew at 2 per cent per year, compared to 1.1 per cent in the middle-income countries (the high-income countries grew at 0.7 per cent per year, reflecting both births and immigration).

Middle-income developing countries show greater variance, with some having achieved lower birth rates closer to those prevailing in rich countries. As seen in Table 1.3, the birth rate is almost three times higher in the low-incoming countries than in the high-income countries.

Developing countries also have higher death rates in each age bracket. However, given their youthful populations, overall death rates are now lower in developing countries (8 per 1,000 population) than in the developed countries (10 per 1,000). As of 2005, the average rate of population growth was about 1.5 per cent in the developing countries (1.8 per cent excluding China).

A major implication of high LDC birth rates is that children under age 15 make up almost 32 per cent of the total population in these countries (35 per cent excluding China) as opposed to 17 per cent of the total population in the developed countries. Thus in most developing countries, the active labour force has to support proportionally almost twice as many children as it does in richer countries. By contrast, the proportion of people over the age of 65 is much greater in the developed nations. Both older people and children are often referred to as an economic dependency burden in the sense that they are nonproductive members of society and therefore must be supported financially by the country's labour force (usually defined as citizens between the ages of 15 and 64). The overall dependency burden (i.e., both young and old) represents only about one-third of the populations of developed countries but almost 40 per cent of the populations of the less developed nations. Moreover, in the latter countries, almost 85 per cent of the dependents are children, whereas only 53 per cent are children in the richer nations.

Fast growing population in the Third World is both a cause and effect of underdevelopment. These countries have effectively brought down the mortality rates but birth rates continue to be high due to wide spread poverty, ignorance and social and religious factors. Due to high birth rate, the dependency burden is about half of the population as against one-fourth in developed countries. The active labour force has to support almost twice as many children as it does in richer countries. Population has been growing in Third World countries in the range of 2 to 3.5 per cent per annum as compared to less than 1 per cent in developed countries. In India, for instance, the rate of growth of population increased from 1.25 per cent per annum in 1951 to 2.5 per cent in 1981. It started declining only thereafter and 1991 census recorded a growth rate of 2 per cent with children under the age 15 forming 38 per cent of the total population. Average annual growth rate during 2000-2007 has been estimated at 1.4 per cent as compared to 0.7 per cent for high income countries, 1.0 per cent for middle income and 2.2 per cent for low income countries (*WDR, 2009*).

We may conclude, therefore, that not only are developing countries characterised by higher rates of population growth, but they must also contend with greater dependency burdens than rich nations.

4. Higher Levels of Inequality and Absolute Poverty

The magnitude and extent of poverty in any country depend on two factors: the average level of national income and the degree of inequality in its distribution. Clearly, for any given level of national per capita income, the more unequal the distribution, the greater the incidence of poverty. Similarly, for any given distribution, the lower the average income level, the greater the incidence of poverty.

Development economists use the concept of absolute poverty to represent a specific minimum level of income needed to satisfy the basic physical needs of food, clothing, and shelter in order to ensure continued survival. A problem, however, arises when one recognises that these minimum subsistence levels will vary from country to country and region to region, reflecting different physiological as well as social and economic requirements. Economists have therefore tended to make conservative estimates of world poverty in order to avoid unintended exaggeration of the problem.

The incidence of extreme poverty varies widely around the developing world. The World Bank estimates that the share of the population living on less than $1 per day is 9.1 per cent in East Asia and the Pacific, 8.6 per cent in Latin America and the Caribbean, 1.5 per cent in the Middle East and North Africa, 31.7 per cent in South Asia, and 41.1 per cent in sub-Saharan Africa. The share of world population living in extreme poverty has fallen encouragingly to an estimated 15 per cent by 2006. As a result, the global incidence of extreme poverty has been increasingly centered in South Asia and sub-Saharan Africa.

Development economists have increasingly focused on ways in which poverty and inequality can lead to slower growth. That is, not only do poverty and inequality result from distorted growth, but they can also be a cause of it.

5. Greater Social Fractionalisation

Low-income countries more often have ethnic, linguistic, and other forms of social divisions, sometimes known as fractionalisation. This is sometimes associated with civil strife and even violent conflict, which can lead developing societies to divert considerable energies to working for political accommodations if not national consolidation. It is one of a variety of governance challenges many developing nations face.

Today, more than 40 per cent of the world's nations have more than five significant ethnic populations. In most cases, one or more of these groups face serious problems of discrimination. Over half of the world's LDCs have recently experienced some form of interethnic conflict. Just in the 1990s, ethnic and religious conflicts leading to widespread death and destruction took place in Afghanistan, Rwanda, Mozambique, Sri Lanka, Iraq, India, Somalia, Ethiopia, Liberia, Angola, Myanmar, Sudan, Yugoslavia, Haiti, Indonesia, and the Democratic Republic of Congo.

Ethnic and religious diversity need not necessarily lead to inequality, turmoil, or instability, and unqualified statements about its impact cannot be made. There have been numerous instances of successful economic and social integration of minority or indigenous ethnic populations in countries as diverse as Malaysia and Mauritius. And in the United States, diversity is often cited as source of creativity and innovation. The broader point is that the ethnic and religious composition of a developing nation and whether or not that diversity leads to conflict or cooperation can be important determinants of the success or failure of development efforts.

6. *Larger Rural Populations but Rapid Rural-to-Urban Migration*

One of the hallmarks of economic development is a shift from agriculture to manufacturing and services. In developing countries, a much higher share of the population lives in rural areas. Although modernising in many regions, rural areas are poorer and tend to suffer from missing markets, limited information, and social stratification. A massive population shift is also under way as hundreds of millions of people are moving from rural to urban areas, fueling rapid urbanisation, with its own attendant problems.

7. *Substantial Dependence on Agricultural Production and Lower Levels of Industrialisation and Manufactured Exports*

The vast majority of people in Third World nations live and work in rural area. Almost 80 per cent are rurally based compared with less than 35 per cent in economically developed countries. The proportion of labour force engaged in agriculture in less developed countries is 66 per cent compared with 21 per cent for developed nations. Moreover, agriculture contributes about 32 per cent to the GNP of the former while it accounts for only 8 per cent of GNP of the latter.

The basic reason for the concentration of people and production in agricultural and other primary production activities in developing countries is the simple fact that for the low income levels, the first priority is for food, clothing and shelter. Agricultural productivity is low not only because of the large number of people in relation to available land but also because in *lower development countries* agriculture is often characterised by primitive technologies, poor organisation and limited physical and human capital inputs.

In India, the predominance of the primary sector is reflected in the contribution of this sector to GDP and employment in the economy. In 1951, the contribution of primary sector to India's GDP was 57 per cent and to employment 73 per cent. Even today, primary sector provides employment to about 60 per cent of the workforce and its contribution to GDP is around 15 per cent as compared with 3 per cent of workforce engaged in primary sector in the UK and 4 per cent in USA contributing about 2 per cent to their GDP. Indian economy has moved from underdevelopment to a developing economy.

One of the most widely used terminologies for the Group of Seven (G-7) countries and other advanced economies such as smaller European countries and Australia is the "industrial countries." Industrialisation is associated with high productivity and incomes and has been a hallmark of modernisation and national economic power. It is no accident that most developing-country governments have made industrialisation a high national priority.

Along with lower industrialisation, developing nations have tended to have a higher dependence on primary exports. Most developing countries have diversified away from agricultural and mineral exports to some degree. The middle-income countries are rapidly catching up with the developed world in the share of manufactured goods in their exports, even if these goods are typically much less advanced in their skill and technology content. However, the low-income countries, particularly those in Africa, remain highly dependent on a relatively small number of agricultural and mineral exports.

8. Underdeveloped Financial and Other Markets

There is a greater prevalence of imperfect markets and incomplete information in developing countries, so that domestic markets, particularly financial markets, have worked less efficiently.

In many LDCs, legal and institutional foundations are either absent or extremely weak. LDCs often lack a legal system that enforces contracts and validates property rights; a stable and trustworthy currency; an infrastructure of roads and utilities that results in low transport and communication costs so as to facilitate interregional trade; a well-developed system of banking and insurance; formal credit markets that select projects and allocate loanable funds on the basis of relative economic profitability and enforce rules of repayment; substantial market information for consumers and producers about prices, quantities, and qualities of products and resources as well as the creditworthiness of potential borrowers; and norms of behaviour that facilitate successful long-term business relationships.

9. Lingering Colonial Impacts

Most developing countries were once colonies of Europe or otherwise dominated by European powers, and institutions created during the colonial period often had adverse effects on development that in many cases have persisted to the present day. Both domestically and internationally, developing countries have more often lacked institutions and formal organisations of the type that have benefited the developed world: Domestically, on average, property rights have been less secure and a smaller segment of society has been able to gain access to and take advantage of economic opportunities.

Decolonization was one of the most important historical and geopolitical events of the post-World War II era. More than 80 former European colonies have joined the United Nations. But the effects of the colonial era linger for many developing nations, particularly the least developed ones.

10. External Dependence

Developing countries have also been less well organised and influential in international relations, with sometimes adverse consequences for development. For example, agreements within the World Trade Organisation (WTO) and its predecessors concerning matters such as agricultural subsidies in rich countries that harm developing-country farmers and one-sided regulation of intellectual property rights have often been relatively unfavourable to the developing world. More generally, developing nations have weaker bargaining positions than developed nations in international economic relations. Developing nations often also voice great concern over various forms of cultural dependence, from news and entertainment to business practices, lifestyles, and social values. The potential importance of these concerns should not be underestimated, either in their directs effects on development in its broader meanings, or indirect impacts on the speed or character of national development.

In contrast, China and India, with over 40 per cent of the developing world's population and recently enjoying high average income growth and expanding international corporate presence, are gaining considerable autonomy in many respects.

Developing nations are also dependent on the developed world for environmental preservation, on which hopes for sustainable development depend. Of greatest concern, although global warming is projected to harm developing regions more than developed ones, both accumulated and even current greenhouse gas emissions still predominately originate from the high-income countries. Thus the developing world endures what may be called environmental dependence, in which it must rely on the developed world to cease aggravating the problem and to develop solutions.

The net effect of all these factors is to create a situation of 'vulnerability' among Third World nations in which forces largely outside their control can have decisive and dominating influences on their overall economic and social well-being.

According to Michael Todaro, the phenomenon of under-development needs to be viewed in a national and an international context. Economic and social forces, both internal and external, are responsible for the poverty, inequality and low productivity that commonly characterise most Third World nations.[18] The successful pursuit of economic and social development will require not only the formulation of appropriate strategies within the Third World but also a modification of the present international economic order to make it more responsive to the development needs of poor nations.

18. "The 157 developing African, Asian, and Latin American member countries of the United Nations often collectively refer to themselves as the Third World. They do this primarily to distinguish themselves from the economically advanced capitalist (First World) and the formerly socialist (Second World) countries of eastern Europe and the Soviet Union—some of which could now justifiably be considered part of the Third World. It is unfortunate that the terms first, second, and third may sometimes be taken to connote superiority or inferiority when in fact they merely reflect the historical sequence of industrialisation" Todaro (2013).

Nature of Indian Economy

Indian economy is in transition from underdeveloped to a developing economy since 1951 when India embarked on a programme of planned economic development of the country.

Indian economy certainly had all the characteristics of an underdeveloped economy at the time of Independence but the planned economic development during the last six decades has definitely brought Indian economy in the category of developing economies, coming closer to middle income category countries. Indeed, in terms of growth, India performed much better than the industrialised countries which experienced a slowdown in growth, the transition economies which did badly, and much of the developing world. And it was only east Asia, particularly China, which performed better.

India has been widely heralded as a success story for globalisation. Over the past two decades, the country has moved into the premier league of world economic growth; high-technology exports are booming and India's emerging middle-class consumers have become a magnet for foreign investors.

Why has accelerated income growth not moved India onto a faster poverty reduction path? Extreme poverty is concentrated in rural areas of the northern poverty-belt states, including Bihar, Madhya Pradesh, Uttar Pradesh and West Bengal, while income growth has been most dynamic in other states, urban areas and the service sectors. While rural poverty has fallen rapidly in some states, such as Gujarat and Tamil Nadu, less progress has been achieved in the northern states.

The deeper problem facing India is its human development legacy. In particular, pervasive gender inequalities, rural poverty and inequalities between states, is undermining the potential for converting growth into human development.

Perhaps the starkest gender inequality is revealed by this simple fact: girls aged 1-5 are 50 per cent, more likely to die than boys. This fact translates into 130,000 'missing' girls. Female mortality rates remain higher than male mortality rates through age 30, reversing the typical demographic pattern. These gender differences reflect a widespread preference for sons, particularly in northern states. Girls, less valued than their brothers, are often brought to health facilities in more advanced stages of illness, taken to less qualified doctors and have less money spent on their health care. The low status and educational disadvantage suffered by women have a direct bearing on their health and their children's. About one-third of India's children are underweight at birth, reflecting poor maternal health.

Translating economic success into human development advances will require public policies aimed explicitly at broadening the distribution of benefits from growth and global integration, increased public investment in rural areas and services and—above all—political leadership to end poor governance and address the underlying causes of gender inequality.

With the objective of inclusive growth taking centre stage, the Government has strengthened its efforts for social sector development in recent years. Expenditures of the Government of India on social services and rural development have more than doubled over the last four years. Impressive outlays on education, health, water supply and housing indicate the emphasis which Government places on these sectors. These expenditures have supplemented sustained high level of economic growth in achieving better social sector performance and improvement in the quality of life. Several initiatives have been launched, especially for the poor. Programmes like the National Rural Employment Guarantee Scheme, Pradhan Mantri Gram Sadak Yojana, Aam Aadmi Bima Yojana and Rashtriya Swasthya Bima Yojana, can go a long way in improving the living conditions of the common man in the remotest part of the country. Proper implementation of these programmes is essential. Consequently, the role of states and district administrations responsible for the implementation of the welfare schemes is vital.

Along with higher economic growth and poverty reduction, there has been an improvement in many important social indicators like life expectancy, infant mortality rate and gross enrolment ratios at primary level of education. However, disparities continue at the state and regional level. The current Twelfth Five Year Plan also aims at reducing poverty and the disparities across regions and communities.

2

Human Development

Human Development

The first *Human Development Report* (HDR) published by the United Nations Development Programme (UNDP) focused on the new paradigm of development that puts people at the centre of development. The concept, developed by Mahbub ul Haq and Amartya Sen, is defined as 'the process of enlarging people's choices', emphasizing the freedom to be healthy, to be educated and to enjoy a decent standard of living. But it also stressed that human development and wellbeing went far beyond these dimensions to encompass a much broader range of capabilities, including political freedoms and human rights.[1] Economic growth is considered only a means of capability expansion and not as an end in itself.

Such a paradigm of development enables all individuals to enlarge their human capabilities to the full and to put these capabilities to their best use in all fields—economic, social, cultural and political. It also protects the options of the unborn generations. It does not run-down the natural resource base needed for sustaining development in the future.

Disadvantaged people are a central focus of human development. This includes people in the future who will suffer the most severe consequences of the risks arising from our activities today.[2]

Human Development Index

The Human Development Index (HDI), used in the HDRs to compare countries in the world, has been designed as an alternative to per capita income, the single most commonly used measure to evaluate

1. UNDP (2010). *Human Development Report 2010.* p.2.
2. UNDP (2011). "Overview", *Human Development Report 2011.* p.1.

development outcomes thus far. The index includes three important choices:

(i) Longevity measured by life expectancy at birth.

(ii) Educational attainment as measured by adult literacy rate and gross enrolment ratio GER (primary, secondary and tertiary level combined).

(iii) Adjusted real GDP per capita—PPP stands for purchasing power parity. PPP GDP is calculated after eliminating price differences among countries.

The HDI value indicates how far a country has gone to attain certain defined goals: an average life span of 85 years, access to education for all and a decent standard of living. The maximum and minimum values for each variable, which are fixed, are reduced to scale between 0 and 1.

Countries are classified into three groups:

(1) High human development countries—Countries with HDI values of 0.800 and above.

(2) Medium human development countries—Countries with HDI values of 0.500 to 0.799.

(3) Low human development countries—Countries with HDI values below 0.500.

Inherent in the human development tradition is that the approach be dynamic, not calcified.

Human development is an evolving idea—not a fixed, static set of precepts—and as the world changes, analytical tools and concepts evolve.

To quote HDR 2010, "Human development is the expansion of people's freedoms to live long, healthy and creative lives; to advance other goals they have reason to value; and to engage actively in shaping development equitably and sustainably on a shared planet. People are both the beneficiaries and the drivers of human development, as individuals and in groups."

The Report further adds, "Human development is not only about health, education and income—it is also about people's active engagement in shaping development, equity and sustainability, intrinsic aspects of the freedom people have to lead lives they have reason to value."

As documented in HDR 2013[2] "Over the past decades, countries across the world have been converging towards higher levels of human development, as shown by the Human Development Index (HDI), a composite measure of indicators along three dimensions: life expectancy, educational attainment and command over the resources needed for a decent living. All groups and regions have seen notable improvement in all HDI components, with faster progress in low and medium HDI countries. On this basis, the world is becoming less unequal. Nevertheless, national averages hide large variations in human experience. Wide disparities remain within countries of both the North and the South, and income inequality within and between many countries has been rising.

Further the HDR 2013 remarks, "Although most developing countries have done well, a large number of countries have done particularly well—in what can be called the "rise of the South". Some of the largest countries have made rapid advances, notably Brazil, China, India, Indonesia, South Africa and Turkey. But there has also been substantial progress in smaller economies, such as Bangladesh, Chile, Ghana, Mauritius, Rwanda and Tunisia.

The South has risen at an unprecedented speed and scale. For example, the current economic takeoffs in China and India began with about 1 billion people in each country and doubled output per capita in less than 20 years—an economic force affecting a much larger population than the Industrial Revolution did. By 2050, Brazil, China and India combined are projected to account for 40 per cent of world output in purchasing power parity terms.

During these uncertain times, countries of the South are collectively bolstering world economic growth, lifting other developing economies, reducing poverty and increasing wealth on a grand scale. They still face formidable challenges and are home to many of the world's poor. But they have demonstrated how pragmatic policies and a strong focus on human development can release the opportunities latent in their economies, facilitated by globalisation.

A Changing World, A More Global South

According to the Report, "The world is getting more connected, not less. Recent years have seen a remarkable reorientation of global production, with much more destined for international trade, which, by 2011, accounted for nearly 60 per cent of global output. Developing

2. UNDP (2013). *Human Development Report 2013*.

countries have played a big part: between 1980 and 2010, they increased their share of world merchandise trade from 25 per cent to 47 per cent and their share of world output from 33 per cent to 45 per cent. Developing regions have also been strengthening links with each other: between 1980 and 2011, South–South trade increased from less than 8 per cent of world merchandise trade to more than 26 per cent".

HDR 2010[3] documented substantial progress over the past four decades. The Human Development Index (HDI) has risen dramatically since 1970—41 per cent overall and 61 per cent in low HDI countries—reflecting strong advances in health, education and incomes. If these rates of progress are sustained, by 2050 more than three-quarters of the world's people will live in countries with an HDI similar to that of very high HDI countries today.

But we cannot assume that average past rates of progress will continue: progress has been far from uniform across countries and over time. And in two key dimensions of human development, conditions have deteriorated. For environmental sustainability, evidence of devastating current and future impacts is mounting. And income inequality has worsened, while disparities in health and education remain significant.

Are there Limits to Human Development[4]?

Most people around the world have seen major improvements in their lives over the last 40 years. But there are major constraints in our capacity to sustain these trends. If we deal decisively with these challenges, we could be on the cusp of an era of historic opportunities for expanded choices and freedoms. But if we fail to act, future generations may remember the early 21st century as the time when the doors to a better future closed for most of the world's people.

We care about environmental sustainability because of the fundamental injustice of one generation living at the expense of others. Poeple born today should not have a greater claim on Earth's resources than those born a hundred or a thousand years from now. We can do much to ensure that our use of the world's resources does not damage future opportunities. Amartya Sen notes that "a fouled environment in which future generations are denied the presence of fresh air ... will remain foul even if future generations are so very rich." The fundamental uncertainty about what people will value in the future

3. UNDP (2011). *Human Development Report 2011,* ch. 1. p.13
4. Ibid: 14.

means that we need to ensure equal freedom of choice, the lynchpin of the capability approach, in part by protecting the availability and diversity of natural resources. Such resources are critical in allowing us to lead lives that we value and have reason to value.

The early HDRs recognized the centrality of the environment. The first report warned of the continuing increase in environmental hazards, including health risks, from Earth's warming, damage to the ozone layer, industrial pollution and environmental disasters. The 1994 HDR asserted "there is no tension between human development and sustainable development. Both are based in the universalism of life claims."

Sustainable development gained prominence with the 1987 publication of Our Common Future, the report of the UN World Commission on Environment and Development, headed by former Norwegian Prime Minister Gro Harlem Brundtland. The report\produced what became the standard definition of sustainable development: "development that meets the needs of the present without compromising the ability of future generations to meet their own needs."

Many problems of resource depletion and environmental stress arise from disparities in economic and political power. An industry may get away with unacceptable levels of water pollution because the people who bear the brunt of it are poor and unable to complain effectively. A forest may be destroyed by excessive felling because the people living there have no alternatives or because timber contractors generally have more influence than forest dwellers. Globally, wealthier nations are better placed financially and technologically to cope with the effects of climatic change. Hence, our inability to promote the common interest in sustainable development is often a product of the relative neglect of economic and social justice within and amongst nations.

Sustainable human development addresses both inter-generational and intra-generational equity—enabling all generations, present and future to make the best use of their potential capabilities. In the final analysis, sustainable human development is *pro-people, pro-jobs and pro-nature*. It gives the highest priority to poverty reduction, productive employment, social integration and environmental regeneration. It accelerates economic growth and translates it into improvements in human lives, without destroying the natural capital needed to protect the opportunities of future generations.

The strongest argument for protecting the environment is the ethical need to guarantee the future generations opportunities similar to the ones previous generations have enjoyed. This guarantee is the foundation of 'Sustainable Development'.

Sustainability, Equity and Human Development[4]

The human development approach recognizes that people have rights that are not affected by the arbitrariness of when they were born. Further, the rights in question refer not only to the capacity to sustain the same living standards but also to access the same opportunities. This limits the substitution that can occur across dimensions of well-being. Today's generation cannot ask future generations to breathe polluted air in exchange for a greater capacity to produce goods and services. That would restrict the freedom of future generations to choose clean air over more goods and services.

A central concern of the human development approach is protecting the most disadvantaged groups. The most disadvantaged are not just the generations that are worse off on average. They are also those who would suffer most from the realizations of the adverse risks they face as a result of our activity. Thus, we are concerned not only with what happens on average or in the most likely scenario but also with what happens in less likely but still possible scenarios, particularly those that entail catastrophic risks.

HDR 2011 defines "sustainable human development" as "the expansion of the substantive freedoms of people today while making reasonable efforts to avoid seriously compromising those of future generations."

Promoting human development entails addressing local, national and global sustainability; this can—and should—be equitable and empowering

What Makes Development Unsustainable?

When increase in GNP is brought about through depletion of resources under unhealthy environmental conditions by the present generation, the future generations will be left with much depleted resource to produce output under polluted environmental conditions adversely affecting their health and efficiency. Under such

---

4. UNDP (2011). *Human Development Report 2011,* ch. 1. p.17.

circumstances, the rate of economic development in future is bound to fall. Thus, when we are producing more at the cost of future generations the present level of development is not sustainable i.e., we will not be able to maintain it in future.[5]

Even when countries progress in the HDI, they do not necessarily excel in the broader dimensions. It is possible to have a high HDI and be unsustainable, undemocratic and unequal just as it is possible to have a low HDI and be relatively sustainable, democratic and equal. These patterns pose important challenges for how we think about human development, its measurement and the policies to improve outcomes and processes over time.

There is no straightforward pattern relating the HDI to other dimensions of human development such as sustainability and empowerment. An exception is inequality, which is negatively related to the value of the HDI, but even that relationship shows wide variation. The lack of correlation can be seen in the large number of countries that have high HDI values but perform poorly on the other variables: about a quarter of countries have a high HDI but low sustainability; we can see a similar though less marked picture for political freedoms.[6]

But perhaps the greatest challenge to maintaining progress in human development comes from the unsustainability of production and consumption patterns. For human development to become truly sustainable, the close link between economic growth and greenhouse gas emissions needs to be severed. Some developed countries have begun to alleviate the worst effects through recycling and investment in public transport and infrastructure. But most developing countries are hampered by the high costs and low availability of clean energy.

Climate change is symbolic of the larger problem—one that is both practical and philosophical—of the dangers inherent in pushing our ecosystems out of balance. Are we pushing our societies and environment too far, too fast? Are we outrunning the regenerative possibilities inherent to our ecosystems? Are we creating social imbalances that cannot be corrected? (*HDR 2010*).

Climate change will be one of the defining forces shaping prospects for human development during the 21st century. Through its impact on ecology, rainfall, temperature and weather systems, global warming will

5. OECD (2010). *Sustainable Development: Linking Economy, Society Environment* by Tracey Strange and Anne Bayley. New Delhi: Academic Foundation.
6. UNDP (2010). *Human Development Report 2010*, ch.1.

directly affect all countries. Nobody will be immune to its consequences. However, some countries and people are more vulnerable than others. In the long term, the whole of humanity faces risks but more immediately, the risks and vulnerabilities are skewed towards the world's poorest people (*HDR 2008*).

Concentrated in fragile ecological areas, drought-prone arid lands, flood-prone coastal areas and precarious urban slums, the poor are highly exposed to climate change risks—and they lack the resources to manage those risks.

The Current State of Human Development[7]

Every Human Development Report has monitored human progress, notably through the HDI, a composite measure that includes indicators along three dimensions: life expectancy, educational attainment, and command over the resources needed for a decent living. Other indices have delved into inequality, poverty and gender deficits.

Over the past decades, countries across the world have been converging towards higher levels of human development. The pace of progress on the HDI has been fastest in countries in the low and medium human development categories. This is good news. Yet progress requires more than average improvement in HDI value. It will be neither desirable nor sustainable if increases in HDI value are accompanied by rising inequality in income, unsustainable patterns of consumption, high military spending and low social cohesion.

In 2012, the global average HDI value was 0.694; Sub-Saharan Africa had the lowest HDI value (0.475), followed by South Asia (0.558). Among developing regions, Europe and Central Asia had the highest HDI value (0.771), followed by Latin America and the Caribbean (0.741).

There are large differences across HDI groups and regions in the components of the HDI—life expectancy, mean years of schooling and income. Average gross national income (GNI) per capita in very high HDI countries is more than 20 times that in low HDI countries (Table 2.1). Life expectancy in very high HDI countries is a third higher than in low HDI countries, while average years of schooling among adults over 25 are nearly three times greater in very high HDI countries than in low HDI countries. However, expected years of schooling, which better reflect changing education opportunities in developing countries, present a much more hopeful picture: the average incoming elementary

7. *Human Development Report 2013*.

TABLE – 2.1

HDI and Components, by Region and HDI Group, 2012

Region and HDI Group	*HDI*	*Life Expectancy at Birth (Years)*	*Mean Years of Schooling (Years)*	*Expected Years of Schooling (Years)*	*Gross National Income Per Capita (2005 PPP $)*
Region					
Arab States	0.652	71.0	6.0	10.6	8,317
East Asia and the Pacific	0.683	72.7	7.2	11.8	6,874
Europe and Central Asia	0.771	71.5	10.4	13.7	12,243
Latin America and the Caribbean	0.741	74.7	7.8	13.7	10,300
South Asia	0.558	66.2	4.7	10.2	3,343
Sub-Saharan Africa	0.475	54.9	4.7	9.3	2,010
HDI group					
Very high human development	0.905	80.1	11.5	16.3	33,391
High human development	0.758	73.4	8.8	13.9	11,501
Medium human development	0.640	69.9	6.3	11.4	5,428
Low human development	0.466	59.1	4.2	8.5	1,633
India	**0.554**	**65.8**	**4.4**	**10.7**	**3,285**
World	0.694	70.1	7.5	11.6	10,184

Note: Data are weighted by population and calculated based on HDI values for 187 countries. PPP is purchasing power parity.

Source: UNDP (2013). *Human Development Report 2013.*

school student in a low HDI country is expected to complete 8.5 years of school, about equal to the current years of schooling among adults in high HDI countries (8.8 years). Overall, most low HDI countries have achieved or are advancing towards full enrolment in elementary school and more than 50% enrolment in secondary school.

Overall, the last decade has seen greater convergence in HDI values, involving accelerated human development among countries with lower HDI values. All HDI groups and regions saw notable improvement in all HDI components, with faster progress in low and medium HDI countries. East Asia and the Pacific and South Asia saw continuing progress from earlier decades, while Sub-Saharan Africa saw more rapid progress in the last decade. The convergence in HDI values has become more pronounced in the last decade.

State of Human Development in India[8]

Over the years, India has made substantial progress in human development. Sustained and high economic growth in the post-reform period reduced the poverty ratio significantly. There was also noteworthy improvement in the literacy rates over time leading to a decline in the absolute number of illiterates.

According to HDR 2013, the HDI for India was 0.554 in 2012 with an overall global ranking of 136 (out of 187 countries) compared to 119 (out of 169 countries) in HDR 2010. The growth rate in average annual HDI of India between 2000-11 is among the highest, a finding also corroborated by the *India Human Development Report (IHDR) 2011* brought out by the Institute of Applied Manpower Research and the Planning Commission. According to the IHDR, HDI between 1999-2000 and 2007-08 has increased by 21 per cent, with an improvement of over 28 per cent in education being the main driver. India is ranked 129 in terms of the gender inequality index (GII) which captures the loss in achievement due to gender disparities in the areas of reproductive health, empowerment, and labour force participation, with values ranging from 0 (perfect equality) to 1 (total inequality). A lot more needs to be done as our GII is higher than the global average of 0.492. The GII value of 0.617 indicates a higher degree of gender discrimination in India compared to countries like China (0.209), Pakistan (0.573), Bangladesh (0.550), Bhutan (0.495), and Sri Lanka (0.419). It is even higher than the global average 0.492. The gross

8. *Economic Survey 2011-12, 2012-13.*

national income (GNI) per capita ranking minus HDI ranking for India is -10 indicating that India is better ranked by GNI than by non-income HDI. As a corollary, India is worse off in its performance of non-income HDI value computed from life expectancy and education.

The existing gap in health and education indicators as compared to developed countries and also many of the developing countries indicates a need for much faster and wider spread of basic health and education. Life expectancy at birth in India was 66.1 years in 2010-11 as against 81 years in Norway, 81.9 years in Australia, 74.9 years in Sri Lanka, and 73.5 years in China and the global average of 69.8 years However, it has increased from 64.4 in 2010 to 66.1 in 2010-11. The other countries referred to are almost stagnant during this period. Similarly, the performance of India in terms of mean years of schooling is not only much below that of countries like Sri Lanka, China, and Egypt which have higher per capita incomes but also below that of Pakistan, Bangladesh, and Vietnam which have lower per capita incomes. It is also much lower than the global average (Table 2.3).

With the objective of inclusive growth taking centre stage, the Government has strengthened its efforts for social sector development in recent years. Expenditures of the Government of India on social services and rural development have more than doubled over the last four years. Impressive outlays on education, health, water supply and housing indicate the emphasis which Government places on these sectors. The Central Government expenditure on social services and rural development (Plan and non-Plan) which contributes to human development has gone up consistently over the years.[9] It has increased from 13.38 per cent in 2006-07 to 18.47 per cent in 2011-12 (BE). These expenditures have supplemented sustained high level of economic growth in achieving better social sector performance and improvement in the quality of life.

Better governance and improved service delivery are essential to ensure that leakages are plugged and the funds under the welfare schemes reach the intended beneficiaries to the maximum extent. Local governments and Panchayati raj institutions as well as social and non-government organisations can play an important role in this area. It is essential that these higher outlays result in better outcomes. To achieve this objective, the Government has taken the initiative of introducing outcome budgets.

---

9. See *Economic Survey 2011-12, 2012-13.*

TABLE – 2.2

Trends in the Human Development Index (HDI) 1980-2011

HDI Rank	*Country*	*1980*	*1990*	*2000*	*2005*	*2009*	*2010*	*2011*	*Avg. Annual HDI Growth Rate (Per cent)*		
									1980- 2011	*1990-* 2011	*2000-* 2011
1	Norway	0.796	0.844	0.913	0.938	0.941	0.941	0.943	0.55	0.53	0.29
2	Australia	0.850	0.873	0.906	0.918	0.926	0.927	0.929	0.29	0.30	0.23
39	Poland	-	-	0.770	0.791	0.807	0.811	0.813	-	-	0.50
61	Malaysia	0.559	0.631	0.705	0.738	0.752	0.758	0.761	1.00	0.90	0.69
66	Russian Fed.	-	-	0.691	0.725	0.747	0.751	0.755	-	-	0.81
84	Brazil	0.549	0.600	0.665	0.692	0.708	0.715	0.718	0.87	0.86	0.69
92	Turkey	0.463	0.558	0.634	0.671	0.690	0.696	0.699	1.34	1.08	0.90
101	China	0.404	0.490	0.588	0.633	0.674	0.682	0.687	1.73	1.62	1.43
97	Sri Lanka	0.539	0.583	0.633	0.662	0.680	0.686	0.691	0.80	0.81	0.80
103	Thailand	0.486	0.566	0.626	0.656	0.673	0.680	0.682	1.10	0.89	0.78
112	Philippines	0.550	0.571	0.602	0.622	0.636	0.641	0.644	0.51	0.58	0.62
113	Egypt	0.406	0.497	0.585	0.611	0.638	0.644	0.644	1.50	1.24	0.88
124	Indonesia	0.423	0.481	0.543	0.572	0.607	0.613	0.617	1.23	1.19	1.17
123	South Africa	0.564	0.615	0.616	0.599	0.610	0.615	0.619	0.30	0.03	0.05
128	Vietnam	-	0.435	0.528	0.561	0.584	0.590	0.593	-	1.50	1.06
134	**India**	**0.344**	**0.410**	**0.461**	**0.504**	**0.535**	**0.542**	**0.547**	**1.51**	**1.38**	**1.56**
145	Pakistan	0.359	0.399	0.436	0.48	0.499	0.503	0.504	1.10	1.12	1.33
143	Kenya	0.420	0.456	0.443	0.467	0.499	0.505	0.509	0.62	0.52	1.27
146	Bangladesh	0.303	0.352	0.422	0.462	0.491	0.496	0.500	1.63	1.69	1.55
	World	0.558	0.594	0.634	0.66	0.676	0.679	0.682	0.65	0.66	0.66

Source: UNDP (2012); *Human Development Report 2011*. *Economic Survey 2011-12* (p.302).

TABLE – 2.3

India's Global Position in Human Development, 2012

Country	*HDI 2012*	*HDI Rank 2012*	*GNI Per Capita (Constant 2005 PPP $) 2012*	*Life Expectancy at Birth (Yrs.) 2012*	*Mean Yrs of Schooling (Yrs) 2012**	*Expected Yrs. of Schooling (Yrs) 2012**
Norway	0.955	1	48,688	81.3	12.6	17.5
Australia	0.938	2	34,340	82.0	12.0	19.6
Poland	0.821	39	17,776	76.3	10.0	15.2
Malaysia	0.769	64	13,685	74.5	9.5	12.8
Russian Fed.	0.788	55	14,461	69.1	11.7	14.3
Brazil	0.730	85	10,152	73.8	7.2	14.2
Turkey	0.722	92	12,246	73.8	6.5	11.7
China	0.699	101	7945	73.7	7.5	11.6
Sri Lanka	0.715	92	5170	75.1	9.3	12.7
Thailand	0.690	103	7694	74.1	6.6	12.3
Philippines	0.654	112	3478	68.7	8.9	11.9
Egypt	0.662	113	5269	73.2	6.4	11.0
Indonesia	0.617	124	3716	69.4	5.8	13.2
South Africa	0.619	123	9469	52.8	8.5	13.1
Vietnam	0.593	128	2805	75.2	5.5	10.4
India	**0.554**	**136**	**3285**	**65.8**	**4.4**	**10.7**
Pakistan	0.515	146	2566	65.7	4.9	7.3
Kenya	0.509	143	1492	57.1	7.0	11.0
Bangladesh	0.5	146	1529	68.9	4.8	8.1
World	0.694	–	10134	70.1	7.5	11.5

Note: * Data refer to 2012 or the most recent year available; PPP is purchasing power parity.

Source: UNDP (2013); *Human Development Report 2013*. *Economic Survey 2012-13* (p.270).

APPENDIX TABLE – A-2.1

Selected Indicators of Human Development for Major States

Sl. No.	*State*	*Life Expectancy[a] at Birth (2006-2010)*			*Infant Mortality Rate (per 1000 Live Births) (2011)*			*Birth Rate (per 1000) (2011)*	*Death Rate (per 1000) (2011)*
		Male	*Female*	*Total*	*Male*	*Female*	*Total*		
1	*2*	*3*	*4*	*5*	*6*	*7*	*8*	*9*	*10*
1.	Andhra Pradesh	63.5	68.2	65.8	40	46	43	17.5	7.5
2.	Assam	61.0	63.2	61.9	55	56	55	22.8	8.0
3.	Bihar	65.5	66.2	65.8	44	45	44	27.7	6.7
4.	Gujarat	64.9	69.0	66.8	39	42	41	21.3	6.7
5.	Haryana	67.0	69.5	67.0	41	48	44	21.8	6.5
6.	Karnataka	64.9	69.7	67.2	34	35	35	18.8	7.1
7.	Kerala	71.5	76.9	74.2	11	13	12	15.2	7.0
8.	Madhya Pradesh	61.1	63.8	62.4	57	62	59	26.9	8.2
9.	Maharashtra	67.9	71.9	69.9	24	25	25	16.7	6.3
10.	Odisha	62.2	63.9	63.0	55	58	57	20.1	8.5
11.	Punjab	67.4	71.6	69.3	28	33	30	16.2	6.8
12.	Rajasthan	64.7	68.3	66.5	50	53	52	26.2	6.7
13.	Tamil Nadu	67.1	70.9	68.9	21	23	22	15.9	7.4
14.	Uttar Pradesh	61.8	63.7	62.7	55	59	57	27.8	7.9
15.	West Bengal	67.4	71.0	69.0	30	34	32	16.3	6.2
	India	64.6	67.7	66.1	43	46	44	21.8	7.1

Note : Bihar, Madhya Pradesh and Uttar Pradesh excludes Jharkhand, Chhattisgarh and Uttarakhand respectivrly..

Source: Sample Registration System, Office of the Registrar General, India, Ministry of Home Affairs; *Economic Survey 2012-13*.

3

India's Economy at Independence

Introduction

The pre-Independence period was a period of near stagnation for the Indian economy. At the time of Independence, Indian economy was caught up in a *vicious circle of poverty* characterised by one of the lowest per capita consumption and income levels among the countries of the world. Low income levels resulted in low levels of saving and capital formation and therefore, low productivity and low level of income and this vicious circle perpetuated poverty in the country. Further, the size of the market being limited because of low incomes, entrepreneurs had little incentive for making investments in diversified fields and therefore, the productivity in the economy continued to be low thereby perpetuating low incomes and mass poverty.

Indian economy at the time of Independence was overwhelmingly rural and agricultural in character with nearly 85 per cent of the population living in villages and deriving their livelihood from agricultural and related pursuits using traditional, low productivity techniques. The backwardness of Indian economy is reflected in its unbalanced occupational structure with 70 per cent of working population engaged in agriculture. Even with this large proportion of population engaged in agriculture, the country was not self-sufficient in food and raw materials for industry. The average availability of food was not only deficient in quantity and quality but also precarious as exhibited in recurrent famines. Illiteracy was as high as 84 per cent; majority of children (60 per cent) in the 6-11 age group did not attend school. Mass communicable diseases were widespread and in the absence of a good public health service, mortality rates were very high (27 per thousand). Thus, the economy was faced with the problems of mass poverty, ignorance and diseases which were aggravated by the unequal distribution of resources between groups and regions.

The India of 1947, under British rule, showed all the signs of what is today called an underdeveloped country.

The Relative Importance of Various Industrial Activities

Composition of National Income

The low degree of economic development can be judged how income is distributed according to each type of industry.

TABLE – 3.1

Distribution of National Income Per Sector

(As Percentage of Total Income) in the Year 1948-49

Agriculture, Forestry and Fisheries (Total)	49.1
Mines, Manufacturing Industries, Small Enterprises (Total)	17.1
Trade, Transport and Communications (Total)	18.5
Professions, Administration, Domestic Services and Other Services (Total)	15.7
Net national product at factor cost	100.12
Transfers abroad	0.2
National income	100.0

Source : Bettleheim, Charles (1968). *India Independent.* p.2.

As can be seen, agricultural activities contributed nearly 50 per cent to India's national income. Mines, factories and small craftsmen's work contributed only one-sixth, even lower than the figure for trade, transport and communications, and hardly greater than that for other services.

The Working Force

The relative importance of the various industrial activities can also be seen from statistics showing the distribution of labour.

Seventy-two per cent of the total working force was occupied in agriculture, whereas the organised industries employed only about 2 per cent, a figure lower than the number of administrative workers (2.7 per cent). Less than 11 per cent of the working force was employed in all the forms of industry, less than 8 per cent in trade and transports and less than 10 per cent in other services. These statistics speak for low level of industrialisation.

TABLE – 3.2

Occupational Structure

Distribution of Labour 1950-51

(Per cent)

1.	Agriculture (Total)	72.3
2.	Industry (Total)	10.7
3.	Trade and Transport (Total)	7.7
4.	Services (Total)	9.3
	Grand Total	**100.0**

Source : Bettleheim, Charles (1968). *India Independent*. p.4.

The high percentage of agricultural workers is obviously not the result of a modern capitalist agricultural system, but is simply evidence of agricultural overpopulation. A large proportion of the Indian peasantry did not own land (or owned practically none) and could not always manage to find employment.

Little industrialisation, low agricultural output, a low figure of national income *per capita*, very sluggish economic progress, considerable unemployment and under-employment: these were some of the main characteristics of India's social and economic situation just after Independence.

The Agrarian Scene

Stagnating Agriculture

Colonialism became a fetter on India's agricultural and industrial development. Agriculture stagnated and even deteriorated over the years, especially during the first half of the 20th century when the full impact of colonialism began to be felt. Per capita agricultural production declined at a rate of 0.72 per cent per year during 1911-1941 (Blyn, 1966). The situation was worse insofar as per capita foodgrain output was concerned: during the same period, it declined by 29 per cent, i.e., at a rate of 1.14 per cent per year. Even though the per capita non-food grain output grew by 14 per cent, it failed to make up for the decline in foodgrain output (Blyn, 1966).[1]

Whatever the absolute growth in agricultural output, it occurred mainly because of the increase in crop-acreage. The rate of increase in

1. Blyn, G. (1966). *Agricultural Trends in India, 1891-1947*. Philadelphia: Pennsylvania University Press.

all-crop yield per acre was near-zero during 1911-1941. While all-crop and food grain yields declined by 0.02 and 0.44 per cent per year, non-food grain yield went up by 1.15 per cent per year (Blyn, 1966). The increase in yield of non-food grains was basically at the cost of food grain yields, as cultivators shifted better and irrigated land and capital resources to commercial crops in order to earn cash.

Causes

(i) Regressive Organic Structure

The stagnation in agriculture is basically explained by the fact that colonialism transformed the agrarian structure in India and made it extremely regressive. As is well-known, the *zamindars* in *zamindari* areas failed to invest in land and relied on rack-renting, while the peasant proprietors fell into the clutches of the moneylenders and lost control over their lands. Sub-infeudation, tenancy and sharecropping increasingly dominated both the *zamindari* and *ryotwari* areas.[2]

(ii) Internal Drain of Capital

Agricultural surpluses were siphoned from agriculture without any *quid pro quo*, thereby subjecting it to an internal drain of capital. Throughout the 18th and 19th centuries, high land revenue demand ate into the peasant's surplus and even his subsistence. But the government spent very little on improving agriculture as was done, for instance, in Japan. The landlords, old or new, took no interest in agriculture beyond collecting rent. They found rack-rent and usury far more profitable than making productive investment in land. The moneylenders and merchants used their increasing share of agricultural surplus to intensify usury or to take possession of land to become landlords.

(iii) Poor Technology

Another reason for the stagnation of productivity in agriculture was the near absence of change in its technological basis or its productive technique and inputs. As Blyn points out, the type of equipment used changed very little till 1941. Modern machinery was conspicuous by its absence. Improved seeds covered about 1.9 per cent of all crop-

2. By 1947, nearly 70 per cent of the total cultivated land in British India was owned by *zamindars* and landlords. According to Nanavati ("Minute of Dissent", in the Famine Inquiry Commission—Final Report, Government of India, Calcutta, 1945), in *ryotwari* areas between 30 to 50 per cent of the land was in the hands of the landlords and most of the rest was heavily under debt. In 1951, 27.8 per cent of rural agricultural families consisted of peasant proprietors while tenants, sharecroppers and labourers made up the remaining families. (Chandra, Bipan (1979). *Nationalism and Colonialism in Modern India*. Delhi: Orient Longman.

acreage in 1922-23 and 11.1 per cent in 1938-39, these being largely confined to non-food cash crops.

It is also to be noted that commercialisation did not change the unit or organisation of productive activity (e.g. capitalist farming) or lead to improved technology—only better soil and available water and other resources were diverted from food crops to commercial crops.

India's Industrial Production and Its Structure

Another aspect of India's economic backwardness was the state of its industry in spite of her vast industrial resources.

India's Industrial Resources[3]

India's iron ore deposits are estimated at 21 thousand million are a quarter of the total world deposits, manganese deposits are the third largest in the world. India also possesses deposits of chromium, gold, bauxite and various non-ferrous metals, which are important raw materials for atomic industries. Finally, gypsum also exists, as does mica, the latter deposit being one of the largest in the world. India is equally rich in her energy potential. India's resources as a whole would give her a leading position in world industry, in particular the steel and engineering industries and the chemical industries based on coal.

Given this potential, we may now examine the state of India's industrial development immediately after Independence.

The Decline of Traditional Industry and the Development of Modern Industry

India's industrial situation in 1948 was the result of a long period of change in which modern industry replaced the traditional crafts.

Foreign trade statistics best show the effects of 'deindustrialisation'. India, still an exporter of manufactured products at the end of the 18th century, becomes an importer. From 1815 to 1832, India's cotton exports dropped by 92 per cent. In 1850, India was buying one quarter of Britain's cotton exports. All industrial products shared this fate.

The ruin of the traditional trades and crafts was the result of the British commercial policy. Restrictions were imposed upon Indians exporting to the West, while favours were granted to British exporters, who flooded the Indian markets.[4]

---

3. Bettleheim, Charles (1968). *India Independent*, ch.3. pp.46-47.
4. Ibid.

Modern industries began to develop during the second half of the 19th century but their progress was exceedingly slow and stunted. Up to the very end of the colonial period, the level of industry and technology remained low. During the 19th century, industrial development was confined to cotton and jute textiles. The iron and steel industry developed after 1907 while the sugar, cement and paper industries and a few engineering firms came up in the 1930s.

Still, as late as 1946, cotton and jute textiles accounted for nearly 30 per cent of all workers employed in factories.[5]

According to the Census of Manufacturing in 1951, which covered the larger enterprises, of the total value added in manufacturing, 56.8 per cent originated in cotton and jute textiles, 6.6 in sugar, 8.4 in engineering, 7.6 in steel, 4.1 in chemicals and 2.1 in cement.[6]

Consequently, even though modern industry developed quite fast after 1918—its rate of growth being 3.8 per cent per annum—it had little impact on the overall economic situation for its share in the national income at the end of British rule at 7.5 per cent was quite insignificant. In 1913, it was 3.8 per cent (CEHI, 1984). Modern industry perhaps barely compensated for the displacement of traditional handicrafts.[7]

In 1951, only about 2.3 per cent of the labour force was employed in modern industries. According to the Planning Commission, the number of persons engaged in processing and manufacturing (including artisanal industries) fell from 10.3 million in 1901 to 8.8 million in 1951, even though the population increased by nearly 40 per cent. Moreover, in 1951, of the total industrial output, at least 60 per cent was by the unorganised, small enterprises.[8]

A very important feature of India's industrial structure was the virtual absence of capital or producer's goods industry. Indian industries had to rely almost wholly on imported machinery and machine tools. In 1950, India met nearly 90 per cent of its need for machine tools through imports.

Similarly, modern banking and insurance were grossly underdeveloped. In 1946, class A and B banks had 4,644 offices or one

---

5. *Cambridge Economic History of India* (CEHI) (1984). Volume 2, Dharma Kumar (ed.), Indian Reprint. Delhi: Orient Longman.
6. Chaudhuri, P. (1979). *The Indian Economy: Poverty and Development*. Delhi: Vikas Publishing House.
7. Jalan, Bimal (1992). *The Indian Economy: Problems and Prospects*. New Delhi: Viking. p.8.
8. Ibid: 10.

office for 90,000 inhabitants. Underdeveloped banking and insurance meant that the Indian entrepreneurs could not mobilise the available capital. Also, British-controlled banks starved Indian industry of funds and favoured British-owned and controlled enterprises.

The growth of foreign trade and the rapid construction of railways which could have been the positive factors, unfortunately became instruments for the underdevelopment of the Indian economy. Under conditions of free trade, imports displaced indigenous handicrafts and artisanal industries and prevented the rise of new industries. In the absence of a simultaneous industrial revolution, railways had only introduced a commercial revolution and further colonialised the Indian economy. The layout of railway lines and the railway freight rates policy promoted the export of raw materials and distribution of imported goods for they encouraged traffic with ports as against traffic between inland centres. The railways also did not have any forward or backward linkages. They had encouraged the steel and machine industry, not in India but in Britain. They had served as a social overhead not for Indian but British industry and their external economies were exported back to Britain.

Till the late 1930s, foreign capital dominated the industrial and financial fields and controlled the foreign trade network as also part of the internal trade that fed into exports.

It is important to keep in view, in this respect, that foreign investment rarely marked a transfer to India of capital from abroad. It was far less than the unilateral transfer of capital or the 'drain' from India. Three other characteristics of foreign investment were important.

(i) It contributed to 'the guided underdevelopment' of India by concentrating on the production and export of raw materials and foodstuff.

(ii) It went into sectors which catered to foreign markets and not to India's home market.

(iii) "The multiplier effects in terms of income, employment, capital, technical knowledge, and growth of external economies of these investments were largely exported back to the developed countries."[9]

We may sum up India's economic profile at the time of Independence as: stagnating per capita national income, abysmal

9. Ibid: 11.

standard of living, stunted industrial development and the bulk of the population dependent on stagnating, low-productivity semi-feudal agriculture.[10]

Some Positive Features

However, during the 1930s and 1940s some major developments occurred in the Indian economy, which imparted it a certain strength and provided a base for post-Independence economic development. These positive features related to the development of a small but independent (Indian owned and controlled) industrial base and the rise of a substantial indigenous industrial capitalist class with an independent economic and financial base.

During and after the First World War, several consumer industries, such as textiles, sugar, soap, matches and paper, underwent a process of rapid import substitution, so that, by 1939, India was more or less self-sufficient in her major consumer goods requirements. There also occurred a certain diversification and sophistication in industrial production. Some intermediate capital goods industries such as iron and steel, cement, basic chemicals, metallurgy and engineering also began to develop. In the 1930s, there was also a significant shift of capital from usury, trade and landlordism to industry. In other words, surplus was increasingly getting into the hands of those who would invest it.

By 1947, India also possessed a core of scientific and technical manpower. Unlike the 19th or early 20th century situation, when managerial as well as technical personnel were mostly foreign even in Indian-owned industries, now, most of them are Indian, exceptions being provided by a small number of highly specialised experts. India also had a small but quite well-developed skilled labour force both in consumer goods industries such as textiles and sugar and in the more sophisticated steel, metallurgical and engineering sectors.

Thus, at Indepedence, there was available, an indigenous entrepreneurial class which could be a major agency for carrying out the developmental plan perspective of the newly independent state unlike several African countries which at Independence although adopted grand plan schemes, often borrowing from the Indian blueprint, but lacked an indigenous agency to carry it through.

---

10. Ibid.

4

Economic Planning

Evolution and Strategy

Evolution of Planning

Just after the attainment of Independence, the Government of India set up the Planning Commission in 1950 to make an assessment of the material, capital and human resources of the country and to formulate a plan for its most effective and balanced utilisation of the country's resources.

The launching of the First Five Year Plan in April 1951 initiated a process of development aimed not merely at raising the standards of living of the people but also opening out to them new opportunities for a richer and more varied life. This was sought to be achieved by planning for growth and social justice.

The First Five Year Plan contains one of the clearest early formulations of the need for planning and of the State's role in it. Planning, it pointed out, involves "acceptance of a clearly defined set of objectives in terms of which to frame overall policies..., formulation of a strategy for promoting the realisation of the ends defined..., and working out a rational solution to problems—an attempt to coordinate means and ends."

At Independence, India was a predominantly agricultural economy, with more than 70 per cent of the population deriving its livelihood from agriculture, and just under 50 per cent of gross domestic product (GDP) originating in agriculture. The Nehruvian view—derived predominantly from Fabian socialism—endorsed the need for rapid development led by state economic activity and planning. The first few years after Independence were naturally focused predominantly on establishing institutions.[1]

Interestingly, the early planning documents regarded the chief barrier to accelerated growth as the then-low savings rate, and set out a 25-year perspective. The Planning Commission documents stated that a major challenge was to raise the savings rate to 20 per cent and concluded that, if that could be attained, India could achieve a satisfactory growth rate of 5 per cent annually.

Role of the State as Visualised in the Fifties[2]

At this time in the early 1950s, it was believed that the State could play a significant role both in raising the domestic rate of savings and in putting it to more productive use. Pre-industrial economies are predominantly rural and agricultural in character. They have land tenure systems in which a substantial part of the surplus over subsistence needs of cultivators and farm labourers gets appropriated by a small class of non-cultivating land owners and intermediaries (especially under the *zamindari* system and other feudal forms of tenure) and used for non-essential consumption. Abolition of such exploitative and socially wasteful land tenure systems could release surplus for productive investment. Land reforms combined with taxation of agriculture (either directly or indirectly by influencing prices of agricultural commodities relative to that of manufactures) are means of exploiting this potential. Both require strong State intervention.

Apart from its role in maintaining law and order, defining and protecting property rights, enforcement of contracts and the like, the State has to take the primary responsibility for providing elementary education, basic health care, safe drinking water and other facilities which are in the nature of basic needs in any civilised society and which, in addition, have beneficial effects on the general level of productivity. The latter effects—which are referred to as external economies—raise questions as to whether the market mechanism can secure the appropriate sharing of costs and benefits. Where externalities (beneficial or otherwise) happen to be significant, direct State intervention is necessary and justified.

Projects (e.g., road networks, major irrigation, steel plants, railways) which call for investments on a scale far beyond the capacity

1. Krueger, Anne O. (ed.) (2002). *Economic Policy Reforms and the Indian Economy*, ch.1. pp.10-11.
2. Kapila, Uma (ed.) (2012). *Indian Economy Since Independence*. 23rd edition, ch.2.

of individual investors and/or are in the nature of natural monopolies (e.g., public utilities) form another category where direct involvement of the State is deemed justifiable. In most cases even if the private sector is allowed to operate, the need for effective mechanisms to define and enforce standards, norms of efficiency, "fair" rate of return on investment and the like is universally accepted. All of this calls for State regulation, though not necessarily direct ownership and operation. During the early phases of Indian planning, given that indigenous industrial entrepreneurs were few in number and had relatively limited resources, the industrialists themselves favoured a large, direct role for the State in many of these activities.

The government can also help development by creating conditions which induce people to save more. Low rates of savings are of course partly a reflection of low levels of income. But those who have relatively large incomes may prefer to spend on current consumption rather than save when there are relatively limited opportunities for investments that offer attractive returns. A relatively stagnant, slow growing economy implies that profitable opportunities for investment are limited. State intervention can help expand such opportunities in several ways.

Public mobilisation of idle labour for creating productive assets especially roads, irrigation, land improvement, schools, rural hospitals, etc., increase the potential productivity of private resources and thereby create profitable private investment opportunities. Under certain conditions, increased public expenditure can enlarge the scope for profitable investment by creating additional demand for goods and services. Both these effects are likely to be considerably strengthened if there is a coordinated programme of investments for 'balanced development' ensuring that supplies of key inputs and services grow in step with the demand for them. This aspect is particularly important in the case of activities which are closely inter-related. With a coordinated programme, the risks of shortages or excesses of particular goods or services are substantially reduced. Reduced risks induce business to invest more.

Finally, strong State intervention is a logical corollary of the goals of social justice and preventing concentration of power which have been explicitly incorporated among the Directive Principles of State Policy in the Constitution. In addition, the Directive Principles lay emphasis on:

1. Securing to all citizens the right to an adequate means of livelihood;

2. Ensuring that distribution of ownership and control of material resources is regulated in a manner which best serves the common good;
3. Preventing the concentration of wealth and means of production; and
4. Protecting children from being forced to work or being exploited on account of economic necessity.

Though these provisions lacked legal sanction, they do reflect the importance attached to 'social justice' and have shaped the scope and nature of State intervention.

Altogether, as the First Plan puts it, whether one thinks of the problem of capital formation or of the introduction of new techniques or of the extension of social services or of the overall realignment of the productive forces and class relationships in society, one inevitably comes to the conclusion that a rapid expansion of the economic and social responsibilities of the State will alone be capable of satisfying the legitimate expectations of the people. This need not involve complete nationalisation of the means of production or elimination of private agencies in agriculture or business and industry. It does however mean a progressive widening of the public sector and a reorientation of the private sector to the needs of a planned economy (First Plan).

Early Experience with Five Year Plans

The First Five Year Plan (1951-52 to 1955-56) was little more than a collection of ongoing public investment projects, most of which were taken from the post-War reconstruction programme evolved before Independence. The Plan aimed at a general increase in the standard of living and also emphasised wider objectives such as full employment and removal of inequalities, but there was no specific analytically directed strategy for development.[3]

The successful completion of the modest first Plan was followed by a very ambitious Second Five Year Plan. The Plan's author, P.C. Mahalanobis, provided an analytical foundation for it with a closed-economy growth model with two sectors, one of which produced consumer goods and the other investment goods, with sector-specific capital as the only factor of production.

3. Ahluwalia, Montek Singh (2012). "Planning", in Kaushik Basu and Annemie Maertens (ed.), *The New Oxford Companion to Economics in India*, Vol.II. Delhi: OUP.

The fundamental insight of this model was that the greater the proportion of investment devoted to increasing the capacity of the investment-goods sector, the faster the long-run growth in consumption and investment. In the strategy based on this model, rapid long-run growth was to be achieved without much sacrifice of short-run consumption by concentrating scarce investment in expanding capital goods-producing (and intermediate goods-producing) heavy industry. Current consumption demand was to be met by employing abundant labour resources to manufacture consumer goods using labour-intensive methods that required little capital (Srinivasan and Tendulkar, 2003).

The Second Plan underlined the political constraints on any radical solutions to redressing inequalities and re-emphasised rapid growth and diversification of economic activity through industrialisation as essential for achieving and maintaining full employment at a rising level of productivity. It went on to define a coherent overall strategy whose central elements included stepping up the rate of investment (but at a more moderate pace than envisaged in the first plan) and a conscious policy of developing an indigenous heavy industry base (comprising metallurgical, chemical and machine building industries) to lay the foundation for accelerated self-reliant growth, with a leading role for the public sector. Accordingly, the 1956 Industrial Policy Resolution emphasised that the state must play a progressive role in the development of industries and as the Resolution puts it, "the adoption of socialist pattern of society as the national objective, as well as the need for planned and rapid development, require that all industries of basic and strategic importance, or in the nature of public utility services, should be in the public sector. Other industries which are essential and require investment on a scale which only the State, in present circumstances, could provide, have also to be in the public sector. The State has, therefore, to assume direct responsibility for the future development of industries over a wider area." The encouragement of labour-intensive forms of producing mass consumer goods was seen to be a potentially important way of reconciling the conflict between emphasis on heavy industry (which would generate faster growth of income and employment in the long run) and the need to generate adequate jobs for the currently unemployed and underemployed in the transitional period.

The dominant growth orientation articulated in the Mahalanobis import substitution based industrialisation strategy of the Second Plan and which was continued into the Third Plan. Thus, the economic growth was expected to take place through the modern industrialisation. The industrialisation in turn, was expected to be a replica of the same process that had taken place in the historical past in the advanced countries. However, the relatively greater emphasis on the long-term growth in an import-substitution oriented strategy required a modification in the industrialisation process. This consisted of a strong accent on the creation of domestic capacity in the direction of producing capital goods to produce more capital goods. In this strategy, the public sector was expected to play a dual role of: (a) promoting the growth of infrastructural facilities and the creation of capacity in the basic and heavy industries, and (b) reducing the concentration of economic power through the expansion of public ownership of means of production.

An attempt was made with a reasonable success in implementing the long-term growth maximising Mahalanobis strategy during the Second and the Third Five Year Plans. There was, as a result, a considerable acceleration in public sector investment in infrastructure (roads, railways, major and medium irrigation) and indirectly productive investments in universal intermediates like steel, coal, power and heavy electrical machinery. Although the encouragement to the cottage, village and small scale industries as a means of providing employment as well as expanding the supplies of consumer goods were conceived as part of this strategy, very little was achieved in this regard. Similar was the fate in regard to the policies towards the reduction of inequalities.

Planning methodology in the 1960s was dominated by two considerations (Ahluwalia, 2012).[4] The first was the perception that certain sectors were of strategic importance and investment resources must be consciously directed towards expanding capacity in these sectors instead of responding to market forces, which were more likely to draw investment into 'non priority sectors' such as consumer goods. The second consideration dominating Indian planning methodology was the perceived need to deal with scarcity of foreign exchange. Export pessimism led to unwillingness to deal with foreign exchange scarcity by depreciating the exchange rate. Instead, a two-fold approach was adopted of mobilising external assistance to meet foreign exchange needs and rationing scarce foreign exchange by restricting import demand through import licensing. Since import licences were not given if domestic production capacity had been set up, it gave tailer-made protection to domestic industry not surprisingly the industrial structure that emerged was high cost and highly inefficient.

As rightly pointed out by Kaushik Basu, "The actual policy regime that India followed in its early days of independence was a mixture of

4. Ibid

the two competing (and almost contradictory) visions. A Soviet-style planning system was developed, but without the state having a monopoly of control over the resources. Capitalism was allowed to flourish, but a large bureaucracy was nurtured. Huge investments were made in basic industries, but at the same time several sectors were protected as belonging to the small-scale sector. Capitalism was criticised but it was also relied upon. Socialism was never practiced, but the rhetoric of socialism was the norm. A burgeoning bureaucracy became the surrogate for socialism."[5]

While India's planning strategy in the 1960s clearly emphasised rapid growth, it did not succeed in generating growth at the level targeted. It can also be argued that it did not pay sufficient attention to

TABLE – 4.1

Growth Targets and Achievements

(% per year)

		Target	*Actual*
1.	First Plan (1951-1956)	2.1	3.6
2.	Second Plan ((1956-1961)	4.5	4.2
3.	Third Plan (1961-1966)	5.6	2.7
4.	Fourth Plan (1969-1974)	5.7	2.1
5.	Fifth Plan (1974-1979)	4.4	4.8
6.	Sixth Plan (1980-1985)	5.2	5.5
7.	Seventh Plan (1985-1990)	5.0	6.0
8.	Eighth Plan (1992-1997)	5.6	6.7
9.	Ninth Plan (1997-2002)	6.5	5.7
10.	Tenth Plan (2002-2007)	8.0	7.1

Note: The growth targets for the first three plans were set with respect to national income. In the Fourth Plan it was net domestic product. In all Plans thereafter it has been gross domestic product at factor cost.

Source: Ahluwalia, Montek Singh (2012). "Planning", in Kaushik Basu and Annemie Maertens (ed.), *The New Oxford Companion to Economics in India*, Vol.II. Delhi: OUP.

5. Basu, Kaushik (ed.) (2004). "The Indian Economy: Up to 1991 and Since", in *India's Emerging Economy: Performance and Prospects in the 1990s and Beyond*, ch.1. Oxford University Press.

examining why growth targets were not being achieved and whether changes in economic policies were needed to achieve the stated objectives. There was constant focus on the need for higher levels of investment, especially in the public sector, but not enough attention was paid to factors affecting the efficiency of investment (Ahluwalia, 2012).

Thus, the first phase spanning roughly over the first three Five Year Plan periods was characterised by fairly sustained growth in per capita incomes, distinct acceleration in public sector investment and in the growth of industrial output. This phase was dominated by the growth-oriented development strategy.

Changing Perceptions

This atmosphere changed dramatically after the drought and the foreign exchange crisis of the mid-sixties. The sudden increase in defence expenditure consequent to the armed conflicts with China and Pakistan and the levelling-off of foreign aid, all in the short span of three years (1962-1965), put the economy under severe strain. A crisis occurred when two consecutive droughts hit the country in 1966 and 1967 and real GDP declined in absolute terms.

The sharp deterioration of the economic situation and the security environment highlighted two main weaknesses of the existing strategy, namely, the relative neglect of agriculture and a critical dependence on foreign aid.

The two-year period 1965 and 1966 witnessed the worst drought in recent memory and consequent famines in large parts of north India. At the same time, all aid was cut off to India by the donor countries on account of the Indo-Pakistan War of 1965, including food aid. The consequence was a virtual collapse of the economy, and recourse had to be taken to extraordinary financing from the International Monetary Fund (IMF) and the World Bank, which were accompanied by stiff conditionalities.

This traumatic experience brought food security into the forefront of our policy imperatives, which was further buttressed by the observation that sustained industrialisation was not possible without adequate provision of wage-goods. The Fourth Plan, conceived after three years of Plan holiday, therefore, had to have food security as its centrepiece.

The Fifth Plan recognised that growth and industrialisation would not necessarily improve the living conditions of the people, particularly the poor. The concepts of "minimum needs" and directed anti-poverty programmes were innovations of this Plan, whatever may have been the success achieved in implementing them effectively. The Fifth Plan also marks the beginning of a period of steady increase in the growth rate of the economy, which continued right through to the Eighth Plan.

The Sixth Plan for the first time recognised that the success of the Mahalanobis heavy industrialisation strategy in raising the savings rate of the country had created a situation where excess capacities were becoming evident in certain industries. A shift in the pattern of industrialisation, with lower emphasis on heavy industries and more on infrastructure, begins here. The Seventh Plan represents the culmination of this shift. In perspective, it may justifiably be termed as the infrastructure plan. It was also during this period that a reappraisal of the import-substitution strategy begins, and a gradual liberalisation of the Indian economy is initiated.

The Eighth Plan was overtaken by the crisis of 1991, and the economic reforms that came in its wake. The dramatic events and policy initiatives of the two-year plan holiday period between 1990 and 1992 demanded a full reappraisal of the planning methodology, and the Eighth Plan represents the first efforts at planning for a market-oriented economy.

Jean Drèze and Amartya Sen (1995)[6] pointed out, "Four decades of allegedly 'interventionist' planning did little to make the country literate, provide a wide-based health service, achieve comprehensive land reforms, or end the rampant social inequalities that blight the material prospects of the underprivileged."

Thus, the Eighth Five Year Plan documents states that, "in the background of our experience of planning for development over the last forty years and under the strong imperatives for change as they have emerged now, a question is generally asked: what will be the role of planning in future?"

Role of Planning in a Market Economy

Can there be a role for centralised planning in a market economy such as India's after liberalisation? The question was debated at some length in the wake of the reforms launched in the nineties to liberate the economy from licensing and controls. It was realised that after

---

6. Drèze, Jean and Amartya Sen (1995). *India's Economic Development and Social Opportunity*. Oxford: Clarendon Press.

liberalisation, planning in the way it was practised in the first four decades after Independence was no longer tenable. In due recognition of this reality, the Eighth Plan (1992-1997), the first to come out after the initiation of the reforms, stated in its preface: "The Plan is indicative in nature". That planning now has to be primarily indicative and the state can at best be a facilitator for private enterprise was reiterated in the two plans that followed, the Ninth and the Tenth.

Following liberalisation, the role of the public sector in the Indian economy has considerably shrunk and is shrinking further. Three-fourths of investments in the economy are now flowing from the private sector. Financial constraints emanating from the fiscal responsibility and budget management law coupled with inefficiency and waste in service deliveries have led to demand for the state to vacate even areas hitherto regarded as the responsibility of the government, like education and health. "Public-private partnership" or PPP is now emerging as the preferred vehicle for initiatives in development, wherever possible. Given this background can or should there be any role for planning? (Bagchi, 2007).[7]

The answer clearly has to be in the affirmative. The reason is twofold. One, when resources happen to be limited—and that lies at the heart of the economic problem of choice—given the objectives, actions must be guided by a well-designed plan. Planning is necessary to provide the information necessary as a guide to action and that applies for both the public and the private sectors. In other words, planning has a very useful "indicative" role. Two, it has to be recognised that even in a market economy the state has to play a vital role not only as a facilitator but also as a provider of basic infrastructure, physical, social and financial (Stiglitz, 1996). In the Indian context, even after the emergence of the private sector as the bigger player in the economy, public sector plays—and will continue to play in the foreseeable future—a vital role as a major investor in several critical areas, particularly infrastructure (Bagchi, 2007).

Not only there has to be a plan of action to achieve desired objectives, a central agency with the requisite expertise is also needed to draw up the plan and set the parameters to guide action in all sectors. An agency is needed also to harmonise and/or coordinate the plans of different ministries and government agencies and monitor results. The

7. Bagchi, Amaresh (2007). "Role of Planning Commission in the New Indian Economy: Case for a Review", *Economic and Political Weekly*, November 3-9.

Planning Commission was created in 1950 to perform precisely these tasks.

Another function of planning is "prescriptive", that is, influencing the behaviour of both public and private agents to serve public goals through "prescription", such as by suggesting appropriate tax policy and measures to create incentives for economic agents to save and invest, to protect the environment, promote employment, ensure the smooth functioning of the common market, and so on. Our Five Year Plan documents are replete with "prescriptions" embracing almost all fields of social and economic policy. That they have not always been heeded is another matter. But the Planning Commission can make valuable contribution in this regard, such as by spelling out the choices in critical policy issues like in goods and services tax (Bagchi, 2007).

That planning can be helpful in a market economy by providing "indication, coordination and prescription" has been acknowledged even in countries avowedly market-oriented, like Korea and France (Kuznets, 1990). However there can be no gain-saying that planning in a largely market-driven economy cannot proceed on the same footing as in an economy that is heavily controlled by the state. In the Indian context, this implies that there has to be a clear shift in the focus of planning now as compared to the past.

Redefining the Role of State

The Approach Paper to the Tenth Five Year Plan stated that an important aspect of the redefinition of strategy that is needed relates to the role of Government. It is now generally recognised that Government in the past tended to take on too many responsibilities, imposing severe strains on its limited financial and administrative capabilities and also stifling individual initiative. An all pervasive government role may have appeared necessary at a stage where private sector capabilities were undeveloped, but the situation has changed dramatically in this respect. India now has a strong and vibrant private sector. The public sector is much less dominant than it used to be in many critical sectors and its relative position is likely to decline further as government ownership in many existing public sector organisations is expected to decline to a minority. It is clear that industrial growth in future will depend largely upon the performance of the private sector and our policies must therefore, provide an environment which is conducive to such growth.

This is not to say that Government has no role to play or only a minimalist role, in promoting development. On the contrary, government has a very important role but a different one from that envisaged in the past. There are many areas, e.g., the social sectors, where its role will clearly have to increase. There are other areas, e.g., infrastructure development, where gaps are large and private sector cannot be expected to step in significantly. In these areas, the role of government may have to be restructured. It will have to increase in some areas of infrastructure development which are unlikely to attract private investment e.g., rural infrastructure and road development. In others e.g., telecommunications, power, ports, etc., the private sector can play a much larger role, provided an appropriate policy framework is in place. Here, the role of the Government needs to change to facilitate such investment as much as possible while still remaining a public sector service provider for quite some time. In all these areas, the role of government as a regulatory ensuring a fair deal for consumers, transparency and accountability, and a level playing field is also extremely important.

Economic planning, according to Ahluwalia (2012), must also pay much greater attention in future to the role of the government in the social sector—health and education—especially in rural areas. India lags behind other developing countries in this respect and corrective steps are urgently needed in this area. Since these are areas where the agencies responsible for delivering services are those of state governments, much of the planning for service delivery must necessarily shift to states and local governments.

According to Kaushik Basu, "There is need now for India to move more strongly forward with the reforms, allow private firms to enter sectors earlier kept reserved for state-owned enterprises (this is more important than privatisation), open the economy further, and, in particular, allow Indian companies to go for larger acquisitions abroad. But one must be aware that there are no panaceas in economic policy. One has to be prepared for flexibility, to experiment with policy but be ready to adjust, alter, and on occasion even do a U-turn, depending on the evidence coming in. To stick with one policy, unbendingly, is to make the same mistake of policy stubbornness that led India to its present predicament."[8]

In the Foreword to the Planning Commission's Macro-Modelling for the Eleventh Five Year Plan (2009), Montek Ahluwalia remarks, "The transition of the Indian economy from a 'planned' economy to a

8. Basu (2004). *op cit.*

more 'market-based economy', and one more integrated with the rest of the world, has seen the role of planning undergoing a change both in terms of priorities as well as instruments. With the growth of a fairly sophisticated private sector with demonstrable entrepreneurial capacity it is felt that government need not try to produce products that can be produced just as well by the market, instead it should devote its scarce resources to providing public goods including especially educational and health services and programmes for social inclusion. Infrastructure development is another priority area since lack of infrastructure is a crucial constraint on the growth of the economy. The role of the government in infrastructure development is obviously critical. The shift to a more open market economy has also created the need to expand modelling capacity to reflect the features of openness including the macroeconomic implications of openness. For all these reasons, the modelling framework needed to undergo a change from being more deterministic and disaggregated to being more aggregative and indicative."[9]

In a later paper relating to the Twelfth Five Year Plan (2011) Montek Ahluwalia points out that there are four critical challenges facing the economy in the Twelfth Plan, which are perhaps more serious than they were at the start of the Eleventh Plan, are the challenges of (a) managing the energy situation, (b) managing the water economy, (c) addressing the problems posed by the urban transformation that is likely to occur, and (d) ensuring protection of the environment in a manner that can facilitate rapid growth. Difficult choices have to be made in each of these areas and both the central government and the states have an important role in bringing about a successful outcome.

9. Planning Commission (2009). *Macro-Modelling for the Eleventh Five Year Plan of India*, (ed.) Kirit S. Parikh, Foreword by Montek Singh Ahluwalia. New Delhi: Academic Foundation.

5

Economic Reform and Liberalisation

ECONOMIC REFORM

Debate on Liberalisation

The most common connotation of the term liberalisation when used in the context of economic policy is that of reducing government regulation of economic activity and the space for state intervention (except in the all-important matter of guaranteeing private property rights) and allowing for the unfettered operation of market forces in determining economic processes.

According to Deepak Nayyar, "Economic liberalisation is about bringing market prices closer to efficiency prices and allowing individuals, households or firms more freedom to make economic decisions. This means a reduced role for the State. But co-ordinating the market through rules that govern may in turn imply a need for more state intervention somewhere and different forms of State intervention elsewhere in the pursuit of development objectives. The belief that markets know best is associated with an unstated presumption that State intervention is not needed or is counterproductive in the process of industrialisation. This is a historical. Experience from the second half of the twentieth century suggests that the guiding and the supportive role of the State has been at the foundation of successful development among late industrialisers. Even among the East Asian countries, which are often cited as success stories that depict the magic of the market place, the visible hand of the State is much more in evidence than the invisible hand of the market. In the earlier stages of industrialisation, State intervention creates the conditions for the development of industrial capitalism by establishing a physical infrastructure through government investment, developing human resources through education or facilitating institutional change through agrarian reform. In the later stages of industrialisation, State intervention is functional or strategic rather than conducive but remains crucial."[1]

The recent focus on economic liberalisation, in India as well as in other developing and formerly socialist countries, has created the widespread impression that this is a qualitatively new approach. Indeed, the arguments in favour of the market-determination of economic processes and resource allocation, and the counter-arguments based on notions of market failure or inadequacy of markets in meeting social goals, are almost as old as the discipline of economics.[2]

The Background

After pursuing an inward-looking development strategy with the state assuming an important role for more than four decades, India decided to take a historic step of changing tracks in 1991. It embarked on a comprehensive reform of the economy to widen and deepen its integration with the world economy as a part of structural adjustment. There seems to be a general consensus on the desirability of reforms to dismantle the bureaucratic regulatory apparatus evolved over the years that may have outlived its utility. However, there has been considerable debate on the contents of the reform package, their sequencing and the pace, their implementation and their impact. The initial hesitant steps in the direction of liberalisation were taken in the 1980s but the reform story really begins with the balance of payments crisis of 1991.

This crisis was a combined effect of a number of events coinciding. These included collapse of the Soviet Union that had emerged as India's major trading partner. The Gulf War that erupted in January 1991 worsened the balance of payments crisis, not only with rising oil prices but also by causing a virtual stoppage of remittances from Indian workers in the Gulf. These events coupled with political uncertainty prevailing in the country led international credit rating agencies to lower India's rating both for short and long-term borrowings. The erosion of international confidence in the Indian economy not only made borrowings in international markets difficult but also led to

---

1. Nayyar, Deepak (1996). "Economic Liberalisation in India: Analytics, Experience and Lessons", *R.C. Dutt Lectures on Political Economy*, 1993. New Delhi: Orient Longman.
2. Ghosh, Jayati (1998). "Liberalisation Debates", in Terence J. Byers (ed.), *The Indian Economy: Major Debates Since Independence*. Delhi: Oxford University Press.

outflow of deposits of non-resident Indians with Indian banks. These developments together brought the country to the verge of default with respect to external payments liability which could be averted by resorting to borrowings from the IMF under the standby arrangements and CCF and by mortgaging gold to the Bank of England. This was complemented by emergency measures to restrict imports.

The Macroeconomic Crisis

The macroeconomic crisis was precipitated mainly by the growth of the public spending through the 1980s that increased the budget deficit as a proportion of our GNP, although external shocks played a contributory role.

The state of our public finances had indeed reached crisis proportions by the end of the 1980s. The public debt-to-GNP ratio increased through the 1980s, going up to almost 60 per cent at the end of the decade, implying a doubling of the ratio at the end of the previous decade. As is now well-known, the proximate reasons for this situation were the failure of the public sector to generate investible resources and the explosive growth of governmental current spending that saw the budget deficit as a proportion of GDP rising from 6.4 to 9 per cent during the 1980s.

According to Bhagwati and Srinivasan, the question must be addressed: Did the microeconomic inefficiencies have anything to do with this, or was "profligacy" the true, final and sole cause of the macroeconomic crisis? To them, it was the former.

The failure of the public sector enterprises to generate profits (and hence their contribution to the macro crisis) is a microeconomic efficiency failure. Because these enterprises have dominated the provision of infrastructure and critical intermediates, their inefficiency has led to downstream inefficiencies in a multiplier fashion. Then again, the restrictive trade and industrial licencing framework, for instance, led to serious loss of efficiency by reducing the scale of output, eliminating effective competition, creating bottlenecks. The result was to reduce the returns from our investments and our growth rate. In turn, surely the revenues raised from the economy, for any given tax rates, were adversely affected, the political ability to raise tax rates in a situation of slowly-growing incomes was impaired, and the necessity to undertake budgetary expenditures to support the creation of public sector jobs and for consumption were also increased—all factors contributing to the budget deficit crisis.

The rise in foreign borrowing was a major component of the fiscal crisis, reflecting in turn the excess of domestic expenditure over income. Thus, as evident from the external public sector debt (and not just the domestic public sector debt) increased greatly as a proportion of GNP during the 1980s, rising to 21 per cent by 1987-88. This increase in external indebtedness meant that debt service as a proportion of exports increased more than threefold to 32 per cent in 1996-97 from 1980-81.

The macro imbalance, fueled by the budget deficit and financed by the external borrowings and the decumulation of reserves, was accompanied by accelerated inflation to double-digit levels.

Given the magnitude of the fiscal and balance of payment problems, there can be no question about the need for structural adjustment. But there were questions about its context as well as viewing it primarily as a means of liberalisation and opening of the economy.

Rationale for the Reforms

As is now well-understood, India faced a macroeconomic crisis that required immediate attention when Prime Minister Rao took office. This crisis had to be attended to forthwith. But, as in many South American countries in the 1980s, the macroeconomic crisis became also the occasion for undertaking substantial microeconomic (or what are sometimes called "structural") reforms that had been long overdue.

In fact, these structural reforms were necessary because we had evidently failed to generate adequate rates of growth of income and of per capita income. Not merely did India's weak performance in this regard fall below her own expectations as defined in the earlier Plans, it also put India behind many other developing countries, and way behind the super performers in the Far East. In fact India had become marginalised in the world economy. Many of our economic policies were also seen as wittingly foolish, senseless bureaucratic controls on production and investment. Perhaps the most compelling reason for reforms was then to clean the house and to restore India eventually to the position of respect in the world economy and polity that she enjoyed during the years of Prime Minister Nehru's stewardship.[3]

3. Bhagwati, Jagdish and T.N. Srinivasan (1993). *India's Economic Reforms*. Paper submitted to Finance Ministry.

Macroeconomic Reforms

The reform package outlined by Manmohan Singh in 1991 had three distinct components:

(1) Fiscal stabilisation to check the growing fiscal deficit and contain it at a much lower level in such a manner that public investments in basic social and economic infrastructure could be substantially stepped up without generating inflationary pressures;

(2) Internal liberalisation to increase competitive pressures, leaving enterprises free to make their production and investment decisions in the light of market conditions and enlarging the scope and freedom for private enterprise;

(3) Integration with the global economy by removing controls on foreign trade and exchange rates, lowering tariffs and rationalising their structure and substantially relaxing regulations regarding external capital flows and a proactive policy for attracting foreign direct investment. This package, it was claimed, would release powerful growth impulses and lift the economy to a high growth trajectory comparable to that of east Asia. This view prevailed and has come to be accepted by successive governments since.[4]

The policy changes brought into force since July 1991 fall broadly into two categories. The first set of measures is part of what is normally known as stabilisation policy. The second set of measures come under the category of structural reform policies. As Rangarajan[5] rightly points out, while the stabilisation policies were intended to correct the lapses and put the house in order in the short term, the structural reform policies were intended to accelerate economic growth over the medium term. Structural reform policies cannot succeed unless a degree of stabilisation has been brought about. But stabilisation by itself will not be adequate unless structural reforms are undertaken to avoid the recurrence of the problems faced in the recent period.

Structural Reforms

Structural reforms were broadly in the area of industrial licencing and regulation, foreign trade and investment and the financial sector.

---

4. Vaidyanathan, A. (2003). *India's Economic Reforms and Development.* New Delhi: Academic Foundation. pp.17-18.
5. Rangarajan, C. (2002). "The New Economic Policy and the Role of the State", in Uma Kapila (ed.), *Indian Economy Since Independence,* 2002-03 edition. New Delhi: Academic Foundation.

Implementation of the Agenda

The implementation of the agenda of the reforms has covered the following:

Industrial Policy Reforms: Although some liberalisation and streamlining of the industrial policy had been effected in the mid-1980s, the New Industrial Policy (NIP) announced on July 24, 1991 and subsequent amendments brought far-reaching changes in the policy regime governing industrial investments. The NIP dismantled the industrial licencing (or approval) system that regulated the industrial investments in the country by abolishing the requirement of obtaining an industrial licence from the government in all except five specified industries. These specified industries need to be regulated in view of environmental hazards, national security or social well-being considerations.

NIP has thrown open new industries and services to private including foreign private sector by pruning the list of 'Industries Reserved for the Public Sector'. Only two industries, are now reserved for exclusive development by public sector, these are atomic energy and railway transport considered sensitive from national security point of view. Thus, a large number of industries and services including infrastructure such as telecommunication, roads, ports, power generation, petroleum refining have become accessible to the private sector. Considering a large requirements of funds for infrastructure, 100 per cent FDI has been allowed in all infrastructure sectors. The emphasis has been on public-private partnership (PPP) as one of the preferred modes for infrastructure project implementation.

In order to instill healthy competition amongst producers, the list of items reserved for the small-scale sector is reviewed from time to time. The definition of small-scale industry (SSI) has been changed to facilitate modernisation and now only 20 items are reserved for the small-scale sector. FDI up to 100 per cent is allowed under the automatic route in most sectors, with a few exceptions. Manufacturers other than small-scale ones may also manufacture these items provided they undertake an export obligation of 50 per cent of the annual production. NIP accords a much more liberal attitude to foreign direct investments (FDI) than ever in post-Independence India. A more favourable treatment is also accorded to non-resident Indian (NRI) investors who are allowed up to 100 per cent ownership priority industries.

In the area of foreign investment, the policy statement abolished the threshold of 40 per cent on foreign equity investment. The concept of automatic approval was introduced whereby the Reserve Bank of India was empowered to approve equity investment up to 51 per cent in the 34 "priority" industries traditionally called "appendix I" industries and now listed in annex III of the new policy. In subsequent years, this policy was considerably liberalised, with automatic approval made available to almost all industries except those subject to public sector monopoly and industrial licensing. Within the context of the new industrial policy, successive governments have steadily opened the Indian economy to foreign investors. Currently, the system operates on a negative list approach such that unless the official DFI policy explicitly spells out specific restrictions, no restriction applies. The current regime prohibits DFI in only four sectors: retail trading (except single-brand product retailing), atomic energy, the lottery business, and betting and other forms of gambling.[6]

A phased programme of disinvestment of public ownership in public sector corporations has been launched. A Disinvestment Commission followed by Department of Disinvestment was set up to make recommendations on the phasing of the disinvestments.

The outward investments by Indian enterprises were also liberalised and proposals fulfilling certain norms could now be granted automatic approval.

Trade Policy Reforms: A major reform of trade policy regime has been effected since 1991. The import licencing system has been dismantled. All non-tariff barriers (NTBs) have been phased out from all tradables except consumer goods. In spite of stiff resistance from rich industrialists on cutting tariffs, all finance ministers starting from Manmohan Singh in 1991, P. Chidambaram, Yashwant Sinha, Jaswant Singh and again P. Chidambaram forcefully fought on the subject of tariff and the tariffs have indeed been substantially done away with. Besides India has also undertaken a major commitment to liberalise its trade regime under WTO Agreement.

Tariffs have come down from a peak rate of 150 per cent in 1990 to a peak non-agricultural rate of 5.8 per cent in 2009-10. Agricultural tariffs remained high till 2007-08 at 19.3 per cent but have fallen drastically in 2008-09 for 4.2 per cent in (MTA 2007-12) and 2.5 per

6. Panagariya, Arvind (2008). *India: The Emerging Giant*. New Delhi: Oxford University Press. p.104.

cent in 2009-10. The reduction in tariffs on non-agricultural products has played an important role in the convergence of Indian to global inflation rates and needs to continue.

Removal of QRs: The process of removal of import restrictions, which began in 1991, has been completed in a phased manner.

Exchange Rate Reforms: The rupee was devalued twice in July 1991 leading to a 20 per cent depreciation in its value. The partial convertibility of rupee on the trade account was announced in the 1992-1993 budget that was subsequently broadened to full convertibility on current account by August 1994.

With respect to capital account liberalisation, India embarked on a gradual and well-sequenced opening up of the capital account. The active capital account management framework was based on a preference for non-debt creating capital inflows like FDI and foreign portfolio investment. The capital account is virtually free for non-residents and resident corporates with some restrictions on financial institutions and higher restrictions on resident individuals.

Capital Market: The Capital Issues Control Act was repealed and the Securities and Exchange Board of India (SEBI) was set up as a watchdog for regulating the functioning of the capital market. SEBI has focused on regulatory reform of the capital market as well as on market modernisation. Online trading and dematerialised trading have been introduced. Companies have been allowed to buy back their own shares subject to the regulations laid down by SEBI.

In September 1992, the government announced guidelines for investments by foreign institutional investors (FIIs) in the Indian capital market. FIIs were now welcome to invest in all types of securities traded on the primary and secondary market with full repatriation benefits and without restrictions on either volume of trading or lock-in-period.

Financial Sector: In January 1993, a package of financial sector reforms was announced that included permission to new private sector banks including foreign joint ventures. The government has also established a policy regime for functioning of private non-banking finance companies (NBFCs) and agencies for rating their credit worthiness.

In the financial sector, the objective was to provide operational flexibility and functional autonomy to banks and other financial institutions so that they could allocate resources more efficiently. Some of the important initiatives in the financial sector were: reduction in statutory pre-emptions so as to release greater funds for commercial lending, interest rate deregulation to enable price discovery, allowing new private sector banks to create a more competitive environment, dilution of government holding in public sector banks and institution of prudential norms such as capital adequacy, income recognition, asset classification, provisioning and exposure norms to strengthen the health of the banking system besides improving transparency and disclosure standards.

Thus, the government since 1991 has undertaken a comprehensive reform of the economy. In addition to the above measures, there has been an emphasis in the government budget-making to restricting budget deficits.

Economic Progress Post-1991[7]

The initiation of economic reforms in the 1990s saw India gradually breaking free of the low growth trap which was euphemistically called the 'Hindu growth rate' of 3.5 per cent per annum. Real GDP growth averaged 5.7 per cent per annum in the 1990s, which accelerated further to 7.3 per cent per annum in 2000s. A feature of the growth acceleration during the period was that while the growth rate of industry and services increased, that of agriculture fell. This was because there was no notable technological breakthrough after the 'green revolution' of the mid-1960s which saw sharp increase in yields of cereal production particularly in northern part of India. By the 1990s, the momentum of 'green revolution' had died down. Consequently, the yield increases in the 2000s were much lower than those experienced even in the 1990s.

Notably, the decade of the 2000s encompassed the inflexion point in the growth trajectory with an annual average GDP growth of about 9 per cent for the five-year period: 2004-2008. Growth in all the sub-sectors of the economy, including agriculture, accelerated during this period. However, this growth process was interrupted by the global financial crisis. Subsequently, the average growth slowed down to 7.8 per cent during 2009-2011 with a noticeable slowdown in both agriculture and industry.

The growth dynamics altered the structure of the Indian economy with a decline in the share of agriculture from 28.4 per cent in the 1990s

7. Kapila, Uma (2012). *Two Decades of Economic Reforms: Towards Faster, Sustainable and More Inclusive Growth*, Ch.2. New Delhi: Academic Foundation.

to about 15 per cent in 2009-2011 (Table 5.1). There was corresponding gain in the share of services, including construction, from 52 per cent to 65 per cent during the same period. What is, however, of concern is that the share of industry has remained unchanged at around 20 per cent of GDP. This suggests that India's growth acceleration during the last two decades has been dominated by the services sector. The pace of average annual industrial growth had nevertheless picked up from 5.7 per cent during the 1990s to 9 per cent during 2004-2008 before being interrupted by the global financial crisis (Mohanty, 2011).

TABLE – 5.1

Real Economy

Item	*1991-2000*	*2001-2010*	*2004-2008*	*2009-2011*
1	*2*	*3*	*4*	*5*
	(Percentage change)			
1. Overall real GDP	5.7	7.3	8.9	7.8
1.1 Agriculture	3.2	2.4	5.0	2.3
1.2 Industry	5.7	7.3	9.0	6.7
1.2.1 Manufacturing	5.6	8.0	10.0	7.1
1.3 Services	7.1	9.0	10.1	9.5
2. Demand-side aggregates				
2.1 Private final consumption expenditure	4.8	6.4	7.4	7.9
2.2 Government final consumption expenditure	6.3	5.8	5.6	10.6
2.3 Gross fixed capital formation	7.2	10.2	15.7	5.8
	(Per cent)			
3. Share in GDP				
3.1 Agriculture	28.4	19.4	18.9	14.9
3.2 Industry	20.1	20.0	20.1	20.1
3.3 Services	51.5	60.6	61.1	65.0

While the share of industry in GDP remained stagnant, there was noteworthy structural transformation in manufacturing over the period. As a process of restructuring, while the gross value added in organised manufacturing increased by 8 per cent per annum at current prices, employment fell by 1.5 per cent per annum during 1995-2003. Subsequently, during 2004-2009, gross value added growth accelerated to 20 per cent per annum at current prices; but significantly, employment also increased by 7.5 per cent per annum.

The structure of Indian economy also underwent a change during this period in terms of openness. The stereotypical view that India is a closed economy has not been borne out by the openness of Indian economy which was increasing rapidly. Exports and imports of goods and services have more than doubled from 23 per cent of GDP in the 1990s to 50 per cent in the recent period of 2009-2011. If the trade flows are considered alongside capital flows, the rise in openness (measured as current receipts and payments plus capital receipts and payments) was more dramatic from 42 per cent of GDP in the 1990s to 107 per cent in the recent period (Table 5.2) Empirical evidence suggests that with increasing openness of the Indian economy, the trade and industrial cycles were getting more synchronised with the global business cycle (Mohanty, 2011).[8]

TABLE – 5.2

Openness Indicators

(As per cent to GDP)

Item	*1991-2000*	*2001-2010*	*2004-2008*	*2009-2011*
1	*2*	*3*	*4*	*5*
1. Exports plus imports of goods & services	22.9	39.2	40.8	49.8
2. Current receipts & payments plus capital receipts & payments	41.9	78.7	83.5	106.5

The high growth phase of 2004-2008 was accompanied by sharp increase in exports and imports as well as capital inflows. Net capital inflows as percentage of GDP more than doubled from 2.2 per cent in the 1990s to 4.6 per cent of GDP during 2004-2008. Subsequently, growth rates in both trade and capital inflows moderated following the global financial crisis. The openness of the Indian economy has been accompanied by improvement in India's external position as the debt to GDP ratio fell from about 29 per cent in the 1990s to 19 per cent in

8. Ibid.

the recent period. The debt service ratio has also declined from 25 per cent to under 5 per cent during the period (Mohanty, 2011).

The openness in the capital account has resulted in two-way movement in capital with a sharp pickup in India's outward FDI since the mid-2000s (Table 5.3). Uptrend in outward FDI mainly reflected the large overseas acquisition deals of Indian corporates to gain market share and reap economies of scale amidst progressive liberalisation of the external payments regime.

TABLE – 5.3

Foreign Direct Investment

(US $ billion)

Year	*Inward*	*Outward*	*Net FDI to India*	*Outward/ Inward (%)*
1	*2*	*3*	*4*	*5*
2000-01	4.0	0.8	3.3	18.8
2001-02	6.1	1.4	4.7	22.7
2002-03	5.0	1.8	3.2	36.1
2003-04	4.3	1.9	2.4	44.7
2004-05	6.0	2.3	3.7	38.0
2005-06	8.9	5.9	3.0	65.9
2006-07	22.7	15.0	7.7	66.2
2007-08	34.7	18.8	15.9	54.2
2008-09	37.7	17.9	19.8	47.4
2009-10	33.1	14.4	18.8	43.3
2010-11	23.4	16.2	7.1	69.4

Source: Reserve Bank of India.

Gradual improvements were also observed in the fiscal position with fiscal deficit moderating sharply during the high growth phase of 2004-2008, which also coincided with a period of switch-over to a rule-based fiscal consolidation process. In fact, the high growth phase of 2004-2008 saw a primary surplus for the Centre enhancing debt sustainability. The deficit indicators, however, have deteriorated in the recent period following crisis induced fiscal expansion (Table 5.4).

TABLE – 5.4

Government Finances

(As per cent to GDP)

Item	*1991-2000*	*2001-2010*	*2004-2008*	*2009-2011*
1	*2*	*3*	*4*	*5*
1. Central government finances				
1.1 Tax revenue	6.8	7.2	7.6	7.4
1.2 Revenue deficit	3.0	3.4	2.3	4.4
1.3 Fiscal deficit	5.9	4.8	3.6	5.8
1.4 Primary deficit	1.6	0.8	-0.2	2.6
2. State finances				
2.1 Gross fiscal deficit	3.1	3.1	2.7	2.6
2.2 Outstanding liabilities	22.3	29.3	30.1	24.8
3. Combined government finances				
3.1 Revenue deficit	4.2	4.4	2.7	4.5
3.2 Fiscal deficit	7.7	7.8	6.3	8.5
3.3 Primary deficit	2.7	2.2	0.7	3.7
3.4 Outstanding liabilities	63.2	75.1	76.5	68.5

The average saving rate also showed a substantial increase from 23 per cent of GDP in the 1990s to about 31 per cent in the 2000s with a peak saving rate of over 33 per cent achieved during the high growth phase of 2004-2008. Fiscal consolidation helped in lifting the overall saving rate as public sector saving rose significantly. The efficiency of capital utilisation also improved as the incremental capital output ratio (ICOR) declined to 3.7 during the high growth phase of 2004-2008 from 5 in the 1990s. Subsequently, however, capital efficiency has declined in the post-crisis period (Table 5.5).

The high growth was achieved in an environment of price stability as headline wholesale price index (WPI) inflation dropped to an annual average of 5.5 per cent in the 2000s from 8.1 per cent in the 1990s. There was also similar drop in consumer price inflation. Subsequently, however, in the post-crisis period the inflation trend has reversed with the headline WPI inflation averaging over 7 per cent and the consumer price inflation crossing double digits during 2009-2011. The uptick in food price inflation was particularly sharp during 2009-2011 (Table 5.6).

TABLE – 5.5

Saving and Investment

Item	*1991-2000*	*2001-2010*	*2004-2008*	*2009-2011*
1	*2*	*3*	*4*	*5*
(As a ratio to GDP at current market prices)				
1. Gross domestic savings	23.0	30.7	33.4	33.0
1.1 Household saving	17.7	23.1	23.4	23.6
1.1.1 Financial assets	9.9	11.0	11.3	11.3
1.1.2 Physical assets	7.8	12.1	12.1	12.4
1.2. Private corporate sector	3.8	6.3	7.2	8.0
1.3. Public sector	1.5	1.3	2.9	1.3
2. Gross domestic capital formation	24.4	31.2	34.3	35.5
3. ICOR*	5.0	4.4	3.7	4.9

Note: *: Ratio of real investment rate and real GDP growth.

TABLE – 5.6

Inflation

Item	*1991-2000*	*2001-2010*	*2004-2008*	*2009-2011*
1	*2*	*3*	*4*	*5*
(Annual average percentage change)				
1. Wholesale price index	8.1	5.4	5.5	7.1
1.1 Food articles	10.2	5.8	5.2	13.3
1.2 Fuel group	10.6	8.9	7.3	7.2
1.3 Non-food manufactured products	6.8	4.0	5.0	4.0
2. CPI- industrial workers	9.5	5.9	5.0	10.6
2.1 CPI- industrial workers food	9.8	6.2	5.5	12.5

Fiscal Adjustment and Stabilisation

A key aspect of the structural adjustment programmes is to restrict the fiscal deficits of the governments. Table 5.7 summarises the trends in budget deficit of the Central government in the late 1980s and 1990s and beyond. In the second half of 1980s, the fiscal imbalance worsened with average fiscal deficit rising to 8.2 per cent of GDP compared to 6.3 per cent in the early 1980s (*Economic Survey, 1992-93*). Compared to this, the average fiscal deficit in the post-reform period has been 5.7 per cent of GDP. This suggests that the government has succeeded in managing the fiscal situation quite well.

TABLE – 5.7

Trends in Central Government Deficit as Percentage of GDP

Year	*Revenue Deficit*	*Fiscal Deficit*
Average		
1985-91	2.6	8.2
1992-99	2.9	5.7
2000-01	4.1	5.7
2001-02	4.4	6.2
2002-03	4.4	5.9
2003-04	3.6	4.5
2004-05	2.4	3.9
2005-06	2.5	4.0
2006-07	1.9	3.3
2007-08	1.1	2.5
2008-09	4.5	6.0
2009-10	5.2	6.5
2010-11 (P)	3.2	4.8
2011-12 (BE)	3.4	4.6

Source: *Economic Survey* 2004-05, 1992-93, 2010-11, 2011-12 and RBI (1999).

Stabilisation of Inflation: An important focus of the stabilisation programme is to bring the rate of inflation under check. Considerable success was also achieved in the post reform decades in stabilising inflation as well as inflationary expectations. The rate of change in wholesale and consumer prices suggest that the overall trend in prices has been on decline since 1992. One striking trend noticeable from Table 5.6 is the growing divergence between the rate of inflation based on wholesale prices and that for consumer price index since 1993-94. Until 1993-94, the two rates generally converged. Since 1995-96, the consumer price index based rate of inflation has exceeded that of one based on wholesale prices by a wide margin. The diverging trend in the wholesale and consumer prices has been explained in terms of the change in the weighting scheme for the two indices. The consumer price index has a 57.0 per cent weight of the food group compared to just 27.5 per cent in WPI. The divergence between the two indices therefore, reflects substantial increases in food prices in the 1990s. Besides, a spurt in prices of housing, medical care and personal care has also contributed to the rise in CPI. The rise in food prices and other goods of mass consumption at a faster rate than prices of other goods also indicates that sharing of burden of adjustment by different sections of society has been uneven and weaker sections may have been affected more.

Impact of Economic Reforms on the Vulnerable Sections

Here, according to Rangarajan, we need to address two sets of issues. One is whether the economic reform measures affects in any way the specific policy measures that we normally undertake in order to improve the conditions of the poor. Second, is there anything in the new economic reform measures which *per se* has an anti-poor bias? It may be emphasised here that the economic reform introduced since 1991 is not the total economic policy of the Government. The new economic policy which may be a convenient expression to refer to the measures introduced since July 1991 is not the total economic policy of the Government. There are many other elements which continue to remain as an integral part of the overall economic policy. Among these are the measures which can be broadly termed as anti-poverty programmes. In the total economic policy there are four elements which can be identified as being meant specifically for poverty alleviation:

“First, since agriculture is the mainstay of the majority of the population, growth in agriculture and, therefore, resources allocated for agriculture are an important part of the attack on poverty. This is not an acceptance of the trickle-down theory. It is common knowledge that in states in which agriculture has made spectacular progress poverty levels have come down. Therefore, allocation of resources for agriculture is an important indicator.

“Second, we have evolved over time a reasonably satisfactory food security system. An integral part of this is the public distribution system. With all its shortcomings, the public distribution system has played a notable role in avoiding acute conditions of scarcity and met to a certain extent the minimum requirements.

"Third, there has been a substantial expansion in programmes which are intended to provide additional employment. The various employment guarantee schemes as well as the credit-related integrated rural development programmes are examples of such programmes.

"Fourth, expenditure on education and health also has an important bearing on reducing poverty levels."

Conclusion

Judged by many of the externally visible signs, the Indian reforms story has been a remarkable success (Nachane, 2011). After a long period of stagnation in the years following independence, growth rates shifted into high gear sometime during the 1980s and in the last decade accelerated sharply, reaching undreamt heights. This growth resurgence has enabled India to move up in the world per capita (PPP-corrected) GDP rankings from 93 (out of a total of 109 countries) in the mid-1970s to 58 by 2004 (Basu and Maertens, 2007). On several other macroeconomic indicators, the country has been doing equally well. Investment as a proportion of GDP, for example, rose from about 10 per cent in the 1950s to about 23 per cent in the early 1980s and is now close to 36 per cent (Rangarajan 2012).[9] Similarly, India today qualifies as an 'open economy' with exports (as a percentage of GDP) amounting to nearly 20 per cent, as compared to less than 5 per cent in the mid-1960s. And finally on the forex front, we have transited from a perennially shortage situation to one that can only be described as an 'embarrassment of riches' (Nachane, 2011). Inflation, always a serious concern in the Indian context, was sharply reined in, in the late 1990s, and even though it has once again shown signs of strong revival in the last year, it is not clear as to what extent it poses a serious threat to the overall success story. All these trends seem to have generated a great deal of optimism about India's future.

However, Basu believes, "Ultimately an economy has to be evaluated in terms of what happens to the poorest and the dispossessed. Everything else, such as a nation's income growth rate, is of instrumental value.[10] Not all economists concur with this view. To many, efficiency, growth, and *aggregate* welfare are the ends that they wish to pursue. Amartya Sen has consistently taken a normative stand where

9. Rangarajan, C. (2012). "The Indian Economy: Current Concerns and Future Prospects", in Uma Kapila (ed.), *Two Decades of Economic Reforms,* ch.3. New Delhi: Academic Foundation.
10. Basu, Kaushik (ed.) (2004). *India's Emerging Economy: Performance and Prospects in the 1990s and Beyond.* Oxford University Press.

TABLE – 5.8

Growth Rates in India over Successive Plan Periods (1951–2010-11)

	Plan Period	*Annual Growth Rate of GDP (Factor Cost) %*	*Average Annual Gross Domestic Capital Formation (as % of GDP at Factor Cost)*
I.	1951-1956	3.6	10.3
II.	1956-1961	4.2	15.4
III.	1961-1966	2.8	15.6
IV.	1969-1974	3.3	17
V.	1974-1979	4.8	20.2
VI.	1980-1985	5.6	21.9
VII.	1985-1990	6.0	25.2
VIII.	1992-1997	6.7	25.4
IX.	1997-2002	5.5	25.9
X.	2002-2007	7.6	27.51
	2005-06	9.5	34.2
	2006-07*	9.6	35.9
	2007-08*	9.3	38.0
	2008-09*	6.8	35.4
	2009-10*	8.0	36.1
	2010-11*	8.6	35.8 (QE)

Source: Basu and Maertens (2007).

these are merely of instrumental value. While Jagdish Bhagwati has argued vigorously for free trade and raising growth, but at the same time he has been categorical: 'As regards the *objective* of development, I should emphasise, as I always have, that growth was seen by me..., from the early 1960s, as simply an instrumental variable, as a means to an end, and the end was clearly the elimination of poverty."[11]

India, unfortunately, still has miles to go, on matters of basic needs and development of the most disadvantaged. Over the last few decades, inequality has been rising, regional disparities have been growing, and poverty and illiteracy continue to be high.

11. Bhagwati, Jagdish (1985). *Essays in Development Economics*. Oxford University Press.

On the overall magnitude of poverty there was, initially, a lot of very confusing data coming in and it was not clear what was happening. The most scientifically convincing study by Deaton (2001), establishes fairly clearly that poverty, after remaining steady through the early 1990s, went in for a definitive dip by 1999. Though the fall in the percentage of people below the poverty line was not as sharp as the government claimed (27.1 per cent for rural areas and 23.6 per cent for urban areas in 1999), it was sufficiently sharp (down to 30.2 per cent and 24.7 per cent in rural and urban areas, respectively) to cause the absolute number of people below the poverty line to fall. This augurs well, but it must not be forgotten that the level of poverty in India continues to be unacceptably high.

Literacy has risen from 52 per cent in 1991 to 65 per cent in 2001. This is, however, not so much a consequence of government policy as people's changing view of the value of education (caused by the greater exposure to the world out there), which has led to parents demanding better education for their children and often willing to pay for that at the expense of great personal hardship. Again, while this trend is heartening, it is tragic that a nation with so much policy devoted to higher education and scientific work still has 35 per cent of its population unable to read and write (Basu, 2004).

"On these fundamental indicators therefore there is reason to be both disappointed at where the nation stands and optimistic about the changes that have taken place" says Kaushik Basu.

Making an overall assessment of reforms one can say that on the growth front reforms have indeed delivered beyond expectations, while simultaneously macro-economic stability has been more or less successfully maintained. But the resultant growth and stability has had a fairly limited impact on poverty and seem to have aggravated both interpersonal and inter-regional inequality. The growth has also had an extremely low employment potential. However, in recent period since 2005, government seems to be seriously concerned with the 'human face' aspect of the reforms and has initiated a number of laudable initiatives. But certainly far more needs to be done on this front (IDR 2011).[12]

The Ministry of Finance has come out with the Index of Government Economic Power (IGEP). The index has been created for

12. Indira Gandhi Institute of Development Research (2011). *India Development Report 2011*, Ch.1.

10 years (2000-2009) covering 112 economies. The IGEP endeavours to capture the ability of a government to project itself in the international sphere. There is also a normative content to this. Since the index shows the extent of charge a government has, it also can be used to determine how much say the government should have in multilateral fora. The index is composed of four variables: government revenues, foreign currency reserves, export of goods and services and human capital. These variables broadly capture a government's ability to raise resources, its creditworthiness and credibility in international financial markets, its influence on global economic activity, and its representational strength, that is how much of the global economy, including global manpower, it can claim to represent (*Economic Survey 2010-11*).

The 2009 results show that the top 10 ranks are occupied by: (1) the United States, (2) China, (3) Japan, (4) Germany, (5) India, (6) Russia, (7) Brazil, (8) France, (9) Italy and (10) the United Kingdom. In 2000, the top 10 places were held by: (1) the United States, (2) Japan, (3) China, (4) Germany, (5) France, (6) the United Kingdom, (7) Italy, (8) Republic of Korea, (9) Canada and (10) India. Among the top ranking economies some of the most dramatic rises in rank have been Brazil's ascent from 13th place in 2000 to 7th in 2009 and India's rise from 10th position in 2000 to 5th in 2009. Japan was replaced by China in the second spot in 2004. The United Kingdom went down from 6th place in 2000 to 10th in 2008 and continued there in 2009. Canada fell from 9th in 2000 to 15th in 2008.

On an analysis of the countries holding the 4th, 9th and 10th positions in 2000 (namely, Germany, Canada and India), India moves from an index value just below Canada in 2000 to one very close to Germany by 2009.

Improved economic performance dramatically altered global perceptions of India's potential. An early recognition of this was a Goldman Sachs report of November 2002, which included India, with Brazil, Russia and China in a new BRIC group of emerging market countries which was predicted to overtake the G-8 in terms of total GDP by 2035. "Continued strong performance in the decade of the 2000s and resilience in the face of a global slowdown, has reinforced this positive assessment."[13] However, the recent deceleration in India's real

13. Ahluwalia, Montek S. (2011). "Prospects and Policy Challenges in the Twelfth Plan", in Uma Kapila (ed.), *op.cit.*

GDP growth has raised questions about the potential growth rate of the economy and the size of the output gap. Based on data from the Central Statistical Office (CSO), India's annual growth rate of real GDP (measured at market prices) has fallen to 7.0 per cent in the calendar year 2011 from 10.5 per cent in 2010: a sharp decline of 3-5 percentage points within one year. The first quarter of 2012 was further marked by a decline in growth to 5.6 per cent. This decline in growth has been accompanied by a slowdown in investment (both gross fixed capital formation and infrastructure investment). In addition, India's ranking in the overall global competitiveness index by the World Economic Forum slipped five positions in 2011-12. In April 2012, Standard and Poor's revised India's credit outlook to negative from stable with a one-third chance of a sovereign downgrade, which would result in India dropping off the list of countries with an investment-grade rating. The scope for reducing interest rates by the Reserve Bank of India (RBI) to boost investment is limited due to high and persistent inflationary pressures, way beyond RBI's comfort zone of 3.5-4 per cent. These developments have created pessimism in the policy circles including the government and the Reserve Bank of India (Mishra, 2013).[14]

The Next Round of Reforms

In order to boost the potential to close to double-digits and regain the momentum as in early 2000s, structural reforms must be hastened. Second, in the shorter term, given that the economy still faces a positive output gap, the RBI should exercise caution in further loosening the monetary policy stance. Given the limited scope for lowering interest rates, there is no substitute to structural reforms for lifting growth rates in the Indian economy (Mishra, 2013).

While much has been written and talked about the next round of reforms, what is not talked about enough but is important to develop is the institution of contracts, without which no modern market can function. This is where government is important: It must play the crucial role of the third party that helps enforce contracts. But contracts are partly a matter of culture without which it is difficult to develop crucial long term market, such as the market for mortgage and long term investment loans, and to take full advantage of globalisation. These, in turn, are key ingredients of fast growth.

---

14. Mishra, Prachi (2013). "Has India's Growth Story Withered?", *Economic and Political Weekly* XLVIII(15), April 13.

According to Kaushik Basu, "There are, fortunately, enough strengths in the Indian economy for it to be a net beneficiary of globalisation. The economy has gone past that critical level where to open up is to risk being cheated and impoverished. Though there are still innumerable important reforms to undertake, the fundamentals of the Indian economy are probably strong enough for it to be able to implement and benefit from another round of market reform and further (though gradual) opening up of the economy. Globalisation and modern markets bring with them many ills. But, on balance, and given the strengths of the Indian economy, these changes will open up rather than close windows of opportunity for India."[15]

15. Basu (2004). *op.cit.*

6

Growth and Structural Changes since 1951

IN this chapter,[1] we analyse the performance of Indian economy since Independence, with reference to the experience of growth, development and structural change in different phases of growth and policy regimes across sectors and regions.

The structure of discussion is as follows:

Section I outlines the growth experience, the turning points in growth rates of national income, the sectoral contributions and comparison with other countries. In Section II, the discussion is on growth performance of different states, the regional contrasts in terms of growth rates and structural changes. Section III draws some conclusions.

Periodisation of Indian Growth Experience[2]

In order to learn lessons from performance it is useful to try a different type of periodisation based on when the policy regime changed substantially. Looked at this way the Indian growth experience can be broken up into the periods indicated in Table 6.1.

The first three plan periods up to the drought and war crisis of 1965-1966 were the foundational years in which the institutional infrastructure and the policy regimes for development were put in place. These were the years when the government launched community development and rural credit cooperatives, industrial and import

1. This chapter is drawn extensively from Kapila, Uma (2013). *Indian Economy Since Independence (24th edition), ch.27.* New Delhi: Academic Foundation.
2. Desai, Nitin (2010). "Sustaining High Growth", in *Sameer Kochhar (ed.), India on the Growth Turnpike (Essays in Honour of Vijay L. Kelkar).* New Delhi: Academic Foundation.

licensing and industrial development banks, IITs and many research establishments, and many other institutional and policy initiatives.

TABLE – 6.1

Periodisation of Indian Growth Experience

Period	*Characterisation*	*GDP Growth (Annual Average)*	*GFCF Percentage (Annual Average)*	*ICOR (Column 4 Divided by Column 3)*
(1)	*(2)*	*(3)*	*(4)*	*(5)*
1951-52 to 1964-65	The foundational years	4.1	11.6	2.8
1965-66 to 1969-70	The crisis years	3.0	14.2	4.7
1970-71 to 1979-80	The turbulent years	2.9	15.7	5.4
1980-81 to 1990-91	The transitional years	5.6	20.4	3.6
1991-92 to 2002-03	The reform years	5.5	22.9	4.1
2003-04 to 2007-08	The high growth years—The best phase in growth	8.8	30.2	3.4

Note: Based on data from Tables 1.4 and 1.6 of the *Economic Survey 2008-09*, Ministry of Finance.

An import substituting heavy industry-oriented strategy was put in place with the Second Plan and large investments were made in public sector projects for steel and machine building, major power and river valley developments and the transport infrastructure. The public sector grew with fresh investment rather than nationalisation. The private sector had ample room to grow and the government was proactive providing technical advice and political support. The growth performance of the economy in this first phase is good in comparision with India's pre-Independence record.

The twin droughts of 1965 and 1966 were a major shock for which the economy was ill-prepared. Food aid prevented large-scale distress but the ambitious development strategy of the foundational years was more or less abandoned. The focus was on agricultural development with substantial results in the form of the green revolution. There was also some liberalisation of licensing for agriculture-related industries. But the overhang of the earlier strategy led to a continued investment in heavy industries, now including fertilisers. This was also the period which saw the real beginnings of the subsidy burden with the growth of the food and fertiliser subsidies.

In terms of policy regimes, 1970-71 is an important break point. By 1970-71, the green revolution had stabilised and India was past the worst when it came to food security. The Congress split was over and Mrs. Gandhi was firmly in the saddle, *garibi hatao* had become the slogan of the day, poverty eradication rather than growth became the dominating consideration in public policy and a public sector-oriented strategy was in place. The MRTP Act was tightened, state trading was actively promoted and for a brief period, the food grain trade was nationalised. The banking system, which was nationalised in 1969, was put under direct bureaucratic control and directed credit with differential interest rates was instituted.

The upheavals of the oil crisis of 1973-74 and the emergency intervened in mid-decade followed by the Janata Party government, which, though more business-friendly, continued to pursue an anti-poverty strategy in the guise of employment orientation. These were the years of turbulence when the state was in charge but the governments in charge of the state were buffeted by political currents that made it difficult for them to steer the economy with any sense of long-term purpose.

These middle years between 1965-66 and 1979-80 were the ones when Indian development performance was at its worst. This can be seen in the low growth rates despite relatively high levels of investment. The public investment programme was poorly managed with delays and cost overruns, inefficiencies imposed by multiple lines of tied credits being used for a single plant and input bottlenecks which could not be relieved through trade because of foreign exchange shortages.

The return of the Congress Party to power in 1980 marks a shift in policy relative to the earlier years. Though the rhetoric of *garibi hatao* continued, there were some changes in policy in Mrs. Indira Gandhi's second administration that signaled a changed attitude to the private sector. A series of high-level committees under leading figures like L.K. Jha, Vadilal Dagli, Abid Hussain and M. Narasimham laid out an agenda for a more pro-private sector and pro-market policy. But the changes made in the eighties are nowhere near as deep and far-reaching as the bonfire of controls in 1991.

Many of the more important substantive changes came later in mid-decade in Mr. Rajiv Gandhi's administration and Mr. V.P. Singh's budgets. The tax reductions that started with the 1985-86 budget conveyed a positive signal to capital markets and may even have led to improved collections as the tax-GDP ratio rose. But public expenditure rose even more rapidly and the combined deficit of the Central and state governments rose from 7.5 per cent in 1980-81 to 9.9 per cent in 1986-1987 and fell only slightly to 9.4 per cent by 1990-91.

India's Growth Turnaround

The shift to a higher growth path during the course of the 1980s is referred to as the Indian growth turnaround. Fast growth in India since the early 1980s has placed it amongst the top nine rapidly growing economies in the world (Ahmed and Varshney, 2009).

The upward shift in India's growth path during the 1980s is significant for two reasons: the turnaround happened well before the BoP crisis of 1991 and the large scale macroeconomic reforms that ensued.

The second puzzling aspect about India's growth turnaround is that is was not driven by manufactured exports and, therefore, has little in common with the East Asian economic miracle. In particular, there was no industrial policy targeted towards developing specific industries. It was the service sector that led the increase in the overall growth rate in the early 1980s. Since many components of services are income related (such as financial services, business services, and hotels and restaurants) and begin to increase only after a certain stage in development, the fact that India's service sector created the impulse for the growth turnaround is puzzling.

The key issue on which all studies agree is that, at some point during the 1980s, there was an increase in growth, which, from the 1990s, was not only of statistical but also of massive economic significance. What has puzzled many contributors to the literature is that analysis of aggregate data suggests a pickup in growth during the early 1980s, before most of the major policy changes.

While there is a reasonable degree of consensus amongst economists on the timing of India's growth turnaround, there is less agreement about its causes. What is indisputable is that something happened during the 1980s that opened the door to a rise in growth. The challenge facing growth economists is to weave a logically consistent story on the timing and causes of India's growth turnaround (Ghate *et al.*, 2012).[3]

---

3. Ghate, Chetan *et al.* (2012). "India's Growth Turnaround", in Kaushik Basu and Annemie Maertens (eds.), *The Concise Oxford Companion to Economics in India*. New Delhi: Oxford University Press

According to Subramanian (2012)[4] a number of plausible explanations can easily be ruled out. External liberalisation could not have been a factor because the Indian trade regime actually became more restrictive during the 1980s, and the full impact of trade reforms implemented in the 1990s was only felt at the end of the 1990s. Very little internal reform, of product and labour markets, was witnessed in the 1980s, and the only serious effort in this areas—the delicensing of Indian manufacturing—started late in the 1980s and was fairly limited in scope; in other words, it was 'too little, too late' to explain the turnaround in performance.

An alternative explanation comprises three elements. First, there was an attitudinal change on the part of the government in the 1980s, signalling a shift in favour of the private sector, with this shift validated in a very haphazard and gradual manner through actual policy changes. Second, this shift and the limited policy changes were pro-business rather than pro-competition, aimed primarily at benefiting incumbents in the formal industrial and commercial sectors. Third, these small shifts elicited a large productivity response because India was far away from its income possibility frontier (Subramanian, 2006).

There were few significant policy changes in the early 1980s, and and the changes later on (beginning in 1985) were restricted largely to some internal liberalisation relating to the relaxation of industrial licensing. The limited nature of these changes, as well as the form that they took, is best understood by appreciating the political logic of Indira Gandhi's (and later Rajiv Gandhi's) efforts. These were aimed to gather support from the business establishment rather than to alienate it. Hence there was more action where business support existed—for example in reducing taxes, easing access to imported capital inputs; or liberalising capacity restrictions—than where it did not—for example in external liberalisation.

We may draw distinction here between a pro-market and pro-business orientation. The former focuses on removing impediments to markets and aims to achieve this through economic liberalisation. It favours entrants and consumers. A pro-business orientation, on the other hand, is one that focuses on raising the profitability of the established industrial and commercial establishments. It tends to favour incumbents and producers. Nevertheless, this shift towards a pro-business orientation was the essential trigger that set off the boom of the 1980s.

4. Subramanian, Arvind (2012). "Growth Experience" in Kaushik Basu and Annemie Maertens (eds.), Ibid.

Another strand of opinion (Ahluwalia, 2000; Srinivasan and Tendulkar, 2003) downplays what happened in the 1980s, arguing that 'the fiscal expansionism of the 1980s, accompanied by some liberalisation of controls on economic activity, generated real GDP growth of more than 5.8 per cent a year. This expansionism, however, was not sustainable and led to the macroeconomic crisis of 1991' (Srinivasan and Tendulkar, 2003-2009).

According to Deepak Nayyar, a convincing explanation must recognise that the acceleration in economic growth, since 1980, was attributable to several factors.

First, expansionary macroeconomic policies which led to an increase in aggregate demand did stimulate an increase in the rate of growth of output.

Second, starting in the late 1970s, there was also a significant increase in public investment which was sustained through the 1980s. Obviously, this contributed to the increase in aggregate demand. However, insofar as such public investment created new infrastructure or improved existing infrastructure, it could have stimulated growth in output by alleviating supply constraints.

Third, trade liberalisation beginning in the late 1970s, combined with some deregulation in industrial policies introduced in the early 1980, also probably contributed to productivity increase and economic growth. In particular, liberalisation of the regime for the import of capital goods and broad-banding which reduced industrial licencing, could have played a contributory role.

The cumulative impact of economic policies or public actions over the preceding 30 years possibly played an important role in the turnaround. Institutional capacities were created. The social institutions and the legal framework for a market economy were put in place. A system of higher education was developed. Entrepreneurial talents and managerial capabilities were fostered. Science and technology was accorded a priority. The capital goods sector was established. Much of this did not exist in colonial India. But it was in place by 1980. All this provided the essential foundation (Nayyar, 2006).

According to Drèze and Sen (2005), the fact that the reasonable growth rates of the 1980s have been sustained and surpassed in the 1990s is a noteworthy achievement. This is all the more so in international perspective, considering that the 1990s have been a period of relatively slow economic growth in many other countries. In the international comparative league, India has recently been among the 'fast growers'.

The important point to recognise is not so much the acceleration of economic growth in the 1990s, compared with the 1980s (that acceleration is quite marginal), but the respectable rates of growth of the Indian economy, by international standards, in *both decades combined*. Indeed, few countries have such a good record of sustained rapid growth over that combined period.

Looking at the average annual growth of per-capita GDP in the 1980s and 1990s together, India ranks among the ten fastest-growing countries in the world, along with China, Vietnam, South Korea, Malaysia, Thailand and Singapore, among others. This achievement is primarily a reflection of the fundamental growth potential of the Indian economy. The economic reforms undertaken so far have helped to enhance that potential in some sectors, but they have not—at least not yet—radically altered it.

Despite a good growth performance why did the Indian economy hit a crisis in 1991? Basically India had not built up a viable relationship with the international economy. Industry remained highly protected and was not subject to competitive pressures though some licensing and MRTP constraints were eased after 1985. Exports had not taken off despite a substantial devaluation of the rupee in the latter half of the decade. Perhaps the large increases in oil production from Bombay High had reduced the sense of urgency. The more immediate reasons for the foreign exchange crisis of 1990-91 were the increase in free foreign exchange needed to replace rupee trade imports lost with the collapse of the Soviet Union, the oil price hike and the inability to go to the IMF before the crisis because of the political upheavals following the break between Rajiv Gandhi and V.P. Singh.

The big change in the policy regime came after the deep foreign exchange crisis of 1991 when the newly elected Congress government, with Dr. Manmohan Singh as Finance Minister reversed four decades of state control on the private sector and high levels of protection with massive changes in the license-permit system and sharp reductions in tariff rates. Along with this, there was a major change in the policy on foreign investment. The policy regime in India now looked more like the regimes in the export-oriented economies of East and South-East Asia. In the financial sector, SEBI was established and the NSE started leading to a sharp shift away from a bureaucratically directed capital market.

2003-2008 The Best Phase in Growth

The best phase in growth was witnessed during 2003-2008 when the annual average growth stood at about 8.5 per cent. India has been among the fastest growing economies in the world during the last decade. According to Nagaraj (2013), "from 2003, the Indian economy enjoyed a boom in growth for five years. The economy grew it a rate close to 9 per cent per year until it was punched by the financial crisis of 2008" Output expansion according to Nagaraj was underpinned by a sharp rise in the investment rate, largely domestically-financed, boosted by an unprecedented influx of foreign private capital under benign macroeconomic conditions. What triggered the boom? According to Nagaraj, from the demand side, a sharp upturn in world trade since 2002, and the technological change in communications (a "revolution", in Alan Blinder's reckoning), combined with the deregulation of the financial sector in the US gave birth to the outsourcing industry, boosting India's services exports. It was a surely an episode of export-led growth, with the export-to-GDP ratio going up by 9 percentage points in five years. The expansion of bank credit, topped by a flood of foreign private capital, enabled the expansion of aggregate supply. The financial crisis and the world economy slump took away the favourable conditions after 2008. However, growth after the crisis was mostly restored, by loosening the monetary policy and stepping up public expenditure, before it turned distinctively adverse by 2012-13 (Nagaraj, 2013).[5]

The boom has two faces: the real sector, and its financial counter part. Prima facie, it was an exceptional phase of growth in the industrial and services sectors for five years. However, on a closer look, according to Nagaraj, the expansion had many dark spots:

(i) A narrow base, with most of the incremental output coming from a few capital-intensive industries like automobiles and a few services like outsourcing and telecoms.

(ii) Incremental investment was skewed in favour of capital and skill-intensive registered manufacturing (especially, the automotive industry), with a marginal rise in infrastructure's share, despite a sharp rise in domestic credit and abundant access to foreign capital.

---

5. Nagaraj, R. (2013). "India's Dream Run, 2003-2008: Understanding the Boom and its Aftermath", *Economic and Political Weekly* XLVIII(20), May 18.

(iii) The growth in power generation capacity improved during the boom, yet it was not adequate to reverse the long-term decline. Modernisation of the national highway network seems satisfactory, but the record of rural road construction (which is also part of Bharat Nirman) was abysmal during the boom, but improved somewhat afterwards.

(iv) By type of assets, share of construction in fixed investment declined, and its composition changed in some notable ways. Residential construction's share in the total declined (despite a sharp rise in housing mortgages), at the expense of non-residential construction.

(v) The financial crisis hit employment in labour-intensive manufacturing. Between 2004-05 and 2009-10, there was no employment growth, but a distinct decline in female labour force participation rates was discernible. However, wages went up across the board, though at rates lower than the rise in per capita income.

Despite a sharp rise in the domestic savings rate, it was a debt-led growth, financed by burgeoning bank credit to the private corporate sector, and boosted by a surge in foreign private capital in three principal streams, namely, FDI, FPI and FCCBs. FDI rose from 0.6 per cent of GDP in 2003-04 to 2.8 per cent of GDP in 2007-08; and, the total capital inflow (sum of FDI, FPI and ECCBs) reached to 10 per cent of GDP just before the financial crisis struck in 2008. While the aggregate FDI inflow was enormous, only about 40 per cent of it went into avenues that could, in principle, augment potential output. PE/VC/HF (the sources with shorter time horizons), and the round-tripped Indian capital that took advantage of tax-free returns, together constituted nearly 60 per cent of the FDI inflows, contributing little by way of technology, or to the economy's long-term growth potential (Nagaraj, 2013).

Disproportionately faster growth of credit and capital inflows, compared to the rate of fixed investment growth, especially in infrastructure, raised corporate leverage. The newer forms of FDI, with shorter time horizons, were invested heavily in newer, and often unlisted, enterprises, which sought to leverage such funds to make it to the big league quickly.

It is hypothesised that such funds have also found their way into asset markets, stoking the prices of stocks, land and property, which have remained stubbornly high, despite the economic slowdown and decline in corporate profitability after the financial crisis. With the decline in external markets, contraction of investment demand and adverse macroeconomic conditions, the corporate debt burden has turned onerous, swelling, in turn, the banking sector's non-performing assets, denting its profitability and restricting its lending potential.

According to Nagaraj (2013), if the foregoing reasoning and evidence are credible and weighty, then one perhaps needs to be cautious in signifying the boom as a new phase of growth acceleration. It was a debt-led boom leading to "rapid monetary expansion, inflationary pressures, real exchange rate appreciation and widening current account deficits", as Calvo *et al.* (1996: 124) cautioned against the perils of capital inflows. The boom appears episodic, which is now gradually deflating, unless, of course, domestic output or export markets turn around dramatically.

According to Ahluwalia (2011), the most striking break from the past is the phenomenal growth in corporate savings from around 4 per cent of GDP at the end of the nineties to 8.8 per cent of GDP in 2007-08. This fuelled a big increase in private sector investment from around 16.5 per cent of GDP at the end of the nineties to 28.1 per cent of GDP by 2007-08. Since then the global crisis has intervened and the growth rates of GDP in 2008-09 fell to 6.8 per cent. However, the contra-cyclical stimulus measures helped the economy to recover to growth rate of 8 per cent and 8.6 per cent in 2009-10 and 2010-11. Even so, the average for the 11th Plan would be 8.2 per cent, a remarkable performance considering that this period saw the greatest economic crisis the world has faced since the great depression.[6]

The moot question is whether and how soon the economy can get back to the 9 per cent growth path projected in the 11th Plan.

Recent Deceleration since 2011

The recent deceleration in India's real GDP growth has raised questions about the potential growth rate of the economy and the size of the output gap. Based on data from the Central Statistical Office (CSO), India's annual growth rate of real GDP (measured at market prices) has fallen to 7.0 per cent in the calendar year 2011 from 10.5 per cent in 2010: a sharp decline of 3-5 percentage points within one year. The first quarter of 2012 was further marked by a decline in growth to 5.6 per cent. This decline in growth has been accompanied

6. Ahluwalia, Montek S. (2011). "Prospects and Policy Challenges in the Twelfth Plan", *Economic and Political Weekly* XLVI(21), May 21.

by a slowdown in investment (both gross fixed capital formation and infrastructure investment. In addition, India's ranking in the overall global competitiveness index by the World Economic Forum slipped five positions in 2011-12. In April 2012, Standard and Poor's revised India's credit outlook to negative from stable with a one-third chance of a sovereign downgrade, which would result in India dropping off the list of countries with an investment-grade rating. The scope for reducing interest rates by the Reserve Bank of India (RBI) to boost investment is limited due to high and persistent inflationary pressures, way beyond RBI's comfort zone of 3.5-4 per cent. These developments have created pessimism in the policy circles including the government and the Reserve Bank of India (Mishra, 2013).[7]

Against this background, Mishra seeks to shed light on potential growth and economic cycle in India. Specifically, (i) What is the potential growth rate for the Indian economy, and how has it changed over time? In particular, to what extent is the deceleration in growth in 2011 structural?

The key message of the paper is that despite the recent slowdown, potential growth in India continues to be high. However, even under optimistic scenario whereby India continues to grow at its peak growth rate of close to 10 per cent in 2007, it would take India 23 years to become an upper middle-income country.

In order to boost the potential to close to double-digits and regain the momentum as in early 2000s, structural reforms must be hastened. Second, in the shorter term, given that the economy still faces a positive output gap, the RBI should exercise caution in further loosening the monetary policy stance. Given the limited scope for lowering interest rates, there is no substitute to structural reforms for lifting growth rates in the Indian economy.

As per the Advance Estimates released by the CSO, the rate of growth in terms of GDP at market prices (at 2004-05 prices) is expected to be 3.3 per cent for 2012-13 as against 6.3 per cent in 2011-12 (Table 6.2). The growth rate declined significantly on account of the reduction in investment rate and lower growth of exports *vis-à-vis* that of imports. The rate of growth of consumption expenditure and particularly that of private final consumption expenditure has generally been more stable than investment, except in 2012-13.

---

7. Mishra, Prachi (2013). "Has India's Growth Story Withered?", *Economic and Political Weekly* XLVIII(15), April 13.

Investment

The growth rate of the economy since 2003-04 has been strongly correlated with investment rate. The investment rate averaged 34.5 per cent between 2003-04 and 2011-12, much higher rate than before. As can be seen from Table 6.2, the real growth rate in the economy averaged 9.5 per cent per annum during 2005-06 to 2007-08, which were also the years when the growth rate of investment in real terms averaged around 16 per cent. Similarly, the average growth rate of the economy was close to 9 per cent per annum in 2009-10 and 2010-11, with the growth rate of investment averaging around 16.2 per cent in these two years. The rate of growth of GDP was lower in the years when growth rate of investment was low, as was the case in 2008-09 and 2011-12.

TABLE – 6.2

Growth in GDP at Constant Market Prices

(Per cent)

	2005-	*2006-*	*2007-*	*2008-*	*2009-*	*2010-11[2R]*	*2011-12[1R]*	*2012-13[AE]*
1. Total final consumption expenditure	8.7	7.7	9.4	7.7	8.4	8.1	8.1	4.1
1.1 Private final consumption expenditure	8.6	8.5	9.4	7.2	7.4	8.6	8.0	4.1
1.2 Government final consumption expenditure	8.9	3.8	9.6	10.4	13.9	5.9	8.6	4.1
2. Gross capital formation	16.2	13.4	18.1	-5.2	17.3	15.2	0.5	3.9
2.1 Gross fixed capital formation	16.2	13.8	16.2	3.5	7.7	14.0	4.4	2.5
2.2 Changes in stocks	26.7	31.6	31.3	-51.4	67.7	29.7	-30.6	47.6
2.3 Valuables	-1.6	13.7	2.9	26.9	57.6	32.4	6.6	-18.1
3. Exports	26.1	20.4	5.9	14.6	-4.7	19.7	15.3	5.1
4. Less imports	32.6	21.5	10.2	22.7	-2.1	15.8	21.5	5.7
Growth in GDP at 2004-05 market prices	9.3	9.3	9.8	3.9	8.5	10.5	6.3	3.3

Notes: 1R: First Revised Estimate, 2R: Second Revised Estimate, AE: Advance Estimate. Totals may not tally due to adjustment for errors and omissions.

Source: CSO.

Economic Survey 2012-13.

The private sector is the major source of investment in the country. Within the private sector there are two categories of investors, *viz.*, the private corporate sector and household sector.

Since 2004-05, the year when the overall investment rate in the economy first exceeded 30 per cent, the share of public investment in total investment (excluding valuables) has remained fairly stable at around 24 per cent for all the years, except in 2008-09 and 2009-10 when it was 27.6 per cent and 26.5 per cent respectively. The increase in these years could be attributed to the fiscal stimulus provided by the government in order to overcome the slowdown in the economy in 2008-09 following the global slowdown (Economic Survey 2012-13).

As per the First Revised Estimates released by the CSO in January 2013, gross domestic capital formation as a ratio of GDP at current market prices (investment rate) is estimated to be 35.0 per cent in 2011-12 as against 36.8 per cent in 2010-11. Both public and private investment declined as a share of GDP. Within private investment, investment by the private corporate sector registered a sharper decline.

The reduction in private investment could be attributed to a number of factors. First is the increase in policy rates (to combat inflation and inflationary expectations). Between March 2010 and October 2011, the RBI raised the repo rate by 375 basis points (bps), thus raising the cost of borrowings in a bid to reduce demand. Another reason for lower private investment could be lower demand for Indian exports from the rest of the world, particularly the advanced countries. A third possible reason for lower corporate investment is policy bottlenecks (such as obtaining environmental permissions, fuel linkages, or carrying out land acquisition, which led to a number of large projects becoming stalled, which may in turn have discouraged new investment. In what follows, the recent trends in various components of investment are discussed to understand the decline in overall investment rate.

Between 2004-05 and 2011-12, on an average, the share of the household sector and the private corporate sector in total private investment has been more or less equal. However, there are large fluctuations from year to year, with the share of the private corporate sector being significantly higher in the high growth years of 2005-06 to 2007-08 and much lower in the years when growth was lower, particularly in 2008-09 and 2011-12. Investment by the private corporate sector, at current prices, was lower by nearly Rs. 90,000 crore in 2011-12 as compared to 2010-11. Consequently, the share of private corporate investment in total investment declined to 29.8 per cent in

2011-12 as against 36.1 per cent in 2010-11. The magnitude of decline was much larger in 2008-09, when private corporate investment declined by nearly Rs. 2,25,000 crore as compared to 2007-08.

Investment in the form of valuables increased by nearly ` 80,000 crore in 2011-12 vis-à-vis that in 2010-11. Valuables include works of art, precious metals, and jewellery carved out of such metals and stones. At current prices, investment in the form of valuables registered a nearly 4.5-fold increase between 2007-08 and 2011-12 and their share in total investment increased from 2.8 per cent in 2007-08 to 7.6 per cent in 2011-12. A part of the increase in this share can be explained by the surge in the prices of gold and other valuables. However, even at constant prices, the share of valuables increased from 2.9 per cent in 2007-08 to 6.2 per cent in 2011-12, thereby pointing to larger acquisition of valuables, including gold (*Economic Survey 2012-13*).

To summarize, overall investment would have slowed further were it not for non-productive investment such as in valuables. Particularly worrisome is the sharp slowing of corporate investment, which is the source of future supply (needed to quell inflation) and of future growth potential. Policies to remove investment bottlenecks as well as structural reforms to encourage productive investment and its financing are essential, as is more accommodative monetary policy, as inflation abates (*Economic Survey 2012-13*).

Growth Prospects

Economic Survey 2010-11 had anticipated that the Indian economy would register growth of around 9 per cent (+ or - 0.25 per cent) in 2011-12, almost reverting to the pre-crisis levels achieved during the three-year period 2005-6 to 2007-8. The optimism was driven in part by the fact that the economy had achieved a growth rate of 8.4 per cent during the years 2009-10 and 2010-11 and the savings and investment rates had begun rising once again. However, during the course of the year it became increasingly clear that economy would fall short of that growth rate by a significant margin for various reasons. This was indeed pointed out in the Mid-Year Analysis for the year 2011-12 that had stated that the Indian economy was expected to register a growth rate of 7.5 per cent during the year. Growth had declerated in the Indian economy through successive quartly of 2011-12, dropping from 9.2 per cent in Q4 of 2010-11 to 5.3 per cent in Q4 of 2011-12.

The *Approach Paper to the Twelfth Plan*, approved by the National Development Council (NDC) in 2011, had set a target of 9 per cent average growth of GDP over the Plan period. That was before the Eurozone crisis in that year triggered a sharp downturn in global economic prospects, and also before the extent of the slowdown in the domestic economy was known. A realistic assessment of the growth prospects of the economy in the Twelfth Plan period is given in chapter 2, Vol.I of the Plan documents.. It concludes that the current slowdown in GDP growth can be reversed through strong corrective action, including especially an expansion in investment with a corresponding increase in savings to keep inflationary pressures under control. However, while our full growth potential remains around 9 per cent, acceleration to this level can only occur in a phased manner, especially since the global economy is expected to remain weak for the first half of the Plan period. Taking account of all these factors, the Twelfth Plan should work towards bringing GDP growth back to an inclusive 9 per cent in the last two years of the Plan, which will yield an average growth rate of about 8 per cent over the entire Plan period. The outcome is conditional on many policy actions as is described in scenario one.

Within the aggregate GDP growth target, two sub-targets are especially important for inclusiveness. These are a growth rate of 4 per cent for the agricultural sector over the Twelfth Plan period and around 10 per cent in the last two years of the Twelfth Five Year Plan for the manufacturing sector.

The Twelfth Plan's strategy for growth depends crucially on productivity gains as one of the key drivers of growth. Productivity is the additional contribution to growth after taking account of the effect of capital accumulation and growth in labour. These traditional sources of growth are not likely to be enough for India in the coming years and we must therefore focus much more on productivity improvements among all constituents: big businesses, MSMEs, farmers and even government. This can be done by improving the business regulatory environment, strengthening the governance capacity of States, investing more in infrastructure rather than subsidies, and by using Science and Technology (S&T) to drive innovation.

Risk Factors and Constraints

While India can sustain high GDP growth and improve its position in the world GDP ranking, the basic question is whether this growth would be inclusive. Inclusive growth is not only desirable from the equity point of view, but is also important for ensuring stable growth. The experience, by and large, is that countries which achieved rapid reduction in poverty are those which combined rapid growth with equity-promoting growth. In such a strategy, public policies influence both the distribution of income and the process of income generation. Excessive focus on redistribution while ignoring growth may undermine the incentive system and also impose constraints on finding resources required for financing the targeted anti-poverty programmes in the absence of growth. Therefore, growth needs to be rapid enough to significantly improve the condition of the poor. Also, for maximum impact, there should be an improvement in the relative position of the poor and the share of poor in the incremental income should be greater than their share in the average.

The overall growth rate can certainly be pushed up by rapid expansion of some favourably placed sectors. Some sectors of the economy, especially those that rely on high skills of the kind that India already has plentifully (such as basic computer proficiency), have been growing fast in recent years and can expand even further. However, to have an impact on India's widespread poverty, what is needed is an expansion on a much broader and more equitable basis (as has happened in, say, South Korea or China), and this would be extremely difficult to achieve without giving much greater priority to the removal of illiteracy, undernutrition, ill health, economic insecurity and other barriers to participatory growth.

The central issue, as has already been stated, is not just the overall growth rate, which may well go up even further in the near future. What we need to emphasise is participatory growth, which is not the same as high achievement in some particular sectors (oriented to more specialised—and more middle-class—skills), nor the same as a high rate of growth of aggregate GNP per head. For example, in the sixties and seventies, the Brazilian economy grew very fast but achieved rather little reduction of poverty, particularly in terms of social backwardness and sectional deprivation. The lack of participatory nature of that growth was extremely important in that outcome. Comparing Brazil's problems with patterns of more inclusive growth processes in East Asia tends to bring out the big difference made by widely-shared, participatory growth, and the specific role of widespread basic education in fostering growth of this kind. There is something quite important in this choice. India can not afford to go Brazil's way. The lessons of East Asia and China (and to some extent also of the more successful states within India) is not just about growth, but about widely-shared growth, assisted by positive state initiatives. The concentration on participatory growth calls for an integrated view of the process of economic expansion—focusing on the significance of economic growth, on the one hand, and on the importance of the participatory character of that growth, on the other (IDR, 2008).[8]

Performance on Inclusiveness

It is more difficult to assess performance on inclusiveness than on growth for three reasons. First, inclusiveness is a multidimensional concept and progress, therefore, needs to be assessed in many different dimensions. Second, the data relating to various aspects of inclusiveness become available only after a considerable lag, and information for the Eleventh Plan period is often not available. Third, most policies aimed at inclusiveness have an impact only over a relatively long term, and this means that even when policies are moving in the right direction, the results may only be evident much later. For example, steps taken to improve education for the poor will improve their earning ability in future, but this impact will only be reflected in actual income earning much later (Ahluwalia, 2011).

Multidimensionality of Inclusion

The multidimensional nature of inclusiveness is best illustrated by listing some of the many dimensions that are relevant. The extent of reduction in the percentage of the population below the poverty line is clearly a very important indicator of progress. However, many families that are above the poverty line in terms of per capita consumption may lack access to basic services such as education, health, clean drinking water and sanitation. Inclusiveness must obviously include progress in delivery of these essential services. Inclusiveness must also extend to addressing concerns about inequality. It is sometimes argued that inequality should not matter as long as the poor are getting better off and it is probably true that a rapid rate of improvement in incomes for the poor may make them willing to accept some increase in inequality. However, large increases in inequality, accompanying only modest improvements in the levels of living of the poor, are unlikely to be acceptable. Inequality in this context relates not only to the distribution of income or consumption across individuals, but also inequality across states, and in some cases, even across regions within states. Inclusiveness in the Indian context also requires a special focus on particular social groups such as the scheduled castes (SC) and scheduled tribes (ST), and also the minorities. Since these groups are concentrated in the lower ranges of the income distribution, it may be thought that an effective

8. Indira Gandhi Development Research Institute (IDR). *India Development Report 2008*. Mumbai,.New Delhi: Oxford University Press.

strategy for reducing poverty or inequality addresses the concerns of these groups. However, if inclusiveness is defined as bringing these groups at par with the rest of the population, it has to address the issue of achieving a fair representation for these groups along the entire income distribution. This is conceptually very different from reduction in overall poverty or inequality, in the sense that it can be achieved leaving the incidence of poverty and the level of inequality unchanged.

The Eleventh Plan explicitly recognised the multidimensional nature of inclusiveness by enumerating 27 monitorable targets of which GDP growth was only one. The others focused on different aspects of inclusion such as growth in agriculture, reduction in poverty, growth of employment opportunities, etc. One consequence of multidimensionality is that the extent of progress in different dimensions will vary. For example, it is perfectly possible for poverty to decline while inequality increases. Similarly, inequality among households in the country as a whole may decrease, or remain unchanged, while inequality across states increases. Any overall assessment of progress on inclusiveness will have to be based on a composite view of all these developments. (Ahluwalia, 2011)

The Need for Faster Growth

Planners are sometimes criticised for focusing too much on GDP growth, when the real objective should be to achieve an improved quality of life of the people across both economic and non-economic dimensions. The Twelfth Plan fully recognises that the objective of development is broad-based improvement in the economic and social conditions of our people. However, rapid growth of GDP is an essential requirement for achieving this objective.

There are two reasons why GDP growth is important for the inclusiveness objective. First, rapid growth of GDP produces a larger expansion in total income and production which, if the growth process is sufficiently inclusive, will directly raise living standards of a large section of our people by providing them with employment and other income enhancing activities. Our focus should not be just on GDP growth itself, but on achieving a growth process that is as inclusive as possible. For example, rapid growth which involves faster growth in agriculture, and especially in rain-fed areas where most of the poor live, will be much more inclusive than a GDP growth that is driven entirely by mining or extraction of minerals for exports. Similarly, rapid growth which is based on faster growth for the manufacturing sector as a whole, including MSME, will generate a much broader spread of employment and income earning opportunities and is therefore more inclusive than a growth which is largely driven by extractive industries.

The second reason why rapid growth is important for inclusiveness is that it generates higher revenues, which help to finance critical programmes of inclusiveness. There are many such programmes which either deliver benefits directly to the poor and the excluded groups, or increase their ability to access employment and income opportunities generated by the growth process. Examples of such programmes are the Mahatma Gandhi National Rural Employment Guarantee Act (MGNREGA), Sarva Siksha Abhiyan (SSA), Mid Day Meals (MDMs), Pradhan Mantri Gram Sadak Yojana (PMGSY), Integrated Child Development Services (ICDS), National Rural Health Mission (NRHM), and so on. This is also relevant for the sustainability objective since programmes aimed at making development more sustainable also involve additional costs.

International Comparisons

The sense that we are exceptional is perhaps unavoidable in any large country and a comparision with others may be considered irrelevant. However, it surely is worth finding out if countries similarly placed in some broad sense have done better or worse (Desai, 2010). Table 6.3 presents data on observed growth rates in developing countries aggregated by continent and a rank for where India would stand in the developing country growth rate league table in each period.

TABLE – 6.3

Growth Rates in a Global Perspective

(Average annual growth in GDP at PPP$ at 1990 prices)

	1951-1964	*1965-1979*	*1980-1990*	*1991-2001*
India	4.11	2.95	5.76	5.63
Asia less Japan	4.76	5.60	5.37	5.61
Latin America	5.15	5.21	-0.07	0.88
Africa	4.21	4.47	2.44	2.79
Rank order of Indian growth	68/108	87/108	13/108	16/108

Note: (1) The growth rates are for GDP calculated at purchasing power parity in 1990 $s.

(2) The rank order in the last row is the rank in the list of countries ordered by the average annual growth rate for the period indicated in the column. The three aggregated figures for 50 small countries were excluded from this ranking.

Source: Author's calculation based on data in Maddison (2003), basic tables 4b/5b/6b. Desai (2010) *op.cit.*

This table shows that the big difference between India and the rest of the developing world was in the 1965-1979 period. This difference cannot be attributed entirely to the droughts of 1965-66, 1972 and 1979 or to the political turbulence of the Emergency and the subsequent restoration of democracy. Nor can one blame the oil shocks of 1973-74 and 1979-80 which affected all oil importing developing countries. At least part of the blame must be laid at the door of the development strategy followed in the early seventies.

An interesting insight is provided by a comparison of growth rates in the South Asian region grouped by policy regimes that is presented in Table 6.4 drawn from the analysis presented by Kirit Parikh (2006).

TABLE – 6.4

Policy Regimes and Growth Rates of GDP in South Asia

Policy Regimes	*India*	*Pakistan*	*Bangladesh*	*Sri Lanka*	*Nepal*
Free market economy; Passive government				1947-1956 3.67%	
Import-substitution; Controlled economy	1950-1967 3.4%	1950-1957 3.1%	1971-1981 2.7%	1956-1965 3.4%	1966-1980 2.3%
Import-substitution Rigid controls; Nationalisation	1967-1980 3.8%	1971-1977 4.7%		1970-1977 2.9%	
Export promotion regulated		1958-1970 6.6%	1981-1989 3.9%		
Deregulation; Import restriction	1980-1990 5.6%	1978-1988 6.1%			1981-1990 4.9%
Liberalisation	1992-1996 6.7% 1997-2000 5.4%	1988-1999 4.4%	1989-1992 6.7% 1992-2000 5.3%	1977-2000 5.0%	1991-2000 5.1%

Source: Parikh, Kirit S. (2006): *Explaining Growth in South Asia*, New Delhi: Oxford University Press.

The analysis presented in the table above suggest that GDP growth was correlated with the orientation of policy on two broad fronts—the stance towards the external economy and towards the domestic private sector. A shift towards export orientation and/or a reduction in controls on the domestic private sector pushed the growth rate.

High growth in East Asia and in South-East Asia was associated with an outward-oriented trade strategy with a strong export bias, based on undervalued exchange rates or export subsidisation. The degree of openness to foreign investment varied. Japan and Korea followed a very restrictive policy on foreign investment while Singapore and Hong Kong based their strategy on attracting foreign investment. Foreign aid may have helped Korea and Taiwan when they were making their transition to outward-oriented growth but not much after that. China and South-East Asia, who came later to the high growth game, are more open but even there the bulk of the investment has been domestic rather than foreign.

Growth and Structural Change

Consistent with the trend observed in other countries, India's growth experience has been characterised by a decline in the share of agriculture in GDP and an increase in the shares of industry and services. Between 1951 and 2000, the share of agriculture in GDP fell from 53 per cent to 22 per cent, while the share of industry and the share of services increased from 16 to 27 per cent, and from 30 to 50 per cent, respectively. Between 2000-01 and 2011-12 while the share of agriculture has declined from 22 per cent to 13.9 per cent and services share increased from 50 per cent to 59 per cent, the share of industrial sector remained stagnant at 27 per cent.

The structure of the economy has also undergone significant changes over time. Between 1950-51 and 1980-81, the industrial sector registered a higher growth rate than the services sector. The converse has been the case since then. This resulted in the share of the industry sector in GDP increasing by around 9 percentage points from 16.6 per cent to 25.9 per cent during the period from 1950-51 to 1980-81. The share of the services sector increased from 30.3 per cent in 1950-51 to 38 per cent in 1980-81. It started growing rapidly thereafter and this phenomenon became more pronounced in the 1990s. Consequently, since 1980-81, the share of the industry sector has remained in the range of 26 to 28 per cent of GDP, while the entire decline in share of agriculture has been balanced by an increase in share of the services sector. Thus, the resilience of the economy to shocks owe to the services sector which has the largest share and most consistent growth performance. The changes in relative shares of these sectors in GDP are shown in the Table 6.5 (*Economic Survey 2011-12*).

TABLE – 6.5

Sectoral Composition of GDP

Year	*Agriculture*	*Industry*	*Services*
1950-51	53.1	16.6	30.3
1960-61	48.7	20.5	30.8
1970-71	42.3	24.0	33.8
1980-81	36.1	25.9	38.0
1990-91	29.6	27.7	42.7
2000-01	22.3	27.3	50.4
2010-11QE	14.5	27.8	57.7
2011-12AE	13.9	27.0	59.0

Source: Calculated from CSO data.

TABLE – 6.6

Growth in Real GDP

(% Per annum)

Period	*Agriculture*	*Industry*	*Services*	*GDP*
1950s	2.7	5.6	3.9	.36
1960s	2.5	6.3	4.8	4.0
1970s	1.3	3.6	4.4	2.9
1980s	4.4	5.9	6.5	5.6
1990s	3.2	5.7	7.3	5.8
2000s	2.5	7.7	8.6	7.2
X Plan (2002-2007)	2.4	9.2	8.8	7.6
XI Plan (2007-2012)	3.3	6.7	9.9	7.9

Source: Central Statistical Organisation.

Growth and Sectoral Shares, Cross-Country Evidence and Indian Experience

The evolution of sectoral shares in output, consumption and employment as economies growth has been studied by economists for well over 50 years. During the 1950s and 1960s, research by Kuznets and Chenery suggested that development would be associated with a sharp decline in the proportion of GDP generated by the primary sector, counterbalanced by a significant increase in industry, and by a more modest increase in the service sector. Sectoral shares in employment were predicted to follow a similar pattern.

With the benefit of more data on development than was available to Kuznets and Chenery, recent literature has tended to emphasise the growing importance of service sector activity (Inman, 1985; Kongsamut, Rebelo and Xie, 2001). For example, Kongsamut *et al.*, (2001) analysed a sample of 123 countries for 1970-1989 and showed that rising per capita GDP is associated with an increase in services and a decline in agriculture both in terms of share in GDP and employment. In other words, the sectoral share given up by agriculture as the economy matures goes more to the services sector and less to industry than the Kuznets-Chenery work had suggested. The modern view is that as an economy matures, the share of services (in output, consumption and employment) grows along with a decline in agriculture. By contrast, the share of industry first increases modestly, and then stabilises or declines. (Gordon and Gupta, 2003)

Such a pattern of growth is visible in the cross-country data on shares in GDP (Table 6.7). These data suggest two stages of development. In the first, both industry and services shares increase as countries move from low income to lower middle income status, while in the second, the share of industry declines and that of services increases as the economy moves to upper middle and higher income levels.

TABLE – 6.7

Sectoral Shares in GDP in 2001, Global Averages

(Per cent of GDP)

	Agriculture	*Industry*	*Services*	
Low income	24	32	45	Stage I
Lower middle income	12	40	48	
Upper middle income	7	33	60	Stage II
High income	2	29	70	

Note: Definition: Low income: per capita GDP<$745; Lower middle-$746-2975; Upper middle-$2976-9205; and high->$9206.

Source: World Bank's WDI, 2003, Table 4.2.

How does the Indian experience fit in with this pattern? In the four decade period, 1950-1990, agriculture's share in GDP declined by about 25 percentage points, while industry and services gained equally. The share of industry has stabilised since 1990, and the entire subsequent decline in the share of agriculture has been picked up by the services sector. Thus, while over the four decades, 1950-1990, the services sector gained a 13 per cent share, the gain in the 1990s alone was 8 percentage points. Consequently, at current levels, India's services share of GDP is higher than the average for other low income countries.

Share of Services in GDP

One of the most remarkable feature of India's recent growth experience relates to the spectacular showing by its services sector. During the last decade and a half (1995-96 to 2009-10), this sector has recorded an average annual rate of growth of 7.55 per cent much in excess of those recorded in agricultural sector (2.63 per cent) and the industrial sector (5.66 per cent). Today, the share of services sector in India's GDP's and 64 per cent with much of the income being at the expense of agricultural sector's share.[9]

What are the Factors behind the Dynamism of the Services Sector in India.

One explanation suggested in the literature for fast growth in services is that the income elasticity of demand for services is greater than one. Hence, the final demand for services grows faster than the demand for goods and commodities as income rises. Another explanation is that technical and structural changes in an economy make it more efficient to contract out services that were once produced in the industry. This type of outsourcing has been called the "splintering" of industrial activity. Splintering results in an increase in net input demand for services from the industrial sector, as well as the services sector growing proportionately faster than other sectors (Gordon and Gupta, 2003).

The set of economic reform measures initiated since 1991 also impacted on the performance of the services sector. First, reforms in the domestic industrial environment which resulted in rising manufacturing growth provided synergies to the services sector in the form of increased demand for producer services. Second, the liberalisation of the financial sector provided an environment for faster

9. *India Development Report 2011*, Ch.1. *op.cit.*

growth of the financial services. Third, reforms in certain segments of infrastructure services also contributed to the growth of services. Consequently, the services sector posted a much higher growth during the reform period as compared with the pre-reform period with its share crossing the 50 per cent mark. Finally, the rapid growth in services sector appears to have benefited from external demand; the typical example of which is the software industry and call centres.

Opinion on the long term prospects of such service led growth differ sharply. The criticism focuses on three special aspects of services growth *viz.*, (i) its dependence on growth in the other sector (especially manufacturing); (ii) its low employment potential, and (iii) its concentration in a few selected sub sectors (construction, hotels & restaurants, communication, finance, insurance, real estate and business services and community and social services). RBI report finds substantial forward linkages of the services sector with the rest of the economy though the backward linkages are week for agriculture and only moderate for industrial sector. The strong forward linkages reflect the crucial dependence of sustained growth in the services sector on the rest of the economy (especially manufacturing) Hence it is difficult to believe that the services sector of itself can be an engine of economic growth (*IDR, 2011*).

Inter-Regional Disparities in Growth and Development

Prior to 1980, the growth rate of the Indian states was mediocre but relatively uniform. After 1980, however, the fortunes of the states diverged considerably.

A study by Montek Ahluwalia[10] on economic performance of the states in the post-reform period brings out that there is considerable variation in the performance of individual states, with some states growing faster than the average and others slower. What is important is that the degree of dispersion in growth rates of SDP (state domestic product) across states increased significantly in the 1990s. The range of variation in the growth rate of SDP in the 1980s was from a low of 3.6 per cent per year in Kerala to a high of 6.6 per cent in Rajasthan. In the 1990s the variation was much larger, from a low of 2.7 per cent per year for Bihar to a high of 9.6 per cent for Gujarat.

10. Ahluwalia, Montek S. (n.d.). "State Level Performance under Economic Reforms in India in A.O. Krign (ed.), *Economic Policy Reforms and the Indian Economy*, The University of Chicago Press.

The differences in performance across states become even more marked when we allow for the differences in the rates of growth of population and evaluate the performance in terms of growth rates of per capita SDP (Table 6.8). The variation in growth rates in the 1980s ranged from a low of 2.1 per cent for Madhya Pradesh to a high of 4.0 for Rajasthan, a factor of 1:2. In the 1990s, it ranged from a low of 1.1 per cent year in Bihar and 1.2 per cent in U.P., to a high of 7.6 per cent per year in Gujarat, with Maharashtra coming next at 6.1 per cent. The ratio between the lowest (Bihar) and the highest (Gujarat) is as much as 1:7.

TABLE – 6.8

Annual Rates of Growth of Gross State Domestic Product (SDP)

(Per cent)

		1980-81 1990-91	*1991-92 1997-98*
1.	Bihar	2.45	1.12
2.	Rajasthan	3.96	3.96
3.	Uttar Pradesh	2.60	1.24
4.	Orissa	2.38	1.64
5.	Madhya Pradesh	2.08	3.87
6.	Andhra Pradesh	3.34	3.45
7.	Tamil Nadu	3.87	4.95
8.	Kerala	2.19	4.52
9.	Karnataka	3.28	3.45
10.	West Bengal	2.39	5.04
11.	Gujarat	3.08	7.57
12.	Haryana	3.86	2.66
13.	Maharashtra	3.58	6.13
14.	Punjab	3.33	2.80
	Combined SDP of 14 States	**3.03**	**4.02**

Source : SDP and population data obtained from the CSO.

The increased variation in growth performance across states in the 1990s reflects the fact that whereas growth accelerated for the economy as a whole, it actually decelerated sharply in Bihar, Uttar Pradesh and Orissa, all of which had relatively low rates of growth to begin with and were also the poorest states. There was also a deceleration in

Haryana and Punjab, but the deceleration was from relatively higher levels of growth in the 1980s, and these states were also the richest.

Six states showed acceleration in growth of SDP in the 1990s. The acceleration was particularly marked in Maharashtra and Gujarat, both of which were among the richer states, but there was also acceleration in West Bengal, Kerala, Tamil Nadu and Madhya Pradesh all belonging to the middle group of states in terms of per capita SDP.

It is important to note that the high growth performers in the 1990s were not concentrated in one part of the country. The six states with growth rates of SDP in the 1990s above 6.0 per cent per year are fairly well distributed regionally i.e., Gujarat (9.6 per cent) and Maharashtra (8.0 per cent) in the west, West Bengal (6.9 per cent) in the east, Tamil Nadu (6.2 per cent) in the south and Madhya Pradesh (6.2 per cent) and Rajasthan (6.5 per cent) in the north.

The performance of Kerala deserves special attention. Kerala has justly celebrated for its achievements in human development but it has also been criticised for under performance in economic growth. It is important to note that its performance in the 1990s showed a marked improvement compared with the 1980s. From an SDP growth rate much below the 14 states average in the 1980s, it accelerated to a growth rate only marginally below the average in the 1990s. However, because of the low population growth, its performance in per capita SDP growth in the 1990s was actually much better than the average.

The fact that Gujarat and Maharashtra grew at rates normally associated with 'miracle growth' economies also deserves special mention. It should be emphasised that if these states have benefited the most in the post-reform period, their superior performance was not the result of any conscious policy of limiting the benefits of liberalisation to these states, as was the case for example in China, where liberalisation was deliberately limited to designated coastal zones. The superior performance of Gujarat and Maharashtra must therefore be attributed to the fact that the states were able to provide an environment most conducive to benefiting from the new policies.

A recent paper on "Growth Experience of States" by Arvind Panagariya[11] brings out that for every single state in the table, growth rate during 2003-2009 exceeded that in every preceding period, however defined. Growth momentum has now penetrated all large states, which account for 93 per cent of the total population as per 2001

---

11. Panagariya (2010). *op cit.*

census. Second and related, with the exception of Jammu and Kashmir and Assam, both of which have been subject to insurgencies, every single large state and Delhi have grown 6 per cent or faster during the last six financial years. Even Jammu and Kashmir and Assam are not far behind, respectively growing 5.7 and 5.5 per cent annually during this period. In comparison, only one state (Delhi) during 1981-1988 and nine states during 1988-2003 grew at rates of 6 per cent or higher. Third, some of the poorest states have shown some of the highest growth rates during 2003-2009. Rajasthan, Orissa and Bihar, all of them

TABLE – 6.9

Annual Average Growth Rates of NSDP at Factor Cost with States Listed in the Descending Order of Per Capita NSDP at Factor Cost in 2005-06

Year	*1981-1988*	*1988-2003*	*2003-2009*	*1981-1992*	*1992-2003*	*1981-2009*
Delhi	7.7	7.8	11.2*	7.9	7.6	8.4
Haryana	4.6	6.6	10.0	5.9	6.1	6.8
Maharashtra	4.2	6.7	8.9*	6.3	5.4	6.5
Punjab	5.5	4.2	6.1	5.3	3.8	4.9
Himachal Pradesh	3.3	6.5	7.5*	4.6	6.6	5.9
Kerala	1.3	6.1	9.4*	3.5	5.8	5.5
Tamil Nadu	4.8	5.5	8.6	5.4	5.1	6.0
Gujarat	2.8	7.8	10.3#	7.0	5.3	6.8
Karnataka	5.1	6.0	7.7	5.5	6.0	6.1
Andhra Pradesh	5.2	6.2	8.6*	5.7	6.0	6.4
West Bengal	4.2	5.9	6.9*	4.4	6.5	5.7
Jammu & Kashmir	0.9	4.7	5.7*	2.9	4.3	3.9
Rajasthan	4.1	6.7	9.4	7.6	3.8	6.6
Assam	4.1	3.0	5.5	3.9	2.6	3.8
Orissa	2.7	3.9	9.4	3.4	3.7	4.8
Madhya Pradesh	3.6	4.3	6.0*	4.1	4.1	4.5
Uttar Pradesh	4.1	3.7	6.1	4.3	3.2	4.3
Bihar	4.3	4.2	8.4	3.3	5.4	5.1

Note: * This growth rate is based on the average of growth rates from 2003-04 to 2007-08 since the NSDP for this state for 2008-09 is still not reported.

This growth rate is based on the average of growth rates from 2003-04 to 2006-07 since the NSDP for this state for 2007-08 and 2008-09 are still not reported.

Source: Author's calculations using state-level data in RBI (2009).
Panagariya, Arvind (2010).

among bottom six states (respectively ranking 13th, 15th and 18th), grew at annual rates of 9.4, 9.4 and 8.4 per cent, respectively. Growth rates in Orissa and Rajasthan exceed those in all states except Delhi, Gujarat and Haryana. Finally, the bottom six states, which account for 41.8 per cent of the population as per 2001 census, have together grown at the annual average rate of 7.1 per cent during 2003-2009. This rate is in contrast to 3.8 per cent during 1981-1988 and 4.0 per cent during 1988-2003. A major breakthrough for the bottom two-fifths of India seems clearly to be in the making.

According to Subramanian (2012),[12] after 1980, some clearer patterns become evident. It appears that two sets of factors played a role. First, different states had different pre-existing capabilities. But these remained latent and could not find expression until the economic environment changed. The trigger—the second set—was the liberalisation begun in 1980, and especially the decentralisation of economic power that was forced by the changing political landscape after 1980. Thus, it was the interaction between pre-existing capabilities and the twin triggers of liberalisation and decentralisation that explains how the different states fared.

What was this pre-existing capability? It turns out that this capability was something more than a state's level of development or educational level or geography. It is best captured by how diversified a state's manufacturing base was. This diversified base is probably a proxy for some generalised capability—human capital, entrepreneurial spirit, organisational capital—that could exploit a favourable economic environment.

Let us now consider the triggers of liberalisation and decentralisation. While the formal reforms at the Centre received tremendous publicity, perhaps less noticed was the growing decentralisation of policy.

Greater economic decentralisation meant states could differentiate themselves, not least in their ability to attract private-sector investment. This was, of course, facilitated by the gradual dismantling of the industrial licencing system that used regional equity as one of the primary criteria guiding industrial investments. Further contributing to differentiation over this period was the rising trend in private investment, as well as the falling trend in public investment, with

12. Subramanian, Arvind (2012). "Growth Experience" in Kaushik Basu and Annemie Maertens (eds.), *op.cit.*

private investment likely to be more sensitive to differences in policies across states.

After all, if the pre-1980s era was about the Centre deciding, for example, where and how much electricity capacity to instal, there is little that the states could have done to affect economic performance within their borders. This is exactly what the evidence shows. For example, when state-level growth is related to state-level policies and institutions, the latter are found to have no role in explaining growth prior to 1980 but a robust role in explaining post-1980s, especially post-1990s, growth.[13]

The Way Ahead

It is clear from the foregoing discussion that for reducing regional disparities in development, improving social and economic infrastructure in the backward regions through greater public investment needs to be given the highest priority in the development strategy. The other two areas of priority action for these regions are: speeding up social transformation through the empowerment of the common people and measures for good governance.

The 11th Five Year Plan (2007-2012) has addressed the challenge of disparities and divides, and that it must seek to bridge these divides as an overarching priority.

While the differences across states have long been a cause of concern but increasingly there is recognition of the problem of severe imbalances within states. Backward districts of otherwise well performing states, present a dismal picture of intra-state imbalance and neglect. The Centre and the states together must deal with this problem on a priority basis. We cannot let large parts of the country be trapped in a prison of discontent, injustice and frustration that will only breed extremism. The spread of Naxalism in more than 100 districts in the country is a warning sign. Pockets of despair where communalism has left scars are also festering with anger. In all areas, despair is the result of visible failures of the state apparatus to ensure good governance and create an environment where the bulk of the people experience the benefit of development.

Special efforts must be made to remove the discontent, dispense justice, instill a sense of fairness among the people and give them dignity and hope. Otherwise, not only will the growth momentum in

13. Ibid.

the rest of the country be disrupted, but we will not attain the dignity and pride of a good society.

In his address at the 54th meeting of the NDC, Prime Minister Manmohan Singh expressed great concern for the growing disparities and divides, "There are States which have adjusted rapidly to the evolving economic circumstances and have benefited from the ongoing growth processes. There are others which are untouched by change and have seen little improvement in their economic conditions. Year after year, one sees the same States at the bottom of the pile on a large number of economic and social indicators. While variations are a natural phenomenon, if they persist over prolonged periods, they can do incalculable harm to the cohesion of our polity. We need therefore to focus our attention on this as a matter of high national priority.

"The other disparity which concerns me is the urban-rural disparity. Often, this is the cause of inter-regional disparity. The quality of life in urban areas is improving more rapidly than in rural areas. This is partly explained by the poor performance of agriculture. While there are limits to which we can raise the growth rate of agriculture, the problem is compounded by the lack of mobility of those employed in agriculture to productive jobs in industry. Therefore, we are faced with this peculiar puzzle whereby on the one side, the growth rate is accelerating to more than 9 per cent but on the other side, the share of agriculture in our GDP has dropped below 20 per cent without any appreciable shift in the proportion of population still dependent on agriculture for livelihood. This is leading to a relative impoverishment of our rural areas. We need to ensure that the rural-urban divide is bridged and take necessary steps to mitigate it."[14]

Growth Prospect: An Assessment

The Indian economy has undisputedly moved to a higher growth path during the last three decades. The break point from the earlier 'Hindu rate' could be placed in the late 1970s to the early 1990s depending on whether one takes a purely statistical approach or looks for policy changes underlying the process to explain the break. Limited reforms and an expansionary fiscal policy helped the economy to achieve an average growth rate of 5.5 per cent in the 1980s, but its sustainability was doubtful. Lack of resilience was evident when a

14. Prime Minister's opening remarks at the 54th meeting of the National Development Council, December 19, 2007. See Uma Kapila (2008). *Indian Economy Since Independence* (19th edition), ch. 3.

macroeconomic crisis occurred in the wake of the Gulf War and the oil price rise in 1990s and 1991. The policies of the 1980s were associated with high levels of domestic and foreign debt leading to fiscal and balance of payments crisis.

Economic reforms initiated in 1991 were wide-ranging, involving abolition of the industrial licensing systems, liberalising trade, and unfreezing the exchange rate among others. The resilience of the economy as it developed in the post-reform period gets reflected in successfully meeting several challenges such as the East Asian crisis in the late-1990s, the Gulf War in early 2000, and severe drought in 2002. As discussed earlier, in the wake of the global economic crisis, economic growth in India slowed down considerably in 2009-09 and recovered partly in the next two years. World trade, which fell by about a quarter in 2009, has not yet recovered to the pre-crisis level of $16 trillion. With new signs of a deepening Euro zone crisis, the global economic scenario does not seem promising at present. Yet, India continues to perform reasonably well in comparison to most other nations.

Attaining above 8 per cent growth consecutively for five years between 2003 and 2007 by the Indian economy attracted world-wide attention and many observers believed that India, like China, was riding on the high road of growth. The post-reform experience shows that India's growth path, unlike that of China, is going to be considerably uneven. Some analysts believe that the high growth story has come to an end and an average growth rate of 5-6 per cent might be more of a rule and see this as the 'new Hindu rate' of growth. Many others, however, are more optimistic and argue that conditions are ripe to maintain an average growth rate of 7-8 per cent as experienced in the last decade. The government has, in fact, targeted an even higher growth rate of 9 per cent during the Eleventh Plan and in the Twelfth Five Year Plan (approach paper). If the realised growth rate will be at the lower end of this spectrum during the 2010s, India's global positioning by GDP criteria might be delayed by a decade or so. Given that current global recessionary conditions might continue till 2013, it would be difficult to achieve a 9 per cent growth rate during the Twelfth Plan period of 2012-17. An average growth rate of 8 per cent could be in the feasible range with bold but mature policy responses.

In the absence of the revival of the manufacturing sector, a higher GDP growth rate cannot be achieved. Given that the nature of the Indian manufacturing sector has been 'idiosyncratic' (Kochhar *et al.,* 2006), it is necessary to create an enabling environment for private investors to cope with business and financial risks in an unprotected environment and meet challenges of global competitiveness. Panagariya (2008) makes a persuasive case that large private firms will not enter into labout-intensive manufacturing without labour market reforms leading to a flexible exit policy. Policy initiatives must also be strengthened to close both physical and human infrastructure gaps, particularly in the backward regions. The Twelfth Five Year Plan approach paper recognises the need for a new policy paradigm for the manufacturing sector so that manufacturing contributes to a quarter of GDP by 2025.

A number of structural factors have contributed to a higher growth rate in the last decade. The rise in the gross capital formation rate from 25 per cent of GDP to 38 per cent during 2002-2008 played an importanty role in rasing GDP growth during this period. As discussed earlier, it dropped by about 3 percentage points after the global crisis, mirroring a similar fall in domestic savings rate which was primarily due to a fall in government savings. Raising government savings will be a critical element in restoring savings and investment levels in the economy. This in turn will depend on: (a) rationalisation and restructuring of government current expenditure, and (b) raising the volume of tax revenue. Non-merit goods subsidies such as those on oil or power once introduced are difficult to reduce or remove in a democratic setup. Yet, the need for a broad agreement among the major political parties on prioritising the subsidies and limiting them to essentials such as food, drinking water, healthy, and education cannot be overemphasised for maintaining macroeconomic stability. Proper monitoring of the several welfare programmes, particularly the centrally sponsored schemes, is another area that can raise efficiency of the programmes and reduce expenditure.

India is often seen as having a soft government in so far as its tax mobilisation efforts are concerned as the tax-GDP ratio has remained below 18 per cent. Going by international standards, there is certainly scope to raise this by a couple of percentage points to provide fiscal support to infrastructure and social sector programmes. Others steps include implementation of the goods and service tax (GST), reducing tax evasions, and expanding the tax base. Finally, the rights and entitlement approach by citizens for several public services must be accompanied by the willingness of society to pay for the services, particularly by those capable of doing so. An entitlement mindset without adequate and stable sources of funding is not viable in the long run. It cripples the government fiscal position in the future leading to a macroeconomic crisis, and the burden of adjustment, when carried out, often falls on the lower income groups in terms of downsizing welfare programmes. The entitlement attitude is evident even among rich households and the corporate sector. An emerging economy must develop growth-oriented social, political, and business norms.

Another factor that may contribute in pushing the long-term growth rate upwards is the so-called demographic dividend. The current age structure of the population is such that the proportion of the working age population to the total population is expected to increase in the coming decades. If the available labour force can be engaged in productive activities without a decline in productivity, it could be a source of additional growth. Creating appropriate employment opportunities for the fast-growing labour force with skill development that matches emerging demand patterns of a growing economy is a major challenge for deriving demographic dividents. Two points may be made in this connection. First, a faster and more stable expansion of labour-intensive industrial sectors, such as agro-processing, could be vital in absorbing the growing labour force since the labour absorption capacity of the services sector has been modest. Second, the working age population also happens to be the major saving class in an economy and the demographic dividend could potentially have a positive feedback effect on household saving rates.

While reforms in the product market have been extensive, the factor markets have remained virtually untouched. Factor market reforms would be essential to fully realise the gains from economic reforms. Labour laws applicable to organised industry in India are too restrictive for the exit of non-viable industries and stand in the way of reallocating factors to take advantage of new technology and changing market conditions. Some of the labour laws meant to protect the interests of the working class in effect protect only a small segment of labourers already employed in the organised sector and go against the interests of the working class as a whole. It is necessary to develop a regulatory framework that permits closure of non-viable units within a reasonable timeframe so that unemployed resources can be re-employed in other productive uses. As Krishna (2012)[15] points out, restrictive labour laws 'have not only reduced employment prospects in organised manufacturing but also constrained its growth by adversely affecting investment and productivity'.

Similarly, the land market is another area that needs immediate attention. Problems with the century-old Land Acquisition Act have

15. Krishna, K.L. (2012). "National Income", in Kaushik Basu and Annemie Maertens (eds.), *op.cit.*

recently attracted attention due to constraints faced by industry and a new land acquisition act is under consideration by the Parliament. A thin land market within agriculture has also been a constraint for the sector's growth. Developing a proper lease market will require a regulatory framework that protects a land-owner's property rights but incentivizes the introduction of technology and investment by ensuring tenancy certainty in the medium run. A proper tenancy registration system will also help tenants to claim benefits in the event of crop failures. Encouraging a contract farming system could help in developing linkages with agro-processing units. Similarly, opening up of the retail market to foreign players could help in developing supply chain and market linkages. The regulatory mechanism must ensure that both small and big players have access to the market on fair terms.

Regional backwardness/disparities is another issue of concern. The differences across states have long been a cause of concern but increasingly, there is recognition of the problem of severe imbalances within states. Backward districts of otherwise well performing states, present a dismal picture of intra-state imbalance and neglect. The Centre and the states together must deal with this problem on a priority basis. We cannot let large parts of the country be trapped in a prison of discontent, injustice and frustration that will only breed extremism. Therefore, special efforts must be made to remove the discontent, dispense justice, instill a sense of fairness among the people and give them dignity and hope.

The growth process must be broad-based so that benefits of growth are widespread. When the benefits accrue to a small group and large sections are left behind, social stability becomes the casualty and the growth process itself comes to a halt. Admittedly, some rise in inequality cannot be avoided in the early stages of development as is evident from the global experience. But unchecked inequality could cause social problems such as those currently noticed in large parts of the tribal belt in the country. The fact that the Scheduled Tribe (ST) and Scheduled Caste (SC) groups have the highest incidence of absolute poverty means that there is a need to reorient welfare programmes towards the STs and SCs. But, ironically, many states are not utilising even the mandated budgetary provisions under ST and SC sub-plans. The state must be an active agent in providing certain basic needs to all its citizens, particularly to those away from the mainstream. Without a new social contract towards this end, the growth process itself might be jeopardized. Developing a broad consensus for balancing the distributional objective with the growth objective requires innovative state craft.

7

Land Reforms

AT the time of Independence, India inherited a semi-feudal agrarian structure with onerous tenure arrangements over substantial areas. The ownership and control of land was highly concentrated in a relatively few landlords and intermediaries. The principal interest of this controlling group in agriculture was to extract maximum rental from tenants, either in cash or in kind. Often tenants of land under intermediary and landlord control sublet their lands in smaller plots to working cultivators, thus smaller holdings increased. Under this arrangement, economic motivation to develop farm land for increased production or to improve the economic conditions of cultivators was lacking. At the same time, working cultivators after paying high rent had no surplus to invest in farm improvement. They had neither resources nor knowledge for increasing agricultural production. Thus, the agricultural land resource of India, along with its operators was gradually impoverished because economic motivation tended toward exploitation rather than toward investment and improvement.

With increasing pressure on land the operating land base of many working cultivators was further reduced. Land occupancy rights became increasingly insecure. Often cultivators were continuously shifted from one plot to another according to the whims of superior holders. Land was divided into small fragments, each owned or leased by cultivators whose objective was subsistence. Over time, a large number of farms became disincentive-ridden due to size disability. A substantial portion of such cultivators sought to supplement their farm income by working as hired labourers competitive with even poorer landless workers. Independent India thus emerged with serious imbalances in man-land relationship among the three principal groups in the agricultural sector, *viz*., proprietors, working cultivators and labourers.

Following Independence, land reform as well as the abolition of intermediaries was considered an essential prerequisite for increasing agricultural production and for establishing an egalitarian society.

In an agrarian economy like India with great scarcity and unequal distribution of land, coupled with a large mass of below poverty-line rural population, there are compelling economic and political arguments for land reform. Not surprisingly, it received top priority on the policy agenda at the time of Independence. In the decades following Independence, India passed several land reform legislations. The Constitution of 1949 left the adoption and implementation of land and tenancy reforms to state governments. This resulted in a lot of variation in the implementation of these reforms across states and over time.[1]

Objectives of Land Reforms

The basic objectives of land reform measures were:

(i) to remove such impediments to increase in agricultural production as arise from the agrarian structure inherited from the past: and

(ii) to eliminate all forms of exploitation and social injustice within the agrarian system, to provide security for the tiller of soil and assure equality of status and opportunity to all sections of the rural population.

Land reform measures consisted of the following:

1. Abolition of Intermediaries who were rent collectors under the pre-independence land revenue system;
2. Tenancy reforms which included three measures: (i) Regulation of Rent (ii) Security of Tenure and (iii) Conferment of ownership rights on tenants.
3. Reorganisation of Agriculture which involved (i) Ceiling on Land Holdings and Redistribution of Land and (ii) Consolidation of Holdings.

Among all the land reform measures abolition of intermediaries is one reform which has been relatively successful. The record in terms of other components is mixed and varies across states. Landowners

1. Ghatak, Maitreesh (2012). "Land Reforms", in Kaushik Basu and Annemie Maertens (ed.), *The New Oxford Companion to Economics in India* (Vol.II). New Delhi: Oxford University Press.

generally resisted the implementation of these reforms and used various methods of evasion and coercion. To evade ceiling on land holdings they transferred land in different names of their relatives. They shuffled tenants on different plots so that they do not acquire occupancy rights which gave their security of tenure. Commenting on the performance of land reforms S.K. Ray remarked "On balance, there seems to be some reasons to conclude that agrarian reorganisation in India has failed to make any considerable impact on the socio-economic conditions of the working cultivators. Indeed, the record so far is so depressing and frustrating that even an able administrator like Appu, who championed and spent a considerable part of his career in administering land reform programmes noted:

> Thus the programmes of land reform implemented since Independence did not lead to any significant re-distribution of land, or, the removal of all the obstacles to increasing agricultural production. Of the three programmes considered in this study, the laws for the abolition of intermediary interests were implemented fairly well. But in the case of tenancy reform and ceilings on holdings, the policies adopted were ambivalent and there were large gaps between policy and legislation and between legislation and implementation. We have seen that as result of the implementation of the tenancy laws, tenants became owners of or acquired rights in only about 4 per cent of the operated area. The enforcement of ceilings led to the redistribution of less than 2 per cent of the operated area. Thus these two measures taken together led to the redistribution of only about 6 per cent of the operated area (Appu, 1995: 217).

Effects of Land Reforms on Productivity and Poverty[2]

According to a study by Besley and Burgess (2000) abolition of intermediaries had a negative effect on poverty but no effect on productivity and ceiling on land holding does not seem to have had much effect on either poverty or productivity, while land consolidation of holding had a positive effect on productivity without having any effect on poverty. Infact how effective a legislation is in terms of achieving its objective depends on how effectively it has been implemented. "A poorly implemented tenancy reform may have a net negative effect on productivity by freezing up the land lease market even through it might improve the productivity as well as the income of some tenants" (Ghatak). A study by Banerjee *et al.* (2002) for West

2. Besley and Burgess (2000) have used state-level data for the sixteen major states of India for the period 1958 to 1962.

Bengal where tenancy reforms were very well implemented give totally different conclusions. There in West Bengal, tenancy reforms improved agricultural productivity as a result of Operation Barga, a programme to implement and enforce tenancy laws that regulated rents and provided security to tenants of sharecroppers.

The broad conclusion is that political factor had a significant effect in the implementation of land reform legislation especially tenancy reforms. It has also been found that the likelihood of reforms increases where land inequality is high and where peasants have greater political power. Thus land reform seems to be driven by political factors. To quote Appu "...If the political will in favour of meaningful land reform was weak at independence and weaker still later on, it is non-existent today. Land reform has practically disappeared from the agenda of most political parties. This, in my view, is the inevitable consequence of the great changes that have taken place in the social and economic fields. With the abolition of intermediary interests the erstwhile superior tenants belonging mostly to upper and middle castes acquired a higher social status. Rise in agricultural productivity, rising land values and higher incomes from cultivation have added to their economic strength. Substantial landowners who wield great authority in rural India are bitterly opposed to ceilings on agricultural holdings. They are able to have their way because no serious efforts have been made to organise the landless and the land poor and enlist their support in favour of reforms. As for tenancy reform is concerned, there is a certain commonality of interest between all landowners - large, medium, small and even marginal. They are all passionately attached to their land and all of them are opposed to conferring benefits on insecure tenants. In the first round of land reform only the intermediaries were adversely affected. They were few in number and were weak politically. They had also made themselves obnoxious by aligning themselves with the colonial power. So it was easy enough to abolish intermediary interests. And it was done without hurting them much. But injuring the interests of the present class of landowners is an entirely different proposition. No political party that wishes to win elections and come to power can afford to do that. At the time of independence this class of landowners did not wield much political and economic power, and with a modicum of political will the reforms could have been implemented. But now it has become almost impossible to carry out the reforms (Appu, 1995: 232-233).

It thus appears that the present policy environment is unlikely to permit drastic changes in the existing land reform legislations. Several measures need to be taken before considering such changes. An appropriate first step in this direction would be the imposition of agricultural income tax and agricultural holding tax. These measures fit well in the newly advocated philosophy for market-friendly approach. They can also help to mobilise the much needed resources for employing the unemployed in the creation of social and physical infrastructure for agricultural development. Moreover, a progressive agricultural holding tax may act as a deterrent against formation of large holdings in the future—while at the same time, it may encourage greater efficiency of farmers who insist on retaining their large holdings.

8

Unemployment and Employment Perspective

TO understand the concept of unemployment it is necessary to understand the concept of labour force, for by definition, one who is not in the labour force cannot be unemployed. By the internationally accepted definitions, all persons who are working (have a job) and though not working, are seeking and are available for work, are deemed to be in the labour force. Correspondingly, all those who are not working and are neither seeking nor available for work are considered outside the labour force and hence do not figure in employment or unemployment statistics.[1]

The growth rate of labour force is determined partly by the age structure of the population and the age and sex specific labour force participation rate that can be expected to obtain.

Concepts and Measurement

The Labour Force Participation Rate (LFPR), Work Participation Rate (WPR) and Unemployment Rate (UR) are a few of the major indicators generally being used to assess labour market conditions. The LFPR is obtained by dividing the number of persons in the labour force with the total population. WPR, on the other hand, is obtained by dividing the number of persons in the workforce with total population. The unemployment rate is obtained by dividing the number of those unemployed with the total number of persons in the labour force.[2]

---

1. Dantwala, M.L. (1999). "Understanding Poverty and Unemployment", in Uma Kapila (ed.), *Indian Economy Since Independence*, 1999-2000 edition, p.865. New Delhi: Academic Foundation.
2. Government of India (2009). *The Challenge of Employment in India: An Informal Economy Perspective*, Report of the National Commission for Enterprises in the Unorganised Sector, Chairman: Arjun K. Sengupta, ch.3. New Delhi: Academic Foundation.

Labour Force and Workforce Participation Rates

Male participation remained higher both in labour and workforce, throughout the period between 1983 and 2004-05. Female participation *per se* in rural areas was much higher than in urban areas. Urban male participation rates (both labour force and workforce) were higher than rural male participation in 1999-2000 and 2004-05 (Table 8.1).

TABLE – 8.1

Labour Force and Workforce Participation

Rates (CDS basis) (Per cent)

	1983	*1993-94*	*1999-2000*	*2004-05*
Labour force participation rates (LFPR)				
Rural male	52.7	53.4	51.5	53.1
Rural female	21.9	23.2	22.0	23.7
Urban male	52.7	53.2	52.8	56.1
Urban female	12.1	13.2	12.3	15.0
Work force participation rates (WFPR)				
Rural male	48.2	50.4	47.8	48.8
Rural female	19.8	21.9	20.4	21.6
Urban male	47.3	49.6	49.0	51.9
Urban female	10.6	12.0	11.1	13.3

Note: LFPR/WFPR represents no. of persons/person days in the labour force/workforce per 1000 persons/person days.

Source: Various rounds of NSSO survey on employment and unemployment/Planning Commission.

Unemployment is measured through labour force surveys that elicit the 'activity' status of the respondent for a given reference period. First, the respondent is identified as not working. Second, for those not working, the typical question in the form is: are you available for work, and have you made some effort to find work during the last x days. Those who answer in the affirmative are the unemployed while those who answer in the negative are the people who have opted out of the labour force. The labour force is the sum of the employed and the unemployed and the rate of unemployment is the proportion of labour force that is unemployed. The reference period could vary from a week to four weeks to a year (Wadhwa and Ramaswami, 2007).[3]

In India, employment-unemployment surveys are conducted by the National Sample Survey (NSS) Organisation. Beginning with the 27th round in 1972-73, labour force surveys have been conducted every five years using standardised concepts and procedures based on the recommendations of the Committee of Experts.

The concepts/procedures presently being used in India for the classification are:

- Usual Principal Status (UPS)
- Usual Principal and Subsidiary Status (UPSS)
- Current Weekly Status (CWS)
- Current Daily Status (CDS)

Usual Principal Status: The labour force, in this context, is typically measured through the usual principal activity status (UPS) which reflects the status of an individual during a reference period of one year. Thus, a person is classified as belonging to labour force, if she had been either working or looking for work during longer part of the 365 days preceding the survey. The UPS measure excludes from the labour force all those who are employed and/or unemployed for a total of less than six months. Therefore, persons who work intermittently, either because of the pattern of work in the household farm/enterprise or due to economic compulsions and other reasons, would not be included in the labour force unless their days at work and unemployment totalled half of the reference year (NCEUS, 2009).

Usual Principal and Subsidiary Status: The UPSS concept was introduced to widen the UPS concept to include even those who were outside the labour force on the basis of the majority time criterion but had been employed during some part of the year on an usual basis. In the NSS 61st Round Survey (NSSO 2006a), all those who were either unemployed or out of labour force but had worked for at least 30 days over the reference year were treated as subsidiary status workers and hence, included in the labour force. UPSS is, thus, a hybrid concept incorporating both the major time criterion and priority to work status.

3. Wadhwa, Wilima and Bharat Ramaswami (2007). "Unemployment, The Measurement of", in Kaushik Basu (ed.), *The Oxford Companion to Economics in India*. New Delhi: Oxford University Press.

The UPSS measure was used on the ground that it was stable and inclusive. It is related to a picture emerging from a long reference period, and even those working for 30 days or more, but not working for the major part of the year, were included.

Current Weekly Status: The concept of CWS has been in use in the labour force surveys in India even before 1970, when the recommendations of the Dantwala Committee became available. It was primarily because the agencies like International Labour Organization (ILO) use estimates of employment and unemployment rates based on weekly reference period for international comparisons. In India, a person is classified to be in labour force as per CWS if s/he has either worked or is seeking and/or available for work at least for one hour during the reference period of one week preceding the date of survey.

Current Daily Status: The Dantwala Committee proposed the use of CDS rates for studying intensity of work. These are computed on the basis of the information on employment and unemployment recorded for the 14 half days of the reference week. The employment status during the seven days is recorded in terms of half or full intensities. An hour or more but less than four hours is taken as half intensity and four hours or more is taken as full intensity. An advantage of this approach is that it is based on more complete information; it embodied the time utilisation, and did not accord priority to labour force over outside the labour force or work over unemployment, except in marginal cases. A disadvantage is that it related to person-days, not persons. Hence, it had to be used with some caution.[4]

It has been observed that the estimates based on daily status is the most inclusive rate of 'unemployment' giving the average level of unemployment on a day during the survey year. It captures the unemployed days of the chronically unemployed, the unemployed days of usually employed who become intermittently unemployed during the reference week and unemployed days of those classified as employed according to the criterion of current weekly status. The Eleventh Five Year Plan has largely used the CDS basis of estimation of employment and unemployment in the country.

4. Government of India (2009). *op.cit.*

Some Characteristics of the Indian Labour Market[5]

India's 520 million workers account for about one-sixth of total workforce of the world. In terms of size, it is next only to China, which accounts for nearly one-fourth of the world's workforce. India has rather a low proportion of workers to total population, mainly due to low participation of women in work. It has a very low sex ratio in its labour force around 28 per cent as compared to 40 per cent in the world. Most of the workers have very low education and skill levels—only about 52 per cent of the workers are educated as compared to 77 per cent in the world as a whole. The average years of schooling of workers is abysmally low—about 4 years as against 6.5 years at global level.

Another important feature of the Indian workforce is that agriculture still accounts for about 53 per cent of the total workforce, the average for the world being only one-third. As in the most developing countries, the open rate of unemployment is quite low. It is around 2.5 per cent on the basis of the UPSS measure. Even using the most comprehensive measure of unemployment, CDS, which takes into account the work performed on daily basis, the rate of unemployment goes upto only around 8 per cent. On the other hand, level of poverty is very high. As per the latest official estimates, the proportion of poor in the country is around 36 per cent. This obviously means that a large proportion of the workers are poor. This is typical of a labour surplus developing economy where most people are engaged in subsistence activities. With about half of the workers engaged as self-employed they share whatever work is available, leading to acute underemployment and poverty. It is not surprising that incidence of poverty was much higher among employed (39%) as compared to the unemployed (27.7%) during 2004-05. Consequently, the unemployed were mostly educated as they could afford to get support from their families. During 2004-05, the average years of schooling of the unemployed were 8.8 years, whereas in case of the employed it was just half of this (4.4 years). Thus, as a whole the unemployed are younger, better educated and economically better off than the employed, on an average.

In such a situation standard definition of employment and unemployment may not be appropriate to capture all the dimensions of labour market in India. It will be better to see the dualism in the labour

5. Papola, T.S. and Alakh N. Sharma (2013). "Labour and Employment in Fast Growing India: Issues of Employment and Inclusiveness", in Uma Kapila (ed.), *Indian Economy Since Independence* (24th ed). New Delhi: Academic Foundation.

market with one large part largely subsistence economy and the other a modern one. The former is what is called unorganised sector and the latter organised sector. The unorganised sector, consisting of both agriculture and non-agriculture, has low productivity and jobs are irregular. More than half of the workers are self employed and about one-third are casual wage workers, working on daily wage basis. A small proportion of workers are full time regular workers but their earnings are also low. This sector is extremely heterogeneous comprising big cultivators and an increasing number of professionals with high earnings on the one hand, and petty producers, small and marginal farmers, hawkers, etc., on the other hand. A part of the sector is linked to organised sector and is more dynamic than the rest. Notwithstanding this heterogeneity, around three-fourth of the unorganised sector workers are poor. The workers in this sector have neither government regulations nor collective bargaining.

On the other hand, employment in the organised sector carries the benefits of social security and other non-wage benefits. Jobs are regular and wages/salaries are determined by collective bargaining and government regulations. Consequently, wage/salary in this sector is much higher than in the unorganised sector.

The broad features of the structure of employment prevailing in India are provided in Table 8.2. As can be seen regular wage employment constitutes less than one–fifth of the total employment. Moreover, more than half of the regular wage employment is informal, either in the organised sector or unorganised sector. A little over one-third of the workers is casual workers and close to half are self employed. Eighty-six per cent of employment is in the unorganised sector and only 14 per cent in the organised sector which employs about 40 per cent informal workers (usual, contract etc.). Thus, the Indian labour market is highly dualistic in nature and this dualism has sharpened over time, more so during the high growth period. Several features of the labour market are in line with the country's GDP growth rate of 8 to 9 per cent and 6.5 to 7.5 per cent annual growth in per capita income growth and aspirations and prospects of becoming a major global economic power in not too far distant a future!

TABLE – 8.2

Structure of Employment, 1983-2009/10

(Persons in age group 15-59 years)

Share (%) in total employment of :	*1983*	*1993/94*	*1999/2000*	*2004/05*	*2009/10*
Regular wage employment	16.1	15.7	16.1	16.5	17.7
Regular-formal	10.2	9.3	6.9	6.7	7.4
Regular informal	5.9	6.4	9.2	9.8	10.3
Casual wage employment	31.6	34.3	35.4	31.1	34.9
Self-employment	52.3	50.0	48.5	52.4	47.4
Casual and self employment	83.9	84.3	83.9	83.5	82.3
Organised Sector	13.6	12.4	11.6	10.9	14.2
Unorganised Sector	86.4	87.6	88.4	89.1	85.8

Source: Calculated by Ajit Ghose at IHD from the various NSSO Surveys.

Trend and Pattern of Employment Growth

Aggregate employment has grown at an average annual rate of two per cent in India during the past four decades since 1972-73. In itself this could be regarded as a significant record, as such an employment growth has not been recorded by many countries historically or in recent periods. However, as mentioned in the earlier section, a large part of this growth of employment simply indicates growth in labour force. The growth of organised sector employment and of formal employment in the organised sector is rather a good indicator of growth of quality employment. Of course, the rise in productivity and earnings of workers in the unorganised sector also denotes improvement in the employment conditions. Employment growth in recent years has, however, not been characterised by these features.

Notwithstanding the quantitative expansion in employment growth, there are a few disconcerting features of employment growth in recent years. First, employment growth has decelerated. Second, employment content of growth has shown a decline. Third, sectors with higher employment potential have registered relatively slower growth. Fourth, agriculture, despite a sharp decline in its importance in gross domestic product, continues to be the largest employer as the non-agricultural sectors have not generated enough employment to affect a shift of workforce. Fifth, most of the employment growth has been contributed by the unorganised, informal sector which is characterised by poor incomes and conditions of work. And, sixth, employment growth in the organised sector which seems to have picked up in recent years, has been mostly in the categories of casual and contract labour.

(i) Growth in Employment, GDP and Employment Elasticity

Although the long-term employment growth over the period of about four decades, as noted earlier, has been around 2 per cent per annum, it has seen a declining trend from one decade to another: it was 2.44 per cent during 1972-73/1983, 2.02 per cent during the next 10 year period and 1.84 per cent during 1993-94/2004-05 (Table 8.3). In between, these decadal periods, some fluctuations were noted in shorter periods of five years. Of these, a sharp rise in employment growth during 2000-2005 to 2.81 per cent over 1.00 per cent during 1993-94/2004-05, is most striking. The most favourable interpretation of this upturn in employment growth in post-2000 period is that the teething troubles of the economic reforms which led to slow growth of employment initially were over by 2000 and globalisation started having its beneficial effect on employment with the start of the millennium. The facts that GDP growth was no better—was, in fact lower—during 2000-2005 than during 1994-2000, that most employment growth recorded during the later period was in the informal sector of which a large part was as self-employment in agriculture. Organised sector employment, in fact, saw an absolute decline, which raises doubts about the high employment growth during 2000-2005 being demand-led and productive. A virtual stagnation in employment during 2004-05/2009-10 as revealed by the latest round of NSSO survey casts further doubt on the veracity of the 2004-05 estimates. This has been largely due to a sharp fall in women work force participation rate due to increase in schooling etc. This period has also seen a significant increase in organised sector employment relative to unorganised sector.

The long-term trend of a decline in the rate of employment growth is, however, a fact that can not be ignored. What is particularly intriguing is that this decline has accompanied an acceleration in the rate of economic growth. Thus when GDP grew at 4.7 per cent per annum during 1972-73 to 1983, employment growth was 2.4 per cent; GDP growth increased to 5 per cent; but employment growth declined to 2.0 per cent during 1983/1993-94; during 1993-94/2004-05 GDP growth accelerated to 6.3 per cent, but employment growth further declined to 1.8 per cent and during the 2004-05/2009-10, when GDP

TABLE – 8.3

Growth of Employment (UPSS) and Employment Elasticity

Sector	Employment Growth					Employment Elasticity				
	1972-73/ 1983	*1983/ 1993-94*	*1993-94/ 2004-05*	*1999-2000 2009-10*	*2004-05 2009-10*	*1972-73/ 1983*	*1983/ 1993-94*	*1993-94/ 2004-05*	*1999-2000/ 2009-10*	*2004-05/ 2009-10*
1	9	10	11	12	8	9	10	11	12	8
Primary Sector	1.70	1.35	0.67	-0.13	-1.63	0.46	0.49	0.26	-0.05	-0.53
Mining & Quarrying	5.92	3.24	-0.08	2.70	3.00	0.86	0.53	-0.02	0.61	0.73
Manufacturing	4.28	2.00	3.17	1.95	-1.06	0.78	0.41	0.47	0.25	-0.11
Utilities	7.86	5.58	-1.86	2.11	1.02	1.00	0.64	-0.32	0.37	0.14
Construction	4.43	5.67	7.19	9.72	11.29	1.44	1.16	0.94	1.06	1.22
Secondary Sector	4.43	2.82	3.97	4.64	3.46	0.87	0.53	0.59	0.60	0.39
Trade, Hotelling etc.	4.62	3.77	5.24	2.54	1.10	0.81	0.67	0.61	0.30	0.12
Transport & Communication etc.	5.88	3.39	5.16	3.68	2.14	0.91	0.56	0.49	0.25	0.13
Financing, Insurance, Real estate & business services	7.43	3.58	7.23	7.68	5.77	1.25	0.39	0.99	0.81	0.47
Community, social and personal services	3.18	3.91	0.40	1.85	0.99	0.71	0.67	0.06	0.28	0.12
Tertiary Sector	4.21	3.77	3.41	2.83	1.59	0.77	0.57	0.43	0.30	0.14
All Non Agricultural	4.30	3.36	3.64	3.61	2.41	0.81	0.55	0.48	0.41	0.23
Total	**2.44**	**2.02**	**1.84**	**1.50**	**0.22**	**0.52**	**0.41**	**0.29**	**0.20**	**0.02**

Source: Estimates based on various rounds of NSS data on employment and unemployment.
Papola and Sharma (2013).

growth was as high as 9 per cent employment grew at an insignificant rate of 0.22 per cent! The declining trend in the employment content of growth is quite clearly seen in terms of the values of employment elasticity (ratio of employment growth to growth in value added) in Table 8.3. It was 0.52 during 1972-73/1983, declined to 0.41 in the next 10-year period and further to 0.29 during 1993-94/2004/05. During 2004-05/2009-10, it declined to almost zero.

The employment growth rates have of course varied across various sectors and activities. In the secondary sector, consisting of mining, manufacturing, electricity, water and gas, and construction, the growth has been relatively high, in fact the highest among the three sectors, during the long period, 1972-73 to 2009-10. It has declined over the period with some fluctuations over the shorter periods, but has shown a significant increase during 1994-2005. Even during 2004-05/2009-10, when overall employment has virtually stagnated, it has grown at around 3.5 per cent in the secondary sector. Employment growth in the tertiary or services sector, has also been relatively high but has consistently declined over the three periods of 10 years each since 1972-1973. Growth of employment in the primary sector, as expected, has been the lowest and seen the sharpest decline. It has, in fact, turned negative in recent years. Slow and declining growth of employment in agriculture, is a result both of slow and declining rate of GDP growth and a decline in employment elasticity. In the secondary sector, a high employment growth despite moderate rates of GDP growth has been possible due to relatively high and rising employment elasticity. But in the tertiary sector, even a high GDP growth has not been able to maintain a high growth in employment due to a steep decline in employment elasticity.

Within the secondary or industry sector, construction experienced a relatively high and increasing rate of employment growth; it was as high as over 7 per cent during 1994-2005, almost similar to its GDP growth. It has recorded 11 per cent employment growth during the 2004-05/2009-10, when total employment has virtually stagnated. Employment growth in manufacturing has also been moderately high, and after declining during 1983/1993-94 over the earlier 10 year period, it registered an increase in the next period, 1994-2005. But it experienced a decline in employment during 2004-05/2009-10. Employment elasticity in manufacturing, has been relatively high except during 2005-2010 when it has, in fact, been negative.

In the services sector, financial services, however, have recorded the highest increase in employment over the longer period 1983-2005 except during 1983/1993-94. Even during 2004-05/2009-10, this sub-sector of services has registered an employment growth of about 6 per cent, while trade and transport sub-sectors experienced only about 1 to 2 per cent growth in employment. All sub-sectors with the possible exception of community, social and personal services have shown reasonably high potential for employment generation. It must, however, be noted that in most sub-sectors of services, while GDP has seen a high and increasing growth rate, employment growth has been on a declining rate. Employment elasticity has, therefore, declined sharply from 0.81 during 1972-73/1983 to 0.30 during 1999-2000/2009-10 in trade, from 0.91 to 0.25 in transport, from 0.71 to 0.28 in community, social and personal, services, although in financial services it increased during 1993-94/2009-10.

Thus, as a whole, it can be concluded that employment content of growth has declined over time. Of course, it has varied across the sectors. Primary sector, consisting of mainly agriculture, has witnessed least employment growth which in itself is not worrisome as this sector is home to the large bulk of surplus labour. The sub-sectors of the tertiary sector such as financial services which are linked to globalisation have witnessed rather faster growth of employment. However, the manufacturing sector which has significant multiplier effects with other sectors has not registered high growth of employment due primarily to low growth of output .

(ii) Organised Versus Unorganised Sector Employment

Organised or formal sector refers to the entire public sector and the private sector enterprises employing 10 or more workers. It accounted for only about 14 per cent of total employment in 1999-2000 as also in 2004-2005. The proportion is found to have slightly increased to 16 per cent in 2009-10. Still that leaves 84 per cent of workers in the 'unorganised' or 'informal' sector, with no job security or social security. Even in the formal sector, over half the workers are in 'informal' category, with no secured tenure of employment, nor any protection against the contingent risks during or after employment. What is further distressing to note is that their proportion has been rising: 'informally' employed workers constituted 42 per cent of those employed in the formal sector in 1999-2000, the figure increased to 47 per cent in 2004-05 and stood at 51 per cent in 2009-10. A small proportion (about half a per cent) of those employed in the informal sector enjoyed a measure of job security and social security. Thus of all the workers in the formal and informal sectors together, 92 per cent were in 'informal' employment. Only 8 per cent were in employment with secured job tenure and with social security against contingent risks of work and life. Their proportion has remained more or less constant during the decade 1999-2000/2009-10. (Table 8.4).

TABLE – 8.4

Percentage Distribution of Workers in Formal/Informal Sectors/Employment

Year	*Informal Workers*			
	Informal Sector	*Formal Sector*	*Total*	
1999-00	93.6	6.4	100	(362.75)
2004-05	93.1	6.9	100	(422.61)
2009-10	91.2	8.8	100	(423.17)
Formal Workers				
1999-00	5.3	94.7	100	(33.64)
2004-05	4.1	95.9	100	(34.85)
2009-10	4.5	95.5	100	(37.25)
Total Workers				
1999-00	86.2	13.8	100	(396.39)
2004-05	86.3	13.7	100	(457.47)
2009-10	84.2	15.8	100	(460.42)

Note: Figures in paranthesis are the absolute number in millions.
Source: NCEUS, 2009 and Kannan, 2012.

Organised sector employment saw a continuous decline for a number of years since mid-1990s. After continuously increasing and reaching the highest figure of 28.3 million in 1997, it recorded a continuous decline since then till 2005, but has shown some increase since 2005. It stood at 28.7 million in the year 2010. It should be noted that the earlier decline has been mainly in public sector employment which has continued to decline even in post-2004 period except during 2009 and 2010. So far as private sector is concerned it showed a small decline during 2001-2004, but has increased to an all time high at 10.8 in 2010. The decline in public sector employment has been in all division of activity namely, manufacturing, construction, transport as well as community, social and personal services. Mining is the only sector where some increase has taken place in public sector employment in recent years.

A decline in public sector employment is a policy-induced phenomenon propelled by the reforms towards economic liberalisation which led to measures like downsizing the government, reduction in overstaffing of public enterprises and withdrawal of government from commercial activities. Employment in all activity segments of the private sector except manufacturing has continuously risen since 1991, and even in manufacturing the trend appears to have reversed with an increase since 2004. While during 2001-2004, the employment of workers as well as employers, declined in manufacturing, there has been reversal during 2005 and 2009 when there is significant growth in employment in both categories. However, here also this employment growth is overwhelmingly because of the employment of contract workers at the expense of regular workers. The analysis of data from the Annual Survey of Industry (ASI) clearly reveals that during the period of 2000-01 to 2008-09, while regular workers increased by around 2.1 per cent, the growth of contract workers has been close to 10 per cent per annum. This has resulted in a significant increase in the share of contract workers from one-fifth during 2000-01 to close to one-third during 2008-09. (Kumar, 2012). In fact, this trend of increasing contractualisation has been evident from early 1990s itself when the economic reforms were initiated. This is quite evident from Figure 8.1 showing the rapid growth of contract workers in the manufacturing sectors.

FIGURE – 8.1

Proportion of Contract Workers in Total Number of Workers in the Organised Factory Sector, 1993-94 to 2008-09

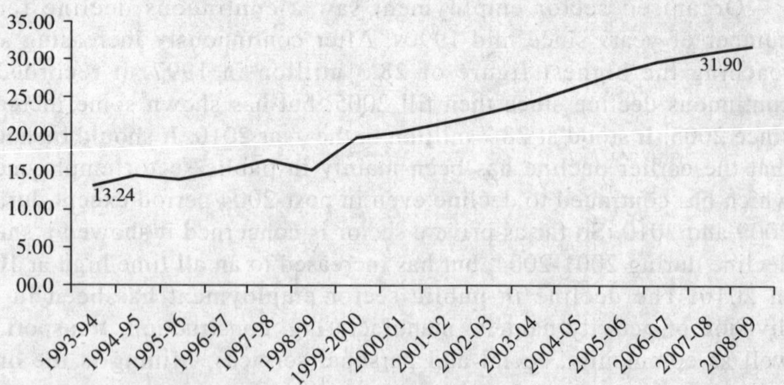

(iii) Sectoral Employment Shares

As is well known, majority of Indian workers are engaged in agriculture and allied activities. With economic development, agriculture is expected to decline in importance in terms of its share in employment and output. Proportion of agriculture in total employment has declined over the years: from 74 per cent in 1972-73 to 68 per cent in 1983, 60 per cent in 1993-94 and to 57 per cent in 2004-05. It has declined further to 51 per cent in 2009-10. But the decline in the employment share of agriculture has been much slower than in its share in gross domestic product (GDP) from agriculture. Thus, while share of agriculture in GDP declined from 41 per cent in 1972-73 to 15 per cent in 2009-10 (Table 8.5), that in employment declined from 74 per cent to 51 per cent. And rate of decline in GDP share has been faster during 1993-94 to 2009-10, from 30 to 15 per cent; while the rate of decline in employment share has been relatively slow, from 64 per cent to 51 per cent.

The decline in employment share of agriculture has been mostly compensated by an increase in the share of secondary sector in the pre-reform period (before 1991), but since the economic reforms the tertiary sector has been the main gainer of the shift in employment. Yet increase in its employment share has not been commensurate with the increase in its share of GDP during 1993-94/2009-10. The share of secondary sector in employment has increased at a relatively faster rate while its share in GDP has remained constant at about one-fourth of the total. Within the secondary sector construction has sharply increased its share in employment. Manufacturing increased its share both in employment and GDP, but rather slowly. In the tertiary sector, trade experienced a fast increase in its share in employment, and a significant though somewhat smaller increases in its share in GDP in the post-reform period but saw only a small increase in its employment share. Financial services registered a fast increase both in its employment and GDP share, though its share in employment is small (2.25) about one-seventh of its share in GDP (15.64%). Community social and personal services which used to be the largest activity in the tertiary sector, both in terms of employment and GDP, in the pre-reform period, saw a marginal decline in their share both in employment and GDP and is now the smallest in regard to GDP, though it continues to be the second largest, after trade, in terms of employment.

The asymmetry in the rate of change in employment and GDP shares of different sectors and divisions, has serious implications in terms of differences in earnings and income between different sectors. In 1972-1973, agriculture employed 74 per cent workers, but it also

TABLE – 8.5

Employment (UPSS) and GDP Share of Major Sectors (%)

Sector	Sectoral share in employment					Sectoral share in employment				
	1972-73	*1983*	*1993-94*	*2004-05*	*2009-10*	*1972-73*	*1983*	*1993-94*	*2004-05*	*2009-10*
1	9	10	11	12	8	9	10	11	12	8
Primary Sector	73.92	68.59	63.98	56.30	51.30	40.92	37.15	30.01	20.20	15.23
Mining & Quarrying	0.43	0.61	0.69	0.56	0.64	1.83	2.25	2.51	2.20	1.74
Manufacturing	8.87	10.66	10.63	12.27	11.50	13.45	14.52	14.46	15.12	15.41
Utilities	0.16	0.28	0.40	0.27	0.28	1.27	1.71	2.43	2.29	2.10
Construction	1.84	2.24	3.24	5.69	9.60	6.77	5.81	5.76	6.62	6.67
Secondary Sector	11.30	13.78	14.96	18.78	22.02	23.32	24.30	25.15	26.24	25.92
Trade, Hotelling etc.	5.11	6.35	7.59	10.89	11.38	10.39	11.51	12.18	15.54	15.53
Transport & Communicationetc.	1.77	2.49	2.87	4.08	4.48	5.05	5.99	6.62	10.25	14.00
Financing, Insurance, Realestate & business services	0.51	0.83	0.97	1.71	2.25	7.35	8.31	12.17	13.53	15.64
Community, social and personal services	7.39	7.96	9.64	8.24	8.57	12.97	12.75	13.86	14.25	13.67
Tertiary Sector	14.78	17.63	21.07	24.92	26.67	35.75	38.56	44.84	53.56	58.84
All NonAgricultural	26.08	31.41	36.02	43.70	48.70	59.08	62.85	69.99	79.80	84.77
Total	**100**	**100**	**100**	**100**	**100**	**100**	**100**	**100**	**100**	**100**

Source: Estimates based on various rounds of NSS data on employment and unemployment. Papola and Sharma (2013).

produced 41 per cent of GDP. Per worker productivity and income in agriculture was significantly lower than in non-agricultural activities even then; the ratio being 1:3.6. In 2009-10, the ratio has gone up to 1:6. Thus there has been a large decline in the relative earnings of agricultural workers. That is partly because agricultural growth has been consistently much lower than that in the non-agricultural sectors, but mainly, because a shift of workers from agricultural to non-agricultural activities as expected in the process of economic development has not taken place. Agriculture has grown at an average rate of 2 to 3 per cent per annum as against 5 to 6.5 per cent growth in the non-agricultural sector during the period under consideration. It is not generally realistic to expect a much higher growth rate in agriculture. But even if it grew at a rate of about 4 per cent per annum, as envisaged in the Eleventh Plan, it cannot employ many more persons productively. In fact, productivity per worker in agriculture is so low that even with a higher growth rate, it would need to reduce its workforce so as to provide a reasonable level of income to those engaged in it. It is precisely for this reason that the Planning Commission projected no increase in the number of workers in agriculture during the Eleventh Plan (2007-2012) and a decline of 4 million during the Twelfth Plan period (2012-2017) (Planning Commission, 2008, Vol. I: 76-77).

Quality of Employment and Disparities

As has been explained earlier, employment growth in a labour surplus economy like India largely denotes growth in the labour force. It is quite evident from the very low rate of open unemployment of around 2 per cent. The fact that nearly 36 per cent of the population is poor according to the new officially adopted poverty line, it points out towards the phenomenon of working poor. While growth in labour force due to the demographic pressure and structural changes in the economy will always necessitate quantitative expansion of employment, the qualitative dimension is more important where about one forth of these employed are poor, the proportion being larger among the casual wage workers. One reason for poverty among the employed workers could be that they do not have full time work and these severely unemployed may need alternative employment. For same groups under employment is quite high. For example, agricultural labourers were reported to be in the labour force on an average for 312 days out of which they were unemployed for 51 days in 2004-05, making the person days of unemployment (or underemployment) to be 16 per cent.

But most often the reason for poverty amongst the employed lies in low earning out of their work-either on a self-employed, or wage/ salary basis. Data on earnings of the self-employed are not available, but according to a survey among farmers who constitute the majority among the self-employed about 48 per cent earned on an average less than the poverty line expenditure of Rs 1,800 per month in 2003 (NSSO, 2005; Bhalla, 2006; Papola, 2010). Average daily earnings of casual workers constituting 31 per cent of all workers and were estimated to be Rs 49 in rural and Rs 58 in urban areas as against per capita per day income of Rs 64 for the entire population in 2004-05. Earnings of a regular worker were relatively higher at Rs 134 in rural and Rs 194 in urban areas. Average daily earnings of casual workers in agriculture were only about 65 per cent of those in non-agriculture. And among the non-agricultural sectors, workers in transport and communications, utilities, and financial and social services earned much better than those in construction, trade and manufacturing. (NCEUS, 2007). The acute disparity is also sharply revealed by the fact that while a rural casual labour earned on average around Rs. 75 in 2009-10, the per capita emoluments of a central public sector enterprises was Rs. 1670 per day.

Levels of earnings in different sectors and activities are, of course, primarily a function of differences in productivity. Utilities, with over eight times the average productivity pay the highest emoluments, followed by financial and social services and transport and communication with about 2.7 times the average productivity. Workers in agriculture with only about one-third of the average productivity level earn the lowest. Ratio between the agriculture and non-agricultural productivity stood at 1:6 in 2009-10. In the unorganised segment of the manufacturing sector productivity per worker was estimated to be as low as Rs 12993 (at constant 1993-94 prices), almost one-twentieth of that in the organised sector (Rs 2.55 hundred thousand) in 2006-07 (Papola *et. al*., 2011). Workers in the unorganised segment of services (excluding trade) are similarly worse off with an average productivity of Rs 35438 (at constant 1993-94 prices) as against the average of about Rs 66995 for the entire sector, in 2006-07 (Papola and Sharma, 2013).

Weaknesses in Past Performance

The basic weakness in our employment performance is the failure of the Indian economy to create a sufficient volume of additional high quality employment to absorb the new entrants into the labour force while also facilitating the absorption of surplus labour that currently exists in the agricultural sector, into higher wage, non-agricultural employment. A successful transition to inclusive growth requires migration of such surplus workers to other areas for productive and gainful employment in the organised or unorganised sector. Women agricultural workers in families where the male head has migrated, also require special attention given the need for credit and other inputs if they are self-employed in agriculture or for wage employment if they do not have land.

The approach to the Eleventh Plan had identified the following specific weaknesses on the employment front which illustrate the general failing just discussed.

(i) The rate of unemployment has increased from 6.1 per cent in 1993-94 to 7.3 per cent in 1999-2000, and further to 8.3 per cent in 2004-05.

(ii) Unemployment among agricultural labour households has risen from 9.5 per cent in 1993-94 to 15.3 per cent in 2004-2005.

(iii) Under-employment appears to be on the rise, as evident from a widening of the gap between the usual status and the current daily status measures of creation of incremental employment opportunities between the periods 1994-2000 and 2000-2005.

(iv) While non-agricultural employment expanded at a robust annual rate of 4.7 per cent during the period 1999-2000 to 2004-05, this growth was largely in the unorganised sector.

(v) Despite fairly healthy GDP growth, employment in the organised sector actually declined, leading to frustration among the educated youth who have rising expectations.

(vi) Although real wages of casual labour in agriculture continue to rise during 2000-2005, growth has decelerated strongly, as compared to the previous quinquennium (1994-2000), almost certainly reflecting poor performance in agriculture. However, over the longer periods 1983 to 1993-94 (Period I) and 1993-1994 to 2004-05 (Period II), the decline is moderate for rural male agricultural casual labour, from 2.75 per cent to 2.18 per cent per annum.

(vii) Growth of average real wage rates in non-agriculture employment in the period 1999-2000 to 2004-05 has been negligible. Seen over the longer period of two decades

(Period I and Period II), the wages have steadily increased at over 2 per cent per annum.

(viii) In respect of entire rural male casual labour, the growth in real wages accelerated from 2.55 per cent (Period I) to 2.78 per cent per annum (Period II).

(ix) Real wages stagnated or declined even for workers in the organised industry although managerial and technical staff did secure large increase.

(x) Wage share in the organised industrial sector has halved after the 1980s and is now among the lowest in the world.

"It is only through a massive effort at employment creation, of the right quality, and decent conditions of work for all sections of population and at all locations that a fair redistribution of benefits from growth can be achieved. This indeed is a stupendous task. Alternative policy measures focusing on different sectors and occupations, and the specific requirements of different target groups are needed to create employment on a sustainable basis" (11th Plan).

According to the Commission (NCEUS), we need to reverse the priority of development agenda from growth first to one of employment first. According to Okun's law, every 1 per cent fall in unemployment would raise GDP by 2.5 per cent. As per the calculations of Minsky for USA, the decreasing unemployment to 2.5 per cent from the level of 5 per cent 'would create 3-5 times the GDP required to raise all households above the poverty line'.

The main findings of the Commission with regard to the likely employment generation may be summed up as in the following three major points: (i) At 7 per cent growth rate, unemployment (MCWS) will more or less remain the same even at the end of 12th Plan. A higher growth at 9 per cent will almost eliminate it (but will still leave the task of providing adequate employment to the under-employed and the part-time employed). A lower growth rate of 5 per cent will increase unemployment. (ii) The share of the informal sector in the total employment will continue to remain around 86 per cent. (iii) There will be increasing informalisation of employment in the economy reflecting the informal nature of the additional employment generated in the formal sector. Therefore, the problem of quality of employment will continue to loom large in the Indian economy.

The generation of productive and gainful employment, with decent working conditions, on a sufficient scale to absorb our growing labour force must form a critical element in the strategy for achieving inclusive growth. Past record in this respect is definitely inadequate and the problem is heightened by the fact that the relatively higher rate of growth achieved during the last decade or so is not seen to generate a sufficient volume of good quality employment (11th Plan).

Employment and Labour Policy

The employment strategy must ensure rapid growth of employment while also ensuring an improvement in the quality of employment. While self-employment will remain an important employment category in the foreseeable future—it accounted for 58 per cent of all employment in 2004-05—there is need to increase the share of regular employees in total employment.

The above analysis implies that the success of labour policy should be seen in terms of the number of regular wage employment opportunities based on some form of a written contract between the employer and the employee, that is, an increase in the number of 'formal' jobs. The potential for creation of formal employment can be fully utilised by making appropriate changes in rules and procedures. It is often said that one of the obstacles to growth of formal employment in the organised sector is the prevalence of excessively rigid labour laws which discourage such employment.

Indian Labour Laws and Labour Markets

Indian labour market is characterised by a sharp dichotomy. A large number of establishments in the unorganised sector remain outside any regulation, while the organised sector has been regulated fairly stringently. It can be reasonably argued that the organised sector has provided too much of job security for too long, while the unorganised sector has provided too little to too many.

Almost all international studies conclude that India's labour regulatory structure does not have the flexibility commensurate with a buoyant, growing economy. For firms in the organised sector having more than a certain critical number of labourers it is extremely hard to retrench workers or downsize the labour force. At first sight this looks like a pro-labour legislation, one that protects the interests of workers. On the other hand, it can be argued that most potential firms are far-sighted enough to realise that, once they become sufficiently large in terms of employment, if they later need to retrench workers because the demand for their product slacks off, they will not be able to do so easily. This is likely to prompt them to remain small or not go into business at all. Hence it is arguable that our labour laws, such as the Industrial Dispute Act of 1947, if appropriately reformed, can lead to a greater demand for labour, and through that improve economic well-being of workers.

Perhaps there are lessons to be learnt from China in the area of labour reforms. China, with a history of extreme employment security, has drastically reformed its labour relations and created a new labour market, in which workers are highly mobile. Although there have been mass layoffs and open unemployment, high rates of industrial growth especially in the coastal regions helped their redeployment. In spite of hardship, workers in China seem to have benefited from wage growth, additional job creation and new opportunities for self employment.

Public Employment Programme for the Unorganised Workers: The Case of NREGA

Programmes to create direct employment opportunities for wage workers through public works have in the past focused on generation of supplementary employment opportunities, especially during lean periods. They have been considered as an important component of the anti-poverty strategy. These programmes are expected to create durable assets for the community and thus, enhance further economic activities. Wage employment programmes also push up demand for labour and thus exert an upward pressure on the market wage rates by attracting people to public works programmes, thereby reducing supply of cheap labour, often at wages that would not even meet their bare basic needs.

Consistent with the approach for an employment-centred development strategy that would level up the informal economy, public employment programmes should be an integral part of planning and policy. Apart from the advantages that would accrue to the unemployed, underemployed and the poorly employed, such programmes will also have a positive macro economic impact via the increase in effective demand from the hitherto poor and vulnerable segments of the population. Viewed in this perspective, the enactment of the National Rural Employment Guarantee Act (NREGA) is a historic step in the Indian context.

The Commission (NCEUS) has viewed NREGA as an important component of an employment-based growth strategy.

An Overview of the Scheme

NREGA has been envisaged from the perspective of 'right to employment' and guarantees 100 days employment at a minimum fixed wage rate, but more importantly it bestows an entitlement. The Act has also identified roles and responsibilities for the Central and state governments, district and block administrations and the *panchayats*. The onus of guaranteeing 100 days of employment rests with the Government and the applicant can demand for unemployment allowance in case he/she does not get work. Apart from creation of work opportunities, the Act also provides for basic facilities at the worksite namely *viz*., crèche, safe drinking water and medical aid.

The salient features revolve around recognition of the right to work and dignity to work. These include:

- A right-based framework, with employment on demand.
- At least one hundred days of guaranteed wage employment in a financial year to every household whose adult members volunteer to do unskilled manual work.
- Wage payment within 15 days.
- Payment of unemployment allowance in case of non-provision of employment within 15 days (unemployment allowance to be at least one fourth of the minimum wage for the first 30 days, and at least one-half of the minimum wages thereafter).
- Work within 5 kilometres of residence (if provided outside 5km, 10 per cent extra wage to meet additional transportation and living expenses).
- Minimum wages to be paid by the state governments.
- Priority for ensuring one-third of workers is women.
- Mandatory basic worksite facilities—drinking water, shade, medical aid and crèche if more than five children below age 6 are present.
- Ban on the use of contractors and machinery and allocation of funds in the ratio of 60:40 for unskilled and skilled/ material components of the work ensure the primacy of labour intensive nature of work.
- Equal wages for men and women.

- Devolution of powers to the Panchayati Raj Institutions.
- Mechanisms of accountability and transparency.
- Creation of durable assets to strengthen the livelihood resource base of the rural poor.

The Performance

Mahatma Gandhi National Rural Employment Guarantee Scheme (MGNREGS), was launched in February 2006 in 200 most backward districts in the first phase and was expanded to 330 districts during 2007-08. The coverage was extended to all rural districts of the country in 2008-09. At present, 619 districts are covered under the MGNREGS.

At national level, the average wage paid under the MGNREGA has increased from Rs 65 in FY 2006-7 to Rs 120 in FY 2011-12 (up to November 2011). This has led to substantial increase in purchasing power leading to strengthening of the livelihood resource base of the rural poor in India. The MGNREGA has successfully raised the bargaining power of agricultural labour, resulting in higher agricultural wages, improved economic outcomes, and reduction in distress migration. However, with better planning of project design and capacity building of the panchayati raj institutions (PRIs), pitfalls in implementation could be plugged to a great extent and the assets so created could make a much larger contribution to increasing land productivity. Many initiatives are being taken for better and more effective implementation of the MGNREGA. The performance of the MGNREGA since its inception has been showing an upward trend in terms of households provided employment, average wages per persondays, and percentage share of women in total persondays generated. Though the share of women has now stagnated at 48 per cent, it is well above the stipulation of 1/3 in the Act. Persondays generated both in absolute terms and average persondays per household however show a slight fall in 2010-11, which may be due to the fact that demand came down owing to a good monsoon. While the overall performance of the MGNREGA has been good, there is scope for improvements like focused planning, shifting to permanent asset and infrastructure building activities, skill upgradation for enhanced employability, reducing transaction costs, better monitoring, avoiding peak seasons in agriculture, and extension to urban areas. (*Economic Survey 2011-2012*)

The performance of the MGNREGA varies significantly across the states. There are some states where MGNREGA has managed to achieve its key outcomes very well and which have indeed innovated in many respects. In others, performance has been unimpressive and lacklustre. Given that the overall framework for the MGNREGA is similar across the states, clearly, the variations in performance depend on factors such as the political and administrative will of the governments, historical background of the state as well as the nature of civil society and public actions around the MGNREGP. But this also suggests that the state governments which have the responsibility of framing the rules as well as overseeing the actual implementation of the scheme on the ground can "own" the scheme and give it a fillip. There is a lot of scope for state governments to innovate and adapt the scheme according to the local requirements. State-specific experiences are important sources for innovations which in turn provide valuable lessons for replication. The relative success of the scheme in some regions, and failure in others highlights the need to properly understand the reasons for inter and intra state variations and to replicate and adopt features of implementation of the better performing states. Below we highlight some of the experiences from the states.

Success Stories

The performance of the scheme in the state of Andhra Pradesh has been laudable because of strong political will and also because the state has had a rural worker and community mobilisation movement. In addition, Andhra Pradesh has successfully employed computerisation and e-governance mechanisms for monitoring the scheme. For example, funds are being transferred electronically; every jobs seeker has got a bank account and wages are paid through bank or post office account; the whole process from job application to registration is computerised.[6]

In Rajasthan, which has the history of drought relief based public employment and active civil society, the success of MGNREGA is more impressive compared to other north Indian states. Dungarpur district was able to make MGNREGA more of a success because of the presence of effective grassroots NGOs and their ability to mobilise the poor.

In Kerala, the MGNREGA implementation pivots around the Kutumbashree (self help groups of poor women). These women are not only involved in identifying the public work projects, but also overseeing the implementation. Besides, Kerala has also used banks and post offices for wage payment. All these have resulted in high

6. Institute of Human Development (2009). "NREGS in India: Impacts and Implimentation Experiences", Report of the conference held on September 16-18, 2008, New Delhi.

participation rate of women and an overall efficient system. Manifold increase in the number of work days, reduction in distress out-migration, enrolment in schools were observed in a study of eight states by Indian School of Women's Studies and Development, New Delhi.[7]

Remaining Gaps

In some states, the scheme has been plagued with teething problems and is yet to take off. Jharkhand faced problems in implementation because of the non-constitution of Panchayati Raj Institutions (PRIs) in the state (Dreze and Bhatia, 2006). Bihar has problems related to shortage of staff, poor infrastructure, low administrative capacity of the state, etc.[8]

Poor awareness levels of workers regarding the scheme and the entitlements can also be cited as a reason for its inability to take off in some regions. In the GBPSSI Study of six states, Rajasthan emerges favourably in this regard, with 90 per cent of workers knowing about the provision of 100 days of work. More than half of the respondents were aware of the minimum wages and the 15 days period within which wage payment should take place. This can be attributed, as already mentioned, to the state's active tradition of public mobilisation, state initiated awareness drives and presence of workers' organisations such as the MKSS. In comparison, the remaining five states where the survey was conducted, less that 50 per cent of the workers exhibited knowledge of the most basic provision of the scheme of employment for 100 days. Further, the demand based nature through which employment is offered under MGNREGA has still got a long way to go in terms of being operationalised, with 71 per cent of the respondents in the study being unaware that an application had to be submitted in order to gain work.

However, within the existing framework and limitations, many of the problems can be substantially overcome if the political and administrative leadership at the state and local levels plays a more pro-active role in implementing the objectives of the MGNREGA.

The Commission (NCEUS) regards the MGNREGA as an important component of the full employment strategy for India. In their assessment, the impact of the MGNREGA in the first three years of its implementation have, on the whole, been positive but given the size and the several inter-related objectives of the scheme, it needs to be

7. Ibid.
8. Ibid.

carefully nurtured and strengthened, especially in the lagging areas and regions.

Employment Perspective

What are the prospects for growth and quality of employment in India in the near future? It is a known fact that a high rate of economic growth has not been able to generate high employment growth, rather the employment growth has slowed down in recent years which has led many economists and others concerned to describe the recent experience as one of 'jobless growth'. Employment elasticities have declined in most sectors, though in some sectors like construction, trade and transport, they continue to be relatively high. A faster growth of these sectors will lead to an increase in overall employment growth. However, their share in employment, is still small as compared to manufacturing which has shown a relatively low employment growth, and low and declining employment elasticity. Although manufacturing still has an employment elasticity of around 0.3 per cent, there are indications to suggest that it may improve. The export-oriented sub-sectors of manufacturing have recently experienced higher employment growth and employment elasticity. During the 1990s, employment in export-oriented industries grew at 3.36 per cent per annum and showed an employment elasticity of 0.48 (Goldar, 2003). A faster growth of manufactured exports, which now constitute over 75 per cent of total exports, as compared to 58 per cent in 1980, therefore, promises to be an important factor in reversing the declining trend in employment growth.[9]

According to Papola and Sharma,[10] new jobs that are required to be created are not likely to be in agriculture, they have to come from the non-agricultural sectors. In a 25 to 30 years perspective, employment structure must be envisioned as consisting of about 30-35 per cent in agriculture and 70-75 per cent in non-agricultural activities as against of 51 per cent in agriculture and 49 per cent in non-agriculture in 2004-05. It would imply that all the new employment opportunities will be located in non-agricultural activities in the coming years.

---

9. Papola, T.S. (2012). "Employment Prospects", in Kaushik Basu and Annemie Maertens (eds.) *The New Oxford Companion to Economics in India* (Vol.I). New Delhi: OUP. pp.427-428.
10. Papola and Sharma (2013) *op. cit.*

9

Poverty in India

THE problem of poverty and unemployment is considered as the biggest challenge to development planning in India. High poverty levels are synonymous with poor quality of life, deprivation, malnutrition, illiteracy and low human resource development. The slogan of poverty eradication has been adopted by all political parties in one form or another and there is a national agreement for the goal of poverty alleviation. The national consensus on poverty alleviation provided the necessary condition for launching various schemes and programmes aimed at achieving this objective. But the persistence of poverty during all these years suggests that the national consensus on objectives did not and could not provide sufficient conditions for poverty alleviation.

Magnitude and Determinants

There is no agreement among scholars on the extent of poverty in India. The question arises why should there be such differences in the extent of poverty when the basic source of data used by all scholars is the same i.e., the various rounds of the NSS?

The Selection of Poverty Lines

The calculation of poverty measures requires two components, a distribution of household expenditure and a poverty line or cut-off that separates poor from non-poor households. Although poverty lines are often linked to the amount of money that households need, to be able to buy a minimally satisfactory diet, the use and long-term survival of poverty lines depends on policy makers and others accepting them as useful.

The starting point for estimating the number of households below the poverty line is a normative nutritional requirement per person per day at some base point. There is a debate on the minimum calorie requirement, and whether it should be the same for all parts of the country. Most acceptable figures are 2,400 calories per person per day in rural areas, and 2,200 calories per person per day in urban areas. The next step is to translate the nutrient requirement into monetary terms. The expenditure level of households which are able to spend the requisite amount to obtain the desired calories serves as the cut-off point, or the poverty line. To adjust the poverty line over a period of time, price variations have to be considered and an appropriate price deflator has to be selected. The problem arises in deciding upon such a deflator.

Thus, the following elements mainly affect the magnitude of the poverty ratio:

(i) the nutrition norm (translated into monetary terms) in the base year;

(ii) price deflator used to update the poverty line; and

(iii) pro rata adjustment in the number of households in different expenditure classes to determine the number of households below and above the poverty line. Different assumptions and methods are used for these three purposes, which accounts for the different estimates provided by scholars.

Multidimensional Poverty Index

The HDR 2010 measures poverty in terms of a new parameter, namely multidimensional poverty index (MPI), which replaced the human poverty index (HPI) used since 1997. The MPI indicates the share of the population that is multidimensionally poor adjusted by the intensity of deprivation in terms of living standards, health, and education. According to this parameter, India with a poverty index of 0.296 and poverty ratios of 41.6 per cent (in terms of PPP $ 1.25 a day) and 28.6 per cent (national poverty line) is not favourably placed when compared with countries like China and Sri Lanka. In fact, the difference in population below the poverty line (BPL) widens substantially in case of India when this indicator is used instead of the national poverty line indicator, while for other countries, there is less of a difference and in some cases even a fall.

According to Subramanian (2012), "India is a country of large absolute and relative deprivations, with a disproportionate burden borne by identifiable sections of the populaiton." There are three useful analytical categories in terms of which deprivation in any society—including India—can be appraised. There are positive freedom, negative freedom, and discrimination. While positive freedom is concerned with 'enablement', negative freedom is concerned with 'absence of restraint' and 'protection from coercion'. A society is subject to the charge of discrimination if it is one that presides over an inequitable distribution of freedoms across individuals on the strength of their group affiliation—where the grouping in question corresponds to some partitioning of the population on the basis, by way of example, of gender or caste or religion or age or geographical sector of origin.[1]

Reduction in Poverty

Table 9.1 summarises the change in poverty between 1993-94 and 2004-05, which is the latest year for which official data are available. The table reports the earlier estimates, based on the Lakdawala Committee method, and also the new poverty estimates based on the recommendations of the Tendulkar Committee. The poverty estimates of the Tendulkar Committee are higher, but both estimates show a decline in the percentage of the population in poverty in the pre-Eleventh Plan period. However the pace of reduction is very modest, about 0.85 percentage points per year using the Lakdawala estimates and slightly lower at 0.81 percentage points per year using the Tendulkar estimates.

TABLE – 9.1

Poverty Ratios

(Per cent)

	Earlier estimates(URP) based on the Lakdawala methodology		*Estimates (MRP)based on the Tendulkar methodology*	
	1993-94	*2004-05*	*1993-94*	*2004-05*
Rural	37.3	28.3	50.1	41.8
Urban	32.4	25.7	31.8	25.7
Total	36.0	27.5	45.3	37.2

Note: URP - Uniform Reference Period; MRP - Mixed Reference Period.
Source: Planning Commission.

According to the latest official estimates of poverty based on the Tendulkar Committee poverty line, as many as 29.8 per cent of the population, that is, 350 million people were below the poverty line in

1. Subramanian, S. (2012). "Poverty", in Kaushik Basu and Annemie Maertens (eds.), *The New Oxford Companion to Economics in India* (Vol.I). New Delhi: OUP.

2009–10. Questions have been raised about the appropriateness of the Tendulkar poverty line which corresponds to a family consumption level of Rs. 3,900 per month in rural areas and Rs. 4,800 per month in urban areas (in both cases for a family of five). There is no doubt that the Tendulkar Committee poverty line represents a very low level of consumption and the scale of poverty even on this basis is substantial. An Expert committee under Dr. C. Rangarajan has been set up to review all issues related to the poverty line keeping in view international practices.

It is well established that the percentage of the population in poverty has been falling consistently but the rate of decline was too slow. The rate of decline in poverty in the period 2004–05 to 2009–10 was 1.5 percentage points per year, which is twice the rate of decline of 0.74 percentage points per year observed between 1993–94 and 2004–05. Normally, large sample surveys used for official estimates of poverty are conducted every five years, but because 2009–10 was a drought year, the National Sample Survey Office (NSSO) felt that it would tend to overstate poverty and it was therefore decided to advance the next large sample survey to 2011–12. The results of this survey will yield an official estimate of the extent of poverty in 2011–12, that is, the position at the end of the Eleventh Plan period, but this will be available only in mid-2013. However, preliminary results from the survey have been published and they suggest that the percentage of the population in poverty will decline significantly compared to 2009–10. According to some non-official estimates, the rate of decline in poverty between 2004–05 and 2011–12 will be close to 2 per cent per year, which was the Eleventh Plan target. If this turns out to be the case, it can be claimed that the Eleventh Plan has indeed delivered on inclusiveness (Planning Commission, 2012).[2]

The Eleventh Plan had set a more ambitious target of reducing poverty by 2 percentage points per year. Abhijit Sen (2010) has estimated that poverty declined sharply from 37 per cent in 2004-05 to 29 per cent in 2007-08, which is much more than 2 percentage points per year.

It is interesting to note that the performance in reducing poverty between 2004-05 and 2009-10 varies considerably across states. The four southern states (Andhra Pradesh, Tamil Nadu, Kerala and to lesser extent Karnataka) all report impressive reduction in poverty, as do Maharashtra, Orissa, Madhya Pradesh and Himachal Pradesh. There is

2. Planning Commission (2012). *Twelfth Five Year Plan* Vol. I.

no improvement in Uttar Pradesh and Bihar, very little improvement in West Bengal and an actual deterioration in Assam. Punjab and Haryana had relatively lower poverty rates to begin with, but do not seem to have improved their position. How far these differences reflect differences in the pace and nature of growth in each state, and how far they reflect differences in the implementation of anti-poverty schemes, is a subject that needs further investigation based on the final official estimates of poverty obtained from unit level data.

TABLE – 9.2

Percentage of Population Below Poverty Line

States	*Lakdawala Methodology*		*Tendulkar Methodology*		*Tentative Estimates1*
	1993-94	*2004-05*	*1993-94*	*2004-05*	*2009-10*
Andhra Pradesh	22.2	15.8	44.6	29.9	20.0
Assam	40.9	19.7	51.8	34.4	39.2
Bihar	55.0	41.4	60.5	54.4	54.8
Gujarat	24.2	16.8	37.8	31.8	26.6
Haryana	25.1	14.0	35.9	24.1	23.8
Himachal Pradesh	28.4	10.0	34.6	22.9	11.7
Jammu and Kashmir	25.2	5.4	26.3	13.2	12.8
Karnataka	33.2	25.0	49.5	33.4	26.5
Kerala	25.4	15.0	31.3	19.7	11.3
Madhya Pradesh	42.5	38.3	44.6	48.6	40.5
Maharashtra	36.9	30.7	47.9	38.1	26.4
Orissa	48.6	46.4	59.1	57.2	46.4
Punjab	11.8	8.4	22.4	20.9	19.3
Rajasthan	27.4	22.1	38.3	34.4	29.4
Tamil Nadu	35.0	22.5	44.6	28.9	18.3
Uttar Pradesh	40.9	32.8	48.4	40.9	40.5
West Bengal	35.7	24.7	39.4	34.3	32.5
All India	36.0	27.5	45.3	37.2	32.2

Note: 1 Estimates for 2009-10 have been made by C. Ravi of the Centre for Economic and Social Studies, Hyderabad based on group data from the 2009-10 NSSO Survey and using the Tendulkar Committee poverty line for 2004-05 adjusting for using the CPIAL for rural areas and the CPIIW for urban areas. These estimates are an approximation of what can be expected when the Tendulkar methodology is applied to the unit level data as will be done by the Planning Commission whebn the unit level data become available.

Source: Ahluwalia, Montek (2011). EPW, May 21, 2011.

Comparison of India and China in terms of Poverty Reduction

Individual country experiences bear out these cross-country trends. China and India have enjoyed historically unprecedented average annual rates of growth of GDP since 1981, as the two countries engaged in opening their economies to foreign trade and investment. To be sure, the effect is not entirely attributable to 'globalisation', as both countries also engaged in domestic economic reforms to varying degrees, allowing a greater role for markets and the private sector in the economy, but integration no doubt played a large role. Growth rates not only accelerated, but the proportion of their populations below national poverty lines declined with the acceleration. Their growth rates and poverty ratios since 1980 are shown in Tables 9.3.

TABLE – 9.3

Growth Rates for China and India

	China	*India*
1980-1990	10.3	6.1
1990-2000	10.6	5.9
2000-2006	9.8	7.4

Source: Srinivasan, T.N. (2009).

Causes of Poverty

During 1950s and 60s Poverty was expected to be tackled by the "trickle down" of growth, with higher growth resulting in larger trickle down and faster decline in poverty.

By the middle of 1970s, the 'trickle down' theory got a severe jolt as a large number of economists questioned it on the basis of the experience of most developing countries over the past two to two and half decades. Most economies grew faster than in the earlier colonial period, but not as fast as expected or envisaged. Yet, poverty continued to be widespread.

The fundamental cause of the failure to achieve a reduction in the proportion of the poor in the total population during this period was, of course, slow growth. With the population growing at more than 2 per cent per year, per capita income grew at just a little above 1 per cent during this period. While sustained growth in per capita income at 3 per cent or more almost always delivers poverty reduction, growth rates of 1 to 2 per cent may or may not lead to such an outcome. At these low growth rates, the pull-up effect may be too weak to pull a larger proportion of the poor at the margin than their average proportion in the population into gainful employment.

According to Panagariya[3] there are perhaps two additional interrelated reasons why poverty did not decline with modestly rising incomes during the first three decades. First, the path to industrialisation that India chose failed to produce rapid growth of labour-intensive industry, which could have generated well-paid jobs for the poor. Even before India had successfully completed the first stage of import substitution, which encourages the production of light manufacturing, such as clothing and footwear, and of the intermediate inptus used in them, it moved into heavy industry.

Reservation of the most labour-intensive products exclusively for production by small-scale units further stunted the growth of export-based, large-scale, labour-intensive industry that could have generated employment for the masses. Small enterprises had at best limited capaicty to meet the quality standards required in the world market at competitive prices.[4]

The mainstream thinking on poverty and approaches towards its alleviation underwent a change: it was considered necessary to attack poverty directly by devising special programmes focused on socio-economic groups identified to be poor or most disadvantageously placed. Recognising that the poor have not gained from growth because they either lacked productive assets or opportunities for gainful employment, the poverty alleviation programmes aimed at direct provisioning of one or both of them (Papola, 2008).[5]

Experiences of programmes of direct attack on poverty have been mixed. It is difficult to assess their impact on poverty reduction separately from such effect of the growth process. But large scale poverty has persisted and that has led many economists to argue that these programmes have not proved effective. The new thinking that has emerged in recent years as part of what has been known as the Washington Consensus, therefore, questions the desirability of large public expenditure on direct poverty alleviation programmes. Instead, it emphasises the need to promote market forces to ensure benefits of growth to the poor as well. In other words, this line of thinking goes

3. Panagariya, Arvind (2008). "Declining Poverty: The Human Face of Reforms", *India: The Emerging Giant*. New Delhi: Oxford University Press.
4. Ibid.
5. Papola (2008).

back to 'trickle-down' theory: it argues that economic growth could be the only significant source for poverty reduction and asserts that market-friendly policies are the only effective way of raising growth.

Early 1990s saw major economic reforms in the Indian economy. In line with the basic principles behind these reforms, the role of government was sought to be reduced in different economic spheres. In respect of the anti-poverty strategy, a greater reliance on growth rather than on direct intervention through expenditure of public funds on targeted programmes was the logical fallout of the new economic policy. So, anti-poverty programmes, continued in modified form in some cases; and a significant addition was made to them in the form of National Rural Employment Guarantee Act (NREGA) in 2005.[6]

In the mean time, the Indian economy has maintained a relatively high growth in the post-reform period. Rates of growth of GDP and per capita income have reached a high of 9 and 7 per cent in recent years. Even if the poverty reducing elasticity of growth is not very high, such high growth rates are certain to make a significant dent on poverty. In the present context, therefore, it is of great significance to assess the role of growth rate, composition of growth and special anti-poverty programmes in poverty alleviation. It is also important to examine the need for universal *vis-à-vis* limited, but well focused and targeted programmes. Equally important is the reexamination of the nature of programmes; in terms of relative merits of focusing on selected geographical areas, emphasis on infrastructure and focus on human development on the one hand, or individual targeting on the other; and in the latter, of the relative suitability and efficacy of self-employment and wage employment programmes.

Growth and Poverty Reduction

Aggregate growth is undoubtedly an instrument for poverty reduction, and it is associated with improvements in the minimum standard of living over some time horizon. The estimates of Besley and Burgess (2003) for the elasticity of poverty with respect to income per capita vary widely across country samples, but all are negative, implying that growth reduces poverty. This association between growth and poverty reduction, however, could take a long time to be seen.

A positive association between growth and reduction in poverty is seen in several large countries with a high incidence of income poverty,

6. See ch.9 for details on anti poverty programmes.

such as China, India, Indonesia (until the financial crisis) and the Philippines. Angus Deaton (2001) estimated the proportion of poor in India's rural (urban) population in 1987-88 to have been 39 per cent (25 per cent). Annual data for earlier years suggests that the rural and urban poverty proportion fluctuated with no downward trend until 1977-1978, when it was 51 per cent. It is no coincidence that significant reductions in poverty since 1980 were associated with a near tripling of per capita GDP growth to an average of around 4 per cent per year during 1980-1990, as compared to 1.25 per cent during 1950-1980, and even higher since 2000.

Growth and Inequality

Poverty reducing impact of growth is influenced by changes in income distribution; a growing inequality will have a negative impact on growth-poverty reduction relationship. In the case of India, it is estimated that poverty reduction could have been higher by about 4 percentage points (12 per cent instead of 8 per cent) during 1993-94/ 2004-05, if inequality had not increased (Dev and Ravi, 2007). Obviously, the benefits of the faster growth have not been proportionately shared by the poor. In other words, growth has not been sufficiently 'pro-poor' or 'inclusive' to use the expression adopted by Planning Commission in its assessment of growth poverty relationship in recent years.

Growth, Employment and Poverty

One of the ways to make growth more 'inclusive' or 'poverty-reduction friendly', is seen in employment growth accompanying it: higher the employment growth generated by economic growth, larger is likely to be the reduction in poverty. Across countries in Asia, high employment growth, with similar rates of per capita income growth, have experienced a higher poverty elasticity of growth and even a slower growth in per capita income has resulted in higher reduction in poverty, if growth was accompanied by faster employment growth. Fast growth (>3.5 per cent per annum) in per capita income showed a poverty reduction elasticity of –1.02 if accompanied by an employment growth of over 2.5 per cent per annum; and, an elasticity of –0.85, if accompanied by lower employment growth. Even a slower per capita income growth had a higher poverty elasticity (–0.91) if accompanied by higher employment growth. Slow per capita income growth accompanied by slow employment growth led to an increase in poverty, elasticity turning positive at 0.53 (Pasha and Palanivel, 2003).

There are, of course, unemployed and underemployed poor for whom new employment opportunities and more work in present activities can provide the way out of poverty. And some of the working poor may, in fact, require alternative employment opportunities because of the non-viable and non-sustainable nature of their activities. But for majority of the poor, the way out of poverty would be in raising productivity and income levels of their current activities by enabling them to have better access to inputs, credit, technology and markets.

Growth Pattern and Poverty

The poverty reducing impact of growth, including that produced by redistribution and employment, depends, to a large extent, on the pattern of growth. A larger contribution of sectors and activities in which poor are mostly engaged, to economic growth, is likely to have higher impact on poverty. In the cases of countries like India, where most poor live in rural areas and are engaged in agriculture, agricultural growth is likely to play a critical role in alleviating overall poverty, not only through direct effect within the rural economy, but also through the indirect effects in the urban economy. Several scholars have attributed the significant decline in poverty during 1960-1980 to Green Revolution. Importance of agriculture for sustaining high growth with faster poverty reduction is well recognised by the Planning Commission in their Approach to the Eleventh Plan (Planning Commission, 2006a; 2008), which targeted for a 4 per cent growth in agriculture during 2007–2012. At the same time, it needs to be emphasised that for the employment route to be effective for poverty reduction, manufacturing sector with relatively high employment elasticity and greater regularity and higher earnings of jobs, is likely to play an increasingly important role this respect in coming years.

Poverty and Inclusive Growth

The National Commission on Enterprises in the Unorganised Sector (NCEUS), in its report, suggested that 77 per cent of the total population of the country in 2004-05, had per capita consumption expenditure of less than Rs. 20 per day. However, it has been observed, based upon calculations on data for 1999-2000 (NSS 55th Round) and 2004-05 (NSS 61st Round) that per capita consumption expenditure of 78.3 per cent of the rural population and 42.5 per cent of the urban population was less than Rs. 20 per day in 1999-2000. For the country as a whole, the per capita consumption expenditure of 68.1 per cent of the population was less than Rs. 20 per day. Per capita consumption expenditure of 71.9 per cent of the rural population and 32.3 per cent of the urban population was less than Rs. 20 per day in 2004-05. For the country as a whole, the per capita consumption expenditure of 60.5 per cent of population was less than Rs. 20 per day.

There is a direct relationship between aggregate poverty and average consumption. Growth of aggregate income/consumption is therefore, a sufficient condition for reduction of overall or aggregate poverty.

NSS consumption data relating to monthly per capita expenditure (MPCE) for three years between 2004-05 and 2006-07 indicates improvement in consumption pattern both across all MPCE levels as well as in rural and urban areas. This is indicative not only of favourable poverty reduction trends but also of the inclusive nature of growth as consumption has improved across the entire distribution in 2005-06 and 2006-07, both for urban and rural population and more so for the latter.

Non-income Poverty Dimensions

Data from the National Family Health Survey (NFHS-3) carried out in 2005-06 and District Level Household Survey on Reproductive Health (RCH) carried out during 2002-2004 show the worst forms of deprivation in India. As high as 46 per cent of children under 3 years of age (NFHS-3) and 49 per cent children under 6 years (RCH) suffered from malnutrition; and 79 per cent of children from anaemia (NFHS-3). These unfavourable child health outcomes could be, *inter alia*, attributable to failures in health care. For instance, 56 per cent of children were not fully immunised and 79 per cent did not receive Vitamin-A dose in the last 6 months prior to the survey (NFHS-3). The position was equally dismal for adolescent girls (10-19 years) and women–33 per cent of ever-married women suffered from chronic energy deficiency, 58 per cent suffered from anaemia, 59 per cent deliveries did not take place in institutional agencies (NFHS-3), and 76 per cent of adolescent girls suffered from severe and moderate anaemia (RCH). The access of households to basic amenities was equally poor. According to NFHS-3, 32 per cent of households did not have electricity, 58 per cent did not have piped drinking water, 55 per cent did not have toilet facility, and 59 per cent did not live in *pucca* houses. These data suggest that the incidence of non-income poverty is much more alarming than the incidence of income poverty. Studies suggest that even if income poverty is eliminated in India, other forms of poverty may persist. NFHS-3 data also reveal rural-urban and intra-household inequalities in nutritional outcomes. For example, the incidence of chronic energy deficiency in rural (urban) women was 38.8 (19.8) per cent among ever-married women and 33.1 (17.5) per cent among men. The performance of India in terms of nutritional outcomes is worse than that of less developed African countries in recent years (UNDP, 2003).

The national averages mask the huge variations in the incidence of child malnutrition across the states of India. In 2005-06, the incidence of child malnutrition varied among the major states from 27 per cent in Punjab and 29 per cent in Kerala and Jammu and Kashmir to 60 per cent in Madhya Pradesh (NFHS-3). It is to be noted that the nutritional status of children and adults in some of the middle-income states such as Kerala and Tamil Nadu was better than that in higher income states such as Maharashtra and Gujarat. This could be attributed to public interventions in the nutrition and health sectors. Factors such as public provision of safe drinking water and health care are also important determinants of nutritional well-being. Analysis of inter-household variations in child nutrition shows that the risk of malnutrition decreases with an improvement in household income, mother's nutritional status, her education and access to health care during child delivery. The mother's present nutritional status, in turn, depends on her childhood nutritional status.

Malnutrition is seriously retarding human development and is hampering further reduction in child mortality. Adults who survived malnutrition in their childhood are less healthy, physically less productive and have poor intellectual abilities. The economic costs of the current scale of malnutrition are enormous. Improvements in incomes of the poor and supply of environmental and health services are the long-term solutions for the eradication of malnutrition. However, in the short run, direct nutrition intervention should be the priority.

Poverty Alleviation Programmes

There is no doubt that growth is important for poverty reduction and pattern of growth has a specific role in this process. At the same time, it is also recognised that growth is necessary but not sufficient for removing poverty. Some poor are able to take up the opportunity offered by a growing economy, while some others are not, due to inadequacy of their capabilities in terms of resource endowment, skills and access to the system providing the opportunities. That is why programmes either to directly redistribute assets and incomes or to increase capabilities through public spending directed towards the poor have always been a part of public policy, not only with a view to alleviating poverty, but also for ensuring social justice and equity. Some of these, such as Integrated Rural Development Programme (IRDP) started in 1978 were designed to encourge self-employment among the poor by providing them assets often in the form of livestock. The IRDP along with other programmes that were subsequently introduced have came together under the banner of Swarnjayanti Gram Swarozgar Yojna (SGSY). A major focus of SGSY has been the promotion of small credit groups known as Self Help Groups. Other programmes include subsidised house construction under the Indira Awas Yojana and Schemes that provide state funds for work on village infrastructure (the Jawahar Rojgar Yojana and more recently the National Rural Employment Programmes.[7]

a. Programme for Socially Disadvantaged

Some of the programmes are targeted at social groups recognised to have been disadvantaged due to historical discrimination and also happen to be among the poorest. Reservation for Scheduled Castes (SC) and Scheduled Tribes (ST) in education and public jobs (and subsequently for the backward classes) and also, special dispensation for them in public programmes of financial and other kinds of support constitute very important parts of programmes in this category.

b. Land Reforms

Among the basic redistributive measures, land reforms can be considered as most important with high potential for poverty alleviation. Abolition of intermediaries and ceiling on landholding and allotment of surplus land to landless were among the early initiatives taken by the governments. These measures and tenancy reforms helped millions of farmers and landless labourers in gaining access to the most valuable asset in rural India, *viz.*, land; consolidation of landholdings, even though not a redistributive land reform measure, was also taken up in several states, leading in increase in private investment and productivity. Operation Barga in West Bengal is among the latest and relatively successful initiative. One would expect that all these

---

7. Somanathan, Rohini (2012). "Poverty and Exclusion", in Kaushik Basu and Annemie Maertens (eds.), *The Oxford Companion to Economics in India* (Vol.II). New Delhi: Oxford University Press.

measures did contribute to poverty reduction, though it is not possible to assess the precise impact they made. Land reforms were however, not seriously pursued and effectively implemented in most of the states and they no longer seem to be on the policy makers' agenda in recent decades.

c. Public Distribution System

Another major initiative in the area of redistributive policy consists of the provision of food at subsidised prices through the public distribution system (PDS). It aims at providing food security to the poor. Viewed initially as a price stabilisation measure, it has over the time been recognised as an important poverty alleviation programme and has been particularly oriented towards this end in the form of targeted PDS since 1997, with special entitlement and prices for the poor.

Programmes specifically designated as anti-poverty programmes have aimed to help the poor raise their incomes through provision of gainful employment. They have broadly been of two kinds: one, assisting the poor to acquire assets and/or start business enterprise to create self-employment, and two, providing wage employment mostly in public works to supplement incomes of the poor.

d. Public Investment in Human Capital and Public Goods

In order that the rapid and pro-poor growth is effective in alleviating poverty, it is important to ensure that enough efforts and investment are made in the areas of human and social development. A basic reason why the poor are not able to participate in and benefit from the rapid growth of the economy lies in their poor human capital endowment. With a relatively meagre public investment in education and health, the poor have very limited chance of augmenting their human capital endowments. Total social sector expenditure by Centre and states together is only around 10 per cent of which share of education and health is only 2.5 and 2.1 per cent respectively. This needs to be increased considerably to make the link between high growth and poverty reduction more effective. Access of people to public goods, education, health, transport, communication services, water and electricity is the most certain means of ensuring 'trickle down' of growth for poverty reduction.[8]

---

8. Ibid

e. A Stronger Welfare System and Improved Social Service Provision are Needed

While broad poverty rates have declined, international evidence suggests that this improvement could have been greater given sustained high economic growth. The comparison with another large emerging economy, Brazil, over the 1990s and 2000s is particularly striking. Measured in terms of the absolute reduction in poverty rates, the average pace of reduction there was similar to India, despite considerably slower economic growth. Measured in proportionate terms the rate of poverty reduction in Brazil was faster (Ravallion, 2011). This reflected falling inequality in Brazil underpinned by a comprehensive social security system with sizeable direct cash transfers to the poor (OECD, 2005). The relative under-performance in poverty reduction in India therefore calls into question the effectiveness of existing welfare safety nets and the provision of essential social services.

Spending on social welfare is relatively high but the system is fragmented and coverage is often poor (Dutta *et al.*, 2010; OECD, 2010a). The lack of a comprehensive safety net leaves the poor vulnerable to economic shocks and reliant on family and other networks. It also limits the effectiveness of government interventions to assist the poor during severe economic downturns as scaling up existing programmes quickly can be difficult. Spending on social programmes is skewed towards food and other subsidies, and towards employment in public works schemes. The single largest initiative is the Public Distribution Scheme (PDS) which provides subsidised food and other items. The scheme is intended to help the neediest but there is considerable evidence of poor targeting and major delivery inefficiencies. A major recent initiative is the NREGS, a workfare scheme that provides a guarantee of a minimum 100 days of employment to rural inhabitants at a minimum wage.

While the NREGS represents a major step in providing more systematic support to the needy, there is no national equivalent for urban residents. Although poverty rates are lower in urban areas, they remain high and urbanisation will continue to draw poor unskilled workers into the cities. Moreover, workfare schemes are ineffective as an instrument for aiding the elderly and incapacitated. The use of conditional cash transfers (CCT) in India is generally limited, despite their growing popularity in other emerging economies and mounting evidence concerning their effectiveness. Some CCT schemes operate at the state level, including the Apni Beti Apna Dhan initiative, which aims to encourage girls to stay in school longer. At the national level, the Janani Suraksha Yojana aims to reduce the number of maternal and neonatal deaths by encouraging women to give birth in a health facility. Since its introduction in 2005, the number of women benefiting from this initiative has expanded rapidly, reaching around 10 million by 2009 compared with 275 million live births (Ministry of Health and Family Welfare, 2010). An evaluation of the scheme by Lim *et al*. (2010) found that it increased the proportion of births in health facilities considerably, highlighting the potential benefit of expanding CCTs in India. There is also evidence from some Indian states that the old-age pension, an unconditional cash transfer, has been effective in supporting intended recipients (Dutta *et al.,* 2010). In addition to a renewed effort to reform subsidies, greater experimentation with new CCT schemes would be advisable. As with schemes operating in other emerging economies these should focus on helping to achieve key health and education objectives and focus on BPL households (Mehrotra, 2010). Administering such schemes will become easier with the introduction of a new identification system, the Unique Identity Number, which is currently being rolled out on a voluntary basis.

Concluding Remarks

Of late, a declining poverty-reducing impact of high growth has become a matter of concern. The argument that high growth may be necessary, but is not sufficient for poverty alleviation has, therefore emerged strongly in the debate on poverty alleviation strategy. Major reliance for poverty reduction can be placed on economic growth, provided its pattern is made to be pro-poor. In the present context, it would imply greater emphasis on agricultural and rural development, on high employment growth through faster growth of labour-intensive manufacturing and accelerating growth in lagging states and areas.

10

Demographic Constraint

Population Change and Economic Development

IN recent years, there has been an increasing focus on the relationship between population growth and economic development. The most difficult problem for such an analysis is to be able to separate cause from effect. Does economic development accelerate or retard population growth or does population growth contribute to or retard economic development? What are the linkages and how strong they are and in what direction do they operate?

Economic Development and Population Growth

The Theory of Demographic Transition

The theory of demographic transition attempts to explain why all contemporary developed nations have more or less passed through the same three stages of population growth. Before their economic modernisation, these countries, for centuries, had stable or very slow growing population as a result of a combination of high birth rate and almost equally high death rate. With economic development resulting in higher incomes, improved public health facilities, there was a marked decline in mortality that gradually raised life expectancy from under 40 years to over 60 years. However, the decline in death rate was not immediately accompanied by a decline in fertility. With declining death rate but birth rate not falling correspondingly, these countries passed through stage two, marking the beginning of demographic transition i.e., transition from stable or slow growing population to rapidly increasing number. Finally, stage three is reached when the forces and influences of modernisation and economic development cause fertility to decline so that eventually falling birth rate converge with lower death rate leaving little or no population growth.[1] Thus, how does economic development affect population growth can be explained through the theory of demographic transition.

The Microeconomic Theory of Fertility

In recent years, economists have begun to look more closely at the micro economic determinants of family fertility. They have utilised the principles of economy and optimisation to explain family size decisions. In deciding whether or not to have additional children, parents are assumed to weigh economic benefits against costs. The principle of benefits are the expected income from child labour usually on the farm and their family support for elderly parents. Balance against these benefits are the two principle elements of costs. (1) The opportunity cost of mother's time, the income she could earn if she were not at home caring for her children. (2) The cost of educating children that is the trade off between having fewer 'high quality' high cost, educated children with high income earning potentials *versus* more 'low quality', low cost, uneducated children with much lower earning prospects.

Statistical studies have shown that birth rates among the poor are likely to fall where there is:

(i) An increase in the education of women and consequent change in their role and status.

(ii) An increase in female non-agricultural wage employment opportunities which raises the price or cost of their traditional child bearing activities.

(iii) A rise in family income through increase in direct employment and earning of husband and wife and or redistribution of income and assets from rich to poor.

(iv) A reduction in infant mortality through expanded public health programme and better nutritional status for both parent and child.

(v) The development of old age and social security systems to bridge the economic dependence of parents on their offsprings.

Thus, efforts to make jobs, education and health more broadly available to poverty groups in Third World countries will not only

---

1. Todaro, Michael (2004). *Economic Development in the Third World* (8th edition). Delhi: Pearson Education (Singapore) Pte. Ltd.

contribute to their income and physical well-being but it can also contribute substantially to their motivation for smaller families which is vital to reducing growth rates.

How does Population Growth Affect Economic Development?

So far we have tried to analyse the effect of economic development on population growth, now let us examine how does population growth affect economic development? We may begin by asking the question how does population growth affect the net national product?

Until recently, the literature of economic demography drew attention to two main relationships through which population growth affect the economy, what we may call : (i) the 'saving effect' and (ii) 'composition of investment effect'.[2] The former of these argues that savings are reduced by population growth because of the so-called burden of dependency. With high fertility and declining mortality in younger and older age groups, the population acquires an increasing proportion of people in the non-working age groups relative to those of working age. Since all must consume, in the absence of increasing output per worker, saving per head must fall. Even if productivity is increasing, savings are less than they would be with a smaller number of dependents per worker.

The investment argument is like this: with increasing population, a share of investible resources has to be devoted to reproducing for additional people unproductive facilities, duplication of social services which would be unnecessary if population were not growing. A number of studies starting with Coale and Hoover have shown through comparison of high and low fertility paths that there have been greater growth of GNP with the lesser rate of population growth. Robert Cassen has raised doubts on the validity of the above saving and investments effect. He argues, if bulk of savings in poor countries come from small wealthy class whose fertility is low and if cost of additional children are met out of consumption rather than saving, the saving cost of additional children would be quite inconsiderable.

The composition of investment argument according to Cassen is really quite general. Wherever population growth requires increase in production, which in turn require investment, a lesser rate of population growth would release investible funds for use elsewhere.

---

2. Cassen, R.H. *India, Population, Economy and Society*, ch.4, p.221.

One fails to understand why past models have concentrated on welfare investment. Food production is in fact the least postponable of all forms of population-related output needs and if agriculture enters a phase of fundamental alteration in production function or in other words changing resource requirements for additional output, this can be a major burden of population growth. India reached this stage since mid-1960s when increases in agricultural output had to be brought out by yield improving technology which is capital-intensive instead of increasing acreage. The biggest problem for India if current trend continues is the increasing share of investible surplus that will be taken up by food needs of the growing population.

According to K. Sundaram, the implications of growing demographic pressures in India for the process of development in general and the progress towards poverty eradication become clearer once we focus on the labour force consequences of population growth.[3] The labour force expansion also puts direct pressure on the single most important natural resource in a predominantly agrarian economy, namely, land. Admittedly, the effective supply of land can be augmented by the use of reproducible capital. Irrigation is the most obvious example making it possible to increase the gross cropped area. The inadequate expansion of gross cropped area and of the irrigated area reflects the fact that the irrigation system has not expanded even up to the limits of currently known irrigation potential. This again is a manifestation of the inadequacy of capital resources.

India's Demographic Transition

Table 10.1 suggest that the country's demographic transition really began, rather hesitatingly, with a reduction in the average death rate during the 1920s and 1930s. These decades saw a decline in the frequency and scale of major famines and epidemics, which previously had made people's lives so incredibly precarious. As a result, there was a modest increase in life expectancy. And, with a prevailing crude birth rate of about 45 per thousand, these small gains in mortality were sufficient to raise the average annual rate of population growth to over one per cent per year during the 1920s, the 1930s and the 1940s.

At the time of its independence in 1947, India's population was about 345 million. Life expectancy was around 33 years and the TFR

---

3. Sundaram, K. (1999-2000). "Demography and Development", in Uma Kapila (ed.), *Indian Economy Since Independence*. New Delhi: Academic Foundation.

TABLE – 10.1

Key Population Statistics of India, 1901-2001[4]

Census Year	*Total Population (million)*	*Average Annual Growth Rate (per cent)*	*Birth Rate*	*Death Rate*	*Rate of Natural Increase*	*Sex Ratio (males per 1000 females)*	*Per Cent of Urban Population*
1901	238.3	0.3	49.2	42.6	6.6	1029	10.8
1911	252.0	0.6	48.1	47.2	0.9	1038	10.3
1921	251.2	N	46.2	36.3	9.9	1047	11.2
1931	278.9	1.1	45.2	31.2	14.0	1053	12.0
1941	318.5	1.3	39.9	27.4	12.5	1058	13.9
1951	361.0	1.3	40.9	22.8	18.1	1057	17.3
1961	439.1	2.0	40.0	17.8	22.2	1063	18.0
1971	548.2	2.2[b]	37.8	15.4	22.4	1075	19.9
1981	683.3	2.2[b]	33.8	12.3	21.5	1071	23.3[a]
1991	846.3	2.1	30.6	10.3	20.3	1067	25.7
2001	1027	1.9	25.8	8.5	13.3	1072	27.8

Notes: a Includes only an estimate for Assam.
b Growth rate for 1961-1971 and 1971-1981 take account of the fact that the reference data of the 1971 Census was 1 April, whereas that of the 1981 Census (like the 1951 and 1961 Census) was 1 March.
N: Negligible.

4. Visaria, Pravin (2008-09). "Demographic Aspects of Development: The Indian Experience", in Uma Kapila (ed.), *Indian Economy Since Independence*. New Delhi: Academic Foundation.

was close to six births. The decades following the 1940s have seen great changes.

The most important change relates to mortality. Immediately after Independence, the Government of India placed great stress upon improving the health of its people. As a result, death rates have fallen almost everywhere, more or less continuously. At the start of the twenty-first century, life expectancy is almost double that of 1947 (about 67 years for females and 64 years for males 2001-2006).

The reduction in the death rate after 1947 resulted in a significant rise in the rate of population growth, which reached almost 2 per cent during 1951-1961. In the following three decades, it remained fairly constant at around 2.2 per cent. The birth rate was more resistant to change than the death rate. It was only during the 1991-2001 intercensal decade that the birth rate fell faster than the death rate—so bringing about a significant decline in the rate of population growth.

Although the 'total fertility rate' (the average number of births per couple) for India as a whole is still well above the 'replacement level' (around 2.1), fertility in India has fallen quite sharply in recent decades, from around 6 in 1961 to 3 in 2001 and 2.9 in 2005.

According to Drèze and Sen (2002), in order to interpret these contrasting trends (continuing rapid population growth on the one hand, and declining fertility rates on the other), population growth has to be placed in the context of the 'demographic transition' from high to low fertility and mortality rates. In the initial phases of this transition, death rates typically fall faster than birth rates so that the rate of population growth increases: in India, for instance, it increased from virtually zero at the beginning of the twentieth century to 2.2 per cent per year in the 1960s and 1970s. As the transition progresses, the rate of decline of birth rates gradually overtakes that of death rates, leading to a decline in the growth rate of population, as began to happen in India about 20 years ago. In some individual states, it happened much earlier.

The decline of population growth, though relatively recent, can be expected to accelerate in the relatively near future, not only due to steadily falling fertility rates but also because of ongoing changes in the age structure of the population. Viewed in the context of this demograpic transition, current patterns of population growth appears, less alarming. Indeed, India is now well into the last phase of its demographic transition, involving falling populaton growth and sustained progresss towards 'population stabilisation' (which is expected to occur around the middle of this century), and there is certainly no evidence that a 'population bomb' is ticking away. This does not, of course, detract from the need for concern about rapid population growth at this time, or from the possibility of accelerating the demographic transition through supportive public policy (Drèze and Sen, 2002).

Causes of High Birth Rate

Social Factors

Social factors like universality of marriage and marriage at young age, joint family system, preference for a son result in high birth rate.

Economic Factors

Economic factors such as widespread poverty, high infant mortality and children as an insurance have also contributed to high birth rate.

Poverty

Among poverty groups not much money is spent on the upbringing of the children and hence, they are not much of a liability. Rather they start earning at an early age by doing some work on farms or take up some odd jobs in urban industrial areas. Hence, they add to family income and prove an asset to the family. Among poor families, additional children do not add to any burden, rather they provide helping hands for the family.

Lack of Social Security

Further, low survival rate among infants also encourages high birth rate. As social security like old age pension is not available to the poor masses in India, they expect their children to look after them in their old age. But since infant mortality rate (death rate among infants or very small children) is very high, people like to raise larger families so that some of them survive to look after parents in the old age. Thus, absence of social security combined with high infant mortality contribute to high birth rate. Because of lack of savings due to poverty, a large number of children act like insurance for their parents.

Illiteracy, Ignorance and Belief in Fate

Illiteracy is widespread in India. Illiterate and ignorant people thus accept every child as a will of God and would never think of interfering with His will. This increases the birth rate in India. Moreover, illiterate population does not realise the problems caused by increasing population or the means to keep family size in reasonable limits.

Ineffective Family Planning

Thus, high birth rate in India is the result of a whole lot of social, economic, religious and cultural factors. Unless a change is brought about in our attitude through social and cultural changes by spread of education and enlightenment or through economic and political pressure, not much decline can be expected in the prevailing high birth rate.

Fertility Rate

Fertility rate is a more scientific explanation of population growth rate than the birth rate. The birth rate, which measures the number of live births per thousand of population, is only a crude measure and thus called crude birth rate. It is crude because it associates the total number of live births with total population, whether young or old, male or female or whether they belong to reproductive age group or not.

Total fertility rate (TFR) on the other hand, measures the average number of children born to a woman up to the end of reproductive period. TFR, which was around 6 during 1951-52 declined to 5.3 during 1970-1972, 4.5 during 1980-1982, and below 4 in 1990-1992. Thus, though there has been some decline in TFR, it has not been large enough to much reduce natural growth rate of population in the face of continued decline in mortality rate. TFR in turn depends upon proportion of the married population, age at marriage and the number of children born per married women in course of her reproductive period.

Fertility rates vary radically across the country—between regions, between states and between districts. The average fertility rate of about 3 children per couple is an amalgam of fertility rates well above 5 children per couple for some districts, while other districts have fertility rates that are quite substantially below the replacement level. For example, for the state of Kerala as a whole—consisting of 14 districts—the average fertility rate is now around 1.8, which is lower than the rates for China and the USA, and comparable with those of some West European countries such as Britain and France. In fact, the fertility rate is also below the replacement level already for Tamil Nadu, and demographic calculations suggest that several other states (including Andhra Pradesh, Himachal Pradesh, Gujarat, Punjab and West Bengal) will have below-replacement fertility rates within the next five years or so.

In general, however, the seriousness of the population issue must not be dismissed. Given the density of pupulation that India already has, the environmental and social implications of further significant expansion can indeed be potentially grave.

Causes of Decline in Death Rate

In the early years of 20th century, death rate was very high. It was 42.6 per thousand during 1901-1910 and further increased to 47.2 per thousand during 1911-1920, but came down slowly to 36.3 per thousand in 1921-1930 and remained above 31 per thousand during 1931-1940. However, since the planned economic development of the country, there is a sharp decline in death rate from about 27 per thousand in 1941-1950 to 8.5 per thousand during 1991-2000. This decline in death rate was slow and gradual in the earlier decades but became progressively sharper after 1951.

Control of Epidemics

In the earlier years of the 20th century, epidemics like plague, smallpox, malaria, etc., took a heavy toll of life. But with increasing availability of effective medicines and improvement in health care facilities, these epidemics have been controlled. This has contributed to a substantial reduction in the death rate.

Control of Famines

Famines which occured in India frequently and with marked regularity, took a heavy toll of life. The Bengal Famine of 1943 for example caused thousands of starvation deaths while millions of people fled to other parts of the country in search of food. With the improvement in the means of transport and communications, spread of famines has been effectively checked. Of course, sometimes famine like conditions do occur in some parts of the country, as had happened during the year 2000 AD in parts of Gujarat and Rajasthan, yet effective measures to make supply of food available in these areas prevented any starvation deaths. Control of famines has been an important factor in the decline of death rate.

Improved Medical Facilities

With the increased investment in health and medical care facilities, many new hospitals have come up and a large number of dispensaries have been opened even in far flung rural areas. Thus, an increasingly greater proportion of population is now being provided medical facilities. This has improved health and prevented deaths due to timely availability of medical aid.

Spread of Maternity Homes

With spread of maternity homes where trained staff looks after child birth, deaths at the time of delivery have been largely prevented.

Impact of Economic Development

Under the impact of development, incomes and living standards of people have improved. This has improved their health and nutritional levels and made them less prone to disease and early death. Improvement in personal hygiene and sanitary conditions which go with better living standard have prevented the spread of communicable diseases. Education has made them aware of preventive measures that ensure disease-free life. Thus, the impact of overall development has been to promote better health and longer life. The life expentancy at birth (number of years a new born child is expected to live) has gone up from 32 years in 1950-51 to nearly 64 years for males and 67 years for females in 2000-01. This shows that now on, an average people live longer. Special programmes aimed at improving income and living standards of the poorer sections of society, provision of basic needs such as pure drinking water, health care facilities, houses for the homeless, etc., have all contributed to better life and lower death rate.

Thus, the social, economic, political, epidemiological and other developments that have underpinned the sustained mortality improvement of recent decades are many and complex. However, the increased control of many infectious and parasitic diseases (e.g. smallpox, malaria, cholera), the spread of immunisation coverage (especially with the Expanded Programme of Immunisation introduced around 1978), general progress in improving sanitation and water supplies, increased levels of education in the population, and a very considerable expansion of health facilities, have all been significant parts of the explanation for the sustained improvement in mortality.

India Vision 2020, Report of the Planning Commission[4] states that India's population would be 1331 million (133 crore) by the year 2020. The current and the projected increase in population growth rate is due to large size of population in the reproductive age group, high fertility rate due to unmet needs of contraception and also high wanted fertility due to high infant mortality rates. Effective steps and appropriate

4. Planning Commission (2003). *India Vision 2020*. New Delhi: Academic Foundation.

policies with regard to these issues thus, need to be devised and implemented to meet the growing population challenge.

Efforts must therefore, be made to reduce the growth rate of population. As there is still some scope for further reduction in death rate in India, therefore, all our efforts are needed to effectively reduce birth rate to stem the tide of rapidly increasing population.

Measures to Reduce Birth Rate

Here, we may just list some of the measures which can help to reduce birth rate and thereby check the growth rate of population.

1. **Spread of education** particularly female education as we have before us the experience of Kerala and Tamil Nadu.
2. **Increase in female wage employment:** Female education and their gainful employment will raise the status of women which will have positive effect on achiveing small family norm.
3. **Provision of old age pension and social security** which will reduce the dependence of parents on their children.
4. **Reduction in infant mortality** i.e., death rate of infants and small children through expanded public health programmes and better nutritional standards by ensuring longevity of life for new born children will help in reducing birth rate.
5. **Family planning:** Family planning means planned parenthood where the parents decide to keep their family small by giving birth to one or two children at proper intervals. The idea is to have a baby by choice and not by chance. Young married couples make use of various birth control devices to limit size of their families. Acceptance of family planning and one or two child norm by a large section of our population in the reproductive age group can help reduce birth rate substantially.
6. **Incentives for small families:** Such incentives as preference in government jobs, housing and other loans at low interest rates, preference in allotment of accommodation to people with small families can have a great impact on cutting down the birth rate. A scheme of disincentive to people with large families can also be devised so that the policy of carrot and stick can yield the desired fall in population growth rate.

Concerns about Population Growth

Although we need not worry about Malthusian fears that population growth in India is outstripping—or will soon outstrip—the growth of food supply but one cannot deny the fact of the widespread prevalence of hunger in India.

The incidence of nutritional deprivation in India is among the highest in the world. General undernourishment—what is sometimes called 'protein-energy malnutrition'—is nearly twice as high in India as in Sub-Saharan Africa on the average. Judged in terms of the usual standards of retardation in weight for age, the proportion of undernourished children in Africa is 20 to 40 per cent, whereas the percentage of undernourished Indian children is very high 40 to 60 per cent. The proportion of 'severely undernourished' children in India is above 20 per cent in the larger north Indian states (based on the weight-for-age criterion).

As Indians acquire greater purchasing power, and as the biases against particular groups (such as young girls) diminish, the size and composition of food consumption per head will have to change. The challenges of food production and food availability in India have to be seen in that light, rather than in terms of the old Malthusian comparison between the growth of total population and that of aggregate food production (Drèze and Sen, 2002).

Second, the pressure on environmental resources is no less serious than perspective of food production and consumption. We have sufficient evidence of rapid deterioration of the local environment across the country (in addition to India's contribution to global environmental degradation), with a wide range of adversities, varying from overcrowding of habitat and increases in manmade pollution to the denuding of forests and vegetation.

Third, rapid population growth leads to excessive pressure not only on the environment but also on the social infrastructure, including sewage systems, hospital facilities, railway networks, power grids, garbage-processing plants, and many other components of the 'stock' of public amenities. When public authorities are constantly racing to bring this stock in line with a larger population, there is much less room for qualitative improvements in public facilities. This phenomenon is clearly visible in some urban agglomerations, the rapid growth of which has gone hand in hand with a qualitative deterioration of the social infrastructure.

"To summarise, concern about population growth must not be simply dismissed as groundless. The size of the Indian population is already large, and its continued rapid expansion can certainly be a source of anxiety for the environment, in addition to the problems it raises for improving the living standard and economic and social well-being of the people. And yet the population situation is not as terrifying as it is sometimes made to look, based on the citation of selectively chosen statistics (or non-statistics). First, food supply has not been falling behind population—quite firmly to the contrary. The possibility of accommodating considerable increases in food consumption per head—both quantitative and qualitative—is still quite favourable. Second, the fertility rate is falling quite rapidly, and may decline faster still with sensible policies, especially related to child health and women's empowerment. Third, the fertility rate varies widely between different regions in India, and there is much to learn from those that have already achieved low fertility rates, and also much evidence that these achievements are indeed spreading to other regions as well" (Drèze and Sen, 2002).

Gender Equity and the Demographic Transition

There is much evidence now, based on inter-country comparisons as well as inter-regional contrasts within India, that women's empowerment (through employment, education, property rights, etc.) can have a very strong effect in reducing fertility rates. Speedy fertility declines in the states of Kerala, Tamil Nadu or Himachal Pradesh in India can be firmly linked to the rapid enhancement of female education and other sources of empowerment of young women. In fact, the principal variables that seem to account for inter-district variations in fertility rates in India are directly linked to women's empowerment, in particular female literacy and women's participation in gainful employment.

Female literacy not only has a strong impact in reducing child mortality rates, which in itself is a great result, it additionally also contributes to reducing fertility. Similarly, the promotion of women's employment opportunities and related sources of empowerment contribute to their security in old age, and offer some protection from the adversities of widowhood. These, again, are important achievements in themselves, and also make a further contribution to fertility decline, insofar as the fear of old-age insecurity often slows down the adoption of small family norms.

Population Policy since 1947

The debate about population growth and family planning received impetus in the late 1940s not only due to the publication of the Bhore Committee Report, but also because of the occurrence of several poor harvests which necessitated the importation of food. Moreover, the 1951 Census revealed significant demographic growth. It was against this background that Nehru announced that India would initiate a national family planning programme. The final document of the First Five Year Plan, presented to Parliament in 1952, referred specifically to a programme for 'family limitation and population control'. Thus, India became the first country in the world to adopt an official national population policy in support of family planning (Caldwell, 1998; Visaria and Jain, 1976).

During the 1950s, the government allocated modest sums of money to the population programme. At that time, many people had reservations about the promotion of modern contraception. Also as India was a *pioneer*, there was little previous experience on which to draw. However, there were other significant developments in the 1950s. There was increasing achievement in promoting contraception in the larger towns. The government of Madras state began endorsing vasectomy with success, and it was soon followed by Kerala, Mysore and Maharashtra. Madras also began making compensation payments to poor people who were sterilised. By the time of the Third Five Year Plan (1961-1966) the 'objective of stabilising the growth of population (within) a reasonable period' was put 'at the very centre of India's planned development'. The Third Plan document also noted the important role that voluntary sterilisation might make towards achieving this. The budgetary outlay was significantly increased. Sterilisation camps began to be used to promote vasectomy. There was also a shift in the emphasis of family planning delivery, from a clinic-based approach to a wider community extension strategy. The late 1960s also saw the increasing adoption of timebound—and often unrealistic—demographic 'targets'. In 1968, a goal was set to reduce the birth rate from 41 to 23 per 1000 within 10 years. But at the start of the twenty-first century, the birth rate was still about 25 (Dyson *et al.*, 2004).

The period of the Fourth Five Year Plan (1969-1974) saw increased concern over the rate of demographic growth. The 1971 Census showed a decadal increment of 109 million. Consequently, there was an increased emphasis upon targets, compensation payments and male sterilisation. This continued into the Fifth Plan, and culminated in the atmosphere of urgency which characterised Indira Gandhi's declaration of Emergency in 1975-1977. The language of the 1976 National Population Policy as quoted in Cassen (1978: 182) is revealing of the time:

"The wait for education and economic development to bring about a drop in fertility is not a practical solution. The very increase in population makes economic development slow and more difficult of achievement. The time factor is so pressing, and the population growth so formidable, that we have to get out of this vicious circle through a direct assault upon this problem as a national commitment."

The Emergency saw a massive increase in vasectomies. But there was later a backlash against the programme, particularly in the northern states, which lasted into the 1980s. Subsequently, although the government family welfare programme has continued to emphasise sterilisation, it has been mainly tubectomy which has been provided.

The rhetoric of population control largely disappeared with the Sixth Plan (1980-1985). Since the Seventh Plan in particular (1986-1990), there has been increasing recognition of the requirements: to tailor the family welfare programme to the conditions prevailing in individual states; to adopt a multi-sectoral approach which recognises the linkages between birth control and programmes in other areas (such as education); and to involve the private sector more in contraceptive delivery. Incentive payments and targets have largely been eliminated. Furthermore, following the 1994 Cairo Population Conference, emphasis has now greater shifted to the reproductive health needs of women.

National Population Policy, 2000

The National Population Policy, 2000 aims at achieving net replacement levels of total fertility rate by 2010 through vigorous implementation of inter-sectoral operational strategies. The long-term objective is to achieve population stabilisation by 2045, at a level consistent with the requirements of sustainable economic growth, social development and environment protection. Crude birth rate has come down, but needs to come down faster in view of the declining crude death rate (Table 10.2).

India is passing through a phase of unprecedented demographic changes. These demographic changes are likely to contribute to a substantially increased labour force in the country. The Census projection report shows that the proportion of working age population between 15 and 59 years is likely to increase from approximately 58 per cent in 2001 to more than 64 per cent by 2021. In absolute numbers, there will be approximately 63.5 million new entrants to the working age group between 2011 and 2016. Further, it is important to note that the bulk of this increase is likely to take place in the relatively younger age group of 20-35 years. Such a trend would make India one of the youngest nations in the world. In 2020, the average Indian will be only 29 years old. Comparable figures for China and the US are 37, 45 for West Europe, and 48 for Japan. This 'demographic dividend' provides India great opportunities, but it also poses a great challenge. It will benefit India only if our population is healthy, educated, and appropriately skilled. Therefore, greater focus on human and inclusive development is necessary to best utilize the demographic dividend. (*Economic Survey 2011-12*, ch.13)

TABLE – 10.2

India: Selected Health Indicators

Sl. No.	*Parameter*	*1951*	*1981*	*1991*	*Current Level*
1.	Crude birth rate (Per 1000 population)	40.8	33.9	29.5	22.8 (2011*)
2.	Crude death rate (Per 1000 population)	25.1	12.5	9.8	7.1 (2011*)
3.	Total fertility rate (TFR) (Per woman)	6.0	4.5	3.6	2.5 (2010*)
4.	Maternal mortality ratio (MMR) (Per 100,000 live births)	NA	NA	NA (1992-93)	212 (2007-2009*)
5.	Infant mortality rate (IMR) (Per 1000 live births)	146 (1951-1961)	110	80	44 (2011*)
	5.1 Male				48
	5.2 Female				29
6.	Child (0-4) mortality rate (Per 1000 children)	57.3 (1972)	41.2	26.5	13.3 (2010*)
7.	Life expectancy at birth:		(1981-85)	(1989-93)	(2006-10)**
	Total		55.5	59.4	66.1
	7.1 Male	37.2	55.4	59.0	64.6
	7.2 Female	36.2	55.7	59.7	67.7

Note: The dates in the brackets indicate years for which latest information is available.

* National Family Health Survey.

** Abridged Life Table 2003-07 to 2006-10, RGI India.

NA: Not Available.

Source: Ministry of Health & Family Welfare and Office of the Registrar General, India; *Economic Survey 2009-10, 2010-11, 2011-12, 2012-13*.

Objectives of National Population Policy

The immediate objective of the NPP, 2000 is to address the unmet needs for contraception, health care infrastructure and health personnel, and to provide integrated service delivery for basic reproductive and child health care. The medium-term objective is to bring the TFR to replacement levels by 2010, through vigorous implementation of inter-sectoral operational strategies. The long-term objective is to achieve a stable population by 2045, at a level consistent with the requirements of sustainable economic growth, social development and environmental protection.

According to the Technical Group on Population Projections constituted by the National Commission on Population, May 2006, annual population growth is expected to gradually decelerate from 1.6 per cent in the five years ending in 2006 to 0.9 per cent in the five years ending in 2026 (Table 10.3). India's population, which is estimated to have gone up from the Census 2001 figure of 1029 million to 1112 million in 2006, is projected to increase to 1400 million by 2026.

TABLE – 10.3

India: Population Projections

(in millions)

Year	*2001*	*2006*	*2011*	*2016*	*2021*	*2026*
Total	1,029	1,112	1,193	1,269	1,340	1,400
Below 15 years	365*(364)	357	347	340	337	327
15-64 years	619*(613)	699	780	851	908	957
Above 65 years	45*(49)	56	66	78	95	116

Notes:* Figures are as per smoothing of age-groups for working out population projections.
Figures in parenthesis are as per Census of India 2001. These figures will not tally with the total since 'age not stated' is excluded.
2001 figures exclude the population of Paomata, Mao-Maram and Purul sub-divisions of Senapati district of Manipur.

Source: Population Projections for India and States 2001-2026 – Census of India 2001: Report of the Technical Group on Population Projections constituted by the National Commission on Population, May 2006.

India is passing through a phase of unprecedented demographic changes. These demographic changes are likely to contribute to a substantially increased labour force in the country. The Census projection report shows that the proportion of working age population between 15 and 59 years is likely to increase from approximately 58 per cent in 2001 to more than 64 per cent by 2021. In absolute numbers, there will be approximately 63.5 million new entrants to the working age group between 2011 and 2016. Further, it is important to note that the bulk of this increase is likely to take place in the relatively younger age group of 20-35 years. Such a trend would make India one of the youngest nations in the world. In 2020, the average Indian will be only 29 years old. Comparable figures for China and the US are 37, 45 for West Europe, and 48 for Japan. This 'demographic dividend' provides India great opportunities, but it also poses a great challenge. It will benefit India only if our population is healthy, educated, and appropriately skilled. Therefore, greater focus on human and inclusive development is necessary to best utilize the demographic dividend. (*Economic Survey 2011-12,* ch.13)

Every fast-growing Asian economy in recent years has accelerated as it underwent a demographic transition. In India itself, Aiyar and Mody (2011) document that the high growth states (Tamil Nadu, Karnataka, and Gujarat) in the period 1991-2001 had a dependency ratio which was 8.7 percentage points lower than that of the low growth states (Bihar, Madhya Pradesh, and Uttar Pradesh) and an average annual growth rate that was 4.3 percentage points higher. Looking ahead, they argue, the low growth states will benefit more from the demographic dividend, as higher incomes and lower fertility alter demographics. Indeed, over the period 2001-2011, the hitherto laggard states have grown at an average of around 5 per cent annually. The difference between their growth and the growth of the leaders in the period 2001-2011 is just 1.5 percentage points. So demographic transition seems to be correlated with growth, with some reasons to believe that causality flows both ways--lower dependency ratios increase growth and higher growth reduces fertility and consequently dependency ratios.

Growth optimists point to another reason for cheer. Cross-country evidence suggests that productivity is an increasing function of age, with the age group 40-49 being the most productive because of work experience (Feyrer, 2007). Nearly half the additions to the Indian labour force over the period 2011-30 will be in the age group 30-49, even while the share of this group in China, Korea, and the United States will be declining. That India will be expanding its most productive cohorts even while most developed countries and some developing countries like China will be contracting theirs in the coming decades can be another source of advantage (*Economic Survey 2012-13*).

The well-known 'demographic dividend' will manifest in the proportion of population in the working age group of 15-64 years increasing steadily from 62.9 per cent in 2006 to 68.4 per cent in 2026. The actual tapping of this demographic dividend will, however, depend a lot on ensuring proper health care and other human resource development such as education.

TABLE – 10.4

India's Global Position in Terms of Socio-demographic Parameters

Country	*Life Expectancy at Birth (years)*	*Under-five Mortality Rate (per 1,000 live births)*	*Infant Mortality Rate (per 1,000 live births)*	*Maternal Mortality Ratio (per 100,000 live births)*
	2010	*2009*	*2008*	*2005*
China	73.5	21	18	45
India	64.4	69	52	450
Nepal	67.5	41	51	830
Pakistan	67.2	89	72	320
Sri Lanka	74.4	93	75	58
Bangladesh	66.9	54	43	570

Note : NA : Not available.

Source : UNDP (2010). *Human Development Report* 2007-08.

In spite of the progress achieved in these parameters of health, family welfare and population growth, we still lag behind some developing countries like China, Sri Lanka and many South Asian countries with regard to social indicators of progress. Thus, for example, life expectancy at birth in the year 2005 was 73 years in China, 71.1 years in Sri Lanka as against 64 years in India. Infant mortality rate in 2008 was only 18 per thousand in China as against 56 per thousand live birth in India. Other parameters of socio-demographic progress show a similar picture.

Among the major states, the states of Kerala and Tamil Nadu have already achieved the replacement level of fertility *viz*., TFR of 2.1, while the states of Andhra Pradesh, Gujarat, Karnataka, Maharashtra, Orissa, Punjab and West Bengal, having a TFR in the range, of 2.2 to 3.0 are in the direction of achieving the replacement level of fertility. There are a few states, namely, Assam, Haryana and Madhya Pradesh, which are having a TFR in the range of 3.1 to 4.0 while the states of Bihar, Rajasthan and Uttar Pradesh have recorded TFRs in the range of 4.1 to 4.7 as per the Sample Registration System, 1999.

The National Population Stabilisation Fund (NPSF) was renamed and registered as Janasankhya Sthirata Kosh (JSK) in June 2003. The objective of JSK is to facilitate the attainment of the goals of National Population Policy (NPP), 2000. The Fund will support projects, schemes, initiatives and innovative ideas, designed to help population stabilisation both in the government and voluntary sectors, and provide a window for canalising monies through voluntary contributions from individuals, industry, trade organisations and other legal entities in furtherance of this national cause. A contribution of Rs. 100 crore has been made out of plan budget.

The Experience of Kerala and Tamil Nadu

The two southern states of Kerala and Tamil Nadu with a population of about 94 million (9 per cent of the total) in 2001 illustrate the alternative ways of reaching a replacement level of fertility.

In Kerala, with its very low infant and child mortality rate, the adoption of a two-child norm has led to a total fertility rate of 2.0; allowing for mortality, its fertility is below (87.8) the replacement level.

An almost universal female literacy and a low level of infant and child mortality, and the high status of women, all intrinsically desirable goals, are considered crucial in the decline in fertility in Kerala. However, other important contributory factors include the very high pressure of population density on land and an associated low proportion of rural male workers engaged in agriculture (the lowest, 54 per cent, among the major states according to the 1987-88 survey of the NSS), a very low proportion of the self-employed and relatively very high rates of open unemployment (the highest in the country). The persistent high level of unemployment has been accompanied by the demonstration by the emigrants to the Middle East of the feasibility of getting out of the vicious circle of poverty. Such a combination of forces favourable to fertility decline through both delayed marriage and control of marital fertility is not easy to find elsewhere in the country.

Tamil Nadu has achieved the largest proportionate reduction in child mortality among all major Indian states other than Kerala. Today, Tamil Nadu has the third-lowest child mortality rate among major Indian states and the second-lowest maternal mortality rate. Over the same period, Tamil Nadu also achieved the largest porportionate reduction in total fertility rate (about 50 per cent). Today, it is the only major state other than Kerala where the total fertility rate is below the 'replacement level'. These achievements are all the more remarkable in view of the fact that

Tamil Nadu has no less income poverty than the Indian average. In fact, the head-count index of poverty is a little higher in Tamil Nadu than in India as a whole.

The decline in fertility in Tamil Nadu has been attributed to the political support for both an increase in the age at marriage and an imaginative programme of information, education and communication (IEC).

Enabling Factors

Recent studies point to a number of enabling factors that have facilitated Tamil Nadu's rapid demographic transition. Commonly-cited factors include a good infrastructure, a rich history of social reform movements, high literacy rates in the younger age groups, wide popular exposure to mass media and strong 'political will'. Less widely discussed is the relatively liberated status of women in contemporary Tamil society. Tamil Nadu has a high female-male ratio, little gender bias in school attendance and high levels of female labour force participation. Also, interesting is some recent information from the second round of the National Family Health Survey (1998-99) relating to different aspects of 'female autonomy'. Whether we look at the proportion of adult women who work outside the household (43 per cent), or who have independent access to money (79 per cent), or who are able to go to the market 'without permission' from other family members (79 per cent again), Tamil Nadu is ahead of all other major states (with one exception—Himachal Pradesh—in the case of 'independent access to money'). Bearing in mind the role of women's agency in the demographic transition, this feature of gender relations is crucial to our understanding of what has happened in Tamil Nadu.

Extensive state initiatives in the fields of child nutrition, health care and social security have also made an important contributon to mortality and fertility decline in Tamil Nadu.

India's Demographic Dividend

Over the past four decades India has undergone rapid demographic changes. The onset and speed of demographic transition—a process of change whereby societies move from a situation of high mortality and fertility to one of low mortality and fertility—differs from region to region within India. As already discussed while the level of fertility in southern Indian states has reached below replacement, it is still high in many states in north India because, though declining, the decline is at a slower pace. There are two important consequences of demographic transition. The first is population explosion due to a rapid decline in mortality rates amidst the maintenance of a high birth rate. This sudden and sustained increase in population size during the initial phase of demographic transition directly impacts the economy.

Another consequence of demographic transition is a shift in the age structure of the population resulting in broader and long-term age structural transition. In the first phase of the demographic transition the number of children increases both in relative and absolute size due to high fertility levels and a rapid fall in mortality. After some time lag as fertility rate starts declining, it contributes to a decline in the relative share of the young population. As children born during different phases of demographic transition move from youth to adulthood, and to old age, the age structure of the population undergoes major changes. During this process, there will be a period of—'window of opportunity' where child dependency ratio (ratio of child population to working age population) declines due to decline in fertility as well as increase in the working age population as children born during the high fertility regime move into working ages. If this window of opportunity is properly exploited, there is greater potential for demographic dividend through increased savings and investment for economic growth (Navaneetham, 2012).[5]

The period of 'window of opportunity' according to Navaneetham can be exploited in three ways to give demographic dividends:

(i) by productive employment of the available labour force, which would raise total gross domestic product (GDP).

(ii) by directing accumulated wealth and savings into productive investments. Households tend to save less when there are more children since a substantial part of the family income is spent on raising them. When fertility declines, the demand on household resources for raising children reduces, allowing households to save more of their income; and

(iii) Fertility decline has immediate and direct impact on the school-going population and provides an opportunity to invest more on their education and health contributing to better-quality human capital in the future. Women with fewer

5. Navaneetham, K. (2012). "Demographic Dividend", in Kaushik Basu and Annemie Maertens (ed.), *The Oxford Companion to Economics in India* (Vol. I). New Delhi: Oxford University Press.

children are more able and often more willing to participate in remunerative work, and are more likely to invest additional income in the health and education of their children.

This would be a one-time only opportunity and its length would be determined by the speed of demographic transition. If appropriate interventions are not made during this period, it would have negative implications for the economy and society. Demographic dividend could explain as much as one-third of the per capita GDP growth rate of the East Asian economies during the period of their economic miracle.

'Window of Opportunity' for India

In India the share of the working-age population (15-64) has been increasing since 1980 and is expected to reach its peak by 2025. Generating new employment opportunities to meet the growing working-age population is a major challenge for India. If it is productively employed it will boost the economy. Among the working-age population, the share of the youth segment (15-24) will decrease from now on while that of the mature labour force will be increasing. There is also rapid decline in the ratio of youth (15-24) to working-age population (25-64) from 2010. This indicates that there will be less pressure on the economy to generate new employment opportunities and that can lead to a possible reduction in unemployment, which can be described as another window of opportunity for India. Further, this would increase the saving ratio as well as tax revenues, which may augment the capacity for investment and funding of social programmes. It is also likely that the increase in the share of middle working-age population (50-64) would contribute to higher saving rates as it tends to have a greater capacity to save due to higher income and reduced consumption. This opportunity would continue even after 2030 and this can be exploited for economic growth (Navaneetham, 2012).

The size and share of the old-age population will continue to increase during the age structural transition. However, the increase would be greater after 2025. The old dependency ratio would also increase rapidly after 2025. Meeting the healthcare and social security needs of the elderly would be a major challenge for India particularly after 2025.

Estimated Demographic Bonus for India

Bhat (2001) estimated that the demographic bonus was negative during the decades (1951-71), as the growth rate of total population was higher than that of working-age population. After 1971, the growth rate of working age population was higher than that of total population, resulting in a positive demographic bonus. He also showed that the demographic bonus would be highest during the decade 2001-11—a contribution of 0.6 per cent GDP growth rate in the total per capita GDP growth rate. The demographic bonus is likely to continue till 2031 and would be negative thereafter.

It may be structural transition would be different in different states. However, the demographic bonus will vary from state to state as the nature of demographic transition is different due to their socio-economic and cultural differences. The bonus would be positive till 2011 among the demographically advanced states such as Kerala, Tamil Nadu, and Punjab and would be negative thereafter. On the other hand the BIMARU states where the process of demographic transition began later than in other states started getting greater dividend from 2001 and would be likely to continue to do so till 2031. As there are regional differences in age structural transition, internal migration could be of critical importance in the future as young workers move from underdeveloped to developed regions. The regional differences in age structural transition may also play an important role in terms of convergence in economic growth among the states in India, provided efforts are made to invest in human capital among the BIMARU states as a large share of labour supply in the future would come from them (Navaneetham, 2012).

The demographic dividend is also likely to accrue from the expected increase in labour-force participation of women due to the shortening of the duration of child-bearing years. The total bonus derived from the labour supply during the period 2001-51 is estimated to be 1 per cent, out of which labour supply effect would be 0.2 per cent and the effect of the expected increase in labour-force participation of women would be 0.8 per cent, keeping labour productivity constant (Bhat, 2001). The savings ratio would increase from 23 per cent in 2001 to 32 per cent in 2031 due to the expected decline in dependency burden, which would contribute to an increase in economic growth rate. It was estimated that the demographic transition would contribute 40 per cent of the per capita GDP growth rate during the period 2001-51. About 13 per cent of this increase would be due to the increase in labour supply, assuming output per worker remained constant, and the remaining 27 per cent would be due to an increase in the savings ratios, assuming per capita consumption did not change (Navaneetham, 2012).

India's Response to 'Window of Opportunity'

The experience of India so far shows that the 'window of opportunity has not been exploited though it has become available since the 1980s (Mitra and Nagarajan, 2005); Chandresekhar *et al.,* 2006). It has been argued that the employment growth rate was low during the 1990s, particularly in the rural areas, and consequently the unemployment rate was high (Chandresekhar *et al.*, 2006). This was the period during which the growth of the youth population was also greater. As new employment opportunities did not grow at the same pace as the numbers of youth, the unemployment rate among the youth increased. But it is encouraging to see that the employment growth rate has increased significantly in both rural and urban areas. It is also likely that the increase in the share of middle working-age population (50-64) would contribute to higher saving rates as it tends to have greater capacity to save due to higher income and reduced consumption. This is likely to continue into the future when the relative share of youth population is expected to decline.

The relative share of childhood population will decline in the future. This provides an opportunity to improve the human capital through public policy measures with respect to nutrition, education, and healthcare. The relatively rapid growth of the labour force would benefit India, if employment opportunities increased with sufficient speed to match the growth in labour supply, maintained growth in labour productivity, and invested in infrastructure. However, the size and share of the elderly population would increase rapidly after 2031 and this will pose several policy and programme challenges. To meet these challenges effectively there will be need for concerted efforts to devise appropriate public and social policies directed at the provision of social security and healthcare and encouraging the development of social networks. In order to meet the challenges in the future and to prepare for them, it is important for India to exploit the window of opportunity available for a short period, a one-time gift from the demographic transition, with appropriate economic and social policies (Navaneetham, 2012).

The Future

According to Dyson[6], during the next few decades India's population will continue to grow, although at a slowing rate; it will continue to urbanise; and it will start to age (though gradually at first).

India's future demographic evolution will also have significant implications for the economy, education and the environment. Economic growth may be enhanced by the 'demographic bonus' deriving from the projected diminishing age dependency ratio. Benefits will arise if there are consequential increases in savings and investment. But such increases cannot be taken for granted. As Mari Bhat argued, there is nothing automatic about such potentially positive relationships (Bhat, 2001). It is virtually certain that the country's working age population is going to grow faster than the total population, and it may be roughly 50 per cent bigger in 2026 compared to 2001.

6. Dyson, Tim (2013). "India's Demographic Transition and its Consequences for Development", in Uma Kapila (ed.) *Indian Economy Since Independence*, 24th edition. New Delhi: Academic Foundation.

SECTION - V

Sectoral Trends and Issues

V.1. Agriculture

11. Agriculture: Role and Growth Performance
12. Agriculture Price Policy, Food Management and Food Security

V.2. Industry and Services

13. Industrial Policy
14. Industrial Growth since 1951
15. Micro, Small and Medium Enterprises (MSMEs)
16. Public Sector in the Indian Economy
17. Services in the Indian Growth Process
18. Foreign Direct Investment

V.3. Financial Sector

19. The Financial Sector: Structure, Performance and Reforms

V.4. External Sector

20. Foreign Trade and Trade Policy
21. Balance of Payments
22. India and the WTO
23. India and the Global Economy

11

Agriculture:
Role and Growth Performance

Importance of Agriculture in National Economy

Agriculture is the mainstay of Indian economy because of its high share in employment and livelihood creation, notwithstanding, its reduced contribution to the nation's GDP. It is the most important sector of the Indian economy from the perspective of poverty alleviation and employment generation. The share of agriculture in national income has been declining from 56.5 per cent in 1950-51 to 39.6 per cent in 1980-1981, 26.3 per cent in 2001-02. As per the 2011-12 advance estimates released by CSO[1] the agriculture and allied sector accounted for 13.9 per cent of the GDP at 2004-05 prices in 2011-2012 as compared to 16.8 per cent in 2007-08 and 14.5 per in 2010-2011.

Agriculture's share in GDP has thus declined rapidly in the recent past. This is explained by the fact that whereas overall GDP has grown by an average of 8.62 per cent during 2004-05 to 2010-11, agricultural sector GDP has increased by only 3.46 per cent during the same period. The role of the agriculture sector, however, remains critical as it accounts for about 58 per cent of employment in the country (as per 2001 census). Moreover, this sector is a supplier of food, fodder, and raw materials for a vast segment of industry. Hence the growth of Indian agriculture can be considered a necessary condition for 'inclusive growth'. More recently, the rural sector (including agriculture) is being seen as a potential source of domestic demand, a recognition that is even shaping the marketing strategies of entrepreneurs wishing to widen the demand for goods and services.

---

1. Central Statistical Organisation, February 29, 2012.

One of the paradoxes of the Indian economy is that the decline in the share of agricultural workers in total workers has been slower than the decline in the share of agriculture in the GDP. While the share of agriculture in total workers declined slowly from 75.9 per cent in 1961 to 59.9 per cent in 1999-2000, the share of agriculture and allied activities in the GDP declined from 57.7 per cent in 1950-51 to 22 per cent in 2002-03 (Mahendra Dev, 2012).[2] According to the advance estimates of 2011-12 agriculture and allied sector accounted for only 13.9 per cent of GDP.

Compared to other countries, India faces a greater challenge, since with only 2.3 per cent share in the world's total land area it has to ensure food security for a population that accounts for 17.5 per cent of world population. This leads to excessive pressure on land and area under foodgrain cultivation has not increased. Increasing agricultural production with limited natural resources in a sustainable manner for ensuring food and nutritional security and providing income security to farmers are major challenges before the government.

Linkage between Agriculture and Other Sectors

The linkages between agriculture and industrial sectors, widely recognised in the literature,[3] focus on the role of agriculture as: (i) supplier of wage goods to the industrial sector, (ii) provider of raw materials to agro-based industries which have a weight of 21.2 per cent in the Index of Industrial Production (base: 1980-81=100) and weight of 17.6 per cent in the index with base 1993-94=100, and (iii) generator of agricultural income that enables rural demand for industrial products to take place. Empirical tests show that a unit increase in agricultural output would have a positive effect on both industrial production and national income. Rangarajan (1982) estimated that a 1 per cent increase in agricultural output tends to raise industrial production by 0.5 per cent and augment national income by 0.7 per cent. The experience in the eighties and nineties also lends support to this. During the eighties, the trend growth rate of 3.2 per cent in agricultural production appeared to have had contributed to accelerated industrial production. The decelerated growth rate in agricultural production seems to have impacted on growth of industrial production in the nineties.

2. Dev, S. Mahendra (2012). "Agriculture Development", in Kaushik Basu and Annemie Maertens (eds.), *The New Oxford Companion to Economics in India* (Vol.I). New Delhi: Oxford University Press.
3. Rudra (1967), Chakravarthy (1974), Raj (1976), Mellor (1976), Mitra (1977), Chakravarty (1979), Krishna (1982) and Rangarajan (1982).

Importance of agriculture in the national economy is indicated by many facts. For example, agriculture is the main support for India's transport system, since railways and roadways secure bulk of their business from the movement of agricultural goods. Internal trade is mostly in agricultural products. Agricultural growth has direct impact on poverty eradication, containing inflation, raising agricultural wages and employment generation.

To quote the *Economic Survey 2009-10*, "Agriculture including crop and animal husbandry, fisheries, forestry and agro processing provides the underpinnings of our food and livelihood security. Agriculture provides significant support for economic growth and social transformation of the country. As one of the world's largest agrarian economies, the agriculture sector (including allied activities) in India accounted for 15.7 per cent of the GDP (at constant 2004-05 prices), in 2008-09, compared to 18.9 per cent in 2004-05, and contributed approximately 10.2 per cent of total exports during 2008-09. Notwithstanding the fact that the share of this sector in the GDP has been declining over the years, its role remains critical as it provides employment to around 52 per cent of the workforce."

Any policymaker trying to alleviate India's poverty cannot neglect the fact that the World Development Report 2008 clearly says that 'GDP growth originating in agriculture is at least twice as effective in reducing poverty as GDP growth originating outside agriculture'.

TABLE – 11.1

Sectoral Composition of GDP

Year	*Agriculture*	*Industry*	*Services*
1950-51	53.1	16.6	30.3
1960-61	48.7	20.5	30.8
1970-71	42.3	24.0	33.8
1980-81	36.1	25.9	38.0
1990-91	29.6	27.7	42.7
2000-01	22.3	27.3	50.4
2010-11QE	14.5	27.8	57.7
2011-12AE	13.9	27.0	59.0

Source: Calculated from CSO data; *Economic Survey 2011-12*.

The power of agriculture in reducing poverty is observable in the Chinese case, especially during 1978-84, the initial years of reform. China began its reform process with agriculture: by moving from the commune-based system to the household responsibility system, and by revising agricultural prices upwards by more than 20 per cent. The results were spectacular. The agricultural growth rate jumped to 7.1 per cent per annum during 1978-1984, up from 2.5 per cent during the pre-reform period of 1966-1977. This was followed by a dramatic reduction of poverty: from 33 per cent to 15 per cent in the early reform period between 1978 and 1984 (Gulati and Fan, 2008: 6). Much of this can be ascribed to the bottom-up approach of reforms adopted by China—that is, starting from the agricultural sector. This is unlike India, which chose a top-down approach—that is, initiating reforms in the non-agricultural sector. As a result, the process of poverty reduction has been held hostage to the 'trickle down' effect.

With 51 per cent of the workforce still dependent on agriculture for their livelihood, agriculture in India has a far-reaching impact on poverty reduction as well as on rural development. Agriculture forms the resource base for a number of agro-based industries. Thus, it would be more meaningful to view agriculture not as farming alone but as a holistic value chain, which includes farming, wholesaling, warehousing (including logistics), processing, and retailing. Also, the fact that an average Indian spends more than 50 per cent of his monthly expenditure on food establishes the centrality of agriculture in the context of food security concerns (GoI 2006a). These factors together determine the critical importance of agriculture in general, and food in particular. Also, for the economy to grow at 9 per cent, it is important that agriculture should grow at 4 per cent.

An important aspect of "inclusive growth" in the Eleventh Five Year Plan (2007–12) and Twelfth Five Year Plan has been its target of 4 per cent per annum growth in GDP from Agriculture and Allied Sectors. This target is not only necessary to achieve the overall GDP growth target of 8 per cent per annum without undue inflation, it is an important element of 'inclusiveness' since the global experience of growth and poverty reduction shows that GDP growth originating in agriculture is at least twice as effective in reducing poverty as GDP growth originating outside agriculture.

Agricultural Growth

Role of Institutional and Technological Factors in Agriculture Growth

It is important, at the very outset, to understand the institutional, demographic and socio-political context within which agricultural growth has been taking place. The prevailing framework had a profound impact on the pattern of agricultural development. This, in turn, has necessitated special strategies and policies for employment generation and poverty removal in rural areas. The thrust of policies, in the first decade of planning (1951-1961) was on institutional and agrarian reforms. In an agrarian economy like India with great scarcity and unequal distribution of land, coupled with a large mass of below poverty line rural population, there are compelling economic and political arguments for land reform. Not surprisingly, it received top priority on the policy agenda at the time of Independence. In the decades following Independence, India passed a significant body of land reform legislation. The Constitution of 1949 left the adoption and implementation of land and tenancy reforms to state governments (Maitreesh Ghatak, 2007). The two basic objectives of land reforms were: (i) to remove such impediments on agricultural production as arise from the character of agrarian structure in rural areas, and (ii) to reduce or eliminate exploitation of landless and small cultivators through measures of land redistribution.

Land reform legislation in India consisted of four main categories: abolition of intermediaries who were rent collectors under the pre-Independence land revenue system; tenancy regulation that attempted to improve the contractual terms for tenants, including crop shares and security of tenure; a ceiling on landholdings with a view to redistributing surplus land to the landless; and finally, attempts to consolidate disparate landholdings.

The New Technology

It was becoming clear by the mid-sixties that there was no alternative to technological change in agriculture for achieving self-sufficiency in food grains. Even those countries in Asia which could carry out radical land reforms and build up an adequate infrastructure for agriculture had taken to the path of modernising agriculture. Japan took the lead in this direction and China followed suit even after successfully experimenting with structural changes and mobilisation of a growing labour force for capital construction in agriculture.

Characteristics of New Technology

The distinguishing characteristic of the new technology lies in the substitution of traditional robust but low-yielding varieties of seed by the so-called high-yielding variety. These seeds have the physiological attribute of being able to turn large amounts of soil nutrients into grain rather than leaf growth. This enables the plant to produce higher yields, especially so if the supply of nutrients in the soil can be increased. This in turn creates the demand for chemical fertilisers to supplement the natural fertility of the soil. Because these contain nutrients in concentrated form, they have to be applied with adequate supplies of water to enable the plant to absorb them without damaging itself. A lack of adequate water supply not only reduces the yield but may do so substantially.

Better Agricultural Practices

This seed-fertiliser-water package in turn calls for better agricultural practices for the effective utilisation of the technology.

First, the plant requires the fertiliser-water input at particular stages of growth to give the best yields.

Secondly, as fertilisers can be absorbed by weeds as well as by the plant, effective weeding is required to prevent waste of expensive fertiliser.

Thirdly, while the HYV seeds give higher yields, they are more prone to damage from excessive watering. For example, shorter-stemmed dwarf varieties are more liable to be flooded. They, thus, require more effective water control and better drainage. The need is for controlled and adequate water supplies.

Fourthly, being relatively new and non-acclimatised strains, they are more prone to local pests and diseases than established indigenous varieties and therefore, require a supply of germicides and pesticides.

Two further physiological characteristics of the new seeds are that they are quicker maturing than the traditional varieties and they are non-photosensitive. On the one hand, these two characteristics give rise to a shorter harvesting period, thus making it possible for farmers to practise multiple cropping, enabling them to use more intensively a given amount of land. Fertilisers, by enabling more production per acre to be achieved, and the quicker maturing HYV seeds, by making it possible to practice double cropping during the year, both act as land-saving innovations. Hence, their attraction to a land-hungry south Asia.

On the other hand, as the crop may be ready for harvesting during the monsoon season at a time when the cloud-cover has not yet dispersed, a possibility of loss of output due to a lack of drying and storage facilities is also opened up.[4]

Thus, the basic technological characteristic of the new technology is the application of a number of inputs which are complementary to each other. The application of these joint inputs yields much larger volumes of output of food grains as a result, largely by increasing yield per acre. However, in order to assess the impact of the technology on Indian agriculture, we have to also take into account some of the economic characteristics of that technology. In an economy where labour is relatively plentiful, it has low opportunity cost.

Economic Aspects of New Technology

The new practices, therefore, are much more expensive to the farmer. This has three implications. First, the extent to which the various inputs are applied in practice depends not on some technologically efficient dosage but on an economically optimum one. This depends in turn on the relative prices of inputs and outputs facing the producer. Minhas and Srinivasan have shown that fertiliser application is subject to diminishing returns, the economically optimum dose being smaller than the technical optimum. As technologically some of the inputs are complementary, the extent to which the application of a particular input can be profitably pushed depends also on the availability of, and the ability to purchase, other inputs. For example, the degree of fertiliser application that is profitable will depend on the availability of water and on the ability of a farmer to purchase the use of both inputs.

Secondly, the new technology is only worthwhile in terms of private benefits, e.g., if the farmer receives yields which are not only larger than traditional varieties but are substantially so, to make up for the additional variable costs of cultivation. This in turn requires, thirdly, a more intensive use of the fixed factor, e.g., land. The new technology opens up the possibility of multiple cropping; the economic imperative drives the farmer to it. This is compounded by the fact that while the new technology yields larger outputs, it is also more subject to risks. We have noted that the HYV seeds are prone to damage from flooding, water scarcity and pests. Moreover, because the farmer is a newcomer

---

4. Choudhary, Pramit (1978). *The Indian Economy: Poverty and Development,* ch.5, pp.121-123. New Delhi: Vikas.

to these practices, he is also ignorant of how to respond if something goes wrong. Additionally, where he is involved in substantial cash outlays in order to utilise the new technology, he bears a liquidity risk. This is reinforced by the fact that very often, the farmer may have to resort to borrowing in order to meet the additional costs of cultivation. A crop failure saddles him with the burden of debt.

These economic aspects of the new technology are as important as its technological characteristics to our understanding of the impact of the 'green revolution' upon the agrarian economy, especially in relation to the problems of mechanisation and of unequal incidence of acceptance and use between large and small farmers. That impact can best be studied in terms of the effects of the new technology on output, employment and the regional and interpersonal distribution of gain arising from the adoption of that technology.

Green Revolution

Three Phases of Green Revolution

Gulati and Fan (2008)[5] identify three phases of the green revolution.

The First Phase, 1966-1972

To end its dependence on P.L. 480, India, prompted by the minister of agriculture at that time, C. Subramaniam adopted a new agricultural strategy to boost grain production accompanied by remunerative support price for farmers. In January 1965, the Agricultural Prices Commission was set up to recommend a MSP, followed by the Food Corporation of India (FCI) to take charge of the logistics of procuring major agricultural commodities (Gulati, 2003). In the same year, India took a bold step by allowing the introduction of new high-yielding seed varieties (HYV) of wheat from Mexico. In 1966, India ordered the import of 18,000 tonnes of HYV wheat seeds that were distributed in the highly irrigated areas of Punjab, Haryana and western Uttar Pradesh where the past investments in irrigation had paid rich dividends.

The new seeds could yield more than double the existing levels and thus had the potential to dramatically increase wheat production and food grain supply. Under the new agricultural policy, the spread of HYVs was supported by public investments in fertilisers, power, irrigation and credit.

5. Gulati, A. and Shenggen Fan (ed.) (2008). *The Dragon and the Elephant—Agricultural and Rural Reforms in China and India*, ch.2. New Delhi: Oxford University Press.

The total amount of food grains harvested increased from 74 mt in 1966-67 to 105 mt in 1971-72, and that year India became self sufficient, with grain imports declining to nearly zero.

These outcomes would not have been possible without the favourable pricing policy that provided farmers with adequate incentives, the dynamism of the national research system that proceeded to indigenise the new seeds to tackle their shortcomings (Gulati, 2003), and the availability of inputs including canal water, fertilisers, power and credit. In view of the strategic importance of these critical inputs, it was the responsibility of the government to ensure that farmers had affordable access to them. Subsidies thus, became an instrument of agricultural policy in the late 1960s and acquired greater importance in the 1970s (Gulati and Narayanan, 2002a). The role of credit began to be important after 1969 following the nationalisation of banks.

Improved agricultural production resulting from modern input and technologies "trickled down" to the poor and led to a rise in farmer income, while output growth and increased grain supplies caused a decline in real food grain prices, benefiting the poor. Thus, rural poverty declined significantly in this phase, from 64 per cent in 1967 to 56 per cent in 1973 (Datanet India Pvt. Ltd., 2006). Several government anti-poverty programmes were also introduced during the Fourth Five-Year Plan in the early 1970s (Gulati and Fan, 2008).

Debacle and the Second Phase, 1973-1980

After the nationalisation of the banks, Prime Minister Indira Gandhi took other steps to extend the role of the state in key areas of economic management. In agriculture, private wholesale traders came under attack because, due to their speculative motives, they were regarded as responsible for fluctuations in food grain prices and supplies. Thus, in 1973-74 the government took over the wholesale trade in wheat, which proved a disaster (Chopra, 1981) and therefore, it was soon abandened. Wheat procurement was hindered by limited supply resulting from droughts in several states in 1972-73.

Following two consecutive droughts in 1972-73, food grain production decreased by 7.7 per cent (India, Ministry of Agriculture, 2003), and India slid back into the trap of food grain imports of an average of about 4 mt a year from the United States between 1973 and 1976.

After the oil shock, the government increased fertiliser subsidies to prevent a drop in consumption following the rise in fertiliser prices. In 1977, the retention price scheme was introduced for urea, the predominant fertiliser in Indian agriculture. During the 1970s, other input subsidies grew in importance within the state budget (Fan, Thorat and Rao, 2004), and the subsidy bill excluding fertilisers grew from Rs. 10 billion at constant prices to Rs. 33.2 billion, or from 0.5 per cent to 4.0 per cent of agricultural GDP between 1973 and 1980 (Gulati and Narayanan, 2002a).

Also during this period, groundwater irrigation increased in importance, with its share rising from 0.55 per cent to 19.5 per cent between 1960 and 1975 (Datanet India Pvt. Ltd., 2006) on account of private investment in tubewells by farmers who reinvested the income from the earlier burst in foodgrain production. As a result, power subsidies for water pumping grew dramatically, reaching 44 per cent of the total input subsidy at the start of the 1980s (Gulati and Narayanan, 2002a).

The extension of HYV technology from wheat to rice, favoured by the growth of tubewells, spread the green revolution to new areas, marking a new phase in the expansion of domestic production. From 1972-73 to 1979-80, production as well as yields of food grains showed remarkable growth, at 3.1 per cent and 2.5 per cent, respectively, and rural poverty declined from roughly 56 per cent to 50 per cent (Ministry of Agriculture, 2004).

The Third Phase, 1981-1990

In the 1980s, India consolidated its status as a food self-sufficient country. Rice production soared to 63.8 mt in 1986, up from 37.0 mt in 1964. Wheat output grew, too, from 12 to 47 mt in 1986, a year in which India had her first 25.4 mt of grain buffer stocks (Ministry of Agriculture, 2004). When in 1987 the "worst drought of the century" struck the country, food needs could be easily met without any loss of lives (Gulati, 2003).

During this phase, the HYV technology spread eastward to states like West Bengal and Bihar, which experienced surpluses in rice, with output over the 1980s growing at 5.0 and 3.7 per cent, respectively (Datanet India Pvt. Ltd., 2006). However, in the rest of the country the green revolution ran out of steam by 1985 once the new seed varieties had been widely adopted in the main producing regions. Yields for rice and wheat that had grown, respectively, by 3.5 per cent and 4.5 per cent per annum between 1967-68 and 1984-85 slowed down to 2.3 and 2.4 per cent per year between 1985-86 and 1999-2000 (IFPRI, 2004). With the HYV technology exhausting its impact in the mid-1980s, input subsidies were steadily increased to continue sustaining food grain production growth. By 1991, input subsidies had grown to 7.2 per cent of agricultural GDP as compared to 4.4 per cent in 1980 and 2.0 per cent of total GDP from 1.5 per cent in 1980 (Gulati and Narayanan, 2002a).

Throughout the green revolution, Indian agriculture laboured under a strictly regulated policy regime characterised by wide restrictions on production through licencing requirements and barriers to entry, as well as controls on pricing, movement and private trading of agricultural produce. On the external front, too, the sector was burdened with various tariff and non-tariff barriers to agricultural trade flows (Gulati and Fan, 2008).

The high level of protection accorded to industry produced high industrial prices and adverse terms of trade (ToT) for agriculture, reducing the relative profitability of the primary sector. Agriculture was overall net taxed (disproteced) on account of the overvalued rupee, which produced an anti-export environment for agriculture. The objectives of this framework were broadly dictated by the dominant strategy of the pre-reform era, that is, food self-sufficiency resulting from domestic supplies, aiming to: (1) ensure inexpensive food for consumers, (2) protect farmers' incomes from price fluctuations, and (3) keep the balance of payments in check (Gulati and Fan, 2008).

Reform Period, 1991 to the Present

Although the reforms were implemented in off-farm activities, they affected agriculture in at least two important ways (Landes and Gulati, 2003). First, the higher rate of economic growth and the consequent rise in per capita incomes resulting from the 1991-1993 reforms had a significant impact on food demand. Higher per capita incomes, growing at 4.5 per cent per annum in this phase as opposed to 3.6 per cent in the 1980s (WDI, 2004), led to the diversification of food demand into non-food grain crops such as fruits and vegetables, as well as meat—mainly poultry—and dairy products. Second, the lowering of industrial protection significantly improved the incentive framework for the sector through improvement in the domestic ToT between agricultural and industrial prices, which rose from 0.9 to 1.2 between 1991 and 2000 (Gulati and Fan, 2008).

Improved ToT for agriculture in turn resulted in an increase in the profitability of the primary sector relative to industry and led to an increase in private investments, which are now double the public investment in agriculture. These were increasingly directed to the production of horticultural produce, poultry, fish, milk and eggs in response to booming consumer demand for these high-value agricultural products, leading to a remarkable growth in output of these commodities during the 1990s relative to the previous decade.

As a result of these developments growth rate of agricultural GDP went up from 3 per cent in the 1980s to 4.1 per cent in the aftermath of reforms between 1991 and 1996.

Deceleration in Agriculture Growth

Growth of agricultural GDP decelerated from over 3.5 per cent per year during 1981-82 and 1996-97 to only around 2 per cent during 1997-1998 and 2004-05 (Table 11.2). This deceleration, although most marked in rainfed areas, occurred in almost all the states and covered almost all the major sub-sectors, including those such as horticulture, livestock and fisheries where growth was expected to be high.

TABLE – 11.2

Average GDP Growth Rates—Overall and in Agriculture

(Per cent Per Year at 1999-2000 Prices)

Period	*Agriculture and Allied Sectors*	*Total Economy*
1. Pre-Green Revolution 1951-52 to 1967-68	2.54	3.69
2. Green Revolution Period 1968-69 to 1980-81	2.44	3.52
3. Wider Technology Dissemination Period 1981-82 to 1990-91	3.52	5.40
4. Early Reforms Period 1991-92 to 1996-97	3.66	5.69
5. Ninth Plan 1997-98 to 2001-02	2.50	5.52
6. Tenth Plan Period 2002-03 to 2006-07	2.47	7.77
Eleventh Plan		
2007-08	4.7	9.2
2008-09	1.6	6.7
2009-10 Revised Estimate	0.2	7.4
Triennium 2009-10 over Triennium 2004-05	**3.4**	**8.6**
Eleventh Plan Average (2007-10)	**2.2**	**7.7**

Source: *Eleventh Five Year Plan 2007-2012*, Vol. III, 2008.
Mid-Term Appraisal Eleventh Five Year Plan, 2010.

States with high percentage of rainfed areas have suffered heavy decline in growth during the period 1995-96 to 2004-05. Also, the instability in output growth is more in states with high percentage of rainfed areas.

There had been a declining trend of acreage for most of the crops during the period 1995-96 to 2004-05, except that for wheat, the acreage of which registered a modest growth of 0.11 per cent per annum. In the decade prior to 1995-96, the area under oilseeds, cotton and sugarcane registered impressive growth but this trend also reversed in later decadal interval. Given the near stagnant net sown area of 140 million hectares and gross cropped area of about 190 million hectares, there was increase in area under certain crops at the expense of declining area under other crops. In the subsequent decade, the scope of increase in area vanished across the crop segments. This trend clearly indicated constraints in availability of land for agriculture due to competing pressure on land demand for non-agriculture sector and rapid urbanisation witnessed in the recent years.

There was sharp decline in the growth rate of productivity of all the crops in the decade of 1995-96 to 2004-05. The productivity growth of rice and wheat, the anchors of Green Revolution in the past, decelerated to 0.82 per cent per annum and 0.56 per cent per annum respectively from 2.40 per cent per annum and 2.61 per cent per annum respectively in the previous decade. The productivity of pulses during 1995-96 to 2004-05 had a declining (negative) trend of 0.07 per cent, reflecting the absence of any technological breakthrough reaching at farmer's end. Only cotton and maize registered productivity growth rate in excess of 2 per cent during 1995-96 to 2004-05. The healthy performance of cotton and maize, the semi-arid crops grown generally outside the traditional green revolution regions, is due to combined response to the technology, delivery and post-harvest linkages (Planning Commission, December 2006).

Performance of the Agriculture Sector during the Eleventh Five Year Plan (2007-2012)

The average annual growth in agriculture and allied sectors realized during the Eleventh Plan Period, is now placed at 3.3 per cent against the targeted growth rate of 4 per cent but is significantly better than the achievement of 2.4 per cent in the Tenth Plan. Failure to reach the target growth is one reason for the high inflation in prices of food and other primary commodities that persist despite the recent slowdown in overall GDP growth. Consequently, although the overall GDP growth target of the Twelfth Plan has been revised down since the Approach Paper, the growth target for agriculture is maintained at 4 per cent.

TABLE – 11.3

Compound Growth Rates of Area, Production, and Yield Indices of Principal Crops during 1980-1990, 1990-2000 and 2000-2011

(Base: TE 1981-82=100)

	1980-81 to 1989-90			*1990-91 to 1999-2000*			*2000-01 to 2011-12**		
	Area	*Production*	*Yield*	*Area*	*Production*	*Yield*	*Area*	*Production*	*Yield*
Rice	0.41	3.62	3.19	0.68	2.02	1.34	0.04	1.72	1.68
Wheat	0.46	3.57	3.10	1.72	3.57	1.83	1.22	2.37	1.14
Coarse Cereals	-1.34	0.40	1.62	-2.12	-0.02	1.82	-0.75	3.01	4.39
Total Pulses	-0.09	1.52	1.61	-0.60	0.59	0.93	1.70	3.47	1.91
Sugarcane	1.44	2.70	1.24	-0.07	2.73	1.05	1.37	1.96	0.58
Total Oilseeds	1.51	5.20	2.43	-0.86	1.63	1.15	2.08	4.45	3.39
Total Foodgrains	-0.23	2.85	2.74	-0.07	2.02	1.52	0.43	2.32	2.91

Notes :* Growth rates are based on the second advance estimates (AE) 2011-12 released on 03 February 2012;Total oilseeds include nine oilseeds, cotton seed, and coconut.

Source : Department of Agriculture and Cooperation.

Although growth trends and targets are subject to high errors due to weather variability (for example, the Eleventh Plan average was pulled down by two successive bad harvests in 2008–09 and 2009-10), there is reason for cautious optimism because the turn-around that began after 2004 appears to be maintaining its momentum. Further, the Twelfth Plan has pointed towards reduction in variability. Based on five-year moving average, the Twelfth Plan document has recorded a growth rate of 3.6 per cent, the highest for any five-year period ever and significantly, growth variability has also reduced to lowest ever.

The reduction in variability is important since claims of acceleration or deceleration make sense only when variability is low. Also, it is a measure of how well the system is able to cope with inevitable bouts of aberrant weather and yet maintain the growth momentum. It should be noted that agricultural growth was positive in 2009–10 despite the worst drought in nearly 40 years. More generally, whereas earlier periods saw at least one and normally two years of negative growth in every five year, there has not been a single year of negative growth of agriculture and allied sectors after 2002–03.

The magnitude of secular decline in growth variability over the last 30 years is also important. This is now less than a third of its peak. A major role must have been played by the increase in irrigation from about 20 per cent of arable area in 1981 to 35 per cent today, based mainly on groundwater. However, since water tables have fallen and temperatures risen, the extent of variability decline is surprisingly large. Even assuming zero variability on irrigated land, this implies that variability on rain-fed land must have reduced very substantially. Clearly factors such as a more diversified agriculture, extended information reach and investments both on-farm and in watershed development, appear to have enabled better responses to depleting natural resources and weather risk. Although there is considerable scope to improve each of these factors further, it is a matter of satisfaction that developments in these areas are having a positive effect (Twelfth Five Year Plan, Vol.II).

However, compared to other countries, India faces a greater challenge, since with only 2.3 per cent share in the world's total land area it has to ensure food security for a population that accounts for 17.5 per cent of world population. This leads to excessive pressure on land and area under foodgrain cultivation has not increased. Increasing agricultural production with limited natural resources in a sustainable manner for ensuring food and nutritional security and providing income security to farmers are major challenges before the government.

Instability in Output

Although the growth rate in food grains output seems to have improved because of the impact of new technology, the growth performance has by no means been smooth. The instability or the year-to-year variation in food grains output has increased in the post-green revolution period. Even within the post-green revolution period, the instability in the last decade (1978-79 to 1988-89) was higher than in the preceding decade. The rural poor, particularly in the drought-prone areas and in the remote areas of the country, continue to suffer from fluctuations in employment and income and inadequate availability of food grains in years of drought.

However, this increase in instability cannot be attributed to new technology. Rather, the instability arises from the adverse agro-climatic conditions in which the technology is used. The new seed-fertiliser technology has raised the response of output to water. Thus, for a given variability in rainfall or moisture conditions, the instability in output would be greater. However, when the new technology is applied under assured irrigated conditions, the increase in output would be on a stable path. This is exactly what has happened in the case of wheat where the new technology has made the maximum impact. The rise in instability is significant for crops like rice, oilseeds and pulses. This is explained by the increasing application of new seed-fertiliser technology for these crops in rainfed areas and under uncertain irrigation in the recent period.

Regional Disparities and Intra-Personal Disparities

Perhaps the most widely debated issue about green revolution is the growing disparities in income between different regions and classes of farmers. The experience after the mid-seventies covering nearly a decade and half reveals trends which are typical of a diffusion process. These trends are: the spread of green revolution to new areas, the increasing adoption of new technology by the small farmers, the decline in the relative prices of food grains and the rise in real wages in agriculture in the less developed regions where new technology is spreading.

New Technology and Environmental Degradation

Pollution of environment due to the intensive use of chemical fertilisers and pesticides has become a major problem in the developed countries. In India, environmental degradation in the rural areas has arisen not so much from the high level of chemical inputs used as from deforestation and extension of cultivation to ecologically fragile areas. Land-saving technological changes by reducing pressure for extension of cultivation and by augmenting biomass, contribute to the conservation of fragile areas and regeneration of forests.

Across different states in India, the extension of area under cultivation and the denudation of forests seem to be high where the progress of yield-increasing technology is slow. In such regions, the levels of agricultural income and wages are low and poverty levels are high. Similarly, the pressure from animals such as goats and sheep on forests and common lands has been increasing in regions where growth in crop production is slow. This is because the rural poor supplement their incomes by rearing these animals.

Major Factors Affecting the Growth Potential

A number of factors are constraining the growth potential of the sector.[6]

i) Lack of Long Term Policy Perspective

On the policy front, there was lack of long-term strategy for agricultural development. One will be surprised to find that only recently the Government has come out with a national agricultural policy. From the very beginning of the planning process in India, especially from the Second Five Year Plan with the sectoral priorities of Mahalanobis model favouring industry, the emphasis has been placed on industry relative to agriculture (Bhide *et al.*, 1998). The policies followed for agricultural development suffers from a number of weaknesses. First, though there was no significant direct taxation of the sector, agricultural sector has suffered from a typical anti-agricultural bias due to the nature of policies followed in other sectors like industry, trade, exchange rate, etc. (Gulati, 1998). Agricultural policies provided little incentives for the farmers, as the agricultural prices were depressed (Indian farmers received lower price than international prices). As there were numerous controls and restrictions, the sector was disprotected *vis-à-vis* other sectors of the economy. The restrictions on agricultural exports were believed to be one of the prime reasons for the disprotection of the sector as compared to the industrial sector. Second, agricultural policies gave little emphasis on agricultural exports as a means of stimulating domestic production (Jeromi, 1997). Third, it has excessive price-based focus than non-price factors like water, infrastructure, research and development (R&D), extension services, etc., which are important determinants of agricultural production in India, a fact highlighted more than three decades back by Dantwala (1967) and recently by Pulapare (2000) and Vaidyanathan (2000). These weaknesses of agricultural policies, *inter alia*, affected the faster growth of the sector and in creating a sound infrastructure base for future growth.

ii) Investment in Agriculture and Subsidies

Elementary growth theory tells us that the growth of a sector depends upon the investments made in that sector, its capital-output ratio, and the efficiency of capital in that sector (Gulati, 2012).

An unfortunate trend over the past two decades has been that expenditure control efforts have led to cutbacks in agricultural

6. Jeromi, P.D. (2002). "Is Indian Agriculture Approaching the Limits to Growth", in Raj Kapila and Uma Kapila (eds.), *Economic Developments in India*. Vol. 58. New Delhi: Academic Foundation.

investment and extension, but not in subsidies. Budgetary subsidies to agriculture have increased from around 3 per cent of agriculture GDP in 1976-1980 to about 7 per cent in 2001-2003. During the same period, public investment in agriculture declined from over 4 per cent of agriculture GDP to 2 per cent.

The public investment in agriculture in real terms has witnessed steady decline from the Sixth Five Year Plan to the Tenth Plan. However, this trend was reversed in the Tenth Plan and the Eleventh Plan.

It is imperative to reduce these subsidies for stepping up public investment in agriculture. However, there is considerable political resistance and, in a democratic polity like India, the process of change towards rational pricing of inputs is bound to be slow. In these days of globalisation and easy flow of information, it is becoming difficult to convince the Indian farmers about the need to reduce such subsidies when their counterparts in the 'market economies' like the United States, European Community and Japan enjoy much higher levels of subsidies. It is not easy to convince the farmers in India that our resources are scarcer and their alternative uses in agriculture are more productive.

As a proportion of the value added by agriculture to GDP, Gross Capital Formation (GCF) in agriculture and allied sectors rose to 20.1 per cent in 2010-11 from 13.5 per cent in 2004-05 at 2004-05 prices (Table 11.4). This is a positive trend. However, the share of agriculture and allied sectors' GCF in overall GCF of the economy at 2004-05 prices shows a mixed trend during the same period.

There is a lively debate in the literature on complementarity between public and private sector capital formation in agricultural sector. Public sector investment has a crucial role to play in creating infrastructure in terms of irrigation, roads, markets, storage facilities, rural electrification and technology development. Private sector capital formation is hard to come in these areas. Private sector capital formation is essentially taking place for short-term asset building and it is mainly in the areas of mechanisation, ground levelling, private irrigation, etc. Therefore, public sector capital formation needed to be augmented with a definite content and targeted focus, especially in case of rain-fed areas, which lack not only in irrigation facilities, but also in other infrastructural facilities. It may also be mentioned here that public spending in agriculture is a common feature in both the developed and developing countries.

TABLE – 11.4

Gross Capital Formation (GCF) in Agriculture, Forestry and Fishing (2004–05 prices)

Year	*GDP from Agriculture and Allied 2004–05 Prices*	*GCF in Agriculture and Allied at 2004–05 Prices*			*GCF in Agriculture as Per cent of GDP from Agriculture*		
		Public Sector	*Private Sector*	*Total*	*Public Sector*	*Private Sector*	*Total*
1	2	*3*	*4*	*5*	*6*	*7*	*8*
Tenth Plan							
2002–03	5,17,559	10,299	63,215	73,514	2.0	12.2	14.2
2003–04	5,64,391	12,683	57,238	69,921	2.3	10.1	12.4
2004–05	5,65,426	16,187	59,909	76,096	2.9	10.6	13.4
2005–06	5,94,487	19,940	66,664	86,604	3.5	11.2	14.6
2006–07	6,19,190	22,987	69,070	92,057	3.7	11.2	14.9
Eleventh Plan							
2007–08	6,55,080	23,257	82,484	1,05,741	3.6	12.6	16.1
2008–09	6,55,689	20,572	1,06,555	1,27,127	3.1	16.3	19.4
2009–10	6,62,509	22,719	1,08,420	1,31,139	3.4	16.4	19.8
2010–11	7,09,103	21,500	1,20,754	1,42,254	3.0	17.0	20.1

Source: Twelfth Five Year Plan 2012-2017, Vol.II.
Central Statistical Organisation National Accounts Division.

There is a view among the agricultural economists that the lagged effect of decline of capital formation during the 80s has been one of the major reasons for the decelerated growth of the sector during the 90s (Dev, 1998). Therefore, the subdued level of capital formation during the 90s could have an impact on agriculture production in the coming years.

The experience of China shows that high rate of investment in agriculture can ensure big spurt in agricultural output (Rao and Gulati, 1994). Many of the problems of agriculture sector *viz.,* low productivity, low employment opportunities, high intensity of poverty, and inadequate infrastructure are attributed to inadequate and progressive decline in public investment in physical capital (irrigation, rural electrification, roads, markets etc.), human capital (health, education and training) and development of non-farm sector. These arguments are reinforced by a recent report by UN World Food Programme (UNWFP) and MSSRF (2009) which recommends more public investment in agriculture, among others, to prevent further fall in agricultural productivity and to ensure a food-secured India (Mahendra Dev, 2013)

In formulating future policy toward public investment in agriculture and rural development, three areas should get priority: rural roads, electricity (including rural electrification), and major and medium irrigation projects (Panagariya, 2008). Rural roads that feed into major highways connect farmers to the market place, and electricity is the critical input in both agricultural and non-agricultural economic activities. The provision of these two critical amenities can go a long way toward allowing farmers to exploit their private entrepreneurial talents. Major and medium irrigation projects provide a key public input into agriculture.

iii) Lagging Research and Development Efforts

Another important factor limiting the growth potential of the sector is the lack of breakthrough in research and development after the green revolution. Perhaps, it may be one of the reasons for the decline of productivity in the nineties. India compares poorly with the productivity levels in major producing countries.

Since there is hardly any scope for further expansion of area under cultivation, the future production prospects depends largely on the improvements in the yield levels. Here what we need is to break the yield barrier and bridge the gap between the potential and actual yield through research and development (R&D) efforts. ICAR studies reveals that there is vast unexplored technological potential for improvement in the yield of crops. In this context, Swaminathan (1999) noted that the "low yield phenomena" in India should be considered as a "yield reservoir" and it should be treated as an asset for future development of the sector. Exploiting the "yield reservoir", *inter alia*, require substantial investment and development and deployment of high yielding seed varieties.

iv) Technology Generation and Dissemination

With availability of land and water fixed, the goal of 4 per cent growth in agriculture can be achieved only by increasing productivity per unit of these scarce natural resources through effective use of improved technology. The research system has so far focused mainly on breeding varieties that increase the yield potential of individual crops by enabling more intensive use of inputs. But although such research did increase potential yields substantially in the past, it puts less emphasis on the efficient and sustainable use of soil nutrients and water and is no longer leading to adequate outcomes.

Unlike the green revolution technology that began with large farmers in resource-rich areas, community-managed sustainable agriculture focusing on marginal and small farmers in resource-poor dry and drought prone areas needs to be promoted.[7]

v) Rising Soil Degradation and Over-Exploitation of Ground Water

Large-scale soil degradation and over-exploitation of groundwater are other important factors putting limits on growth of the sector. Around 40 per cent of India's total geographical area are officially estimated as degraded (some other estimates put the figure at 50 per cent).

The emergence of rice-wheat crops system in states like Punjab and Haryana, on account of continuous increase in procurement prices, has resulted in over-exploitation of natural resource base. An ICAR study found that soil health is deteriorating in Punjab and Haryana and this is a major cause of decline or stagnation in productivity of cereals, particularly of rice and wheat. The study revealed that the organic carbon content in the soils in Punjab and Haryana has declined to 0.2 per cent in 1995 from 0.5 per cent in the sixties. Soils with low phosphorus content have also increased to 73 per cent from only 3.5 per cent in 1975 in Haryana. Similarly, soils with high potash category have scaled down from 91 per cent in 1975 to 62 per cent in 1995. Further, consequent to the decontrol of prices of phosphorus and potash, there was decline in the application of these fertilisers. This caused nutrient imbalance in the soils. Now farmers have to apply more fertilisers to get the same yield as they were getting with less fertiliser 20-30 years ago. In case of groundwater, the study found that the rapid increase in the number of tubewells during the last three decades in the region has resulted in over-exploitation of groundwater. This decline forces the farmers to lower the pumps further deeper in the wells, which results in the use of irrigation with saline water.

As the present agricultural development strategy in India is centred mainly on the irrigated areas and the yield levels of crops in many

7. Mishra and Reddy (2011). "Persistence of Crisis in Indian Agriculture", in D.M. Nachane (ed.), *India Development Report 2011*. Oxford and Indira Gandhi Institute of Development Research: New Delhi.

irrigated areas are plateauing, there is a growing realisation that agricultural production cannot be increased beyond a point.

vi) Degradation of Natural Resources

The pressing need to accelerate agriculture growth should not be at the cost of sustainability of our natural resource base, which is starkly limited. This is compounded by degradation of soil and over-exploitation of groundwater. Deforestation has affected both soils and water. Action on these environmental fronts cannot wait, especially in the face of a possibly looming adverse climate change due to global warming.

Rural Distress in Post-Reform India

A recent nationwide survey (NSS 59th Round, Report 498, 2005) brings out the grave agrarian situation in terms of farmer indebtedness. Almost 50 per cent of the farming households are indebted, but the proportion is much higher in states like Andhra Pradesh (82.0 per cent), Tamil Nadu (74.5 per cent), Punjab (65.4 per cent) and Kerala (64.4 per cent), which are also states with relatively higher investment. More than 50 per cent of the borrowing is for investment in agriculture, but it is much higher in Andhra Pradesh (77 per cent), Karnataka (73 per cent) and Maharashtra (83 per cent). Institutional sources account for about 50 per cent on an average, but it is much lower at 30 per cent in states like Andhra Pradesh, where the remaining 70 per cent comes from informal sources (*IDR, 2008*).[8]

There has been a steep increase in the costs of farming across the country, which is substantially due to the reforms. The fertiliser price index increased from 99 in 1990-91 to 228 in 1998-99 at a compound annual growth rate of 11 per cent (Acharya, 2004). And one estimate, across the crops and country, suggests that fertilisers presently account for 29 per cent of farmers' inputs costs (Acharya, 2004). There have also been increases in the water charges in many states. One of the often cited reasons for agricultural trade liberalisation is that it provides access to higher prices in the global markets. However, there has actually been a decline in global prices of some of the agricultural commodities such as rice and cotton for which India enjoyed comparative advantage.

There is the steep rise in cost of living in rural areas as indicated by the CPI for agricultural labour (CPIAL) while the farmers' income

8. Radhakrishna, R. (2008). *India Development Report 2008*. ch.3. *op.cit.*

languishes. This is a familiar scissors crisis in agriculture often resulting in pauperisation of the peasantry. This has also resulted in widening of disparities between agricultural and non-agricultural incomes (Table 11.5). The disparities have doubled over the last two and a half decades, leaving agriculture way behind (*IDR, 2008*).

TABLE – 11.5

Per Worker Income in Agriculture and Non-agriculture Sectors in India

(1993-94 prices)

Period	*Income Per Worker (rupees)*		*Ratio of Non-agriculture to Agriculture*	*Growth Rates in the Last Decade (per cent)*	
	Agriculture	*Non-agriculture*		*Agriculture*	*Non-agriculture*
1978-99 to 1983-84	9961	28,430	2.85	-	-
1988-89 to 1993-94	11,179	39,355	3.52	1.16	3.31
1998-99 to 2003-04	11,496	59,961	5.22	0.28	4.30

Source: Chand (2006).

The persistence of distress in Indian agriculture has two intertwined dimensions—the agricultural and the agrarian. On the one hand, there is an agricultural developmental crisis arising out of poor designing of programmes and inadequate allocation of resources. This has adversely affected the production and productivity. Withdrawal of the state, manifested in insufficient public investments, poor availability of credit, and the failure of research and extension to address the needs of dry land/rain-fed agriculture, increased the risk and vulnerability in farming. On the other hand, there is an agrarian crisis threatening the mass of small-marginal farmers and agricultural labourers. The ratio of share of employment in agriculture to share of agricultural GDP is increasing. Incidence of calorie poor is higher than expenditure poor among cultivators and agricultural labourers, and the average calorie and protein consumption among farmers and agricultural labourers has been decreasing. The irony is that the hands that produce food do not get adequate amounts to consume. A symptom of the larger crisis is the increasing incidence of farmers' suicides (*IDR, 2011*).

National Policy for Farmers, 2007

Based on the recommendations of the National Commission on Farmers and in consultation with the concerned Central Ministries/ departments and the states, the Government of India has adopted the National Policy for Farmers, 2007. Major policy provisions include provisions for asset reforms, water use efficiency, use of technology, inputs and services like soil health, good quality seeds, disease free planting material, support services for women, credit, insurance etc. Provisions have also been made for National Agricultural Bio-security System, setting up of farm schools in the fields of outstanding farmers to promote farmer to farmer learning and to strengthen extension services and expanding food security basket to include nutritious crops like *bajra*, *jowar*, *ragi* and millets mostly grown in dry land areas. A comprehensive National Social Security Scheme for the farmers for ensuring livelihood security by taking care of insurance needs on account of illness, old age is included.

High Value Commodities: The Future Sources of Growth in Agriculture[9]

The agricultural production basket comprises of (a) food grains (wheat, rice, coarse cereals, and pulses) and commercial or cash crops (cotton, sugarcane, oilseeds, and other crops); and (b) high value commodities such as fruits and vegetables, livestock (milk, meat, poultry, and eggs), and marine products. As compared with food grains, commercial crops—particularly cotton and sugarcane (more than 355 million tons of sugarcane as per the final estimates for 2006-07—have performed well over time. For cotton in particular, the technology breakthrough with Bt has worked wonders. In 2007-08, cotton exports reached an unprecedented level of 8.3 million bales (Cotton Corporation of India 2007).

The production of cotton has been growing at the rate of 13.2 per cent during 2002-03 to 2007-08, and production more than doubled from 13.6 million bales in 2002-03 to 31.5 million bales in 2007-08 (Cotton Corporation of India 2007). As a result of this blistering growth, India has emerged as the second largest producer of cotton in 2006-2007—next only to China and having overtaken the US. India has also emerged as the second largest exporter of cotton (worth nearly $ 2

9. This section is drawn from Gulati, Ashok. "Accelerating Agricultural Growth: Moving from Farming to Value Chains", in Acharya, Shankar and Rakesh Mohan (eds.) (2010), *India's Economy: Performance and Challenges*, New Delhi: OUP.

billion of cotton exports in 2007-08)—the highest ever in the sixty-year history of independent India. The area under Bt cotton reached 7.6 million hectares in 2008, covering almost 65 per cent of the area under cotton and also accounting for more than 80 per cent of the hike in yields (James 2008). A similar technology breakthrough in other crops can help overcome stagnation, and invigorate the growth potential of the agricultural sector.

Thus, the high value segment holds the key to future sources of growth. This is primarily due to their higher expenditure elasticity compared to food grains. The share of high value agriculture in total agriculture (crops, livestock, and fisheries) has increased from 37.2 per cent in TE 1982-93 to 46.8 per cent in TE 2007-08, indicating a distinct shift in production pattern.

Although the share of food grains in value of output of total agriculture is 24.9 per cent (TE 2007-08), it comprises of nearly 64 per cent of the gross cropped area (TE 2004-05). This is in contrast to fruit and vegetables that comprise less than 6 per cent of the gross cropped area but constitute 16 per cent of the total agriculture during the same periods. Dairy in India is a classic example that has steered India to the number one position in milk production (more than 100 million tons), and is still based primarily on small holders. With the amendment of Milk and Milk Products Order (MMPO) in March 2002, private sector participation has increased in a significant way.

Changing tastes and preferences towards high value food commodities are the rationale for diversification towards this segment. The westernization of diets is a phenomenon that is being experienced by almost all South and Southeast Asian countries (Pingali, 2006). The average per capita consumption of food grains has exhibited a negative growth during 1991-2005, and there is clear indication that the plate is skewed in favour of high value commodities.

Given the fact that the markets for these products are by and large free, and the demand is income elastic, changing demographics, and socio-economic indicators will ensure higher returns. In India, cereals are being increasingly overtaken by fruits, vegetables, milk, eggs, and poultry. While the percentage of food to total expenditure has declined over time, the share of high value products within food expenditure is increasing.

Per capita per month consumption of cereals has come down from 14.9 kg. in 1983 to 12.1 kg. in 2004-05 in rural areas, while urban areas saw a decline from 11.6 kg. to 9.9 kg. during the same time period. In other words, the weighted share of cereal consumption has declined from 14.1 kg. to 11.5 kg. during the same time period.

Rapid economic growth, rising income levels, and changing demographics have triggered a significant change. The rising number of nuclear families and the increasing number of women professionals are fuelling the change in consumption habits and preferences in favour of semi-processed and processed foods, as well as setting trends in eating out. It is being projected that, in the years to come, nearly 80 per cent of the consumption boom is likely to come from rising income levels (McKinsey and Company 2007).

The food processing sector in India is still in a nascent stage with only eight per cent of the produce being processed as against 80-98 per cent in case of high income countries (Government of India, 2008). The food processing sector is now receiving the boost with the annual growth of 13.2 per cent in registered food processing units during 2004-2010 (Government of India, 2011a). In the above backdrop, there is a great need to strategically handle the situation in order to facilitate a self-sustainable and long run growth of the agriculture sector, which is possible by focussing on what is termed as secondary agriculture. Though not a panacea for all ailments of the primary sector, it can definitely drive the growth (Chengappa, 2013).[10]

Potential of Secondary Agriculture

The secondary sector is regarded as a sunrise sector for the Indian economy, owing to its immense untapped potential. The impetus for development of secondary agriculture has been due to increasing consumers demand for value added goods like ready-to-eat, ready-to-serve, convenience food. This is again favoured by the growth of organised retail which makes the processed food easily available to the consumers. Secondly, the fast depletion of natural resources used for industries has created a demand for utilisation of non-conventional renewable agro-bioresources. Thus, demand-side factors are key drivers for creating market opportunities for end products of primary agriculture through the growth of secondary sector (Chengappa, 2013).

10. Chengappa, P.G. (2013). "Secondary Agriculture: A Driver for Growth of Primary Agriculture in India", in *Indian Journal of Agricultural Economics*, Vol.68, No.1. January-March 2013.

Reforming the Three 'I's: Investments, Incentives, and Institutions

Thus, in response to new demand patterns, developed markets and infrastructure, and a change in approach from farming towards a new agri-system will be needed. New investments will be needed to become the driving force in today's agriculture. While India has a large production base, the lack of infrastructure and organised market structure stand in the way of successful diversification. A World Bank (2007b) study shows that for horticulture produce, farmers typically receive about 12 to 15 per cent of the price paid by the retail consumer in the export market. Further studies conducted by the World Bank (2007c) on value chains of mango and litchi in Bihar show that a significant amount of the consumer price is lost in transport and wastage, and farmers receive 34 and 42 per cent of that price, respectively. This can be further increased if the supply chain can be compressed and the wastage minimised (Gulati, 2010).

If one looks at the overall public resources being spent on agriculture, one is amazed to observe that three-fourths of the resources go primarily as subsidies on inputs like fertilisers, irrigation, and power. Only one-fourth of the resources go as public investment in agricultural, and roughly 90 per cent of this is on major and medium irrigation. Moreover, over time, input subsidies in real terms have gone up much faster than investments in agriculture. This has severe implications for policy regarding the allocation of public resources (Gulati, 2010).

The IFPRI research on marginal returns in terms of agricultural GDP from a unit of public expenditure across various categories within agriculture reveals that the returns are the highest on public expenditures devoted to agriculture R&D, followed by rural roads, education, and irrigation, and lowest from fertiliser subsidies. Yet, the fertiliser subsidy in 2008-09 is more than Rs. 99,000 crore, indicating a huge inefficiency in the allocation of public expenditure. In fact, the fertiliser subsidy has remained a hard nut to crack for policymakers since the beginning of the reforms in 1991 (Gulati, 2010).

It is interesting to note that while public investment in agriculture is critical and important, in reality it forms only less than 25 per cent of the total investment in agriculture; 75 per cent comes from the private sector (GoI, 2008d). Moreover, the private sector responds much better to the incentive structures in agriculture. Thus, reforming the incentives in agriculture is as, if not more, important as public investments in agriculture. Thus, private investments should be encouraged to be the spur that can transform agriculture (Gulati, 2010).

Reforming Incentives

Price and Marketing Policy

Gulati maintains to reform incentives in agriculture, the first policy action has to be getting the 'prices right'. While the reduction of tariffs on manufactured products, the correction of exchange rate of the rupee, and the relaxation of export controls on several agricultural products since 1991 have helped reduce ‘implicit taxation’ on agriculture (Pursell *et al.,* 2009), there are still occasional interventions by the government (like export bans on wheat and rice, or limits on the stocking of grains by private trade in 2008) that dissuade the private sector to invest in agri-system. However, the main government intervention in agricultural markets currently comes through its policy of minimum support prices (MSP) for some twenty-four odd crops, although in practice this mainly works for rice, wheat, sugarcane, and cotton, wherein there is some significant degree of procurement. Over time, this MSP has become de facto a procurement price, and discourages farmers to diversify into high value crops that do not have such a support/procurement price. To make the system more market oriented, it is critical to de-link the support price from procurement price, where the latter can be changed (up or down) depending upon market conditions, and in full competition with private trade within the same marketing year. This call for the abolition of all levies (on rice or sugar); the free movement of goods across the country; and the abolition of stocking limits, export bans, bans on future markets, etc., on private trade.

Reforming Institutions

While rationalising subsidies and incentives can pave the way towards greater investments, both public and private, it is important to bring about certain institutional reforms that create an enabling environment for private sector participation with a view to promoting efficiency.

Marketing and Warehouse Facilities

Improving marketing conditions and encouraging private sector participation require reforming the Agricultural Produce Marketing Committee (APMC) Act and abolishing the Essential Commodities Act (ECA). What started as a protective regime to restrict the exploitation of farmers in marketing their produce and ensuring a fair price has resulted in excessive government control. Cleaning up these archaic provisions can trigger private sector investment in developing regularised markets, logistics and warehouse receipt systems, futures markets, and in infrastructure (such as cold storage facilities, quality certification, etc.) for imports and exports. This is particularly relevant for the high value segment that is currently hostage to high post harvest losses and weak farm-firm linkages.

Reforming Land and Credit Markets

The land and credit markets are intricately linked, and improving the marketability of land will enhance access of farmers to institutional credit. According to the 2003 estimates of NSSO, farmer households with less than 2 hectares of land accounted for 80 per cent of the indebted farmer households, and availed nearly 50 per cent of their loan requirements from non-institutional sources. What aggravates their plight is that nearly 38 per cent of it is acquired at a staggering interest rate of 30 per cent (GoI, 2007b). One could think of bringing the traditional moneylenders into the organised network as Non-Banking Financial Intermediaries (NBFIs), wherein NABARD can take the responsibility of refinancing them—suppose at an interest rate of 7 per cent, while they can still charge farmers p to 12 per cent rate of interest.

High value agriculture is more income augmenting and has the potential to create both farm and off-farm employment opportunities.

Thus agriculture can no longer be confined to farming, and needs to be integrated with other segments of the agri-food system such as input supply, logistics and warehousing , processing, and retailing/ wholesaling. This shifts the focus towards backward linkages that delivers inputs, extension services, market information, and the like. Herein, the role of institutional arrangements such as rural or agri business hubs coordinated by public-private-panchayat partnerships and contract farming led by cooperatives, corporates, or producers' organisations need to be explored.

To sum up "two decades of economic reforms have at least corrected two things that are critical to agriculture: (i) that the so-called 'anti-agriculture bias' emanating from overvalued exchange rates and high rates of protection to industry has been largely removed, and this was done very early in the reform process; and (ii) the gross capital formation in agriculture, which had dipped to its lowest levels to 6.99 per cent of agri-GDP in 1994-95, was revived and it touched a high of 20 per cent during 2008-09 and 2009-10. These are commendable achievements of the reform process and will go a long way to strengthen the base of Indian agriculture.

The third noteworthy feature of Indian agriculture in an open economy environment is its gradual integration with the global economy. The exports plus imports of agricultural commodities as a percentage to agri-GDP increased steadily from about 5 per cent in 1991-92 to roughly 13 per cent in 2010-11. Though still much below the economy as a whole, this was done with a log to hesitation in changing trade policies. Nevertheless, the fact is that Indian agriculture today is almost three times more integrated with the global economy than it was 20 years back. Exports of agri-goods in 2010-11 were more than Rs 120 thousand crore, while imports were only about Rs 56 thousand crore, giving a large trade surplus in agriculture. This is not a mean achievement for a sector that was largely inward looking and wedded to import substitution. The trade surplus reflects the competitive strength of India's agri-sector.

The challenge for agriculture tomorrow comes not as much from opening it up to global markets, as from policies that still use severe export controls (be it rice, wheat, sugar, or even cotton) and do not permit a single unified national market for agri-produce. Other concerns are the high and distorted structure of taxes and fees on agri-goods in certain states, levies that are still distorting the evolution of markets, the failure to give a clear signal on market reforms that can connect the farmers' organisations to organised processors and retailers without going through the anarchic *mandi* system, and failure to give the right signals to agri-scientists and entrepreneurs on new technologies related to GM crops for commercialisation. These reforms imply institutional reforms, and require strong political will at the Centre. Only then can one hope that Indian agriculture will cross the barrier of 4 per cent growth on a sustainable basis and being much-needed prosperity in rural areas.

Farm profitability is central to achieving rapid and inclusive agricultural growth. The reports of the Commission on Agricultural Costs and Prices show low net farm revenue for many crops, particularly rain-fed. Diversification towards higher value crops and livestock remains the best way not only to improve farm incomes and accelerate growth, but also to reduce stress on natural resources which form farmers' production base. This needs better infrastructure and emphasis on integrated farming systems, combining crops and livestock, including small ruminants, for different location-specific endowments. This also requires innovative institutional and contractual arrangements so that smallholders have the requisite technology and market access (Twelfth Five Year Plan, Vol.II).

Challenges and Outlook

The agriculture sector faces challenges on various fronts. On the supply side, the yield of most crops has not improved significantly and in some cases, fluctuated downwards. The scope for increase in the net sown area is limited and farm size has been shrinking. In the case of certain crops like sugarcane, extreme variability in the acreage and production over the years has been a matter of concern. On the other hand, in the case of pulses, production has just not kept pace with the requirement leading to a rise in prices given that its availability in the international markets is limited.

Therefore, there is clearly a need for a renewed focus on improving productivity; at the same time, to step up the growth of allied activities and non-farm activities that can help improve value addition. The current focus on developing rural infrastructure particularly rural roads needs to be maintained as it would go a long way in providing connectivity that is essential for movement of agricultural produce. The irrigation sector requires a renewed thrust both in terms of investment as also modern management. There is considerable scope for development of micro-irrigation systems and watersheds and in the use of a participatory approach for achieving the same.

The 4 per cent target for growth in agriculture, which will be missed in the Eleventh Plan, must be achieved in the Twelfth Plan as it is critical for inclusiveness. Fortunately, this is technically feasible as there is ample evidence that productivity per hectare can be increased by 80% to 100% for many crops in large areas by applying modern agronomic practices based on existing technology. However, achieving these increases in productivity requires action on several fronts, most of which lie in the domain of state governments.

Since most of the growth in agriculture in future will come not from foodgrains, but from sectors such as horticulture, dairying and fisheries, where the produce is perishable, much greater attention needs to be paid to the logistics of transporting produce from the farm to the consumer, with minimum spoilage. This requires active involvement of the private sector. To facilitate such involvement, state governments must amend the Agricultural Produce Marketing Committee (APMC) Acts which at present prevent private sector buyers from dealing directly with producers. Some states have amended their APMC Acts, but the rules are either not notified, or are not designed to encourage entry of private players. For example, giving licences to operate outside the mandi only for a year at a time, as is the case in some states, discourages any serious long-term private sector investment. There is an overwhelming case for exempting horticultural produce entirely from the APMC Act. Much of the reluctance to make these changes reflect the operation of vested interests who control the mandis. Establishing better road connectivity in rural areas helps market access and the Pradhan Mantri Gram Sadak Yojana is an important intervention in this regard (Ahluwalia, 2012).[11]

Another area for policy intervention by state governments is the reform of laws relating to leasing of land. As holdings are subdivided and become uneconomic, very small and marginal farmers may be better off leasing out their land to more viable farmers, while seeking paid employment themselves. They would be more willing to do this if they felt that they could lease out their land and get it back when they want. Yet, leasing is not legal in some states. Where it is allowed, the law is biased towards the tenant, whereas the need of the hour is to protect the interest of the small farmers leasing out land.

Unfortunately, despite the importance of agriculture for rural prosperity very few state governments have taken up the challenge of bringing about the multifaceted transformation that is needed. There is too much focus on delivering a variety of subsidies in power, seeds, and credit, and not enough on bringing about a change in farming practices and adoption of new technology that would actually raise land productivity and enable farmers to become less dependent on subsidies in the long run (Ahluwalia, 2012).

As international trade in agricultural commodity is likely to be liberalised further, a greater preparedness is required to face the competition in the international market. In order to compete in the world trade and exploit the full potential of trade liberalisation, India should streamline its domestic reforms, infrastructure and institutions (Mahendra Dev, 2012).

The rural economy needs to be viewed as comprising of a continuum of interrelated economic activities. Farming needs to be dovetailed with viable off-farm and non-farm activities. Farmers need to be facilitated to take up value addition such as processing of agricultural produce, horticulture, pisciculture, poultry, development of non-farm rural enterprises. The future sources of growth in agriculture

11. Ahluwalia, Montek Singh (2012). "Prospects and Policy Challenges in the Twelfth Plan", in Uma Kapila (ed.), *Two Decades of Economic Reforms,* ch.8, New Delhi: Academic Foundation.

lie in the high value segment and reforming the Three 'I's—Investments, Incentives and Institutions.

To revive farming as also the farmer, it is necessary to have alternative technology and institutional structures. There is a need to do away with input-intensive cultivation in favour of cost-reducing knowledge-centric technology that builds on local resources and further strengthens the existing social capital. The latter is possible through structures that empower the farmers at the grassroots and organise them into federations so that they can aggregate different things at different levels. In short, the need of the hour is innovation in institutions (like federation of SHGs), government structure that facilitates empowerment (not the current line departments that have become burdened under their own weight), and technologies that reduce costs/risks (not the input-intensive production practices) if we have to revive farming and save farmers. And the successful experiments indicate that this is possible (*IDR, 2011*). These efforts will in time rejuvenate agriculture sector and bring about inclusive growth of the economy (*Economic Survey 2011-12*).

12

Agriculture Price Policy, Food Management and Food Security

Agricultural Price Policy[1]

The Government's price policy for agricultural commodities seeks to ensure remunerative prices to the growers for their produce with a view to encouraging higher investment and production, and to safeguard the interests of consumers by making supplies available at reasonable prices. The price policy also seeks to evolve a balanced and integrated price structure in the perspective of the overall needs of the economy. Towards this end, the Government announces minimum support prices (MSPs) each season for major agricultural commodities and organises purchase operations through public and cooperative agencies. The designated Central nodal agencies intervene in the market to undertake procurement operations with the objective of ensuring that market prices do not fall below the MSPs fixed by the Government.

The Government decides the support prices for various agricultural commodities after taking into account the recommendations of the Commission for Agricultural Costs and Prices (CACP), the views of State Governments and Central Ministries as well as such other relevant factors as considered important for fixation of support prices.

The objectives of price policy as propounded from time to time are multiple and often conflicting. The price policy was evolved in the context of relative shortage of agricultural products, particularly of food

1. Kapila, Uma (2013). "Developments in Indian Agriculture: Major Issues", in Uma Kapila (ed.), *Indian Economy Since Independence (Ch.9)*. New Delhi: Academic Foundation.

grains. Thus, we had the overriding objectives of the price policy as achieving self-sufficiency in food grains (understood as the availability of adequate food grains from domestic production) and protection of consumer from scarcity-induced speculative price rise. As V.S. Vyas points out, "The main function of prices, i.e., to act as signals for allocation of resources has been made subservient to income parity and food security objectives."

Apart from the consideration of income transfers, the policy is also directed to increase agricultural production by offering higher 'incentive' prices. A discriminatory price policy can be used to encourage inter-crop shifts in resource use. However, when it comes to aggregate agricultural output, greater reliance has to be placed on 'non-price' factors, e.g., generating and extending more efficient technologies. The available studies clearly bring out that aggregate supply response of agriculture is very weak. Thus, any attempt to use high prices to encourage agricultural production can bring in its wake irreparable distortions in the price structure.

These limitations of price policy are not very often recognised. Also, the strength of price policy in affecting desirable shift in cropping pattern fully exploited. As Vyas remarks, "In a mixed economy like ours an important objective of the price policy could be to give directions to the cropping pattern not only on the basis of the existing demand supply situation but also to take into account a qualitatively superior crop mix, e.g., to provide a price advantage to nutritionally superior crops or to the crops where the country may have comparative advantage. In fact, in this respect we seem to be regressing. In the 1970s price policy was used as an effective tool to encourage production of crops where superior technology was available" (Vyas, 1989). In recent years, we have largely neglected this aspect of price policy.

Further, there has been no clarity on the priority to be assigned among these numerous objectives, or the trade-off involved in pursuing these objectives simultaneously. If we are to go by the public pronouncements, the objectives sought to be achieved by the price policy include, ensuring: (i) reasonable prices for the growers, (ii) reasonable prices for the grains released from public distribution system, and (iii) reasonable prices in the open market. A moment's reflection will show that in most of the circumstances, these aims conflict with each other. The price policy cannot resolve all conflicts in the society.

It must be recognised that price policy taken by itself is a weak instrument in giving directions to agricultural economy, more so as an instrument of income transfer. While the objective of providing an insurance cover in terms of guaranteed minimum prices to a large section of agricultural producers could be a worthy objective, but until and unless required resources are available and administrative machinery is in place, mere announcement of minimum prices for a large number of commodities may not serve any purpose. It may, in fact, do more harm with an erosion of the credibility of the government. In view of this, it is suggested that the support prices should be applicable only for a limited number of crops. Crops which can be considered as price leaders or the crops, for which technological breakthrough is imminent ought to be covered under the price guarantees. The other crops to be considered for support are the crops grown under high risk environment and there also it should be a transient measure i.e., till a viable crop insurance programme is evolved.

Along with limiting the scope for price policy is the need for a discriminatory and flexible approach to price interventions. By covering a large number of commodities on the one hand and by ensuring minimum prices in the guise of procurement prices on the other, not only government's commitment has enhanced to an unmanageable extent, it has also led to serious distortions in agricultural economy.

V.S. Vyas remarks, "The time has come to take a serious look at the scope, instruments and institutions of agricultural price policy. There is a need to recognise that the price policy is a weak instrument for income transfers; our capacity to offer minimum support prices for a large number of commodities is limited; need for dovetailing agriculture and trade policies is urgent. Instrument of minimum support prices has to be used sparingly; procurement operations need to be made more business like; CACP should retain its expert character rather than trying to be representative of various interests, FCI should be decentralised and debureaucratised and the states should be made major stakeholders."

National minimum support prices (MSPs) for food grains and other major commodities are recommended by the Commission for Agricultural Costs and Prices (CACP), but are actually set by a committee chaired by the Prime Minister. CACP recommendations are based on several factors, but key factors are assessments of costs of production (CoP) and domestic and global market conditions. Historically, the MSPs for wheat and rice were generally increased at rates below inflation, and remained well under import parity prices. Although intended to be a national programme covering all major crops, the MSPs are generally defended by GoI purchases only for wheat and rice in the major surplus areas of Punjab, Haryana, western Uttar Pradesh and Andhra Pradesh (rice only) (Landes and Gulati, 2004).[2]

Beginning in the late-1990s, the MSPs set for wheat and rice became increasingly out of step with domestic market conditions. One key factor was (and still is) that the CoP concept used in setting the price became a "full cost" measure that, in addition to variable input costs, included the rental value of land, the imputed value of family labour, and a return to management. Another was pressure to compensate farmers for the price swings associated with changes in India's rice and wheat export policy during 1995 and 1996. For rice, higher market prices resulting from the initial removal of export restraints later created pressure for higher MSPs when world prices fell. Similarly for wheat, lower market prices following the re-imposition export restraints led the government to compensate farmers with higher MSPs. With these developments, the MSPs became disconnected from domestic market conditions and— when world prices fell from a temporary spike in 1996-1997—from competitive world market prices. The tendency for MSPs to be increased has likely been compounded as MSP benefits boost land rental, labour and management costs, thus leading to higher CoP.

An important factor affecting MSP policy in the 1990s concerns the changing political dimensions of the policy when India entered an era of coalition governments and the farm lobby became more influential. During 1995-96–2001-02, just before and during the accumulation of surpluses, the government set MSPs above the CACP recommendation in four out of seven years for rice and five out of seven years for wheat (Parikh *et al.,* 2002). Another key dimension is that the MSP mechanism is one of the few levers available to Indian policy makers and there is a tendency to try to use it to achieve multiple policy goals, including both price stabilisation and income support.

The failure of price policy to successfully adapt to the new environment has had a number of impacts. First, breaking with the historical pattern, domestic wheat and rice prices have tended to strengthen relative to both world and domestic prices, and to move above domestic market clearing levels. While benefiting the relatively few producers receiving wheat and rice MSPs, higher consumer prices have undoubtedly had negative impacts. Per capita wheat and rice

---

2. Landes, Rip and Ashok Gulati (2004). "Farm Sector Performance and the Reform Agenda", in K.L. Krishna and Uma Kapila (eds.) (2009), *Readings in Indian Agriculture and Industry*. New Delhi: Academic Foundation.

consumption has actually declined in recent years, as higher procurement and prices contributed to decline in consumption of open market supplies that have not been offset by subsidised distribution. A recent study of the economy-wide impacts of increasing the wheat and rice MSPs when they are above market clearing levels found that reduced consumption and investment associated with higher prices actually reduced incomes, both in aggregate and for most rural and urban income groups (Parikh *et al.*, 2002).

Second, by maintaining high prices, the government has become responsible for the storage and transport of most of the marketed surplus of FAQ—grade wheat and rice in the country—what some observers have termed a "*de facto* nationalisation" of grain trade. In addition to raising budgetary costs, the policy provides little incentive for private investment in grain storage, handling or distribution, with the exception of the fees traders can earn in the export of subsidised grain allocated by the government.

Third, by focusing on supporting relatively high prices only for wheat and rice in a few regions, MSP policy has not been made an effective tool for stabilising producer prices for other crops and supporting the diversification of agriculture.

Fourth, the budgetary cost of FCI operations under current policies has now reached about $5.5 billion. When policies support domestic prices above market clearing, much of this subsidy accrues to producers rather than consumers. Combined with the cost of subsidies on fertiliser and other inputs, the subsidy bill has burgeoned to about 43,668 crore annually, far exceeding both public and private capital formation in agriculture. Subsidy outlays are crowding out new investment needed to boost productivity and marketing efficiency.

Finally, the policy of maintaining high wheat and rice prices has contributed to emergent environmental problems, particularly associated with the intensive wheat-rice cropping system in northern India. When combined with the low cost of irrigation water—much of which is either free, stolen, or subsidised—the strong price incentives for wheat and rice are contributing to the rapid deterioration of groundwater resources, and rising concern with deteriorating soil fertility in some areas.

In more recent period since 2008, two issues have been the subject of much debate: the unprecedented increase in global prices of agri-commodities, and how Indian policymakers can make sure that their people do not suffer. Several factors—ranging from energy prices, diversion of grains and oils for bio-fuels, supply shocks from Australia and the EU, growing demand from Asia and Africa, export controls by certain countries (including India), and speculative funds in commodity markets—are supposed to be pushing global agricultural prices (Abbott *et al.,* 2008; ADB, 2008; Chand, 2008; FAO, 2007; OECD–FAO, 2008; Rosegrant, 2008; Von Braun *et al.,* 2008). Most of these studies paint a gloomy picture with respect to global prices. They suggest that the era of low agricultural prices is over, and that they are likely to remain high in the next five to ten years. However, all these studies, despite their sincere efforts, remain weak on diagnostics, especially in terms of nailing down the relative importance of various factors that have driven the prices so high in 2008. Policymakers need to avoid knee jerk reactions as India's buffer stocks are comfortable and Indian food price inflation, though high, is way below the global food price inflation. However, in the long run, investments in agricultural research and development (R&D), infrastructure, and markets have to be increased in order to augment food supplies as also to accelerate the rates of growth in Indian agriculture (Gulati, 2010).

Food Management

Food management in India has three basic objectives: procurement of food grains from farmers at remunerative prices, distribution of food grains to the consumers particularly the vulnerable sections of the society at affordable prices, and maintenance of food buffers for food security and price stability. The instruments for food management are the Minimum Support Price (MSP) and Central Issue Price (CIP). The focus is on incentivising farmers by ensuring fair value for their produce through the Minimum Support Price mechanism, distribution of food grains at subsidised rates to 6.52 crore BPL families, covering all households at the risk of hunger under Antyodaya Anna Yojana (AAY), establishing grain banks in chronically food-scarce areas and strengthening the Public Distribution System (PDS). The nodal agency which undertakes the procurement and distribution and storage of food grains is the Food Corporation of India (FCI). The procurement under the current system is open-ended at MSP, while the distribution is governed by the scale of allocation and its offtake by the beneficiaries. Rice and wheat are predominant cereals in procurement of food grains.

Food Procurement Policy

The main objectives of food management are procurement of foodgrains from farmers at remunerative prices, distribution of foodgrains to consumers, particularly the vulnerable sections of society, at affordable prices, and maintenance of food buffers for food security and price stability. The instruments used are MSP and central issue price (CIP). The nodal agency for procurement, distribution, and storage of foodgrains is the Food Corporation of India (FCI). Procurement at MSP is open-ended, while distribution is governed by the scale of allocation and its offtake by beneficiaries. The offtake of foodgrains is primarily under the targeted public distribution system (TPDS) and other welfare schemes of the GoI.

Procurement of food grains by FCI continues to be higher in states such as Punjab, Haryana, Uttar Pradesh and Andhra Pradesh. These four states accounted for 69.7 per cent in 2006-07, 69.46 per cent in 2007-2008 and 67.47 per cent in 2008-09. Punjab and Haryana which accounted for 91.1 per cent of procurement of wheat for the Central Pool in 2007-08, accounted for 66.88 per cent in 2008-09 and 69.53 per cent in 2009-10, indicating an increased share in procurement by other states. Increased MSP along with various other steps taken by the Government has resulted in higher levels of procurement of foodgrains. This has paved the way for comfortable levels of food stocks to meet the TPDS needs and buffer stocks norms. Offtake of wheat and rice from the Central pool for the TPDS and other welfare schemes) has gone up in the last many years.[3]

Price and Distribution Controls in the Food Grain Market

The major elements of the food policy are procurement of grain at Minimum Support Prices (MSP), maintenance of buffer stocks and distribution at subsidised rates through the Public Distribution System (PDS). The Government of India (GoI) allocates grains to states at Central Issue Price (CIP) for distribution to consumers. The Food Corporation of India (FCI), an agency of the GoI, handles procurement, storage and transportation of grains to states. The states in turn distribute to consumers at subsidised prices through a network of more than 4,60,000 fair price shops (FPSs). The 'food subsidy' comprises the cost of procurement incurred by the GoI net of sales realisation (for rice, wheat, and sugar) and the carrying costs for maintaining the central pool of buffer stock incurred by the FCI and reimbursed by the GoI (Jha, 2012).[4]

The policy is effective for rice and wheat in major surplus states. For wheat, the government offers to buy all grain that comes forth for

3. Government of India, *Economic Survey 2010-11*.
4. Jha, Shikha (2012). "Food Procurement Policy", in Kaushik Basu and Annemie Maertens (eds.), *The New Oxford Companion to Economics in India*, Vol.II. *op.cit.*

sale at the announced MSP. In the case of rice, part of the procurement is in the form of paddy at the MSP, which is custom milled and the rest, which is the major part, is procured as rice in the form of a statutory levy imposed by all major rice-producing states on rice millers/dealers. The levy percentage varies widely from 10 per cent in Pondicherry to 75 per cent in Haryana, Punjab and Orissa. Rice millers are paid levy rice prices fixed by the state government. The Commission for Agricultural Costs and Prices (CACP) recommends levels at which the MSP should be fixed based on several considerations. These include cost of cultivation, the overall shortage of grains as reflected by the trend in wholesale prices, and the need to keep in check the rate of inflation in the consumers' interest (Jha, 2012).

Although the MSP is fixed supposedly based on a cost-plus formula, the actual price offered in practice is higher and influenced by high expectations of rich farmers represented by politically strong farm lobbies (Rao, 2001). The high and rising MSPs provided by the GoI for wheat and more recently, for paddy increased profitability of these crops and motivated farmers to shift greater area to these crops from coarse cereals, pulses and oilseeds. Moreover, the income transfers accrued disproportionately to large farmers confined mainly to surplus states. Price distortions in the output market combined with distorted prices of inputs such as fertilisers, power and irrigation had an added detrimental effect not only on the production of other crops but also on the environment such as decline in water tables. The policy also led to an accumulation of buffer stocks of grains and the credit blocked in these stocks put pressure on interest rates and possibly crowded out more productive investment. These adverse fiscal and environmental implications led to increased recognition of the need to reform farm support policies (Jha, 2012).

Apart from supporting farmer prices, the government's policy of procurement helps supply grain to the PDS, the scheme to distribute subsidised grain to consumers. In order to reduce the budgetary costs of this scheme as well as to redirect subsidy mainly to the poor (people below the poverty line), the government shifted from a universal PDS to a Targeted PDS (TPDS) in 1997. However, in general the TPDS suffers from several deficiencies such as urban bias in coverage, leakage and diversion of grain to the open market due to lack of transparent and accountable delivery systems. The move by the government to decentralise the procurement and PDS operations to states is in part meant to rectify these problems.

Public Distribution System (PDS)

The PDS has attracted considerable debate in recent years on the ground that the benefits of PDS are not reaching the poor on account of poor targeting and leakages in the system, despite its restructuring in 1997. It has also been argued that despite the huge food subsidy and

TABLE – 12.1

Procurement, Offtake, Stocks and Food Subsidy

Year	*Procurement (Million Tonnes)*	*Off-take (Million Tonnes)*	*Stocks (Million Tonnes)*	*Food Subsidy (Rupees Crore)*
1	2	*3*	*4*	*5*
1993-94	26.40	18.61	20.54	5537
1994-95	24.99	19.44	26.80	5100
1995-96	22.24	24.35	20.82	5377
1996-97	20.03	25.63	16.41	6066
1997-98	23.82	18.96	18.12	7500
1998-99	24.22	20.73	21.82	8700
1999-2000	31.43	23.05	28.91	9200
2000-01	35.43	17.95	44.98	12010
2001-02	41.91	16.15	59.14	17494
2002-03	35.46	45.60	—	24176
2003-04	37.29	45.13	—	25160
2004-05	43.48	44.4	24.4 (Jan.)	25800
2005-06	42.45	42.3	21.7 (Jan.)	23071
2006-07	34.3	36.8	17.4 (Jan. 07)	23826
2007-08	39.8	37.4	19.2 (Jan. 08)	312.60
2008-09 (Prov.)	56.8	39.5	35.8 (Jan. 09)	43668
2009-10	57.4	49.7	47.7	58242
2010-11	56.7	52.0		63844
2011-12	63.3	56.38	55.2 (Jan. 2012)	72822
2012-13 (upto Dec., 2012)	52.8	47.16	62.9	85000

Note: B.E : Budget Estimate

Source: *Economic Survey 2003-04, 2004-05, 2006-07, 2007-08, 2008-09, 2010-11, 2011-12*, 2012-13.

the large-scale of intervention, the food security of many households is still marginal or insufficient. In recent years, there has been a substantial rise in procurement of food grains by the public sector agencies on account of consistent increases in Minimum Support Prices (MSP), despite the recommendations of the Commission for Agricultural Cost and Prices to freeze the same. It is argued that consistent increases in the MSP have distorted relative prices between alternate agricultural activities, land use patterns as well as the consumption of inputs.

Procurement higher than the offtake had resulted in a build-up of excessive stocks of food grains since 2001-02 (Table 12.1).

Food Subsidy

The difference between the economic cost of food grains and the issue price is reimbursed to FCI. Provision of minimum nutritional support to the poor through subsidised food grains and ensuring price stability in different states are the twin objectives of the food security system. By fulfilling the obligation towards distributive justice, the Government incurs food subsidies. Food subsidy showed an annual increase of above 30 per cent during each of the three years namely, 2000-01, 2001-02 and 2002-03. The same trend is seen since 2007-08 (Table 12.2).

TABLE – 12.2

Growth of Food Subsidy in India (other than sugar)

Year	*Food Subsidy (Rs. crore)*	*Annual Growth (%)*	*Year*	*Food Subsidy (Rs. crore)*	*Annual Growth (%)*
2000-01	12,010.00	30.54	2007-08	31,259.68	31.19
2001-02	17,494.00	45.66	2008-09	43,668.08	39.69
2002-03	24,176.45	38.20	2009-10	58,242.45	33.38
2003-04	25,160.00	4.07	2010-11	63,844.00	9.20
2004-05	25,746.45	2.33	2011-12	72,822.00	14.10
2005-06	23,071.00	-10.39	**2012-13**	**85,000.00**	**16.70**
2006-07	23,827.59	3.28			

Source : *Economic Survery 2009-10, 2011-12, 2012-13.*
EPW, June 8, 2013, p.127.

Food subsidy being the difference between the economic cost of wheat and rice and their issue prices for different groups of beneficiaries are linked to the increase in the economic cost and the issue prices. While the economic cost of wheat and rice has gone up due to an increase in MSP, the issue price has been kept unchanged since July 1, 2002 (Table 12.3).

TABLE – 12.3

MSP and Issue Price for Wheat and Rice under TPDS

Marketing Season	*Minimum Support Price (MSP)*		*Central Issue Price (CIP)*					
			Wheat			*Rice*		
	Wheat	*Paddy*	*APL*	*BPL*	*AAY*	*APL*	*BPL*	*AAY*
2002-03	620[a]	530[a]	610	415	200	830	565	300
2003-04	630	550	610	415	200	830	565	300
2004-05	640	560	610	415	200	830	565	300
2005-06	650[b]	570	610	415	200	830	565	300
2006-07	750[d]	580[c]	610	415	200	830	565	300
2007-08	1,000	645[e]	610	415	200	830	565	300
2008-09	1,080	850[f]	610	415	200	830	565	300
2009-10	1,100	1000[g]	610	415	200	830	565	300
2010-11	1,170	1000[g]	610	415	200	830	565	300
2011-12	1285	1080	610	415	200	830	565	300
2012-13	1350	1250	610	415	200	830	565	300

Notes: a One-time special drought relief of Rs20 per quintal was given in the case of paddy over and above the existing MSP and Rs10 per quintal for wheat.

b An incentive bonus of Rs50 per quintal over the MSP given for wheat procured in RMS 2006-07 during the period 20.3.06 to 30.6.06.

c An incentive bonus of Rs40 per quintal over the MSP allowed for paddy procured in KMS 2006-07 till 31.3.2007. Applicability of bonus was extended up to 30.9.2007 for the states of Andhra Pradesh, Tamil Nadu, Orissa, West Bengal and Chhattisgarh. For Bihar and Kerala, it was extended up to 31.5.2007.

d An incentive bonus of Rs 100 per quintal over the MSP given for wheat procured in RMS 2007-08.

e An incentive bonus of Rs 100 per quintal over the MSP allowed for paddy/rice procured in the entire KMS 2007-08.

f An incentive bonus of Rs50 per quintal allowed over the MSP of paddy for KMS 2008-09.

g An incentive bonus of Rs50 per quintal allowed over the MSP of paddy for KMS 2009-10.

Source: Economic Survey 2009-10, 2010-11, 2011-12, 2012-13, Economic & Political Weekly Vol XLVII(23). June 8, 2013.

The government also spends around 35 per cent more beyond the MSP in the form of incidental and distribution costs. These incremental costs are direct cost. There may be indirect cost also. So for these obvious reasons, total food subsidy (for all crops) has gone up from Rs. 25,746 crore in 2004-05 to around Rs. 72,000 in 2011-12 and the fertiliser subsidy from Rs. 15,662 crore to Rs. 54,976 crore in 2010-11.

India's agriculture sector is also facing cost-push inflation. In the last two years, food production costs have gone up between 15 and 19.67 per cent. One of the most important reasons for higher food inflation has been the increase in the minimum support price (MSP). But given the overall rise in farmers' production costs, the government will be forced to raise the MSP further. So, in the best case scenario, food inflation may only moderate.

Buffer Stock

The years 2001-02 and 2002-03 witnessed high levels of stock build-up in the central pool. Food grains stocks reached a peak of 64.7 million tonnes, an all time record, in June 2002. The year 2003-04 witnessed a general easing in the food grains stocks with relatively lower procurement of rice and wheat following a bad agricultural year in 2002-03 and relatively high off-take of food grains, especially for drought-related relief operations and under the welfare schemes.

The steady reduction in stocks prompted the Government to stop fresh allocation of rice and wheat for export with effect from August 2003, which has continued till date. The year 2004-05 started with a much lower stock of 20 million tonnes on April 1, 2004, down from 32.8 million tonnes on April 1, 2003. Stocks, however, remained consistently higher than the buffer requirement in the subsequent years.

The stock position of foodgrains in the central pool as on 1 February, 2012 was 55.2 million tonnes comprising 31.8 million tonnes of rice and 23.4 million tonnes of wheat, which is adequate for meeting the requirements under the TPDS and welfare schemes during the current financial year (Table 12.4).

TABLE – 12.4

Buffer Stock Norms and Actual Stocks

(lakh tonnes)

As on	*Wheat*		*Rice*		*Total*	
	Minimum Buffer Norms	*Actual Stock*	*Minimum Buffer Norms*	*Actual Stock*	*Minimum BufferNorms*	*Actual Stock*
January 2009*	112	182.12	138	175.76	250	357.88
April	70	134.29	142	216.04	212	350.33
July	201	329.22	118	196.16	319	525.38
October	140	284.57	72	153.49	212	438.06
January 2010	112	230.92	138	243.53	250	474.45
April	70	161.25	142	267.13	212	428.38
July	201	335.84	118	242.66	319	578.50
October	140	277.77	72	184.44	212	462.21
January 2011	112	215.40	138	255.80	250	471.20
April	70	153.64	142	288.20	212	441.84
July	201	371.49	118	268.57	319	640.06
October	140	314.26	72	203.59	212	517.85
January, 2012	112	256.76	138	297.18	250	553.94

Notes: * Buffer norms include Food Security Reserve of 30 lakh tonnes of wheat from 1 July 2008 and 20 lakh tonnes of rice from 1 January 2009 onwards.
Source: *Economic Survey 2010-11, 2011-12.*

Recent Policy Initiatives

In the last few years, the government initiated steps to encourage private participation in grain markets. The role of the FCI is proposed to be restricted to timely sales and purchases to maintain stability in food prices. In a scenario of trade liberalisation, however, this needs to be complemented with appropriate trade and tariff policies. As part of a new strategy, the government plans to promote exports through long-term credit, removal of export restrictions, establishment of Agricultural Export Zones, and transport subsidies for export of wheat and rice from government warehouses. But it also needs to improve facilities for grading and measuring standards, and address quality problems. In order to take full advantage of growing exports, the exporters would need to have better ports and other domestic infrastructure facilities, which are currently very meagre. The ports are highly congested, have obsolete equipment, are managed by government-controlled port trusts, and marred by bureaucracy. Undertaking reforms in these areas would allow India to take on competition from major exporting countries such as Vietnam and Pakistan for rice and the United States for wheat.

Domestic marketing reforms also need to be undertaken so that there is one integrated market for food within India and restrictions do not prevent inter-regional flows in a timely and efficient manner. The private sector should be allowed to operate more freely in the market and to trade and store grains based on its expectations from the market. The public sector needs to play a facilitating role by providing the appropriate economic environment and creating a level playing field for private operators and traders. Several government committees have recommended the abolition of statutory and nonstatutory charges such as *mandi* charges and purchase tax to reduce transaction costs and encourage free movement of grains domestically.

The high costs of maintaining public stocks can be reduced through encouraging private storage, which plays a complementary role to public storage. Support price should not be fixed at unduly high levels. The level of the MSP should be such that it provides protection against distress sales during surplus situations and not a guarantee for fixed returns on the costs incurred. The costs of operation of the FCI can be reduced by decentralising procurement to local market, carrying out storage operations at state level (Jha and Srinivasan, 2005). Decentralisation would help to ensure market efficiency and reduce the economic costs of running the PDS. Efficient functioning of a decentralised system would, however, require support and cooperation from state governments. Reforms to the GoI's food procurement policy in these directions would help achieve its twin objectives more effectively (Jha, 2012).

Food Security and Future Sources of Growth in Agriculture

From the chronic shortage of food grains and virtually 'ship-to-mouth' existence in the mid-1960s, India has made considerable strides towards achieving food security. Thanks to the green revolution, the country has not only achieved self-sufficiency in food grains, but has become a net exporter. For the first time in the history of independent India, the country has been a net exporter of food grains consecutively for the last seven years. What is more, the Food Corporation of India (FCI) had, by 2002, accumulated over 60 million tonnes of food grains—nearly three times the normal requirement for buffer stocks and the public distribution system (PDS). There has been a significant decline in the incidence of poverty since the mid-1960s. Even then, according to the latest official estimates (NSSO 61st Round) in 2004-2005, 27.5 per cent of the population was still below the poverty line. This implies that despite the availability of food grains for meeting the requirements of the entire population, we are still far from generating the necessary purchasing power or effective demand from the poor to satisfy their needs. Since effective food security implies achievement of both physical and economic access to food, a large section of our population can still be considered to be suffering from food insecurity.

In terms of its performance, the food economy of India reveals three distinct phases. The first phase from the beginning of the plan period to the mid-1960s was characterised by severe imbalances between the demand for food and its domestic supply. Over the post-green revolution period from about the mid-1960s to the close of the 1980s, the country achieved near self-sufficiency in the availability of food and experienced an improvement in effective food security insofar as there was a significant reduction in the incidence of poverty, especially in the 1980s. As such, this second phase itself warrants sub-grouping into the 1970s characterised by the emergence of inter-regional and inter-crop imbalances in agricultural growth and the 1980s when crops such as rice, oilseeds and pulses registered high growth, especially in the eastern and central regions where poverty is widespread and which were largely bypassed in the early phase of the green revolution. The third phase is represented by the post-economic reform period of the 1990s when a series of measures for macroeconomic stabilisation and structural adjustment were launched. The immediate or short-run consequences of these reforms for the food economy were negative.

Pre-Green Revolution

Food grains production in the pre-green revolution period barely kept pace with population growth, the annual growth rate in per capita output being negative in the 1960s (Rao and Radhakrishna, 1997). Growth in food grains output in this period was achieved mainly through the increase in area under cultivation by using traditional technology. The imports of food grains increased reaching a level of 14 per cent of domestic availability in 1966. The droughts of 1965 and 1966 and the rising prices of food highlighted the imbalance in India's food economy: sluggish growth in productivity with slow rise in the use of inputs like irrigation, fertilisers and high yielding seeds in the face of growing demand for food on account of rapid growth of population and rise in per capita income.

Green Revolution

This crisis prompted the government to accord an overriding priority to the goal of achieving self-sufficiency in food grains by launching the green revolution. Public investment in irrigation and agricultural research was stepped up. As a result of this and the rise in total factor productivity, the per head growth rate in the output of food grains was close to 1 per cent in the first decade of the green revolution and accelerated further to slightly over 1.5 per cent during the 1980s (Rao and Radhakrishna, 1997). Consequently, the dependence on imports declined in the post-Green Revolution period. Net imports of food grains were either negative or less than 1 per cent of domestic availability over much of this period. The relative prices of food grains showed a decline after the mid-1970s and there was a rise in real wages of farm labour.

Post-Reform Revolution

In the post-reform period of the 1990s, however, the growth rate in food grains output at around 1.7 per cent has been lagging behind the population growth rate of 1.9 per cent. The rate of inflation was high, at 10 per cent or more, consecutively for four years in the first half of the 1990s, the rise in the prices of food grains being even higher. As such, there was a rise in poverty and inequality in the immediate post-reform period (Gupta, 1995), and slower reduction in poverty thereafter.

Public intervention in the food grains market assumed greater significance in the post-green revolution period, both for ensuring remunerative prices for the farmers and for stabilising consumption. Procurement of foodgrains by the government increased steadily from well below 5 per cent of output over much of the pre-green revolution period to well above 10 per cent and 15 per cent of output in the 1980s and the 1990s. Correspondingly, the volume of public distribution of food grains increased significantly—exceeding 10 per cent of domestic availability in the post-green revolution period. As a result of procurement operations, the terms of trade for agriculture improved (Radhakrishna and Rao, 1995), the annual fluctuations in the per capita availability of food grains declined during the 1980s and the 1990s when compared to the previous period (Rao and Radhakrishna, 1997), and there was a decline in the seasonal as well as regional variation in the prices of food grains (Bhalla, 1995).

The foregoing overview suggests that the most important problem concerning food management in India is to overcome chronic or long-term food insecurity by ensuring adequate nutrition to the whole population on a sustainable basis (Radhakrishna, 1996). This would require augmentation of food supplies to meet the expanding food basket which, as discussed in the previous chapter, is getting increasingly diversified on account of changing tastes and preferences. The experience of the green revolution demonstrates that with necessary investments in agricultural infrastructure and research and an appropriate policy environment, it should be possible to achieve the desired growth in the availability of food.

However, the real challenge is to ensure adequate purchasing power in the hands of those suffering from chronic food insecurity. As argued in this chapter, the ongoing economic reforms, given appropriate content and sequencing, can be expected to generate productive employment necessary to overcome chronic food insecurity. Public support to poverty alleviation programmes and subsidised food for the vulnerable sections will have to continue but, basically, as supplementary to the broad-based, employment-oriented growth. As discussed later, the focus of such interventions in the future should be on better targeting of the beneficiaries and on cost-effective delivery systems.

There seems to be a dramatic decline in the rate of growth in the value of food grains output from 3.6 per cent during 1992-93 to 1996-1997 to 1.3 per cent in 1997-98 to 2001-02, and then to 1.4 per cent during 2002-03 to 2006-07. These numbers have raised concerns regarding our population growth (GoI, 2007a). Several researchers have cited technology fatigue, a deteriorating natural resource base, and policy neglect as some of the reasons behind the stagnating yields of several food grain crops. This has led the media to create a 'hype' about our food security being compromised, leading to dire consequences.[5]

However, all this 'hyped' concern about food security dilutes if we include 2007-08 in our calculations, and see the grain output in tonnage rather than in the value of output. In tonnage terms, the food grain production in 2007-08 has been estimated at 230.78 million tons, up

5. Gulati, Ashok (2010). *op.cit.*

from 217.3 million tons for 2006-07—a growth rate of 6.2 per cent. This has raised the growth rate of production of food grains to 2.1 per cent for the period 2002-03 to 2007-08—which is higher than the rate of growth of population (about 1.6 per cent). Also, one should not forget that, even when the food grain growth rate (in value of output terms) was 1.3 per cent during 1997-2001, it led to a huge accumulation of stocks of 63 million tons in 2002, indicating shifting demand patterns away from cereals. It is worth remembering that, historically, grain production has often shown a sort of 'step function'—that is, stagnating for a few years and then taking a sudden jump, as in a stair case. The growth patterns of the value of output of the crop, livestock, and fisheries sectors over three distinct time periods indicate a growing diversification of the production basket. The average annual growth rate of value of output of food grains is much less than that of the non-food grain sector which is comprised of high value and commercial crops. These trends suggest that the major sources of future growth in agriculture will not come from grains but from commercial and high value agriculture.

The 'hyped' concern about food security has often overshadowed the fact that India has been a net exporter of cereals for more than a decade, and more than 28 million tons of rice and wheat were exported between 2002-03 and 2005-06. Not many are aware of the fact that even in 2006-07—when India imported 6.1 million tons of wheat worth roughly Rs. 5,850.5 crore (about $ 1.3 billion)—India exported 4.7 million tons of rice, the value of which was Rs. 7,036 crore (about $ 1.6 billion). And, in the so-called 'global food crisis' year 2007-08, India exported about 9.7 million tons of cereals, 6.5 million tons of rice, and about 3 million tons of corn in particular against an import 1.8 million tons of wheat. In most of these years, India's grain stocks have been way above buffer stock norms (see Table 12.4).

Bulging food stocks have resulted in a huge food subsidy bill, budgeted at Rs. 629 billion for the year 2010-11 as a result of increasing procurement levels and declining off-take. The fiscal outgo is expected to be more once the National Food Security Bill already passed by an ordinance on July 6, 2013 is implimented.[6]

---

6. The States of Delhi, Haryana, Uttarakhand launched the programme under the Act on August 20, 2013.

BOX – 12.1

National Food Security Bill

The National Food Security Bill was introduced in the Lok Sabha on 22 December 2011. As per the provisions of the Bill, it is proposed to provide 7 kg. of foodgrains per person per month belonging to priority households at prices not exceeding Rs. 3 per kg of rice, Rs. 2 per kg of wheat, and Rs. 1 per kg of coarse grains and to general households not less than 3 kg of foodgrains per person per month at prices not exceeding 50 per cent of the MSP for wheat and coarse grains and derived MSP for rice. It will benefit up to 75 per cent of rural population (with at least 46 per cent belonging to priority households) and up to 50 per cent of urban population (with at least 28 per cent belonging to priority households), besides providing nutritional support to women and children and meals to special groups such as destitute and homeless, emergency and disaster affected, and persons living in starvation. Pregnant and lactating women will also be entitled to maternity benefit of Rs. 1,000/per month for six months. In case of non-supply of foodgrains or meals, entitled persons will be provided food security allowance by the concerned state/UT governments. Provisions for reforms in the TPDS such as doorstep delivery of foodgrains, application of information and communication technology (ICT) including end to end computerization, leveraging 'aadhaar' for unique identification of beneficiaries have also been made in the Bill. Provisions have also been made for transparency and accountability including disclosure of records relating to the PDS, social audits, and setting up of vigilance committees besides an elaborate grievance redressal mechanism.

13

Industrial Policy

The Industrial Scene at Independence

The main features of the industrial scene in India on the eve of planning (1950) were as under:

(i) There was the preponderance of consumer goods industries *vis-à-vis* producer goods industries resulting in lopsided industrial development. In 1953, the ratio of consumer goods to producer goods worked out to be 62:38.

(ii) The industrial sector was extremely underdeveloped with a very weak infrastructure.

(iii) The lack of government intervention in favour of the industrial sector was considered as an important cause of under-development.

(iv) Export orientation had been against the country's interests.

(v) The structure of ownership was highly concentrated.

(vi) Technical and managerial skills were in short supply.

As a result, the national consensus was that economic sovereignty and economic independence lay in rapid industrialisation including particularly the promotion of industrial infrastructure.

Organised thinking concerning the direction of industrial development in India may be traced to the Statement of Industrial Policy, 1945; the Industrial Policy Resolution of 1948; the enactment of the Industries (Development and Regulation) Act, 1951; the First and Second Five Year Plan documents; and the Industrial Policy Resolution of 1956.

The First Five Year Plan stated that the objective of industrial planning was to make good the deficiencies in production of key industrial items and to initiate development which would enable the cumulative expansion of such basic production. The scope and need for the development of India's industries was felt to be so great that it was necessary for the public sector to develop those industries 'in which private enterprise is unable or unwilling to put up the resources required and to run the risk involved'. The idea was that the rest of the field could be left free for private enterprise.

The Industrial Policy Resolution of 1948 had identified a small number of industries to be reserved for production by the public sector. The production of arms and ammunition, production and control of atomic energy and ownership and management of railways were to be the sole preserve of the Central government. However, coal, iron and steel, aircraft manufacturing, ship-building, manufacture of telegraph and wireless equipment (except radios) and minerals were reserved for production by Central or state government undertakings.

The thinking concerning the public sector had changed during the course of the 1950s. As far as can be ascertained, the original thinking was concerned with the use of the public sector investment in industries which the private sector would find difficult to invest in. By 1956 this had changed towards an explicit preference for state ownership of industries that were termed as capturing the 'commanding heights of the economy'.

Industrial Control Regime 1950s to 1970s

The system of Indian industrial licensing, therefore, has its origins in a combination of thinking resulting from the exigencies and requirements of a war situation, Indian nationalistic aspirations and the socialistic leanings of some of the founding fathers of the country. The leaders of the private sector of the time were also in favour of strong governmental assertion. The industrial licensing system has operated in the country with the simultaneous operation of other schemes of governmental allocations and controls such as:

(i) Five Year Plan documents

(ii) Import and export controls

(iii) Control of capital issues

(iv) Control of foreign exchange

(v) Transport controls including allocation of raw materials

(vi) Price controls

(vii) Allocations of credit

This suggests that the planners and policymakers in India understood the need for using a wide variety of instruments and controls to steer Indian industrial development in a desired direction. However, there has always been a mismatch between the intentions expressed and the licensing instruments available for realising these planning intentions. It should also be noted that, whereas the original intention of licensing was to use this power selectively for the promotion of selected important industries, it was later used to control almost all industries with the result that *regulation rather than development became the more important feature of the system.*

Performance of the Industrial Licensing System

Until the recent industrial and trade policy reforms, the establishment and operation of an industrial enterprise in India required approvals from the Central government at almost every step.

In addition to these approvals, since the enactment of the MRTP Act in 1969, the firms covered under this needed to obtain separate MRTP clearances from the Department of Company Affairs. Further, resulting from the desire to promote small-scale industries, 836 items have been reserved for production in small-scale enterprises. Since 1956, there has also been a list of industries reserved for exclusive production in the public sector. Since 1977, there has also been a ban on the location of industries in the largest 20 to 30 cities. In 1988, this ban was extended to include municipal areas of all towns and cities and to specified areas of influence around the largest 21 cities.

That this system was unsuited for directing investments has been well understood since the early 1960s. The most comprehensive description, evaluation and indictment of this system is that by Bhagwati and Desai (1970). The government appointed one committee after another in the 1960s to examine the industrial licensing system (The Swaminathan Committee, 1964; the Mahalanobis Committee, 1964; the Hazari Report, 1967; the Dutt Committee Report, 1969; and the Administrative Reform Commission, 1969). Despite the findings of most of these early committees, that the licensing mechanism was not serving its purpose of channelising investments into desired directions, there seems to have been a continuing inability of the government, until recently, to bring any substantative changes to the industrial licensing system.

India's import tariffs were among the highest in world with duty rates of above 200 per cent being fairly common. Imports of manufactured goods were completely banned. Policies towards foreign investment were quite restrictive reflecting the general protectionist thrust of industrial policy (Ahluwalia, 2012).[1]

It seems the promotion of a sheltered home market had a common appeal to the bureaucratic authoritarian state, urban manufacturers and multinationals that supplied technology and capital. Protection also met the state's objectives pursuing revenue and expenditure maximising activities through maximum revenue tariffs and export tariffs.

Thus, the interests of politicians, bureaucrats, multinationals as well as domestic industrial houses all coincided to keep Indian industry sheltered through the operation of the industrial control system.

Industrial Policy Reforms 1980s

Industrial policy changes of the 1980s represented a response to the heavily felt need for domestic deregulation. Experiments with industrial delicensing, weakening of MRTP provisions to provide larger scope for large industrial houses, incentives for modernisation of capital stock, policies for major industries such as textiles and sugar, gradual introduction of price decontrol for cement and aluminum, etc., were some of the major steps taken in the direction of domestic deregulation. A move away from physical controls to a system of financial incentives and disincentives and from discretionary to more market-oriented regulation formed the underlying thrust of the industrial policy changes of the 1980s.

A major exception to this thrust was the continuation of the policy of reservation of production for the small-scale sector particularly since it constituted an important hurdle in the way of developing export capability in sectors such as garments, leather products, sports goods etc., where India has a comparative advantage. Industrial policy in the 1980s also paid little attention to facilitating the restructuring of the industrial sector by removing the numerous barriers to exit. The labour laws, the bankruptcy laws, the laws relating to rent control and urban

1. Ahluwalia, Isher Judge (2012). "Industry", in Kaushik Basu and Annemie Maertens (eds.), *The New Oxford Companion to Economics in India* (Vol.I).

land ceiling were some of the major legislative barriers which came in the way of moving resources away from the unproductive and economically non-viable sectors to the more vibrant sectors.

The Policy Regime in the 1990s

A process of reflection and debate on the need for a change in policies had been set in motion in India in the second half of the 1970s, i.e., about the same time that China was preparing for a major change in policy. It is worth noting that China went ahead with full force towards market orientation and doubled its GDP between 1978 and 1991. By contrast, India used the decade of the 1980s for hesitant experimentation in domestic deregulation, while retaining its highly protectionist trade policy regime and keeping its loss-making public sector intact. The reform on the industrial policy front, however, coincided with a sharp deterioration in the fiscal accounts of the government. As the Government of India's policies became increasingly expansionary to support growing levels of current government expenditures on sharply rising interest payments, defence and subsidies, the gross fiscal deficit of the government increased from 6.2 per cent of GDP in 1980-81 to 8.3 per cent by 1990-91.

While the reorientation of industrial and trade policies evoked a better productivity response and led to substantially higher industrial growth in the 1980s, the deteriorating fiscal position and growing macroeconomic imbalances posed a serious challenge to the sustainability of the higher growth of the 1980s. The Gulf War of 1990 provided the trigger, which brought the underlying economic crisis to the force.

New Economic Policy 1991

As Rangarajan has rightly stated, the year 1991 is an important landmark in the economic history of post-Independent India. The country went through a severe economic crisis triggered by a serious balance of payments situation. The crisis was converted into an opportunity to introduce some fundamental changes in the content and approach to economic policy. The response to the crisis was to put in place a set of policies aimed at stabilisation and structural reform. While the stabilisation policies were aimed at correcting the weaknesses that had developed on the fiscal and the balance of payments fronts, the structural reforms sought to remove the rigidities that had entered into the various segments of the Indian economy. The structural reforms introduced in the early 1990s broadly covered the areas of industrial licensing, foreign trade, foreign investment, exchange rate management and the financial sector. From the point of view of industrialisation, changes in the areas of licensing and foreign trade and investment had important implications. Even before the onset of reforms, the problems associated with industrial licensing were well recognised. The approach document of the Eighth Plan (1991-1996) submitted in May 1990 had remarked: "A return to the regime of direct, indiscriminate and detailed controls in industry is clearly out of question. Past experience has shown that such control system is not effective in achieving the desired objective. Also the system is widely abused and leads to corruption, delays and inefficiency" (Government of India, 1990).

Without going into details, the common thread running through the various policy measures introduced since 1991 has been the improvement of the efficiency of the system. The thrust of the New Economic Policy has been towards creating a more competitive environment in the economy as a means to improving the productivity and efficiency of the system. This was to be achieved by removing the barriers to entry and the restrictions on the growth of firms. The private sector was to be given a larger space to operate in as much as some of the areas, reserved exclusively earlier for the public sector were now to be opened to the private sector. In these areas, the public sector would have to compete with the private sector, even though the public sector might continue to play the dominant role in the foreseeable future. What was sought to be achieved was the improvement in the functioning of the various entities, whether they were in the private or in the public sector.

The 10 years from 1991 to 2001 therefore, marked a significant transition for the Indian economy from a policy regime with very high rates of protection and all-pervasive quantitative restrictions to moderate rates of protection and removal of quantitative restrictions. The degree of tariff protection, however, was still higher than in most developing economies.

Opening up to Foreign Investment

The reforms of the 1990s marked a significant break with the past in respect of the policy towards foreign investment. From a policy which was restrictive and selective and supported mainly technology transfers, foreign investment policy in the 1990s became more open and more proactive as the rules were liberalised over time with a view not only to gain better access to technology but also to build strategic alliances to penetrate world markets. Besides enlarging the scope for automatic approval over the years, the Foreign Investment Promotion Board was set up to expedite other applications for foreign investment. Specifically, liberal conditions were set up for attracting foreign investment in infrastructure sectors and export-oriented sectors.

Public Sector Reforms and Privatisation

Public sector reform remained an area of darkness in the 1990s. A significant practical approach was adopted in which the better performing PSUs were given the freedom to access capital markets on the strength of their own performance. They were also given more autonomy in shaping their future. The non-performing PSUs, on the other hand, languished for want of budgetary support or reform.

Privatisation was not pursued as an option in the early phase of reforms. Instead, government policy concentrated on selective disinvestments of public sector equity with a view to finance fiscal deficits rather than address the issue of improving the returns on the capital invested. In 1997, the Government of India set up the Disinvestment Commission. The Commission gave a series of reports analysing the 50 or so cases of PSUs, which were referred to it and made detailed recommendations. Subsequently, the Commission was wound up and a Department of Privatisation was created. While there have been some major privatisations, e.g., BALCO, VSNL, Maruti and IPCL, it remains a highly contentions issue.

There is no getting away from the need for reforming the public sector as the case of power sector makes it amply clear. For example, the pricing policy, which does not cover the cost of producing the infrastructure services is eroding the economic viability of public sector infrastructure and stands in the way of attracting private investment into infrastructure. Since infrastructure services such as electric power, roads, ports, railways and telecommunications are crucial for industrialisation and these services can not be imported, adequate investments (public or private) and efficient use of existing and new investments in these sectors are essential prerequisites for any strategy which seeks to accelerate the pace of economic growth. Unless public sector reforms are undertaken and economic viability of infrastructure operations ensured, private sector investment will not be attracted to these sectors.

Industrial Policy: Recent Policy Initiatives

Industrial licensing had already been substantially dismantled. At the end of the Tenth Five Year Plan period, only the following manufacturing activities needed industrial license:

- distillation and brewing of alcoholic drinks;
- cigars and cigarettes of tobacco and manufactured tobacco substitutes;
- electronic aerospace and defence equipment;
- industrial explosives;
- specified hazardous chemicals.

Entrepreneurs are free to select the location for setting up industry. Approval is required from the government for locating an industrial unit within 25 km of the periphery of cities having a population of more than one million according to the 1991 census, provided that is not within an industrial area designated before 24 July 1991. However, these locational restrictions are not applicable for electronics, computer software, printing industries and other non-polluting industries that may be designated from time to time.

The Foreign Direct Investment (FDI) policy was also successively liberalised during the Tenth Five Year Plan. Following a comprehensive review in 2006 it was further liberalised, particularly by allowing FDI under the automatic route for manufacture of industrial explosives and hazardous chemicals and making it easier for new investments by foreign investors who had entered into joint ventures with Indian partners earlier. At the end of the Plan period, FDI upto 100 per cent was permitted in all manufacturing activities except where the foreign investor had an existing joint venture/technical collaboration/trademark agreement in the same field of activity (11th Plan).

Industrial Policy Eleventh Plan

The major focus areas for improving the industrial climate during the Eleventh Plan are:

- Creation of world class infrastructure and devising regulatory mechanisms to reduce transaction costs.
- Promotion and facilitation of industrial investments, particularly Foreign Direct Investment (FDI), non-resident investment and foreign technology transfers/collaborations.

- Improvement in business regulatory environment of Central and State Governments
- Development of industrial infrastructure through PPP initiatives
- Removal of regional industrial imbalance
- Development of industry relevant skills
- Addressing environmental issues emerging out of industrial activities

According to *Mid-Term Appraisal, Eleventh Five Year Plan* (MTA) during the first two years of the Plan, the following important policy modifications were carried out.

i. The earlier restriction on location of industry in cities with population of one million and above (1991 census) has been done away with. Entrepreneurs are now free to select the location for setting up of industry subject to permissibility in zone/land use regulations and environmental legislations.

ii. In order to instil healthy competition amongst producers, the list of items reserved for small scale sector is reviewed from time to time. At present only 21 items are reserved for the small scale sector. Manufacturers other than small scale manufacturers may also manufacture these items provided they undertake export obligation of 50% of the annual production.

iii. Government has put in place a liberal and transparent regime, where FDI upto 100 per cent is allowed in most of the sectors and activities.

Commenting on the policy approach of the 11th Plan and earlier Plans, the Twelfth Five Year Plan remarks, "The Eleventh Five Year Plan as well as Plans that preceded it aimed at establishing a strong manufacturing sector but this has not happened. This suggests that a radical change in the policy approach is needed".

Comparison with the performance of other countries shows that the countries that managed to catch up with the earlier industrialised, high-income countries were the ones whose governments proactively promoted structural change. Industrial policy, and with a special focus on manufacturing, is back on the national agendas of many countries and we need to consider what lesson we can draw given our particular circumstances. In other words, the critical question now is not whether there should be an industrial policy but what should be the architecture of the industrial policy (*Economic Survey 2012-13*).

Quoting the Twelfth Five Year Plan, "Industrial policies, where they have succeeded, have generally not been an outcome of Centrally planned economies but of economies that have had the active involvement of private enterprises and other non-governmental stakeholders. Successful strategies evolve from ongoing productive interactions between government and producers. Therefore, the government must improve the process of interaction, collaboration and learning amongst producers and itself. This is very different from the paradigm of Indian industrial policy prior to India's economic reforms commencing in the 1980s. In that era, industrial planning was a topdown control activity with Government determining who should produce what, where and how much and also what technology they should use. The roadmap for the Twelfth Plan and beyond can definitely not be a return to this type of planning".

Industrial Policy Objectives for the Twelfth Plan and Beyond[2]

According to the Twelfth Plan document, in order to create a paradigm shift in the manufacturing sector, it is essential to consider the objectives over a longer time frame, such as 15 years. The National Manufacturing Policy, which was introduced in 2011, states these objectives and these are the underlying objectives that the Plan aims to achieve as well. These objectives are:

1. Increase manufacturing sector growth to 12–14 per cent over the medium term to make it the engine of growth for the economy. The 2 to 4 per cent differential over the medium term growth rate of the overall economy will enable manufacturing to contribute at least 25 per cent of the national GDP by 2025.
2. Increase the rate of job creation in manufacturing to create 100 million additional jobs by 2025. Emphasis should be given to creation of appropriate skill sets among the rural migrant and urban poor to make growth inclusive.
3. Increase 'depth' in manufacturing, with focus on the level of domestic value addition, to address the national strategic requirements.

2. This section is drawn from Twelfth Five Year Plan 2012-2017, Vol.II, Ch. 13.

4. Enhance global competitiveness of Indian manufacturing through appropriate policy support.
5. Ensure sustainability of growth, particularly with regard to the environment.

The Architecture of a Strategy to Accelerate Growth of Manufacturing

Manufacturing enterprises, unlike IT and financial services enterprises, involve the production and movement of material goods. They, therefore, require good physical infrastructure to be competitive and this means improving transportation, uninterrupted power and adequate land to build. Moreover, the materiality of manufacturing activities also results in more regulations—of safety, pollution, factory inspections, labour conditions—and hence a more complex administration structure too. The quality and efficiency of the physical and administrative infrastructure is a basic requirement for productive manufacturing enterprises. This is a major weakness in India at present. The thrust in Government's New Manufacturing Policy (2011) to create good infrastructure for manufacturing enterprises along transportation corridors is, therefore, overdue.

Good physical infrastructure and smoothly functioning administrative infrastructure are threshold requirements for Twenty-first century manufacturing enterprises to compete in the international arena. However, these will not be sufficient. Competitive manufacturing, requires the development of complex capabilities—technologies, skills and management abilities to coordinate diverse interactions and processes of learning. Such capabilities can be learned and improved. Continuous improvement in these capabilities is the key to sustainable competitive advantage. Therefore, the thrust of Government strategy must be on the enrichment of the composition of these capabilities in the country's manufacturing ecosystem.

Three Components of India's Manufacturing Strategy and Plan

India's Manufacturing Plan strategy in the Twelfth Plan must be built around three components.

The first are capabilities and processes that go across many, if not all sectors of manufacturing, and that build into the ecosystem the processes for rapid learning and building of capabilities.

The second component has to be the plans to strengthen the performance of selected sectors. The selection of these sectors is done by a combination of top-down and bottom-up analysis. From the top, certain sectors appear more important to meet the goals of the Plan for more employment, for example, to produce goods that India needs for its strategic security. On the other hand, the capabilities created by Indian entrepreneurs in some sectors provide potential for more growth, and they should be supported. For example, the pharmaceutical and auto parts sectors. Thus the Plan, at present, has identified 18 such sectors.

India's sectoral strategy has to be broad-based, covering many sectors, to achieve the large-scale growth that India needs in manufacturing. India cannot achieve its goals by 'picking winners'. In each of these sectors, a sector strategy is required to grow capabilities and relieve constraints. Such sector strategies should be formulated jointly by the associations of producers in the sector (and other principal stakeholders too) and the relevant Government department. They should describe the opportunity for the sector and the actions required from the producers themselves, along with support from Government policies.

The third, vital, component of the Strategy is the institutional ability for effective consultation and collaboration between producers and public policymakers and implementers and the systemic reform of existing systems and processes within the Government. The strength of this process has been found to be the common factor in the success stories of all countries that have built large, competitive manufacturing sectors.

Lack of co ordination amongst government ministries, and the relatively poor quality of interaction between business associations and government—which is constrained by the competition amongst associations, and the orientation, by and large, towards lobbying and financial sops—prevents improvement in the process of collaborative learning and capability building that India needs to grow its manufacturing sector.

The challenges to developing and implementing a cohesive manufacturing strategy in democratic India are many. Cohesion can be brought about through more effective coordination amongst agencies, and more effective consultation amongst stakeholders. Apart from this, the Government will also require specialised skills such as consensus building and programme management to manage this process. Government should consider a 'Backbone Organisation (BBO)' to facilitate this process (Twelfth Five Year Plan, Ch.13).

14

Industrial Growth since 1951

Industrial Growth

Having looked into the industrial control regime and the performance of the industrial licensing system under different policy regimes and the trade liberalisation and industrialisation policy reforms of the 90s in the previous chapter, let us now look at the industrial growth since Independence—the rate and pattern of growth and the structural changes.[1]

Phases of Industrial Growth

One can identify four distinct phases of industrial growth in India since the planning era. The first phase of rapid growth is from 1956-1965. The second phase of slow growth or deceleration extends from 1965-66 to 1979-80. The third phase is a phase of recovery and revival of growth since 1980s and the fourth phase starts with economic policy reform since 1991. Krishna[2] has summarised the various explanatory hypotheses and has also reviewed the available empirical evidence bearing upon the alternative hypotheses.

During the period 1959-60 to 1965-66, value added in organised industry grew at the rate of 8.0 per cent per annum. The growth rate declined to 5.7 per cent in the period 1966-67 to 1989-90. The corresponding growth rates for the registered manufacturing were 7.6 and 5.5 per cent. In capital goods and basic goods, the decline was very pronounced from 15.4 to 6.6 and 11.0 to 5.0 per cent per annum, respectively. Consumer goods and its sub-category consumer non-durables experienced slight acceleration. In intermediate goods and

1. Kapila, Uma (2013). "Industrial Development and Policies since Independence", in *Indian Economy Since Independence*, ch. 15, 24th edition. New Delhi: Academic Foundation.
2. Krishna, K.L. (2008). "Industrial Growth and Diversification" in Uma Kapila (ed.), *Indian Economy Since Independence* (ch.15), 19th edition, New Delhi: Academic Foundation.

consumer durables, there was mild deceleration. Thus, deceleration was largely confined to heavy industry which accounted for about 50 per cent of value added in industry in 1979-80.

According to Isher Ahluwalia (2012)[3], Indian Industry experienced slow growth and poor productivity performance during the period from 1950 to 1980. The policy regime had strong preference for the public sector, extensive controls over private investment, a highly protective trade policy, and inflexible labour laws (especially after the mid-1970s). Promotion of the small-scale sector and regional balance were additional objectives of the industrial policy regime. Up to the mid-1960s, policy instruments were aimed at purposive diversification within the industrial sector and increased public investment. The period after the mid-1960s witnessed a marked deepening of the import-substitution regime and strengthening of domestic regulatory structures. This period witnessed a significant deceleration in growth to 4 per cent per annum compared to 6.1 per cent in the period from 1950 to 1965.

Ahluwalia (1985) after empirically examining different hypotheses identified four factors:

(i) slowdown in public investment,

(ii) poor management of the infrastructure sector,

(iii) slow growth of agricultural incomes, and

(iv) restrictive industrial and trade policies.

However, Ahluwalia did not carry out any econometric exercise to establish her thesis. Rangarajan (1982), Lahiri *et al.* (1984), Ray (1991) Mukhopadhyay (1992), Kavita Rao (1993) and Balakrishnan (1995) conducted econometric exercises to verify the various hypotheses. These exercises established that one or more of the following factors, public investment, agricultural performance, infrastructure, the policy of import substitution and domestic terms of trade turned out to be significant for the different industry groups. The overall inference from the various studies is that the demand constraints were more important than supply constraints (Krishna, 2008).

The decade of the 1980s according to Ahluwalia (2012) witnessed some experimentation with domestic deregulation that yielded handsome dividends in productivity gains and acceleration in growth to 7 per cent per annum.

---

3. Ahluwalia, Isher Judge (2012). "Industry" in Kaushik Basu and Annemie Maetrey (eds.) The New Oxford Companion to Economics in India, Vol.II, p.371-375. New Delhi: OUP.

In the 1980s, the industrial sector fared impressively in this decade, compared to the preceding 15-year period. The annual rates of growth for manufacturing, registered manufacturing and unregistered manufacturing were 7.0, 8.1 and 5.8, respectively.

In the first six years of the eighties, consumer durables recorded a growth rate of 14.2 per cent, while capital goods recorded a relatively modest growth of 7.8 per cent per annum.

Empirical evidence suggests that the explanations for the resurgence of growth in the 1980s are similar to those for the deceleration after the mid-sixties.

The manufacturing sector witnessed an upward trend in growth rates registering a growth rate of 8 to 9 per cent in the second half of 80s.

The Pre-Reform Regime

The pre-reform industrial policy regime relied heavily on the development of a public sector to cater to the infrastructure needs of development and to provide direction to the process of industrial development within a mixed economy framework. Besides 'reserving' certain strategic areas of industrial production, for example, iron and steel, coal, transport, power, mineral oils, atomic energy, arms and ammunition, and allied items of defence equipment, in the public sector, the state also acted as the leading entrepreneur in machine tools, non-ferrous metals, fertilisers, etc. Nevertheless, the private sector was expected to play a major role, especially in the provision of consumer goods and building up the small-scale sector.

Industrial licensing was a major instrument of control of the private sector under which central government permission was needed for both investment in new units and for substantial expansion of capacity in existing units. Licensing also controlled technology, output mix, capacity location, and import content. Large industrial houses needed separate permission for investment or expansion under the Monopolies and Restrictive Trade Practices (MRTP) Act so as to prevent the concentration of economic power. There were price and distribution controls in industries such as fertilisers, cement, aluminium, petroleum, and pharmaceuticals. Almost 800 items were reserved for production by small-scale units as a way of protecting the small-scale sector from competition the large-scale units. There were also barriers to industrial restructuring and exit of firms.

India's import tariffs were among the highest in the world, with duty rates above 200 per cent being fairly common and tariff rates being highly dispersed. Imports of manufactured consumer goods were completely banned. For the rest, only some goods were freely importable, and for most items where domestic substitutes were being produced, imports were only possible with import licences. The criteria for issuing these licences were non-transparent, delays were endemic, and corruption unavoidable. Policies towards foreign investment were quite restrictive, reflecting the general protectionist thrust of industrial policy.

The period from 1950 to 1980 experienced stagnant industrial growth at the rate of 5.5 per cent per annum. However, significant diversification of the industrial structure was achieved. But total factor productivity (a measure of the efficiency with which labour and capital are used in generating value added in the manufacturing sector) is estimated to have stagnated/declined during the period from 1960 to 1980. The high-cost industrial structure resulting from the heavily protectionist policy regime created an anti-export bias in the industrial sector. The erosion of competitiveness could be seen in the secular decline of India's share in global exports of manufactured goods from 1 per cent in 1950 to 0.4 per cent in 1980.

Industrial Growth in the 90s

In 1991, in response to a major balance-of-payments crisis, India made a radical shift away from its long-standing policy of inward orientation, and the subsequent reforms have moved the policy regime significantly towards market orientation, deregulation, and liberalisation. Indian industry has responded to the increased competition—domestic as well as foreign—with significant restructuring, although the constraints arising from poor infrastructure, largely unreformed public sector, slowly reforming banking sector, inflexible labour laws, and other barriers to exit stand in the way of faster adjustment to the new and emerging policy regime which is inspired by market orientation.

Economic reforms of the 1990s had the dual objective of macroeconomic stabilisation and enhancing the growth potential of the economy. The industrial policy reforms during the 1990s were bold in doing away with numerous barriers to entry, for example removal of industrial licensing for investment, opening up all but a few strategic areas to other than the public sector, and, more recently, replacing the earlier MRTP Act with a new Competition Law to regulate anti-competitive behaviour. Even on the policy of reservation for the small-scale sector, a beginning was made by dereserving a number of items, although the task remains essentially unfinished. Also, the microeconomic reforms and judicial reforms which would make the factor markets more flexible and enable individual firms to benefit from the more competitive environment were slow to come.

Trade policy reforms made a radical break with the past by discontinuing with the complex system of import licensing and making an open commitment to lowering the tariff rates on imports. At the outset, import licensing was dispensed with for most goods other than consumer goods, thereby removing a major source of corruption and inefficiency. In 2001 India finally began to remove the quantitative restrictions on consumer goods and agricultural products over a three-year period.

In the 1990s the FDI rules were liberalised with a view to gain improved access to technology and world markets and also to help release the resource constraints on investment. Many industries were deregulated and opened to FDI (Ahluwalia, 2012).[4]

Telecommunications is the area where reforms have been most successful, helped by the fact that pricing of telecom services (unlike that of power) was not uneconomic. Access to telecom services has expanded greatly, costs have come down, and quality improved as a handful of strong private-sector telecom service suppliers are competing effectively with the public-sector companies. Private investment has also been attracted in ports and more recently in airports.

Policies to promote competition both within the economy and from imports were expected to contribute to cutting costs, improving quality and enhancing competitiveness of Indian industry. A proactive policy of attracting foreign investment was expected not only to ease the resource constraint for investment on account of the deteriorating fiscal situation but also to release critical supply constraints for industry, e.g., in the infrastructure sectors. If the growth of public investment was restrained or at times negative because of the compulsions of macroeconomic stabilisation, the expectation was that private investment could fill this void as it would respond to a much improved investment outlook in the economy. The private sector was given more room for greater participation in the process.[5]

The 1990s have certainly been an eventful period for the industrial economy of India. Crisis, reform, adjustment, recovery, rapid growth and then a downward slide—this decade has seen it all. The collapse from a growth rate of 8.5 per cent in value added of manufacturing in the decade

4. Ibid.
5. Ibid

1981-1991 to –2.3 per cent in 1991-92 was followed by a rapid and perhaps unprecedented recovery in such adjustment episodes. The three years from 1993-94 to 1995-96 saw an average growth of 13 per cent per annum (not reported in the table). Even though a major slowdown began in 1996-97, the average growth of value added in the period 1991-1992 to 1997-98 was still as high as 9.1 per cent per annum, higher than the rapid growth of the early phase of Indian industrialisation in the first half of the 1960s. However, by 1999-2000, the average growth for the decade (not reported in the table) had declined to 8.0 per cent, based on the data for value added in manufacturing from National Accounts, which are available for more recent years.

Among the two-digit industry groups, the fastest growing industries for the period up to 1997-98 were basic metal industries, footwear, chemicals and chemical products, rubber products and transport equipment. Growth of value added in textiles at 7.2 per cent per annum in the 1990s was quite a bit higher than in the 1980s but the industry experienced more fluctuations in the 1990s compared to earlier years.

Table 14.1 presents the growth of value added for the use-based sectors. Capital goods emerges as the laggard sector. After its golden period in the first half of the 1960s, the capital goods sector in the Indian economy never really recovered from the setback. A long period of stagnation after the mid-60s was followed by only a modest improvement in the 1980s and some further increase in the growth rate in the 1990s. By contrast, the consumer non-durables sector was a slow

TABLE – 14.1

Trends in Growth in Value Added Used-based Sectors

(Per cent per annum)

	Share in Value Added (1990-91)	*1960-61 to 1965-66*	*1965-66 to 1980-81*	*1980-81 to 1990-91*	*1991-92*	*1991-92 to 1997-98*
Manufacturing	100.0	8.5	4.3	7.8	-3.8	9.3
Capital goods	19.8	15.9	6.7	8.2	1.3	9.2
Intermediate goods	35.5	10.8	3.9	8.6	-4.3	11.4
Consumer durables	4.6	11.1	8.1	11.0	5.8	12.9
Consumer non-durables	40.1	5.1	4.0	10.7	3.9	11.0

Source: Annual Survey of Industries.

growing sector pretty much till the end of the 1980s. The process of domestic deregulation of the 1980s provided a major stimulus to the growth of this sector. The recovery of this sector after 1991-92 was also robust as the sector recorded an average growth of 11 per cent.

After a relatively modest performance during 1996-97 to 1998-99, the Indian industry experienced a turnaround. Several macroeconomic and business indicators were showing signs of a broad-based industrial recovery. The cumulative growth of industrial production, as measured by the Index of Industrial Production (IIP), was 6.2 per cent for April-December 1999, significantly higher than the 4.0 per cent of April-December 1998. The higher growth in the 1999-2000 has been largely contributed by the 7.0 per cent growth in manufacturing and the 7.7 per cent growth in electricity.

Comparative Growth Rates in the 80s and the 90s

The average growth rate of the industrial sector (measured by the Index of Industrial Production) during the period 1992-93 to 1999-2000 was lower than that observed during the period 1980-81 to 1991-92. The growth rate was lower in all the three sectors i.e., manufacturing, mining and electricity. In terms of use-based classification also, there was a lower growth rate in basic and capital goods. However, the GDP from manufacturing sector at constant prices showed higher growth rates during the period 1992-93 to 1999-2000 when compared to the period 1980-81 to 1991-92 at the aggregate (total) level and amongst both registered and unregistered segments (Table 14.2).

Relative Contribution of Sectors to Total Production

Changes in the relative contribution of different sectors to the general Index of Industrial Production reflect another dimension of the structural changes in industrial production. Data presented in Table 14.2 reveal that the relative contribution of the manufacturing sector rose from 70.0 per cent during the eighties to 81.6 per cent during the nineties. However, in case of mining and quarrying, there was a noticeable decline. This was reflected in the changes in the weights assigned to different sector in the construction of IIP series. The weight for the manufacturing sector rose from 77.1 per cent in the earlier series of IIP with base 1980-81=100, to 79.36 per cent in the current series with base 1993-94=100. Correspondingly, the relative weights of mining and quarrying and electricity sectors declined from 11.46 per cent and 11.43 per cent in the old series to 10.47 per cent and 10.17 per cent, respectively, in the new series (Table 14.3).

TABLE – 14.2

Comparative Growth Rates in the Industrial Sector 1980-2000

Parameter	*Avg. Annual Growth Rate (1980-81 to 1991-92)**	*Avg. Annual Growth Rate (1992-93 to 1999-2000)**
Index of Industrial Production		
General	7.8	6.0
Manufacturing	7.6	6.3
Mining	8.4	3.3
Electricity	9.0	6.6
Use-based classification		
Basic goods	7.4	6.1
Capital goods	9.4	5.9
Intermediate goods	4.9	9.1
Consumer goods	6.0	6.3
of which:		
(i) Consumer durables	10.8	11.2
(ii) Consumer non-durables	5.3	5.1
GDP-Manufacturing at 1993-94 Prices		
Total	6.1	7.4
Registered	6.8	8.1
Unregistered	5.0	6.2

Note : * Simple average of the annual growth rates.
Source : *Economic Survey, 2000-01.*

TABLE – 14.3

Relative Contribution of Sectors to the Industrial Production

(*Per cent*)

Sector	*1981-82 to 1990-91 (Average)*	*1992-93 to 1998-99* (Average)*
1	*2*	*3*
i) Manufacturing	70.0	81.6
ii) Electricity	14.4	14.4
iii) Mining and quarrying	15.6	4.0
General Index	**100.0**	**100.0**

Note :* The data relating to 1991-92 were excluded in this period because production was almost stagnant.

During the nineties, while the relative contributions of basic and capital goods sectors declined, there was a rise in those of intermediate and consumer goods sectors (Table 14.4). In the new series (Base: 1993-1994=100), the weights of basic and capital goods sectors were reduced and those of intermediate goods and consumer goods sectors were raised.

The relatively low contributions of the basic and capital goods sectors to overall industrial output in the nineties reflect, among others, the impact of trade liberalisation, particularly imports, and of financial liberalisation that enabled the corporate sector to make financial gains through 'other income', as also the lack of competitiveness requiring industrial restructuring and modernisation of technologies in a number of industries.

TABLE – 14.4

Relative Contribution of Sectors to Industrial Production (Use-based Classification)

(Per cent)

	Sector	*1981-82 to 1990-91 (Average)*	*1992-93 to 1998-99* (Average)*
	1	2	3
i)	Basic goods	43.6	35.8
ii)	Capital goods	25.0	7.1
iii)	Intermediate goods	14.6	35.2
iv)	Consumer goods	16.8	21.9
	General Index	**100.0**	**100.0**

Note :* The data relating to 1991-92 were excluded in this period because production was almost stagnant.

The Manufacturing Slowdown (1996-2002)

The loss of momentum in manufacturing growth, which occured in the latter part of 1996, has since continued during the second phase of the reform period. At the disaggregated two-digit level, the manufacturing sector witnessed substantial deceleration in 11 industry groups with a combined weight of 64 per cent in the manufacturing production. Six industry groups with a combined weight of 36 per cent withstood the slowdown and posted an accelerated growth during 1996-2002. However, in view of their relatively low weight, the manufacturing sector, as a whole, registered a slowdown.

Factors Causing the Slowdown: Some Hypotheses

A number of hypotheses in terms of cyclical and structural factors have been put forward to explain the slowdown in the manufacturing activity during this period.[6] The explanations provided, however, fall short of giving a satisfactory answer to what has led to the manufacturing slowdown and its persistence. The onset of slowdown is often attributed to the saturation of the pent-up domestic demand of 'once-for-all' nature for a host of import-intensive goods, which could be domestically assembled or produced following trade liberalisation (Chandrasekhar and Ghosh, 2002). The short-run increase in domestic demand was seemingly facilitated by easy access to credit, including consumer credit in the wake of financial liberalisation. Once that pent-up demand of transitory nature was satisfied, industry entered the phase of slowdown in the absence of demand support—domestic or exports.

Another hypothesis on the onset of slowdown relates to the 'credit crunch' which, it is argued, triggered off the manufacturing slowdown (Sen *et al.,* 1997 and Desai, 2001). The unexpected and temporary tightening of liquidity in money markets during 1995-96, resulting from large dollar sales by the Reserve Bank to contain volatility in the forex market, was mistaken to be an expression of deflationary credit policy (Acharya, 2002).

Yet another factor was the role of the corporate sector. The proportion of corporate funds locked up in inventories and receivables went up steadily, leading to a scarcity of working capital (Sen *et al.,* 1997). Further, the proportion of funds invested in financial instruments, which had hovered around 5 per cent during 1985-1993, crossed the level of 10 per cent subsequently. The depressed stock market conditions in 1995-1996 inhibited the redemption of financial instruments. The rising interest rates may also have been prohibitive for new projects and investment, particularly, in the informal sector which has limited access to funds (Shetty, 1997a and 2001b). Reinforced by the increased borrowings by the Government, the weighted average lending rate of scheduled commercial banks rose to 17.1 per cent in 1995-96 from 16.1 per cent in 1994-95. In real terms, the rate shot up to 8.5 per cent in 1995-96 from an all-time low (for the 1990s) of 3.9 per cent in the preceding year.

---

6. RBI *Report on Currency and Finance 2001-02.*

Infrastructure Constraints in the Industrial Sector

The industrial performance continues to be hampered by physical infrastructure bottlenecks with the demand-supply imbalances persisting and growing during the reform period.

The deteriorating infrastructure services represent a direct fall out of shrinkage in infrastructure investment in the context of grossly inadequate internal resources of public infrastructure entities and dwindling Plan outlay for infrastructure. The real capital formation in electricity, gas and water supply declined to 2.6 per cent of GDP during the 1990s from 2.9 per cent during the preceding decade. A similar trend was observed for railways. Within the 1990s also, there was a decline in the real gross capital formation in sectors like electricity, gas and water supply, and the railways between the first and the second half. The investment in infrastructure sector as a whole has shown clear decline of one percentage point of GDP between the first and the second halves of the 1990s. This decline can be attributed to declining government investment on infrastructure—a fall out of the prevailing fiscal situation—which was a major contributing factor for the economic slowdown in the latter part of the 1990s.

The pace of public investment in infrastructure slowed down substantially during this period on account of rising fiscal imbalances of the Government, both at the Centre and the states. As a result, public investment in major infrastructure sectors declined in real terms during the reform period. The rates of return from infrastructure services extended by the Government continue to be abysmally low, constraining the ability to generate internal resources for investment. For instance, the rate of return on investment for the state power sector deteriorated from (-)12.7 per cent in 1991-92 to (-)32.8 per cent in 2001-02.

Recovery in Industrial Growth since 2002-03

The industrial recovery in 2002-03 (5.7 per cent), which consolidated during 2003-04 (7.0 per cent), has gathered momentum since then reaching 8.4 per cent in 2004-05, 8.2 per cent in 2005-06 and 11 per cent in 2006-07.

The double-digit growth since 2003-04 in capital goods sector indicates the capital formation taking place in the industrial sector, which can help in strengthening the upswing. The ongoing growth process, which is investment-led and fairly evenly spread within manufacturing sector, reflects the medium and long-term optimism on the part of investors.

TABLE – 14.5

Growth Rates

	CAGR in Ninth Plan	*2002-03*	*2003-04*	*2004-05*	*2005-06 (QE)*	*2006-07 (RE)*	*CAGR in Tenth Plan*
GDP	5.5	3.8	8.5	7.5	9.0	9.4	7.6
Agriculture, forestry, and fishing	2.0	–7.2	10.0	0.0	6.0	2.7	2.1
Industry	4.5	6.8	6.0	8.4	8.0	11.0	8.0
(manufacturing)	(3.8)	(6.8)	(6.6)	(8.7)	(9.1)	(12.3)	(8.7)
Services#	8.1	7.4	8.9	10.0	10.3	11.0	9.5

Note : # Construction is included in services;
QE = Quarterly Estimates. Figures in parentheses relate to manufacturing.
Source: Central Statistical Organisation.
Government of India (2008). *Eleventh Five Year Plan 2007-2012*, Planning Commission.

Measured by investment, the manufacturing sector's share in total fixed investment (gross fixed capital formation) has gone up from around 27 per cent in 1980s to about 40 per cent in the current decade. (Nagaraj, 2011)[7]

The rising demand in both domestic and external markets was a major contributory factor but the impressive performance of manufacturing was due in no small measure to the cumulative effect of industrial and fiscal policy changes carried out since the economic reforms of 1991-92. The competitive environment created by the reduction of external barriers to trade finally started to bear fruit. Against a CAGR of 6.3 per cent in the Ninth Five Year Plan, exports of manufactures registered a CAGR of more than 19 per cent during the Tenth Five Year Plan.[8]

A major feature of the performance of industry was the remarkable increase in the export share of manufacturing sustained during the entire Plan period. Against a CAGR of 6.3 per cent achieved during the Ninth Plan, exports of manufactured products had a CAGR of 19.9 per cent during the Tenth Five Year Plan.

7. Nagaraj, R. (2011). "Industrial Performance, 1991-2008: A Review", in D.M. Nachane (ed.), *India Development Report 2011*. Indira Gandhi Institute of Development Research, New Delhi.
8. Government of India (2008). *Eleventh Five Year Plan 2007-2012*. Planning Commission.

Recent Industrial Growth

Recent industrial growth, measured in terms of IIP, shows fluctuating trends. Growth had reached 15.5 per cent in 2007-8 and then started decelerating. Initial deceleration in industrial growth was largely on account of the global economic meltdown. There was, however, a recovery in industrial growth from 2.5 per cent in 2008-9 to 5.3 per cent in 2009-10 and 8.2 per cent in 2010-11. Fragile economic recovery in the US and European countries and subdued business sentiments at home affected the growth of the industrial sector in the current year. Overall growth during April-December 2011 was 3.6 per cent compared to 8.3 per cent in the corresponding period of the previous year. Growth of IIP in terms of its major components is indicated in Table 14.6.

TABLE – 14.6

Volatility of IIP Growth

	Mean growth	*Standard deviation*	*Coefficient of variation*
Overall IIP	8.3	6.5	78.0
Mining	4.1	4.1	99.4
Manufacturing	9.3	8.0	85.6
Electricity	6.1	3.1	50.5
In terms of Use-based classification of industries			
Basic goods	6.1	3.3	54.2
Capital goods	18.0	23.2	128.6
Intermediates	5.6	5.7	101.4
Consumer goods	9.8	8.6	88.5

Source: Economic Division, Department of Economic Affairs. Economic Survey 2011-12.

In terms of use-based classification of the IIP, in the 2011-12 year (April-December) basic goods with a growth of 6.1 per cent and consumer nondurables with a growth of 6.1 per cent had relatively better growth compared to the corresponding period of the previous year. There was moderation in growth in other segments of the IIP and negative growth was observed in the capital goods and intermediates segments. The highest contribution to growth in the current year was from the basic goods segment, which at 65.7 per cent exceeded its weight in the IIP. The contribution of consumer non-durables at 28.1 per cent also exceeded its weight in the IIP. However, the capital goods sector sustained negative growth in the last six quarters. Growth in the consumer durable sector continued to fluctuate, turning negative in Q4 of 2011-12, 0.7 per cent in Q2 and 3.2 per cent in Q3 of 2012-13. Pickup in growth in October was generally broad based with consumer goods, capital goods, and intermediates showing improvement in performance. The growth of consumer durables 16.9 per cent was the highest in the last 20 months.

Volatility in growth has been seen across all the broad sectors of the IIP. IIP growth during April 2006 to December 2011 varied from 7.2 to 20.0 per cent, with a mean growth of 8.3 per cent and standard deviation of 6.5. While different sectors had different volatility spectrums, capital goods and intermediates were the most volatile. In fact, volatility of the manufacturing sector was largely on account of extreme fluctuations in growth in the capital goods and intermediates segments. In case of capital goods, growth varied from - 26.5 per cent to 65.1 per cent, with a mean growth of 18.0 per cent and standard deviation of 23.2 (Table 14.6).

Commenting on the Industrial performance in the most recent period 2009-10 to 2012-13, Economic Survey 2012-13 remarks "After recovering to a growth of 9.2 per cent in 2009-10 and 2010-11, growth of value added in industrial sector, comprising manufacturing, mining, electricity and construction sectors, slowed to 3.5 per cent in 2011-12 and to 3.1 percent in the current year. The manufacturing sector, the most dominant sector within industry, also witnessed a decline in growth to 2.7 per cent in 2011-12 and 1.9 per cent in 2012-13 compared to 11.3 per cent and 9.7 per cent in 2009-10 and 2010-11, respectively. The growth in electricity sector in 2012-13 has also moderated. The growth of the mining sector in 2012-13 is estimated at 0.4 per cent, though it showed an improvement over a negative growth of 0.63 per cent recorded in 2011-12. With improved business sentiments and investor perception and a partial rebound in industrial activity in other developing countries, industrial growth is expected to improve in the next financial year". However, the first quarter of 2013-14, has not witnessed the expected improvement.

Thus, according to Krishna (2013)[9] the industrial growth in last six decades, the period since 1951 may be divided into five phases as in Table 14.7, according to policy regime:

- 1951-52 to 1966-67: Evolution of Industrial Development Strategy

9. Krishna, K.L. (2013). "Industrial Development and Policies since Independence: Growth without Employment", in Uma Kapila (ed), *Indian Economy Since Independence (Ch. 16)*, 24th edition. New Delhi: Academic Foundation.

- 1967-68 to 1980-81: Inward orientation and Industrial Stagnation
- 1981-82 to 1990-91: Deregulation, and Acceleration of Growth
- 1991-92 to 2010-11: Economic Reforms and Service-led Growth.
- 2001-02 to 2010-11: Growth Resurgence and Global Crisis.

TABLE – 14.7

Annual Average Growth Rates of GDP and Major Sectors

	1900-01 to 1929-30	*1930-31 to 1946-47*	*1951-52 to 1966-67*	*1967-68 to 1980-81*	*1981-82 to 1990-91*	*1991-92 to 2000-01*	*2001-02 to 2010-11*
Agriculture and Allied	0.5	0.2	1.8	3.3	3.5	2.7	2.9
Industry	0.9	1.2	6.3	4.1	7.1	5.7	7.8
Services	1.6	1.7	4.8	4.3	6.8	7.6	9.4
GDP	0.8	0.8	3.4	3.8	5.6	5.6	7.9
GDP per Capita	0.4	-0.5	1.4	1.5	3.4	3.7	6.2

Source: Acharya *et al.* (2006), Table 6 and Krishna (2012), Table 1.

Data Sources: Sivasubramonian (2000) and Central Statistical Organisation (2001) and EPW (2011).

Index of Industrial Production (IIP)

The index of industrial production (IIP), released each month, is the key indicator of industrial performance. The new IIP series with 2004-2005 as base was released in June 2011 replacing the earlier IIP series with base 1993-94. Since the IIP is a fixed weight and fixed base series, a dated base often has limitations in reflecting the industrial scenario. The new series not only has a more recent base, it has a larger and more representative product basket and weights that appropriately reflect the relative importance of the sectors, products, and product groups.

The IIP provides data for 22 sub-groups of the manufacturing sector. Cumulatively during April- December 2012, four manufacturing sub groups with a weight of 14.5 per cent in the IIP recorded a growth in excess of 5 per cent. Seven sub-groups with a weight of 37.0 per cent had a positive growth and eleven sub-groups with a weight of 24.0 per cent had a negative growth, the highest negative growth of 14.6 per cent being shown by electric machinery and apparatus. Negative growth has persisted in tobacco products, office accounting and computing machinery and wood and wood products. On the positive side, however, growth in some of the labourintensive industries particularly textile has shown improvement in the last three quarters. Growth has also turned significantly positive for leather and food products in the Q3. Growth, as with the broad groups of the IIP, has varied across manufacturing subgroups and over time.

TABLE – 14.8

Contribution to IIP Growth–April-December

(Per cent)

	Weight	*2008*	*2009*	*2010*	*2011*
Mining	14.16	6.4	32.1	9.4	-8.3
Manufacturing	75.53	89.4	46.8	85.6	85.6
Electricity	10.32	4.2	21.2	5.0	22.6
In terms of Use-based classification					
Basic goods	45.68	16.2	64.8	27.8	65.7
Capital goods	8.83	52.2	-52.9	30.2	-12.0
Intermediates	15.69	3.7	24.1	13.6	-3.3
Consumer Goods	29.81	28.0	64.0	28.4	49.4
Durables	8.46	32.7	67.3	23.0	21.3
Non Durables	21.35	-4.8	-3.3	5.5	28.1

Source: Economic Division, Department of Economic Affairs; *Economic Survey 2011-12*.

Why has Growth Moderated since 2011-12?

According to *Economic Survey 2012-13* the moderation in industrial growth, particularly in the manufacturing sector, is largely attributed to sluggish growth of investment, squeezed margins of the corporate sector, deceleration in the rate of growth of credit flows and the fragile global economic recovery.

Investment in the Industrial Sector

Investment in industry has generally been buoyant and witnessed an increase in its share in overall GCF of the economy. The share peaked to reach 56.2 per cent of total GCF in the economy in 1995-6 in the post reform period. The rate of growth of GCF, however, moved with the rate of growth of industry. This sector has continued to allocate a significantly high share of its income to the capital formation.

Together with a deceleration in growth of investment (investment in the overall industry sector actually declined in 2011-12), excess capacity in aggregate appears to have persisted, which depicts de-trended growth of the IIP and capacity utilization clearly indicates that with moderation in IIP growth, there has also been a decline in capacity utilization. Capacity utilization as measured by the 19th round of the Order Books, Inventories and Capacity Utilization Survey (OBICUS) of the Reserve Bank of India (RBI) shows a continuous decline until Q1 of 2012-13 and a moderately upward trend in Q2. There is a broad co-movement between capacity utilization and de-trended IIP.

Credit Flow to the Industrial Sector

Moderation in investment was largely because of two factors: decline in profitability and deceleration in the rate of growth of credit to the industrial sector. Overall rate of growth of credit flow to industry moderated from 26.48 per cent on an average in 2010-11 to an average15.52 per cent in Q3 of 2012-13. The moderation in the growth was even shaper for the construction sector with overall growth in credit disbursement declining from 16.3 per cent in 2010-11 to 6.6 per cent in Q3 of 2012-13. Mining and electricity sectors also suffered a decline in the growth of credit disbursement.

The lower corporate profitability and moderation in the growth of credit flow to industry also had its impact of the performance of capital goods sector, which in turn affected overall industrial growth. Post global financial crisis, the IIP-based growth rate of the capital goods sector was robust at 14.8 per cent in 2010-11, thereafter the sector has continued to experience a sustained recession. The output of the capital goods sector contracted by 10.1 per cent during April-December 2012.

Deceleration in investment, import substitution in the machinery and electrical machinery segments, and a decline in the number of new projects adversely impacted the capital goods sector. The dip in the transport segment after robust growth in 2009-2011 has mainly been due to the decline in domestic demand for commercial vehicles and three wheelers. During 2010-11 and 2011-12 imports of capital goods increased by 28 per cent and 32 per cent respectively. Imports of machinery, electrical machinery, machine tools and project goods saw a major spurt. However, due to depreciation of the rupee and depressed domestic demand during the current financial year, the import of key capital goods has declined. The share of capital goods in overall imports during 2010-11, 2011-12 and 2012-13 (Apr-Dec) ranged between 18-20 per cent. Total import of capital goods during April-December 2012-2013 was about $68.35 billion out of the total imports of $365 billion.

Why did Manufacturing Sector's Share in Total Employment Stagnate?[10]

Despite a respectable trend growth of over 6.5 per cent per year manufacturing sectors' share in total employment has been stagnating. Prima facie, it represents the failure of the reforms to promote labour-intensive manufacturing in spite of doing away with the import substitution bias in the industrial policy. Partly, growing capital intensity of production in general perhaps explains the employment stagnation, as it has become much easier to import the latest labour-saving equipment in an open trade regime with modest tariffs (if any).

With economic reforms it had been expected that the industrial sector would emerge as the key to additional employment opportunities for the labour force. There has been significant increase in employment opportunities in the industrial sector, though most of these additional opportunities have been created in the construction sector. In 2009-10, the construction sector employed 9.6 per cent of the workforce as against a 7.9 per cent share in GDP. There has also been an increase in employment opportunities in the mining sector. However, in the manufacturing sector, overall employment opportunities have declined in 2009-10 compared to 2004-05 (Table 14.9).

TABLE – 14.9

Employment in the Industrial Sector

	Persons Employed (million)			*Share in employment (%)*			*Share in GDP (%)*		
	1999-2000	*2004-2005*	*2009-2010*	*1999-2000*	*2004-2005*	*2009-2010*	*1999-2000*	*2004-2005*	*2009-2010*
Mining	2.3	2.6	2.9	0.6	0.6	0.6	3.0	2.9	2.3
Manufacturing	43.8	56.1	52.4	11.0	12.2	11.4	15.1	15.3	16.0
Electricity	1.0	1.2	1.3	0.3	0.3	0.3	2.3	2.1	2.0
Construction	17.5	26.1	44.2	4.4	5.7	9.6	6.5	7.7	7.9
Industry	64.6	85.9	100.7	16.2	18.7	21.9	26.9	27.9	28.1

Note: Employment as per usual principal and subsidiary status (UPSS) basis.
Source: *Economic Survey 2011-12*.

There could, however, be some deeper structural reasons as well, with increasing sub-contracting (outsourcing) of manufacture of parts

10. Nagaraj (2011) *op.cit.*

and auxiliary services to the unorganised sector, and forging of close supply-chain networks. Such an organisation of production is quite the opposite of the vertically integrated production structures that were common in the early years of industrialisation. After the reforms, with increased competitive pressure, under the liberalised rules of resource use, and with lax enforcement of labour laws, firms have apparently restructured their production processes by shedding labour. Conceivably, some of the employment lost in the organised sector would have reappeared in the unorganised sector, though no direct evidence for it is available. Therefore, while the stagnation of the industrial employment share is a cause for concern, it perhaps represents an outcome of the changing market conditions, organisation of production, and technology in an open labour-surplus economy.

Table 14.10 presents growth rates of GDP and employment in manufacturing and the total economy for four sub-periods of the long period 1972-73 to 2009-10.

TABLE – 14.10

Growth of GDP and Employment (UPSS) in Manufacturing: 1972-73 to 2009-10

(Per cent per annum)

	1972-73 to 1983	*1983 to 1993-94*	*1993-94 to 1999-00*	*1999-00 to 2009-10*
(1)	*(2)*	*(3)*	*(4)*	*(5)*
		GDP		
Manufacturing	5.5	4.9	6.9	8.0
Total economy	4.7	5.0	6.5	7.5
		Employment		
Manufacturing	4.3	2.0	1.6	1.9
	(0.61	(0.41)	(0.24)	(0.25)
Total economy	2.4	2.0	1.0	1.5
	(0.56)	(0.41)	(0.16)	(0.20)

Note: Figures in parantheses are employment elasticities (EE).
Source: Papola and Sahu (2012), Tables 1, 2 and 3.

As may be seen in Table 16.6, manufacturing GDP growth has accelerated from 4.9 per cent per annum during 1983 to 1993-94 to 6.9

per cent during 1993-94 to 1999-2000 and further to 8.0 per cent during 1999-2000 to 2009-10. But employment growth in the manufacturing sector has decelerated from 2.0 per cent during 1983 to 1993-94 to 1.6 per cent 1993-94 to 1999-2000. Although it has accelerated to 1.9 per cent in the first decade of the 21st century, it is much lower than the GDP growth in manufacturing and much lower than the employment growth rate during 1972-73 to 1983. The employment elasticity declined from 0.61 to 0.41. It has been around 0.25 in the post-reform period.

Much of the growth in employment in manufacturing during the past two decades seems to have occurred in the unorganized segment of the sector (See Goldar, 2009: Table 1). Basu and Maertens (2010) deal with the issue of job creation for the large labour force in South Asia. Drawing on the experience of growth in manufacturing and services sectors in South Asian countries, they note the disappointing outcome in terms of creation of good jobs which has limited the poverty reduction impact of rapid growth. They trace the disappointing outcome in India to the restrictive labour laws. Those laws have not only reduced employment prospects in organized manufacturing but also constrained its growth by adversely affecting investment and productivity. In all South Asian countries including India, inadequate and weak infrastructure has also constrained the expansion of the manufacturing sector and job creation. The policy conclusions are quite obvious.

Other Aspects of Industrial Change

The reforms have increased the effective competition in the domestic market with easier imports and entry of new firms, though it would be hard to quantify these effects. Perhaps, for the first time, there is a buyers' market in industrial goods, with improved quality, variety, and after-sales service—as evident from the decline in the relative price of capital goods, making fixed investment more productive (Nagaraj, 2011).

The growing strength and stature of Indian industry and enterprise are also evident from their ability to acquire and manage factories and firms in developed economies in relatively advanced 'manufacturing industries. For instance, Tata group's exports apparently account for 15-20 per cent of its sales, and (as per the group's website) it earned 61 per cent of its annual revenue from international operations. Moreover, the growing outward foreign direct investment (FDI) by large private Indian firms in the recent boom, estimated at $17.6 billion cumulative stock as in 2008 (UN, 2009)—to leverage their domestic manufacturing capability and use it as a short-cut to acquire technology—is yet another testimony of the coming of age of Indian business (Nagaraj, 2006a; Nayyar, 2008).

Why did the Reforms Fail to Deliver the Expected Results?

Still, the principal question remains unanswered: why did the speeding up of the reforms after 1991 not yield faster output, employment, and labour-intensive growth? The protagonists would contend that the reforms have remained incomplete, with the persistence of the labour market rigidities (lack of entrepreneurial freedom to hire and fire workers at will), infrastructure bottlenecks, and incomplete financial integration, including full convertibility of the currency (Kocchar *et al.*, 2006; Panagariya, 2008; Krueger, 2009, among others).

Based on cross-country analysis, Kocchar et al. argue that India has followed idiosyncratic policies in promoting skill-intensive industries, discouraging labour-intensive manufactures—a pattern that has not changed after the reforms because of the labour market rigidities. These scholars also contend that on average Indian firms tend to be small because workers cannot be fired, preventing them from reaping the advantages of economes of scale in production. But, since skilled workers and professionals are outside the purview of trade unions, India has specialised in skill-intensive industries.

What then are the facts of the matter? The average factory size in registered manufacturing in 2004-05 was 35 workers per factory, declining steadily over the last half century from over 140 workers (Nagaraj, 1985). At the other end of the scale, household manufacturing has become marginal with the expansion of smaller-sized workshops and factories. These are long-term trends of industrial change, unaffected by the reforms.

India's Unique Pattern of Development[11]

We now take up the uniqueness aspect of Indian industrial development. In a very insightful analysis of Indian industrialization since Independence, Kochhar *et al.* (2006) argue that India pursued a "idiosyncratic" pattern of development which resulted in direct shift of labour from agriculture sector to the service sector, bypassing the intermediate stage (industrial sector) to a considerable extent. Within manufacturing, India has emphasized skill-intensive rather than labor-intensive industries and industries with typically higher average scale.

11. Krishna (2013) *op.cit.*

Analyzing the pattern of growth of fast-moving Indian states in the reform era, they come to the conclusion that it is unlikely that India will adopt the pattern of development followed by other countries. This prediction has serious implication for the employment potential of the manufacturing sector in the years to come.

OECD (2007) notes that India has followed a unique development path with the share of manufacturing in total GDP not increasing with economic growth, and attributes this feature to "deeply rooted problems" in the manufacturing sector constraining its growth, although some of these have been eased with reforms. Manufacturing firms were not able to fully exploit their comparative advantages of low-labour costs and have remained very small in scale—yet capital-intensive-limiting productivity gains as well as job creation. In recent years, there has been some employment expansion due to some liberalisation of labour laws, but many of the new jobs are of low quality. Large firms still face obstacles to restructuring employment, constraining their ability to compete effectively.

Labour Market Rigidity Hypothesis

The reformists believe that India's labour laws are the most protective of the organised labour, which makes firing of workers almost impossible, rendering labour a quasi-fixedcapital, leading to substitution of capital for labour, yielding little employment growth. Such a reading of the labour law is perhaps facile as it overlooks the 'fine print' of exemptions and loopholes that are build into them. By now, there is abundant evidence to question such a simplistic view. Perhaps it is suffice to present the telling evidence that between 1997 and 2004, 1.3 million workers, or 1 in 6 workers in registered manufacturing, lost their jobs without a murmur of protest or industrial unrest (Nagaraj, 2004). Moreover, in the current economic crisis (since 2008), the labour ministry's quick surveys reported on its website show that during the last financial year (2008-09) 3.7 lakh workers lost their jobs, mostly in export-oriented textiles and gems and jewellery industries—an ample testimony to the fallacy of the labour market rigidity hypothesis, at least in the aggregate.

Infrastructure Bottlenecks

That infrastructure bottlenecks are throttling industrial progress is undisputed. But on how to overcome them and why the progress is so meagre despite much official rhetoric, there can be widly differing diagnoses and prescriptions. Until 1991, public sector provided much of the infrastructure, as in most industrialising economies. But its poor supply was often blamed on lack of resources, enormous cost and time overruns in project completion, and poor public management in general.

Attributing these problems to public ownership, the reforms have encouraged entry of private and foreign capital in these industries. Infrastructure services, by definition, have a long gestation period and are capital intensive, with low rates of return spread over a long period. They are often networked industries, where efficiency of an individual plant or a firm depends on the preformance of the entire network, and financial returns depend on output pricing, which are public policy decisions. In such industries, foreign investment is fraught with risk, as evidence world over can testify (Wells and Gleason, 1995). Closer home, the nation has paid dearly for the misadventures like the Enron's Dabhol power project.

The Cost of Doing Business

Two other challenges that beset manufacturers in India illustrate the nature of solutions required to attract more investments into manufacturing. The ‘cost of doing business’ is much higher in India than in other countries due to the plethora of forms and inspections that manufacturers have to comply with, some of them arising out of legislations long pending review, such as the Factories Act. The streamlining of these requires action by government agencies in the states and in the Centre. Action has begun and thereby some states are becoming more attractive for investments.

Another challenge is to provide more flexibility to employers to adjust employment levels along with more fairness and security to employees. The solution cannot be restricted merely to modifying laws such as the Industrial Disputes Act to permit hire and fire. New institutional arrangements are required to provide security for employees before existing legal safe-guards for them can be reduced or altered. The evolution of such institutions, as well as development of employee-employer contracts founded on new principles, requires wider stakeholder involvement and consensus. At the national and state levels, unions and employers’ associations must engage in a well-conducted constructive dialogue to build trust and find new institutional solutions. Such solutions can take the forms of unemployment insurance and staffing companies. Institutionalised processes of consultation between managers and workers within manufacturing units, as exist in several enterprises, must be widely applied in all units. The quality and conduct of representation institutions on both employers’ side and employees' side must be strengthened too. In short, the solution to the fairness-flexibility conundrum is not only in changes in laws but also in building and strengthening institutions.

The Annual Survey of Industries (ASI) provides information on the organized factory sector (employing 10 or more workers if using power) in terms of a variety of parameters. Technological depth of organized manufacturing, defined in terms of increase in share of value added, indicates a worsening trend in organized manufacturing during the post-reform period. The share of inputs as per cent to output actually increased from 77.2 per cent during 1981-91 to 77.3 per cent during 1991-2001 and further to over 80 per cent in the last decade. This indicates that the growth of Indian industry in general, particularly the organized manufacturing sector, was largely driven by increase in use of inputs. There has, however, been significant improvement in use of energy. The ratio of expenditure on fuel to output declined from 8.2 per cent during 1981-91 to 7.0 per cent during 1991-2001 and further to 4.3 per cent in 2009-10. Industry is becoming increasingly conscious of energy efficiency (Table 14.11).

TABLE – 14.11

Some Key Parameters of Organised Manufacturing in India

CHARACTERISTICS	*1981-1991*	*1991-2001*	*2001-2006*	*2006-2007*	*2007-2008*	*2008-2009*	*2009-2010*
Number of factories	101905	127431	132419	144710	146385	155321	158877
Value of output (Rs billion)	1450	6469	13923	24085	27757	32728	37228
In per cent							
Input/ output	77.20	77.26	81.04	80.89	80.09	81.32	81.54
Fuel/output	8.21	7.01	5.76	4.99	4.67	4.65	4.34
Capital invested/labour (Rs '000)	133	498	872	1037	1225	1355	1638
Emoluments/output	8.75	6.18	4.35	3.68	3.80	3.96	3.95
Profit/output	3.52	5.58	7.44	10.02	10.72	9.07	8.67
Interest Rate	11.90	15.31	11.96	9.64	11.34	12.80	11.06

Source: *Economic Survey 2011-12.*

The number of persons engaged in organized manufacturing also increased from an average of 7.95 million in 1981-91 to an average of 8.98 million during 1991-2001 and further to 11.79 million in 2009-

2010. This is in contrast to a decline in workforce in manufacturing as a whole, covering both the organized and unorganized sectors. However, the ratio of total emoluments to output declined from 8.75 per cent during 1981-91 to 3.95 per cent in 2009-10, the most recent year for which ASI data is available. There has been an increase in profitability in organized manufacturing, with the ratio of profit to output increasing from 3.52 per cent in 1981-91 to 10.72 per cent in 2007-08. However, thereafter there has been a moderation in the ratio of profit to output to 8.67 per cent in 2009-10. Profitability of organized manufacturing seems to be considerably dependent on the rate of interest on its outstanding credit and emoluments paid to workers. A trend of moderating interest rate from 1998-99 until 2007-08 resulted in the ratio of profit to output increasing from 6 per cent to 10.7 per cent. Hardening of interest rates in 2008-09 substantially reduced the ratio of profit to output. The decline in rate of interest, however, did not result in any improvement in profit/output ratio in 2009-10.

What Should be Done Now?

It is argued that the reforms failed to deliver because they ignored the demand factors.[12] Careful analytical work and econometric evidence have suggested that long-term industrial growth in India is constrained by supply as well as demand factors, which, it seems, runs on the twin engines of public investment and agriculture productivity (Chakravarty, 1979; Storm, 1993). Moreover, in a large agrarian economy, public investment removes constraints on productivity growth in agriculture, creating demand for industrial goods—a crucial insight that the writings on the reforms have inadequately appreciated—a view also endorsed by Krueger (2009). Surely, the creative function of competitive industrial structure is to spur efficiency, but it need not necessarily translate into faster and labour-intensive growth, as argued in the mainstream economic literature. As the experience of the 1980s has demonstrated, gradual deregulation of industrial markets, along with stepping up of public infrastructure investment and rising agriculture productivity perhaps provided the right demand and supply conditions for industrial turnaround.

Arthur Lewis famously said that if a nation wants to industrialise, it should enrich its farmers. But farmers have got impoverished after the reforms as the growth rate of crop production has decelerated. This seems to get reflected in the widespread phenomenon of farmers

12. Nagaraj (2011) *op.cit.*

committing suicide (under debt burden), which is not just a crisis of production but also a serious humanitarian problem. The agrarian distress has also manifested itself in a political crisis, fuelling rural violence, as evident from the spread of left-wing radical movements, engulfing nearly one-third of the districts in the country.

Balanced Growth

Proponents of the reforms would probably contend that agriculture has lost the capacity to absorb labour and, in any case, India is saddled with excess food stocks. Both are probably half-truths, at best. India's land productivity in all major crops is a modest fraction of the world average, so the argument that agriculture has little scope for absorbing labour to increase productivity is simply incorrect. As is widely acknowledged, overflowing food stocks are not a measure of food self-sufficiency when a large proportion of the poor cannot demand food for lack of purchasing power. So, the argument that agriculture cannot absorb labour is patently false. If we believe that the pace of workforce transformation depends on agriculture productivity to sustain non-agricultural employment, then poor agricultural growth is surely retarding industrial progress.

Therefore, what is needed, as Lewis argued long ago, is balanced growth. Surely, rising demand from rural economy can boost industrial output, but unless industry modernises to augment exports, economy may face external imbalance. Therefore, what is also required after reaching a certain level of economic development, as Kaldor (1967) argued, is growing exports of manufactures to meet finance import requirements. As India has more or less completed import substitution phase, what it now needs to vigorously pursue is export of labour-intensive goods to finance its burgeoning import requirements (especially of oil) to lubricate the engine of domestic market-led growth. This requires modern infrastructure and long-term credit at reasonable interest rates.

Integrating into Global Networks

Building protective walls for shielding Indian manufacturers is neither an appropriate nor a feasible strategy in a world where trade is open. India's manufacturing strategy must build upon its competitive advantages in a changing global manufacturing landscape. Abilities to work within networks (and also to design and engineer rapidly) have become critical sources of competitive advantage. Scale remains an advantage no doubt. But in many industries, scale can be obtained by growing networks rather than building massive factories. In fact, the smallness and nimbleness of Indian manufacturers, supported by software, can be their sources of strategic advantage in the new world of manufacturing, where competitiveness is in the 'scope' of a networked enterprise, not the 'scale' of its units (Planning Commission, 2011).

Improving Physical Infrastructure

A significant part of the supportive framework to enable manufacturing to expand rapidly in line with both domestic and overseas demand is the rolling out of adequate physical infrastructure support including electric power, railways, roads and ports. Poor infrastructure, especially power, is a major constraint on competitiveness especially of SMEs who cannot afford to build their own infrastructure.

But we are now in a peculiar situation: even after steady improvement in the financial performance of public sector enterprises (PSEs) over the last two decades (Nagaraj, 2006b), rising tax—GDP ratio, and a steep increase in domestic saving rate (Nagaraj 2008), policymakers continue to favour private sector over public sector in infrastructure development due to fiscal orthodoxy. It is true that in the period after the mid-1960s to 1980, excessive and discretionary regulation stifled private initiative. However, it is equally true that leaving infrastructure to private initiative after the reforms did not lead to faster investment and output growth. Therefore, what is needed, as Hazari (1985) insightfully noted, is a judicious rebalancing between the babu and bania, to achieve the national goals—a balance that needs to be pragmatically reassessed from time to time (Nagaraj, 2011).

National Manufacturing Policy (NMP) Nov. 2011

The report of the Prime Minister's Group, constituted to look into the measures for ensuring growth of the manufacturing sector, submitted in 2008 had recommended the putting in place a well structured manufacturing-sector policy to attain sustained 12-14 per cent growth in this sector. The government released the NMP on November 4, 2011 for bringing about a quantitative and qualitative change with the objectives to: (i) increase manufacturing sector growth to 12-14 per cent over the medium term; (ii) enable manufacturing to contribute at least 25 per cent of GDP by 2022; (iii) create 100 million additional jobs in the manufacturing sector by 2022; (iv) create appropriate skill sets among the rural migrant and urban poor for their easy absorption in manufacturing; (v) increase domestic value addition and technological depth in manufacturing; and (vi) enhance global competitiveness of Indian manufacturing (*Economic Survey 2011-12*).

The NMP was finalised after extensive consultations with the stakeholders and inputs from industry, state governments, and experts in the field of manufacturing, technology development, and business environment. The NMP envisages simplification of business regulations without diluting their intent. Recognising the importance of small and medium enterprises (SMEs) in the country's economy, the policy contains dedicated interventions for SMEs in addition to other interventions for manufacturing industry generally. These interventions relate primarily to technology upgradation; adoption of environment-friendly technology; and equity investments. Skill development, to make young people employable, has been given high priority in the policy through fiscal incentives for the private sector and government schemes. National investment and manufacturing zones (NIMZs) are also provided for on lands which are degraded and uncultivable. NIMZs are envisaged as integrated industrial townships with world class physical and social infrastructure. The NMP, which is the first such dedicated policy measure for the manufacturing sector in the country, is expected to change the manufacturing landscape of the Indian economy through increased capital formation; industrial infrastructure of global standards; technology upgradation; creation of innovation and vocational skill development infrastructure; and industry, worker, and environment-friendly regulations.

In order to ensure effective implementation of the NMP, manufacturing policy review mechanisms will be instituted. The NMP also provides for constitution of a high-level Manufacturing Industry Promotion Board (MIPB) to ensure coordination amongst central ministries and state governments.

Conclusions

Ending the strategic role of the state-led import-substituting industrialisation, the two decades of industry and trade policy reforms have dismantled the output and investments controls. Quality and variety of goods produced have improved; relative price of capital goods has declined (enhancing the productivity of fixed investment), although the import content in domestic production has risen. The unintended boom in the export of information technology and related services can be clearly seen as a consequence of early investments in heavy industry and scientific and technical education. A growing number of Indian firms have gained technical expertise to run factories and firms across the globe, leveraging their domestic competence and, in turn, to acquire technology to enhance their domestic cababilities. (Nagaraj, 2011)

Yet, these achievements have not translated into faster and labour-intensive industrial growth or growth in industrial exports, as compared to the 1980s. As a result, the services sector has replaced manufacturing as the economy's leading sector. Though India did not witness de-industrialisation, as the critics of the reforms apprehended, industry's share of domestic output and employment has stagnated; its share in merchandise export has declined, with rising exports of primary exports (mainly of iron ore). Why did the reforms fail to deliver a faster and equitable industrial growth? In other words, why did the reforms fail to promote labour-intensive growth and manufactured exports, as in East Asia and China?

With rapid changes of technologies in various industries and open international trade environment within which domestic manufacturers must compete, response by producers and policymakers must be dynamic. Recent studies of the manufacturing strengths of countries reveal that, while the industries they focussed on and the policies they adopted differed, all the successful countries had one thing in common. They had a very good process for consultation between producers and policymakers and for establishing coordination amongst the policy-makers. Thus, the paradigm of policy planning in manufacturing must shift from 'planning as allocations' to 'planning as learning'; and from budgets and controls towards improving processes for consultation and coordination. In India we have already given up the paradigm of allocations and quotas and there is no question of reverting to it. However, having not mastered the other paradigm yet, we are not able to grow our manufacturing sector as fast as we could.

According to Nagaraj, the principle drawback of the reforms is its exclusive focus on removing supply constraints at the neglect of demand. There is a growing consensus on the need to raise agriculture productivity to find markets for industrial goods.

First, on the global front, there are tendencies by some trading partners to indulge in what may possibly be termed as dumping into the Indian market. The response will have to be calibrated by balancing the need to achieve input cost advantages while protecting the legitimate interests of the Indian industry. Given the possible global restructuring of industry underway, it is critical for Indian industry to consciously build and maintain cost advantages.

Second, the size of the Indian market and the unmet demand for industrial products provide reasonable hope that demand would not be a constraining factor by itself. There is an increasing realisation that the industry should make conscious efforts to reach out to the bottom of the pyramid. To be able to do so, the industry will need to deliver products that give value for money in a cost effective way.

Third, the large pool of scientific manpower and research labs, especially in the public domain, provide a potential for innovation that could create such products which can open up new market segments . However, for innovation to become a key driver of growth, the industry and the research fraternity need to actively collaborate in a time-bound and result-oriented fashion.

The inherent strength of Indian industrial corporate sector with strong entrepreneurial abilities provides a hope that they will continue to display the dynamism by adjusting to the current changes. This dynamism needs to be tempered with good corporate governance that adheres to the best standards of ethics in business and industry.

Fourth, the large investment plans made for infrastructure during the Eleventh Five Year Plan and beyond are expected to ameliorate the infrastructural constraints that bind the industry. The challenge rests in ensuring that such investments in infrastructure projects fructify quickly, for, growth in infrastructure not only alleviates supply side constraints, but also stimulates additional domestic demand required for industrial growth.

At the same time, a balance needs to be struck between the immediate priorities for the Indian economy and the long-term concerns that include environmental and security concerns.

In the short run, revival of investment in industry and key infrastructure sectors is the key challenge. Industrial sector has been hit hard by the deceleration in investment for the second successive year. As per the latest first revised estimates of GDP, gross capital formation in the manufacturing sector in 2011-12 (at 2004-05 prices) had declined by 18.8 per cent as compared to 2010-11. Lower foreign direct investment inflows in key industry and infrastructure sectors during April-October 2012 at $ 6.19 billion as against the inflow of $18.66 billion during the same period of the previous year have further constrained investment in these sectors. Investment intentions indicated in the industrial entrepreneur memorandum (IEMs) filed, which are lead indicators of likely investment flows to industry, also declined in 2011 and 2012. Notwithstanding a marginal pickup in the gross bank credit deployment into industrial sector in recent months, year on year increase in gross bank credit deployment as on end December 2012 has been 13.8 per cent as compared to 19.8 per cent a year ago.

Apart from weak investment climate, industrial sector performance remained subdued due to infrastructure bottlenecks. Industrial growth rate moderated due to sharp decline in output of natural gas; subdued performance of the coal sector and its resultant impact on thermal power generation; and slow pace of project implementation in rail, road, and ports sectors. In the medium term it is therefore crucial to accelerate the output of core sectors and speed up implementation of crucial big ticket projects.

As discussed in detail in the earlier sections, the key underpinning cause of the recent industrial slowdown has been the manufacturing sector. India's manufacturing value-added (MVA) as share of GDP, has remained sticky at around 15 per cent. As per the latest competitive industrial performance index (CIP) compiled by UNIDO for the year 2009, India was placed 42nd out of the 118 countries. India's low CIP ranking hints at the underlying weaknesses and vulnerabilities despite being one of the top ten manufacturing nations. India's manufacturing sector therefore needs to acquire dynamism and technological sophistication to become one of the leading manufacturers. From the long term point of view, low level of R&D and inadequate availability of skilled manpower would adversely affect India's competitiveness and the manufacturing growth.

Countries that have performed better than the others in terms of thriving business have, to a great extent, done so on account of the quality of the business regulatory environment, which is an important factor distinguishing better performing countries from others. The key objectives of streamlining of business activities through the regulatory framework should be:

- Low compliance cost for doing business in India
- Simple regulatory environment, saving time and energy for the businesses; and
- Ensuring fair competition

The country must improve regulations and implementation in many subjects to make India generally a more attractive country for doing business. These include land and environmental regulations, labour laws and their administration and so on. It should be noted that, in the context of India's federal structure, the ability to mandate specific reforms to the regulatory framework from any centralised apex body is fairly constrained. Therefore, while nodal agencies may be set up to focus attention on matters that must be attended to across the country, and this section and others mention some, it is imperative that the role of such agencies in the process of making improvements across the country fits the country's federal and decentralised political structure. Such agencies cannot and must not usurp local authority.

Cohesion can be brought about through more effective coordination amongst agencies, and more effective consultation amongst stakeholders. The success of the Indian auto sector can be attributed significantly to the long term plan prepared a few years ago, collaboratively by the Society of Indian Automobile Manufacturers, the Association of Component Manufacturers of India, and the Ministry of Heavy Industry, involving other agencies too. Such plans are required in other sectors too (Twelfth Five Year Plan, Vol.II, Ch.13).

To conclude on a positive note, the current global and domestic scenario presents Indian industry with major challenges. At the same time, there are a number of positive factors that make the industrial outlook in the medium-term bright for India both in its own right as also in relation to most other countries.

15

Micro, Small and Medium Enterprises (MSMEs)

SMALL industry has been one of the major planks of India's economic development strategy since Independence. Today, small industry occupies a position of strategic importance in the Indian economic structure due to its significant contribution in terms of output, exports and employment.

The Micro, Small and Medium Enterprises (MSME) sector has emerged as a highly vibrant and dynamic sector of the Indian economy over the last few decades. It is estimated that this sector contributes about 45 per cent of manufacturing output and 40 per cent of total exports of the country and employs about 69 million persons in over 29 million units throughout the country. Within the MSME Sector there is a significant concentration of Micro Enterprises, both in terms of working enterprises and employment. There are over 6,000 products ranging from traditional to high-tech items manufactured by the MSMEs. The sector also covers the enterprises established in khadi and village industries and coir sector (Planning Commission, 2012).[1]

The MSEs are, however, more than just GDP earners; they are instruments of inclusive growth which touch upon the lives of the most vulnerable, the most marginalised—women, Muslims, SCs and STs—and the most unskilled. Being the largest source of employment after agriculture, the MSE sector in India enables 650 lakh men, women and children living in urban slums, upcoming towns, remote villages and isolated hamlets to use indigenous knowledge, cultural wisdom and entrepreneurial skills for the sustenance of their lives and livelihoods (Planning Commission, 2008).[2]

1. Planning Commission (2012). *Twelfth Five Year Plan (2012-2017)*, Vol.II, Ch.13.
2. Planning Commission (2008). *Eleventh Five Year Plan 2007-2012*, Vol. III.

Role of SMEs in Global Economy: International Scenario

Worldwide, MSMEs have been recognised as engines of economic growth.

The overall contribution of small firms—formal and informal—to the GDP and employment remain about the same across low, middle and high-income group countries. As income increases, the share of the informal sector decreases and that of the formal SME sector increases. In Brazil, MSEs represent 20 per cent of the total GDP. Of the country's 4.7 million registered businesses, 96.8 per cent are MSEs and—along with the other 9.5 million informal enterprises—they employ 59 per cent of the economically active population. Similarly, informal and micro enterprises account for 39 per cent of labour force and contribute to 24 per cent of the GDP in South Africa; SMEs employ 27 per cent of the labour force and contribute 32 per cent to the GDP; while large enterprises employ 34 per cent people and account for 44 per cent of GDP. SMEs comprise over 90 per cent of all industrial units in Bangladesh contributing between 80 per cent and 85 per cent of the industrial employment and 23 per cent of the total civilian employment. They contribute three-quarters of the household income in both the urban and the rural areas. In Japan, SMEs employ more than 70 per cent of the wage earners, contributing over 55 per cent of value added in the manufacturing sector. In Thailand in 2003, there were 2006528 enterprises of which 99.5 per cent were SMEs. These SMEs generated products worth 38.1 per cent of GDP and in 2003 they employed 60.7 per cent of Thailand's working population.

The real importance of the SMEs, however, can be seen in China where over 68 per cent of the exports come from the SMEs. China has created more SMEs in the last 20 years than the total number of SMEs in Europe and the US combined. Their numbers have increased from about 1 million private sector SMEs in the 1990s to 40 million in 2004. In China, an industrial SME is defined as having up to 2000 employees, while a small business has less than 300 employees and a medium-size business has employees between 301 and 2000 (Planning Commission, 2008).

Defining MSEs—MSMED Act, 2006

There is no globally accepted definition of MSMEs. Different countries use different criterion; most of the definitions are based on investment ceiling and number of people employed. In India, the Micro,

Small and Medium Enterprises Development (MSMED) Act, 2006 defines MSMEs. It introduces the concept of 'enterprise' as opposed to the earlier concept of industry. According to the Act, MSMEs are classified into the following: (i) enterprises engaged in the manufacture or production of goods pertaining to any industry specified in the first schedule to the Industries (Development and Regulation Act, 1951) and (ii) enterprises engaged in providing or rendering services. Table 15.1 defines the MSMEs in both these sectors:

TABLE – 15.1

Definition of MSMEs

	Manufacturing Sector
Enterprises	Investment in plant and machinery (original cost excluding land and building and the items specified by the then ministry of small scale industries, vide its notification No. S.O.1722(E) dated 5 October 2006)
Micro enterprises	Does not exceed Rs. 25 lakh
Small enterprises	More than Rs. 25 lakh and less than Rs. 5 crore
Medium enterprises	More than Rs. 5 crore and less than Rs. 10 crore
	Service Sector
Enterprises	Investment in equipments
Micro enterprises	Does not exceed Rs. 10 lakh
Small enterprises	More than Rs. 10 lakh and less than Rs. 2 crore
Medium enterprises	More than Rs. 2 crore and less than Rs. 5 crore

Source : Micro, Small and Medium Enterprises Development Act, 2006.
Planning Commission (2008). *Eleventh Five Year Plan 2007-2012*.

The Act also provides for a statutory consultative mechanism at the national level with a balanced representation of all the sections of stakeholders and with a wide range of advisory functions. Establishment of specific funds for promotion, development and enhancement of the competitiveness of these enterprises; notification of schemes/ programmes, progressive credit policies and practices; preference to products and services of MSEs in the government procurement; more effective mechanisms for mitigating the problems of delayed payments; and a scheme for easing the closure of business by these enterprises are some features of the Act.

Role of SMSEs in Indian Economy

To Generate Large-Scale Employment

As countries develop, the share of agriculture in providing employment and in GDP decreases. According to the Australian economist Chris Hall, the SMEs contribute about 70 per cent of net new jobs across the globe, while larger firms tend to be job destroyers.

The MSE sector in India has grown significantly since 1960, when there were only 12376 MSEs providing employment to 10 lakh people—of which, direct employment was 1.85 lakh; annual production level was Rs. 875 crore. At the beginning of the Tenth Plan, 249 lakh people in the rural and urban areas were employed in 105.21 lakh MSEs. This has increased to 295 lakh people in 128 lakh units now; an average annual growth rate of 4.4 per cent in the number of these units and 4.62 per cent in employment. If the units in the *khadi* industries, village industries and coir industries are taken into account, the employment is estimated to be over 332 lakh. With the inclusion of handlooms, handicrafts, wool and sericulture, the total job in the MSE sector in India goes up to 650 lakh. The employment intensity of the registered units indicates that an investment of Rs. 0.72 lakh is required for creating one employment in MSME sector as against Rs. 5.56 lakh in the large organised sector.

Not only do MSEs generate the highest employment per capita investment, they also go a long way in checking rural–urban migration by providing villagers and people living in isolated areas with a sustainable source of employment. Among the MSEs in India, the dispersed food products sector generates maximum employment (13.7 per cent of total employment in the MSE sector), followed by non-metallic mineral products (10.9 per cent) and metal products (10.2 per cent). In chemicals and chemical products, machinery parts except electrical parts, wood products, basic metal industries, paper products and printing, hosiery and garments, repair services, and rubber and plastic products, the contribution ranges from 9 per cent to 5 per cent. In all other industries, the contribution is less than 5 per cent.

Per unit employment is highest (20) in units engaged in beverages, tobacco and tobacco products. Next come cotton textile products (17), non-metallic mineral products (14.1), basic metal industries (13.6), and electrical machinery and parts (11.2). Per unit employment is highest (10) in the metropolitan areas and lowest (5) in the rural areas. Non-metallic products contribute 22.7 per cent to the employment generated in the rural areas, followed by food products (21.1 per cent), wood products, and chemicals and chemical products. As for the urban areas, food products and metal products almost equally share 22.8 per cent employment. Machinery parts except electrical, non-metallic mineral products, and chemicals and chemical products between them account for another 26.2 per cent employment. Metal products, machinery and parts except electrical, and paper products and printing (total share being 33.6 per cent) are the leading industries in metropolitan areas (Planning Commission, 2008).

To Sustain Economic Growth and Increase Exports

According to 11th Plan estimates in order to achieve the target of 10 per cent growth in the Eleventh Plan, the MSE sector needs to grow at 12 per cent.

Non-traditional products account for more than 95 per cent of the SSI exports. The performance of garments, leather, and gems and jewellery units has been remarkable in the last decade. The SSI sector dominates in export of sports goods, readymade garments, woollen garments and knitwear, plastic products, processed food and leather products. The US, Europe and West Asia are the major export destinations.

There is tremendous potential to expand the quantum of exports from traditional MSEs because they are handcrafted and hence eco-friendly and exclusive. Further, while MSEs are unable to take advantage of economies of scale, they are ideal for meeting small order quantities—a bonus in industries such as readymade garments, home furnishings, etc.

MSEs often act as ancillary industries for LSIs providing them with raw materials, vital components and backward linkages. For instance, large cycle manufacturers of Ludhiana rely heavily on the small MSEs of Malerkotla which produce cycle parts. MSEs also promote eco-friendly growth, especially in difficult terrains and the ecologically sensitive areas. In large tracts of barren desert land in Barmer and Kutch, in the scattered *dhani*s of Udaipur, in the hilly hamlets of J&K, Ladakh, Himachal and the Northeast, in the tribal hinterlands of central India, they are the only source of livelihood.

For Making Growth Inclusive

The MSE sector is a microcosm of all vulnerabilities—it touches upon the lives of women, children, minorities, SCs and STs in the villages, in the urban slums and in the deprived pockets of flourishing towns and cities. For many families, it is the only source of livelihood. For others, it supplements the family income. Thus, instead of taking a welfare approach, this sector seeks to empower people to break the cycle of poverty and deprivation. It focuses on people's skills and agency.

Different segments of the MSE sector are dominated by different social groups. Women are mostly found in the unregistered sector—food processing enterprises, manufacturing enterprises and weaving—and often work part time in the family enterprises. Women and small children roll *bidis*, make *agarbattis*, do *zari* and sequin work for meagre wages. Large number of Muslims are found in the unorganised weaving sector and in powerlooms. In the Northeast, most women weave. In states like Tripura, 50 per cent of rural men and 35 per cent rural women are engaged in MSEs. In Nagaland and Mizoram, over 68 per cent of urban men are with MSEs (Planning Commission, 2008).

The 12th Plan has listed the following as the objectives for the MSME Sector:

- Promoting competitiveness and productivity in the MSME space
- Making the MSME Sector innovative, improving technology and depth
- Enabling environment for promotion and development of MSMEs
- Strong presence in exports
- Improved managerial processes in MSMEs

Globalisation and Small Industry Performance[3]

The overall performance and contribution of small industry to the Indian economy is generally described in terms of its absolute growth in units, employment, production and exports. Equally important is its relative contribution, which can be analysed in terms of small industry share in national income, total exports and total organised sector employment. Thus, the growth performance of small industry can be evaluated in two ways:

---

3. Subrahmanya Bala, M.H. (2009). "Small Industry and Globalisation: Implications, Performance and Prospects", in K.L. Krishna and Uma Kapila (eds.), *Readings in Indian Agriculture and Industry*. New Delhi: Academic Foundation.

(1) To compare the growth rates of units, employment, output and exports of small industry in the 1990s with that of the 1980s.

(2) To ascertain the change in small industry's relative contribution to GDP, exports and organised sector employment in the 1990s with that of the 1980s.

This according to Bala Subrahmanya will reveal how the sector is coping with challenges and changes in the intensifying competitive environment emerging since 1990-91. The growth rates of small industry in terms of units, employment, output and exports for the 1980s and 1990s are presented in Table 15.2. It is clear that the growth of small industry in the transitional period of 1990s has come down not only in terms of units and employment but also output. This could be an indication that increasing competition in the globalisation period does affect the growth of Indian small industry adversely. However, the growth rate of exports has actually increased marginally. To probe the growth pattern further, growth rates are estimated for five-year periods for both the 1980s and 1990s. They also broadly correspond to India's five year plans, namely, the Sixth, Seventh, Eighth and Ninth Five Year Plans. The scenario does not differ much, except for exports (Table 15.2). The growth rates of units and employment have steadily come down. But the growth rates of output and more importantly, exports have fluctuated. In fact, the growth rate of output increased in the late 1980s compared with the early 1980s but then declined in the early 1990s and further in the late 1990s. Whereas the growth rate of exports increased steadily till the early 1990s but then declined considerably.

TABLE – 15.2

Growth of Small Industry: 1990s *vs* 1980s

	Period	*Units**	*Employment**	*Output**	*Exports**
I.	1980s	18.40	5.84	18.66	19.38
	1990s	5.62	4.00	15.31	20.62
II.	1980-81 to 1985-86	9.18	6.21	16.88	11.00
	1985-86 to 1990-91	7.63	5.47	20.46	28.40
	1990-91 to 1995-96	6.88	4.02	18.05	30.42
	1995-96 to 2000-01	4.37	3.99	12.62	11.56

Note: * Figures represent compound average rate of growth (CARG).

Source : SIDBI (1999); GoI (2002); Bala Subrahmanya (2009).

The other dimension of small industry performance is its relative contribution to national income (GDP), exports and employment. The contribution of small industries is considered for three periods of time: 1980-81, 1990-91 and 2000-01 (Table 15.3). The share of small industry in national income increased in the protection period of the 1980s but declined considerably in the transitional period of the 1990s. The share of small industry in exports and its employment in relation to organised sector employment have consistently increased both in the protection period and in the transitional period. But the increase in the share of small industry in total exports was more significant in the protection period of the 1980s than in the transitional period of the 1990s. However, the increase in the relative share of small industry employment was more significant in the 1990s than in the 1980s. Small industry employment (which included partly unorganised manufacturing sector employment as well) was equivalent to about 31 per cent of the total organised sector employment in 1980-81. It went up to nearly 48 per cent of the organised sector employment in 1990-91. By 2000-01, small industry employment increased to two-thirds of the organised sector employment. That is, though the growth rate of small industry employment has come down in the 1990s, it has increased more than proportionately in the period of globalisation compared with the protection period, with respect to other sectors of the Indian economy. As a result, its size relative to organised sector employment has gone up.

TABLE – 15.3

Small Industry in National Income, Exports and Employment

(Per cent)

Year	*National Income*	*Exports*	*Employment*
1980-81	9.2	24.5	31.0
1990-91	11.0	29.7	47.6
2000-01	7.8*	30.9	66.4

Note: * For the year 1997-98.

Source : GoI (1998, 2002); RBI (2001); EPW Research Foundation (2002); Bala Subrahmanya (2009).

On the whole, small industry performance does indicate that the sector faces a tough challenge for its survival and growth in the period of globalisation.

The pertinent issue is, *why should liberalisation and globalisation affect Indian small industry to such an extent?* The reasons are not far to seek.

Infrastructure

A substantial majority of Indian small industry does not have access to reliable and efficient infrastructure even today, which in turn impedes small industry competitiveness. According to Kulkarni and Parishwad (2001), about 40 per cent of the 2.6 lakh small industry units in Karnataka have been closed due to infrastructural bottlenecks and lack of orders from PSUs, among others. In Peenya Industrial Estate, Bangalore, which is considered to be the largest in south and south-east Asia, only about 2,000 units function out of the total 3,500 units, and lack of infrastructure and competition are considered to be the major causal factors (Menon and Raghunandan, 2003).

The infrastructural constraints confronted by small industry can be broadly classified as economic, technological, marketing and financial.

Economic

Stable and reliable economic infrastructure such as power, water, transport and communications are a prerequisite for the efficient functioning of any economic activity, including small industry. Inadequate economic infrastructure is a major factor that affects the performance and competitiveness of small industry.

Technological

Technological obsolescence has been a characteristic of small industry in India across a wide variety of sectors. In the early 1990s, two survey-based studies showed that technological obsolescence in the small industry affects quality and productivity adversely.

However, the need for improving the competitive strength of small industry through technology improvement and modernisation was recognised as early as in the 1950s, with the setting up of the Small Industries Development Organisation (SIDO) and a network of small industries service institutes (SISIs), National Small Industries Corporation (NSIC) and National Research Development Corporation (NRDC). Since then, over a period of time, particularly in the 1990s, exclusive technology infrastructure has come up for small industry to facilitate technology transfer (Bala Subrahmanya *et al.*, 2002). Thus, policy makers in India have considered technology development in small industry only from a single dimension, that is, through institutional technology transfer. This implies that small industry in India is perennially external-technology dependant.

Financial

Timely availability of adequate finance is another issue that crucially determines the survival and growth of small firms. Small firms are largely dependent on bank credit to meet their financing requirements, while large firms have alternative sources of finance (RBI, 2003). To ensure better financial infrastructure, SIDBI was set up in 1990. Today, SIDBI operates through the head office, five regional offices and 36 branch offices across the country (SIDBI, 2002). In addition, based on the recommendations of the Nayak committee, set up by RBI (1992), 370 exclusive bank branches for small industry were set up by public sector banks by 1998 (DCSSI, 1999). Further, as per the Nayak committee recommendations, the Reserve Bank of India has directed banks to meet the working capital needs of small industry at the rate of 20 per cent of annual output subject to an individual upper limit of Rs. 20 million (DCSSI, 1999). However, despite the development of exclusive financial infrastructure for small industry, growth in the amount of bank credit extended to small industry declined in the 1990s from that in the 1980s. In fact, the decline in growth rate was more pronounced relative to total priority sector, medium- and large-scale industry sector and total non-food bank credit. As a result, credit to small industry as a percentage of non-food gross bank credit increased marginally from about 14 per cent in 1980-81 to 15.14 per cent in 1990-91 but declined to 13 per cent in 2000-01. Further, the total bank credit extended to small industry as a percentage of small industry output declined marginally from about 9.4 per cent in 1993-94 to 8.7 per cent in 2000-01. This shows that despite policy support, credit flow to small industry has actually declined relatively in the 1990s (Bala Subrahmanya, 2009).

Lending to micro enterprises, which is stipulated at 60 per cent of the total credit to MSE sector, has fallen from 51.2 per cent in 2002–2003 to 45.1 per cent at the end of 2005-06. Moreover, difficulty in arranging collaterals or third-party guarantees continues to be a problem. Though the RBI had issued instructions to advance collateral free loans up to Rs. 5 lakh, at the end of 2005-06, only 24 per cent of the total outstanding loans under Rs. 5 lakh were without collaterals. The high cost of credit to MSEs also impacts the competitiveness of their products.

Marketing

Marketing has been identified as one of the major problem areas of the small-scale sector and it has been ranked, according to the second census of small-scale industries, as the second-most important reason for the closure of small industry units (SIDBI, 2002). It is quite logical and obvious. If small firms do not have access to reliable and efficient economic infrastructure, suffer from technological obsolescence and credit flow is not sufficient, they will not be able to produce quality goods and productivity will not be high either. In such a case, small firms will not be able to penetrate markets, national or international, even if marketing support is forthcoming from government agencies.

Most MSEs do not have money to invest in market research and are unable to carry out design and technical improvements to keep up with market demands. Unlike big businesses, they cannot invest in advertising and packaging. This limits their ability to tap markets and attract consumers.

Future Prospects of Small Industry

The central issue of concern for the growth of small industry is how to strengthen its competitiveness. First of all, if small industry has to thrive steadily, infrastructural bottlenecks must be overcome to enable it to compete on its own based on inherent potential. And it is the responsibility of the government to remove any structural bottleneck in small industry performance especially when market forces are given prominence through the removal of 'protective elements'. It is essential to provide the much-needed 'level playing field' to small enterprises through infrastructure development. But overcoming infrastructural bottlenecks for small enterprises is easier said than done.

Small enterprises in India have come up in an unplanned, uncontrolled and haphazard manner. They have emerged anywhere and everywhere—closer to the location of resources as well as markets—in clusters as well as in a dispersed manner, in industrial, commercial and residential areas. A considerable majority of these clusters are based on natural and traditional skills. By and large, these clusters lack reliable and efficient infrastructural facilities such as power, road, water, transportation and communications, information and technical inputs. But the infrastructural problem is more acute in case of units that are located in a dispersed manner. How does one promote infrastructure to support small industry development?

The state governments along with industry associations should involve the private sector in the development of infrastructure in existing industrial estates and clusters and permit provision of infrastructural services on payment. Similarly, private sector investment should be encouraged for the development and management of existing as well as new industrial parks/clusters/estates (Hussain, 1997). Development of industrial parks/estates/clusters should be treated on par with infrastructure development and state governments should prepare guidelines for private investments. These steps would go a long way in strengthening the infrastructure for small industry development in India.

Further, subsequent to the recommendation of the Planning Commission's expert committee on small scale enterprises (Planning Commission, 2001), the government has now decided to cover the entire country by integrated infrastructure development (IID) schemes. This is a welcome development. But the government has not set up any time frame for its completion.

There is a need to explicitly recognise and exploit the 'innovation potential' of small enterprises. In developed countries small enterprises are promoted, among others, as the 'seed bed' of innovation (Bala Subrahmanya *et al.,* 2002). Small enterprises have the specific advantages of flexibility, concentration and internal communications for carrying out technological innovations. Technological innovations contribute to competitiveness. Even in the Indian context, a significant number of small firms do carry out technological innovations and thereby, enhance their competitiveness (Bala Subrahmanya *et al.,* 2002). Therefore, it is appropriate to incorporate schemes in the existing policy and institutional network to provide technological and financial assistance to in-house technological innovations at the district level and make it easily accessible to small enterprises.

There is a need to create R&D fund at the state level for disbursement as margin money through DICs to small industry units to encourage them to undertake formal an R&D and technological innovations. In addition, the Department of Science and Technology (DST) may allocate funds to universities and engineering institutions, which could provide institutional infrastructure for R&D or conduct R&D for small industry units at the regional level (Bala Subrahmanya *et al.,* 2002).

These schemes are not to undermine the significance of the present strategy of 'technology transfer'. It is essential to pursue with more intensity the existing strategy of technological upgradation and modernisation by involving local governments and small industry associations, particularly with a focus on small industry clusters. However, it needs to be emphasised that the technological transformation of Indian small industry is a gigantic task and that government alone cannot achieve this objective, however extensive its infrastructure may be. Therefore, the major initiative has to come from small industry itself, particularly through their associations.

The increase in the competitiveness of small industry will also be determined by the availability and quantum of finance. The demand for finance, implicit as well as explicit, from small industry will be substantial considering its size, structure, growth pattern, need for restructuring and technology development (Bala Subrahmanya, 2002a). Particularly, the investment demand for finance from small industry will increase considerably due to technology upgradation and modernisation, expansion (of efficient ones), quality improvement, R&D and technological innovations, and environment-related investments (industry-specific). To meet the growing and diversified investment demand requirements, it is essential to broaden financial infrastructure, specifically to take care of the technological transformation of small industry and lay more thrust on adequate flow of finance to the sector (Bala Subrahmanya, 2002a).

Globalisation and liberalisation need not affect Indian small industry only adversely. It would have created beneficial opportunities as well. The removal of quantitative restrictions and the reduction of import duties, particularly after the setting up of WTO in 1995, have opened up foreign markets to Indian small industry as much as the Indian market has opened up to foreign goods. Many efficient and export-oriented small firms would have gained out of this development. Such opportunities should act as an incentive to many a small firm in India to enhance their competitiveness to penetrate the global market. This could also be achieved by small firms becoming vendors or subcontractors to foreign large-scale industries. The trend is outsourcing of supplies by TNCs and they are always on the lookout for firms that could supply reliable and quality products (Sabade, 2001).

In fact, outsourcing is the major factor contributing to the growth of the Indian software industry (MoF, 2001) and business process outsourcing (BPO). After software and BPO, auto parts is being mentioned as the site of the next big outsourcing wave likely to bring in a clutch of investors looking for a low-cost, high quality production base. A number of the world's largest automobile and equipment-makers have already announced plans to source parts from Indian companies or expand their own production operations in the country, especially for export. This trend is likely to gain further momentum as a recession-hit global automotive industry struggles to cut production costs. Such opportunities should be exploited with concerted efforts in other industries as well by the government, small industries and their associations working together.

Finally, irrespective of the degree of support extended by the government and irrespective of the amount of effort put in by small industries and their associations, India is going to experience the emergence of the small industry sector, which is qualitatively superior, technologically vibrant and internationally competitive, in the next 5-10 years because the 'inefficient ones' are likely to vanish gradually. The objective of the policy makers as well as small industry associations should be to enable the sector to be vibrant and competitive without a considerable reduction in its size and thereby, enable it to make a sustainable contribution to national income, output and exports. (Bala Subrahmanya, 2009).

New Initiatives

The Small Industries Development Organisation now called Micro, Small and Medium Enterprises Development Organisation has a network of more than 3000 technically qualified personnel working through its small industries service institutes (and branch SISIs), testing centres and autonomous organisations such as the tool room, product and process development centres, etc.

The Prime Minister appointed a high level task force in 2009 to examine ways to overcome the handicaps in the growth of this sector. The task force's recommendations are now being implemented. They address the critical issues that organisations in this sector face—credit flow, improvement of skills, access to markets and raw materials, and coping with a multiplicity of regulations and inspectors. High level committees have also been set up to monitor the progress of these recommendations.

To ensure enhanced credit flow to the sector, in terms of the recommendations of the Prime Minister's Task Force on Micro, Small and Medium Enterprises (MSMEs) constituted by the Government of India, banks were advised to achieve a 20 per cent year-on-year growth in credit to MSEs; the allocation of 60 per cent of the MSE advances to the microenterprises is to be achieved in stages *viz.*, 50 per cent in the year 2010-11, 55 per cent in the year 2011-12 and 60 per cent in the year 2012-13 and achieve a 10 per cent annual growth in number of microenterprise accounts. The Reserve Bank is closely monitoring the achievement of targets by banks on a quarterly basis. The matter is followed up with the laggard banks to know their constraints and impress upon them the need to devise strategies to gear up the credit mechanism for the sector (Chakrabarty, 2012).[4]

Further, based on the recommendations of the Working Group constituted by the Reserve Bank of India to review the Credit Guarantee Scheme (CGS) of the Credit Guarantee Fund Trust for Micro and Small Enterprises (CGTMSE), the limit for collateral free loans to the MSE has been increased from the present level of Rs 5 lakh to Rs 10 lakh and it has been made mandatory for banks. The implementation of the Recommendations of the Working Group should result in enhanced usage of the guarantee scheme and facilitate increase in quality and quantity of credit to the presently included, as well as excluded, MSEs, leading eventually to sustainable inclusive growth

All SCBs have also been advised to review and put in place MSE loan policy, restructuring/rehabilitation policy and non-discretionary One Time Settlement scheme for recovery of non-performing loans duly approved by their Board of Directors (Chakrabarty, 2012).

In line with the overall target set by the Prime Minister's National Council on Skill Development, the Ministry of MSME has taken up skill development as a high priority area. The Agencies under the Ministry aim to train 4.78 lakh trainees in the year 2011-12 through its various programmes for the development of self-employment opportunities as well as wage employment opportunities in the country.

A flexible growth stimulating and artisancentric scheme named Market Development Assistance (MDA) to promote production and sales of khadi and polyvastra has been introduced from 2010-11. The scheme provides for assistance up to 20 per cent of the value of production to be shared among artisans, producing institutions, and selling institutions in the ratio 25:30:45.

The Government has tied up financial aid from the Asian Development Bank (ADB) amounting to US$150 million over a period of three years for implementing a comprehensive Khadi Reform Programme worked out in consultation with the ADB and Khadi and Village Industries Commission (KVIC). Under this reform package, it

4. Chakrabarty, K.C. (2012). "Empowering MSMEs for Financial Inclusion and Growth: Issues and Strategies", in Uma Kapila (ed.), *Two Decades of Economic Reforms*. New Delhi: Academic Foundation.

is proposed to revitalize the khadi sector with enhanced sustainability of khadi, increased incomes and employment for artisans, and artisans' welfare and to enable the KVIC to stand on its own with gradually decreasing dependence on Government grants. Initially, the programme will be initiated in 300 khadi institutions keeping the needs of regional balance, geographical spread, and inclusion of backward areas in view.

Summary and Conclusions

Small industry in India has found itself in an intensely competitive environment since 1991, thanks to globalisation, domestic economic liberalisation and dilution of sector-specific protective measures. As a result, its growth in terms of units, employment, output and exports has come down. This has resulted in a less impressive growth in its contribution to national income and exports, though not in terms of employment, in the 1990s. Lack of reliable and stable economic infrastructure, reduced growth of credit inflow and technological obsolescence, which together would have led to inferior quality and low productivity are the major bane of small industry in India.

But at the same time, international and national policy changes have thrown open new opportunities and markets for the Indian small industry. Concerted effort is needed from the government and small industry to imbibe technological dynamism. Technological upgradation and in-house technological innovations and promotion of inter-firm linkages need to be encouraged consciously and consistently. The benefits and need to go for technology development, through either technology transfer or technological innovations or inter-firm linkages should be emphasised in the light of the dimensions of global competition and its negative fallouts as well as opportunities, to small industry entrepreneurs through seminars and workshops at the local level. Financial infrastructure needs to be broadened and adequate inflow of credit to the sector be ensured taking into consideration the growing investment demand, including the requirements of technological transformation. Small industry should be allowed to come up only in designated industrial areas for better monitoring and periodic surveys through DICs which should enable policy corrections from time to time. A technologically vibrant, internationally competitive small industry should be encouraged to emerge, to make a sustainable contribution to national income, employment and exports. It is essential to take care of the sector to enable it to take care of the economy.[5]

---

5. Subrahmanya (2009). *op.cit.*

16

Public Sector in the Indian Economy

THE declared social objective of the Indian development strategy since Independence has been growth with social justice which was sought to be achieved within the democratic political framework and for which India adopted the concept of mixed economy. The expansion of the public sector was considered to be a major instrument with which the state in a mixed economy can influence the pace as well as the composition of economic activity with a view to pursuing the social objective.

The Rationale

In India, the rationale for the public sector has been explicit or implicit in all plan documents as well as policy statements, although the emphasis has changed in degrees depending upon the constraints faced and the emerging major issues of the time.

Tracing the chronological developments in this connection, we find that as far back as 1948, the Industrial Policy Resolution declared, "A dynamic national policy must... be directed to a continuous increase in production by all possible means, side by side with measures to secure its equitable distribution." For this purpose, while recognising that the "State must play a progressively active role in the development of industries," it was conceded that in the conditions then prevailing "the mechanism and the resources of the State may not permit it to function as widely as may be desirable." The First Five Year Plan that followed did not have a clear-cut strategy of development and hence, it did not contain any operational statements on the public sector.

It was in the context of the Mahalanobis strategy that the approach to the public sector got further crystallised. The long-term growth orientation in an import-substitution dominated strategy required that the domestic capacity creation be biased in the direction of producing capital goods to produce more capital goods. According to Prof. Tendulkar,[1] the distinct preference for the public sector in this strategy can be traced to the following reasons.

First, the concentration of economic power that would result from the uncontrolled operation of the market forces can be reduced through the extension in the public ownership of means of production.

Secondly, private investors may demand a higher risk premium for investment in certain industries than would be socially justified. Off-shore drilling of oil is one example in this connection.

Thirdly, the scale of investment efforts in certain heavy industries may be beyond the capital-raising capacity of the private sector e.g., steel mills, heavy electrical machinery.

Fourthly, the public sector, through the appropriate price policy for its output will generate investible surpluses for further investment in the economy.

Fifthly, by production as well as distribution of certain universal intermediate inputs like coal, steel, electricity etc., the State will be able to control the composition of private economic activity in a socially desirable direction.

Finally, the public sector would assume the role of a model employer and its employment and wage policies would have a moderating influence on the corresponding policies in the private sector.

Analysing these reasons, one finds that public sector was expected to fulfil varied and sometimes conflicting objectives. The generation of investible surplus was bound to conflict with subsidies involved in keeping the prices of certain universal intermediates at low levels as well as the public sector's role as a model employer.

In the sixties and seventies, the public sector policy has been largely guided by the Industrial Policy Resolution of 1956 which gave the public sector a strategic role in the economy. Massive investments have been made over the past four decades to build a public sector which had a commanding role in the economy. Many key sectors of the economy are today dominated by mature public enterprises that have

1. Tendulkar, S.D. "Approach to the Public Sector in the Context of an Overall Development Strategy", in Uma Kapila (ed.), *Indian Economy Since Independence* 2000-01 edition. New Delhi: Academic Foundation.

successfully expanded production, opened up new areas of technology and built up a reserve of technical competence in a number of areas.

As a result, the country's ranking in terms of industrialisation with other developing countries is quite high. India's comparative advantages such as a large pool of well-trained workforce, technical skills in manufacturing and chemical industries primarily stem from the public sector.

Over the years, the size of the public sector has increased and currently, there are 473 central PSUs including banks and insurance companies. Out of these, 104 are listed and 369 unlisted; while at the State level there are 1,160 State PSUs. It is estimated by informed financial analysts that the valuation of the central PSUs on P/E basis for the listed companies and P/B basis for the unlisted companies is now placed at $ 450-$500 billion or 40-45 per cent of the country's GDP.[2]

The public sector in India, in its broadest measure as recorded in the National Accounts Statistics (NAS), currently contributes to about a quarter of the gross domestic product (GDP) increasing from slightly less than one-tenth in 1960-61 (the earliest year with firm estimates). The gross value added of the administrative departments, broadly representing Adam Smith's "duties of the sovereign", account for 8 to 9 per cent of GDP; natural monopolies such as the railways and the postal system add another 3 to 4 per cent. But the largest share of public sector gross value added, 12 to 13 per cent of GDP, comes from the non-departmental enterprises (NDEs), producing many private goods and services, but mainly from utilities and infrastructure, owned and operated by the Central, state and local governments. NDEs are further disaggregated into: (a) financial enterprises that are part of the financial sector (including the Reserve Bank of India), and (b) the non-financial enterprises, which account for much of the growth in public sector output during the last half century.[3]

However, according to the latest CMIE data, the net profits of the Central PSUs works out to be only 2.2 per cent of their total assets. It is true that this ratio is higher for the oil companies such as ONGC and

2. Kelkar, Vijay (2010). "On Strategies of Disinvestment and Privatisation", (26th Sir Purshotamdas Thakurdas Memorial Lecture, January 29, Mumbai) in Uma Kapila (ed.), *Indian Economy Since Independence* (24th edition). New Delhi: Academic Foundation.
3. Nagaraj, R. (2008). "Public Sector Performance since 1950", in K.L. Krishna and Uma Kapila (eds.), *Readings in Indian Agriculture and Industry*. New Delhi: Academic Foundation.

Oil India, but in general, the net return on the capital employed in PSUs seems to be lower than for the India's private corporate sector. If one includes the State level PSUs, then the private corporate sector would show significantly higher returns on the capital employed. While the public sector or the state-led entrepreneurship played an important role in triggering India's industrialisation, our evolving development needs, comparatively less than satisfactory performance of the public sector enterprises, the maturing of our private sector, a much larger social base now available for expanding entrepreneurship and the growing institutional capabilities to enforce competition policies would suggest that the time has come to review the role of public sector, particularly the structural composition of the portfolio of public sector or in other words, of the country's "public capital assets".[4]

Performance of Central Public Sector Undertakings

There were altogether 260 CPSEs under the administrative control of various ministries/departments as on 31 March 2012. Out of these, 225 were in operation and 35 were under construction. The share of industrial CPSEs in the total investment in CPSEs in terms of gross block, stood at 77.46 percent during the year. The latest complete results are available for the year 2011-12. CPSEs in the mining sector registered the highest increase in net profit (29.45 per cent) in 2011-2012. CPSEs in manufacturing sector recorded a decline of 22.65 per cent in net profit in 2011-12 despite 27.73 per cent increase in their turnover. The electricity sector recorded growth of 16 per cent in turnover and 13.42 per cent in profit (*Economic Survey 2012-13*).[5]

Output and Capital Formation

According to Nagaraj,[6] with the acceleration of the domestic output growth rate after 1980-81, the public sector has contributed to the additional output growth in equal measure (Nagaraj, 1991). In spite of industrial deregulation and growing import competition, the public sector has broadly maintained its share in domestic output in producing private goods and services, and its composition has also remained roughly the same.

4. Kelkar (2010). *op.cit.*
5. Govt. of India (2013). *Economic Survey 2012-13.*
6. Nagaraj (2008). *op.cit.*

TABLE – 16.1

Macro View of Central Public Sector Enterprises

(Rs. Crore)

	2001-02	*2002-03*	*2003-04*	*2004-05*	*2005-06*	*April-Sept. 2005*	*April-Sept. 2006*
Number of operating CPSEs	231	226	230	227	225		
Profit before interest, tax, and EP (PBITEP)	63190	72539	95039	108420	106533	64962	73169
Capital employed	289934	417160	452336	504407	581250		
Turnover	478731	572833	630704	744307	832584	377370	468221
Net profit	25978	32344	52985	64963	70288	27235	35465
Net profit as % of turnover	5.4	5.6	8.4	8.7	8.4	7.2	7.6
Profit of profit-making CPSEs	36432	43316	61606	74433	76240		
Loss of loss-incurring CPSEs	10454	10972	8522	9356	5952		
Profit-making CPSEs (nos.)	120	119	139	138	157		
Loss-incurring CPSEs (nos.)	109	105	89	79	58		

Source : Public Enterprise Survey 2005–06 and Mid-Year Review of CPSEs for 2006–07, Department of Public Enterprises (DPE).
Government of India, *Eleventh Five Year Plan*, Planning Commission.

In contrast, however, the public investment ratio, after peaking at 12.5 per cent of GDPfc in 1986-87 nearly halved to 6.4 per cent by 2001-02, taking the ratio back to the level where it was in the mid-1950s. Clearly, what took the "big planners" three decades to accomplish, the "reformers" undid in less than two decades!

Whether the fall in the share of public investment by design (market-oriented reforms), or by default (the fiscal imbalance) is a moot point. But, undisputedly, the public sector has managed to deliver roughly an unchanging share of the accelerating domestic output for nearly 20 years, even when its investment share was halved—an impressive record of productivity growth by any yardstick, at least so far. Corroborating the finding, also there is a steady decline in the public sector's average capital output ratio (ACOR) in constant prices, from 7.0 in 1981-82 to about 4.4 in 2001-02. This holds true for most (1-digit) sectors of the economy as well (EPWRF, 2004).

It is arguable that the decline in ACOR could mean a shift in public investment to less capital-intensive activities. But this is not the case. In fact, the share of infrastructure (sum of mining, electricity, gas and water, and transport and communication) in public sector gross capital formation—representing capital-intensive industries—has increased from 33.3 per cent in 1973-74 to over 53.5 per cent in 2001-02; the manufacturing sector's share has declined. Infrastructure's share in public sector output narrowly fluctuated around 30 per cent; the manufacturing sector's share has tumbled from 23.7 in 1974-75 to 5.5 per cent in 2001-02. Thus, there is little basis to suggest a shift in public investment into less capital-intensive sectors; on the contrary, the investment composition has moved in the desired direction of infrastructure that is capital-intensive, away from (much contested) manufacturing.

Thus, the public sector has shown remarkable progress that has gone virtually unnoticed. What could account for the improvement? It suggests a decline in what Harvey Leibenstein called X-inefficiency (in production and in organisation), and a deceleration in investment and employment. There is evidence of both (Nagaraj, 2008).

Fall in Public Sector Employment Growth

A bloated workforce, often employed on non-economic considerations, is widely cited as a source of public sector inefficiency. But the evidence suggests that despite such pressures, the growth rate in public employment has declined drastically: from about 6 per cent per year in the mid-1970s to a negative 1 per cent in 2002-03 in public sector enterprises owned and managed by the Central government (central PSEs, for short), in quasi public sector, and in the public sector as a whole as well. Without denying the need for further rationalisation of the workforce, what can certainly be claimed is that public sector employment growth has got drastically reduced in spite of the compulsions to the contrary, contributing to the improved productivity.

Central PSEs' Profitability

What is the correct measure of profitability? It depends upon the purpose. From the view point of a private individual, the ratio of net profits to equity capital (or net worth) may be appropriate, but it may be unsuitable to measure a PSE's contribution to the economy, for many reasons. One, PSEs usually have a high depreciation cost since they have to invest not only in plant and machinery, but also on social overhead capital, for which budgetary provisions are made. Second, a PSE's capital structure is not aimed to maximise return on shareholders' investment, but provision of goods and services that the market has not (or inadequately) succeeded in supplying—the argument of "missing market". Third, very often PSEs start with a high proportion of debt as government expects a certain interest on its loans. When the enterprise commences production it is often saddled with a high debt-equity ratio, which is usually renegotiated to make the enterprise commercially viable. Finally, for the economy, what matters is not the capital structure but return on total capital employed. Thus, gross profit to total capital employed is a better measure of public sector profitability, which we have used below (Nagaraj, 2008).

Thus measured, according to Nagaraj, profitability of the central PSEs has increased from around 8 per cent in the mid-1970s to 21 per cent in 2003-04—a respectable figure by any reasonable reckoning. Such rosy estimates may conceal the effect of high mark-up, cost-based administered pricing in the performance of petroleum companies. Surely, net of the petroleum sector, the profitability is lower, but with an unmistakable rising trend, at 18 per cent return on gross capital employed in 2003-04.

Thus, the central PSEs as a source of NDNFEs' poor financial position is ruled out, leaving us mainly with the utilities and infrastructure services at the state level—that is, state electricity boards (SEBs) and road transport corporations (RTCs). In principle, public irrigation would belong to this category, as it accounts for a sizeable share of plan expenditure in most states.

According to Nagaraj, the real culprit of poor public sector saving is not the central PSEs (that have been the subject of much of reforms) but inadequate pricing of the utilities and infrastructure services, and lack of recovery of user charges for the services rendered. Perhaps a telling evidence of the problem, in the aggregate, is the movement of the public sector price deflator, relative to the GDP deflator since 1960-61. Over the last 40 years, public sector prices never exceeded the overall price level, and in 2003-04 the relative price stood just 83 per cent of what it was in 1960-61. In other words, public sector prices have risen since 1951 at a slower rate than the overall prices in the economy over the long-run, adversely affecting its financial position. However, as these are decreasing cost industries, their prices can be expected to rise relatively slowly. But they are also capital-intensive industries, where the principle of access to these services on social considerations raises the cost of provision. Moreover, the public sector, being an instrument of public policy is often made to shoulder many social responsibilities, increasing its expenditure, which needs to be recovered from reasonably pricing the output or from the budget. With a growing fiscal imbalance, reasonable pricing is the only avenue to compensate for the services rendered.

The main findings according to Nagaraj are:

(1) There is a distinct improvement in the efficiency of resource use in the public sector in the aggregate since the second half of the 1980s, and a corresponding fall in the average capital-output ratio.

(2) Improvement in physical efficiency, in part, may reflect a fall in public sector employment growth (however, measured).

(3) Thermal power plants in India that account for the bulk of electricity generation (and a sizeable share of public investment) show an uninterrupted rise in efficiency.

(4) These trends are, however, inadequately reflected in public sector financial performance, despite a sustained improvement in profitability of the central PSEs (even excluding the petroleum enterprises).

(5) Thus, the source of financial distress is the utilities and infrastructure services, like the SEBs, RTCs and the railways.

(6) The SEBs' revenue-cost ratio deteriorated since the 1990s; the same is true of the railways and the RTCs.

(7) That inadequate pricing of the output public sector utilities is the main reason for their deteriorating financial position is illustrated by a 17 percentage point fall in the public sector price deflator output relative to the GDP deflator over the last 40 years since 1960-61.

Reasons and Implications

What accounts for the changes in the performance of the public sector? Arguably, the market-oriented reforms since the 1980s could have induced the desired effect. But, such an explanation would seem too facile to be taken seriously, in the absence of a casual explanation between the reforms and the observed improvement (Nagaraj, 2008).

But probably what has perhaps been happening is: (i) a hardening of the budget constraint, accompanied by a greater managerial autonomy, and (ii) a growing competition in the product market. In NDNFEs, between 1960-61 and 2002-03, government's budgetary support (sum of equity capital and loans) declined, and the share of internal resources (depreciation and net saving) rose, both as a proportion of gross fixed capital formation. In 1963-64, budgetary support was 97.6 per cent of fixed capital formation, which came down to as little as 16.9 per cent in 1996-97; the share of internal resource went up from 11.2 per cent in 1960-61 to 73 per cent in 2002-03. Changes in market conditions and financial governance could have ensured greater accountability and cost consciousness. But these advantages could not get translated into improved financial results, as pricing and recovery of user charges continued to remain a matter of public policy. The problems of inadequate electricity pricing, incomplete metering of power usage and recovery of user charges are too well known to be recounted here.

According to Nagaraj, the real problem is not the lack of efficiency in production, but one of pricing and collection of user charges. Hence, unless these problems are squarely addressed, public sector finances are unlikely to shape up.

Public Sector and 1991 Industrial Policy

To improve the performance of the public sector, the Government of India announced in July 1991 the new Industrial Policy which contained the following decisions pertaining to the public sector.

(i) Portfolio of public sector investments will be reviewed with a view to focus the public sector on strategic, hi-tech and essential infrastructure. Whereas some reservation for the public sector is being retained, there would be no bar for area of exclusivity to be opened up to the private sector selectively. Similarly, the public sector will be allowed entry in areas not reserved for it.

(ii) Public enterprises which are chronically sick and which are unlikely to be turned around will, for the formulation of revival/rehabilitation schemes, be referred to the Board for Industrial and Financial Reconstruction (BIFR), or other similar high level institutions created for the purpose. A social security mechanism will be created to protect the interests of workers likely to be affected by such rehabilitation packages.

(iii) In order to raise resources and encourage wider public participation, a part of the government's share-holding in the public sector would be offered to mutual funds, financial institutions, general public and workers.

(iv) Boards of public sector companies would be made more professional and given greater powers.

(v) There will be a greater thrust on performance improvement through the Memoranda of Understanding (MoU) system through which managements would be granted greater autonomy and will be held accountable. Technical expertise on the part of the Government would be upgraded to make MoU negotiations and implementation more effective.

The Industrial Policy 1991 provides a new approach to public enterprises. The new policy emphasises that measures must be taken to make these enterprises more growth oriented and technically dynamic. According to the New Industrial Policy, the priority areas for growth of public enterprises in the future will be the following: Essential infrastructure goods and services; exploration and exploitation of oil and mineral resources; technology development and building of manufacturing capabilities in areas which are crucial in the long-term development of the economy and where private sector investment is inadequate; manufacture of products where strategic considerations predominate such as defence equipment.

Government will strengthen those public enterprises which fall in the reserved areas of operation or are in high priority areas or are generating good or reasonable profits. Such enterprises will be provided a much greater degree of management autonomy through the system of memoranda of understanding.

Policies toward CPSEs and their Implementation

In accordance with the mandate in the NCMP, the two main elements of the GoI policy have been devolution of full managerial and commercial autonomy to successful, profit-making companies and modernisation and restructuring of sick PSUs (as well as sell-off or closure of chronically sick CPSEs).

Policy developments for CPSEs mainly relate to increased delegation of financial and operational powers and revival of CPSEs. With a view to delegating enhanced financial and operational powers to CPSEs, the government introduced the Navratna Scheme in July

1997. In December 2010, the Government introduced the Maharatna Scheme enhancing financial delegation to CPSEs. Coal India Limited and Neyveli Lignite Corporation Limited were conferred Maharatna and Navratna status respectively in 2011 and the number of CPSEs under these categories increased to 5 and 16 respectively. In December 2004, the government established a Board for Reconstruction of Public Sector Enterprises (BRPSE) to advise on revival/restructuring of sick and loss-making CPSEs. The BRPSE has made recommendations in respect of 62 CPSEs until 31 October 2011. The government, in turn, has approved proposals for revival of 43 CPSEs and closure of two. The total assistance approved by the government in this regard up to 31 October 2011 is Rs. 25,104 crore (Rs. 3,873.86 crore as cash assistance and Rs. 21,230.67 crore as non-cash assistance). Out of the 43 CPSEs approved for revival by the government, 13 turnaround CPSEs have posted profit before tax (PBT) consecutively for three or more years (*Economic Survey 2011-12*).

Privatisation

There has been a significant move towards privatisation in economies across the globe. Several industrial countries have embraced it as have most of the transition economies for East Europe and large parts of the developing world. In India, privatisation or disinvestment of the public sector emerged as a major public policy option after the country embarked on a process of economic reforms in 1991.

Privatisation may be broadly defined as the transfer of various activities from the public to the private sphere. Specifically, it could mean the sale by government or state-owned enterprises (SOEs) to private economic agents. It could refer to a sale that is effected in full or in part. It can also mean a partnership between the public and private sectors through a transfer of responsibilities from the public to private sector. In terms of broad political economy, it could also simply mean a shrinking of the welfare state (Nayak, 2012).[7]

Privatisation: Indian Experience since 1991

In 1991, when the government embarked on a comprehensive process of economic reform and liberalisation, the public sector in India accounted for more than one-fifth of the country's GDP. Since a large number of public-sector enterprises (PSEs) regularly showed negative

7. Nayak, Pulin (2012). "Privatisation", in Kaushik Basu and Annemie Maertens (ed.), *The Oxford Companion to Economics in India*. Vol. II, *op.cit*.

profit margins the government was keen on a programme of privatisation, calling it disinvestment instead.

In the interim budget of 1991-92, the government took a policy decision to disinvest up to 20 per cent of the equity in selected PSUs in favour of mutual funds and financial or investment institutions in the public sector. The disinvestment, which was to broad base the equity, was to improve management and enhance the availability of resources for these enterprises. The Rangarajan Committee report on the Disinvestment of Shares in PSEs in April 1993 emphasised the need for substantial disinvestment, and recommended that the percentage of equity to be divested could go up to 49 per cent for industries especially reserved for the public sector. It recommended that in exceptional cases, such as enterprises that had a dominant market share or where separate identity had to be maintained for strategic reasons, the target public ownership level could be kept at 26 per cent, that is disinvestment could take place to the tune of 74 per cent. In all other cases, it recommended 100 per cent divestment of the government stake. Holding of 51 per cent or more equity by the government was recommended only for six scheduled industries, namely: (i) coal and lignite, (ii) mineral oils, (iii) arms, ammunitions, and defence equipment, (iv) atomic energy, (v) radioactive minerals, and (vi) railway transport.

In 1996, the government set up the Disinvestment Commission with a view to formulate procedures so that any decision to disinvest would be taken and implemented in a transparent manner. The revenues generated from such disinvestment were to be allocated for education and health and for creating a fund to strengthen PSEs. By August 1999, the Disinvestment Commission made recommendations on 58 PSEs. The recommendations indicated a shift from public offerings to strategic/trade sales, with transfer of management. The Commission also observed that the essence of a long-term disinvestment strategy should be not only to enhance budgetary receipts, but also to minimise budgetary support to unprofitable units while ensuring their long-term viability. By 1998, government was of the view that 'in the generality of cases its shareholding in PSEs will be brought down to 26 per cent'. In PSEs involving strategic considerations, namely arms and ammunitions, atomic energy and railway transport, government was to retain majority voting.

By 2000-01, the government's policy regarding privatisation and public-sector restructuring comprises the following considerations: restructure and revive potentially viable PSEs, close down PSEs that cannot be revived, bring down government equity in all strategic PSEs to 20 per cent or lower, if necessary, and fully protect the interests of workers. The entire receipt from disinvestments and privatisation was to be used for meeting expenditure in social sectors, restructuring of PSEs and meeting public debt.

The Ministry of Disinvestment was converted into a Department under the Ministry of Finance with effect from 27 May 2004 after the UPA (United Progressive Alliance) government headed by Dr. Manmohan Singh as Prime Minister assumed office. From this point on, the disinvestment programme had to be in conformity with the National Common Minimum Programme. All privatisations were from now on to be considered on a transparent and consultative case-by-case basis. It was made explicit that the UPA would retain the existing *navaratna* companies, which include the BHEL (Bharat Heavy Electricals Limited), in the public sector and that these will be permitted to raise resources from the capital market. The government constituted a 'National Investment Fund' in January 2005 into which the realisation from sale of minority shareholding of the government in profitable PSEs would be channelised. This fund would be maintained outside the Consolidated Fund of India and the income from this Fund would be used for the following purposes: (i) invest in social sector projects that promote education, health care and employment and (ii) capital investment in selected profitable and revivable PSEs that yield adequate returns, in order to enlarge their capital base to finance expansion or diversification (Nayak, 2012).[8]

According to Kelkar[9] disinvestment is an area of economic policy with multiple objectives. The most important objective should be that of increasing the efficiency with which the labour and capital, that is in existing PSUs, is converted into GDP. In addition, other auxiliary goals include enhancing investment in the country, creating new traditions of corporate governance catering to consumer interests by maximising competition in product markets, and reducing the stock of public debt. An important positive impact of disinvestment upon our fiscal problems would flow through a higher GDP growth.

Policies on disinvestment must be particularly mindful of its ramifications to the political economy. The disinvestment process can lead to dispersed share ownership amongst millions of households. This

8. Ibid.
9. Kelkar (2010). *op.cit.*

would disperse wealth in the country. It would help create a middle-class constituency which has a stake in the profits of PSUs and (more generally) in the economic well-being of the country. This could have larger ramifications for the reforms programme. The design of disinvestment policy needs to cater to these multiple goals. In particular, a narrow focus upon maximising proceeds is unlikely to yield sound policies on disinvestment.

Regarding the policy for deployment of resources generated through disinvestment/privatisation which is currently channelised from the National Investment Fund, Kelkar argues that this is a restrictive policy and we should liberalise this fully by allowing the government to use these resources as a part of the budgetary resources to create new public capital assets—whether in the form of better urban infrastructure by providing capital grants to our cities or for revamping the country's energy base through an ambitious solar energy programme or the expansion of rural road network or for recharging the country's depleting water bodies and cleaning of rivers. This would require the Union government sharing the proceeds from disinvestment or privatisation with the State governments on a systematic basis on the lines of the Finance Commission's devolution formula for the sharing of union taxes with the States.

For coming decades, water, environment and urban infrastructure are going to be the key binding constraints on India's growth ambition. To remove these binding constraints, we will require large investments to accelerate the country's march towards high quality growth. Disinvestment and privatisation policy has now assumed strategic importance in our country.

According to Kelkar (2010), "India's future lies in building a new institutional architecture with government as regulator and with the private sector doing investment. If we think of the next 25 years, a very substantial portion of the investment in all regulated industries in India is going to come from the private sector. It makes more sense for the government to reorganise itself, shifting into the role of the umpire and away from the role of the player.

We need a bold and imaginative programme for disinvestment and privatisation calling for restructuring of the portfolio of the country's "public capital assets". It does not mean a retreat of the State but essentially a re-engineering of its portfolio of public capital assets. This will help our country meet the challenges of the first half of the 21st century just like our PSUs helped the country in the second half of the 20th century to overcome our industrial backwardness (Kelkar, 2010).[10]

In conclusion, we may quote Minhas (1991)[11] which is very relevant even today.

"The choice between the public sector enterprises and private firms is not a simple either/or question. While there may be eminently good reasons for promoting public sector production under certain circumstances, nevertheless there is no basis whatever for the doctrine of the so-called commanding heights. The Indian economy is struggling in the deep swamps of inefficiency. Its deliverance from this inefficiency trap can be vastly facilitated if both the public sector and private firms are exposed more and more to global competition and the arbitrary bureaucratic controls for the regulation of entry and freedom of exit of firms are substantially rolled back."

There is certainly no clear superiority of private *vis-à-vis* public ownership from the standpoint of economic theory. More than ownership, it would seem that the degree of competition and the regulatory environment are more relevant to productive efficiency. The empirical evidence presents a mixed picture. As the world environment gets more competitive, it would be necessary to put the sizeable assets of the PSEs in countries like India to more productive use. Ultimately, it is this consideration that should be of relevance rather than the simplistic presumption that the public sector is necessarily inefficient or that privatisation is an all-purpose panacea (Nayak, 2012).[12]

---

10. Kelkar, Vijay (2010). *op.cit.*
11. Minhas, B.S. "Public *versus* Private Sector: Neglect of Lessons of Economics in Indian Policy Formulation", in Uma Kapila (ed.), *Indian Economy Since Independence*, 19th edition, 2008-09 (Ch. 18), New Delhi: Academic Foundation.
12. Nayak, Pulin B. (2012). *op.cit.*

17

Services in the Indian Growth Process

India stands out for the size and dynamism of its services sector. The contribution of the services sector to the Indian economy has been manifold: a 55.2 per cent share in gross domestic product (GDP), growing by 10 per cent annually, contributing to about a quarter of total employment, accounting for a high share in foreign direct investment (FDI) inflows and over one-third of total exports, and recording very fast (27.4 per cent) export growth through the first half of 2010-11 (*Economic Survey 2010-11*).

THE services sector covers a wide range of activities from the most sophisticated information technology (IT) to simple services provided by the unorganized sector, such as the services of the barber and plumber. National Accounts classification of the services sector incorporates trade, hotels, and restaurants; transport, storage, and communication; financing, insurance, real estate, and business services; and community, social, and personal services. In World Trade Organization (WTO) and Reserve Bank of India (RBI) classifications, construction is also included.The phenomenal expansion of services worldwide led to services being regarded as an engine of growth and even as a necessary concomitant of economic growth. Development economics suggests that development is a three-stage process. The dominance of the services sector in the growth process is usually associated with the third stage of growth. During the 1980s and 1990s, services accounted for a share of about 70 per cent of GDP in industrialised countries and about 50 per cent in developing countries.

In India growth of services picked up in the 1980s, and accelerated in the 1990s, when it averaged 7.5 per cent per annum, thus providing an impetus to industry and agriculture, which grew on average by 5.8

per cent and 3.1 per cent respectively. Growth in the services sector has also been less cyclical and more stable than the growth of industry and agriculture (in the sense of having the smallest coefficient of variation).

Importance of the Services Sector for India

The importance of the services sector can be gauged by looking at its contributions to different aspects of the economy.

Services GDP

The share of services in India's GDP at factor cost (at current prices) increased from 33.5 per cent in 1950-51 to 55.1 per cent in 2010-2011 and to 56.3 per cent in 2011-12 as per Advance Estimates (AE). If construction is also included, the service sector's share increases to 63.3 per cent in 2010-11 and 64.4 per cent in 2011-12.

The acceleration in the overall growth rate (compound annual growth rate [CAGR]) of the Indian economy from 5.7 per cent in the 1990s to 8.6 per cent during the period 2004-05 to 2009-10 was to a large measure due to the acceleration of the growth rate (CAGR) in the services sector from 7.5 per cent in the 1990s to 10.3 per cent in 2004-05 to 2009-10. The services sector growth was significantly faster than the 6.6 per cent for the combined agriculture and industry sectors annual output growth during the same period. In 2009-10, services growth was 10.1 per cent and in 2010-11 it was 9.6 per cent (AE). India's services GDP growth has been continuously above overall GDP growth, pulling up the latter since 1997-98.

Services Employment in India

Although the primary sector (agriculture mainly) is the dominant employer followed by the services sector, the share of services has been increasing over the years while that of primary sector has been decreasing. Between 1993-94 to 2004-05, there was a sharp fall in the share of the primary sector in employment. The consequent rise in share of employment of the other two sectors was almost equally divided between the secondary and tertiary sectors. In 2007-08 compared to 2004-05, though the trend was similar, the fall in employment in primary sector was less (at -1.1 per cent) with a small commensurate rise in employment in the other two sectors, which was again almost equally divided between the other two sectors (Table 17.1)

TABLE – 17.1

Share of Broad Sectors in Employment (UPSS)

Sectors	*Shares*			*Change in shares*		
	1993-94	*2004-05*	*2007-08*	*2004-05 over 1993-94*	*2007-08 over 2004-05*	*2007-08 over 1993-94*
Primary	64.5	57.0	55.9	-7.5	-1.1	-8.6
Secondary	14.3	18.2	18.7	3.9	0.5	4.4
Tertiary	21.2	24.8	25.4	3.6	0.6	4.2

Source: *Economic Survey 2010-11.*

A notable feature of the structural transformation of the services sector has been the growth of skill intensive and high value added sectors, i.e., software, communication and financial services. The rapid growth of services can be attributed, *inter alia*, to the advent of information technology (IT) and the knowledge economy. This has enhanced the growth of the high productivity segment of the services sector as well as a variety of service activities involving low productivity activities catering to a large mass of people. The phenomenal growth of low skilled service activities has occurred due to reduced opportunities in the manufacturing sector, particularly in the unorganised sectors.

Some of the activities in the services sector are multidimensional, being part of industry as well as services, such as information technology and construction. Service statistics in most countries including India provide information on value-addition of various activities of business services, hotels, trade, financial services, etc. For an empirical analysis, sub-sectors including trade, transport and communication, financing, insurance, real estate and business services can be categorised as producer services with hotels and restaurants and other services as consumer services. Government services comprise public administration and defence services. During 1999-2000, producer services accounted for about 70 per cent of the total services followed by consumer services (17 per cent) and government services (13 per cent). The high share of producer services reflects the strong inter-linkages between services and goods producing sectors of the economy.

Even though India has experienced profound changes in output shares, the same is not true for employment shares (Table 17.2). A striking feature of India's development is that in contrast to the substantial decline in the share of agriculture in GDP, there has been rather little change in the share of employment in agriculture.

India's relatively jobless service sector growth is unlike the experience of other countries, where the service sector has also tended to gain a larger share of employment over time. When compared with other countries India has an exceptionally low share of services employment.

TABLE – 17.2

India, Sectoral Shares in GDP, 1950-2006
(Per cent of GDP)

	Agriculture	*Industry*	*Services*	
1950	58	15	28	
1980	38	24	38	Stage I
1990	33	27	41	
2000	24	27	49	Stage II
2003-04	22	26	53	
2004-05(P)	20	26	54	
2005-6(Q)	20	26	54	
2006-07(R)	19	27	55	

Source : Central Statistical Organisation.

Rapid growth of the service sector is not unique to India. The existing literature shows that as an economy matures the share of services in output increases consistently. To begin with, the increase occurs along with an increase in the share of industry. Thereafter, the service share grows more rapidly, accompanied by a stagnant or declining share of the industrial sector. Cross-country experience suggests that the first stage occurs until the country reaches lower middle income status, while the second stage commences once it becomes an upper middle income country.

Growth and Sectoral Shares, Cross Country Evidence and Indian Experience

The evolution of sectoral shares in output, consumption and employment as economies growth has been studied by economists for well over fifty years. During the 1950s and 1960s, research by Kuznets and Chenery suggested that development would be associated with a sharp decline in the proportion of GDP generated by the primary sector, counterbalanced by a significant increase in industry, and by a more modest increase in the service sector. Sectoral shares in employment were predicted to follow a similar pattern.

With the benefit of more data on development than was available to Kuznets and Chenery, recent literature has tended to emphasise the growing importance of service sector activity (Inman 1985, Kongsamut, Rebelo and Xie, 2001). For example, Kongsamut *et al.* (2001) analyse a sample of 123 countries for 1970-1989 and show that rising per-capita GDP is associated with an increase in services and a decline in agriculture both in terms of share in GDP and employment. In other words, the sectoral share given up by agriculture as the economy matures goes more to the services sector and less to industry than the Kuznets-Chenery work had suggested. The modern view is that as an economy matures, the share of services (in output, consumption, and employment) grows along with a decline in agriculture. By contrast, the share of industry first increases modestly, and then stabilises or declines (Gordon and Gupta, 2003).

Such a pattern of growth is visible in the cross-country data on shares in GDP (Table 17.3). These data suggest two stages of development. In the first, both industry and services shares increase as countries move from low income to lower middle income status, while in the second, the share of industry declines and that of services increases as the economy moves to upper middle and higher income levels.

TABLE – 17.3

Sectoral Shares in GDP in 2001, Global Averages (Per cent of GDP)

	Agriculture	*Industry*	*Services*	
Low income	24	32	45	Stage I
Lower middle income	12	40	48	
Upper middle income	7	33	60	Stage II
High income	2	29	70	

Source : World Bank's WDI, 2003, Table 4.2. Definition: Low income: per capita GDP<$745; Lower middle-$746-2975; Upper middle-$2976-9205; and high->$9206.

How does the Indian experience fit in with this pattern? In the four decade period, 1950-1990, agriculture's share in GDP declined by about

25 percentage points, while industry and services gained equally. The share of industry has stabilised since 1990, and the entire subsequent decline in the share of agriculture has been picked up by the services sector. Thus, while over the four decades, 1950-1990, the services sector gained a 13 per cent share, the gain in the 1990s alone was 8 percentage points. Consequently, at current levels, India's services share of GDP is higher than the average for other low income countries.

Services GDP: International Comparison

Among the top 12 countries with highest overall GDP in 2010, India ranks 8 and 11 in overall GDP and services GDP respectively. While countries like the UK, USA, and France have the highest share of services in GDP at above 78 per cent, India's share of 57 per cent is much above that of China at 41.8 per cent. In 2010 compared to 2001, India is the topmost country in terms of increase in its services share in GDP (7 percentage points) followed by Spain and Canada (5.3 percentage points each), the UK (4.5 percentage points), and Italy (3.2 percentage points). In terms of compound annual growth rate (CAGR) for the period 2001-2010, China at 11.3 per cent and India at 9.4 per cent show very high services sector growth. Russia at 5.5 per cent and Brazil at 4.0 per cent are a distant third and fourth respectively. While India's growth rate of the services sector at 10.1 per cent in 2009 was higher than that of China at 9.6 per cent, in 2010 it has decelerated to 7.7 per cent while China's has remained constant (Table 17.4). All this highlights the prominence of the services sector for India. Despite the higher share of services in India's GDP and China's dominance in manufacturing over services, the hard fact, however, is that in terms of absolute value of services GDP and also in terms of growth of services, China is still ahead of India in 2010.

State-wise Comparison of Services

A comparison of the share of services in the gross state domestic product (GSDP) of different states and union territories (UTs) in 2009-2010 shows that the services sector is the dominant sector in most states of India. States and UTs such as Tripura, Nagaland, West Bengal, Mizoram, Maharashtra, Bihar, Tamil Nadu, Kerala, Delhi, and Chandigarh have higher than all-India shares. Chandigarh with an 86 per cent share and Delhi with 81.8 per cent top the list. Other than Chhattisgarh (34.8 per cent) and Himachal Pradesh (39.6 per cent), services in all other states individually hold a share of more than 40 per cent in the GSDP. Thus, the services revolution in India seems to

TABLE – 17.4

Performance in Services Growth of Top 12 Countries

	Country	Rank		Overall GDP (US$ billion)		Share of Services (% of GDP)			Services Growth Rate (%)			
		Overall GDP	*Services GDP*	*At Current Prices 2010*	*At Constant Prices 2010*	*2001*	*2009*	*2010*	*2001*	*2009*	*2010*	*CAGR 2001-10*
1	US	1	1	14447.1	13017.0	77.0	79.0	78.2	2.9	-1.4	1.2	1.8
2	Japan	2	2	5458.9	4578.5	69.8	71.7	70.0	2.0	-4.8	2.9	0.6
3	China	3	3	5739.4	3883.5	39.8	42.1	41.8	10.3	9.6	9.6	11.3
4	Germany	4	4	3280.3	2945.8	69.7	73.7	72.5	2.1	-1.6	2.3	1.4
5	France	6	5	2559.8	2208.6	76.5	78.9	78.1	1.7	-1.1	0.2	1.4
6	UK	5	6	2253.6	2330.0	73.9	78.8	78.4	3.5	-3.2	1.1	2.0
7	Italy	7	7	2051.3	1744.0	70.1	73.6	73.3	2.3	-2.9	1.2	0.6
8	Brazil	11	8	2089.0	1092.6	65.3	67.6	66.8	1.8	3.0	4.8	4.0
9	Spain	10	10	1407.3	1180.7	65.7	70.5	71.0	3.4	-1.0	0.7	2.7
10	Canada	9	9	1577.0	1203.9	64.9	70.7	70.2	3.6	0.1	2.5	2.8
11	India	8	11	1722.3	1251.6	50.0	56.5	57.0	7.5	10.1	7.7	9.4
12	Russia	12	12	1479.8	905.2	63.3	62.0	61.5	3.2	-5.6	2.9	5.5
	World	–	–	63064.0	51040.5	68.1	68.7	67.8	2.9	-0.9	2.5	2.6

Note : Rank is based on current prices.
Growth rates are based on constant prices (US$).
CAGR is estimated for 2001-10.
Construction sector is excluded in services GDP.

Source: UN National Accounts Statistics accessed on 8 February 2012; *Economic Survey 2011-12.*

be becoming more broad based rather than being concentrated in only a few States.

Important Services for India

Some services have been particularly important for this improving performance in India. Software is one sector in which India has achieved a remarkable global brand identity. Tourism- and travel-related services and transport services are also major items in India's services. Besides these, the potential and growing services include many professional services, infrastructure-related services, and financial services.

CSO's classification of the services sector falls under four broad categories, namely a) trade, hotels, and restaurants; b) transport, storage, and communication; c) financing, insurance, real estate, and business services; and d) community, social, and personal services. Among these, financing, insurance, real estate, and business services; and trade, hotels and restaurants are the largest groups accounting for 16.7 per cent and 16.3 per cent respectively of the national GDP in 2009-10. The community, social, and personal services category accounts for a 14.4 per cent share, while transport, storage, and communication accounts for a 7.8 per cent share. Construction, which is a borderline services inclusion, has a share of 8.2 per cent.

Which Services have Grown Rapidly?

The two fast-growing broad services categories are: a) financing, insurance, real estate and business services; and b) transport, storage, and communication. The latter overtook the former in 2009-10 with a high growth of 15 per cent. A third category, growth of trade, hotels, and restaurants, slowed in 2008-09 and has recovered moderately in 2009-10. The fourth category, community, social, and personal services, saw a sudden jump in 2008-09 to overtake the growth of all other categories, reflecting the high growth in public administration and defence. This category has continued to grow rapidly in 2009-10, despite a slowdown in growth in public administration and defence (with the commitments for pay arrears under the new revised scale for Government employees coming down), due to the offsetting rise in growth of other services reflecting the fiscal stimulus to social sector activities. Among the subcategories, in 2008-09, double-digit growth was registered by communication (25.8 per cent), public administration, and defence (20.2 per cent), banking and insurance (14 per cent) and storage (10.5 per cent). Negative growth was registered only by hotels and restaurants (-3.1 per cent). Among business services, the two important categories are computer-related services and the category consisting of many services like R&D services, market research, business and management consultancy, architectural engineering, and advertising, with shares of 3.26 per cent and 0.88 per cent respectively in the GDP. While computerrelated services, which grew by 21.2 per cent in 2008-09, registered a moderate growth of 5.2 per cent in 2009-2010 due to the global crisis, R&D services registered good growth of 19.6 per cent and 19.9 per cent in 2008-09 and 2009-10 respectively. Among other services, the two important ones in terms of share of GDP are education and medical health, with the former growing at 13.9 per cent and the latter at 5.3 per cent in 2009-10. All other services are of minor importance in India's GDP. While total services including construction grew by 9.7 per cent, total services excluding construction grew by 10.1 per cent in 2009-10. In 2010-11(AE), they grew by 9.4 per cent and 9.6 per cent respectively.

A comparison of the different indicators related to different services in India shows good performance in services like telecom, aviation, and railways.

Factors Underlying the Services Growth

What are the factors behind the dynamism of the services sector in India. One explanation suggested in the literature for fast growth in services is that the income elasticity of demand for services is greater than one. Hence, the final demand for services grows faster than the demand for goods and commodities as income rises.

A rising share of services in GDP is regarded as an outcome of higher income elasticity of demand for services. The empirical studies have shown that the income elasticity of demand for services could be greater than or equal to unity. Income elasticity of demand for services increases with rising income which favours the fulfilment of more sophisticated desires. During the development process, distribution of GDP and employment register sectoral shifts. Such shifts may occur on account of the hierarchy of needs, distinguished into basic needs for food and shelter and needs for other material and non-material goods including services (Maslow, 1970). According to this view, income elasticity of demand depends on per capita income and differs across various sectors.

The empirical estimates of price and income elasticity for various categories of services in India are summarised in Table 17.5. It is important to mention that the actual behaviour of the services sector in real GDP depends on the relative strength of the coefficients of income and price elasticity.

TABLE – 17.5

Income and Price Elasticities for the Services Sector

Sector	*Income Elasticity*	*Price Elasticity*
1	*2*	*3*
Services	1.20 *	-0.68 *
1. Producer Services	1.22 *	-0.78 *
2. Consumer Services	1.00 *	-0.10
3. Government Services	1.41 *	-1.05 *

Note : * : Statistically significant at 1 per cent.

The income elasticity of demand is greater than unity and price elasticity is negative and significant for the total services, producer services and government services. In other words, demand for overall services rises with increase in per capita GDP and decreases with increase in prices of services. The higher income elasticity of demand in the case of producer services underscores its forward linkages. This is corroborated by the emergence of producer services comprising advertising, publicity, marketing and other IT-related activities in the recent period as important service industries in India. Therefore, producer services can be regarded as a major source of economic growth.

Another explanation is that technical and structural changes in an economy make it more efficient to contract out services that were once produced in the industry. This type of outsourcing has been called the "splintering" of industrial activity. Splintering results in an increase in net input demand for services from the industrial sector, as well as the services sector growing proportionately faster than other sectors.

The empirical evidence presented in Gordon and Gupta (2003) shows that while splintering and high income elasticity of demand for services have served to stimulate services growth in India, it is necessary to look beyond these factors to fully explain the growth acceleration since the 1990s. In particular, important roles also seem to have been played by economic reforms, the advent of the IT era, and growing external demand for services exports. Industrial sector reforms have also been carried out in India and the question arises why the industrial sector has not experienced the same sustained high level of growth that the service sector has experienced. This could be because industrial growth is more dependent on infrastructure development (such as roads and ports), which have acted as a bottleneck to growth. Labor restrictions and small-scale reservations may also have disadvantaged industry more than services. In addition, the faster growing services activities seem to be more intensive in skilled labor, with which India is well endowed.

A number of studies have attempted to explain the fast growth in the share of service activity observed in cross country data. The literature draws a distinction between demand and supply factors.

On the supply side, the share of services can be boosted by a switch to a more service-input intensive method of organising production. Such a change in production methods can arise as a result of increasing specialisation as the economy matures. For example, over time, industrial firms may make greater use of specialist sub-contractors to provide services that were previously provided by the firms themselves. Legal, accounting, and security services are obvious candidates to be contracted out. Bhagwati (1994) calls this process of specialisation splintering. Kravis (1982) points out that splintering will lead to growth in the share of services in GDP, even when GDP itself is not growing.

On the demand side, an increase in the output share of services can arise from rapid growth in the final demand for services. This could be from domestic consumers with a high income elasticity of demand for services, or from foreign consumers with a growing demand for the country's service exports. Demand-led growth of this type is likely to result, at least initially, in higher prices of services, as well as a shift of resources into the production of services.

With the advent of the IT revolution, it has become possible to deliver services over long distances at a reasonable cost, thus trade in services has increased world wide. India has been a particular beneficiary of this trend. In India, the exports in services (in dollar) grew in average at 15 per cent a year in the 1990s, compared with 9 per cent in the 1980s, and at 21 per cent a year in the second half of the 1990s. Cumulatively, services exports increased four fold in the 1990s and reached US$ 25 billion in 2002.

The increase in exports has been most dramatic in software and other business services (included in the miscellaneous category), but there has also been growth in the export of transport, and travel services. As a result, the composition of services has changed dramatically in favor of miscellaneous services, which includes software exports.

Service activity can also be stimulated by *technological advances*, whereby new activities or products emerge as a result of technological breakthrough—such advances are likely to be particularly relevant in the case of the IT sector (e.g. the internet), telecommunication (cellular phone services) and to some extent in financial services (credit cards, ATMs etc.).

Economic reform measures initiated since 1991 also impacted on the performance of the services sector. First, reforms in the domestic industrial environment which resulted in rising manufacturing growth provided synergies to the services sector in the form of increased demand for producer services. Second, the liberalisation of the financial sector provided an environment for faster growth of the financial services. Third, reforms in certain segments of infrastructure services also contributed to the growth of services. Consequently, the services sector posted a much higher growth during the reform period as compared with the pre-reform period with its share touching the 50 per cent mark.

World Trade in Services Sector

The US$ 3.7 trillion world exports of commercial services are dominated by the developed western countries in terms of share except for China, India, and Singapore which also appear in the list of top traders of services. While the United States, Germany, the United Kingdom, China, and Japan represent a third of world trade in commercial services, Europe alone accounts for 45 per cent of total trade in commercial services. While in terms of share, the developed western countries are the major traders, in terms of growth the Asian countries are the leaders with their exports of commercial services expanding on an average by 13 per cent annually since 2008. While world merchandise exports bounced back strongly in 2010 and increased by 14 per cent in volume terms, world exports of commercial services grew by only 9 per cent in 2010, to reach US$ 3,695 billion according to International Trade Statistics, 2011. However, both world merchandise and services exports have not reached the pre-crisis (2008) level. The recovery has not been even across regions. The most rapid growth of commercial services has been in Asia, where exports rose by 22 per cent in 2010, led by India and China. EU exports grew by only 3 per cent. Exports of commercial services from Central and South America and the Caribbean as well as from the Commonwealth of Independent States grew by 12 per cent; North America by 9 per cent; and Africa by 10 per cent.

India's Services Trade

India's Services Exports

For more than a decade, Indian growth story has been dominated by the services sector. This domination was also evident from the trend in export of services (receipts) which grew at a CAGR of 23.4 per cent during 2000-01 to 2010-11 while merchandise exports grew at a CAGR of 18.6 per cent during the same period. Having recorded a contraction of 9.4 per cent in 2009-10 due to the global financial crisis, services exports bounced back to grow by 38.4 per cent to US$ 132.9 billion in 2010-11. However, growth in exports of services moderated during the first half of 2011-12 to 17.1 per cent compared to 32.7 per cent during the first half of 2010-11 (Table 17.6).

India's growing presence in global BPO services is based on its huge labour endowment, varied skill sets and low-cost but quality manpower coupled with a rapidly growing domestic IT industry. According to the *Financial Times*, half of the world's largest 500 companies and many government agencies contract out information technology and business process work to India across a wide range of services, including medical and legal transcriptions, customer support, human-resource management and administration, financial and accounting processes, technical support, logistics, sales, and research and development, to name a few. According to a 2004 AT Kearney report, India ranks highest among offshoring destinations (Chanda, 2012).[1]

Apart from software and BPO services, there are emerging export opportunities in various other services, such as health, education, and tourism. There are concerted efforts underway to establish India as a hub for medical tourism services. Similarly, there is growing interest among Indian higher-education institutions in exporting education services through establishment of offshore campuses as well as twining and partnership arrangements. It is again worth noting that trade data

1. Chanda, Rupa (2012). "Services—Let Growth", in Kaushik Basu and Annemie Maertens (eds.), *The New Oxford Companion to Economics in India* (Vol.II). New Delhi: Oxford University Press.

TABLE – 17.6

India's Exports of Services

	Commodity Group	*Share (per cent)*				*CAGR*	*Growth rate**			
				April-September		*2000-01 to*			*April-September*	
		2000-01	*2010-11*	*2010-11*	*2011-12*	*2008-09*	*2009-10*	*2010-11*	*2010-11*	*2011-12*
1	Travel	21.5	11.5	10.9	12.9	15.3	8.9	28.8	26.2	38.7
2	Transportation	12.6	10.7	11.0	12.8	23.8	-1.2	27.7	26.5	36.1
3	Insurance	1.7	1.5	1.5	1.7	23.1	11.9	22.5	10.2	38.8
4	GNIE	4.0	0.4	0.4	0.4	-6.2	13.4	21.3	9.5	30.6
5	Miscellaneous	60.3	75.9	76.2	72.1	30.4	-12.4	42.1	35.3	10.7
	a) Software services	39.0	41.7	42.7	45.2	28.2	7.4	11.6	11.6	24.1
	b) Non-software services	21.3	34.2	33.5	26.9	33.8	-40.3	113.0	85.6	-6.3
	Of which:									
	i) Business services	2.1	18.1	18.5	15.9	65.3	-39.4	112.4	111.4	0.3
	ii) Financial services	2.1	4.9	5.2	4.2	37.5	-16.6	76.3	64.9	-6.7
	iii) Communication services	7.0	1.2	1.3	1.1	9.2	-46.6	27.2	2.3	1.1
	Total services exports	100.0	100.0	100.0	100.0	26.4	-9.4	38.4	32.7	17.1

Note: * Growth rate in US dollar terms.

Source: *Economic Survey 2011-12*.

on services are subject to problems of coverage and classification. Information is not available from the balance of payments at a sufficiently disaggregated level, particularly in the category of other services, to gauge trends and prospects for individual activities.

There are, however, numerous domestic and external barriers to India's services exports. The main domestic barriers are in the form of infrastructural, financial, regulatory, technical, and standard-related constraints. The main external barriers are in the form of immigration and labour-market regulations, which limit India's ability to deliver on-site services. In addition, there has recently been a backlash against outsourcing in key markets like the US and introduction of domestic regulations such as data privacy laws, which could affect India's BPO exports (Chanda 2012).[2]

India's Services Imports

Import growth of services rebounded in 2010-11 with growth at 40 per cent. But in the first half of 2011-12 it grew by only 1.0 per cent as against 48.3 per cent in the first half of 2010-11. Growth deceleration in import of services was mainly on account of lower imports of miscellaneous services in the first half of 2011-12. Within miscellaneous services, imports of software and business services declined by 47.5 per cent and 1.7 per cent respectively during the first half of 2011-12 as against a growth of 39.9 per cent and 62.6 per cent respectively in the first half of 2010-11. In the first half of 2011-12, import growth of financial and transportation services moderated to 21.1 per cent and 14.5 per cent respectively. However, travel services import growth more than doubled to 39.7 per cent.

India's Balance of Trade in Services

A consistent increase in surplus on account of India's services exports has been a cushioning factor for financing a large part of the trade deficit on the merchandise account in recent years. During 2005-2006 to 2009-10, surplus in services exports, on average, financed around 41 per cent of merchandise trade deficit. Net services surplus which was increasing over the years registered a dip in 2009- 10 with services exports falling due to the global economic crisis but services imports increasing. However, in 2010-11, net services surplus again increased and was at US$ 48.8 billion. During the first half of 2011-2012, a surplus of US$ 31.1 billion has been recorded in net services

2. Ibid

which is 44.7 per cent higher than that recorded during the first half of 2010-11 (Table 17.7). Going forward, downward risks to export of services cannot be ruled out as certain weaknesses have re-emerged in the global economy, particularly the crisis in the euro zone and slowdown in the US economy.

TABLE – 17.7

India's Exports, Imports and Balance of Trade in Services

(US $ billion)

	Exports	*Imports*	*Balance*
2000-01	16.3	14.6	1.7
2001-02	17.1	13.8	3.3
2002-03	20.8	17.1	3.6
2003-04	26.9	16.7	10.1
2004-05	43.2	27.8	15.4
2005-06	57.7	34.5	23.2
2006-07	73.8	44.3	29.5
2007-08	90.3	51.5	38.9
2008-09	106.0	52.0	53.9
2009-10	96.0	60.0	36.0
2010-11	132.9	84.1	48.8
2010-11 (Apr.-Sept.)	58.1	36.6	21.5
2011-12 (Apr.-Sept.)	68.0	36.9	31.1

Source : *Economic Survey 2011-12.*

FDI in India's Service Sector

FDI plays a major role in the dynamic growth of the services sector though the ambiguity in classifying various activities under the services sector poses difficulty in the measurement of FDI inflows into this sector. The combined FDI share of financial and non-financial services, computer hardware and software, telecommunications, and housing and real estate can be taken as a rough estimate of FDI share of services, though it could include some non-service elements. This share is 41.9 per cent of the cumulative FDI equity inflows during the period April 2000-December 2011. With the inclusion of the construction sector (6.5 per cent), the share of services in FDI inflows increases to 48.4 per cent. If the shares of some other services or service-related sectors like hotels and tourism (2.02 per cent), trading (1.94 per cent), information and broadcasting (1.60 per cent), consultancy services (1.21 per cent), ports (1.04 per cent), agriculture services (0.91 per cent), hospital and diagnostic centres (0.72 per cent), education (0.30 per cent), air transport including air freight (0.27 per cent), and retail trading (0.03 per cent) are included then the total share of cumulative FDI inflows to the services sector would be 58.4 per cent. Following the general trend in FDI inflows, FDI inflows to the services sector (top five sectors including construction) have also slowed down in 2009-10 and 2010-2011, with negative growths of -7.5 per cent and -42.5 per cent respectively in rupee terms. In 2011-12 (April-December), again following the trend of overall FDI inflows, which increased by 50.8 per cent to reach US$ 24.19 billion, FDI inflows to the top five service sectors (including construction) also increased by 36.8 per cent to US$ 9.3 billion Services (financial and non-financial), telecommunications, and construction, are the leading sectors in FDI inflows to the services sector in 2011-12 (April-December). The inflows to the other two service sectors are comparatively low.

Services are also accounting for a growing share of outward FDI flows from the Indian economy. Services constituted 45 per cent of total FDI outflows for the 1999-2003 period, with non-financial services, namely communication, software and business services, being the main source sectors (*World Investment Report, 2004*: 6). In segments like software and health services, Indian firms are increasingly emerging as exporters of capital, setting up overseas subsidiaries, establishments and networks in developing and developed economies (Chandra, 2007).[3]

Thus, there is considerable scope for further opening up of many parts of India's service sector.

Liberalisation of Services in India

Evidence suggests that services that have been liberalised most have typically experienced higher growth rates. Areas such as business services (mainly IT and IT-enabled services), communication, banking, and insurance, which have been liberalised, have exhibited higher growth rates, with wider efficiency and growth benefits to the rest of the economy. On the other hand, services where there has been limited opening, like air-transport, legal, and real-estate services have grown much more slowly, with likely adverse effects on economy-wide competitiveness and growth performance (Chanda, 2012).

3. Ibid

India and Trade Negotiations in Services

The preceding discussion clearly highlights that the service sector has not only outperformed other sectors of the Indian economy, but has also played an important role in India's integration with world trade and capital markets. There is, however, growing debate within the country about the sustainability of a services-led growth process. No country in history has been able to grow rapidly in a sustained manner based on services alone. The manufacturing sector has always been part of the growth success. Hence it remains to be seen whether this model of growth also holds for India or not. The prevailing view today is that India needs broad-based growth as its service sector is largely driven by external demand. If high growth is to be sustained within services, then creation of internal demand is necessary and this is only possible with a vibrant manufacturing sector. Also, More broad-based growth within the service sector is required. Services such as trade and distribution, tourism, and construction, which has high employment intensities and large backward and forward linkages with other sectors need to grow more rapidly. In this regard, further infrastructural and regulatory reforms and FDI liberalisation in services can help diversify the sources of growth within India's service sector and provide the required momentum (Chanda, 2012).

India Moving towards a Services-led Export Growth

As per balance of payments (BoP) data of the RBI, India's services exports grew at a CAGR of 20.6 per cent during the period 2004-5 to 2010-11, compared to the 19.7 per cent CAGR of merchandise exports in the same period. Within the services sector, CAGRs of financial services (52.8 per cent) and business services (29.2 per cent) were higher, while that of software at 21 per cent was low. In terms of size, software is a major services export category, accounting for 41.7 per cent of total services exports in 2010-11. The CAGR for import of services was 20.2 per cent compared to the CAGR of merchandise imports at 21.4 per cent. Among services imports, nonsoftware services (22.6 per cent) and transportation (20.5 per cent) had high CAGRs. The overall openness of the economy reflected by total trade including services as a percentage of GDP showed a higher degree of openness at 50.3 per cent in 2010-11 compared to 25.4 per cent in 1997-98. Openness indicator based only on merchandise trade is at 37.5 per cent in 2010-11 compared to 21.2 per cent in 1997-98 (*Economic Survey 2011-12*).

Given the difficult situation arising out of the global economic crisis, which also affected services trade, the Government took some specific measures for the services sector, besides the general measures related to liquidity and trade finance. Some such specific policy measures in the Union Budget and Foreign Trade Policy include extension of the 10A sunset clause for Software Technology Parks of India (STPI) for the financial year 2010-11 and exemption from service tax for certain services linked to exports. Well-thoughtout policy measures could give a further boost to this sector. While policies like disinvestment of services' PSUs and easing domestic regulations can create the conducive atmosphere, liberalization of foreign investment-related policies could also help as trade in services is usually accompanied by foreign investment in services due to the high intra-firm trade of multinational parent firms with affiliates. These should be complemented by specific trade policies including tariff, tax and credit-related policies for services.

Challenges and Outlook

This dominant sector in terms of both shares and growth is a growth engine not only for the national economy but also for many states. It is second only to agriculture in terms of employment both in the national economy and in the majority of states. Unlike the unskilled or semi-skilled nature of jobs in the agriculture sector, this sector provides myriad job opportunities ranging from highly skilled to unskilled in a variety of activities, Hence, services along with a revival in manufacturing activity, can be major drivers of overall employment. Unlike the merchandise sector, the services sector is a net foreign exchange earner with exports of some services growing exponentially. It is also the major FDI-attracting sector with the five services topping the list of sectors attracting FDI to the country. Thus India's services sector is like an uncharted sea with plenty of opportunities and also new challenges.

However, the challenges are also many.[4] One of the challenges in this area is to retain India's competitiveness in those sectors where it has already made a mark such as IT & ITeS and Telecommunications. Their deeper and broader use in the domestic sectors would also have a dramatic potential to increase the efficiency and productivity of other goods and services. The second challenge lies in making inroads into some traditional areas such as tourism and shipping where other

4. Kapila, Uma (ed.) (2013). *Indian Economy since Independence* (24th edition), Ch.20. New Delhi: Academic Foundation.

countries have already established themselves, but where the potential for India is nevertheless very high.

The third challenge is to make some of the fair-weather services like business and financial services more stable and less vulnerable to external shocks. While these sectors cannot be fully insulated from external shocks in this highly globalized world, efforts are needed to make them at least as stable as software and telecom services. This can be done by both piggybacking on the progress of the software and telecom sectors and also making inroads in the domestic economy where opportunities are aplenty.

The fourth challenge is to retain and expand our competitive advantage in those services where we have already made a mark. The present advantage in services may not continue forever, with new competitors from other developing countries making rapid strides even in areas where we had the initial advantage as in the case of software services. Further expansion of established services like software and telecom into new markets and greater usage of these services domestically can not only increase services growth but also propel growth in other sectors with greater efficiency in these sectors using knowledge- and technology-based services.

Removing or easing domestic regulations is another challenge. While removal of market barriers in the form of domestic regulations in other countries depends on multilateral and bilateral negotiations, the myriad restrictions and regulations in the different services domestically need immediate attention. Removing or easing them can lead to dynamic gains for the Indian economy.

The services sector is an uncharted sea throwing up many daunting challenges as well as opening up many exciting opportunities. While many hitherto non-tradable services including those in the government and social sectors are becoming domestically tradable, many services hitherto confined within national borders (like telemedicine) have become internationally tradable. Addressing the challenges of the diverse services sectors and seizing the new opportunities can lead to multiple gains for the services sector and the economy (*Economic Survey 2012-13*).

18

Foreign Direct Investment

Introduction

FDI, being a non-debt capital flow, is a leading source of external financing, especially for the developing economies. It not only brings in capital and technical know-how but also increases the competitiveness of the economy. Overall it supplements domestic investment, much required for sustaining the high growth rate of the country. Since 2000, significant changes have been made in the FDI policy regime by the government to ensure that India becomes an increasingly attractive and investor-friendly destination.

Role of FDI

Growth impulses originating from FDI are primarily ascribed to superior technology and greater competition that generally accompany FDI. Local firms of many developing host countries also do not invest enough on R&D to offer and sustain competition with Transnational Corporations (TNCs). Investment on R&D by TNCs in foreign affiliates is, however, found to be low, accounting for as little as 1 per cent of the total R&D investment even though TNCs are generally viewed as R&D intensive (UNCTAD, 1999). Despite the usual concerns that inappropriate technology is generally transferred to the foreign affiliates, empirical assessments suggest that technology—both public and private—that accompany FDI are complementary and inter-firm collaboration helps in augmenting growth. In such cases also, FDI may augment growth in a country if its initial technology gap is higher and openness to FDI is significant.

This chapter is drawn extensively from Kumar, Nagesh (2013). "Foreign Direct and Portfolio Investments Flows and Development: A Perspective on Indian Experience", ch. 24 in Uma Kapila (ed.) *Indian Economy Since Independence (24th edition)*. New Delhi: Academic Foundation.

Whether FDI promotes competition or facilitates development of oligopolistic structures depends upon whether FDI crowds-out or crowds-in domestic investment. FDI can potentially displace domestic producers by preempting their investment opportunities. It is possible, however, that the adverse growth effect emanating from crowding-out could be more than offset by the increase in productivity resulting from advanced technology that often accompanies FDI.

Since trade is an important vehicle for growth, FDI could also contribute to growth by promoting exports. For sustaining an export-led growth strategy, it becomes important to attain dynamic shifts in comparative advantage and FDI can play a major role in imparting the desired dynamism on account of its global marketing network.

In India Foreign direct investment (FDI) directly impacts on output growth by augmenting the available investible capital. However, a far more important impact of FDI is through externalities leading to higher efficiency and productivity. FDI typically serves to increase competition in markets, bring new technology into India, and foster skill acquisition amongst domestic labour. FDI by international corporations is also central to the process of India being utilised as a platform for global production chains, which would pave the way for strong exports growth.

FDI Policy: A Historical Perspective

Over the last five decades, there have been significant changes in approaches and policies relating to FDI in India in tune with the developments in the industrial policies and also foreign exchange situation, from time to time. There is a view in the literature that the attitude and approach to FDI reflected the under current of balance of payments crisis in the respective periods. Depending upon the thrust and direction of the policies at different time period, one can identify four distinct phases in the evolution of the policies:

i) first phase from 1950 to 1967—characterised by receptive attitude or cautious welcome;

ii) second phase from 1967 to 1980—marked by restrictive and selective policies;

iii) third phase from 1980 to 1990—gradual liberalisation; and

iv) fourth phase from 1991 till date—paradigm shift to open door policy (Jain, 1994; Subrahmanian *et al.,* 1996; Kumar, 1998). Major features of FDI policies during the above four phases are reviewed below. Exhibit 1 provides the major features of FDI policies during the four phases.

EXHIBIT – 18.1

Major Features of FDI Policies during the Four Phases

Phase I 1950-1967	*Phase II 1967-1980*	*Phase III 1980-1990*	*Phase IV 1991 Onwards*
Receptive Attitude or Cautious Welcome	*Restrictive Attitude*	*Gradual Liberalisation*	*Open Door Policy*
• Non-discriminatory treatment to FDI.	• Restriction on FDI without technology.	• Higher foreign equity in export-oriented units allowed.	• Liberal policies relating to technology collaboration, foreign trade and foreign exchange.
• No restrictions on remittance of profits and dividends.	• Above 40 per cent stake not allowed.	• Procedure for remittance of royalty and technical fees liberalised.	• Encouraging FDI in core and infrastructure industries.
	• Allowed only in priority area.		• FERA replaced with FEMA.
• Ownership and control with Indians.	• FDI controlled by FERA.	• Fast channel for FDI clearance.	• Procedures transparent.
			• Liberal approach for NRI investments.
	• Discretionary power in sanctioning the projects.		• FDI need not be accompanied by technology.
			• FDI through mergers and acquistions.
			• FDI in services and financial sector-banks, NBFCs, insurance.

After pursuing a restrictive policy towards FDI for over four decades with a varying degree of selectivity, India changed tracks in 1990s and embarked on a broader process of reforms designed to increase her integration with the global economy. Among the reform measures implemented included a departure from the restrictive policy towards FDI, a much more liberal trade policy besides reforms of capital market and exchange controls. The New Industrial Policy (NIP) announced on 24 July 1991, marked a major departure with respect to FDI policy with the abolition of industrial licensing system except where it is required for strategic or environmental grounds, creation of a system of automatic clearance of FDI proposals fulfilling the conditions laid down, such as the ownership levels of 50 per cent, 51 per cent, 74 per cent and 100 per cent foreign equity and opening of new sectors such as mining, banking, insurance, telecommunications, construction and management of ports, harbours, roads and highways, airlines, and defence equipment, to foreign owned companies subject to sectoral caps. Foreign ownership up to 100 per cent is permitted in most manufacturing sectors—in some sectors even on automatic basis—except for defence equipment where it is limited to 26 per cent and for items reserved for production by small-scale industries where it is limited to 24 per cent. The dividend balancing and the related export obligation conditions on foreign investors, which applied to 22 consumer goods industries, were withdrawn in 2000 (Kumar, 2005a). In September 2012, India allowed FDI in multibrand retail and in civil aviation. Sectoral caps were revised upwards in July 2013 in some sectors like telecom to 100 per cent, in insurance to 49 per cent, and in defence equipment beyond 26 per cent on a case by case basis (Kumar, 2013).[1]

In September 1992, the Indian government announced guidelines for investments by FIIs in the Indian capital market. FIIs were now welcome to invest in all types of securities traded on the primary and secondary market with full repatriation benefits and without restrictions on either volume of trading or lock-in-period. This liberalisation has led to considerable inflows of portfolio inflows making the country most exposed to portfolio inflows. In June 2013, FII investments were reclassified as FPI which is subject to their holding in a company within 10 per cent of its equity. Any holdings beyond 10 per cent will qualify as FDI (Kumar, 2013).

Recognising the importance of outward investment for competitiveness of enterprises, the policy governing outward FDI has also been liberalised since 1991. With the build up of foreign exchange reserves, the limits for outward investments have been gradually relaxed and Indian enterprises are now permitted to invest abroad up to 100 per cent of their net worth on automatic basis (Kumar, 2013).

1. Kumar (2013).

India has also entered into 65 Double Taxation Avoidance Treaties, and Bilateral Investment Promotion and Protection Agreement (BIPAs) with 58 countries (Kumar, 2013).

The current phase of FDI policy is characterized by negative listing, permitting FDI freely except in a few sectors indicated through a negative list. Under the current policy regime, there are three broad entry options for foreign direct investors. In a few sectors, FDI is not permitted (negative list); in another small category of sectors, foreign investment is permitted only till a specified level of foreign equity participation; and the third category, comprising all the other sectors, is where foreign investment up to 100 per cent of equity participation is allowed. The third category has two subsets—one consisting of sectors where automatic approval is granted for FDI (often foreign equity participation less than 100 per cent) and the other consisting of sectors where prior approval from the Foreign Investment Approval Board (FIPB) is required. FDI policy changes increasingly reflect the requirements of industry and are based on stakeholders' consultation. Upfront listing of negative sectors has helped focus on reform areas, which are reflected in buoyant FDI inflows.

Trends in FDI Inflows

FDI inflows to India have been growing since 1991 but the big break came in 2006 when annual inflows to the country nearly tripled in one year from $ 7.6 billion to $ 20 billion and increased from that level peaking to $ 43 billion in 2008 before declining to $ 24 billion in 2010 in the wake of the global financial crisis but recovering to $31.5 billion in 2011 (Table 18.1). India's share in global FDI inflows nearly doubled over 2005-06 and again between 2006-2009 to nearly 2.97 per cent before declining to 2.1 per cent in 2011 (Table 18.1). The relative importance of the flows in relation to gross fixed investment, has also risen from 2.9 per cent in 2005 to 6.6 per cent in 2006. The share of FDI in gross fixed investments in India has been lower than other developing countries, but was catching up. In 2008 when FDI inflows peaked in India, this ratio at 10.1 per cent was quite close to that for developing Asia at 10.4 per cent. Afterwards it has declined in the wake of financial crisis indicating the potential for a rise in the future (Table 18.1B).

TABLE – 18.1

Inward Foreign Direct Investment Flows, Annual: 2001-2011,

Million US$

A. Inward FDI Flows, Annual 2001-2011

	World	*Developing economies*	*Developing Asia*	*India*	*Share of India in Developing*	*Share of India in Developing*	*Share of India in World*
2001	827617	216865	115968	5478	4.72	2.53	0.66
2002	627975	173283	100083	5630	5.62	3.25	0.9
2003	586956	190125	123707	4321	3.49	2.27	0.74
2004	744329	291866	177983	5778	3.25	1.98	0.78
2005	980727	327248	218420	7622	3.49	2.33	0.78
2006	1463351	427163	290907	20328	6.99	4.76	1.39
2007	1975537	574311	349412	25506	7.3	4.44	1.29
2008	1790706	650017	380360	43406	11.41	6.68	2.42
2009	1197824	519225	315238	35596	11.29	6.86	2.97
2010	1309001	616661	384063	24159	6.29	3.92	1.85
2011	1524422	684399	423157	31554	7.46	4.61	2.07

B. FDI Inflows as a per cent of Gross Fixed Capital Formation

	2001	*2002*	*2003*	*2004*	*2005*	*2006*	*2007*	*2008*	*2009*	*2010*
India	4.7	4.6	2.8	2.7	2.9	6.6	6.2	10.1	8.1	4.5
World	12.2	9.1	7.6	8.3	9.9	13.3	15.7	12.9	9.5	9.5
Developing Economies	13.5	10.2	9.8	12.4	11.8	12.9	14.1	13.2	10.1	10.1
Developing Asia	10.3	8	8.4	9.9	10.4	11.7	11.5	10.4	7.9	8
South Asia	4.5	4.7	3	3.1	3.7	7.3	6.9	10.3	7.8	4.6

Source: Authors compilation from UNCTAD online data base (2012), *www.unctad.org*

Investment Climate and Prospects for FDI Inflows

The empirical studies of determinants of FDI inflows have found an important role of market size, extent of urbanisation, quality of infrastructure, geographical and cultural proximity with major sources of capital, and policy factors, e.g., tax rates, investment incentives, performance requirements, among other factors (Kumar, 2000). In the light of these findings, while India's large population base may be an advantage, relatively low income levels, low levels of urbanisation and relatively poor quality of infrastructure are disadvantages. Furthermore, India also does not have the benefit of geographical and cultural proximity with major sources of FDI such as the US, Europe or Japan. However, over time the relative attractiveness of the country is improving with rapid growth that is expanding market size and other aspects of macroeconomic performance. A recent inter-temporal analysis for India has found a broad correspondence between the industrial growth rates in a year and FDI inflows received in the following year (Kumar, 2005a). Apparently, good industrial performance tends to crowd-in FDI inflows as well.

The recent rise in FDI inflows since 2006 reflects improving investment climate in India with the acceleration of growth rate since 2003, the rise of a sizeable middle class with purchasing power, and with the recognition of India's comparative advantage in knowledge-based industries. This is not only evident from the rising magnitudes of FDI inflows but also from investor surveys conducted by global consultancy organisations. In the FDI Confidence Index published by AT Kearney, a global consultancy organisation, covering 25 top destinations for FDI, India has moved up from 6th place in 2003 to 2nd in 2005 and stayed there before swapping the 3rd rank with the United States in 2010 (Table 18.2). In 2012, it again regained the second position in the global rankings (AT Kearney, 2012). In 2013, India moved down to the 5th rank globally as the US moved up to the 1st rank as the prospects for growth improved and as their natural resources bases helped Brazil (3) and Canada (4) move up. Among the Asian developing countries, India continues to remain 2nd after China. Similar upgrading in India's ranks has been reported by the surveys of investors conducted by the Japanese Bank of International Cooperation (JBIC) as well as in UNCTAD's *World Prospects Survey 2013-2015*, where India is ranked as the 3rd most preferred FDI location (UNCTAD, 2013). Recent reforms adopted by the country to allow FDI in multibrand retail and civil aviation and large infrastructure projects such as Delhi-Mumbai Industrial Corridor (DMIC) are also likely to help in realising its potential for FDI inflows. This is in sharp contrast to the World Bank's studies on *Ease of Doing Business* based on perception surveys that tend to put India at a very poor rank of 132. It is clear therefore that foreign investors get attracted to a country by the potential of benefiting from its dynamism and are willing to put up with hardships rather than going to countries with easier business conditions but with poorer prospects of making profits. FDI inflows may also assist in manufacturing oriented structural transformation of the economy and technological upgrading of exports that India needs by bringing technologies and other resources working together with local entrepreneurs.

TABLE – 18.2

Select Asian Ranking in FDI Confidence Index

	2003	*2004*	*2005*	*2007*	*2010*	*2013*
China	1 (1.97)	1 (2.03)	1 (2.19)	1 (2.21)	1 (1.93)	2 (2.02)
India	6 (1.04)	3 (1.4)	2 (1.95)	2 (2.09)	3 (1.64)	5 (1.85)
Thailand	16 (0.83)	20 (0.87)	20 (1.05)	..	..	17 (1.63)
Singapore	28 (0.91)	18 (1.07)	18 (1.75)	7 (1.19)	24 (1.77)	10
Malaysia	23 (0.67)	15 (0.92)	..	16 (1.63)	21 (1.22)	25 (1.60)
Hong Kong	22 (0.69)	8 (0.99)	10 (1.21)	5 (1.78)	14 (1.28)	– –

Note: Index values are in parentheses.

Source: Author based on A.T. Kearney, *Foreign Direct Investment Confidence Index*, different years.

Quality of FDI Inflows

There can be several indicators of quality of FDI inflows (Kumar, 2002). In what follows, we discuss India's performance in terms of a few such indicators.

Sectoral Composition

One of the indicators of quality is the sectoral composition of FDI inflows. It matters whether FDI is going to the modern technology intensive sectors and building productive capabilities or to conventional sectors crowding out domestic investments. In terms of the sectoral composition of FDI inflows, there is a shift since 1991 in India's case. Earlier the bulk of FDI inflows used to be directed to manufacturing especially the high technology industries through a selective policy. After the liberalisation, a substantial proportion of FDI inflows has been directed to services. Manufacturing has accounted for only about 40 per cent of inflows in the post-1991 period with services accounting for about 35 per cent share. Furthermore, among the manufacturing subsectors, FDI stock in post-1991 period is also more evenly distributed between food and beverages, transport equipment, metals and metal products, electricals and electronics, chemicals and allied products, and miscellaneous manufacturing. This stands in contrast to the situation prior to 1990 when there was a very heavy concentration in relatively technology intensive sectors *viz.*, machinery, chemicals, electricals and transport equipment (Kumar, 2005a).

In China, on the other hand, the bulk of FDI inflows have been directed by the government policy to manufacturing (of the export-oriented type) and very little has gone to services (Yongding, 2006). Of the FDI in manufacturing in China, 11 per cent has gone in electronics and telecommunication equipment helping it emerge as the leading producer and exporter of these products. A policy guiding FDI inflows to manufacturing has helped in China's emergence as a global factory. Therefore, FDI inflows in China have been directed to assist in its industrial development that has made China a global factory generating in the process billions of dollars of output and exports and millions of jobs.

Impact of FDI on Growth and Domestic Investment

FDI inflows could contribute to growth rate of the host economy by augmenting the capital stock as well as with infusion of new technology. However, high growth rates may also attract more FDI inflows by enhancing the investment climate in the country.

The empirical studies on the nature of the relationship between FDI and domestic investments suggest that the effect of FDI on domestic investment depends on host government policies. Governments have extensively employed selective policies and imposed various performance requirements such as local content requirements (LCRs) to deepen the commitment of MNEs to the host economy. The Indian government has imposed a condition of phased manufacturing programmes (or local content requirements) in the auto industry to promote vertical inter-firm linkages and encourage development of the auto component industry (and crowding-in of domestic investments). A case study of the auto industry where such a policy was followed shows that these policies (in combination with other performance requirements *viz.*, foreign exchange neutrality), have succeeded in building an internationally competitive vertically integrated auto sector in the country (see Kumar, 2005).

FDI and Export-Platform Production

A number of developing countries have used FDI to exploit the resources of MNEs such as globally recognised brand names, best practice technology or by increasing integration with their global production networks, among others, for expanding their manufactured exports. In this respect, China has had a considerable success in exploiting the potential of FDI for export-oriented production. A very substantial (55%) proportion of manufactured exports of China are undertaken by foreign invested enterprises, which account for as much as 80 per cent of all technology intensive exports (UNCTAD, 2005). Foreign enterprises while setting up export-oriented production bases created 23 million jobs by 2003 making China a global factory. Export-oriented FDI also helps in bringing world's best practice technology as the affiliate has to compete globally right from the beginning. It also enhances the chances of FDI inflows crowding in domestic investments and reducing the chances of crowd-out as the foreign affiliate would be mainly catering to the outside markets rather than eating into domestic firms' markets. It would also create fresh possibilities of market information spillovers for domestic firms on export possibilities.

Unlike the East Asian countries, India has not been able to exploit the potential of FDI for export-oriented production. The bulk of FDI inflows in India are market-seeking coming for tapping the domestic market with the share of foreign affiliates in exports around 10 per cent. Therefore, the quality of FDI in respect of export-orientation is poorer compared to FDI received by East Asian countries. In this respect two observations can be made. The first is that recent studies of export-performance are beginning to indicate a relatively superior performance of foreign enterprises in terms of export orientation compared to early studies suggesting a poorer performance of foreign companies (see Kumar and Joseph, 2007). Therefore, MNEs are beginning to exploit the potential of India as base for export-oriented production (Kumar, 2013).

Export-obligations have also been employed fruitfully by many countries to prompt MNE affiliates to exploit the host country's potential for export platform production. For instance, in China which has succeeded in expanding manufactured exports with help of MNE affiliates, regulations stipulate that wholly owned foreign enterprises must undertake to export more than 50 per cent of their output (Rosen, 1999: 63-71). As a result of these policies, the proportion of foreign enterprises in manufactured exports has steadily increased to over 55 per cent as observed above (Kumar, 2013).

FPI Inflows and their Impact

FII inflows rose to a sizeable $ 27 billion in 2007-08 that led to not only stock prices booming, with BSE Sensex more than doubling from under 10,000 to 20,000, but also the rupee exchange rate appreciating sharply from 47 Rupees in year in 2006 to 38 Rupees to a US dollar in 2008. In 2008-09, in the wake of global financial crisis, there was a net outflow of FII to the tune of $14 billion dollars that brought down the BSE Sensex from nearly 20,000 points to less than 9,000 points in the early part of 2009. Much more importantly it led to a sharp depreciation of rupee by nearly 25 per cent in early 2009. The depreciation would have been greater if the Reserve Bank of India (RBI) had not intervened in the market by selling dollars. This depleted the RBI's foreign exchange reserves by $58 billion to about $252 billion from $310 billion from 2007-08 to 2008-09. However, as FIIs returned rapidly to the market with the onset of recovery and the FII inflows to the country in 2010 were of the order of $ 32 billion bringing the Sensex back above 20,000 points in October 2010. Despite the RBI's market intervention to offset the subsequent exchange rate pressure, the rupee appreciated by nearly 8 per cent although foreign exchange reserves were augmented to about $284 billion. FII inflows have become primary determinants of the movements in the stock exchange indices and the exchange rate of the rupee (see Kumar, 2011). As there are sharp movements in these inflows linked to global developments, they become channels of transmission of instability to the country's financial system. As a result, the rupee has been on a roller coaster ride: from Rs 44 per dollar in January 2007 to Rs 39 in January 2008 to increase again to Rs 49 per dollar in January 2009 to Rs 44 in October 2010. The rupee fluctuated around Rs 54 in 2012 and early 2013 and after May 2013 depreciated sharply to cross Rs 60 to a dollar, as there was outflow of FIIs in anticipation of roll back of quantitative easing policy by Federal Reserve in the US and as concerns about India's rising current account deficit mounted.

Besides the volatility, FII inflows have a very high servicing burden. Among foreign resources such as FDI, foreign borrowings, non-resident Indian (NRI) deposits, American Depositary Receipts (ADRs/), global depositary receipts (GDRs), FII investments are most expensive in terms of servicing burden (Kumar, 2011). This is because they come to chase primarily good returns at the stock markets and exchange rate speculation. In 2007-08, Indian stock markets were giving around 44 per cent return. That means for every dollar India received in FII flows, it became liable to pay $1.44 in one year. As they are stock price makers rather than takers, they manage to exit safely before major crashes of markets thereby precipitating the declines.

One may argue that FII inflows help a country to build foreign exchange reserves. What is not appreciated very well is the fact that exposure to these inflows also enhances the need to have large foreign exchange reserves due to their highly volatile nature. Therefore, developing countries such as India should rely for their foreign resource needs more on FDI inflows and where possible raise ADRs/GDRs and deposits from NRIs rather than relying on the FIIs. In view of their high cost and their other deleterious effects such as volatility, a number of emerging economies such as Brazil, South Korea, and Indonesia have recently imposed capital controls to moderate their volatility (Kumar, 2013).

TABLE – 18.3

FDI and Foreign Portfolio Investment Flows to India

	Gross inflows/ Gross Investments	*Direct Investments to India*	*FDI by India*	*Net Foreign Direct Investment*	*Net Portfolio Investment*	*Total (in million USD)*
2000-01	4029	4029	759	3270	2590	5860
2001-02	6130	6125	1391	4734	1952	6686
2002-03	5035	4976	1819	3157	944	4101
2003-04	4322	4322	1934	2388	11377	13765
2004-05	6051	5986	2274	3712	9291	13003
2005-06	8961	8900	5867	3033	12492	15525
2006-07	22826	22739	15046	7693	6947	14640
2007-08	34843	34727	18836	15891	27434	43325
2008-09	41873	41707	19364	22343	-14032	8311
2009-10	37745	33108	15143	17965	32396	50361
2010-11	34847	27829	16524	11305	30292	41597
2011-12	46553	32955	10950	22006	17171	39177

Source: Extracted from RBI's *Handbook of Statistics on Indian Economy, 2012*. *www.rbi.org.in*

India as an Emerging Source of FDI Outflows

Another important emerging trend with respect to FDI in India is its emergence as a significant source of FDI outflows. Like FDI inflows, the major turnaround in their outflows came in 2006 when outflows more than quadrupled in one year to $ 14 billion and peaked to nearly $ 20 billion in 2007 before declining to around $ 15 billion in subsequent years in the wake of global financial crisis (Table 18.4). The big break came with Indian enterprises using their outward investments to acquire larger companies in the advanced economies as a part of their effort to augment their bundles of strategic assets including known brand names, proprietary knowledge and global marketing networks in order to jump start their global orientation. The past few years have seen several multibillion-dollar acquisitions of western firms by Indian companies including Tata Steel-Corrus, Tata Motors-Jaguar/Land Rover, Handalco-Novelis among others.

TABLE – 18.4

Foreign Direct Investment (FDI) Outflows Originating in India

(Million USD)

	World	*Developing Economies*	*Developing Economies: Asia*	*India*
2001	747657	83087	49155	1397
2002	528496	47484	34987	1678
2003	570679	46668	23961	1876
2004	925716	122792	91404	2175
2005	888561	132507	86425	2985
2006	1415094	239336	151400	14285
2007	2198025	316863	228154	19594
2008	1969336	328121	223116	19257
2009	1175108	268476	210925	15927
2010	1451365	400144	273033	13151
2011	1694396	383754	280478	14752

Source: Extracted from UNCTAD database 2012.
Kumar, 2013

Concluding Remarks and Policy Lessons

Although starting from a low base, India has also been able to increase its share in FDI inflows received by developing countries especially in the past few years and is catching up with Southeast Asian countries in terms of share of these inflows in capital formation. India is also attracting large magnitudes of portfolio equity flows from FIIs which are highly volatile.

The above discussion also shows that even though India may be attracting increasing magnitudes of FDI inflows, they are yet to harness their development potential fully. The empirical studies suggest that the country has received FDI inflows of mixed quality and the developmental impact has been uneven. India can learn a great deal from the experiences of China and other Southeast Asian countries in this regard. China has had a much greater success in harnessing the potential of FDI for building high technology export-oriented industrial base using a variety of policy instruments and performance requirements. On the other hand, India is getting exposed in a significant manner to the FPI flows that are not only highly volatile and are expensive in terms of servicing burden.

Policy Lessons

In general, the above analysis brings out the role of government policy in attracting and benefiting from FDI inflows for development. In light of this discussion, we may now draw a few policy lessons for the region and other similarly placed developing countries.

First of all, liberalisation of FDI policy may be necessary but not sufficient for expanding FDI inflows. The overall macroeconomic performance continues to exercise a major influence on the magnitude of FDI inflows by acting as a signalling device for foreign investors about the growth prospects for the potential host economy. Hence, paying attention to macroeconomic performance indicators such as growth rates of industry through public investments in socio-economic infrastructure and other supportive policies and creating a stable and enabling environment would crowd-in FDI inflows. Studies have shown that policies that facilitate domestic investments also pull in FDI inflows. While investment incentives may not be efficient, active promotion of FDI by developing certain viable projects and getting key MNEs interested in them could be useful in attracting investments in desirable directions.

The evidence suggests that the government policies play an important role in determining the quality or developmental impact of FDI and in facilitating the exploitation of its potential benefits by host country's development. The various performance requirements such as phased manufacturing programmes, export performance requirements and domestic ownership requirements have also been employed by the governments to achieve their developmental policy objectives.

Even with liberalised policy some policy direction to FDI is desirable as has been demonstrated by the case of East Asian countries.

Another sphere where governmental intervention may be required to maximise gains from globalisation is in diffusion of knowledge brought in by foreign enterprises. An important channel of diffusion of knowledge brought in by MNEs in the host economy is vertical inter-firm linkages with domestic enterprises. Many governments—in developed as well as developing countries alike—have imposed local content requirements on MNEs to intensify generation of local linkages and transfer of technology (see Kumar, 2005b for evidence). The host governments could also consider employing proactive measures that encourage foreign and local firms to deepen their local content as a number of countries, e.g., Singapore, Taiwan, Korea and Ireland have done so successfully.

Changes in Sectoral Composition

In tune with the government's priorities with respect to FDI, sectoral composition of FDI has undergone significant changes during the last two decades. Till 1990, the government policy was to channel FDI inflow in technology-intensive branches of manufacturing. Thus, more than four-fifth of FDI stock in 1990 was in the manufacturing industries. The share of petroleum and power and service sectors were only marginal. However, with the changes in the FDI policies in the nineties, the share of manufacturing has been more than halved to 40.1 per cent. Within the manufacturing industries, FDI is shifting away from heavy capital goods industries to light industries. With the opening up of the infrastructure industries, on the other hand, the share of petroleum and power sector rose substantially to 30.6 per cent in 1999 from just 0.1 per cent of FDI stock in 1990. Similarly, the share of service sector rose to 27.8 per cent from just 5.2 per cent, respectively, during the above period (Kumar, 2009).

Three high priority industries, namely, power, telecommunication and oil refinery accounted for nearly half of the total amount of FDI approvals during 1991 to 1999. Among the different industries, power and telecommunication accounted for the highest share (17.5 per cent each) of FDI approvals during the nineties. They are closely followed by oil refinery, which accounted for 13.1 per cent of FDI approvals.

Transportation industry and financial sector were the other two prominent sectors accounting for larger share of FDI approvals. Thus, what is noticeable in the nineties is the rise of FDI inflows in the priority infrastructure sectors like power, telecommunication, oil refinery, transportation, finance and banking. Perhaps, this is on account of the opening up of these industries for FDI in recent times. (Kumar, 2009).

Changes in the Sources of FDI

Over the years, there has been diversification of sources of FDI. Until 1990, European countries have been the major sources of FDI inflows in India. They accounted for nearly two-third of total stock of FDI in 1990. However, their share drastically declined to around one-fifth during the nineties. Among the European countries, the decline was significantly high in case of the UK from 48.8 per cent in 1990 to just 7.6 per cent during the nineties. The share of European countries, America and Japan taken together accounted for nearly 90 per cent of total stock of FDI in 1990, however, it has declined to 46.6 per cent during the nineties. The decline in the share of the above group is essentially due to the rise in the inflows from other countries. What is more striking is the fact that after USA, Mauritius is the second largest source of FDI in India. Because of lower taxes in Mauritius, they are able to attract foreign capital from different parts of the world, which is in turn invested in countries like India.

From April 2000 to November 2007, Mauritius remained the predominant source country for FDI to India accounting for 44.24 per cent share of the cumulative total, followed by the United States (9.37 per cent), the United Kingdom (7.98 per cent) and the Netherlands (5.81 per cent). Country-wise, investment routed through Mauritius remained the largest component of FDI inflows to India in 2010-11 followed by Singapore and the Netherlands. Outward FDI increased from US$ 15.1 billion in 2009-10 to US$ 16.5 billion in 2010-11. With lower inward FDI and rise in outward FDI, net FDI (inward minus outward) to India stood considerably lower at US$ 9.4 billion during 2010-11 (US$ 18.0 billion a year earlier).

FDI Outlook

Liberalisation of FDI policy may be necessary but not sufficient for expanding FDI inflows. The overall macroeconomic performance continues to exercise a major influence on the magnitude of FDI inflows by acting as a signalling device for foreign investors about the growth prospects for the potential host economy. Hence, paying attention to macroeconomic performance indicators such as growth rates of industry through public investments in socio-economic infrastructure and other supportive policies and creating a stable and enabling environment would crowd-in FDI inflows.[2] Studies have shown that policies that facilitate domestic investments also pull in FDI inflows. While investment incentives may not be efficient, active promotion of FDI by developing certain viable projects and getting key MNEs interested in them could be useful in attracting investments in desirable directions.

2. Kumar, Nagesh (2012). "FDI", in Kaushik Basu and Annemie Maertens (eds.), *The New Oxford Companion to Economics in India* (Vol.I). New Delhi: Oxford University Press.

19

The Financial Sector

Structure, Performance and Reforms

THE financial sector plays a major role in the mobilisation and allocation of savings. Financial institutions, instruments and markets which constitute the financial sector act as a conduit for the transfer of financial resources from net savers to net borrowers, i.e., from those who spend less than they earn to those who earn less than they spend. The gains to the real sector, therefore, depend on how efficiently the financial sector performs this function of intermediation.[1]

Efficient and developed financial markets can lead to increased economic growth by improving the efficiency of allocation and utilisation of savings in the economy. Empirical evidence across countries prove a strong and positive link between the functioning of the financial system and long-term economic growth.[2]

Growing Importance of Finance in India

Indian economy has witnessed rapid economic growth during the last 20 years or so. There has also been a sharp rise in rate of saving and investments. This has inevitably involved a substantial role for finance as the intermediary between household and firms. Over the last 10 years or so, India moved up from being medium size developing country with an aggregate GDP of $ 396 billion in 1998-99 to being a member of the G-20 with an aggregate GDP of $ 1.13 trillion in 2009-2010 i.e., roughly tripling of the aggregate GDP. Along side the saving rate increased from 24.13 per cent to 34.65 per cent. Gross capital

1. Rangarajan, C. and Narendra Jadhav (1992). "Issues in Financial Sector Reforms", in Bimal Jalan (ed.), *The Indian Economy: Problems and Prospects*. New Delhi: Viking.
2. Krishnan, K.P. (2012). "Financial Sector Reforms", in Kaushik Basu and Annemie Maertens (eds.), *The New Oxford Companion to Economics in India* (Vol.I).

formation by the private corporate sector grew from 7.67 per cent of GDP to 14.53 per cent of GDP over this decade. As a result of all this, financial system has begun to play a more prominent role in the economy (Krishnan, 2012).

According to Rangarajan (2013)[3], Financial sector development and economic development have a mutually interacting beneficial effect. The one helps the other. With respect to financial sector development and more particularly banking development, there are two possible scenarios. One is supply leading and the other is demand following. In the first case, banking institutions come first into existence and then create the demand for their services. In the second scenario, banking institutions are set up to meet an emerging and existing demand. In the banking development of our country, we have seen both types of phenomena operating.

Financial Sector Development in India

The Indian financial system comprises an impressive network of banks and financial institutions and a wide range of financial instruments. There is no doubt that there has been a considerable widening and deepening of the Indian financial system, particularly in the last two decades. The extension of banking and other financial facilities to a larger cross-section of people stands out as a significant achievement. As a ratio of GDP at current prices, bank deposits increased from 18 per cent in 1969–70 to 45.3 per cent by end-March 1995, and now stand at 73 per cent. All indicators of financial development, such as the 'finance ratio', 'financial interrelations ratio' and 'intermediation ratio', have significantly increased, highlighting the growing importance of financial institutions in the economy and the growth of financial flows in relation to economic activity (Rangarajan, 2013).

Institutional Structure

At present, the institutional structure of the financial system is characterised by: (a) banks, either owned by the government, the RBI, or the private sector (domestic or foreign) and regulated by the RBI; (b) development financial institutions and refinancing institutions, set up by a separate statute or owned by the Government, RBI, private, or

3. Rangarajan, C. (2013). "The Indian Banking System: Some Issues (Ch.4)", in Uma Kapila (ed.), *Indian Financial Reforms: Priorities and Policy Thrust Post Global Financial Crisis*. New Delhi: Academic Foundation.

other development financial institutions under the Companies Act and regulated by the RBI; and (c) non-bank financial companies (NBFCs), owned privately and regulated by the RBI.

Provision of short-term credit is entrusted primarily to commercial and cooperative banks. Of late, commercial banks have diversified into several new areas of business such as merchant banking, mutual funds, leasing, venture capital, factoring and other financial services. In addition, there is a wide network of cooperative banks and cooperative land development banks at state, district and subdistrict levels.

Medium-term and long-term finance is provided primarily by a few large all India development banks together with a spectrum of state level financial institutions. While the Industrial Development Bank of India (IDBI), the National Bank for Agriculture and Rural Development (NABARD), the Export-Import Bank of India (EXIM Bank) and the National Housing Bank (NHB) serve as apex agencies in their respective areas of concern, there are also other financial institutions which specialise in areas like tourism and the small-scale industry.

Besides these, there are investment institutions, which include the Unit Trust of India (UTI), the Life Insurance Corporation (LIC) and the General Insurance Corporation (GIC). In recent years, a number of public sector mutual funds have been set up by banks and financial institutions. In addition, a large number of private sector non-bank financial companies undertake para-banking activity mainly in the area of hire-purchase and leasing.

The capital market has witnessed a remarkable growth in the paid-up capital of listed companies and market capitalisation in recent years. It has emerged as one of the important markets in the developing world. The Securities and Exchange Board of India (SEBI) has been established to regulate the capital market.

Capital Markets

The 1990s have been remarkable for the Indian equity market. The market has grown exponentially in terms of resource mobilisation, number of stock exchanges, number of listed stocks, market capitalisation, trading volumes, turnover and investors' base. Along with this growth, the profile of the investors, issuers and intermediaries have changed significantly. The market has witnessed a fundamental institutional change resulting in drastic reduction in transaction costs and significant improvement in efficiency, transparency and safety (NSE, 2002). In the 1990s, reform measures initiated by SEBI, market determined allocation of resources, rolling settlement, sophisticated risk management and derivatives trading have greatly improved the framework and efficiency of trading and settlement. Almost all equity settlements take place at the depository. As a result, the Indian capital market has become qualitatively comparable to many developed and emerging markets.

The liberalisation and consequent reform measures have drawn attention of foreign investors and led to rise in the FIIs investment in India. During the first half of the 1990s, India accounted for a larger volume of international equity issues than any other emerging market (IMF Survey, 1995). Presently, there are nearly 500 registered FIIs in India, which include asset management companies, pension funds, investment trusts and incorporated institutional portfolio managers. FIIs are eligible to invest in listed as well as unlisted securities.

Indian security market has had may firsts to its credit including

(i) establishing one of the first demutualised exchange in the world and

(ii) corporatisation and demutualisation of all stock exchanges.

India ranked 13 in the world in terms of total market capitalisation and total value traded in 2008 (*Global Markets Facebook 2009*). The explosive growth of the Indian equity markets is well capitalised in the market capitalisation to GDP ratio which stood at 92.64 per cent as at end December 2010 (Krishnan, 2012). In fact there has been a rapid evolution of a modern securities market in India and SEBI has emerged as a tough and effective regulator over a rather short period of time.

To develop the government securities market, an active internal debt management policy has been pursued since 1991.

The reforms in the government securities market have facilitated the active use of open market operations (OMO) as a tool of market intervention through auctions. The sale of government securities by the RBI increased from Rs. 14 billion in 1995-96 to Rs. 416 billion in 2003-2004. Market-related rates, both in the primary auction as well as the OMO, have also helped achieve diversification of the investor base, with the share of non-captive investors increasing, though—statutorily—commercial banks, insurance companies, and provident funds continue to invest in government securities.

The reforms in the securities market were accompanied by two important developments in the economy. First, the statutory liquidity ratio (SLR), requiring the commercial banks to invest a specific proportion of their deposits in approved securities, mainly government, was reduced in quick phases to the lowest prescribed under the Banking Regulation Act. Second, market-related interest rates have increasingly been adopted in various sectors of the economy, including money markets, government securities, bank deposits and credit, public-sector bonds, and small (postal) savings. the dismantling of the administered interest rate regime raised the efficiency of the intermediation process and ensured financing of projects based on commercial considerations.

Money Markets

The short-term money market which has links with the entire spectrum of the financial system, comprises five segments:

- the call money market,
- the inter-bank term deposit market,
- the bills re-discount market, and
- the Treasury bill market
- the inter-corporate funds market

In recent years, new money market instruments such as Certificates of Deposits (CDs), Commercial Paper (CP) and 182 days Treasury bills have been introduced so as to impart liquidity and depth to the money market. Moreover, a specialised money market institution, named the Discount and Finance House of India (DFHI), has been established with the objective of providing liquidity to money market instruments, thereby helping to develop an active secondary market.

Major reforms in the money market were introduced from 1991 onwards, though some measures had been initiated in 1987. The reforms included the introduction of new participants, instruments (commercial paper, certificates of deposit, and inter-bank participation certificates), and maturities of Treasury Bills. To regulate short-term liquidity in the system, the RBI introduced repurchase transactions (repo) on December 10, 1992 and a liquidity adjustment facility (LAF) on June 5, 2000 under which it absorbs (repo) or injects liquidity (reverse repo) in the system each day. The repo rate has become an important signalling instrument for the financial markets, and the LAF has succeeded in reducing volatility in the call rate.

The Reserve Bank of India is the most important constituent of the money market. Money market falls under the direct purview of regulation of the Reserve Bank owing to its implications for conducting monetary policy. The primary objective of the Reserve Banks operations into the money market has been to ensure that short term interest rates and liquidity are maintained at levels consistent with overall monetary policy objective.

"Monetary policy (understood broadly, to include financial regulatory policy) is of such importance in part because the financial sector is so important: the financial sector has been likened to the brain of an economy, and if the financial sector does not work well, the economy does not work well. In many countries around the world-including the US and the EU—the financial sector has not done what it should have done and done what it should not have done; the costs of their failures in the US alone amount to trillions of dollars" (Stiglitz, 2013).[4]

1991 and After: The Reform Years[5]

The reform in the financial sector was attuned to the reform of the economy, which now signified opening up. Greater opening up underscores the importance of moving to international best practice quickly since investors tend to benchmark against such best practices and standards. Since 1991, the Indian financial system has undergone radical transformation. Reforms have altered the organisational structure, ownership pattern and domain of operation of banks, DFIs and Non-Banking Financial Companies (NBFCs). The main thrust of reforms in the financial sector was the creation of efficient and stable financial institutions and markets. Reforms in the banking and non-banking sectors focused on creating a deregulated environment, strengthening the prudential norms and the supervisory system, changing the ownership pattern, and increasing competition.

The policy environment was stanced to enable greater flexibility in the use of resources by banks through reduced statutory pre-emptions. Interest rate deregulation rendered greater freedom to banks to price their deposits and loans and the Reserve Bank moved away from micromanaging the banks on both the asset and liability-sides. The idea was to impart operational flexibility and functional autonomy with a view to enhancing efficiency, productivity and profitability. The

4. Kapila, Uma (ed.) (2013). "Introduction", *Indian Financial Reforms: Priorities and Policy Thrust Post Global Financial Crisis.* New Delhi: Academic Foundation.
5. This section has been drawn extensively from Mohan, Rakesh (2004). "Globalisation: The Role of Institution Building in the Financial Sector: The Indian Case", in Uma Kapila (ed.), *Economic Developments in India*, Vol. 74. New Delhi: Academic Foundation.

objective was also to create an enabling environment where existing banks could respond to changing circumstances and compete with new domestic private and foreign institutions that were permitted to operate. The Reserve Bank focused on tighter prudential norms in the form of capital adequacy ratio, asset classification norms, provisioning requirements, exposure norms and improved level of transparency and disclosure standards. As the market opens up, the need for monitoring and supervising becomes even more important systemically. The greater flexibility and the prudential regulation were fortified by 'on-site inspections' and 'off-site surveillance'. Furthermore, moving away from the closed economy objectives of ensuring appropriate credit planning and credit allocation, the inspection objectives and procedures, have been redefined to evaluate the bank's safety and soundness; to appraise the quality of the Board and management; to ensure compliance with banking laws and regulation; to provide an appraisal of soundness of the bank's assets; to analyse the financial factors which determine bank's solvency and to identify areas where corrective action is needed to strengthen the institution and improve its performance. A high-powered Board for Financial Supervision (BFS) was constituted in 1994, with the mandate to exercise the powers of supervision and inspection in relation to the banking companies, financial institutions and non-banking companies. Currently, given the developing state of the financial system, the function of supervision of banks, financial institutions and NBFCs rests with the Reserve Bank.

Role of Competition

It is generally argued that competition increases efficiency. Competition has been infused into the financial system by licensing new private banks since 1993. Foreign banks have also been given more liberal entry. While these banks have increased their share in the financial system, their presence has improved the efficiency of the financial system through their technology and risk management practices and provided a demonstration effect on the rest of the financial system.

Capital Adequacy and Government Ownership in the Banking Sector

In a globalised system, banks tend to get rated if they have to enter the market to raise debt or equity. Internationally, banks follow the Basel norms for capital adequacy. Banks were required to adopt these norms for maintaining capital in a phased manner in order to avoid any disruption. However, as a result of past bad lending, a few banks found it difficult to maintain adequate capital. The Government had contributed Rs. 4,000 crore to the paid-up capital of banks between 1985-86 and 1992-93. Subsequently, over the period 1992-93 to 2002-2003, the Government contributed over Rs. 22,000 crore towards recapitalisation of nationalised banks. In view of the limited resources and the many competing demands on the fisc, it became increasingly difficult for the Government to contribute any substantial amount required by nationalised banks for augmenting their capital base. In this context, Government permitted banks that were in a position to raise fresh equity to do so in order to meet their shortfall in capital requirements; the additional capital would enable banks to expand their lending.

Since the onset of reforms, there has been a change in the ownership pattern of banks. The legislative framework governing public-sector banks (PSBs) was amended in 1994 to enable them to raise capital funds from the market by way of public issue of shares. Many public-sector banks have accessed the markets since then to meet the increasing capital requirements.

Conclusion

The Indian financial system today has a wide network of institutions. The commercial banks have their presence in the most remote parts of the country. The development of the different segments of the financial system is, however, uneven. The cooperative credit system is effective only in certain parts of the country. But new institutions have come on the scene. The capital market has also become more active, with both primary and secondary markets showing strong upward movement.

The Indian financial development is a classic illustration of the 'supply leading' phenomenon under which financial institutions come into existence first and then create the demand for their services. The geographical spread of the Indian banking system was a conscious policy decision. Regional disparities in the provision of financial services have come down even though some states do complain of inadequate provision of credit in relation to deposits mobilised in their states. The involvement of banks and financial institutions in the schemes for providing credit to select segments of the society is very active. Banks are also closely associated with credit linked poverty alleviation programmes such as the Integrated Rural Development

Programme (IRDP), the Self-Employment Programme for Urban Poor (SEPUP) and Self-Employment Scheme for Educated Unemployed Youth (SEEUY). The experience with the poverty alleviation programmes has been mixed, as revealed by many studies. Even where such programmes have succeeded in raising the incomes of the beneficiaries, the recovery performance has not been that good.

Reform efforts in terms of strengthening of prudential norms, enhancing transparency standards and positioning best management practices are an ongoing process. Organised banking has made its presence felt in remote parts of the country. Insurance, hitherto a public sector monopoly, has since been transformed into a competitive market in both life and non-life segments. Strengthening corporate governance in cooperative banks has been making headway. Disclosures standards have been strengthened for non-banking financial companies. DFIs are also restructuring themselves in an era of global competition. A great deal of reforms has been undertaken in most areas of financial sector, reflected in the growing sophistication of the financial system. The resilience of the system is reflected in terms of absence of any major crisis in the financial system, a sustainable and broadbased growth environment, lower levels of inflation and strong external sector position. No doubt, the institutional framework in the financial sector had a major role to play in this process and the globalisation process in the financial sector has been beneficial for the economy. At the same time, the stance of the authorities has been proactive, reacting to the macroeconomic policy stance, global challenges and constantly endeavouring towards international best practices.

The basic emphasis of the Indian approach remains the creation of an enabling environment so as to foster deep, competitive, efficient and vibrant financial institutions and markets, with emphasis on stability. A number of measures have been initiated to achieve convergence with international best practices. Keeping in view the fast pace of technological innovations in the financial sector and product development at the international level, the focus has been to bring the Indian financial system at par with such standards. However, while adapting to international standards and trends, special attention is being devoted so as to customise norms and standards keeping in view various country-specific, including institution-specific considerations.

The global financial crisis has shown how misguided were policies of financial market liberalisation and deregulation. "These are policies that served special interests well and the voices of those special interests are often heard more loudly than the voices of these that are hurt by these policies" (Stiglitz, 2013).

According to K.C. Chakrabarty,[6] While India's financial sector remained resilient in the face of global shocks, there are a number of areas where the reforms would be needed to promote stability and generate growth impulses for the real economy. In the wake of turbulent global financial environment, banks and financial entities have to grapple with growing complexities and risks associated with their businesses. Against this backdrop, the policy initiatives such as adoption of tighter capital and liquidity standards, improved risk management practices and sound compensation practices are required to place the Indian banking system on a strong footing and enhance the banking sector's ability to absorb shocks arising from any financial and economic stress and encourage prudent risk taking.

Moreover, in India, while broader institutional reforms have taken place at the macro level, the internal reforms among banks and financial institutions are yet to take place. Thus, there is a need to go for second generation reforms, particularly focusing on bringing down the cost of banking services, strengthening the credit delivery mechanism, improving customer service, reforming the human resources management systems and enhancing the financial outreach to hitherto unbanked areas (Chakrabarty, 2013).

In India, growth with equity has been the central objective right from the inception of the planning process. The objective of financial inclusion is to provide financial services at affordable cost to those who are excluded from the formal financial system. This is vital for sustaining long term equitable development, since a large proportion of the households/areas do not have access to basic banking facilities, notwithstanding the existence of vast institutional framework in the country. An important challenge is to channelise more savings to the financial system, particularly in rural areas and from the urban informal sector. This would need further penetration of the banking system. The Reserve Bank's emphasis on financial inclusion is important in attaining this objective over time. There is also enormous potential for extending finance in semi-urban and rural areas for productive activities, which may require strengthening the banking correspondent (BC) relationship, simultaneously enhancing the risk assessment and risk management

6. Chakrabarty, K.C. (2013). "Indian Economy: Imperatives for Second Generation Reforms (Ch.2)", in Uma Kapila (ed.), *Indian Financial Reforms: Priorities and Policy Thrust Post Global Financial Crisis*. New Delhi: Academic Foundation.

capacities in order to maintain credit quality and sustain the credit growth in these sectors. Besides benefiting the unbanked masses, this will also ensure viability and scalability of banks' financial inclusion initiatives (Chakrabarty, 2013).

20

Foreign Trade and Trade Policy

Constraints Arising from Foreign Trade and Import Substitution-based Policies

Indian economic development strategy, particularly relating to industrialisation had been driven by perceived foreign exchange scarcities and the desire to ensure that scarce foreign exchange is used only for purposes deemed 'essential' from the perspective of development. Industrialisation and self-sufficiency in essential commodities have been important objectives of policy because of the fear that dependence on other, more powerful countries, for imports of essential commodities would lead to political dependence on them as well.

Far from viewing foreign trade as an engine of growth, Indian planners sought to minimise import demand and viewed exports more or less as a necessary evil mainly to generate the foreign exchange earnings to meet that part of the import bill not covered by external assistance. They created an elaborate administrative regulatory machinery in an attempt to control investment and resource allocation in the economy and ensure their consistency with five year plan targets. Controls over imports and exports were also part of this regulatory system.

This Chapter is extensively drawn from Uma Kapila (ed.) (2013). *Indian Economy Since Independence* (24th edition) (Ch.22). New Delhi: Academic Foundation.

FOREIGN TRADE PERFORMANCE

Exports and Imports: Broad Trends

Exports

1. 1950 to early 70s - Import substitution became the keystone of development strategy in the late 1950s. Consequently, exports were neglected by the Government. The value of exports as a percentage of GDP at market prices declined from an average of over 6 per cent (1950-1951 to 1955-56) to less than 4 per cent in the period following. This declining trend in the value of exports continues till 1971-72. The decline is in spite of the introduction of many incentive scheme for the exporters in the sixties. The sixties can be seen as the period of induction of export orientation through incentive schemes for exports along with import substitution. With the decision to devalue the rupee in 1966, changes in tariffs and export subsidy policy, it was evident that the policy makers were trying to use fiscal measures to step up exports and curb imports. But the incentives given to exporters could not offset the bias against exports which was implicit in the over valued exchange rate (except for 1966 devaluation) and the prevalent level of import restrictions.

2. Early 70s to late 80s - The value of exports as a percentage of GDP at market prices picked up after 1971-72 and increased till end of seventies. Eighties again shows a declining trend in value of exports with a recovery to over 6 per cent level only in the last couple of years in eighties (Table 20.1). It was realised after the first oil shock of 1973 that India had to step up exports simply to finance the rising import bill on account of an increase in oil prices.

Eighties can be viewed as a period of growing uneasiness with the policies of excessive protectionism. The Abid Hussain Committee on import and export policies (1985-1988) recommended more liberal access to imports by exporters. The second major recommendations of the Committee was that the real exchange rate of the rupee should not be allowed to appreciate and it should be maintained at a level considered appropriate for ensuring the competitiveness of exports.

3. 1990s - The 1990s have witnessed an increase in the value of exports as a percentage of GDP at market price to over 8 per cent from over 6 per cent level. After the payment crisis of 1990-91, when the foreign exchange reserves had fallen drastically and were enough to pay for two weeks of imports, the process of economic reforms was started in 1991. The chief elements of reforms are devaluation of the rupee, liberalisation of import licensing, reduction in tariffs, abolition of cash subsidies for exports, introduction of partial convertibility of the rupee on the current account and later full convertibility of the rupee on the current account.

TABLE – 20.1

Value of Exports and Imports—1950-51 to 2011-12

(US $ Million)

Year	*Exports*	*Imports*	*Trade Balance*	*Rate of Change*	
				Exports	*Imports*
1950-51	1269	1273	-4	24.9	-1.5
1960-61	1346	2353	-1007	0.3	16.7
1970-71	2031	2162	-131	8.8	3.5
1980-81	8486	15869	-7383	6.8	40.2
1990-91	18143	24075	-5932	9.2	13.5
2000-01	44560	50536	-5976	21.0	1.7
2005-06	103092	149167	-46076	23.4	33.8
2006-07	126360	185747	-59387	22.6	24.5
2007-08	163132	251654	-88522	29.0	35.5
2008-09	185295	303696	-118401	13.6	20.7
2009-10	178751	268373	-109622	-3.5	-5.0
2010-11	251136	369769	-118633	40.5	28.2
2011-12(P)[a] (April-Dec.)	217664	350936	-133272	25.8	30.4

Note: P: Provisional; a: Growth rate on provisional over revised basis.
Source: Government of India, *Economic Survey, 2011-12*, A-81.

After three successive years of robust growth at an annual average of 19.7 per cent (in US dollars) during 1993-94 to 1995-96, export momentum slowed down since 1996-97, with exports registering a modest growth of 5.3 per cent and decelerating further to 1.5 per cent in 1997-98. Both global and domestic factors have contributed to the slowdown in export growth in India since 1996-97. The share of east Asian countries in India's exports was around one-sixth before the crisis. India could not escape the fallout from the import compression in these countries. The slump in global trade and continued recessionary phase has caused not only import contraction, but has also triggered protectionist measures.

Amongst the domestic factors that continue to hamper exports infrastructure constraints, high transaction costs, SSI reservations, labour inflexibility, quality problems and quantitative ceilings on agricultural exports remain problematic.

Unlike many other countries, the global recession only slightly jolted the continued upward growth in India's export sector with exports rising at a reasonable rate of 13.6 per cent in 2008-09. The compound annual growth rate (CAGR) for India's merchandise exports for the five-year period 2004-05 to 2008-09 increased to 22 per cent from the 14 per cent of the preceding five-year period. However, in 2009-10 export growth was negative at (-)3.5 per cent, partly reflecting the effect of global recession and partly the higher base effect due to lagged export data of 2008-09. Despite this negative growth, India's ranking in the leading exporters in merchandise trade which slipped marginally from 26th in 2007 to 27th in 2008 improved to 21st in 2009.

Bolstered by the measures taken by the government to help exports in the aftermath of the world recession of 2008 and also the low base effect, India's export growth in 2010-11 reached an all time high of 40.5 per cent since Independence. Though it decelerated in 2011-12 to 21.3 per cent, it was still above 20 per cent and higher than the compound annual growth rate (CAGR) of 20.3 per cent for the period 2004-5 to 2011-12. After registering very high growth of 56.5 per cent in July 2011, export growth started decelerating with a sudden fall to single digits in November 2011 as a result of the emerging global situation and then to negative figures from March 2012. Monthly export growth rates in 2012-2013 (April-December) were negative except for a marginal positive growth in April 2012. For three months in 2012-13, exports declined YOY by double digits with the largest decline recorded in July 2012 at -15.1 per cent. In January, 2013, there is a marginal positive growth of 0.8 per cent (*Economic Survey 2012-13*).

Export growth in dollar terms was negative at -4.9 per cent in 2012-2013 (April-January), compared to 21.3 per cent growth in 2011-12 (full year). In rupee terms, it was positive at 9.1 per cent, though here too, there was a deceleration from the 28.3 per cent in 2011-12 (full year) (*Economic Survey 2012-13*).

India's share in world merchandise exports which had started rising fast since 2004, reached 1.3 per cent in 2009 and 1.5 per cent in 2010. It increased to 1.9 per cent in the first half of 2011, mainly due to the relatively higher Indian export growth of 55 per cent compared to the 23.1 per cent export growth of the world (Table 20.2). The increase in China's share in world exports between 2000 and 2010 at 6.5 percentage points is 48 per cent of the total increase in the share of emerging and developing countries over this period, while India's rise in share of 0.8 percentage points forms only 6 per cent of the total increase. However,

China's export growth rate at 31.3 per cent in 2010 and 24 per cent in the first half of 2011 was relatively lower than that of India.

TABLE – 20.2

Export Growth and Share in World Exports: India and Other Selected Countries

Country	*Value (US$ billion) 2010*	*Growth Rate (%) CAGR 2000-2008*	*Growth Rate (%) Annual 2009*	*Annual 2010*	*Annual 2011 (Jan-June)*	*Share in World Exports (%) 2000*	*2009*	*2010*	*2011 (Jan-June)*	*Changes in Shares 2010/2000*
China	1578	24.4	-15.9	31.3	24.0	3.9	9.7	10.5	10.1	6.5
Korea	466	11.9	-14.3	29.0	24.2	2.7	2.9	3.1	3.2	0.4
Hong Kong	390	7.6	-12.2	22.5	15.3	3.2	2.6	2.6	2.4	-0.6
Russia	400	20.6	-35.7	32.0	31.5	1.7	2.5	2.7	2.9	1.0
Singapore	352	11.9	-20.2	30.4	21.9	2.2	2.2	2.3	2.3	0.2
Mexico	298	7.3	-21.3	29.8	21.3	2.6	1.9	2.0	2.0	-0.6
Taiwan	275	7.1	-20.1	34.8	NA	2.3	1.6	1.8	NA	-0.5
India	223	21.0	-15.2	35.1	55.0	0.7	1.3	1.5	1.9	0.8
Malaysia	199	9.9	-24.9	26.2	17.6	1.5	1.3	1.3	1.3	-0.2
Brazil	202	17.3	-22.7	32.0	32.6	0.9	1.2	1.3	1.4	0.5
Thailand	195	12.4	-13.6	28.6	17.3	1.1	1.2	1.3	1.3	0.2
Indonesia	158	9.9	-14.4	32.1	27.6	1.0	1.0	1.0	1.1	0.0
South Africa	82	13.9	-26.0	30.6	29.2	0.5	0.5	0.5	0.5	0.1
EDEs	5894	18.0	-24.4	28.4	29.2	25.4	37.1	39.1	39.8	13.6
World	15087	12.2	-22.7	21.9	23.1	100.0	100.0	100.0	100.0	-

Note: EDEs: Emerging and Developing Economies.
Source: IFS November, 2011, IMF; *Economic Survey 2011-12*.

Composition of India's Exports

Compositional changes in India's export basket have been taking place over the years. While the share of primary products in India's exports fell over the years from 16 per cent in 2000-01, in April-November 2012-13 it regained the share of 16 per cent mainly due to the export of agricultural items like rice and guar gum meal. The share of manufacturing exports whose share rose from 45 per cent in 1950-1951 to 71 per cent in 1990-91 and 78.8 per cent in 2000-01 fell drastically to 66.1 per cent in 2011-12 and further to 64.5 per cent in 2012-13 (April-November) mainly due to the fall in shares of traditional items like textiles and leather and leather manufactures even though the share of engineering goods and chemicals and related products increased. Share of gems and jewellery fell marginally. Share of petroleum, crude & products exports, which also include refined items, increased from 4.3 per cent in 2000-01 to 18.3 per cent in 2011-12 and 18.6 per cent in 2012-13 (April-November) (*Economic Survey 2012-13*).

BOX – 20.1

India's Major Manufactured Exports

The top four items in India's manufactured exports are engineering goods, gems and jewellery, chemicals and related products, and textiles (see Table). Since 2007-8, electronic goods have displaced leather and manufactures from fifth place with the share of the former increasing and the latter decreasing. There has been a gradual shift in India's manufactures exports from labour-intensive sectors like textiles, leather and manufactures, handicrafts, and carpets to capital- and skillintensive sectors.

Engineering goods exports has seen an almost steady rise in shares from 1999-2000 to the first half of 2011-12 and high growth rates of 84 per cent and 43.6 per cent in 2010-11 and the first half of 2011-12 respectively mainly due to the high growth rates of two major items machinery & instruments and transport equipments besides residual engineering items with very high growth rates. The major markets for Indian engineering exports in 2010-11 were China, the USA, the UAE, Singapore, Saudi Arabia, South Africa, Germany, Sri Lanka, and the UK. All these markets showed tremendous export growth with China topping at 409 per cent.

TABLE

Performance of Top Four Items in India's Manufactured Exports

	Shares				*CAGR*	*Growth rate*		
	1999-2000	*2010-11*	*2010-11 Apr.-Sept.*	*2011-12*	*1999-2000 to 2008-09*	*2009-10*	*2010-11*	*2011 11 (Apr.-Sept.)*
1. Engineering Goods	11.9	23.8	21.7	22.2	28.0	-18.7	84.0	43.6
2. Gems & Jewellery	20.4	14.7	14.3	16.1	15.9	3.7	27.0	58.4
3. Chemicals & Related Products	13.4	11.5	12.2	11.6	19.3	0.9	26.5	34.2
4. TEXTILES	25.0	8.7	9.6	8.7	8.6	-1.2	17.1	27.0

...contd...

With the highest growth rate among manufactures at 58.4 per cent in the first half of 2011-12,gems and jewellery, the second major export item, has retained its share of around 16-17 per cent since 2000-1. In 2010-11, this sector accounted for 14.7 per cent of India's total merchandise exports. India is the largest cutting and polishing centre for diamonds in the world. Of the global polished diamond market, India's share is estimated to be 70 per cent in terms of value, 85 per cent in terms of volume, and 92 per cent in terms of pieces. As per the Gem and Jewellery Export Promotion Council (GJEPC), this sector as a whole supports about 34 lakh jobs. The gems and jewellery manufacturing sector consists of large number of small and medium enterprise (SME) units, employing skilled and semi-skilled labour, almost entirely in the unorganized sector.

The share of chemicals and related products has fallen marginally over the years mainly because of the fall in shares of basic chemicals, pharmaceuticals, and cosmetics. The growth in 2010-11 and the first half of 2011-12, however, have been higher by 26.5 per cent and 34.2 per cent respectively. The steady fall in share of the textiles sector to single digits since 2000-1 is mainly due to a fall in shares of ready-made garments and cotton, yarn, fabrics, made-ups, etc. Clearly, India has not been able to utilize the opportunity provided by the phasing out of the Multi Fibre Agreement (MFA) in 2005.

The rise of the electronics sector, though long overdue, is a welcome sign. This is due to the recent policies of the government to help this sector like including many electronic items in the Focus Product Scheme and customs duty exemption to many electronic components. The Tsunami in Japan which led to disruption of supply chains in Japan could also have benefitted India at a time when support measures were taken by India for this sector.

Economic Survey 2012-13.

Export growth was high in 2010-11 and the first half of 2011-12 in case of agriculture and allied products due to export growth in cereals, meat preparations, oil meals, and coffee.Among manufactured exports, engineering goods, gems and jewellery, and chemicals and related products registered high growth, while textiles export growth was moderate. Export growth of petroleum, crude, and products was also very high due to the high prices of crude oil and also due to increase in refining capacity.

Diversification of exports constitutes an important element of India's export promotion strategy. Reflecting the policy thrust as also the evolving pattern of industrial development, India has gradually transformed from a predominantly primary products exporting country into an exporter of manufactured goods. The commodity composition within the major groups has also undergone a considerable transformation. Within the 'primary products' group, the share of 'ores and minerals' in total exports has declined while the share of 'agricultural and allied products' remained almost unchanged at around 18 per cent between 1990-91 and 1998-99 but declined thereafter to 13.4 per cent in 2000-01. The falling share of 'ores and minerals' has been offset by the increase in share of 'engineering goods' within the manufactured products group—an indication of upward movement of India's exports in the value-addition chain.

Direction of Exports

Destination-wise analysis of the Indian exports indicates an unchanged position in respect of the Organisation for Economic Cooperation and Development (OECD) group being the largest market, increasing prominence of the Organisation of Petroleum Exporting Countries (OPEC) and the developing countries (Asia, Africa and Latin America), and a steep erosion in the relative position of the Eastern Europe. With the break-up of the Soviet Union, the share of the East European countries fell dramatically from 17.9 per cent in 1990-91 to just 2.9 per cent in 2001-02, primarily on account of the termination of Rupee trade and its adverse impact on exports of agricultural products such as tea, tobacco and spices to this region. The loss of this market share was, however, made up by increasing the shares in developing countries and the OPEC region, both of which doubled between the years 1987-88 and 2001-02.

The reason for India's export growth in 2012-13 (April-November) being more negative than in 2009-10 in the aftermath of the global recession can be seen from India's commodity-country export performance. India's exports to EU and China have been more negative during the recent global slowdown than in 2009-10, while its performance to USA has been better for most of the sectors except gems and jewellery. The performance of India's exports to EU of textiles and readymade garments, gems and jewellery and ores: and to China of manufactures, engineering goods, chemicals gems and jewellery and ores was worse off in 2012-13 (April-November) compared to 2009-10. India's POL export growth to all major markets also decelerated in 2012-13 (April-

November) compared to 2009-10. Thus, the Euro Zone crisis and the Chinese slowdown have affected India's exports more during the recent slowdown than in 2009-10 (*Economic Survey 2012-13*).

Export Diversification

In 2011, India had a global export share of 1 per cent or more in 53 out of a total of 99 commodities at the two-digit harmonized system (HS) level. While noticeable changes can be seen in India's market diversification, the same is not the case with its export basket diversification (Box 20.2) (*Economic Survey 2012-13*).

BOX – 20.2

Market vs Product Diversification

India has been fairly successful in diversifying its export markets from developed countries like the US and Europe to Asia and Africa, which has helped to a great extent in weathering the global crisis of 2008 and the recent global slowdown (Table 1).

Table – 1

Region-wise Share of India's Exports:

	2000-1	*2005-6*	*2011-12*	*2012-13 (Apr.-Nov.)*
1) Europe	25.9	24.2	19.0	18.7
2) Africa	5.3	6.8	8.1	9.6
3) America	24.7	20.7	16.4	19.5
4) Asia	37.4	46.9	50.0	50.4
5) CIS & Baltics	2.3	1.2	1.0	1.3

Source: Computed from DGCI&S data.

However, in terms of product diversification a lot more needs to be done as can be seen from the following:

- In the top 100 imports of the world at the four-digit HS level in 2011, India has only 6 items in the top 50; it has only 5 items with a share of 5 per cent and above and 18 items with a share of 2 per cent and above (Table 2), with 6 new items with high export growth (India) entering the list and 3 going out of the list in 2011 compared to 2010. The new items are medicaments consisting of mixed or unmixed products for

contd...

...contd...

therapeutic use; other articles of iron and steel; men's or boys' suits, ensembles; cruise ships, excursion boats, ferry-boats, cargo ships, barges and similar vessels; cane or beet sugar and chemically pure sucrose in solid form; and maize.

Table – 2

Export Items of India with 2 per cent and above Share in Top 100 World Imports at Four-digit level

Rank# World 2011	*HS4*	*Items*	*India share in world 2011*	*Growth rate in 2011*	
				India (Export)	*World (Import)*
2	2710	Petroleum oils and oils obtained from bituminous minerals, etc.	6.7	49.0	39.4
7	3004	Medicaments consisting of mixed or unmixed products for therapeutic use	2.1	36.0	5.7
11	2601	Iron ores and concentrates, including roasted iron pyrites	2.3	-32.3	37.8
14	7102	Diamonds, whether or not worked, but not mounted or set.	23.8	44.7	14.7
34	7403	Refined copper and copper alloys, unwrought	3.2	-53.7	12.2
39	8803	Parts of goods of heading no. 88.01or 88.02.	3.5	45.4	1.2
51	6403	Footwear with outer soles of rubber	3.1	23.0	9.2
52	6204	Women's or girls' suits, ensembles, jackets, blazers, dresses	4.9	34.8	9.2
55	7210	Flat-rolled products of iron or non-alloy steel	2.8	0.8	12.2
56	7113	Articles of jewellery and parts thereof, of precious metal	28.5	83.6	13.4
61	2902	Cyclic hydrocarbons.	4.4	47.8	27.8
68	7326	Other articles of iron or steel.	2.0	97.9	13.9
69	3902	Polymers of propylene or of other olefins, in primary forms.	2.8	46.0	17.3

contd...

...contd...

72	6203	Men's or boys' suits, ensembles, jackets, blazers, trousers, etc.	2.3	31.5	16.4
92	6109	T-shirts, singlets & other vests, knitted or crocheted	6.0	22.1	12.1
97	8901	Cruise ships, excursion boats, ferry-boats, cargo ships, barges, and similar vessels	2.2	40.0	-25.8
99	1701	Cane or beet sugar and chemically pure sucrose, in solid form.	6.0	123.1	20.1
100	1005	Maize	3.4	103.1	34.1

Note: # Rank is in top 100 world imports.
Source: Computed from UN Comtrade data extracted on 9 January 2013.

- India has a very high export share in world imports in the case of only two four-digit HS items, jewellery and diamonds. While India can increase its shares further in the other 16 items given in the table, there are many other simple items in the top 100 world imports with high demand where India has developed its competence. Most of the items come under the three Es, electronic, electrical, and engineering items and some textiles items. Greater focus on these items could lead to a perceptible increase in India's share of exports in world imports.

Source: Internal study, Economic Division, Department of Economic Affairs. *Economic Survey 2012-13.*

Imports

1. **1950 to early 1970s** - The value of imports as a proportion of GDP at market prices, fluctuated through the 1950s (around 6 to 9.8 per cent) and thereafter declined slowly till the early 1970s (from 6.8 per cent in 1960-61 to 4.2 per cent in 1972-1973.

   The severe foreign exchange crisis of 1956-57 led to the adoption of strict measures for import controls. The import licensing system was intensified in the late fifties and early sixties. After a brief attempt at using fiscal measures instead of physical controls in mid-sixties, the import licensing was intensified. Import policy became increasingly restrictive and complex. The quantitative restrictions were used to provide protection to any domestic activity that substituted for imports. The decline in public investment and industrial growth after the mid-1960s also contributed to reducing the pressure on imports.

2. **Early 1970s to late 1980s** - After 1972-73, the value of imports as a proportion of GDP showed a distinct increase. The import needs became stronger as the industrial growth recovered in mid-seventies and showed an accelerating trend in the 1980s. The eighties is marked with a clear shift in the trade strategy towards reduction of quantitative restrictions on imports. The number of items in the category of OGL—that is, a licence to import but with no quantitative restrictions—increased substantially in this period. The rise in the value of imports as a proportion of GDP at market prices is in spite of the sharp increase in tariffs in eighties. The value of imports as a proportion of GDP increased from a level of 4.6 per cent (1973-74) to over 6 per cent in the remaining years of seventies. It was around 8 to 9 per cent in the decade of eighties.
3. **1990s** - The value of imports as a proportion of GDP at market prices show a distinct increase in the 1990s except for 1991-1992. The decline in 1991-92 was due to severe import curbs introduced after the payment crisis of 1990-91. The value of imports as a proportion of GDP increased from 8.8 per cent in 1990-91 to 12.5 per cent in 1997-98 and 13 per cent in 2000-2001.

Composition of Imports

The commodity-structure of India's imports has also shown marked changes, reflecting, *inter alia*, the impact of trade policy, the movements in international prices and the pattern of domestic demand. The share of oil imports in India's total imports increased from 17.1 per cent during 1987-1990 to 23.9 per cent during 1992-1997 and further to 27.2 per cent in 2001-02. While the share and absolute value of these imports showed sharp fluctuations over the years mainly on account of the large movements in international crude prices, the volume of such imports has grown significantly on account of increase in domestic consumption and the stagnation in domestic crude oil production. Given the large swings in international crude prices, as also a trend rise in the oil import bill, there is a need for a comprehensive review of energy policy of the country covering the demand-supply aspects, as well as the price policy. Renewed efforts to improve energy supply from domestic sources by encouraging explorations, and

TABLE – 20.3

Commodity Composition of Imports

Commodity Group	Percentage share					CAGR	Growth rate[a]			
	2000-01	*2010-11*	*2011-12*	*2011-12 (Apr.-Nov.)*	*2012-13 (Apr.-Nov.)*	*2000-01 to 2009-10*	*2010-11*	*2011-12*	*2011-12 (Apr.-Nov.)*	*2012-13 (Apr.-Nov.)*
I. Food and allied products, *of which*	**3.3**	**2.9**	**3.1**	**3.1**	**3.5**	**22.7**	**2.2**	**44.4**	**38.0**	**11.6**
1. Cereals	0.0	0.0	0.0	0.0	0.0	24.3	15.8	-34.2	-46.6	6.8
2. Pulses	0.2	0.4	0.4	0.4	0.4	38.3	-23.1	27.2	11.3	9.2
3. Edible oils	2.6	1.8	2.1	2.1	2.5	17.2	19.0	57.7	55.3	18.0
II. Fuel, of which	**33.5**	**30.9**	**37.4**	**34.3**	**38.0**	**21.0**	**22.4**	**59.7**	**52.3**	**9.8**
4. POL	31.3	28.7	31.7	30.7	34.6	21.0	21.6	46.2	50.6	11.7
III. Fertilizers	**1.3**	**1.9**	**2.4**	**2.3**	**2.2**	**29.0**	**4.8**	**72.1**	**32.2**	**-6.8**
IV. Capital goods, of which	**10.5**	**13.6**	**14.1**	**12.6**	**11.9**	**26.1**	**19.2**	**36.9**	**25.6**	**-6.5**
5. Machinery except electrical & machine tool	5.9	7.0	7.2	6.7	6.3	24.4	24.0	35.8	28.2	-5.8
6. Electrical machinery	1.0	1.0	1.0	1.0	0.9	22.7	25.1	33.1	26.6	-5.5
7. Transport equipment	1.4	3.1	3.0	2.5	2.3	36.4	-0.9	31.8	13.1	-8.3
V. Others, of which	**52.5**	**49.6**	**49.0**	**47.6**	**44.3**	**19.3**	**43.2**	**30.8**	**29.6**	**-7.6**
8. Chemicals	5.9	5.2	5.1	5.0	5.1	19.5	29.6	31.8	24.3	1.1
9. Pearls, precious, semi-precious stones	9.7	9.3	6.1	6.1	4.1	14.0	116.9	-13.3	4.3	-32.3
10. Gold & silver	9.3	11.5	12.6	13.0	10.5	23.0	43.0	44.5	59.2	-20.4
11. Electronic goods	7.0	7.1	7.1	7.0	6.5	21.6	28.4	31.7	22.2	-7.7
Total Imports	**100.0**	**100.0**	**100.0**	**100.0**	**100.0**	**21.5**	**28.2**	**32.3**	**36.2**	**-0.8**

Note: a Growth rate in US dollar.
Source: *Economic Survey* 2012-13.

stepping up of production and refining capacities are necessary to bring about a structural change in this area.

Reflecting the impact of a series of policy measures undertaken in the post-reform years starting with the repeal of the Gold Control Order in 1991 for liberalising the imports of gold and silver, these imports showed a sharp pick-up from 1992-93. The imports of gold and silver (including passenger baggage) rose from a meagre US $ 6 million in 1991-1992 to US $ 1.3 billion in 1992-93 and further to US $ 5.9 billion in 1997-98. A large part of the increase in these imports could be due to a switchover from the unofficial channel to the official channel, initially through the Non-Resident Indian (NRI) baggage route and subsequently through the OGL route. In the subsequent years, however, these imports have stabilised and, in fact, declined to US $ 4.6 billion in 2001-02.

There have been some significant compositional changes in India's import basket in recent years. The share of POL imports increased from 28.7 per cent in 2010-11 to 31.7 per cent in 2011-12 (with a very high growth rate) and 34.6 per cent in 2012-13 (April-November). The share of gold and silver imports increased from 9.3 per cent in 2000-1 to 12.6 per cent in 2011-12 with a high import growth rate of 44.5 per cent. However, in part due to policy measures like raising import duty on gold, there was a moderation in gold and silver imports in 2012-13 (April-November) with its share falling to 10.5 per cent following a negative growth of -20.4 per cent. The import share of pearls, precious and semiprecious stones also fell sharply in 2011-12 to 6.1 per cent following a negative growth of -13.3 per cent and further to 4.1 per cent in 2012-13 (April- November), with a high negative growth rate of - 32.3 per cent. Another important development is related to the share of capital goods imports which increased from 10.5 per cent in 2000-1 to 13.6 per cent in 2010-11 and further to 14.1 per cent in 2011-12, declining thereafter to 11.9 per cent in 2012-13 (April-November) following a negative growth rate of - 6.5 per cent. Among capital goods, the import shares of all items machinery except electrical and machine tools, transport equipment, project goods, and electrical machinery fell, clearly signaling a slowdown in industrial activity. The share of electronic goods, which includes both consumer electronics and capital goods, also fell in 2012-13 (April-November) (*Economic Survey 2012-13*).

Direction of Trade

There has been significant market diversification in India's trade. Region-wise, while India's exports to Europe and America have declined, its exports to Asia and Africa have increased (See Box 20.1). However, in 2012-13 (April- November), the share of India's exports to the USA increased to 13.5 per cent. Within Asia, while the share of North East Asia (consisting of China, Hong Kong, Japan) and ASEAN (Association of South East Asian Nations) fell from 14.8 per cent and 12.0 per cent in 2011-12 to 13.1 per cent and 10.3 per cent respectively in 2012-13 (April- November), there was a noticeable rise in the share of West Asia-GCC (Gulf Cooperation Council) countries from 14.9 per cent in 2011-12 to 17.7 per cent in 2012-13 (April- November).

In 2012-13 (April- November), compared to 2000-01, the share of India's imports from Europe has declined to 16.7 per cent from 27.6 per cent, while that from Asia has increased substantially to 61.1 per cent from 27.7 per cent. The share of America in India's imports also increased to 11.5 per cent from 7.9 per cent. India's top 15 trading partners have nearly 60 per cent in share in its trade with the top three contributing nearly half of this share. While Iran and UK are out of this top 15 list in 2011-12, Iraq and Kuwait are the new entrants (*Economic Survey 2012-13*).

At 10 per cent in 2011-12 India's trade deficit as a per cent of GDP is one of the highest in the world. Export-import ratios reflecting the bilateral trade balance show that among its top 15 trading partners, India had bilateral trade surplus with four countries in 2011-12, viz. the UAE, USA, Singapore, and Hong Kong. In 2012-13 (April- November), India's trade balance with the UAE has turned slightly negative while it has improved further with the USA and Hong Kong. Another important trend is the growing trade deficit of India with China and Switzerland, increasing from US$ 28 billion and US$24.1 billion in 2010-11 to US$ 39.4 billion and US$ 31.3 billion respectively in 2011-12. In 2012-13 (April-November), the export-import ratio with China worsened further to 0.23 from 0.31 in 2011-12 (*Economic Survey 2012-13*).

World Merchandise Trade: Global Recession

The deepening world recession had profound impact on world trade. The US$16 trillion global trade of 2008 collapsed, reaching US $ 5.8 trillion in the first half of 2009 compared to US$8.2 trillion in the corresponding period of 2008. As a result, growth of world output and trade volume of goods and services fell to (-) 0.8 and (-) 12.3 per cent respectively in 2009 according to the International Monetary Fund's (IMF) World Economic Outlook (WEO) January 2010.

World trade value, which fell sharply from US$ 16 trillion in 2008 to US$ 12.4 trillion in 2009, recovered to US$ 15.1 trillion in 2010 though it was still below the pre-crisis level.

World merchandise trade value surpassed the pre-crisis (2008) level of US $ 16 trillion, reaching US $ 18.26 trillion in 2011 after an interregnum of two years. However, world trade volume decelerated sharply to 2.8 per cent in 2012 from 5.9 per cent in 2011 and 12.6 per cent in 2010 (Table 20.4).

World exports fell by 0.2 per cent in the first three quarters of 2012 over the corresponding periods of 2011 as per World Trade Organization (WTO) statistics. As per the January 2013 update of the IMF, world trade volume is projected to grow by 3.8 per cent in 2013 which is down 0.7 percentage points compared to its October 2012 update. Import and export volume growth rates of emerging market and developing economies are however projected to be higher than those of advanced economies. Global economic uncertainty including doubts about the ultimate resolution of the crisis in the euro area, doubts about the pace of fiscal withdrawal in the US, challenges to sustaining growth after the earthquake reconstruction rebound in Japan and trade disruptions with China, though of a passing nature, continue to cast their shadows on the trade growth of emerging and developing economies (EDEs) including India.

TABLE – 20.4

Trends in Growth in Trade Volumes
(per cent change)

				Projections	
	2010	*2011*	*2012*	*2013*	*2014*
World Trade Volume (Goods and Services)	12.7	5.9	2.8	3.8	5.5
Imports					
Advanced Economies	11.5	4.6	1.2	2.2	4.1
Emerging and Developing Economies	15.0	8.4	6.1	6.5	7.8
Exports					
Advanced Economies	12.2	5.6	2.1	2.8	4.5
Emerging and Developing Economies	13.8	6.6	3.6	5.5	6.9

Source: IMF:WEO, January 2013.
Economic Survey 2011-12, 2012-13.

Services Trade

In recent years, the focus of services trade has shifted away from just facilitating trade in goods as the sector has emerged as an independent entity in itself. With the spread of telecommunications and computer technologies, virtually all commercial services have become tradable across borders. The trend of globalisation, reinforced by liberalisation policies and the removal of regulatory obstacles, has fuelled steady growth of international investment and trade in services. (for details, see ch.17)

Special Economic Zones (SEZs)

Another major policy issue in the trade sector which created a lot of heat was that of SEZs. The SEZ Act, 2005, supported by SEZ Rules, came into effect on February 10, 2006. The main objectives of the SEZ Act are generation of additional economic activity, promotion of exports of goods and services, promotion of investment from domestic and foreign sources, creation of employment opportunities and development of infrastructure facilities. Various incentives and facilities are offered to both—units in SEZs for attracting investments into SEZs (including foreign investment) as well as for SEZ developers. These incentives and facilities are expected to trigger a large flow of foreign and domestic investment in SEZs, particularly in infrastructure and productive capacity, leading to generation of additional economic activity and creation of employment opportunities. The SEZ Rules provide for different minimum land requirements for different classes of SEZs. Every SEZ is divided into a processing area where alone, the SEZ units are set up and a non-processing area where the supporting infrastructure is to be created. The SEZ Rules also provide for simplified procedures for development, operation and maintenance of the SEZ and setting up units in SEZs, single window clearance both relating to Central as well as state governments for setting up of an SEZ and units in a SEZ and simplified compliance procedures/ documentation with emphasis on self-certification.

The performance of SEZs is mainly examined in three areas, exports, employment, and investment.

Exports: A total of 130 SEZs are already exporting. Out of this 75 are information technology (IT)/ IT enabled services (ITES), 16 multi-product and 39 other sector specific SEZs. The total number of units in these SEZs is 3139. When the whole world including India was reeling under the effects of the global recession, growth in exports from SEZs was 121 per cent in 2009-10 compared to a paltry 0.6 per cent growth in total exports from India. Exports during the first three quarters of the current year have been to the tune of Rs. 2,23,132 crore. The share of SEZs in India's total exports has increased consistently from 4.7 per cent in 2003-04 to 26.1 per cent in 2009-10 and 29.7 per cent in the first three quarters of 2010-11 (Table 20.5).

Employment: Out of the total employment of 6,44,073 persons in SEZs, an incremental employment of 5,09,369 persons was generated after February 2006 when the SEZ Act came into force. At least double this number obtains indirect employment outside the SEZs as a result of the operations of SEZ units. This is in addition to the employment created by the developer for infrastructure activities.

Investment: The total investment in SEZs till 31 December 2010 is approximately Rs. 1,95,348 crore including Rs. 1,91,313 crore in the newly notified zones. In SEZs 100 per cent FDI is allowed through automatic route.The Government's role has been more as a facilitator by fast tracking the approvals rather than providing any direct monetary support. SEZs being set up under the SEZ Act 2005 are primarily private investment driven.

TABLE – 20.5

Exports from Special Economic Zones

Year	*Value of Exports from SEZs (Rs Crore)*	*Growth Rate (%) (Over the Previous Year)*
2003-04	13,854	39
2004-05	18,314	32
2005-06	22,840	25
2006-07	34,615	52
2007-08	66,638	93
2008-09	99,689	50
2009-10	220711	121.4
2010-11 (April-Dec.)	223132	-

Source: *Economic Survey 2010-11*.

Challenges and Outlook

The challenges for India on the trade front are many. Some are due to the current emerging global situation and some are systemic and long term in nature. If the global situation worsens, the pressure for stimulus measures could again resurface and protectionist measures from trading partners could increase. Thus a lot needs to be done on the trade facilitation front. While India has achieved a fair amount of stability in software services exports, there is less stability in business services exports. Despite the rhetoric in India on the potential of tourism services exports, results on the ground could improve further. Finally, while there are no signs of any meaningful conclusion of WTO negotiations in the near horizon, India's push towards regional and bilateral agreements should result in meaningful and result-oriented FTAs and CECAs.

The recent global slowdown has thrown up new challenges for India with its export growth being continuously negative since May 2012 compared to very high growth rates of even above 50 per cent in some months of the previous year. With limited fiscal space available for the government and with protectionist measures of trading partners showing signs of rising, the policy options left are more at the micro level as indicated in Box 20.3.

Thus there are many micro, port-specific and sector-specific issues that need urgent attention. These are related to infrastructure, trade facilitation, tax and tariffs, and credit, and can realistically be addressed in the short and medium term. Addressing these issues, as is currently being done by the government, can exponentially promote India's export growth.

BOX – 20.3

Reviving and Accelerating India's Trade: Micro, Sector- and Port-specific issues

Some trade-related issues and suggested policies at the micro, sector-specific and port-specific levels are as follows:

Infrastructure Related: Even the best of Indian ports do not have state-of-the-art technology as in Singapore, Rotterdam, and Shanghai. Port Infrastructure issues include poor road conditions and port connectivity, congestions, vessel berthing delays, poor cargo handling techniques and equipment., resulting in multiple handlings, increased lead time, high transaction costs and thus loss of market competitiveness.

Port-specific infrastructure issues include restriction in port access points to Chennai Port, various surcharges like congestion surcharge and Chennai trade recovery charge on the users of Chennai Port, container relocation

contd...

...contd. ...

charges, imbalance surcharge, etc. levied without any legal sanction with the charge on the trade component being very low and port congestion at the Jawaharlal Nehru Port Trust (JNPT) Port at Mumbai, entry gates closing prematurely resulting in export consignments being dumped in the buffer yard at a very high cost and delay in shipments, and many vessels bypassing the JNPT Port carrying containers to be delivered at their next voyage thereby delaying vital raw materials for the industry.

Trade Facilitation Measures: While India is ranked 132 in the 'ease of doing business', on 'trading across borders' India is ranked 127 with Singapore at first rank and China at 68th as per the World Bank and IFC 'Doing Business 2013'. India requires 9 export documents to be cleared, while China needs 8, with good practice economies like France needing 2. Time to export is 16 days for India and five for Denmark. Cost to export is $1120 per container, compared to $580 in China and $435 in Malaysia. Number of import documents that need clearance is 11 in India, 5 in China, and 2 in France. Time to import is 20 days in India and 4 in Singapore. Cost to import is $1200 per container in India, $615 in China, and $439 in Singapore. There are many trade facilitation measures that can help the export sector without any cost to the government exchequer. These include simplification of the multiple documentation procedures as on an average an Indian exporter is required to sign at about 130 places to complete an export transaction (from pre-shipment till receiving export related benefits) as per the Federation of Indian Export Organisations (FIEO). These procedures and costs need to be reduced to the barest minimum.

Other procedural and documentation reforms include abolishing the system of printing and certifying export promotion(EP) copies of shipping bills, implementing 24x7 system for Container Freight Stations (CFSs) , reducing unnecessary paper work related to renewal of letters of undertaking (LUT) for export without payment of duty, discouraging the practice of insistence by banks for L/Cs through their branches in foreign countries, merging or streamlining the Market Access Initiative (MAI) & Marketing Development Assistance (MDA) schemes, removing the annual average export performance condition under the EPCG scheme, and addressing the issue of trade litigations.

Some port-specific trade facilitation measures include addressing the issues of high terminal handling charges (THC) and increase in cut-off time resulting in containers missing the intended vessels and non-availability of electronic data interchange (EDI) facility inside the International Container Transhipment Terminal (ICTT) in Vallarpadam

contd. ...

...contd. ...

Port; and streamlining the timing of the Customs office at the Precious Cargo Customs Clearance Centre (PCCC), Mumbai, as it is open till 1.30 p.m. while the timing for receiving goods/parcels for exporting is till 4.00 p.m..

Tax and Customs Duty Related: These include fixing a time limit for disbursal of duty drawback, service tax refunds, and central excise rebate claims to the exporters as delays in the release of these claims adversely affect working capital, making them less competitive; crediting payment of central excise rebate claims directly to the bank account of the exporter; introducing value added tax (VAT) refund system for purchases in India by foreigners which can increase purchases in India by foreign tourists; and reviewing inverted duty structure under the India-Thailand FTA as finished jewellery imports from Thailand are cheaper than primary gold (raw material) available in India.

Source: H.A.C. Prasad, (2012). 'Emerging Global Economic Situation: Its impact on India's Trade and some Policy Issues', Working paper No 1/2012-DEA, Ministry of Finance.

Economic Survey 2012-13.

BALANCE OF TRADE

APPENDIX TABLE – A-20.1

Balance of Trade

Balance of trade, simply defined is, the difference between the value of export of goods and the value of import of goods or more generally between exports and imports or (X-M) where X denotes value of exports and M, value of imports.

When value of exports is more than value of imports (i.e., X > M), balance of trade (BoT) is said to be favourable or positive. On the other hand, when exports are less than imports (X < M) or imports more than exports (M > X), the balance of trade (BoT) is said to be unfavourable or negative, or there is said to be a deficit in the balance of trade.

Since goods are also called merchandise, the balance of trade or trade balance is also called balance of merchandise account.

India's Balance of Trade

Ever since the beginning of planning era in 1951, India has continued to suffer from an unfavourable balance of trade. The only exceptions to this trend have been the years 1972-73 and 1976-77 when the country had a positive trade balance of Rs. 104 crore and Rs. 68 crore, respectively.

In the early years after Independence, the value of India's exports as well as imports were low and the difference between them was small. This resulted in comparatively lower magnitude of deficit in trade balance. From Rs. 174 crore in 1951-52, average annual deficit rose to an annual average of Rs. 626533 (April-December 2011-12, Economic Survey 2011-12 Table 7.1(A)). Thus, the trade deficit has not only persisted since 1951 but has increased widely over the years.

Causes of Unfavourable Balance of Trade

Continued excess of imports over exports has perpetuated the unfavourable balance of trade since 1950-51. To begin with, the trade deficit was small, but it widened over time, more particularly from the Sixth Plan onwards, it rose sharply to assume serious dimensions during and after the Eighth Five Year Plan. This has happened because exports from India have not been able to keep pace with the high growth rate of imports.

contd. ...

...contd. ...

India's Balance of Trade

(Rs. Crore)

Plans		*Average Annual*		*Trade Balance*
		Exports	*Imports*	
First Plan	(1951-1956)	605	735	-130
Second Plan	(1956-1961)	606	973	-367
Third Plan	(1961-1966)	753	1,240	-487
Annual Plans	(1966-1969)	1,238	1,998	-760
Fourth Plan	(1969-1974)	1,810	1,973	-163
Fifth Plan	(1974-1979)	4,728	5,538	-810
Annual Plans	(1979-1980)	6,418	9,143	-2,725
Sixth Plan	(1980-1985)	8,967	14,683	-5,716
Seventh Plan	(1985-1990)	17,382	25,112	-7,730
Annual Plans	(1991-1992)	38,297	45,525	-7,278
Eighth Plan	(1992-1997)	86,557	97,609	-11,352
Ninth Plan	(1997-2002)	1,68,400	2,04,763	-36,363
Tenth Plan	(2002-2007)	20,52,041	26,58,294	-6,06,253
Eleventh	(2007-08)	6,55,864	10,12,312	-3,56,448
Plan	(2008-09)	8,40,755	13,74,436	-5,33,680
	(2009-10)	8,45,534	13,63,736	-5,18,202
	(2010-11)(P) (Apr-Dec.)	7,51,633	11,86,513	-3,74,880

Note : P: Provisional

Source : Compiled from *Economic Survey, 2003-2004, 2005-06, 2007-08* and *2010-11.*

Large Increase in Imports

In terms of value, India's imports have increased sharply between 1950-51 and 2009-10 from a level of Rs. 608 crore to estimated Rs. 1363736 crore in 2009-2010. Some of the factors that have contributed to this massive import growth are as below:

(i) Large Increase in Developmental and Other Imports: Under planned economic development of the country starting with the First Plan, there has been a continuous expansion in imports of capital goods, machinery equipment, etc. Also with globalisation and liberalisation, imports of all kinds have increased.

(ii) Large Increase in Import of Petroleum: Petroleum, oils and lubricants (POL) have registered more than 500-fold increase between 1960-61 and 1991 as the value of POL imports increased from Rs. 69 crore to Rs. 4,11,649 crore

contd. ...

...contd. ...

in 2009-10. Petroleum is a major source of energy used in industry and in surface as well as air transport.

(iii) Fertiliser Imports: In spite of increased domestic production, fertilisers are imported to meet their fast growing consumption requirements. Thus, import of fertilisers has gone up from Rs. 13 crore in 1960-61 to Rs. 3,034 crore in 2000-01 and Rs. 31,755 crore in 2009-10.

(iv) Import of Pearls and Precious Stones: The import of unfinished and finished/worked precious and semi-precious stones has increased from Rs. 1 crore in 1960-61 to Rs.76,678 crore in 2009-10.

Modest Growth in Exports

Growth of exports was quite low and insignificant till the Third Five Year Plan. The total value of exports increased from Rs. 606 crore in 1950-51 to Rs. 810 crore in 1965-66. However, the growth of exports picked up after the 3rd Plan to reach the level of Rs. 36,711 crore in 1980-1981 and Rs. 32,553 crore in 1991. The policy of liberalisation following the economic reforms resulted in marked improvement in export performance. In the year 2000-01, the total value of exports was Rs. 2,03,571 crore which jumped to Rs. 8,45,534 crore in 2009-10.

Inspite of this large increase in exports, the gap between the value of imports and value of exports not only persisted but also widened particularly during the last decade. Both external and the internal factors are responsibles for this.

Some of the external factors are: low world demand for our products due to continuing recession and downturn in many countries; low income and price elasticity of demand for some of our exports; import restriction on our goods entering foreign countries and disintegration of the Soviet Union—our largest trading partners providing a big market for Indian goods.

Among the internal factors, the important ones are: increasing domestic demand not leaving large surplus for export and low quality and high cost of production.

Measures to Correct Deficit in Balance of Trade

The Government of India has been adopting and implementing various policies for restricting imports and promoting exports to reduce trade deficit.

Restrictions on Imports

Following measures have been taken to regulate imports:

(i) Licensing of Imports: For quite a long time, the import of non-essential consumer goods was not permitted while the importers of capital goods essential for country's development were given import licences. However, now under the liberalised trade policy, licensing requirements for most of the goods have been abolished; only a small negative list of import items remains under licensing system.

contd. ...

...contd. ...

(ii) Tariff Restrictions: For the goods that are permitted to be imported under licence from the government, further restrictions are imposed by way of custom duties or import duties also called import tariffs. This means a tax is imposed on the goods which arrive at the Indian ports and thus the price of such goods becomes higher for the Indian buyers. The higher the rate of custom duty, the greater is the price that Indian buyers need to pay for imported goods. These high prices of imported goods are expected to reduce their demand in the domestic market and thereby to restrict imports.

(iii) Quantitative Restrictions: The government may determine the total import quota of goods, i.e., the total amount of goods that can be imported and allot this quota to various importers. Nothing beyond the quota is allowed to be imported. This naturally limits the quantity of imports. However, under an agreement with the World Trade Organization (WTO), such quantitative restrictions have been removed.

Export Promotion

With the continuing large deficits in India's balance of trade and limited scope for imports reduction, the only long-term solution to the problem lies in promotion of exports to earn sufficient foreign exchange to pay for our growing imports. Export promotion measures opening up wider international market for our entrepreneurs will stimulate industrial development in the country under the incentive of larger world demand for our goods.

Export Promotion Measures

The export promotion measures adopted by the Government of India include monetary and non-monetary incentives, fiscal reliefs, credit facilities, establishment of institutions to help exporters as well as strict quality controls and inspection of goods meant from export. Some of the major steps in this direction are as below:

(i) Devaluation: In July 1991, the rupee was devalued by about 20 per cent in terms of major world currencies. This was expected to cheapen our goods to foreign buyers, thereby encouraging our exports.

(ii) Cash Assistance: Under this scheme, cash assistance is given to exporters to compensate them for indirect taxes (e.g., custom duties) levied on the imported inputs that are used in production of goods for exports.

(iii) Income Tax Concessions: Income from exports is given several concessions under the income tax laws. For example, profits from exports are totally exempted from income tax.

(iv) Import Concessions: Several concessions in imports of machinery, equipment and technology are given to export production units. Export-oriented units are allowed duty-free imports of machines, raw materials and technology. Exporters are also allocated foreign exchange for import of raw materials used in production of export goods.

contd. ...

...contd. ...

(v) Concessional Bank Credit to Exporters: For financing production meant for exports and also for financing exports themselves, banks give credit to exporters at concessional terms.

(vi) Import Licences to Exporters: Since imported goods fetched very high prices in the domestic market as their imports were highly restricted, the exporters were granted licences for import of goods up to a certain percentage of value of goods exported by them. This was expected to provide added incentive for exports.

(vii) Issue of Exim Scrips: The system of granting import licences to exporters was later replaced by exim scrips. The exporters were given exim scrips equivalent to 30 per cent of value of their exports. These exim scrips could be used to import a large variety of items. The exim scrips could also be sold in the market. Since these enjoyed a premium, the exporters could make additional profits from their sale. This could act as a great incentive to exporters.

(viii) Convertibility of the Rupee: The system of exim scrips was also replaced by partial convertibility of rupee in March 1992. Under this scheme, exporters, who earlier had to surrender their entire foreign exchange earnings to the Reserve Bank of India (RBI) at a rate fixed by it, were now obliged to sell only 40 per cent of their exchange earnings at the official rate to the RBI. The rest, they were free to sell in the market at the market determined rate, which was obviously higher than the official rate. This indeed was a great liberalisation measure and a bigger incentive. In March 1997, even this was replaced by a system of full convertibility of rupee on the trade account.

(ix) System of Advanced Licensing: Exporters are given advance licences for duty-free import of goods used in production of export items.

(x) Relaxation of Controls on Exports and Simplification of Procedures: Controls on exports have been relaxed. Exports of many items have been decontrolled while export procedures and formalities have been simplified.

(xi) Export Processing Zones: Many export processing zones have been set up. The units operating there are allowed free trade with other countries. They also enjoy various concessions like five-year tax holiday.

(xii) Export Promotion Organisations: Some such organisations are Export Advisory Council, Export Promotion Councils, Directorate of Export Promotion, etc.

(xiii) Export-Import Bank: The EXIM Bank provides financial services to exporters and importers and coordinates the work of other institutions engaged in financing export trade. It pays special attention to export of capital goods.

TRADE POLICY: AN OVERVIEW

Import Substitution based Strategy

As we embarked on a period of planning, during the fifties, import substitution came to constitute a major element of India's trade and industrial policies. Planners, more or less chose to ignore the option of foreign trade as an engine of India's economic growth. This was primarily due to the highly pessimistic view taken on the potential for export earnings. A further impetus to the inward orientation was provided by the existence of a vast domestic market. In retrospect, it is now abundantly clear that the policy makers not only under-estimated the export possibilities but also the import intensity of the import substitution process itself. As a consequence India's share of total world exports declined from 1.91 per cent in 1950 to about 0.53 per cent in 1992.

India's participation in world markets declined steadily during the second half of the twentieth century, with only a marginal improvement following the reforms of the 1990s. Its share of world merchandise exports was 2.2 per cent in 1948, higher than China's 0.9 per cent or Japan's 0.4 per cent. It fell to one-fifth its initial level, 0.5 per cent in 1983 and recovered only marginally to 0.7 per cent in 2000. Japan, in contrast, progressively increased its share from 0.4 per cent in 1948 to a peak of 10.0 per cent in 1993. China's share first increased to a high of 1.3 per cent in 1963, then fell to a low of 1.0 per cent in 1973, later recovering dramatically after its opening to the world economy in 1978 to 4.0 per cent in 2000.

India's inward orientation has had significant economic costs in lower overall growth and stagnating living standards. Japan's rapid export growth was associated with very rapid GDP growth and improvements in living standards. Its export sector became more efficient over time. Its image as a producer of low-cost, low-quality imitative products shifted to that of a world leader in producing high-quality high-technology goods. Though China's internal market is large, international trade has played a powerful instrumental role in its growth process. The country achieved an average annual growth rate of more than 10 per cent during the period 1980-2000 (World Bank, 2002) and its real GDP and exports have grown even more rapidly since 1980.

India's GDP growth rate, in contrast, averaged 3.75 per cent a year from 1950 to 1980, putting it in the category of a low-income, slow-growing economy among the 41 "Third World" countries examined by Reynolds (1985).

India's international trade policy had the direct effect of limiting its participation in world trade. It sought to minimise imports by supporting indigenous production and according priority to domestic use in the disposition of production. Import tariffs, based on the recommendations of the Tariff Commission, were initially used to provide infant-industry protection to selected industries. The ambitious investment in heavy industries at the start of the Second Five Year Plan (1956-1961) led to a significant spurt in import demand and a rapid depletion of foreign exchange reserves, and it precipitated a balance of payments crisis in 1957.

Quantitative restrictions (QRs) on imports were initially imposed to meet the crisis but continued until early 2001 in varying intensities. Graded import tariffs (highest on "least essential" consumer goods, lower on industrial intermediate inputs, and the lowest on capital goods deemed "essential" for development) were also introduced in the 1960s in an effort to contain balance of payments deficits.

Persistent deficits in the balance of payments were mitigated by increases in tariff levels and in the severity of QRs rather than by devaluation of the rupee.

Towards Efficient Import Substitution

Foreign trade policy issues became the subject of intensive discussion in early eighties. It came to be realised that a scheme of import licensing under which imports were permitted only to the extent that domestic production fell short of domestic demand irrespective of difference in cost and prices, could only lead to inefficiency. The view gained ground that a more liberal policy of imports of capital goods and technology would enable India to reap the benefits of international division of labour. *The attempt therefore was to move away from import substitution per se towards efficient import substitution,* so that considerations relating to cost and efficiency were incorporated in the overall policy framework. It also became increasingly clear that production for export could not be isolated from production for the home market and that trade policy had to be integrated with the policy for domestic industrialisation.

With the realisation of the drawbacks of the excessively inward-looking trade strategy on the one hand and the need for modernisation and technology upgradation of the Indian industry on the other, certain policy measures in the direction of trade liberalisation were initiated in the late seventies. The strategy towards a greater integration of the Indian economy with the rest of the world has been pursued since then. The liberalisation process remained somewhat slow during the first-half of the eighties and it gathered momentum during the second half of the decade.

The policy changes have been influenced, *inter alia*, by the recommendations of a number of Committees, which were set up during the 'seventies and the eighties. In this context, mention may be made about two prominent Committee Reports—the Report of the Committee on Import Export Policies and Procedures (Chairman: P.C. Alexander, 1978) and the Report of the Committee on Trade Policies (Chairman: Abid Hussain, 1984). The Alexander Committee recommended simplification of the import licensing procedure and provided a framework involving a shift in the emphasis from 'controls' to 'development'. Following the recommendations of the Alexander Committee, selective import liberalisation measures were initiated in the late seventies primarily aiming at making the import of capital goods easier. Imports of certain raw materials that were not available indigenously were also placed under the Open General License (OGL) List. The emphasis of the policy efforts was also to simplify the procedures governing India's foreign trade. During this period, special measures were initiated to boost the export of project goods.

The Abid Hussain Committee envisaged "growth-led exports" rather than "export-led growth" and stressed upon the need for harmonisation of foreign trade policies with other economic policies arguing for a phased reduction of effective protection. The Committee also favoured announcement of trade policies for longer periods in order to impart a degree of continuity and facilitate long-term planning of export business. In line with these recommendations, long-term trade policy was introduced with the announcement of an import export policy covering the period 1985-1988. The policy was formulated with the aim of boosting exports and encouraging efficient import substitution.

While the signs of liberalised trade policy became visible in the latter half of eighties, it was only in 1991 that the country embarked on a truly liberalised trade policy with a short negative list of exports and imports and with quantitative controls over imports withdrawn for all, except consumer goods. It was recognised that trade, exchange rate and industrial policies must form part of an integrated policy framework if the aim was to improve the productivity and efficiency of the economic system.

Trade Policy since 1991

Outward Orientation Focusing on Export Promotion

The trade policy changes in the post-1991 period sought to minimise the role of quantitative restrictions and substantially reduce the tariff rates on the lines suggested by the Tax Reforms Committee (Chairman: Raja J. Chelliah). The developments in India's trade policy during this period needs to be viewed in conjunction with policy reforms initiated in other spheres of the economy. The devaluation of the Rupee in July 1991 and the transition to the market-based exchange rate regime deserve mention in this regard. These measures were aimed at enhancing the price competitiveness of exports. The policies governing foreign investment and foreign collaboration also have undergone significant change, which have a bearing on trade performance. Apart from unilateral measures, the liberalisation of India's trade policies also reflects the multilateral commitments of the country to the World Trade Organization (WTO).

The focus of these reforms has been on liberalisation, openness, transparency and globalisation with a basic thrust on outward orientation focusing on export promotion activity and improving competitiveness of Indian industry to meet global market requirements. In early 2002, the Government presented a Medium-Term Export Strategy (MTES) for 2002-2007 providing a vision for creating a stable policy environment with indicative sector-wise targets, with a mission to achieve one per cent of global trade by 2007. The Export and Import (EXIM) Policy framed for the period 2002-2007 and unveiled on 31 March 2002 also sought to usher in an environment free of restrictions and controls.

Trade policy reforms in the recent past, have provided an export-friendly environment with simplified procedures for trade facilitation. Such continued trade promotion and trade facilitation efforts of the Government have also aided the current strengthening of export growth. On August 31, 2004, a new Foreign Trade Policy for the period 2004-2009, replacing the hitherto nomenclature of EXIM Policy by Foreign Trade Policy (FTP) was announced. A vigorous export-led growth strategy of doubling India's share in global merchandise trade in the next five years, with a focus on the sectors having prospects for export expansion and potential for employment generation, constitute the main plank of the Policy. These measures are expected to enhance international competitiveness and aid in further increasing the acceptability of Indian exports.

The year 2008-09 was marked by adverse developments in the external sector of the economy, particularly during the second half of the year, reflecting the impact of global financial crisis on emerging market economies including India. Emerging economies were affected in varying degrees depending upon the extent of openness and the dependence on capital flows as the external environment deteriorated on account of slowdown in global demand, reversal of capital flows and reduced access to external sources of finance in the face of adverse global credit market conditions (*Economic Survey 2008-09*).

With gradual deepening of the global financial crisis, its impact was transmitted from the financial sector to real economic activity in advanced countries and then to emerging economies through the trade and financial channels.

The effect on the Indian economy was not significant in the beginning. The initial effect of the subprime crisis was, in fact, positive, as the country received accelerated Foreign Institutional Investment (FII) flows during September 2007 to January 2008. This contributed to the debate on "decoupling," where it was believed that the emerging economies could remain largely insulated from the crisis and provide an alternative engine of growth to the world economy. The argument soon proved unfounded as the global crisis intensified and spread to the emerging economies through capital and current account of the balance of payments (BoP). The net portfolio flows to India soon turned negative as Foreign Institutional Investors (FIIs) rushed to sell equity stakes in a bid to replenish overseas cash balances. This had a knock-on effect on the stock market and the exchange rates through creating the supply-demand imbalance in the foreign exchange market. The current account was affected mainly after September 2008 through slowdown in exports. Despite setbacks, however, the BoP situation of the country continues to remain resilient.

Recent Trade Policy Measures

Trade policy measures taken by the Government and the RBI this year focused on mitigating the adverse impact of the global recession on the Indian economy and on checking inflation. Many measures were taken including three stimulus packages announced in 2008-09, measures by the RBI and the Government in the Union Budget 2009-2010 and the Foreign Trade Policy (2009-14) to help the export sector in general and the employmentintensive sectors affected by the world recession in particular.

Trade policy measures taken by the Government and the RBI in 2009-2010 and 2010-11 focused on reviving exports and export-related employment. The Government followed a mix of policy measures including fiscal incentives, institutional changes, procedural rationalization, and enhanced market access across the world and diversification of export markets. Improvement in infrastructure related to exports; bringing down transactions costs, and providing full refund of all indirect taxes and levies, were the three major areas of focus.

Annual Supplement 2012-13 to the Foreign Trade Policy 2009-2014 (June 5, 2012)

Faced with uncertain global environment, the Central Government, announced a slew of measures, including extension of two per cent interest subsidy by one year, as part of seven-point strategy to achieve 20 per cent increase in exports to $360 billion in the current fiscal.

The measures announced included the following: The export promotion capital goods scheme that allows duty-free import of machines and has stood the test of time has been extended to the end of the current fiscal and widened in scope by covering more sectors/ exporters and introducing a new post-export variant. The 2 per cent interest subvention will now be available to exporters of toys, sports goods, processed farm goods and readymade garments, in addition to sections which currently enjoy the benefit-handlooms, handicrafts, carpets and SMEs.

The scrips for duty-free imports by exporters under various schemes will be allowed to be used for excise duty payment as goods are procured from the domestic market. The compliance burden on exporters from North Eastern states for the variant of EPCG scheme that allows import of capital goods at concessional import duties, has been reduced. Exporters from the region will have to meet only 25 per cent of the export obligation norm under the scheme. In another significant step, the government allowed export shipments from Delhi and Mumbai through post, courier or through e-commerce to be entitled for export benefits. This would benefit the fast-growing e-commerce segment immensely.

As part of the seven-point strategy to boost exports, the government has accepted the key demand of industry to extend the two per cent interest subsidy till March, 2013 and expand its coverage to include other labour-intensive sectors.

Seven Point Strategy:

- Zero-duty EPCG scheme for technology upgrade extended till March 31, 2013
- Compliance burden on exporters from northeastern states reduced to 25 per cent.
- Export benefits for shipments from Delhi, Mumbai via post/courier/e-comm
- Single bank guarantee for different exports, focus market scheme expanded
- Utilisation of duty-free scrips for buys from local market for payment of excise duty
- Easier export obligations for building 16 identified green technology products
- Ahmedabad, Kolhapur and Shaharanpur named new towns of export excellence

Over the last two decades the world has witnessed rapid expansion of global trade and reduction in tariff rates both through the multilateral arrangement under the WTO as well as various types of trade cooperation agreements including FTAs. However, at the same time developed countries are increasingly resorting to the use of non-tariff measures (NTMs) to protect their domestic industries.

BOX – 20.4

Trade Policy Reforms: Some Challenges for the Medium and Long Term

Some important challenges for India's trade sector in the medium and long term are the following:

Challenge of becoming a major player in world trade: The challenge for India is to achieve a share in world trade commensurate with its size. Despite making great strides in its export growth with 20 per cent plus growth continuously from 2002-03 to 2007-08, India has not made much progress in terms of the share in world trade. While India's exports were higher than those of China till 1954, they started lagging thereafter. In 1990, shares in world exports of China and India were 1.8 per cent and 0.5 per cent respectively and in 2009, their respective shares stood at 9.7 per cent and 1.3 per cent. If India can attain at least half of China's share in world exports, the impact on its employment and manufacturing activity will be enormous. While trade policy measures, shift in focus to some markets and some products, trade facilitation, tariff reforms, etc. have helped in some measure, if India has to achieve a substantial share in world exports, a big push will be needed.

Challenge of real diversification of India's exports: While India has diversified its export basket as well as export markets over the years, substantial diversification in tune with world demand has not taken place. This can be seen by matching India's exports with the top 100 imports of the world at the six-digit HS level. The exercise based on PCTAS data 2010(data for 2008) shows that India's presence in these top items of world demand is negligible except for a few items such as diamonds and jewellery, oil cakes, t-shirts, mens/boys trousers, flat rolled iron products, and maize (corn). There are many electronic, electrical, and engineering items (the three Es) in the top 100 imports of the world where India's presence is negligible.

Challenge of increasing export competitiveness: India's export competitiveness is being challenged not only from China and the South East Asian countries but also from the newly emerging Asian countries, less developed countries like Bangladesh, and small countries like Vietnam in items like textiles. At macro level, the two major determinants of export competitiveness are the exchange rate and inflation reflected in the real effective exchange rate (REER).

contd. ...

...contd. ...

Challenges related to tariff reforms: India has been progressively lowering peak customs duty. The fall in peak duty has not led to the feared collapse in revenue collections. The duty cuts have neither wiped out the domestic manufacturing sector nor resulted in large-scale unemployment as forecasted by many. The data show that progressive peak duty cuts have been accompanied by rise in customs duty collections. However, further bold tariff reforms with minimum revenue loss are needed to reach levels comparable to those in ASEAN both for peak rate as well as total duty.

Challenges related to FTAs/Comprehensive Economic Cooperation Agreements (CECAs) in the absence of successful WTO negotiations. The proliferation of FTAs in the world is characterized as the 'spaghetti bowl' in which trade crisscrosses in a complex fashion between countries based on tariff differentials and complicated rules of origin. In recent years, India too is a part of many regional and bilateral groupings. While there are benefits from these FTAs for Indian exports, in some cases the benefits to the partner countries are much more, with net gains of incremental exports from India being small or negative. The policy challenge related to FTAs/CECAs should take note of specific concerns of the domestic sector and ensure FTAs do not mushroom. Instead they should lead to higher trade particularly higher net exports from India.

Challenges related to services trade: Services trade is uncharted territory with plenty of opportunities and challenges. A more conducive environment for trade in services can be created by liberalizing FDI in services as FDI inflows and trade in services have a close relationship given the nature of intra-firm trade of multinational parent firms with affiliates; rationalizing taxes in services like shipping and telecom; going forward with totalization agreements; streamlining domestic regulations like licensing requirements and procedures, technical standards, and regulatory transparency which can help in the growth and export of services; and continuing with the focus on services in multilateral and bilateral negotiations. These, along with systematic marketing of services, collection and dissemination of market information by setting up a portal for services, streamlining the services data system, and a more focused, coordinated, and synchronized policy by the different agencies involved, could help the services sector make further strides.

Source: *Economic Survey 2010-11.*

21

Balance of Payments

Concepts

Balance of payments (BoP) is a systematic record of all economic transactions between the residents of a country and the rest of the world. Like all double-entry book keeping accounts, it always balances i.e., Sum of credit entries = Sum of debit entries.

There are two types of accounts in BoP, namely: (i) Current Account and (ii) Capital Account.

Under current account of the BoP, transactions are classified into merchandise (exports and imports) and invisibles. Invisible transactions are further classified into three categories, namely: (a) Services–travel, transportation, insurance, Government not included elsewhere (GNIE) and miscellaneous, which latter encompasses communication, construction, financial, software, news agency, royalties, management and business services, (b) Income, and (c) Transfers (grants, gifts, remittances, etc.) which do not have any *quid pro quo*.

Capital inflows can be classified by instrument (debt or equity) and maturity (short or long term). The main components of capital account include foreign investment, loans and banking capital. Foreign investment comprising foreign direct investment (FDI) and portfolio investment represents non-debt liabilities, while loans (external assistance, external commercial borrowings and trade credit) and banking capital including non-resident Indian (NRI) deposits are debt liabilities.

A current account deficit is financed through net inflow of capital on the capital account and the change in the Government's foreign exchange reserve position.

India's Balance of Payment Trends: 1950-51 to 2011-12[1]

According to Deepak Mohanty, India's BoP evolved reflecting both the changes in our development paradigm and exogenous shocks from time to time. In the 60 year span, 1951-52 to 2011-12, six events had a lasting impact on our BoP: (i) the devaluation in 1966; (ii) first and second oil shocks of 1973 and 1980; (iii) external payments crisis of 1991; (iv) the East Asian crisis of 1997; (v) the Y2K event of 2000; and (vi) the global financial crisis of 2008.

The first phase can be considered from the 1950s through mid-1960s. In the early 1950s, India was reasonably open. For example, in 1951-52, merchandise trade, exports plus imports, accounted for 16 per cent of GDP. Overall current receipts plus payments were nearly 19 per cent of GDP. Subsequently, the share of external sector in India's GDP gradually declined with the inward looking policy of import substitution. Moreover, Indian export basket comprised mainly traditional items like tea, cotton textile and jute manufactures. Not only the scope of world trade expansion in these commodities was less but additionally India had to face competition from new emerging suppliers, such as Pakistan in jute manufactures and Ceylon and East Africa in tea.

During this period, policy emphasis was on import saving rather than export promotion, and priority was given to basic goods and capital goods sector. It was argued that investment in heavy industries would bring in saving in foreign exchange, as output from such industries would replace their imports in the long-run. Import-substituting strategies were expected to gradually increase export competitiveness through efficiency-gains achieved in the domestic economy. But this did not happen. Hence, exports remained modest. In fact our external sector contracted in relation to GDP from the level observed in the early 1950s. By 1965-66, merchandise trade was under 8 per cent of GDP and overall current receipts and payments were below 10 per cent of GDP.

Notwithstanding the contracting size of the external sector, as imports growth outstripped exports growth, there was persistent current account deficit (CAD). Emphasis on heavy industrialisation in the second five year Plan led to a sharp increase in imports. On top of this, the strains of Indo-China conflict of 1962, Indo-Pakistan war of 1965 and severe drought of 1965-66 triggered a major BoP crisis. India's international economic relations with advanced countries came under stress during the

1. This section is drawn extensively from Deepak Mohanty's paper (Dec. 7, 2012). "Perspectives on India's Balance of Payments", in Raj Kapila and Uma Kapila (ed.), *Economic Developments in India*, Vol.180. New Delhi: Academic Foundation.

TABLE – 21.1

Balance of Payments : Summary

(US$ million)

Sl. No.	*Items*	*1990-91*	*2000-01*	*2007-08*	*2008-09*	*2009-10*	*2010-11 (PR)*	*2011-12P (P)*	*2011-12 H1 Apr-Sep. 2011 (PR)*	*2012-13 H1 Apr-Sep. 2012 (P)*
I	**Current Account**									
1.	Exports	18477	45452	166,162	189,001	182,442	256,159	309,774	158,202	146,549
2.	Imports	27915	57912	257,629	308,520	300,644	383,481	499,533	247,739	237,221
3.	Trade Balance	-9438	-12460	-91,467	-119,519	-118,203	-127,322	-189,759	-89,537	-90,672
4.	Invisibles (net)	-242	9794	75,731	91,604	80,022	79,269	111,604	53,103	51,699
	a. Non-factor Services	980	1692	38,853	53,916	36,016	44,081	64,098	30,409	29,572
	b. Income	-3752	-5004	-5,068	-7,110	-8,038	-17,952	-15,988	-7,587	-10,510
	c. Transfers	2069	12854	41,945	44,798	52,045	53,140	63,494	30,281	32,637
5.	Goods and Services Balance	—	—	-52,614	-65,603	-82,187	-83,241	-125,661	-59,128	-61,100
6.	Current Account Balance	-9680	-2666	-15,737	-27,914	-38,181	-48,053	-78,155	-36,433	-38,973
II	**Capital Account**									
	Capital Account Balance	—	—	106,585	7,395	51,634	63,740	67,755	43,490	39,989
7.	External Assistance (net)	2204	410	2,114	2,439	2,890	4,941	2,296	640	15
8.	External Commercial Borrowings (net)	2254	4303	22,609	7,861	2,000	12,160	10,344	8,388	1,726
9.	Non-Resident Deposits (net)	1537	2316	179	4,290	2,922	3,238	11,918	3,937	9,397
10.	Foreign Investment (net) of which:	103	5862	43,326	8,342	50,362	42,127	39,231	17,087	18,608
	a. FDI (net)	97	3272	15,893	22,372	17,966	11,834	22,061	15,741	12,812
	b. Portfolio (net)	—	—	27,433	-14,030	32,396	30,293	17,170	1,346	5,796
11.	Other Flows (net)	2283	-3740	10,847	-6,016	-13,259	-12,484	-7,008	-8,278	-4,769
III	**Reserves change [increase (-) / decrease (+)]**	**1278**	**-5842**	**-92,164**	**20,080**	**-13,441**	**-13,050**	**12,831**	**-5,719**	**-363**

Note: a Includes, among others delayed export receipts and errors and omissions. PR: Partially Revised. P: Preliminary

Source : *Economic Survey 2010-11, 2011-12, 2012-13*

Indo-Pak conflict. Withdrawal of foreign aid by countries like the US and conditional resumption of aid by the Aid India Consortium led to contraction in capital inflows. Given the low level of foreign exchange reserves and burgeoning trade deficit, India had no option other than to devalue. Rupee was devalued by 36.5 per cent in June 1966.

Though India's export basket was limited, the sharp devaluation clearly increased the competitiveness of India's exports. Concurrently, India had to undertake a number of trade liberalising measures. Even though the net impact of devaluation was a contentious issue among the leading economists, data show that exports growth, though modest, outpaced imports growth.

In fact, the current account turned into a surplus in 1973-74 as not only the exports growth was significant but invisible receipts also showed a sharp turnaround from deficit to surplus mainly on account of official transfers which largely represented grants under the agreement of February 1974 with the US Government on the disposition of PL 480 and other rupee funds. Since surplus in current account balance (CAB) was used for repaying rupee loans under the same agreement with the US, accretion to reserves was only marginal.

The BoP position deteriorated once again in 1966-67. In 1965, the United States suspended its aid in response to the Indo-Pakistan war and later refused to renew the PL 480 agreement on a long-term basis. There was a concerted effort by the United States, the World Bank and the IMF to use external assistance as an instrument to induce India: (a) to adopt a new agricultural strategy, and (b) to devalue the rupee. The rupee was devalued by 36.5 per cent in June 1966, and tariffs and export subsidies were simultaneously rationalised, on the understanding that the inflow of aid would be substantially increased.

The BoP improved after 1966-67 but largely because of the decline in imports. Exports performed indifferently despite the devaluation.

First and Second Oil Shocks of 1973 and 1980

India's balance of payments remained comfortable during the seventies. The adjustment to the first oil shock of 1973-74 was rendered smooth by a happy combination of buoyant exports, spurt in private transfer receipts and increased inflow of aid. Exports, benefited by the expansion in global trade, rose at an annual rate of 6.8 per cent in volume terms and by 15.6 per cent in US dollar terms during the decade. An effective depreciation of the rupee occurred due to the link with Pound Sterling until 1973 and later, because of the lower growth in prices in India relative to other countries. Private transfers rose seven-fold from $ 296 million in 1974-75 to $ 2175 million in 1979-80 and in fact, in the post first oil shock period, financed roughly 80 per cent of the trade deficit. Within two years of the shock, the current account balance turned into surplus and it was only in 1978-79 that a deficit of about 0.2 per cent of GDP appeared. The utilisation of aid was significant and was substantially higher than the financing requirement for the decade, allowing for a build-up of reserves. At the close of the decade, the foreign exchange reserves stood at $ 7361 million providing cover for over 7 months of imports.

During the eighties, issues relating to the balance of payments came to occupy the centre stage in terms of India's macroeconomic management. The impact of the second oil shock of 1979, the full effects of which spilled over into the eighties, was more severe than of the 1973-74. Between 1978-79 and 1981-82, imports almost doubled. The increase in POL imports accounted for a little over half the increase in the overall imports. This was followed by the second-round effects on non-POL imports. Export performance was depressed by the severe international recession of 1980-1983 and recorded a volume growth of just a little over 3 per cent. Net invisible receipts continued to provide support to the balance of payments, largely in the form of earnings from tourism and the sustained buoyancy of private transfers. However, the sharp widening in the merchandise trade deficit resulted in a turnaround in the current account balance from a surplus in 1977-78 to a deficit in 1981-1982 of the order of US $ 3,166 million or 1.8 per cent of GDP. Adjustment efforts consisted essentially of an Extended Fund Facility (EFF) negotiated with the IMF, although there were also intensified efforts to improve domestic production of crude petroleum.

During the 1980s, BoP again came under stress. The second oil shock led to a rapid increase in imports in early 1980s. Oil imports increased to about two-fifths of India's imports during 1980-83. At the same time, India's external sector policy was changing towards greater openness. Various measures were undertaken to promote exports and liberalise imports for exporters during this period. However, several factors weighed against external stability. First, despite a number of export promotion measures, the subdued growth conditions in the world economy constrained exports growth. Second, the surplus on account of invisibles also deteriorated due to moderation in private transfers. Third, the debt servicing had increased with greater recourse to debt creating flows such as external commercial borrowings (ECBs) and non-resident Indian (NRI) deposits. Fourth, deterioration is the fiscal position stemming from rising expenditures accentuated the twin deficit risks.

External Payment Crisis of 1991

The Crisis: 1990-1992

In 1991, India found itself in its worst balance of payments crisis since 1947. That there was a crisis in the making during the second half of 1980s had been evident for a long time. The inflow of foreign borrowing had increased at a rapid rate during the late 1980s. This was due to the excess domestic expenditure over income—the fiscal deficit of the Centre and the states soared to over 11 per cent in 1991. During this period, total public debt as a proportion of GNP doubled reaching the level of 60 per cent and foreign currency reserves were depleted rapidly.

Matters were made worse by an accompanying double-digit inflation in 1990-91. The oil price increase resulting from Iraq's invasion of Kuwait in August 1990 reinforced the crisis-like situation in India.

India's credit rating got downgraded as, for the first time in its history, India was on the verge of defaulting on its international commitments and was denied access to external commercial credit markets. A net outflow of Non-Resident Indian (NRI) deposits commenced in October 1990 and continued during 1991. The only way left for India was to borrow against the security of its gold reserves transported abroad.

But something good emerged out of the BoP crisis of 1991—the long overdue economic reforms. Apart from an immediate programme of macroeconomic stabilisation, structural reforms were also introduced in the industrial and trade policy regimes with a view to improving the efficiency, productivity and international competitiveness of India's economy.

The broad approach to reform in the external sector was laid out in the Report of the High Level Committee on Balance of Payments (Chairman: C. Rangarajan, 1993).

The impact of policy changes was reflected in lower CAD and its comfortable financing in subsequent years. India could manage the external shocks that emanated from the East Asian crisis in 1997 and subsequently, the rise in international oil prices and bursting of dotcom bubble in 1999-2000. Indeed, the Indian economy remained relatively insulated from the East Asian crisis owing to the reforms undertaken in previous years and proactive and timely policy measures initiated by the

Reserve Bank to minimise the contagion effect. Monetary tightening coupled with flexible exchange rate and steps to bolster reserves through issuance of Resurgent India Bonds (RIBs) helped in stabilising the BoP.

The BoP came under some stress again in the first half of 2000-01 due to a sharp rise in oil prices and increase in interest rates in advanced countries. At the same time, India's software exports got a boost following the demands to address the Y2K challenges. This also encouraged migration of Indian software engineers to the advanced countries. As a result, the surplus in the services exports and remittance account of the BoP increased sharply which more than offset the deficit in the trade account. Software exports rose from 0.9 per cent of GDP in 1999-2000 to a peak of 3.8 per cent of GDP by 2008-09. Private remittances also rose from 2.7 per cent of GDP to 3.8 per cent during this period. Thus, in the 2000s software exports and private remittances emerged as two main financing items for the current account mitigating to a large extent the merchandise trade deficit (Tables 21.2 and 21.3).

TABLE – 21.2

Trend in Net Invisibles

(Per cent of GDP)

	1950-1980	*1980-1990*	*1990-2000*	*2000-2009*	*2009-2012*
1. Services (Net)	0.3	0.4	0.3	2.1	3.0
2. Software (Net)	-	-	-	2.3	3.3
3. Other Services (Net)	0.3	0.4	0.3	-0.2	-0.3
4. Private Transfers (Net)	0.4	1.1	2.2	3.2	3.5
5. Total Invisibles (Net)	0.7	1.4	1.6	4.6	5.6

Source: Mohanty (2012).

TABLE – 21.3

Composition of Current Account Balance

(Percent of GDP)

Period	*1970s*	*1980s*	*1990s*	*2000-2009*	*2009-2012*
1. Oil TB	-1.2	-1.7	-2.0	-3.5	-4.5
2. Non-Oil TB	0.4	-0.9	0.6	-0.8	-3.9
3. Non-oil CAB	1.1	-0.1	0.8	3.3	1.3
4. CAB	-0.1	-1.8	-1.3	-0.3	-3.3

Note: TB: Trade Balance, CAB: Current Account Balance, (-): Implies deficit.
Source: Mohanty (2012).

Owing to a combination of factors, in fact, the current account recorded a surplus during 2001-04. Subsequently, as international oil prices started rising and domestic growth picked up, deficit in current account re-emerged during 2004-05 to 2007-08 albeit remained range bound.

After a period of stability, India's BoP came under stress in 2008-2009 reflecting the impact of global financial crisis. As capital inflows plummeted, India had to draw down its foreign currency assets by US $ 20 billion during 2008-09. Stress since the collapse of Lehman Brothers largely emanated from decline in India's merchandise exports and deceleration in growth in services exports. Though there was some improvement during 2010-11 on the back of a strong pick-up in exports mainly led by diversification of trade in terms of composition as well as direction, it proved to be short-lived.

India's BoP during 2011-12

India's BoP was under stress during 2011-12, as the trade and current account deficit widened. Though capital inflows increased, it fell short of fully financing current account deficit, resulting in drawdown of foreign exchange reserves. The trade deficit increased to US$ 189.8 billion (10.2 per cent of GDP) in 2011-12 as compared to US$ 127.3 billion (7.4 per cent of GDP) during 2010-11. This increase of 49.1 per cent in trade deficit in 2011-12 was primarily on account of higher increase in imports relative to exports. Net invisible balances showed significant improvement, registering 40.7 per cent increase from US$ 79.3 billion in 2010-11 to US$ 111.6 billion during 2011-12. Net invisible balance as per cent of GDP improved to 6.0 per cent in 2011-12 from 4.6 per cent in 2010-11. The current account deficit widened to US$ 78.2 billion (4.2 per cent of GDP) as compared with US$ 48.1 billion (2.8 per cent of GDP) in 2010-11. Net capital inflows were higher at US$ 67.8 billion (3.6 per cent of GDP) in 2011-12 as compared to US$ 63.7 billion (3.7 per cent of GDP) in 2010-11, mainly due to higher FDI inflows and NRI deposits. As the capital account surplus fell short of financing current account deficit, there was a drawdown of reserves (on BoP basis) to the extent of US$ 12.8 billion during 2011-12 as against an accretion of US$ 13.1 billion in 2010-11.

As per the latest available data for the first half (H1- April-September 2012) of 2012-13, India's balance of payments continued to be under stress. This is reflected in the higher current account deficit in H1 (April-September) of 2012-13 than the corresponding period of the previous year, mainly due to worsening of trade deficit reflected in sharper decline in exports than the imports and lower invisibles surplus.

The net capital flows in absolute term, were also lower during H1 of 2012-13 *vis-à-vis* the corresponding period of 2011-12). Current Account during 2011-12 (*Economic Survey 2012-13*).

Current Account during H1 of 2012-13

In the first Half (H1 - April-September 2012) of 2012-13, there was a steep decline in exports to US$ 146.5 billion, registering a 7.4 per cent decline over US$ 158.2 billion in H1 of 2011-12. Like exports, there was decline of 4.2 per cent in imports to US$ 237.2 billion in H1 of 2012-13 from US$ 247.7 billion during the corresponding period in previous year. The steep fall in exports than that in imports was responsible for widening of trade deficit to US$ 90.7 billion (10.8 per cent of GDP) in H1 of 2012-13 *vis-à-vis* US$ 89.5 billion (9.9 per cent of GDP) in H1 of 2011-12.

During H1 (April-September 2012) of 2012-13, net surplus under invisibles showed a decline of 2.6 per cent as outflows on account of payments under invisibles increased considerably. Growth in invisible receipts decelerated to 4.7 per cent, mainly due to lower growth in exports of services, private transfers and decline in investment income.

As per the latest data available from the Ministry of Commerce, exports of US$ 214.1 billion during April-December 2012, registered a decline of 5.5 per cent over export of US$ 226.6 billion during the same period in 2011-12. Imports of US$ 361.3 billion recorded a marginal decline of 0.7 per cent during April-December 2012 over the figure of US$ 363.9 billion during the corresponding period of previous year. As a result of steeper decline in exports than imports, trade deficit increased by 7.2 per cent to US$ 147.2 billion during April-December 2012 as compared to US$ 137.3 billion in April- December 2011 (Economic Survey 2012-13).

Sustainability of Current Account

One of the factors underlying the external payments crisis of 1991 was the high levels of current account deficit (CAD) maintained during the 1980s which at the time of the crisis had reached 3.1 per cent of GDP, well above the sustainable level for India (Cerra and Saxena, 2002). Concerted efforts directed at imparting strength and stability to the external sector emphasised a policy of maintaining the CAD within a sustainable level of about 2 per cent. This is broadly in line with the recommendations of the High Level Committee on Balance of Payments (RBI, 1993), which recommended that CAD-GDP ratio could be sustainable at 1.6 per cent. The current account deficit averaged only about 1.0 per cent of GDP during the last decade (1992-2002), as compared with 1.8 per cent in the 1980s, and recorded a surplus in 2001-02 after a period of 23 years. Among the components of current account, while the trade deficit (BoP basis) declined marginally from 3.2 per cent of GDP during the 1980s to 3.0 per cent during 1992-2002, the invisibles surplus increased significantly from 1.4 per cent of GDP to 2.1 per cent over the same period. With the narrowing of the current account deficit in the recent years, there is a need for revisiting the issue of sustainability of current account in the Indian context.

It has been noted that developing countries typically run CAD in their early stages of development to supplement their domestic saving to achieve higher level of investment and growth. This process enables recipient countries to achieve higher growth without cutting their current consumption; at the same time, higher productivity of capital in developing countries benefits foreign lenders by earning higher returns on their capital. This raises the question of an optimal CAD level for a country which, however, needs to be circumscribed by a sustainable level of capital flows. The external payments problems faced by India in 1991 and the East Asian crisis in 1997 have highlighted, *inter alia*, the role of large current account deficits and the consequent build-up of external debt, in precipitating the crisis (Rangarajan, 1993; RBI, 1999 and 2002a).

The current account sustainability depends upon external as well as domestic macroeconomic factors (Ghosh and Ostry, 1994; Milesi-Ferretti, Gian and Razin, 1997). Accordingly, a sustainable level of CAD would have elements of time and country specificity. Ultimately, it is determined by the foreign investors' confidence in the domestic economy, depending upon the various external and domestic factors identified above. While a ratio of CAD-GDP of 8 per cent or so turned out to be unsustainable in the case of Thailand, the same ratio continues to remain sustainable in the case of New Zealand. This level of deficit need not be a cause for alarm as long as transparent and consistent policies remain (Brash, 1998).

India's current account particularly remains vulnerable to developments in the trade account. It is evident from the size of trade deficit growing from 0.5 per cent of GDP during 1951-55 to 8.7 per cent during 2007-12. In 2011-12, the current account deficit has widened to a record 4.2 per cent of GDP. Over the years, current account derived some resilience from surplus generated by invisibles, particularly software exports and private transfers, but trade deficit continues to dictate the overall trend in the current account. Whenever trade account worsens reflecting downswings in the global business cycle or rise in international oil prices, the current account also comes under stress as is evident in the present context. Going forward, since India's linkage with the world economy, in terms of trade and finance, is likely to grow further, it is important that resilience in its trade account is built up mainly by promoting productivity based export competitiveness and improving domestic fundamentals that are supportive of least costly non-debt creating flows, particularly foreign direct investment (FDI). In this context, I make a few suggestions.

According to Mohanty, the current level of CAD is far above the level sustainable for India as Rangarajan (2013) has estimated, at a nominal growth rate of about 13 per cent, the sustainable current account to GDP ratio is 2.3 per cent. Reserve Bank's own research shows that economy can sustain CAD of about 2.5 per cent of GDP under a scenario of slower growth (RBI, 2012). A slowing global economy and protracted high levels of unemployment in advanced economies make it difficult to boost services exports in the short run. If the slowdown continues, it could also have an adverse impact on inward remittances. Hence, there is a need to reduce imports and boost merchandise exports to bring the CAD to sustainable levels, remarks Mohanty (2013).

Capital Account

Capital inflows can be classified by instrument (debt or equity) and maturity (short-term or longterm). The main components of capital account include foreign investment, loans, and banking capital. Foreign investment comprising FDI and portfolio investment represents non-debt liabilities, while loans (external assistance, ECBs, and trade credit) and banking capital including NRI deposits are debt liabilities. In India, FDI is preferred over portfolio flows as the FDI flows tend to be more stable than portfolio and other forms of capital flows. Rupee-denominated debt is preferred over foreign currency debt and medium- and long-term debt is preferred over short-term.

Capital inflows, as a proportion of GDP, were on an uptrend during 2003-04 to 2007-08. They reached a high of 9.3 per cent of GDP in 2007-08 after a modest growth of 3.1 per cent in 2005-06 and 5.1 per cent in 2006-07. Capital inflows were lower at 1.8 per cent of GDP during 2008-09 (April-December) due to the global financial crisis.

In 2010-11, both gross inflows of US$ 499.4 billion and outflows of US$ 437.4 billion under the capital account were higher than gross inflows of US$ 345.8 billion and outflows of US$ 294.1 billion in the preceding year. In net terms, capital inflows increased by 20.2 per cent to US$ 62.0 billion (3.7 per cent of GDP) in 2010-11 *vis-à-vis* US$ 51.6 billion (3.8 per cent of GDP) in 2009-10 mainly on account of trade credit and loans (ECBs and banking capital).Push and pull factors explain international capital flows.

Push factors are external to an economy and inter alia include parameters like low interest rates, abundant liquidity, slow growth, or lack of investment opportunities in advanced economies. Pull factors like robust economic performance and improved investment climate as a result of economic reforms in emerging economies are internal to an economy.

Inward FDI showed a declining trend while outward FDI showed an increasing trend in 2010-11 *vis-à-vis* 2009-10. Inward FDI declined from US$ 33.1 billion in 2009-10 to US$ 25.9 billion in 2010-11.

As per the latest available information on capital inflows, FDI flows to India stood at US$ 22.2 billion during April-December 2012, which is 22.1 per cent lower than US$ 28.5 billion during April-December 2011. Up to December 2012, net FII flows amounted to at US$ 16.0 billion (US$ 2.7 billion during the corresponding period of 2011-12). FII flows in recent months witnessed improvement, reflecting the impact of various reform measures announced by the Government.

External Debt

India's external debt stock at end-March 2012 stood at US$ 345.4 billion (Rs. 1,765,333 crore) recording an increase of US$ 39.5 billion (12.9 per cent) over end-March 2011 level of US$ 305.9 billion (Rs 1,365,929 crore). Component-wise, long-term debt increased by 10.9 per cent to US$ 267.2 billion at end-March 2012 from US$ 240.9 billion at end-March 2011, while short-term showed an increase of 20.3 per cent to US$ 78.2 billion from US$ 65.0 billion at end-March 2011. India's external debt stock increased by about US$ 20.0 billion (5.8 per cent) to US$ 365.3 billion at end-September 2012 over the level at end- March 2012. The rise in external debt is largely due to higher NRI deposits, short-term debt and commercial borrowings. NRI deposits alone accounted for 42.1 per cent of the rise in total external debt at end-September 2012 over the level of end- March 2012, while short-term debt and commercial borrowings together accounted for 52.6 per cent of the rise in debt during the period.

The maturity profile of India's external debt indicates the dominance of long-term borrowings. Long-term external debt at US$ 280.8 billion at end-September 2012 accounted for 76.9 per cent of the total external debt, while the remaining 23.1 per cent was short-term debt. Long-term debt at end-September 2012 increased by US$ 13.6 billion (5.1 per cent) over the level at end-March 2012, while short-term debt increased by US$ 6.3 billion (8.1 per cent). Within long-term, components such as commercial borrowings, NRI deposits and multilateral borrowings taken together, accounted for 62.1 per cent of total external debt at the end of September 2012 while other long-term debt components (viz. bilateral borrowings, export credit, IMF and rupee debt) accounted for 14.8 per cent of total external debt.

The currency composition of India's total external debt shows that the share of US dollar denominated debt continued to be the highest in external debt stock at 55.7 per cent at end- September 2012, followed by Indian rupee (22.9 per cent), Japanese yen (8.6 per cent), SDR (8.1 per cent) and euro (3.2 per cent). The currency composition of Government (sovereign) debt indicates pre-dominance of SDR denominated debt (36.6 per cent), which is attributable to borrowing from International Development Association (IDA) i.e., the soft loan window of the World Bank under the multilateral agencies and SDR allocations by the IMF. The share of US dollar denominated debt was 26.2 per cent followed by Japanese yen denominated (19.3 per cent), Indian rupee (14.3) and euro (3.6). At end-September 2012, Government (sovereign) external debt was US$ 81.5 billion. It accounted for 22.3 per cent of India's total external debt. Non- Government external debt amounted to US$ 283.9 billion which was 77.7 per cent of total external debt at end-September 2012 (*Economic Survey 2012-13*).

Over the years, India's external debt stock has witnessed structural change in terms of composition. The share of concessional in total debt has declined due to shrinking share of official creditors and the Government debt and the surge in non-concessional private debt. The proportion of concessional in total debt declined from 42.9 per cent (average) during the period 1991-2000 to 28.1 per cent in 2001-2010 and further to 13.2 per cent at end-September 2012. The rising share of nongovernment debt is evident from the fact that such debt accounted for 65.6 per cent of total debt during the decade of 2000s, vis-a-vis

45.3 per cent in 1990s. Non-Government debt accounted for over 70 per cent of total debt in the last five years and stood at 77.7 per cent at end-September 2012 (*Economic Survey 2012-13*).

The key external debt indicators are presented in Table 21.4. India's foreign exchange reserves provided a cover of 80.7 per cent to the total external debt stock at end-September 2012 *vis-à-vis* 85.2 per cent at

TABLE – 21.4

India's Key External Debt Indicators

(Per cent)

Year	*External Debt (US $ billion)*	*Total External Debt to GDP*	*Debt-Service Ratio*	*Foreign Exchange Reserves to Total External Debt*	*Concessional Debt to Total External Debt*	*Short-term External Debt* to Foreign Exchange Reserves*	*Short-term External Debt* to Total Debt*
1	2	3	4	5	6	7	8
1990-91	83.8	28.7	35.3	7.0	45.9	146.5	10.2
1995-96	93.7	27.0	26.2	23.1	44.7	23.2	5.4
2000-01	101.3	22.5	16.6	41.7	35.4	8.6	3.6
2005-06	139.1	16.8	10.1#	109.0	28.4	12.9	14.0
2006-07	172.4	17.5	4.7	115.6	23.0	14.1	16.3
2007-08	224.4	18.0	4.8	138.0	19.7	14.8	20.4
2008-09	224.5	20.3	4.4	112.1	18.7	17.2	19.3
2009-10	260.9	18.2	5.8	106.8	16.8	18.8	20.1
2010-11	305.9	17.5	4.3	99.6	15.5	21.3	21.2
2011-12	345.4	19.7	6.0	85.2	13.9	26.6	22.6
2012-13							
End-June 2012 PR	348.8	-	5.9	83.1	13.5	27.8	23.1
End-Sept. 2012 QE	365.3	-	-	80.7	13.2	28.7	23.1

Notes: - Not worked out for the broken period

PR: Partially Revised QE: Quick Estimates..

*: Short-term debt is based on original maturity.

#: Works out to 6.3 per cent, with the exclusion of India millennium deposits (IMDs) repayments of US$ 7.1 billion and prepayment of US$ 23.5 million.Debt-service ratio is the proportion of gross debt service payments to external current receipts (net of official transfers).

Source: Ministry of Finance, Government of India and Reserve Bank of India. *Economic Survey 2012-13*.

end-March 2012. The ratio of short-term external debt to foreign exchange reserves was at 28.7 per cent at end-September 2012 as compared to 26.6 per cent at end-March 2012. The ratio of concessional debt to total external debt declined steadily and worked out to 13.2 per cent at end-September 2012 as against 13.9 per cent at end-March 2012.

India's external debt has remained within manageable limits as indicated by the external debt to GDP ratio of 19.7 per cent and debt service ratio of 6.0 per cent in 2011-12. The active external debt management policy of the Government of India has helped in containing rise in external debt and maintaining a comfortable external debt position. The policy continues to focus on monitoring long and short-term debt, raising sovereign loans on concessional terms with longer maturities, regulating external commercial borrowings through end-use, all-in-cost and maturity restrictions; and rationalizing interest rates on non-resident Indian deposits (*Economic Survey 2012-13*).

BOX – 21.1

Changing Composition of India's External Debt

India's external debt stock has witnessed structural change in terms of composition over the years. The share of concessional in total debt has declined due to shrinking share of official creditors and the Government debt and the surge in non-concessional private debt. The proportion of concessional in total debt declined from 42.9 per cent (average) during the period 1991-2000 to 28.1 per cent in 2001-2010 and further to 15.6 per cent at end-March 2011. The rising share of non-government debt is evident from the fact that such debt accounted for 65.6 per cent of total debt during the decade of 2000s, *vis-à-vis* 45.3 per cent in 1990s. Non-Government debt accounted for over 70 per cent of total debt in the last five years and stood at 74.4 per cent at end-March 2011..

Component-wise, the share of multilateral and bilateral credit in total external debt are showing decline while the commercial borrowings reflect rising trends over the years. The share of commercial borrowings in total debt increased from 15.6 per cent in the decade of 1990s to 23.4 per cent during the decade of 2000s and further to 28.9 per cent at end-March 2011. The rising share of commercial borrowings reflects maturing market economy and the increasing role that corporate sector is playing in sustaining high growth rate.

BOX – 21.2

Changing Composition of India's External Debt

India's external debt stock has witnessed structural change in terms of composition over the years. The share of concessional in total debt has declined due to shrinking share of official creditors and the Government debt and the surge in non-concessional private debt. The proportion of concessional in total debt declined from 42.9 per cent (average) during the period 1991-2000 to 28.1 per cent in 2001-2010 and further to 15.6 per cent at end-March 2011. The rising share of non-government debt is evident from the fact that such debt accounted for 65.6 per cent of total debt during the decade of 2000s, *vis-à-vis* 45.3 per cent in 1990s. Non-Government debt accounted for over 70 per cent of total debt in the last five years and stood at 74.4 per cent at end-March 2011..

Component-wise, the share of multilateral and bilateral credit in total external debt are showing decline while the commercial borrowings reflect rising trends over the years. The share of commercial borrowings in total debt increased from 15.6 per cent in the decade of 1990s to 23.4 per cent during the decade of 2000s and further to 28.9 per cent at end-March 2011. The rising share of commercial borrowings reflects maturing market economy and the increasing role that corporate sector is playing in sustaining high growth rate.

BOX – 21.3

Trends in India's External Debt Indicators

India's external debt has remained within manageable limits despite the increase in absolute debt numbers. The external debt to GDP ratio was 17.3 per cent in 2010-11, compared with 38.7 per cent in 1991-92 and 22.5 per cent in 2000-01. This is an indication of active external debt management policy followed by the Government of India, the main planks of which are monitoring long and short-term debt, raising sovereign loans on concessional terms with longer maturities and regulating external commercial borrowings.

The ratio of foreign exchange reserves to total external debt has also shown a steady uptrend from a level of 7 per cent in 1990-91 to as high as 138 per cent at end-March 2008. At end-March 2011, foreign exchange reserves provided almost 100 per cent cover to the India's external debt

Source: Ministry of Finance, August 2011.

TABLE – 21.5

Creditor Classification of External Debt

(Per cent)

Sl. No.	Category	2005	2006	2007	2008	2009	2010 (PR)	2011 (QE)	2012 (PR)
		at end-March							
1	*2*	*3*	*4*	*5*	*6*	*7*	*8*	*9*	*10*
1.	Multilateral	23.7	23.4	20.5	17.6	17.6	16.4	15.8	14.6
2.	Bilateral	12.7	11.3	9.3	8.8	9.2	8.7	8.5	7.7
3.	IMF	0.8	0.7	0.6	0.5	0.5	2.3	2.1	1.8
4.	Export Credits	3.8	3.9	4.2	4.5	6.5	6.5	6.1	5.5
5.	Commercial Borrowings	19.7	19.0	24.0	27.8	27.8	27.1	28.9	30.4
6.	NRI Deposits	24.4	26.1	23.9	19.5	18.5	18.3	16.9	17.0
7.	Rupee Debt	1.7	1.5	1.1	0.9	0.7	0.6	0.5	0.4
8.	Long-term Debt (1to7)	86.8	85.9	83.6	79.6	80.7	80.0	78.8	77.4
9.	Short-term Debt	13.2	14.1	16.4	20.4	19.3	20.0	21.2	22.6
10.	Grand Total (8+9)	100	100	100	100	100	100	100	100

Note: PR: Partially Revised, QE: Quick Estimate.
Source: Various *Economic Survey* including 2012-13.

The share of official creditors in total external debt has declined over the years. The private creditors have accounted for over 70 per cent of total external debt in recent years. The ratio of official and private creditors that was about 40:60 per cent in 2005 changed to 27:73 per cent in 2011 (Table 21.6).

The external debt management policy of the Government of India continues to focus on raising sovereign loans on concessional terms with longer maturities, regulating ECBs through end-use and all-in-cost restrictions, rationalizing interest rates on NRI deposits and monitoring long as well as shortterm debt.

TABLE – 21.6

Share of Official and Private Creditors in External Debt (per cent)

At end-March	*Official Creditors*	*Private Creditors*
2005	39.7	60.3
2006	37.7	62.3
2007	32.2	67.8
2008	28.4	71.6
2009	28.5	71.5
2010 PR	28.6	71.4
2011 QE	27.4	72.6

Note: PR: Partially Revised;

QE: Quick Estimates.

(1) Official creditors include multilateral and bilateral sources of finance, loans and credits obtained from IMF, export credit component of bilateral credit, export credit for defence purposes and rupee debt. (2) Private creditors denote sources of loans raised under ECBs, NRI deposits, export credits (other than those included under official creditors) and short-term debt.

Source: Ministry of Finance, 2011

International Comparison

A cross country comparison of external debt of twenty most indebted developing countries, based on the data given in the World Bank's "Global Development Finance, 2010", showed that India was the fifth most indebted country, after the Russian Federation, China, Turkey, and Brazil, in 2008 in terms of stock of external debt. The ratio of India's external debt stock to gross national income (GNI) as of 2008 at 19.0 per cent was the fourth lowest with China having the lowest ratio at 8.7 per cent. The element of concessionality in India's external debt portfolio was fourth highest after Pakistan, Indonesia and the Philippines (Table 21.7).

In terms of the cover of external debt provided by foreign exchange reserves, India's position was fourth highest at 111.6 per cent after China, Thailand and Malaysia. A comparison of the share of short term debt in total external debt across countries reveals that India's position was tenth lowest with Pakistan having the lowest ratio.

TABLE – 21.7

International Comparison of Top 20 Developing Debtor Countries, 2011

Sl. No.	*Countries*	*Total External Debt Stock (US$ million)*	*Total Debt to GNI (per cent)*	*Short-term to Total External Debt (per cent)*	*Foreign Exchange Reserves to Total Debt (per cent)*
1	2	3	4	5	6
1	China	685,418	9.4	69.6	467.3
2	Russian Federation	542,977	31.1	12.9	83.6
3	Brazil	404,317	16.6	10.4	86.7
4	India	334,331	18.3	23.3	81.1
5	Turkey	307,007	40.1	27.3	25.5
6	Mexico	287,037	25.2	17.9	50.2
7	Indonesia	213,541	26.0	17.9	49.9
8	Ukraine	134,481	83.3	24.3	22.6
9	Romania	129,822	72.3	22.9	33.1
10	Kazakhstan	124,437	77.9	7.2	20.2
11	Argentina	114,704	26.3	14.5	37.7
12	South Africa	113,512	28.4	16.6	37.5
13	Chile	96,245	41.0	17.8	43.6
14	Malaysia	94,468	34.8	46.3	139.5
15	Thailand	80,039	24.0	56.2	209.1
16	Colombia	76,918	24.3	14.1	40.8
17	Philippines	76,043	33.6	9.2	88.5
18	Venezuela	67,908	21.8	24.6	14.6
19	Pakistan	60,182	27.3	4.2	24.1
20	Vietnam	57,841	49.1	17.2	23.4

Note: Countries are arranged based on the magnitude of debt presented in Column 3 in the Table.

Source: *World Bank's International Debt Statistics 2013.*

Foreign Exchange Reserves: Approach, Developments and Issues[2]

Approach

The subject of foreign exchange reserves has received renewed interest in recent times in the context of increasing globalisation,

2. This section is drawn extensively from Uma Kapila (ed.) (2013). *Indian Economy Since Independence* (24th edition).*op.cit*.

acceleration of capital flows and integration of financial markets. The debt-banking-financial crises in several countries have also necessitated the need for an international financial architecture in which the management of foreign exchange reserves has emerged as one of the critical issues.

The motives for holding reserves may be broadly classified under three categories, *viz*., transaction, speculative and precautionary. International trade gives rise to currency flows, which are assumed to be handled by banks driven by the transaction motive. Similarly, speculative motive is left to individuals or corporates. Central bank reserves, however, are characterised primarily as a last resort stock of foreign currency for unpredictable flows, which is consistent with precautionary motive for holding foreign assets. Precautionary motive for holding foreign currency, like the demand for money, can be positively related to wealth and the cost of covering unplanned deficit, and negatively related to the return from alternative assets. Furthermore, foreign exchange reserves are instruments to maintain or manage the exchange rate, while enabling orderly absorption of international capital flows. Official reserves are mainly held for precautionary and transaction motives keeping in view the aggregate of national interests, to achieve balance between demand for and supply of foreign currencies, for intervention, and to preserve confidence in the country's ability to carry out external transactions.

The objectives for maintaining reserves are:

(i) maintaining confidence in monetary and exchange rate policies;

(ii) enhancing capacity to intervene in foreign exchange markets;

(iii) limiting external vulnerability by maintaining foreign currency liquidity to absorb shocks during times of crisis including national disasters or emergencies;

(iv) providing confidence to the markets, including credit rating agencies, that external obligations can always be met (thus, reducing the overall costs at which foreign exchange resources are available to all the market participants); and

(v) adding to the comfort of the market participants, by demonstrating the backing of domestic currency by external assets.

India's approach to reserve management, until the balance of payments crisis of 1991 was essentially based on the traditional approach, i.e., to maintain an appropriate level of import cover defined in terms of number of months of imports equivalent to reserves. For example, the import cover of reserves shrank to three weeks of imports by the end of December 1990, and the emphasis on import cover constituted the primary concern say, till 1993-94. The approach to reserve management, as part of exchange rate management, and indeed the overall external sector policy underwent a paradigm shift with the adoption of the recommendations of the High Level Committee on Balance of Payments, 1993 (Chairman: C. Rangarajan). The Committee had recommended that the foreign exchange reserve targets be fixed in such a way that they are generally in a position to accommodate imports of three months.

With the introduction of market determined exchange rate, a change in the approach to reserve management was warranted and the emphasis on import cover had to be supplemented with the objective of smoothening out the volatility in the exchange rate, which has been reflective of the underlying market condition.

An important issue which has figured prominently in the current debate on foreign exchange management is the question of appropriate policy for management of foreign exchange reserves. In a regime of free float, it can be argued that there is no need for reserves. In the light of volatility induced by capital flows and self-fulfiling expectations that this can generate, there is now a growing consensus among emerging market economies to maintain 'adequate' reserves (Jalan, 2002). Therefore, while focusing on prudent management of foreign exchange reserves in recent years, the 'liquidity at risk' associated with different types of flows has come to the fore. With the changing profile of capital flows, the traditional approach to assessing reserve adequacy in terms of import cover has been broadened to include a number of parameters which take into account the size, composition and risk profiles of various types of capital flows as well as the types of external shocks to which the economy is vulnerable. A sufficiently high level of reserves is necessary to ensure that even if there is prolonged uncertainty, reserves can cover the liquidity at risk on all accounts over a fairly long period. Taking these considerations into account, India's foreign exchange reserves have reached a very comfortable level.

Developments

In India, reserves have been steadily built up by encouraging non-debt creating flows and de-emphasising debt creating flows, particularly short-term debt. This strategy, coupled with the maintenance of an acceptable level of current account deficit and market determined exchange rate regime was the cornerstone of the policy of external sector management. In the context of the changing interface with the external sector and the importance of the capital account, reserve adequacy is now evaluated by the Reserve Bank in terms of several indicators and not merely through conventional norms, such as, the import cover. As a matter of policy, as far as possible, foreign exchange reserves are kept at a level which is adequate to withstand both cyclical and unanticipated shocks.

Beginning from a low level of US$ 5.8 billion at end March 1991, India's foreign exchange reserves gradually increased to US$ 25.2 billion by end March 1995, US$ 38.0 billion by end March 2000, US$ 113.0 billion by end March 2004, and US$ 199.2 billion by end March 2007. The reserves stood at US$ 314.6 billion at end May 2008, before declining to US$ 252.0 billion at the end of March 2009. The decline in reserves in 2008-09 was inter alia a fallout of the global crisis and strengthening of the US dollar *vis-à-vis* other international currencies. During 2009-10, the level of foreign exchange reserves increased to US$ 279.1 billion at end March 2010, mainly on account of valuation gain as the US dollar depreciated against most of the major international currencies. In fiscal 2010-11, foreign exchange reserves have shown an increasing trend and reached US$ 304.8 billion at end March 2011, up by US$ 25.7 billion from the US$ 279.1 billion level at end March 2010, mainly on account of valuation gain as the US dollar depreciated against most of the major international currencies. In fiscal 2010-11, the reserves again showed an increasing trend, reaching US$ 304.8 billion at end-March 2011. In fiscal 2011-12, they reached all-time high of US$ 322.0 billion at end-August 2011. However, they declined thereafter and stood at US$ 294.4 billion at end-March 2012.

In 2012-13, the reserves increased marginally by US$ 0.4 billion from US$ 294.4 billion at end-March 2012 to US$ 294.8 billion at end-September 2012. Of this total increase, US$ 0.3 billion was on BoP basis and US$ 0.1 billion was on account of valuation effect. A summary of changes in the foreign exchange reserves since 2007-08, with a breakdown into increase/decrease on BoP basis and valuation effect is presented in Table 21.8.

In the current fiscal, foreign exchange reserves on month-on-month basis remained in the range of US$ 286.0 billion (at end-May 2012) to US$ 295.6 billion (at end-December 2012). At end- December 2012, reserves stood at US$ 295.6 billion, indicating a marginal increase of US$ 1.2 billion from US$ 294.4 billion at end-March, 2012. At this level, reserves provided about seven months of import cover.

A summary of changes in the foreign exchange reserves since 2006-2007, with a breakdown into increase /decrease on BoP basis and valuation effect is presented in Table 21.8.

TABLE – 21.8

Summary of Changes in Foreign Exchange Reserves

(US$ billion)

Sl. No.	*Year*	*Foreign exchange reserves at the end of financial year (end March)*	*Total Increase(+)/ decrease(-) in reserves*	*Increase/ decrease in reserves on a BoP basis*	*Increase/ decrease in reserves due to valuation effect*
1	*2*	*3*	*4*	*5*	*6*
1	2007-08	309.7	110.5	92.2 (83.4)	18.3 (16.6)
2	2008-09	252.0	-57.7	-20.1 (34.8)	-37.6 (65.2)
3	2009-10	279.1	27.1	13.4 (49.4)	13.7 (50.6)
4	2010-11	304.8	25.7	13.1 (51.0)	12.6 (49.0)
5	2011-12	294.4	-10.4	-12.8 (123.0)	2.4 (-23.0)
6	2012-13 (up to Sept. 2012)	294.8	0.4	0.3 (75.0)	0.1 (25.0)

Note: Figures in parentheses indicate percentage share in total change.
Source: *Economic Survey 2012-13*.

In terms of various adequacy indicators, India's reserves remain comfortable. As regards trade-related indicators, reserves are well-above the conventional criterion although the import cover came down from 16.9 months in 2003-04 to 10 months at the end of December 2010.

A comparative picture of foreign exchange reserves and import cover, as measured by the ratio of foreign exchange reserves to import of goods and services for select country groups and countries including India, is presented in Table 21.9. The ratio of reserves to import of goods and services of 'Emerging and Developing Economies' witnessed an improvement from 75.5 per cent in 2006 to 109.1 per cent in 2009 before declining to 102.4 per cent in 2010. Among the country groups, the ratio of 'Developing Asia including China and India' increased from

89.5 per cent in 2006 to 145 per cent in 2009, before declining to 131.2 per cent in 2010. In case of 'Middle East and North Africa' the ratio has improved steadily from 104.3 in 2006 to 118.9 in 2010.

TABLE – 21.9

International Comparison of Foreign Exchange Reserves (US$ billion) and Ratio of Reserves to Imports of Goods and Services

Sl. No.	*Country/ Country Group*	*2006*	*2007*	*2008*	*2009*	*2010*	*2011 (Projection)*	*2012 (Projection)*
1	*2*	*3*	*4*	*5*	*6*	*7*	*8*	*9*
I	**Country**							
1	Russia	296.2 (141.7)	467.6 (165.5)	412.7 (112.3)	417.8 (164.8)	454.5 (141.6)	527.4 (129.4)	582.5 (130.2)
2	China	1069.5 (125.4)	1531.3 (148.0)	1950.3 (158.2)	2417.9 (217.2)	2889.6 (190.0)	3479.5 (188.4)	4112.7 (195.4)
3	India	171.3 (75.5)	267.6 (95.1)	248.0 (71.3)	266.2 (73.8)	291.5 (66.4)	319.7 (62.1)	354.9 (60.3)
4	Brazil	85.2 (70.7)	179.5 (113.8)	192.9 (87.6)	237.4 (135.9)	287.5 (117.7)	366.1 (120.3)	412.9 (128.0)
5	Mexico	76.3 (27.4)	87.1 (28.5)	95.1 (28.5)	99.6 (38.7)	120.3 (36.8)	140.3 (35.9)	150.3 (37.1)
II	**Country Group**							
1	Developing Asia (excluding China & India)	248.7 (42.6)	330.0 (49.1)	335.8 (41.7)	393.9 (60.6)	488.0 (58.3)	581.3 (58.2)	658.2 (60.6)

Note :1. Reserves are based on official holding of gold valued at SDR 35 an ounce. This convention results in a marked underestimation of reserves for countries that have substantial gold holdings.

2. Figures in parentheses indicate ratios of reserves to imports of goods and services.

Source : *World Economic Outlook Database*, September 2011; *Economic Survey 2011-12*

India continues to be one of the largest holders of foreign exchange reserves. Country-wise details of foreign exchange reserves reveal that India is the eighth largest foreign exchange reserves holder in the world, after China, Japan, Russia, Switzerland, Brazil, Republic of Korea and China P R Hong Kong (Table 21.10) at end-December 2012.

TABLE – 21.10

Foreign Exchange Reserves of Some Major Countries

Sl. No.	*Country*	*Foreign Exchange Reserves (End December 2012) (US$ billion)*
1	*2*	*3*
1	China	3310.0[a]
2	Japan	1304.1
3	Russia	538.6
4	Switzerland (November 2012)	531.7
5	Brazil	373.1
6	Republic of Korea (November 2012)	326.2
7	China P R Hong Kong (November 2012)	305.2
8	India	295.6 [b]
9	Germany (November 2012)	259.4
10	France (November 2012)	211.0
11	Italy	185.6
12	Thailand	184.2

Source: IMF; *Economic Survey 2012-13*.

a : As per PBC, at end-December 2012, China's foreign exchange reserves stood at US$ 3.31 trillion (*source*: *http:/www.pbc.gov.cn)*.

b : RBI

In additional foreign exchange reserves of Taiwan are shown at US$ 403.2 billion (Q4) as per *The Economist* January 31, 2013.

Issues

Foreign Exchange Rate Policy

The exchange rate policy is guided by the broad principles of careful monitoring and management of exchange rates with flexibility, while allowing the underlying demand and supply conditions to determine its movements over a period in an orderly manner. Subject to this predominant objective, RBI intervention in the foreign exchange market is guided by the goals of reducing excess volatility, preventing the emergence of destabilizing speculative activities, maintaining adequate levels of reserves, and developing an orderly foreign exchange market.

During 2010-11, the average monthly exchange rate of the rupee against the US dollar appreciated by 1.2 per cent from Rs 45.50 per US dollar in March 2010 to Rs 44.97 per US dollar in March 2011. Similarly, on point-to-point basis, the average exchange rate of the rupee [average of buying and selling rate of the Foreign Exchange Dealers Association of India (FEDAI)] appreciated by 1.1 per cent from Rs 45.14 per US dollar on 31 March 2010 to Rs 44.65 per US dollar on 31 March 2011. This was mainly on account of weakening of the US dollar in the international market in 2010-11.

On an annual average basis, the rupee appreciated against major international currencies except the Japanese yen in fiscal 2010-11. The annual average exchange rate of the rupee was Rs 47.44 per US dollar in 2009-10, appreciating by 4.1 per cent to Rs 45.56 per US dollar in 2010-11. Similarly, the annual average exchange rate of the rupee in 2009-10 was Rs 75.76 per pound sterling and Rs 67.03 per euro, which appreciated by 6.9 per cent and 11.3 per cent to Rs 70.87 per pound sterling and Rs 60.21 per euro respectively during 2010-11. The annual average exchange rate of the rupee per Japanese yen however depreciated by 4.1 per cent from Rs 51.11 per 100 Japanese yen in 2009-10 to Rs 53.27 per 100 Japanese yen in 2010-11.

In the current fiscal, there are two distinct phases in the exchange rate of the rupee. The rupee continued exhibiting a two-way movement with an appreciating trend till about July 2011, after which the trend reversed and it started declining sharply from September 2011 onwards, due to factors relating to the uncertain global economy.

A sharp fall in rupee value may be explained by the supply-demand imbalance in the domestic foreign exchange market on account of slowdown in FII inflows, strengthening of the US dollar in the international market due to the safe haven status of the US treasury, and heightened risk aversion and deleveraging due to the euro area crisis that impacted financial markets across emerging market economies (EMEs). Apart from the global factors, there were several domestic factors that have added to the weakening trend of the rupee, which include increasing CAD and high inflation.

Exchange Rate of Other Emerging Economies

Currency depreciation during 2011-12 was not specific to India. The currencies of other emerging economies, such as the Brazilian real, Mexican peso, Russian rouble, South Korean won, and South African rand, also depreciated against the US dollar, reflecting the increased demand for the US dollar as a safe haven asset in the wake of the sovereign debt crisis in the euro zone. Between July and November 2011, the Brazilian real has depreciated by 11.9 per cent, Russian rouble by 9.3 per cent, South Korean won by 6.2 per cent, and South African rand by 17.63 per cent.

Nominal Effective Exchange Rate (NEER) and Real Effective Exchange Rate (REER)

The NEER and REER indices are used as indicators of external competitiveness of the country over a period of time. NEER is the weighted average of bilateral nominal exchange rates of the home currency in terms of foreign currencies, while REER is defined as a weighted average of nominal exchange rates, adjusted for home and foreign country relative price differentials. REER captures movements in cross-currency exchange rates as well as inflation differentials between India and its major trading partners. The RBI has been constructing six-currency (US dollar, euro for euro zone, pound sterling, Japanese yen, Chinese renminbi, and Hong Kong dollar) and 36-currency NEER and REER indices.

The six-currency trade-based NEER (base: 2004-05=100) depreciated by 2.1 per cent between March 2010 and March 2011 and by 13.5 per cent between March 2011 and December 2011. As compared to this, the monthly average exchange rate of the rupee appreciated by 1.2 per cent between March 2010 and March 2011, while in the current fiscal it depreciated by 14.6 per cent against the US dollar from ` 44.97 per US dollar in March 2011 to Rs 52.68 per US dollar in December 2011.

The six-currency trade-based REER (base: 2004-5=100) of the rupee appreciated by 4.1 per cent between March 2010 and March 2011. During 2011-12 (up to December 2011), the six-currency index showed depreciation of 10.8 per cent over March 2011 largely reflecting depreciation of the rupee in nominal terms, which mainly happened during the period August-December 2011.

The indices of nominal effective exchange rate (NEER) and real effective exchange rate (REER) is used as indicators of external competitiveness of the country over a period of time. NEER is the weighted average of bilateral nominal exchange rates of the home currency in terms of foreign currencies. REER is defined as a weighted average of nominal exchange rates adjusted for relative price differential between the domestic and foreign countries. REER captures movements in cross-currency exchange rates as well as inflation differential between India and its major trading partners. RBI has been constructing six currency (US dollar, euro for eurozone, pound sterling, Japanese yen, Chinese renminbi and Hong Kong dollar) and 36 currency indices of NEER and REER.

Exchange Rate Management

In India, the exchange rate system has undergone a paradigm shift from a system of fixed exchange rate (until March 1992) to a market determined regime in March 1993.

The unified market determined exchange rate regime replaced the dual regime on March 1, 1993 and since then "the objective of exchange rate management has been to ensure that the external value of the Rupee is realistic and credible as evidenced by a sustainable current account deficit and manageable foreign exchange situation. Subject to this predominant objective, the exchange rate policy is guided by the need to reduce excess volatility, prevent the emergence of destabilising speculative activities, help maintain adequate level of reserves, and develop an orderly foreign exchange market" (Jalan, 1999). In order to reduce the excess volatility in the foreign exchange market, the Reserve Bank has undertaken market clearing sale and purchase operations in the foreign exchange market to moderate the impact on exchange rate arising from lumpy demand and supply as well as leads and lags in merchant transactions. Such interventions, however, are not governed by any predetermined target or band around the exchange rate.

The experience with the market determined exchange rate regime has been satisfactory, although the exchange rate management had to occasionally contend with a few episodes of volatility. The Reserve Bank has been responding through appropriate intervention supported by monetary and other administrative measures like variations in the bank rate, repo rate, cash reserve requirements, refinance to banks, surcharge on import finance and minimum interest rates on overdue export bills. These measures helped in curbing destabilising speculation, while at the same time allowing an orderly correction in the value of the Rupee.

Concluding Remarks

The widening of the trade deficit to more than 10 per cent of GDP and the CAD crossing 4 per cent of GDP in 2011-12 and the first half of 2012-13 have been matters of concern. In recent years, net invisible balance reduced the need for financing, while capital inflows were sufficient to finance the CAD safely. In the current fiscal, the growth in invisibles is insufficient to narrow the growing trade deficit. Besides, the CAD is financed by volatile capital flows, which has led to financial fragility and is reflected in rupee exchange rate volatility.

The room to increase exports in the short run is limited, as they are dependent upon the recovery and growth of partner countries, especially in industrial economies. This may take time. The main focus has to be on curbing imports, mainly by making oil prices more market determined, and curbing imports of gold. At the same time, further measures to ease the inflow of remittances and steps to diversify software exports could help reduce financing needs. Greater emphasis on FDI including opening up sectors further can help increase the quantum of safe financing. FII flows need to be targeted towards longer term rupee instruments so as to minimize the 'reversal' of capital during risk-off phases. Finally, external commercial borrowing needs to be monitored carefully so that entities without access to foreign exchange revenues do not leave significant exposures unhedged.

With the gradual external liberalisation of Indian economy, not only the size of BoP has increased manifold, but the pattern of current and capital account has changed. Even though the reform process has strengthened resilience of India's external sector, at the same time vulnerabilities arise with greater exposure of the economy to the rest of world through liberalised trade and investment environment.

India's current account particularly remains vulnerable to developments in the trade account. It is evident from the size of trade deficit growing from 0.5 per cent of GDP during 1951-55 to 8.7 per cent during 2007-2012. In 2011-12, the current account deficit has widened to a record 4.2 per cent of GDP. Over the years, current account derived some resilience from surplus generated by invisibles, particularly software exports and private transfers, but trade deficit continues to dictate the overall trend in the current account. Whenever trade account worsens reflecting downswings in the global business cycle or rise in international oil prices, the current account also comes under stress as is evident in the present context. Going forward, since India's linkage with the world economy, in terms of trade and finance, is likely to grow further, it is important that resilience in its trade account is built up mainly by promoting productivity based export competitiveness and improving domestic fundamentals that are supportive of least costly non-debt creating flows, particularly foreign direct investment (FDI). In this context. Mohanty has made the following suggestions.

First, the current level of CAD is far above the level sustainable for India. As per estimates, at a nominal growth rate of about 13 per cent, the sustainable current account to GDP ratio is 2.3 per cent (Rangarajan, 2012). Reserve Bank's own research shows that economy can sustain CAD of about 2.5 per cent of GDP under a scenario of slower growth (RBI, 2012). A slowing global economy and protracted high levels of unemployment in advanced economies make it difficult to boost services exports in the short run. If the slowdown continues, it could also have an adverse impact on inward remittances. Hence, there is a need to reduce imports and boost merchandise exports to bring the CAD to sustainable levels.

Second, structural policy measures are needed to reduce vulnerability emanating from high oil and gold imports. While oil has been a major component of India's imports, the sharp increase in demand for gold has put an additional pressure. During 2008-09 to 2011-12, on average, the net gold imports stood at about 2 per cent of GDP, almost double the level recorded during 2004-05 to 2007-08. Thus, during the same period, CAD-GDP ratio, excluding net gold imports, would seem less problematic at 1.1 per cent as compared to a surplus of 0.2 per cent. In addition to the traditional motive of gold demand for jewellery, gold seems to have become a safe investment asset and a hedge against inflation as is observed in other advanced economies. Its dematerialisation like any other financial product can reduce its physical imports (Gokarn, 2012). Furthermore, inflation indexed bonds could also be another option to offer investors the inflation linked returns and detract them from gold investments. In the case of oil, we need to become more energy efficient to reduce our dependence on oil imports. Stepping up of production of electricity could reduce oil demand from backup generation systems. Moreover, the domestic pricing of oil should be aligned further to the international prices to rationalise oil consumption.

Third, current policies towards further diversification of India's export basket, both destination and products, needs to be stepped up. Indian exporters need to accelerate efforts to move up in the value chain at the global lcvcl.

Fourth, given the global uncertainties and volatility in capital flows, the resilience of capital account needs to be further enhanced by encouraging FDI inflows.

To conclude, the Indian economy is much more open and globalised now than ever before. The periodic pressures on BoP have been addressed through policy changes. While the BoP has again come under stress since 2011-12 as emphasised by Governor Dr Subbarao, the situation is not as serious as it was in 1991. This is because the structure of the economy has changed in a fundamental way with flexible exchange rate and greater depth in financial markets, besides much larger foreign exchange reserves than those in 1991. However, there is a need to bring the CAD to sustainable levels in the short run and over the medium-term to accelerate efforts towards structural reforms that help boosting our competitiveness, raise growth potential and bring in more stable flows into the economy.

22

India and the WTO

World Trade Organization

The World Trade Organization (WTO) is an international organisation that oversees the operation of the rules-based multilateral trading system. The WTO is based on a series of trade agreements negotiated during the Uruguay Round (1986-1994), the eighth and final trade round conducted under the General Agreement on Tarriffs and Trade (GATT). The Treaty of Marrakesh established the WTO at the close of the Uruguay Round in 1994. The WTO began operations on January 1, 1995, it was comprised of 148 members. The WTO is one of the Big Three international organisations that oversee economic relations among nations, joining the International Monetary Fund (IMF) and the World Bank. The WTO's headqurters is located in Geneva, Switzerland. Pascal Lamy of France, current WTO Director General, began a four-year, renewable term of office on September 1, 2005.

The WTO's main function is to monitor and enforce trade rules in the global economy. The WTO administers the complex trade agreements listed in the WTO agreement. Article 1 of the WTO agreement, the General Agreement on Tariffs and Trade, deals with rules of merchandise trade. The General Agreement on Tariffs and Trade in Article 1 is often called GATT 1994 to distinguish it from the original GATT agreement of 1947. Article 2, the General Agreement on Trade in Services (GATS), pertains to the trade of commercial services. Article 4, the Agreement on Trade-Related Aspect of Intellectual Property (TRIPS), provides uniform legal protections for scientific, technological and artistic achievements. In addition, the WTO is a forum for trade negotiations, a dispute settlement mechanism, a source

---

This Chapter is drawn from Uma Kapila (ed.) (2013). *Indian Economy Since Independence* (24th edition) (Ch.25). New Delhi: Academic Foundation.

of technical expertise on trade and development for the world's poorer countries and a sister organisation to the World Bank and IMF. Unlike the World Bank and IMF, the WTO does not make loans to countries.

The WTO inherited many of GATT's guiding principles. These fundamental principles are incorporated in the numerous agreements that comprise the Agreement Establishing the World Trade Organization. In its *Understanding the WTO* (2003), the World Trade Organization identified five core principles.

The first principle is "trade without discrimination," which involves most-favoured-nation (MFN) status and national treatment. MFN states that a trade concession granted to one WTO member automatically applies to all members. National treatment guarantees equal treatment of imported goods with domestically produced output in nations' markets.

The second principle is freer trade through the progressive liberalisation of trade regimes.

The third principle is the predictability of trade rules. Predictability, in this context, prevents governments from arbitrarily raising existing tariffs or non-tarriff trade barriers.

The fourth principle is fair competition. Fair competition attempts to level the playing field in international trade and minimise the market distortions caused by export subsidy, dumping and other disruptive trade practices.

The fifth principle is economic development through trade. Economic development for the world's poorer countries should be enhanced by trade assistance and increased market access through preferential trade arrangements.

The WTO's dispute settlement process is the enforcement arm of the organisation. The WTO's apparatus for dispute settlement is stronger and more defined than GATT's dispute settlement procedures. The WTO's dispute settlement process is the essence of multilateralism. That is, a country or group of countries can air trade grievances in a global forum. A trade complaint is made to the WTO's Dispute Settlement Body (DSB), which consists of the entire WTO membership. The DSB, in turn, establishes a panel of three to five experts to hear the evidence and render a ruling. The panel's ruling can only be reversed by a unanimous vote of the DSB. Under normal conditions, the entire process takes one year or less to complete. One or both sides in the dispute can appeal the panel's decision. A seven-member Appellate Body considers an appeal and renders a decision. Again, only a unanimous vote of the DSB can reverse the Appellate Body's ruling. The appellate process could add as much as three months to the dispute settlement process. A member country found guilty breaking WTO trade rules is required to correct the violation with due speed. The DSB is empowered to initiate retaliatory tariffs or other trade sanctions for non-compliance with a WTO ruling.

According to Pascal Lamy[2], the institutional structure that was created in 1995 as a result of the Uruguay Round (UR) has served as a solid basis for global trade. Since the establishment of the WTO, international trade has seen a boost and its expansion rate for the period 1990-2008 has been six per cent on average. The rules and functions of the WTO have been of paramount importance in keeping markets open and resisting protectionism, especially in times of crisis. During the recent financial and economic crisis, the WTO responded by establishing a surveillance mechanism to track trade policy responses and restrictive measures put in place by governments. We feared that weak recovery of the global economy and high unemployment rates would put pressure on governments to turn to inward-looking policies.

While a number of trade restrictive measures have been adopted, it is important to note that, overall, WTO Members have refrained from high intensity protectionism, reconfirming the organisation's role as an anchor for trade policies. But the trade-restrictive measures introduced by governments since the beginning of the crisis show that there are still gaps and loopholes that members can exploit to the detriment of their trading partners. The launch of the Doha Development Round in 2001 was an attempt at correcting these imbalances and locking in and expanding members' commitments. Over 10 years later, negotiations are stalled and the political, economic and social environment in which the WTO operates appears once again changed.

Over the past 20 years, the world has experienced a significant economic and geopolitical shift. Developing countries' participation in international trade has risen considerably faster than world trade. WTO figures for 2011 show that their share of trade rose to 47 per cent on the export side and 42 per cent on the import side, the highest levels ever recorded since 1948. This growing share of trade is led by

2. Lamy, Pascal (2013). "WTO: Building a Global Trading System for the 21st Century", in Nitin Desai and Rajiv D. Mathur (eds.), *Growth and Equity: Essays in Honour of Pradeep Mehta*. New Delhi: Academic Foundation. pp.57-63.

emerging countries such as India, China, Brazil, Malaysia or Mexico, all of which have become drivers of economic growth and are now asserting their role in global governance. These countries have made the most of their trade opening opportunities and their vibrant economies make them increasingly attractive markets for trade and investment. They are also proving relatively resilient to external shocks.

While the current crisis continues to frustrate demand and growth in industrialised countries, emerging economies recovered faster than the rest of the developed world and became sources of both demand and supply for other developing countries. China overtook Germany as the world's leading merchandise exporter in 2009 but more importantly, it recorded the fastest growing share of imports in 2011. The dynamism of emerging economies is shifting the axis of trade from North-South to South-South, and from West to East, with China taking up the role that until recently had been of the US and the European Union as a major export destination (Lamy, 2013).

Emerging economies' dynamism and the level of competitiveness they have achieved, require the definition of a new equilibrium in international trade relations. According to Lamy (2013), as the gap between developed and emerging economies narrows, it requires a new balance of rights and obligations, of contributions between countries at different levels of development. Developed countries are growing more reluctant to make concessions to emerging economies that are in direct competition with them. On the other hand, developing countries are reluctant to accept much higher levels of commitments while they still face development challenges. This dichotomy is proving a hard challenge for the trading system and is stalling progress in multilateral negotiations, much as it is stalling progress in climate change or on the quota and voice within the International Monetary Fund (IMF).

Another challenge for the multilateral trading system in the 21st century is the rise of preferential trade arrangements (PTAs). The stalling of the Doha Development Round and the uncertainty it brings about has led countries to seek trade openings bilaterally or regionally. As of January 2012, over 500 regional trade agreements had been notified to the WTO, of which more than 300 are currently in force. The proliferation of PTAs demonstrates an appetite for trade opening and can be a blessing for the multilateral trading system as they can be the forerunners of further opening at the multilateral level. However, as their number increases, the risk also grows that members of different trade agreements would implement increasingly divergent regulatory systems. As the global economy becomes more integrated, regulatory divergence poses further obstacles for businesses that seek more coherent and predictable rules that can only be achieved multilaterally (Lamy, 2013).

In addition to structural changes in trade dynamics, new emerging issues—often dubbed as '21st century issues'—are changing the perception of international trade. As the reality of trade is decoupling from the mere consideration of exchanges in goods and services, its linkages to other areas of international co-operation are becoming more evident. Some of the issues that the WTO is being called to look upon include the relationship between trade and climate change, exchange rate policies, food security, energy policies, competition and investment (Lamy, 2013).

Although some of these issues are not entirely new, their implications for the multilateral trading system are taking new forms as more challenging and complex links emerge. In this context, some observers are wondering whether the WTO should not step up its engagement in the debate about the future structure of global governance. Indeed, the organisation has achieved considerable progress since its establishment. The interest shown by acceding countries in joining the organisation speaks volumes about the value of its rules and agreements. With Russia becoming a WTO member, about 97 per cent of world trade will be under the aegis of the WTO, making it even more attractive to the present and prospective members. Even as the mere repository of trade rules, the WTO will continue to play a role in global governance, but its relevance would be greatly diminished if it fails to keep up with this changing trade environment (Lamy, 2013).

A successful conclusion of the Doha Development Round would certainly be the best overhaul for the multilateral trading system. The issues contained in the negotiating agenda, including disciplines for trade-distorting agriculture subsidies, elimination of export subsidies, reduction of industrial tariff peaks, efficient customs procedures, further opening in services and deeper integration of least-developed countries in the trading system, are as relevant today as they were 10 years ago. These issues need to be resolved. However, currently the Doha Round is at an impasse. At the Eighth WTO Ministerial Conference in December 2011, WTO members recognised the need to strengthen the WTO and to look at innovative ways of solving the negotiating impasse without striding away from the original Doha mandate. Amongst the suggested approaches, there have been calls for a pragmatic, step-by-step approach that would deliver small but steady results, thus reinstating confidence in the multilateral trading system (Lamy, 2013).

The WTO should also continue to press for building trade capacity in developing and least developed countries through 'Aid for Trade', which in reality should be renamed 'Investment for Trade'. For many countries the trade opportunities that the WTO offers can only be transformed into realities if an investment is made through development assistance, to build trade capacity at home.

Further, Lamy remarks, inaction is not an option. For the WTO to remain relevant in the new century, it needs to keep advancing. The world of the 21st century needs a global trading system that is relevant, dynamic and comprehensive; a system that is responsive to the needs of its members and to the expectations of the world citizens that it serves; a system that contributes to development, poverty alleviation and growth through enhanced economic opportunities, a system for the 21st century that is able to lead the world out of the stalemate that it is in and reinject trust and confidence in international cooperation. Even in the 21st century, the WTO needs to be able to make a difference in the world economy for the benefit of all, especially for the poorest amongst us. "The difference between rich and poor is not wealth, but opportunity," says Nobel Laureate Prof Muhammad Yunus. By equipping the WTO with a 21st century software, the organisation will continue to contribute to global prosperity by ensuring that the new opportunities created by a changing global context are available to all.

India and the WTO

India was one of the 23 founding Contracting Parties to the General Agreement on Tariffs and Trade (GATT) that was concluded in October 1947. India has often led groups of less developed countries in subsequent rounds of multilateral trade negotiations (MTNs) under the auspices of the GATT.

Despite being a founder member of GATT, India was never very active in various negotiating rounds until late eighties. Since the Indian economy followed the import-substitution led growth strategy during sixties and seventies, gaining from the import liberalisation at principal export markets (the EU and US) was never a prime objective. In addition, a considerable proportion of India's trade was directed to the Soviet bloc countries, and the presence of this assured market weakened the incentive to search for newer outlets. On the other hand, opening the domestic market to foreign competition through progressive tariff cuts was perceived harmful for the local industries. Instead, the country was more willing to discuss trade and development related issues at UNCTAD forums in collaboration with other developing countries like Brazil (primarily through the G-77 network). Despite adoption of a proactive approach at WTO, India still feels comfortable to discuss trade-related issues at UNCTAD forums for coalition building among developing counries on areas pertaining to mutual interest.

India's Participation in WTO Meetings

Table 22.1 illustrates India's participation in WTO meetings (Sengupta, 2006).[3]

During the Seattle-Doha period, India, for the first time, started communicating its dissatisfaction over several issues and sharing its position with other countries at various appropriate forums of WTO and other international bodies. Broadly speaking, a clearly distinguishable and proactive stand emerged before the Doha ministerial, and India became particularly concerned with: (i) non-realisation of anticipated benefits (e.g., Agreement on Textiles and Clothing and Agreement on Agriculture), (ii) inequities and imbalances in WTO (TRIPSs, Subsidies, Anti-dumping, etc.), and (iii) non-binding nature of special and differential provisions (market access, DSB, etc.). In short, India strongly objected to the inclusion of any new issue in the negotiating agenda before realisation of Uruguay round promises, the non-implementation of which was costly to developing countries.

Buoyed by the success achieved at Doha, India tried to utilise the two-year period before Cancun in a much productive manner and coalition-formation experience with other developing countries were fruitful not only for general agreements that affected merchandise and services trade, but also in case of institutional arrangements like dispute settlement. The movement towards a proactive strategy at the WTO was accompanied towards implementing an increasingly WTO compatible regime at home and frustration mounted at not obtaining the desired level of market access in principal export destinations. In Cancun, India principally negotiated over liberalisation of agricultural trade and trade in services.

In addition, the intensity of proactive approach was further noticed in the sharp increase in the number of joint submissions at WTO, ranging from agriculture to services. Interestingly, the Indian

3. Sengupta, Dipankar, Debashis Chakraborty and Pritam Banerjee (eds.) (2006). "India at the WTO: The Story so Far", in *Beyond the Transition Phase of WTO: An Indian Perspective on Emerging Issues.* New Delhi: Academic Foundation.

submissions to WTO, both joint and individual, stressed both export promotion (enhancement of market access) and domestic protection (e.g. provision of special products, special safeguard mechanism in agriculture) much vigorously. On the other hand, domestic reforms have been regularly undertaken in order to enhance compliance with WTO.

TABLE – 22.1

India at the WTO Meetings

No. of Ministerial	*Place of Occurrence*	*Year*	*Outcome*	*India's Role*
1.	Singapore	1996	Information Technology Agreement was signed. In addition, four new issues were discussed, Trade and Investment, Competition Policy, Transparency in Government Procurement, and Trade Facilitation.	Mere presence.
2.	Geneva	1998	Global E-commerce Agreement was signed. Also, the implementation issues were discussed.	Mere presence.
3.	Seattle	1999	The negotiations failed as several developed countries wanted to incorporate environmental and labour-standard related issues under the wings of WTO. The move was strongly opposed by developing countries.	Was vocal against introduction of environmental and labour-standard related issues under WTO.
4.	Doha	2001	A new round was launched and the concerns for developing countries like India (e.g. TRIPS and Public Health) were attended. The market access and implementation issues were also given due notice.	Mostly singled out in its protest. However, made its presence and position felt for the first time.
5.	Cancun	2003	The members could not arrive at a common viewpoint even on the last date of the conference. The ministerial decided to take stock of progress in negotiations and other work under the Doha Development Agenda. The developing country solidarity at the ministerial was formed for the first time.	Actively protested against EU-US draft on agriculture jointly with other developing countries.
6.	Geneva	2004	Five member countries came forward to create an atmosphere for initiating multilateral negotiations once again.	Played a constructive role in the process while protecting developing countries' interests.

Source: Compiled from WTO Ministerial Declarations and other documents.

WTO Negotiations and India[4]

The Doha Round of trade negotiations at the WTO has been under way since 2001. The negotiations cover several areas such as agriculture, market access for non-agricultural products, traderelated intellectual property rights, rules (covering anti-dumping and subsidies) and trade facilitation. The conduct, conclusion and entry into force of the outcome of the negotiations are parts of a single undertaking, that is "nothing is agreed until everything is agreed".

While the years 2007 and 2008 saw intensive discussions in the WTO and progress achieved on several complex subjects, the negotiations were slow to resume following the December 2008 break at the WTO.

The Doha Round of trade negotiations in the WTO effectively made very little progress after 2008. Throughout 2009 and 2010, discussions continued but no headway was made on any substantive issue in the negotiations. (A summary of India's stand on key negotiabing issues is given in Box 22.1). However, the subject featured on the agenda of almost every major international meeting and there were strong affirmations of political support for an early conclusion of the Doha Round. Discussions continued in Geneva during March and April 2011, in a variety of formats. Reports on each area of the negotiations were issued on 21 April 2011. These documents provided an overview of the status of negotiations in each area covered in the Doha Development Agenda. While they indicated significant progress in many areas, they also captured the wide gaps remaining on many issues.

In October-November 2011, concerted efforts were made by some of the developed country members of the WTO to use the G20 Leaders Summit in November 2011 to advance an agenda for the Eighth WTO Ministerial Conference scheduled to be held in Geneva in December 2011. Specifically, they wanted to set the stage for plurilateral agreements on selected issues in the WTO negotiations (rather than multilateral agreements); get WTO members to agree to a commitment abjuring the use of export restrictions; and introduce new issues for negotiation, namely climate change, energy security, and food security. The weeks preceding the Eighth WTO Ministerial Conference saw hectic activity in the WTO as some members attempted to put various issues on the agenda for ministerial decision. These proposals, however, did not receive support amongst WTO members. At the Eighth

4. Government of India (2010). *Economic Survey 2009-10.*

BOX – 22.1

India's Stand on Key Negotiating Issues: A Summary

Agriculture

- Substantial and effective reductions in overall trade-distorting domestic support (OTDS) of the US and EU;
- Self-designation of an appropriate number of special products (SPs);
- An operational and effective Special Safeguard Mechanism (SSM);
- Simplification and capping of developed country tariffs.

Non-Agricultural Market Access (NAMA)

- Adequate and appropriate flexibilities for protecting economically vulnerable industries;
- Participation in sectoral initiatives only on a non-mandatory and good faith basis without prejudgment of the final outcome, with substantial special and differential treatment provisions for developing countries;
- Serious consideration of non-tariff barrier (NTB) textual proposals with wide support such as the horizontal mechanism.

Services

- Need for qualitative improvement in the revised offers especially on Modes 1(cross-border supply) and 4 (movement of natural persons);
- Appropriate disciplining of domestic regulations by developed countries.

Rules

- Tightening of disciplines on anti-dumping (deletion of zeroing clause and reiteration of the lesser duty rule)
- Effective special and differential treatment for developing countries on fisheries subsidies.

Trade-related Aspects of Intellectual Property Rights (TRIPS)

- Establishing a clear linkage between the TRIPS Agreement and the Convention on Bio-diversity (CBD) by incorporating specific disclosure norms for patent applications;
- Enhanced protection for geographical indications (GIs) other than wines and spirits.

Source: *Economic Survey 2011-12.*

Ministerial Conference from 15 to 17 December, ministers adopted a number of decisions on intellectual property (IP), electronic commerce, small economies, LDCs' accession, a services waiver for LDCs, and trade policy reviews. A number of members expressed strong reservations about plurilateral approaches. Many members stressed that any different approaches in the work ahead should conform to the Doha mandate, respect the single undertaking, and be truly multilateral, transparent, and inclusive. In looking at future work, a large number of ministers stressed the centrality of development. Many underlined the need to give priority to issues of interest to LDCs, including cotton. Many mentioned the importance of all three pillars in the agriculture negotiations. Many also mentioned trade facilitation, special and differential (S&D) treatment, S&D monitoring mechanism and NTMs. In an unprecedented display of unity, a coalition of more than a hundred developing countries, including India, Brazil, China, and South Africa, met on the sidelines of the Conference and issued a declaration emphasizing the development agenda. They roundly criticized suggestions for plurilateral agreements to replace decision making by multilateral consensus.

In order to promote transparency and provide better understanding of the trade policies and practices of its members, the WTO has a mechanism for regular review of their trade policies. Depending upon its share in world trade, each member's trade policy is reviewed by the WTO at fixed periodic intervals. India's TPR is carried out every four years. The TPR offers an opportunity to other WTO members to ask questions and raise concerns on different aspects of policies and practices of the country under review. The Fifth TPR of India was held on 14 and 16 September 2011 in the WTO. Before the meeting, the WTO Secretariat circulated a compilation of India's written replies to 886 advance questions raised by 26 WTO members. During the review, most of the members commended the resilience of the Indian economy that smoothly withstood the adverse effects of global financial crisis without taking recourse to protectionist measures. Members appreciated India for using its trade policy to promote sustainable development and inclusive growth. Members also noted India's positive engagement in Doha Round negotiations. Some of the members, notably the US, raised concerns in certain areas, namely tariffs and duties, licensing and restrictions, trade defence measures (antidumping), SPS & TBT, government procurement, incentive schemes to promote investments and exports and protect agriculture, tariff protection on agriculture, services and investments. Responses to the issues raised were provided in India's Closing Statement on 16 September 2011.

During the current year, some of the developed country members of the Information Technology Agreement (ITA) of WTO viz. the USA, European Union, and Japan, have proposed expansion of the agreement (called ITA-2) to increase the coverage of IT products on which customs duty would be bound at zero, addressing non-tariff measures, and expanding the number of signatory countries to include new signatories such as Argentina, Brazil, and South Africa. The proponents of ITA expansion have prepared a consolidated list containing around 350 IT products (combining products of interest to all proponents of ITA-2) on which tariff reductions are being sought. This is under active discussion in the WTO and India is carefully examining the proposal.

BOX – 22.2

Fifth Trade Policy Review: Issues Raised and India's Responses

The Openness of India's Trading Regime: Questions were asked about the openness of India's trading regime. In response India pointed out that year after year, India's imports had outpaced exports. In terms of percentage of GDP, the country's merchandise trade deficit is one of the highest in the world. India has been autonomously reducing its tariffs over the years. The simple average most favoured nation (MFN) tariff rate declined from 15.1 per cent in 2006-7 to 12 per cent in 2010-11. Both the average agricultural and industrial average tariffs have declined over time. The tariffs on 71 per cent of India's tariff lines are between 5 and 10 per cent.

Gap between India's Bound and Applied Rates on Agricultural Products: Some members mentioned the large gap between India's bound and applied rates on agricultural products. India responded that the large gap reflected India's steady and continued autonomous tariff liberalization. During the four years since the last TPR, the tariffs on some agricultural commodities had to be adjusted in the face of high volatility in food prices. In most cases tariffs have been brought down and have stayed down. In a few instances they have been raised again but never above their original levels.

Export Incentives: Questions were asked about export promotion schemes. It was explained that India's export promotion schemes are based on the concept of duty neutralization and providing a level playing field. These schemes are reviewed regularly.

FDI Policy: To a number of questions on FDI policy, India explained that the continuing thrust, during the period since India's last TPR in

contd...

...contd...

2007, has been on making the FDI policy more liberal and investment friendly. The FDI guidelines have been significantly rationalized, simplified, and consolidated, with the aim of providing a single policy platform for reference of foreign investors. Several new sectors, such as petroleum and natural gas and civil aviation were either opened up to foreign investment or significantly liberalized during this period. Efforts were also being made to streamline and simplify the business environment and make regulations conducive to business.

India's IP Policies and Enforcement: On questions related to India's IP policies, India replied that a number of initiatives have been taken to enhance IP protection and enforcement. The changes proposed in the Copyright and Trademark Acts would enhance protection to intellectual property rights (IPRs) in digital technology particularly with regard to the dissemination of protected material over digital networks. These have been supplemented by administrative as well as judicial measures to strengthen the IPR regime. The provisions on IP protection in these laws are further supplemented by border measures to prevent the import of goods involving copyright piracy and counterfeit trademarks. Another initiative taken by Indian customs is the facility for online registration by the right holders through the web-based Automatic Recordation and Targeting for IPR Protection System.

Government Procurement: On this subject, India explained that the procurement of high tech items and high value tenders, above US$ 50,000 is generally open to international bidders. Major reforms are on the anvil for increasing coverage, improving transparency and efficiency, and better enforcement, which are triggered by domestic concerns relating to enhancing the value for money. An omnibus procurement law applicable to the entire country and to all procuring entities, including public-sector enterprises, is being deliberated upon.

Sanitary and Phyto-sanitary (SPS) and Technical Barriers to Trade (TBT) measures: In response to question on India's SPS and TBT measures, India explained that specific trade concerns raised against India have been largely addressed. Regulations adopted in the past have been on the basis of scientific risk analysis.

Export Restrictions: There were some questions on India's use of export restrictions. India responded that export restrictions have been used on some occasions for purposes of domestic supply management but these have been purely on a temporary basis. The ban on the export

contd...

...contd...

of rice and wheat had to be extended in 2009 due to a dislocation in production and again in 2010 due to the severest drought in the country in the last forty years. However, the export of wheat and non-basmati rice is now completely free. The export of basmati rice is and has always been free. Restrictions on cotton exports were imposed for only a brief period last year. Cotton yarn exports have been made completely free. Similarly, cotton is also freely exportable.

Other Issues: There were questions related to customs valuation, tariffs, and other charges, internal taxation, import licensing, and the use of trade remedies. In response it was pointed out that India cannot be accused of protectionist intent in its use of trade remedies. If that were the case, then the easy route of increasing the tariffs up to the bound rates could have been used; that has not been done. Anti-dumping measures are legitimate instruments against unfair trade practices. Investigations are carried out in a fair and transparent manner and subjected to strict scrutiny. As a rule India only imposes the lesser duty and not the full dumping margin as is done by some WTO members. This underscores the fact that trade remedies are not used as a protectionist tool. Despite the fact that many members, with very deep pockets, use subsidies as part of their trade policy, India has not imposed a single anti-subsidy measure. As on date, there is only one safeguard duty in force. In the wake of the economic crisis, there was a spurt in application of safeguard investigations in 2009. A total of 14 applications were received but in nine cases, investigations were either terminated or a decision was taken not to impose any safeguard duty. Duties were imposed only in five cases and those too have since been withdrawn. Moreover, India has never taken recourse to quantitative restrictions as safeguard measures. Import licensing affects only a few restricted items primarily on grounds of protection of human, animal, and plant life and the environment. The licensing regime is open and transparent. Licences are granted on a non-discriminatory basis. The relevant regulations are all available in the public domain and the DGFT acts as the nodal agency.

Source: *Economic Survey 2011-12.*

To conclude, while India, so far, may not have been able to gain a lot from the negotiations, it certainly came out of seclusion during the Doha Ministerial (2001) and is currently leading the developing country coalitions at WTO. Furthermore, expansion of the negotiating agenda (e.g., environmental services) in recent years depicts an evolving learning curve, which is no less important. A similar 'learning through trading' is observed in the case of several other developing countries as well. On the other hand, the aversion of several developed countries towards ensuring free trade is becoming quite obvious in recent years.

Presenting the Annual Supplement 2010-11 to the Foreign Trade Policy 2009-2014 (August 23, 2010) the Commerce Minister stated, "India remains committed to the successful conclusion of the Doha Development Round. We are in favour of establishing a rule-based, fair and equitable global trading regime, which has development as its core objective, and which must respond to the aspirations of millions of people of the developing world.

23

India and the Global Economy

> The big story of the last decade for India has been its arrival on the global scene. The Indian economy had broken free of the low-growth trap from the early 1980s. By the mid-1990s, following the economic reforms of 1991-3, India began to appear as a player of some significance in the global economy. Then, following the East Asian crisis of the late 1990s, and from the first years of the first decade of the 21st century there was no looking back. India's exports began to climb, its foreign exchange reserves, which for decades had hovered around 5 billion dollars, rose exponentially after the economic reforms and in little\ more than a decade had risen to 300 billion dollars. Indian corporations that rarely ventured out of India were suddenly investing all over the world and even in some industrialized countries. When, in 2009, the Group of 20 (G-20) was raised to the level of a forum for leaders, India was a significant member of this global policy group (*Economic Survey 2011-12*).

THE globalisation of India has given rise to new opportunities but it has also brought with it new challenges and responsibilities. It means that the global economy can no longer be viewed from a spectator's standpoint. What happens there has large implications for India. And, in turn, the rise and fall of India's growth rate has an impact on global growth and there is need for India to take this responsibility seriously. This chapter, examines the state of the global economy and India's position therein. It analyses the current global slowdown and eurozone crisis, what this means for India and the policy challenges that these international matters give rise to on domestic soil. The chapter also discusses G-20 imperatives and India's role as a constructive player in the evolving global order.

State of the Global Economy

The developments over the last two years in major economies of the world have not been encouraging. There is an apprehension that the process of global economic recovery that began after the financial crisis of the 2008 is beginning to stall and the sovereign debt crisis in the eurozone area may persist for a while. The US economy has shown some improvement but economic growth remains sluggish.

The predominant reason for the subdued growth in advanced economies remains the sovereign debt crisis that started in the peripheral economies of the eurozone, but from the latter half of 2011, started to adversely affect the major economies there, as well. Issues relating to medium-term fiscal consolidation, the exposure of European banks to public and private debt, and recurring differences in the ways to resolve the crisis have continued to weigh on the global economic outlook as the eurozone accounts for close to one-fifths of global GDP.

Volatility in capital flows resulting from the spillover effects of monetary policy choices and other uncertainties in the advanced financial markets further impacted exchange rates and made the task of macroeconomic management difficult in many emerging economies. This has brought out a new dimension of globalization in the post financial crisis world, where easy monetary policy in one set of countries may result in inflation elsewhere due to cross-border capital flows.

Unemployment situation in advanced economies in general, and the peripheral economies of the eurozone in particular, which had deteriorated in the wake of global crisis has not improved. The OECD Employment Outlook 2011 observed that with the recovery stalling, OECD unemployment remained high, with close to 44.5 million persons unemployed. The extent of unemployment has been varied across OECD countries, with Spain exhibiting the highest unemployment rate (21.7 per cent). As per the OECD report, the main losers have been youth and temporary workers, some of whom have been getting out of the job market. The unemployment rate in the US has shown some improvement (8.7 per cent in Q4 2011 compared to 9.1 per cent in Q3 2011), but nevertheless remains high. The persistently high rates of unemployment in advanced countries, especially in the crisis affected countries of the eurozone, the inherent contradiction of fiscal consolidation (without worsening the contractionary tendencies) is having a social fallout in the peripheral economies and has sharply polarized public debate on the appropriate economic policies to be adopted.

TABLE – 23.1

Growth of the GDP (%) (Y-o-y)

	World	*Advanced economies*	*US*	*EU*	*UK*	*Eurozone*	*Germany*	*Japan*	*B*	*R*	*I*#*	*C**	*S*
2010	5.2	3.2	3.0	2.0	2.1	1.8	3.6	4.4	7.5	4.0	9.9	10.4	2.9
Q1			2.2	1.0	1.2	1.0	2.4	5.0	9.3	3.0	9.4	11.9	1.6
Q2			3.3	2.2	2.5	2.1	4.1	4.5	8.7	5.2	8.8	10.3	3.0
Q3			3.5	2.4	3.0	2.1	4.0	5.2	7.0	3.4	8.9	9.6	3.3
Q4			3.1	2.2	1.7	2.0	3.8	3.2	5.3	4.4	8.3	9.7	3.6
2011	3.8	1.6	1.8	1.6	0.9	1.5	3.0	-0.9	2.9	4.1	7.4	9.2	3.1
Q1			2.2	2.4	1.6	2.4	4.6	0.1	4.2	3.8	7.8	9.7	3.7
Q2			1.6	1.7	0.5	1.6	2.9	-1.7	3.3	3.5	7.7	9.5	3.3
Q3			1.5	1.4	0.4	1.3	2.6	-0.6	2.2	4.9	6.9	9.1	2.9
Q4			1.6	0.9	0.7	0.7	2.0	-1.0	na	na	6.1	8.9	na
2012 (P)	3.3	1.2	1.8	-0.1	0.6	-0.5	0.3	1.7	3.0	3.3	7.0	8.2	2.5

Notes : P: Projection from IMF World Economic outlook January 2012 update.

na: not available. Growth rates may not necessarily correspond to country sources.

* Country website. Y-o- y is year-on-year. EU is European Union. B,R,I,C,S stand for the separate countries of the BRICS grouping, i.e. Brazil, Russia, India, China, and South Africa. Q1, Q2, Q3, and Q4 stand for the first, second, third, and fourth quarters Aggregations for World and Advanced Economies use purchasing power parity weights.

\# India¡¦s GDP growth is in terms of factor cost whereas for other countries it is in terms of market prices.

Source: Organization for Economic Cooperation and Development (OECD) Principal Global indicators and IMF WEO.

BOX – 23.1

The Eurozone : A Crisis after a Crisis

The eurozone crisis: The eurozone (a currency union of 17 European countries) has been going through a major crisis which started with Greece but spread rapidly to Ireland, Portugal, and Spain and subsequently Italy. While it got sparked off by fear over the sovereign debt crisis in Greece, it went on to impact the peripheral economies as well, especially those with over-leveraged financial institutions. These economies (especially Greece) have witnessed downgrades in the ratings of their sovereign debt due to fears of default and a rise in borrowing costs.The sovereign debt crisis has made it very difficult for some of these countries to re-finance government debt. The banking sector in these countries also stands adversely affected.

Good times: After the launch of the euro, the eurozone witnessed not only a decline in long-term interest rates (especially from 2002 to 2006), but an increasing degree of convergence in the interest rates of member countries. A common currency, similar interest rates, and relatively strong growth provided a basis for a rise in public and private borrowing with crossborder holdings of sovereign and private debt by banks.

Trigger: In the aftermath of the global financial crisis in 2008, sovereign debt levels started to mount. The revelation that the fiscal deficit in Greece was much higher than stated earlier set off serious concerns in early 2010 about the sustainability of the debt. The downgrade of ratings led to a spiral of rising bond yields and further downgrade of government debt of other peripheral eurozone economies as well, that had high public debt or a build-up of bank lending or both.

How it spread: Concerns intensified in early 2010 as cross-border holdings of sovereign debt and exposure of banks came to light. The financial markets quickly transmitted the shocks which not only led to a sharp rise in credit default swap (CDS) spreads but later impacted capital flows elsewhere.

Underlying weaknesses: The crisis has been difficult to resolve due to certain specificities:

- The eurozone lacks a single fiscal authority capable of strict enforcement;

contd...

...contd...

- Economies with different levels of competitiveness (and fiscal positions) have a single currency;
- These economies cannot adjust through a depreciation of the currency;
- There is no lender of last resort, i.e. a full-fledged central bank.

Steps to resolve it: In May 2010, the European finance ministers agreed on a rescue package worth Rs. 750 billion to ensure financial stability by creating the European Financial Stability Facility (EFSF). In October 2011, the eurozone leaders agreed to a package of measures that included an agreement whereby banks would accept a 50 per cent write-off of Greek debt owed to private creditors, an increase in the EFSF to about Rs. 1 trillion, and requiring European banks to achieve 9 per cent capitalization. The date for starting the European Stability Mechanism was brought forward to July 2012. To restore confidence in Europe, EU leaders also agreed to a fiscal compact with a commitment that participating countries would introduce a balanced budget amendment. In December 2011, the European Central Bank (ECB) took the step of offering a three-year long-term refinancing operation (LTRO) at highly favourable rates to alleviate funding stress which helped bring down the yields somewhat during January and February 2012. But overall uncertainty about the effectiveness of all these measures and how further resources would be raised, their adequacy, and doubts about sovereign debt levels coming down and the ability of Greece and other economies to undertake further fiscal austerity remain, especially due to the low-growth scenario.

The Euro zone and India: The eurozone, though distinct from the European Union (EU) is a major subset of the EU. The eurozone and EU account for about 19 and 25 per cent respectively of global GDP. The EU is a major trade partner for India accounting for about 20 per cent of India's exports and is an important source of foreign direct investment (FDI). The IMF has forecast that the eurozone is likely to go through a mild recession in 2012. A slowdown in the eurozone is likely to impact the EU and the world economy as well as India.

There are early signs of a turnaround in the global economy. A series of measures by the euro zone authorities and the European Central Bank have allayed fears of an imminent meltdown. The change is reflected in the equity market boom in advanced and emerging economies. However doubts still exist about the sustainability of the recovery. The eurozone still faces problems such as the continuing recession; the existence of a monetary union without fiscal union; the slow progress of the proposed European banking union; the continuing need for austerity in many advanced economies. In addition, fiscal tensions in the United States might re-surface in the next few months. Japan has still to find a reasonable way out of its decade long slump. Emerging markets continue to face problems of overheating. All these cast a shadow on the prospects of the global economy.

The International Monetary Fund (IMF), in its January 2013 *World Economic Outlook Update*, reduced global growth forecast for the year 2012 to 3.2 per cent from its October 2012 estimate of 3.3 per cent. Advanced economies are expected to grow at 1.4 per cent in 2013, while emerging and developing economies are projected to grow at 5.5 per cent in 2013 (*Economic Survey 2012-13*).

The World Bank in its publication 'Global Economic Prospects January 2013' highlights that the uncertainty over future policy and necessary fiscal and financial restructuring would continue to be a drag on growth in many countries. The downside risks to the global economy include: a stalling of progress on the euro-area crisis, debt and fiscal issues in the United States, the possibility of a sharp slowing of investment in China, and a disruption in global oil supplies. However, the likelihood of these risks and their potential impact has diminished, and that of a stronger-than-anticipated recovery in highincome countries has increased.

Going forward, global recovery will depend upon how the risks emanating from US fiscal adjustment and euro area are managed. In the euro area, despite several rescue packages over the last two years, the crisis has become deep, structural and multifaceted, posing a major downside risk to the global outlook. Some of the important measures which are needed to stabilize the euro area include mapping out the role of European Stability Mechanism; creating a single supervisory mechanism and a more integrated banking system; progress with the ratification of the Fiscal Compact; and further structural reforms in euro area member States (*Economic Survey 2012-13*).

TABLE – 23.2

Overview of World Economic Outlook Projections

Percentage change year over year

	Projections			
	2011	*2012*	*2013*	*2014*
World Output	**3.9**	**3.2**	**3.5**	**4.1**
Advanced economies	**1.6**	**1.3**	**1.4**	**2.2**
United States	1.8	2.3	2.0	3.0
Euro Area	1.4	-0.4	-0.2	1.0
Japan	-0.6	2.0	1.2	0.7
United Kingdom	0.9	-0.2	1.0	1.9
Emerging and developing economies	**6.3**	**5.1**	**5.5**	**5.9**
China	9.3	7.8	8.2	8.5
India	7.9	4.5	5.9	6.4
World Trade Volume (goods and services)	**5.9**	**2.8**	**3.8**	**5.5**

Source: World Economic Outlook Update, January 2013. IMF. *Economic Survey 2012-13.*

Locating India in the New Global Economy

India has over the years become a more open economy. The total share of imports and exports accounts for close to 50 per cent of GDP while that of capital inflows and outflows measures up to 54 per cent of GDP. Yet economic outcomes and their impact on growth and development arising from the interaction between the domestic and external economies are contingent on a large number of factors. Though economic outcomes are to some extent contingent on choosing policies appropriate to the conditions characterizing an economy, the relative position of an economy vis-à-vis other countries in a global setting could facilitate (or even constrain) policy choices. This section flags a few features that characterize India that may be relevant in its further engagement with the global economy as also for its future development.

India has moved up the Ranks but is still the poorest among the G-20: India has emerged as the fourth largest economy globally with a high growth rate and has also improved its global ranking in terms of per capita income (as mentioned earlier). Yet the fact remains that its per capita income continues to be quite low (at current US $ 1527 in 2011). Addressing this is perhaps the most visible challenge. Nevertheless, India has a diverse set of factors, domestic as well as external, that could drive growth well into the future.

Demographics: With over 1.2 billion people, India accounts for nearly one-sixth of global population. While the rate of growth of population has consistently declined, India's population increased by nearly 180 million persons during 2001-11 (the highest in the world in absolute terms). However, India is also passing through a phase when its dependency ratio will decline from an estimated 74.8 in 2001 to 55.6 in 2026 with a corresponding increase in the share of persons in working-age group. With labour being a key factor of production, a demographic dividend is a clear positive for growth. It has, however, been pointed out that much of the growth in population will occur in states that are currently poor. Therefore, for this dividend to accrue, it will be necessary to build human capital in adequate measure.

On this count, India has shown some improvement in terms of its human development index (HDI). The UNDP's HDI, which captures the progress of a country in terms of economic indicators as well as education and health indicators increased from 0.344 in 1980 to 0.547 in 2011 with an overall global ranking of 134 (out of 187 countries) compared to 119 (out of 169 countries) in HDR 2010. The growth rate in average annual HDI of India between 2000-11 is among the highest, a finding also corroborated by the India Human Development Report (IHDR) 2011 brought out by the Institute of Applied Manpower Research and the Planning Commission. According to the IHDR, HDI between 1999-2000 and 2007-8 has increased by 21 per cent, with an improvement of over 28 per cent in education being the main driver. India is ranked 129 in terms of the gender inequality index(GII) which captures the loss in achievement due to gender disparities in the areas of reproductive health, empowerment, and labour force participation, with values ranging from 0 (perfect equality) to 1 (total inequality). A lot more needs to be done as our GII is higher than the global average of 0.492. Even neighbours like Pakistan (115), Bangladesh (112), and Sri Lanka (74), have performed better in terms of this indicator. The gross national income (GNI) per capita ranking minus HDI ranking for India is -10 indicating that India is better ranked by GNI than by non-income HDI. As a corollary, India is worse off in its performance of non-income HDI value computed from life expectancy and education. Even though India's score has improved, her HDI rank has not moved very significantly. A possible reason could be that some other countries may have registered faster improvement in these indices. India therefore needs to benchmark her achievements (on various fronts) not only in absolute terms but also in relation to other countries.

Exports and External Demand: The process of globalization has been marked by a rising share of exports (as also imports) that reached 27.9 per cent for the world as a whole in 2010, with some countries showing much higher dependence of exports. A stylized fact of the so called East Asian miracle economies was that an export-led, investment-fuelled strategy propelled growth and helped them acquire manufacturing capabilities. This strategy was supported by a favourable exchange rate, cheap credit, and relatively low wages which helped to gain competitive advantage. Global demand for goods, particularly in the advanced markets, lent support to this growth strategy. As a result, these economies moved up the value chain in manufacturing (Table 23.2).

TABLE – 23.2

Exports of Goods and Services (% of GDP)

Year	*World*	*High income*	*USA*	*UK*	*EU*	*EA*	*Germany*	*Japan*	*B*	*R*	*I*	*C*	*S*
1980	19.1	19.9	10.1	27.1	25.5	24.7	20.2	13.5	9.1	na	6.2	10.6	35.4
1990	19.2	19.3	9.6	24.0	27.0	27.1	24.8	10.4	8.2	18.2	7.1	16.1	24.2
2000	24.7	24.3	11.0	27.6	35.8	36.7	33.4	11.0	10.0	44.1	13.2	23.3	27.9
2005	26.7	25.6	10.4	26.4	36.9	38.0	41.3	14.3	15.1	35.2	19.3	37.1	27.4
2010	27.9	27.8	12.6	29.4	39.7	40.6	46.8	15.2	11.2	30.0	21.5	29.6	25.5

Source : World Bank Database.

This leads to the question of how far export can be a driver of growth for India at this point in time. With a slowdown in advanced economies, the prospect of their growth fuelling demand for imports (i.e. exports from other countries), seems somewhat bleak at this juncture. Second, the large build-up of capacity in some countries (including China) suggests that they might act as barriers to new entrants for some time. Third, the costs of energy are rising and there are growing concerns about climate change.

In this regard, India's export (of goods and services) to GDP ratio increased from 6.2 per cent in 1990 to 21.5 per cent in 2010. Yet India accounts for only 1.5 per cent of world exports. India's exports are also evenly balanced between merchandise and services. Moreover, the change in direction of exports suggests that India has been diversifying the destination of its exports away from traditional markets.

There is therefore some scope for exports to grow, particularly to the fast growing economies, many of which are in Asia and Africa and to some extent Latin America, while some of the mature markets may remain important, albeit with declining shares on the whole for the group. Moreover, the main advantage of a presence in the global market is of being able to benchmark to global standards and therefore worth pursuing in its own right. Additionally, the advantage of having the twin engines of domestic and export demand is that it lends the economy greater resilience to fluctuations in global demand.

Investing in Research and Development (R&D) and Innovation: The World Bank Study titled 'Unleashing India's Innovation' (2007) observed that India had increasingly become a top global innovator in high–tech products and services. Yet the country is underperforming in terms of its innovation potential. India spends less than 0.9 per cent of its GDP in the area of R&D, which covers basic research, applied research, and experimental development. This fact emerges from the OECD Fact Book 2010 that lists 41 countries with Israel topping the list on this count and most developed countries spending over 2 per cent of their GDP on R&D. While more resources into R&D would be needed, equally critical would be to harness existing institutions and organizations set up for formal R&D and also to encourage grass-roots level innovation.

Given the increasing acceptance of the fact that land, water, and energy are likely to be in short supply and environment a major concern, India is well placed to advance through the route of frugal innovation and devising of specific applications suited to the bottom of the pyramid that would not only open new market segments within India but also in other countries in the developing world. That apart, with regard to frontier areas, India is well placed to take advantage of its vast diaspora to jump-start its R&D efforts. Strategically positioning India as a hub for FDI in R&D may well be a way for it to leapfrog into the next generation of technologies and products.

Energy Security and Growth: India is characterized by a relatively lower energy intensity of GDP as compared to China, South Africa, and Russia but higher than that of Brazil. Advanced countries, in particular EU countries and Japan, have been witnessing a decline in the energy intensity of GDP due, apart from technological improvements, to various factors, the main one being a shift in the structure of their economies towards services.

As regards dependence on imported energy sources, at an overall level, India' energy dependence appears modest at 25.7 per cent in terms of total energy usage. However, this masks the fact the around 80 per cent of the crude oil consumed is imported, whereas the bulk of coal is domestically produced. Even with respect to coal, the country is importing on the margin to meet domestic demand. On the other side, there is a large fraction of population that has little or no access to commercial sources of energy and depends on traditional sources.

A rise in the price of oil in international markets has mostly been a source of vulnerability for the macroeconomy of India on account of its impact on the current account deficit. High international prices of fossil fuels also result in a higher import bill, which either gets passed on to the consumers or results in higher subsidy thereby affecting fiscal health. That apart, the growing tensions in many oil- producing economies are a source of vulnerability for the energy security of India. In this one area, the strategic advantage for India would lie in diversifying its energy sources.

Resources for Development and the Availability of Capital: A case is often made for the virtues of a minimalist state and the need to disengage from a number of activities. The actual facts speak otherwise. India's general government expenditure in relation to GDP is actually lower even in comparison to many market economies by a factor of at least half. More importantly, the ratio of general government revenues to GDP at 17.6 per cent is one of the lowest in emerging economies and certainly very low vis-à-vis the advanced economies. Therefore, even if fiscal consolidation is needed, the priority has to be on raising resources. Recent developments in the developed economies reveal how important it is to maintain the revenue base and keep government finances in shape. As India becomes more exposed to the external economy, its fiscal strength based on a large revenue base would become even more critical.

FDI—Playing Strategically: Many of the advanced economies, with deep technological strengths, are now aging societies and need to invest overseas and rely on factor incomes. At the stage at which India is placed, there is the need for sustained investment. There is an inherent complementary relationship between India's requirement for more 'real' investment and the need for some of the advanced economies, including some of the Asian industrialized economies, to invest in production facilities in friendly countries overseas in order to diversify their supply chains.

An Economy in a Democratic Framework: The global economic crisis opened afresh the debate on the relative role of the market and the state as also the relative advantages of democratic vis-à-vis state-led economies. The challenge of managing a mixed economy within a democratic and federal system is a complex task. However, the challenge of transiting from a stateled monolith to a more representative system may be even more daunting. In either case, for a system to thrive, economic outcomes need to be tangible. The critical question is therefore not of state versus markets but, rather, of how to maximize market outcomes (minimize market failures) and have effective governance (i.e. minimize government failure) with a democratic system as the political basis for governance.

Engaging the World

It is said that India has entered a 'critical decade'. India has emerged as a large and systemically important economy on the global stage. It enjoys the unique advantage of having many economic indicators in its favour, particularly a large domestic market, robust investment-to-GDP ratio, and demographic advantage. However, all of these will need to be leveraged to get the full advantage out of them. Undoubtedly this requires India to address its internal challenges, which include the long-standing problem of poverty and the development of its social and physical infrastructure.

Challenges and Outlook

The recent global slowdown has thrown up new challenges for India with its export growth being continuously negative since May 2012 compared to very high growth rates of even above 50 per cent in some months of the previous year. With limited fiscal space available for the government and with protectionist measures of trading partners showing signs of rising, the policy options left are more at the micro level (*Economic Survey 2012-13*).

The widening of the trade deficit to more than 10 per cent of GDP and the CAD crossing 4 per cent of GDP in 2011-12 and the first half of 2012-13 have been matters of concern. In recent years, net invisible balance reduced the need for financing, while capital inflows were sufficient to finance the CAD safely. In the current fiscal, the growth in invisibles is insufficient to narrow the growing trade deficit. Besides, the CAD is financed by volatile capital flows, which has led to financial fragility and is reflected in rupee exchange rate volatility.

The room to increase exports in the short run is limited, as they are dependent upon the recovery and growth of partner countries, especially in industrial economies. This may take time. The main focus has to be on curbing imports, mainly by making oil prices more market determined, and curbing imports of gold. At the same time, further measures to ease the inflow of remittances and steps to diversify software exports could help reduce financing needs. Greater emphasis on FDI including opening up sectors further can help increase the quantum of safe financing. FII flows need to be targeted towards longer term rupee instruments so as to minimize the 'reversal' of capital during risk-off phases. Finally, external commercial borrowing needs to be monitored carefully so that entities without access to foreign exchange revenues do not leave significant exposures unhedged (*Economic Survey 2012-13*).

Given its size and its profile in the global economy, India will inevitably need to play an active role at global level, not just in debates about how to resolve the continuing crisis and prevent the recurrence of similar crises in the future, but in influencing the rules for the global economy on overarching macroeconomic issues such as trade, capital flows, financial regulation, climate change, and governance of global financial institutions.

It may be argued, and in some ways it may seem the easy option, that India should take a passive stance in the current global debate and just wait out the period of crisis. But that option is no longer realistically feasible. India is already too much a part of the global economy and polity; developments in the world will affect India deeply and what India does will affect the world. There is, therefore, a need for India to engage with the world in terms of action and ideas.

This Chapter is extensively drawn from Uma Kapila (ed.) (2013). *Indian Economy Since Independence* (24th edition) (Ch.26). New Delhi: Academic Foundation.

QUESTIONS

SECTION I
(Chs. 1-2)

Section-I: Basic Issues in Economic Developments

Chs. 1–2

1. (a) "Economic growth is necessary but not sufficient condition for Economic development." Comment.

   B.Com (Hons.) 2013

   OR

   (b) What are the environmental concerns in Economic Development? Explain the concept of sustainable development.

   B.Com (Hons.) 2013

2. (a) Distinguish between growth and development.

   (b) Explain Human Development Index as a measure of economic development.

   OR

   (a) Explain the features of underdeveloped countries.

   (b) Explain GOULETS three core values of development.

   B.Com (Hons.) 2012

3. "Growth is necessary but not sufficient condition for development." Explain. What are the factors affecting economic development of a country? *B.Com (Hons.) 2011, 2007*

4. Explain the meaning of underdevelopment and discuss some common features of the underdeveloped countries.

5. "Economic growth is the means to achieve the end which is the improvement in the quality of life of human beings". Comment. What other factors/conditions are required besides economic growth for achieving an improved quality of life? *B.Com (Hons.) 2010*

6. Explain the concept of Human Development as distinguished from economic development. What is the Human Development Index (HDI)? Comment on India's HDI. *B.Com (Hons.) 2009*

7. What is meant by sustainable development? What measures should a developing country like India take to protect its environment?

   B.Com (Hons.) 2008

SECTION II
(Ch. 3)

Section-II: Basic Features of Indian Economy at Independence

Note: No question to be asked.

SECTION III
(Chs. 4-5)

Section-III: Policy Regimes

(a) ***The Evolution of Planning and Import Substituting Industrialisation***

(b) ***Economic Reform and Liberalisation***

Chs.4 & 5

1. What was the rationale behind economic reforms initiated in India in 1991? Discuss the impact of these reforms on India's economy.
B.Com (Hons.) 2013

2. Why did the government adopt import substitution strategy of industrialisation after independence. Why was this strategy changed and how? *B.Com (Hons.) 2011*

SECTION IV
(Chs. 6-10)

Section-IV: Growth, Development and Structural Change

(a) ***The Experience of Growth, Development and Structural Change in different phases of Growth and Policy Regimes across sectors and Regions***

(b) ***The Institutional Framework***

(c) ***Changes in Policy Perspective***

Section-IV(a)—Ch.6

1. Describe the structural changes in Indian Economy since Independence.
B.Com (Hons.) 2013

2. Analyse briefly the changes in the sectoral composition of national income and workforce in India. Do these changes reflect economic growth? *B.Com (Hons.) 2011*

3. (a) Discuss the interegional disparities in growth and development in India.

   (b) Analyse the change in occupation distribution of working population in India. *B.Com (Hons.) 2012*

4. Analyse briefly the changes in the sectoral composition of national income and workforce in India. Do these changes reflect economic growth? *B.Com (Hons.) 2011*

5. Describe trends in inter-regional disparities in growth and development. What are their implications? What changes are observed in the occupation structure of India. *B.Com (Hons.) 2011*

6. Write an essay on the growth performance of India's economy under different policy regimes since 1951. *B.Com (Hons.) 2010*

7. Describe trends in inter-regional disparities in growth and development. What are their implications? *B.Com (Hons.) 2009*

8. Discuss the changes in sectoral composition of GDP. *B.Com (Hons.) 2008*

9. Analyse briefly the changes in the sectoral composition of national income. Do these changes reflect economic growth? *B.Com (Hons.) 2007*

10. Discuss the main changes in the relative contribution of various sectors to GDP since 1950-51. Are these changes in conformity with the development process?

11. What is meant by Economic Reforms in India? Outline the various reform measures undertaken in India since the 1990s. *B.Com (Hons.) 2009*

Ch. 7

12. (a) Write short note on Land Reforms in India. *B.Com (Hons.) 2013*

Section-IV(d): Growth and Distribution; Unemployment and Poverty

Chs. 8 to 10

13. Do demographic changes in India since 1951 reflect development of the economy? *B.Com (Hons.) 2013*

14. "Despite impressive rates of GDP growth in India over the last two decades, the level of poverty and unemployment has remained unacceptably high." Do you agree? *B.Com (Hons.) 2013*

15. What are the special programmes of Government to fight poverty and unemployment in India. *B.Com (Hons.) 2012*

16. Discuss the nature, extent and causes of poverty and unemployment in India. Briefly review the policy of the government to solve this problem. *B.Com (Hons.) 2011*

17. Suggest measures to reduce poverty and unemployment in India. *B.Com (Hons.) 2010*

18. Discuss:

    Poverty Line in India *B.Com (Hons.) 2009*

19. Write a short note on National Rural Employment Guarantee Programme (NREGP).

20. 'Poverty and unemployment are closely related'. Comment. Discuss the poverty alleviation programmes which address the issue of employment generation. *B.Com (Hons.) 2008*

Section-IV(e): Demographic Constraints—Ch. 10

21. "The ongoing demographic transition poses challenges and opportunities," comment. Discuss briefly the possible pathways to a faster decline in fertility highlighting the experience of Kerala and Tamil Nadu. *B.Com (Hons.) 2011*

22. "Population growth is not a cause but a result of poverty." Do you agree? Explain in the light of India's experience in this regard. *B.Com (Hons.) 2010*

23. Explain the reasons why Birth Rate still continues to be high in India while there has been a relative decline in Death Rate. Critically examine the measures taken to control the rate of growth of population. *B.Com (Hons.) 2009*

24. 'The relationship between population and economic development is a two sided relationship.' Explain the statement in the light of India's experience since 1951. *B.Com (Hons.) 2008*

SECTION V
(Chs. 11-22)

Section-V: Sectoral Trends and Issues

Section V.1: Agriculture—Chs. 11-12

Ch. 11

1. Write a short note on:
   (b) Green Revolution
   (c) Food Security in India *B.Com (Hons.) 2013*

2. Discuss why the new agricultural strategy was necessary. What has been the impact of Green Revolution on regional imbalances? *B.Com (Hons.) 2011*

   Or

   Comment on the new agricultural strategy. Evaluate technological and institutional reforms for agriculture in India. *B.Com (Hons.) 2012*

3. What do you understand by "Green Revolution"? How did it try to overcome the slow progress of land reforms in India?
B.Com (Hons.) 2011

4. Write a short note on:
Major factors responsible for the deceleration of growth in agriculture production in the last 15 years. *B.Com (Hons.) 2010*

Ch. 12

5. Write a short note on:
Role of agricultural price policy in food security.
B.Com (Hons.) 2010

6. Discuss:
Public Distribution System in India. *B.Com (Hons.) 2013, 2009*

Section–V.2: Industry and Services—(Chhs. 13-18)

Ch. 13

7. What have been the major changes in Industrial Policy in India since 1951? What has been the impact of these on the growth of industrial sector?. *B.Com (Hons.) 2013*
8. Identify the phases of industrial growth since independence highlighting the profile of industrial growth and the factors causing the slowdown since 1990s. *B.Com (Hons.) 2011*
9. Examine the challenges and outlook for the industrial sector in India. What policy measures would you suggest for this sector so that it may help in resolving the critical problems of poverty and unemployment in our country. *B.Com (Hons.) 2010*
10. Identify the phases of India's industrial growth since Independence highlighting the profile of industrial growth and factors causing the slowdown since the 1990s.

Ch. 15

11. Write short note on role of small scale industries in India.
B.Com (Hons.) 2011

Ch. 16

12. Role of Public Sector in Indian Economy. Explain.
B.Com (Hons.) 2013
13. Discuss the performance of Public Sector Enterprises in India. How has liberalisation affected this performance ? *B.Com (Hons.) 2009*
14. Write short notes:
Disinvestment programme in India. *B.Com (Hons.) 2011*

Ch. 17

15. Write a short note on "role, performance and growth of the services sector in India". *B.Com (Hons.) 2010*

Ch. 18

16. Write short on shift in Government's policy towards Foreign Direct Investment (FDI) since 1991. *B.Com (Hons.) 2011*
17. Discuss:

    Foreign Direct Investment (FDI) in India after 1991.

    B.Com (Hons.) 2009

Ch. 19

18. Explain: Financial Sector Reforms *B.Com (Hons.) 2013*

Section–V.4: Foreign Trade and Balance of Payment—(Chs. 20-22)

Ch. 20

19. Examine the impact of liberalisation measures on external sector (foreign trade, capital inflows etc.) in India since 1991. You may use the data in Table 1. *B.Com (Hons.) 2013*
20. Write a short note on role played by the external sector in India's economic development. *B.Com (Hons.) 2010*
21. Write short note:

    Composition and direction of exports and imports in India
22. Discuss: Changes in the composition of foreign trade since 1991.

    B.Com (Hons.) 2008
23. Examine the trends in India's foreign trade during the last two decades. Evaluate the impact of liberalisation measures adopted by the Government for the foreign trade sector in India.

Ch. 21

24. Analyse the trends in India's balance of trade, Balance of current account and Balance of payments over the last two decades. Refer to Table 1. *B.Com (Hons.) 2013*
25. Describe the trends in India's balance of payments since 1990-91. Discuss any two indicators of the external sector.

    B.Com (Hons.) 2009

Ch. 22

26. Write short notes:

    (a) WTO

    (b) Shift in Government policy towards Foreign Direct Investment (FDI) since 1991. *B.Com (Hons.) 2011*

TABLE – 1

Balance of Payments: Summary 1990-91 to 2011-12

(US $ Million)

Sl. No.	*Items*	*1990-91*	*2000-01*	*2007-08*	*2008-09*	*2009-10*	*2010-11*
1.	Exports	18477	45452	166162	189001	182442	250468
2.	Imports	27915	57912	257629	308520	300644	381061
3.	Trade Balance	-9438	-12460	-91467	-119519	-118202	-130593
4.	Invisibles (net)	-242	9794	75731	91604	80022	84647
	Non-factor services	980	1692	38853	53916	36016	48816
	Income	-3752	-5004	-5068	-7100	-8038	-17308
	Transfers	2069	12854	41945	44798	52045	53140
5.	Goods and Services Balance	–	–	-52614	-65603	-82186	-81777
6.	Current Account Balance	-9680	-2666	-15736	-27915	-38180	-45946
7.	External Assistance (net)	2204	410	2114	2439	2890	4941
8.	External Commercial Borrowings (net)	2254	4303	22609	7861	2000	12506
9.	Non-resident Deposits (net)	1537	2316	179	4290	2922	3238
10.	Foreign Investment (net) *of which*	103	5862	43326	8342	50362	39652
	(i) FDI (net)	97	3272	15893	22372	17966	9360
	(ii) Portfolio (net)	–	–	27433	-14030	32396	30293
11.	Other Flows (net)	2283	-3740	10969	-5916	-13162	-10994
12.	Reserves [increase(-)/ decreases (+)]	1278	-5842	-92164	20080	-13441	-13050

Glossary of Selected Terms

Absolute advantage. Occurs when a nation or other economic region is able to produce a good or service more efficiently than a second nation or region.

Absorptive capacity. The ability of a country to absorb foreign private or public financial assistance (to use the funds in a productive manner).

Acquisition. Occurs when one firm buys controlling interest in a target firm; acquisitions of foreign firms by transnational corporations are an important form of foreign direct investment.

Advanced economies. The twenty-nine richer, more industrialised countries in the world; also called the developed countries.

Agenda 21. A landmark document that established guidelines for global sustainable economic development; *Agenda 21* was adopted at the Rio Earth Summit in 1992.

Age structure of the population. The age composition of a given population. For example, in LDCs, the age structure of the population is typified by a large portion of population under 15 years old, a slightly smaller proportion aged between 15 and 45 years, and a very small proportion above 45 years old.

Agricultural sector. An economic sector comprised of farms, dairies, poultry and livestock farms, forestry, and fishing and shellfish industries.

Asian Development Bank (ADB). A regional development bank that serves Asia and the Pacific region.

Balance of payments (BoP). A summary statement of a nation's financial transactions with the outside world.

Balance of trade. The difference between the value of a nation's total imports and total exports in a given period of time.

Bank for International Settlements (BIS). An international organisation designed to promote international monetary and financial cooperation among central banks, and serves as a bank for central banks and international organisations.

Basic economic questions. The universal questions that all economies, past and present, have answered, including what, how, and for whom to produce.

Big Three. The dominant multilateral organisations that oversee economic relations among countries—the International Monetary Fund, World Bank, and World Trade Organization.

Bottlenecks. Sectors in the economy where the development process leads to a more rapid expansion of demand than supply in the goods or factor markets.

Brain drain. The emigration of highly educated and skilled professional and technical manpower from the developing to the developed countries.

Buffer stocks. Stocks of commodities held by countries or international organisations to moderate the commodities' price fluctuations.

Bretton Woods System. The institutions and operation of the international monetary system from 1946 to 1973.

Business cycle. A recurring, but irregular pattern of upswings and downswings in economic activity on the national, or global levels.

Calorie requirement. The calories needed to sustain the population at normal levels of activity and health, taking account of its age and sex distributions, average body weights, and physical environment.

Capital account. The portion of a country's *balance of payments* that shows the volume of *private foreign investment* and public *grants* and *loans* that flow into and out of a country over a given period, usually one year.

Capital deepening. Occurs when the real capital per worker increases in a country over time.

Capital flight. The excessive cross-border transfers of financial capital, often an outflow of funds from developing countries to more stable advanced economies.

Capital formation. The process of increasing the amount of capital goods in a country; capital formation stems from savings and productive investments.

Capital goods. The items that are designed to produce other goods; a factor of production.

Capital-intensive production. A method of producing goods and services that relies on the use of sophisticated capital goods.

Capitalism. A type of economic system based on the private ownership and control of the factors of production—natural resources, human resources, and capital goods.

Capital markets. The institutions that channel surplus money into medium- and long-term productive investments, investments of at least one year in duration.

Capital-output ratio. A ratio that shows the units of capital required to produce a unit of output over a given period of time.

Capital stock. The total amount of capital goods in a country.

Cash crops. Agricultural output produced for sale in domestic or global markets rather than for the household's consumption; examples are cotton, rubber and coffee.

Civil society organisations (CSOs). A variety of non-governmental and non-profit groups, or citizen's associations, that work to improve society and the human condition.

Closed economy. An economy in which there are no foreign trade transactions or any other form of economic contacts with the rest of the world.

Collusion. An agreement among producers to limit the supply, market share, and price of a good; used by producer cartels.

Command economy. A highly centralised economic system in which the government owns or controls the factors of production—natural resources, human resources, and capital goods; viewed as an economic model.

Common market. A type of regional trade agreement that creates a free trade area, uniform external trade policy, and other types of regional economic integration.

Communism. An economic system based on government ownership and control of the factors of production—and on the theories of Karl Marx.

Comparative advantage. Occurs when a nation or economic region is able to produce a product at a lower opportunity cost compared to another nation or region.

Competition. The economic rivalry that exists among producers of a similar product.

Competitiveness. The factors that influence economic performance in a nation's macroeconomy and microeconomy.

Concessional terms. Favorable credit terms on loans, including a low interest rate and extended repayment period; offered by some multilateral development institutions to the poorest developing countries.

Conditionality. The requirement imposed by the *International Monetary Fund* that a borrowing country undertake fiscal, monetary, and international commercial reforms as a condition to receiving a *loan* for *balance of payments* difficulties.

Consumer price index (CPI). Measures the percentage change in the price of a uniform market basket of goods and services every month; the CPI is used to calculate the inflation rate.

Cooperative. A voluntary association of people who jointly own and control a productive enterprise to satisfy the economic, social, or cultural needs of members; also called a co-op.

Corporation. A type of business that is owned by stockholders, but typically run by professional managers.

Corruption. The abuse of the public trust for personal gain.

Crude birthrate. The number of children born alive each year per 1,000 population (a crude birthrate of 20 per 1,000 is the same as a 2 per cent increase).

Deathrate. The yearly number of deaths per 1,000 population—an annual crude deathrate of 15 per 1,000 would involve 1.5 per cent of the population.

Debt-service ratio. The ratio of interest and principal payments due in a year to export receipts for that year.

Decile. A 10 per cent portion of any numerical quantity; a population divided into deciles would be divided into 10 equal numeric groups.

Default. Occurs when a government refuses to make scheduled payments on its debts.

Deforestation. The clearing of forested land.

Democracy. A type of political system in which political authority is derived from the people, either directly or through freely elected representatives.

Democratic socialism. A type of economic system in which core socialist beliefs guide national economic policy, and democratic institutions govern the nation.

Demographic transition. The phasing-out process of population growth rates from a virtually stagnant growth stage characterised by high *birthrates* and *death rates*, through a rapid-growth stage with high birthrates and low death rates, to a stable, low-growth stage in which both birth and death rates are low.

Dependency burden. The proportion of the total population aged 0 to 15 and 65+, which is considered economically unproductive and therefore not counted in the labour force.

Devaluation. A government action that lowers the value of its currency relative to other countries' currencies.

Developing countries. The poorer, less industrialised countries in the global economy.

Developed World. The now economically advanced capitalist countries of Western Europe, North America, Australia, New Zealand, and Japan. These were the first countries to experience sustained long-term *economic growth*.

Developing countries. The present countries of Asia, Africa, the Middle East, Latin America and East Europe and the Former Soviet Union, mainly characterised by low *levels of living*, high rates of *population growth*, low *income per capita*, and general economic and technological *dependence* on developed economies.

Digital divide. The information and communications technologies (ICTs) gap between the "have" and "have not" countries.

Doha Development Agenda (DDA). A 2001 World Trade Organization statement pledging support for fair trade and sustainable economic development.

Dumping. An illegal trade practice that occurs when a company from one nation sells its output in a second country at a price lower than its production costs, or lower than the price charged in its own domestic market.

Economic freedom. The ability of individuals and businesses to freely choose how to use their private property in an economy.

Economic growth. The steady process by which the productive capacity of the economy is increased over time to bring about rising levels of national output and income.

Economic infrastructure. The physical capital that underpins economic growth and development; examples include transportation and communications systems, public utilities, and courts.

Economic integration. The merging to various degrees of the economies and economic policies of two or more countries in a given region.

Economic planning. A deliberate and conscious attempt by the state to formulate decisions on how the *factors of production* shall be allocated among different uses or industries, thereby determining how much of total *goods* and *services* shall be produced in one or more ensuing periods.

Economic policy. A statement of objectives and the methods of achieving these objectives (policy instruments) by government, political party, business concern, etc. Some examples of government economic objectives are maintaining *full employment,* achieving a high rate of *economic growth*, reducing *income inequalities* and regional development inequalities, and maintaining price stability. Policy instruments include fiscal policy, monetary and financial policy, and legislative controls (e.g., price and wage control and rent control).

Economic sanctions. Any restrictions on trade, investment, or foreign aid that are intended to pressurise a country to change a policy or action.

Economic system. Represents all economic activity in a country; different types of economic systems answer the basic economic questions in different ways.

Economies of scale. The decline in the average cost of producing a good as the rate of output rises; highlights the advantages of bigness.

Ecosystems. Systems consisting of organic and inorganic matter and natural forces that interact and change; basic ecosystems include grasslands, forests, agricultural areas, freshwater, and coastal.

Embargo. A type of economic sanction often designed to influence a domestic or international policy in a second country; embargoes can be comprehensive or selective.

Emerging market economies (EMEs). Refers to countries that have made significant strides toward capitalism and sustainable economic development.

Empowerment of women. The idea that giving women power over their economic, social, and *reproductive choices* will raise their status, promote development, and reduce population growth.

Entrepreneur. A person who starts a new business, develops a new product, or devises a new way to produce a product; a risk-taker and innovator.

Environmental degradation. A wide variety of human-induced and naturally occurring stresses on the natural environment.

Euro. The common currency of the European Union; the euro replaced the national currencies of 12 EU countries in 2002.

European Union (EU). A unique intergovernmental organisation that coordinates economic, foreign, security, and judicial policies among its 25 member nations.

Exchange rates. The value of one currency compared to a second currency.

Export processing zone (EPZ). An industrial area that offers special incentives to attract foreign direct investment, and in which export industries produce products.

Export promotion. Governmental efforts to expand the volume of a country's exports through *export incentives* and other means in order to generate more *foreign exchange* and improve the *current account* of its *balance of payments*.

Expropriation. The government's seizure of private physical assets or financial assets without compensation to the previous owner.

External Debt. The money owed by a nation to a foreign government or commercial bank, a multilateral organisation, or other creditor; also called foreign debt.

Factors of production. The resources used to produce goods or services, including natural resources, human resources, and capital goods; entrepreneurship is often considered a fourth factor of production; also called productive resources.

Fertility rate. The yearly number of children born alive per 1,000 women within the childbearing age bracket (normally between the ages of 15 and 49 years). The total *fertility rate* (TFR) is the number of children that would be born to a woman if she were to live to the end of her childbearing years and bear children at each age in accordance with the prevailing age-specific fertility rates.

Final goods. Commodities that are consumed to satisfy wants rather than passed on to further stages of production. Whenever a final good is not consumed but is used as an *input* instead, it becomes an *intermediate producer good*.

Fixed exchange rate system. A system of converting nations' currencies at a rate tied to gold or to the US dollar; the fixed exchange rate system was an important feature of the Bretton Woods System from 1946 to 1973.

Flexible exchange rate. The exchange value of a national currency that is free to move up and down in response to shifts in demand and supply arising from international trade and finance.

Foreign aid. A grant of money, technical assistance, food, capital equipment, or other assistance from one country to another.

Foreign direct investment (FDI). Overseas investments by private multinational corporations.

Foreign exchange gap. Exists when the planned merchandise *trade deficit* exceeds the value of capital inflows thus causing output growth to be limited by inadequate *foreign exchange*.

Foreign exchange market. A network of commercial banks, investment banks, brokerage houses, and other financial institutions that buy and sell currencies for profit; also called the forex market.

Foreign reserves. The value of a country's holdings of foreign currencies, gold, and IMF special drawing rights (SDRs); the reserve is sometimes tapped to make international payments.

Free trade. Refers to international trade that is not restricted by trade barriers—such as tariffs and import quotas—or other distortions such as subsidies.

Free trade area. A type of regional trade agreement that eliminates trade barriers among members.

General Agreement on Tariffs and Trade (GATT). A multilateral agreement that established rules for international trade from 1948 to 1994.

Global economy. The international network of individuals, businesses, governments, and multilateral organisations, which collectively make decisions about the production, consumption, and distribution of goods and services.

Globalisation. The freer cross-border movements of goods and services, labour, technology, real capital, and financial capital to create an integrated and interdependent global economy.

Global warming. The gradual warming of world surface temperatures over time, due mainly to the greenhouse effect.

Good governance. The honest, competent administration of governments, businesses, civil society organisations, multilateral organisations, and other decision-making bodies in the global community.

Government failure. Situation in which government intervention in an economy worsens outcomes.

Gradualism. A cautious approach to economic transition, based on experimentation and the gradual infusion of successful market reforms.

Green revolution. The boost in grain production associated with the scientific discovery of new *hybrid seed* varieties of wheat, rice, and corn that have resulted in high farm yields in many LDCs.

Green technologies. Environmentally friendly technologies that promote the efficient use of resources and reduce waste and pollution.

Gross domestic product (GDP). The total money value of all newly produced final goods and services in an economy in a given year.

Gross national income (GNI). The people's total income derived from domestic and foreign sources; the broadest measure of national income; previously called the gross national product (GNP).

Group of Eight (G8). An organisation of eight industrialised economies that discuss and form common policies on matters of global concern; comprised of the G7 plus Russia.

Group of Seven (G7). The seven leading industrialised developed nations (the United States, Canada, Great Britain, France, Germany, Japan, and Italy), who meet annually to discuss global economic issues.

Group of Seventy-seven (G77). A coalition of 133 developing countries; originally formed to promote economic justice in the global economy.

Group of Twenty (G20). A forum comprised of advanced economies, and emerging market and developing countries; designed to strengthen the global financial architecture and promote sustainable economic development.

Hard currency. The currency of a major advanced economy, such as the US dollar, Japanese yen, or EMU euro; used in many types of international transactions.

Human capital. Workers whose abilities and skills have been enhanced by education, training, apprenticeships, or other means.

Human development. Reflects the realistic range of choices that people have to live happy and productive lives.

Human Development Index (HDI). An index of people's well-being; an annual HDI is published by the United Nations Development Program.

Human resources. The people involved in production; human resources is a factor of production.

Import substitution. A trade strategy that challenges domestic businesses to produce substitute goods for items normally imported; designed to reduce the country's dependence on foreign goods.

Indicative planning. A collaborative, inclusive economic planning process employed by some democratic socialist economies.

Industrial Revolution. The economic transition from small-scale labour-intensive production to large-scale capital-intensive production in factories and mills; the Industrial Revolution began in Great Britain during the 1700s.

Infant industry. A newly formed industry in a country; the infant industry argument is used to defend protectionist trade policies, such as tariffs and import quotas.

Infant mortality rate. Deaths among children between birth and 1 year of age per 1,000 live births.

Inflation. An increase in the overall price level in an economy; two types of inflation are demand-pull and cost-push inflation.

Inflation rate. Measures the percentage increase in the overall price level over time.

Informal economy. Refers to business activity that is not reported to the government.

Innovation. The process of converting scientific discoveries and technological advances into profitable business ventures, products, or production processes.

Intellectual property rights. Refers to legal codes and structures to protect people's creative endeavours, including industrial property and copyrights.

International Bank for Reconstruction and Development (IBRD). A member-owned development institution that provides low-interest loans and technical assistance mainly to middle-income developing countries; part of the World Bank Group.

International Labor Organization (ILO). A specialised agency of the United Nations that promotes worker rights and decent work in the global economy.

International Monetary Fund (IMF). An international financial institution (IFI) designed to promote global financial and economic stability, growth and development; a specialised agency in the United Nations System.

International trade. The cross-border exchange of goods or services; occurs when an individual, business, government, or other entity imports or exports products.

Investment goods. Items not designed for present consumption, including capital goods, inventories, and residential housing.

Inward-looking development policies. Policies that stress economic *self-reliance* on the part of LDCs, including the development of indigenous *appropriate technology*, the imposition of substantial protective *tariffs* and *nontariff trade barriers* to promote *import substitution,* and the general discouragement of *private foreign investment*.

Joint venture. A business agreement between two or more companies to produce or sell a product; usually short-term in nature.

Labour force. Consists of individuals of employable age, who have a job or are actively seeking employment.

Labour-intensive production. A method of producing goods or services that relies on physical labour; often associated with production in the developing countries.

Land reform. A deliberate attempt to reorganise and transform existing *agrarian systems* with the intention of improving the distribution of agricultural incomes and thus fostering *rural development*.

Least developed countries (LDCs). Refers to 50 of the world's poorest developing countries; most low-income developing countries are LDCs.

Life expectancy at birth. The number of years newborn children would live subject to the *mortality* risks prevailing for the cross section of population at the time of their birth.

Literacy. The ability to read and write.

Literacy rate. The percentage of the population age 15 and over able to read and write. Literacy rates are often used as one of the many social and economic indicators of the state of development of a country.

Market economy. A type of economic system in which the private sector owns and controls the factors of production—natural resources, human resources, and capital goods; viewed as an economic model.

Market failure. A phenomenon that results from the existence of market imperfections (e.g., *monopoly* power, lack of *factor mobility*, significant *externalities,* lack of knowledge) that weaken the functioning of a free-market economy—it fails to realise its theoretical beneficial results. Market failure often provides the justification for government interference with the working of the *free market*.

Market mechanism. The interaction of supply and demand in free markets to determine prices and allocate resources without government intervention.

Merger. Occurs when two or more firms combine their assets, or equity, to form a single larger firm; mergers of firms headquartered in different countries is a type of foreign direct investment.

Mergers and acquisitions (M&As). Occur when two existing companies are legally joined under single ownership; M&As are a type of foreign direct investment.

Microeconomic theory of fertility. An extension of the theory of consumer behaviour of individual couples. The central proposition of this theory is that family formation has costs and benefits and hence the size of families formed will depend on these costs and benefits. If the costs of family formation are high relative to its benefits, the rates at which couples will decide to bring forth children will decline, and *vice versa*.

Millennium Development Goals (MDGs). The eight specific objectives for human and economic development in the global economy, established by the United Nations in 2000.

Mixed economy. An economy that combines features of the market economy and command economy models; in common usage, mixed economies refer to economic systems that lean toward the market model.

Most favored nations (MFN). Agreement that a trade concession granted by one World Trade Organization member to another member automatically applies to all members; a basic principle of the General Agreement on Tariffs and Trade and the WTO.

Multilateral environmental agreements (MEAs). The formal protocols, conventions, treaties, or declarations negotiated by countries to protect or restore the natural environment.

Nationalisation. The government's seizure of private productive assets with compensation to the previous owner.

Newly industrialising countries (NICs). A small group of countries at a relatively advanced level of economic *development* with a substantial and dynamic industrial sector and with close links to the international trade, finance, and investment system (Argentina, Brazil, Greece, Mexico, Portugal, Singapore, South Korea, Spain, and Taiwan).

New protectionism. Wide range of non-tariff trade barriers erected by developed countries against the manufactured exports of developing nations; typically as quotas or 'voluntary' export restrain by LDCs.

Non-Governmental organisation (NGO). A special interest group that conducts research, disseminates information, and advocates for change at the national and international levels.

Non-renewable resources. Resources that are consumed during production and cannot be replenished, such as oil and natural gas.

Offshoring. Occurs when a producer from one country outsources production to another country.

Organization for Economic Co-operation and Development (OECD). A thirty-member intergovernmental organisation that collects and analyses statistical data, discusses global trends and issues, and forms binding and non-binding economic and social policies.

Organization of the Petroleum Exporting Countries (OPEC). An eleven-member producer cartel comprised of major petroleum-producing countries.

Paradigm. Implicit assumptions from which theories evolve; a *model* or framework of analysis.

Political will. A determined effort by persons in political authority to achieve certain economic objectives, such as elimination of inequality, poverty, and unemployment through various reforms of social, economic and institutional structures. Lack of political will is often said to be one of the main obstacles to *development* and one of the main reasons for the failure of many *development plans.*

Private property rights. The legal codes and other protections that guarantee people's right to own, control, buy, sell, and profit from private property.

Private sector. The part of an economy whose activities are under the control and direction of non-governmental economic units such as households or firms. Each economic unit owns its own *resources* and uses them mainly to maximise its own well-being.

Privatisation. Selling public assets (corporations) to individuals or private business interests.

Protectionism. The government's use of import controls, such as tariffs and import quotas, and export subsidies to protect local industries and jobs.

Public consumption. All current expenditures for purchases of *goods* and *services* by all levels of government: includes capital expenditures on national defence and security.

Public good. An entity that provides benefits to all individuals simultaneously and whose enjoyment by one person is in no way diminished by that of another.

Public Sector. The portion of an economy whose activities (economic and noneconomic) are under the control and direction of the state.

Purchasing power parity (PPP). The purchasing power of a country's currency: the number of units of that currency required to purchase the same basket of goods and services that a US Dollar would buy in the United States.

Quality of life. The overall conditions under which people live.

Quota. A physical limitation on the quantity of any item that can be imported into a country, such as so many automobiles per year. Also a method for allocating limited school places by noncompetitive means—for example, by income or ethnicity.

Recession. A period of slack general economic activity as reflected in rising unemployment and excess productive capacity in a broad spectrum of industries.

Redistribution policies. Policies geared to reducing *income inequality* and expanding economic opportunities in order to promote *development*. Examples include *progressive income tax policies*, provision of services financed out of such taxation to benefit persons in the lower-income groups, *rural development* policies giving emphasis to raising *levels of living* for the rural poor through *land reform* and other forms of asset and wealth redistribution.

Regional trade agreement (RTA). An agreement that creates preferential trade concessions among member countries.

Remittances. Money earned by foreign-born or immigrant workers in one country but sent to family, friends, business associates, or others in the home country; sometimes viewed as a type of foreign aid.

Renewable resources. Resources that can be replenished, such as sunlight and forests.

Replacement fertility. The level of *fertility* at which childbearing women have just enough daughters to replace themselves in the population. This keeps the existing population size constant through an infinite number of succeeding generations.

Reproductive choice. Argument that women should be able to determine on an equal status with their husbands and for themselves how many children they want and what methods to use to achieve their desired family size.

Research and development (R&D). Scientific investigation with a view toward improving the existing quality of human life, products, *profits, factors of production*, or knowledge. There are two categories of R&D: basic R&D (without a specific commercial objective) and applied R&D (with a commercial objective).

Scale-neutral. Unaffected by size; applied to *technological progress* that can lead to the achievement of higher output levels irrespective of the size (scale) of a firm or farm, making it equally applicable to small- and large-scale production processes. An often-cited example is the *hybrid seeds* of the *green revolution*, which can theoretically increase yields on both small and large farms (if *complementary resources* such as fertiliser, irrigation, and pesticides are available).

Self-esteem. The feeling of worthiness that a society enjoys when its *social, political*, and *economic systems* and *institutions* promote human respect, dignity, integrity, self-determination, etc.

Social capital. A country's broad infrastructure; social capial is provided by the government for the collective welfare of the people.

Socialism. A type of economic system based on public ownership and control of key resources and industries; strands range from democratic socialism to communism.

Special Drawing Rights (SDR). The International Monetary Fund's unit of account, roughly comparable to the European Union's euro, the US dollar, or other national unit of account.

Statism. An economic philosophy that supports active government intervention in the economy, including the nationalisation of key industries.

Subsidy. A government payment to a business, mainly to support domestic producers; viewed as a type of protectionism in international markets.

Subsistence agriculture. An agricultural system designed to satisfy the personal consumption needs of households rather than to produce surpluses for export.

Supply chain. A network of businesses that are collectively responsible for the production and distribution of a product.

Subsistence economy. An economy in which production is mainly for personal consumption and the standard of living yields no more than the basic necessities of life—food, shelter, and clothing.

Subsistence farming. Farming in which crop production, stock rearing, and other activities are conducted mainly for personal consumption, characterised by low productivity, *risk*, and *uncertainty*.

Sustainable development. Pattern of *development* that permits future generations to live at least as well as the current generation.

Sustainable economic development. Occurs when an economy achieves sustained economic growth and substantive improvements in people's quality of life.

Sustenance. The basic *goods* and *services*, such as food, clothing, and shelter, that are necessary to sustain an average human being at the bare minimum *level of living*.

Tariff. A fixed percentage tax on the value of an imported commodity levied at the point of entry into the importing country.

Technological progress. Increased application of new scientific knowledge in form of inventions and *innovations* with regard to both *physical* and *human capital*. Such progress has been a major factor in stimulating the long-term *economic growth* of contemporary developed countries.

Technology transfer. The sharing of advanced technology between transnational corporations and their affiliates or other related firms.

Tenant farmer. One who farms on land held by a *landlord* and therefore lacks secure ownership rights and has to pay for the use of that land, for example, by surrendering part of his output to the owner. Examples are found in the Latin American and Asian *agrarian systems.*

Terms of trade. A measure of the relative prices of a country's exports and imports.

Trade barrier. Government policies designed to discourage or prohibit imports, such as import tariffs and import quotas.

Trade deficit. Occurs when the value of a country's imports is greater than its exports.

Trade liberalisation. Refers to government policies that result in freer trade; includes the removal of trade barriers and business subsidies.

Trade-off. The necessity of sacrificing (trading off) something in order to get more of something else— for example, sacrificing consumption now for consumption later by devoting some present *resources to investment*.

Trade-Related Aspects of Intellectual Property (TRIPS). An international agreement designed to protect intellectual properties in global markets; administered by the World Trade Organization.

Trade surplus. Occurs when the value of a country's exports is greater than its imports.

Traditional economy. An economic system that relies on custom or tradition to answer the basic economic questions.

Transition countries. The 28 countries of eastern and central Europe and central Asia that are in the process of transforming from communism to capitalism, and from totalitarianism to democracy; also called transition economies.

Transnational corporation (TNC). A company that is based in one country, but owns or controls other companies, called affiliates, in one or more additional countries.

Transparency. Refers to a free flow of information; transparency promotes accountability of governments, transnational corporations, multilateral organisations, and others; it also promotes inclusion of the marginalised in global decision making.

Trickle-down theory of development. The notion that *development* is purely an economic phenomenon in which rapid gains from the overall growth of *gross national product* and *income per capita* would automatically bring benefits (trickle down) to the masses in the form of jobs and other economic opportunities. The main preoccupation is therefore to get the growth job done while problems of *poverty*, unemployment, and *income distribution* are perceived to be of secondary importance.

Two-gap model. Theoretical *foreign aid* model comparing *savings* and *foreign exchange* gaps to determine which is the binding constraint on *economic growth*.

Underemployment. Occurs when workers are employed at jobs beneath their skill level, at jobs that do not fully utilise their skills, or at jobs that offer insufficient work hours.

Unorganised money market. The informal and often usurious credit system that exists in most developing countries (especially in rural areas) where low-income farms and firms with little collateral are forced to borrow from *moneylenders* and loan sharks at exorbitant rates of *interest*.

Unsustainable debt. A country's inability to service, or make payments on, its external debt without decimating its domestic economy.

Urbanisation. The process of becoming more urban; the shift of population and economic activity from rural areas to cities.

Venture capital. Money invested to create new businesses; also called risk capital.

Vicious cycle. A self-reinforcing situation in which factors tend to perpetuate a certain undesirable phenomenon—for example, low incomes in poor countries lead to low consumption, which then leads to poor health and low *labour productivity* and eventually to the persistence of *poverty*.

Wage-price spiral. *Vicious cycle* in which higher consumer prices (e.g., as a result of *devaluation*) cause workers to demand higher wages, which in turn cause producers to raise prices and worsen inflationary forces.

World Trade Organization (WTO). An international organisation that oversees the operation of the rules-based multilateral trading system.

Select Bibliography

Acharya, Shankar (2009). *India and Global Crisis*. New Delhi: Academic Foundation.

———. (2007). *Can India Grow without Bharat?* New Delhi: Academic Foundation.

———. (2006). *Essays on Macroeconomic Policy and Growth in India*. New Delhi: Oxford University Press.

———. (2003). *India's Economy: Some Issues and Answers*. New Delhi: Academic Foundation.

Acharya, Shankar and Rakesh Mohan (2010). *India's Economy: Performance and Challenges (Essays in honour of Montek Singh Ahluwalia)*. New Delhi: OUP.

Ahluwalia, I.J. (2005). "Trade Liberalisation and Industrial Performance in India", in S.D. Tendulkar *et. al.,* (eds.), *Industrialisation in a Reforming Economy*, Essays for K.L. Krishna. New Delhi: Academic Foundation.

Ahluwalia, Montek S. (2011). "Prospects and Policy Challenges in the Twelfth Plan", in *Economic & Political Weekly,* May 21, Vol. XIVI, No. 21.

———. (2000). "Economic Reforms: A Policy Agenda for the Future", in *Economic Developments in India*, Vol. 25. New Delhi: Academic Foundation.

Baijal, Pradip (2002). *Privatisation: Compulsions and Options for Economic Reform, EPW*, (Oct 12).

Bala Subrahmanya, M.H. (2008). "Small Industry and Globalisation: Implications, Performance and Prospects", in K.L. Krishna and Uma Kapila (eds.) *Readings in Indian Agriculture and Industry*. New Delhi: Academic Foundation.

Basu, Kaushik (ed.) (2004). "The Indian Economy: Up to 1991 and Since", *India's Emerging Economy, Performance and Prospects in the 1990s and Beyond*, Ch.1, OUP.

———. (ed.) (2007). *The Oxford Companion to Economics in India*. New Delhi: Oxford University Press.

Bhagwati, Jagdish (1998). "The Design of Indian Development", in Ahluwalia I.J. and Little I.M.D (eds.), *India's Economic Reforms and Development*. Essays for Manmohan Singh. New Delhi: Oxford University Press.

Bhagwati, J. and P. Desai (1970). *India Planning for Industrialisation*. London: Oxford University Press.

Bhagwati, Jagdish and T.N. Srinivasan (1993). "India's Economic Reforms", Ministry of Finance, GoI, New Delhi. Reproduced in Uma Kapila (ed.), *Indian Economy Since Independence* (2001 edition). New Delhi: Academic Foundation.

Bisaliah, S., S. Mahendra Dev and Syed Saifullah (2013). *Investment in Indian Agriculture: Macro and Micro Evidences*. New Delhi: Academic Foundation.

Byres, Terence J. (ed.) (1998). *The Indian Economy, Major Debates Since Independence*, Oxford University Press.

Cassen, R.H. (1978). *India: Population, Economy and Society*, Ch. 4.

Cassen, Robert and Joshi, Vijay (eds.) (1995). *India: The Future of Economic Reform*. New Delhi: Oxford University Press.

Chakravarthy, Sukhamoy (1987a). *Development Planning: The Indian Experience*, Oxford University Press.

Charles, Bettleheim, *India Independent*, Chs. 1,2,3.

Commission on Growth and Development (2008). *The Growth Report, Strategies for Sustained Growth and Inclusive Development*.

Dandekar, V.M. "Forty Years After Independence" in Bimal Jalan (ed.), *Indian Economy: Problems and Prospects*. New Delhi: Viking.

Dantwala, M.L. (1981). *Understanding Poverty and Unemployment*, Artha Jignasa, (April-June). Bombay: Indian Merchants Chamber.

Debroy, Bibek and Debashis Chakraborty (2006). *The Trade Game Negotiation Trends at WTO and Concerns of Developing Countries*. New Delhi: Academic Foundation..

Debroy, Bibek (2004). *India: Redeeming the Economic Pledge*. New Delhi: Academic Foundation.

Desai, A.V. (2001). "A Decade of Reforms", in *Economic Developments in India*, Vol. 47. New Delhi: Academic Foundation.

Desai, Nitin and Rajeev D. Mathur (2013). *Growth and Equity: Essays in Honour of Pradeep Mehta*. New Delhi: Academic Foundation.

Deshpande, R.S., *et al.* (eds.) (2008). *Glimpses of Indian Agriculture: Macro and Micro Aspects* (A set of 2 vols.). New Delhi: Academic Foundation.

Dev, Mahendra S. and N. Chandrasekhara Rao (eds.) (2009). *India: Perspectives on Equitable Development*. New Delhi: Academic Foundation.

Drèze, Jean and Amartya Sen (2002). *India: Development and Participation*, Oxford University Press.

Dyson, Tim (2008). "India's Demographic Transition and its Consequences for Development", Third Lecture in the Golden Jubliee Series, Institute of Economic Growth, Delhi. Reprinted in Uma Kapila (ed.), *Indian Economy Since Independence*, 2008 edition.

EPW Research Foundation (2013). *India: A Pocket Book of Data Series 2013*, New Delhi: Academic Foundation.

Gordon, Jim and Poonam Gupta (2003). "Understanding India's Services Revolution", Paper prepared for the IMF-NCAER Conference, *A Tale of Two Giants: India's and China's Experience with Reform*, November 14-16.

Government of India. *Economic Survey*, various issues including 2012-13, (Ministry of Finance) New Delhi.

———. (2001). "Report of the Task Force on Employment Opportunities", (Chairman: M.S. Ahluwalia), Reproduced in Planning Commission *Reports on Labour and Employment*. New Delhi: Academic Foundation.

Gulati, Ashok (2012). "Reforming Agriculture", in Uma Kapila (ed.), Two Decades of Economic Reforms. New Delhi: Academic Foundation.

Gulati, A. and Shenggen Fan (2008). *The Dragon and the Elephant—Agricultural and Rural Reforms in China and India*. New Delhi: Oxford University Press.

Hashim, S.R. *et al.*, (eds.) (2009). *Indian Industrial Development and Globalisation* (Essays in Honour of Professor S.K. Goyal). New Delhi: Academic Foundation.

Helpman, Elhanan (2005). *The Mystery of Economic Growth*. New Delhi: Academic Foundation.

Jalan, Bimal (ed.) (1992). *The Indian Economy: Problems and Prospects*. New Delhi: Viking Penguin, India.

———. (1996). *India's Economic Policy—Preparing for the 20th Century*, Viking Penguin, India.

James, K.S. (2008). "Glorifying Malthus: Current Debtate on 'Demographic Dividend' in India", *Economic and Political Weekly*, Vol. XLIII, No. 25, June 21-27.

Jha, Veena (2012). *India Emerging: The Reality Checks*. New Delhi: Academic Foundation.

Jayaram, N. and R.S. Deshpande (eds.) (2008). *Footprints of Development and Change*. New Delhi: Academic Foundation.

Joshi, Vijay and I.M.D. Little (1997). *India's Economic Reforms: 1991-2001*, Oxford University Press.

Joshi, Seema (2008). *Growth and Structure of Tertiary Sector in Developing Economies*. New Delhi: Academic Foundation.

Kapila, Raj and Uma Kapila (2002). *A Decade of Economic Reforms in India*. New Delhi: Academic Foundation.

———. (2006). *India's Economy: A Journey in Time and Space*. New Delhi: Academic Foundation.

———. (eds.) (2009). *Economic Developments in India*, (various volumes); latest volume: Vol. 184 (monthly update). New Delhi: Academic Foundation.

Kapila, Uma (ed.) (2013). *Indian Financial Reforms: Priorities and Policy Thrust Post Global Financial Crisis*. New Delhi: Academic Foundation.

Kapila, Uma (ed.), *Indian Economy Since Independence*, New Delhi: Academic Foundation (Various editions 1989 to 2012 edition).

———. (2010). *India's Economic Development Since 1947*, New Delhi: Academic Foundation, (5th edition).

———. (2012). *Two Decades of Economic Reforms*, New Delhi: Academic Foundation.

Kelkar, Vijay (2010). "On Strategies for Disinvestment and Privatisation", (26th Sir Purshotam Das Thakur Das Memorial Lecture, Jan, 2010) in Sameer Kochhar and M. Ramachandran (eds.), *Building from the Bottom: Infrastructure and Poverty Alleviation*. New Delhi: Academic Foundation.

———. (2001). "Economic Reforms Agenda: Micro, Meso and Macro Economic Reforms", in *Economic Developments in India*, Vol. 44. New Delhi: Academic Foundation.

Kindleberger Charles P. and Bruce Herrik (1977). *Economic Development*, 3rd (ed.) International Students Edition.

Krishna, K.L. (2013). "Industrial Development and Policies since Independence: Growth without Employment", in Uma Kapila (ed.), *Indian Economy Since Independence (24th edition)*. New Delhi: Academic Foundation.

———. (2008). "Industrial Growth and Diversification", in Uma Kapila (ed.), *Indian Economy Since Independence*. New Delhi: Academic Foundation.

Krishna, K.L and Uma Kapila (2009). *Readings in Indian Agriculture and Industry*. New Delhi: Academic Foundation.

Krishnaji, N. (1990). "Agricultural Price Policy: A Survey with Reference to Indian Foodgrains Economy", in Uma Kapila (ed.), *Indian Economy Since Independence* (2001-02 edition). New Delhi: Academic Foundation.

Kochhar, Sameer (ed.) (2013). *An Agenda for India's Growth: Essays in Honour of P. Chidambaram*. New Delhi: Academic Foundation.

———. (2012). *Policymaking for Indian Planning: Essays on Contemporary Issues in Honour of Montek S. Ahluwalia*. New Delhi: Academic Foundation.

ILO (2012). *World of Work Report 2012: Better Jobs for a Better Economy*. New Delhi: Academic Foundation.

Krueger, O. Anne (2002). *Economic Policy Reforms and the Indian Economy*. New Delhi: Oxford University Press.

Kumar, Nagesh (2009). "Liberalisation, Foreign Direct Investment Flows and Development: Indian Experience in the 1990s", in K.L. Krishna and Uma Kapila (eds.) *Readings in Indian Agriculture and Industry*. New Delhi: Academic Foundation.

Meier, G. (1995). *Leading Issues in Economic Development*, 6th Ed. Ch. I-A pp., 7-9.

Mohan, Rakesh (2008). "Growth Record of Indian Economy 1958-2008", *Economic and Political Weekly*, Feb. 14, 2008.

———. (2002). *Facets of the Indian Economy*. New Delhi: Oxford University Press.

———. (1992). "Industrial Policy and Controls", in Bimal Jalan (ed.), *The Indian Economy: Problems and Prospects*. (Viking Penguin), India.

Mohanty, Deepak (ed.) (2012). *Regional Economy of India: Growth and Finance*. New Delhi: Academic Foundation.

Mujumdar, N.A. (2011). *India's New Development Agenda: Building a Value-based Society*. New Delhi: Academic Foundation.

———. (2007). *Inclusive Growth: Development Perspectives in Indian Economy*. New Delhi: Academic Foundation.

———. (2004). *Economic Reforms Sans Development*. New Delhi: Academic Foundation.

Mujumdar, N.A. and Uma Kapila (eds.) (2006). *Indian Agriculture in the New Millennium* (two volumes set). New Delhi: Academic Foundation.

Nachane, D.M. (ed.), India Development Report 2011. Indira Gandhi Institute of Development Research, Mumbai, Oxford, New Delhi.

Nagaraj, R. (2005). *Aspects of India's Economic Growth and Reforms*. New Delhi: Academic Foundation.

———. (2008). "India's Recent Economic Growth: A Closer Look", *Economic and Political Weekly*, Vol. XLIII, No. 15, April 12-18.

———. (2009). "Public Sector Performance Since 1950: A Fresh Look", in K.L. Krishna and Uma Kapila (eds.) *Readings in Indian Agriculture and Industry*. New Delhi: Academic Foundation.

National Commission for Enterprises in the Unorganised Sector, Govt. of India (2009). Chairman: Arjun K. Sengupta. *The Challenge of Employment in India: An Informal Economy Perspective*, Vol. I and Vol. II. New Delhi: Academic Foundation.

Nayyar, Deepak (2006). "Economic Growth in Independent India", *Economic and Political Weekly*, April 15-21.

———. (1996). *Economic Liberalisation in India: Analytics Experience and Lessons*. Orient Longman.

Nurul Islam (2005). *Exploration in Development Issues*. New Delhi: Academic Foundation.

OECD Insights (2010). *Sustainable Development: Linking Economy, Society, Environment* (Tracey Strange & Anne Bayley). New Delhi: Academic Foundation.

OECD Economic Surveys: India 2011. New Delhi: Academic Foundation. June.

———. Economic Surveys: India 2007. New Delhi: Academic Foundation.

Panagariya, Arvind (2010). "India on the Growth Turnpike: No State Left Behind", in Sameer Kochhar (ed.), *India on the Growth Turnpike (Essays in honour of Vijay L. Kelkar)*. New Delhi: Academic Foundation.

———. (2008). *India: The Emerging Giant*. New Delhi: Oxford University Press.

Planning Commission (2010). *Mid-term Appraisal of the Eleventh Five Year Plan*.

———. (2009). *Macro-Modelling for the Eleventh Five Year Plan of India*, edited by Kirit S. Parikh. New Delhi: Academic Foundation.

———. (2006). *Approach Paper to the 11th Plan*.

———. (2005). *Mid-term Appraisal of the Tenth Five Year Plan*.

———. (2006). *Tenth Five Year Plan* 2002-07.

———. (2008). *Eleventh Five Year Plan* 2007-2012.

———. (2012). *Twelfth Five Year Plan* Approach Paper.

Pursell, Garry and Ashok Gulati (1993). "Liberalising Indian Agriculture: An Agenda for Reform", Working Paper, Policy Research Department, The World Bank (September), WPS 1172, reproduced in (ed.) Uma Kapila, *Indian Economy Since Independence*. New Delhi: Academic Foundation.

Radhakrishna, R. (ed.) (2008). *India Development Report 2008*, Indira Gandhi Institute of Development Research. New Delhi: Oxford University Press.

Radhakrishna, R., S.K. Rao, S. Mahendra Dev and K. Subbarao (eds.) (2006). *India in a Globalising World: Some Aspects of Macroeconomy, Agriculture and Poverty* (Essays in Honour of C.H. Hanumantha Rao). New Delhi: Academic Foundation,

———. (2006). "Food Trends, Public Distribution and Food Security Concerns", Ch. 10, in N.A. Mujumdar and Uma Kapila (eds.), *Indian Agriculture in the New Millennium, Volume 2*. New Delhi: Academic Foundation.

Raghavan Srinivasa, T.C.A (ed.) (2012). *On the Turnpike: Indian Economy since 1947 & Indian Economic Service at 50*. Ministry of Finance, Govt. of India. New Delhi: Academic Foundation.

Rangarajan, C. (2009). *India: Monetary Policy Financial Stability and Other Essays*. New Delhi: Academic Foundation.

———. (2003). *Select Essays on Indian Economy*. New Delhi: Academic Foundation.

———. (2003). "India's Balance of Payments: The Emerging Dimensions", in (ed.), Uma Kapila, *Indian Economy Since Independence* (2003 edition). New Delhi: Academic Foundation.

Rao, C.H.H (2005). *Agriculture, Food Security, Poverty, and Environment: Essays on Post-reform India*. New Delhi: Academic Foundation.

———. (2005). *Essays on Agricultural Growth, Farm Size and Rural Poverty Alleviation in India*. New Delhi: Academic Foundation.

———. (2005). *Essays on Development Strategy, Regional Disparities and Centre-State Financial Relations in India*. New Delhi: Academic Foundation.

———. (2003), *Reform Agenda for Agriculture*, EPW, Feb 15.

Rao, C.H.H, B.B. Bhattacharya and N.S. Sidharathan (ed.) (2005). *Indian Economy and Society in the Era of Globalisation and Liberalisation*. New Delhi: Academic Foundation.

Rao, C.H.H and Ashok Gulati (1994c). "Indian Agriculture Emerging Perspectives and Policy Issues', EPW Dec. 31. Reproduced in (ed.) Uma Kapila, *Indian Economy Since Independence*. New Delhi: Academic Foundation.

Rao, V.M. and P.D. Jeromi (2000). "Modernising Indian Agriculture, Priority Tasks and Critical Policy", Study No. 21, DRG, DEAP, Reserve Bank of India, reproduced in Uma Kapila (ed.), *Indian Economy Since Independence*. New Delhi: Academic Foundation.

Reserve Bank of India (2004). *Report on Currency and Finance 2003-04* and various issues.

Sen, Amartya (2000). *Development as Freedom*. New Delhi: Oxford University Press.

Sengupta, Dipankar, Debashis Chakraborty and Pritam Banerjee (2006). *Beyond the Transition Phase of WTO: An Indian Perspective on Emerging Issues*. New Delhi: Academic Foundation in association with Centre de Sciences Humaines.

Sengupta, Jaishree (2007). *A Nation in Transition: Understanding the Indian Economy*. New Delhi: Academic Foundation.

Srinivasan, T.N. (2009). *Trade, Growth and Poverty Reduction*. New Delhi: Academic Foundation.

———. (2000). *Eight Lectures on India's Economic Reforms*. Oxford University Press.

———. (2003). "Foreign Trade Policies and India's Development", reproduced in Uma Kapila (ed.), *Indian Economy Since Independence* (2003 edition). New Delhi: Academic Foundation.

———. (1991). "Reform of Industrial and Trade Policies", *EPW* (Sept. 14), Vol. XXVI, No. 37.

Srinivasan, T.N. and S.D. Tendulkar (2003). *Reintegrating India with the World Economy*. New Delhi: Oxford University Press.

Sundaram, K. (2008). "Employment and Poverty in India, 2000-2005", *Economic and Political Weekly*, Vol. XLII No. 30, July 28-August 3.

Singh, Surjit and V. Ratna Reddy (eds.) (2009). *Changing Contours of Asian Agriculture: Policies, Performance and Challenges* (Essays in Honour of Professor V.S. Vyas). New Delhi: Academic Foundation.

Tarapore, S.S. (2012). *Financial Policies and Everyday Life: The Indian Context*. New Delhi: Academic Foundation.

Tendulkar, S.D. .(1981). *Indian Development Strategy: Compulsions and Constraints*, Working Paper No. 23, (1 June), Delhi School of Economics, reproduced in Uma Kapila (ed.), *Indian Economy Since Independence* (2001 edition). New Delhi: Academic Foundation.

Todaro, M., *(2008). Economic Development, 8th edition. Delhi: Pearson Education (Singapore) Pvt. Ltd.*

UNDP (2013). *Human Development Report 2013: The Rise of the South: Human Progress in a Diverse World*. UNDP/Academic Foundation.

———. (2011). *Human Development Report 2011.*

———. (2010). *Human Development Report 2010.*

———. (2008). *Human Development Report 2007-08.*

United Nations (2008). *Trade and Development Report*. New Delhi: Academic Foundation.

Vaidyanathan, A. (2013). *India's Evolving EconomyPuzzles and Perspectives.* New Delhi: Academic Foundation.

Vaidyanathan, A. (2003). *Economic Reforms and Development*. New Delhi: Academic Foundation.

Virmani, Arvind (2006). *Propelling India from Socialist Stagnation to Global Power*, (Two volume set). New Delhi: Academic Foundation.

———. (2004). *Accelerating Growth and Poverty Reduction: A Policy Framework for India's Development*. New Delhi: Academic Foundation.

Vyas, V.S. (2005). *Food Security in Asian Countries in the Context of Millennium Goals*. New Delhi: Academic Foundation.

World Bank (2012), *World Development Report*. New Delhi: Oxford University Press.

———. *World Development Report* 2011, 2009, 2008, 2007, 2006, 2005, 2002. New Delhi: Oxford University Press.

———. (2002). *Globalisation, Growth, and Poverty: Building an Inclusive World Economy*. A World Bank Policy Research Report. New Delhi: Oxford University Press.